OUTDOOR BOOKS & MAPS

(800) 660-5107 (303) 660-3307 Fax: (303) 688-4388
4WDbooks.com

ACKNOWLEDGEMENTS

We thank the following agencies for their assistance to make this guide possible.

Colorado Division of Wildlife
Colorado State Parks
U.S. Forest Service
National Parks Service

Front Cover Photo
Brand X Pictures
Inside Photos
Photo Disk

ISBN 0-930657-41-1

TABLE OF CONTENTS

The guide is divided into sections, each section has an index map and table of contents.

Front Range Section 8
Colorado State Parks Section... 46
State Trust Lands Section... 77
State Wildlife Areas Section 83
Larimer County Parks 252
Wolford Reservoir 254

NATIONAL FORESTS SECTION

Colorado National Forest Index Map 96
Arapaho/Roosevelt National Forest 98
Grand Mesa National Forest 124
Gunnison National Forest 150
Pike National Forest 170
Rio Grande National Forest 178
Routt National Forest 193
San Isabel National Forest 204
San Juan National Forest...216
Uncompahgre National Forest 229
White River National Forest 234

NATIONAL PARKS AND RECREATION AREAS

Arapaho National Recreation Area 99
Rocky Mountain National Park.......................................100
Curecanti National Recreation Area (Blue Mesa) 165

HOW TO USE THIS GUIDE 2
Map Symbol Explanation 2
How To Catch Colorado Fish 3
Fish You are Likely to Catch 7
Appendix, alphabetical listing of contents 255

How to Use This Guide

HOW TO USE THIS GUIDE
Guide Sections

The guide has been divide into sections by managing agencies except the Front Range Section. The Front Range Section includes managing agencies from Metro Denver area and Forest Service.

Front Range Section has over150 lakes within a one-hour drive from the Metro Denver area. Fishing information for nearby mountain lakes and streams and a variety of fishing in urban ponds. Divided into three sections, Urban Lakes, Mountain Lakes and Streams. Information includes fish species present, maximum depth, directions and USGS topographic map name for mountain lakes.

Colorado State Parks Section describes maps and locates thirty-one state parks located throughout Colorado. A locator index map is in front of section. Except for Arkansas River, Lower Colorado River and Yampa River, State Parks offer lake fishing. State Parks have the best facilities for camping and other water related activities. Most State parks provide campgrounds with RV hook-ups, restrooms, water, RV dump stations, and picnic areas. Map symbols locate facilities for each park. Daily or annual parks pass is required and an overnight camping fee.

State Trust Lands and State Wildlife Areas are managed by the Colorado Division of Wildlife and are located throughout Colorado. A locator index map is in front of each section. Properties are located in urban and remote areas and have few facilities. Some properties provide solitude and great fishing. Camping is permitted on some properties, most have vault toilets and a few have water. A couple wildlife areas have entrance fees, no camping fee where camping is permitted.

National Forests Section comprises ten Colorado National Forests, Rocky Mountain National Park, Arapaho National Recreation Area and Curecanti National Recreation Area. National Forests cover millions of acres of Colorado and contain its wilderness areas and a large portion of the cold water fishing.

Campgrounds are rustic most have tables, vault toilets and water. Rocky Mountain National Park has entrance and camping fees. National forest and recreation areas do not have entrance fees, there are camping fees for established campgrounds. Physical features such as the Continental Divide or a mountain range separate National Forests and determine boundaries.

Information

State Wildlife Areas and State Trust Lands have a state locator index map with numbered locations. Numbers correspond to text following the index map. Number on map represents number of county in text, a lower case letter next to represents sequence under county heading. Exact location of property in state is from numbers in text heading. Numbers and character refer to page number and map coordinates in Pierson Guides Colorado Road Atlas. ISBN 1-928721-04-4.

State Parks are located from directions in park text provided with individual state park maps.

National Forests have a numbered map index in front of each forest. Numbered maps are accompanied with text locating fishing areas. Numbers on individual maps following locator map corresponds to fishing text.

Information contained in this guide has been carefully researched by Outdoor Books & Maps. Source of information was Colorado governmental agencies and other reliable sources. Some distances used in the directions to destinations are estimated, verify before attempting trip.

Information contained in this guide has been checked for accuracy but can contain errors. Contact us with comments, corrections or if you are critcal of the content.

The Publisher is not responsible for mishaps are injuries caused by use of this guide for other than its intended use. The intended use of this guide is for trip planning only.

MAP SYMBOL EXPLANATION

P	Parking Area		Forest Service Facility	(285)	U.S. Highway		National Forest Area
	Picnic Area		Fishing Area	(126)	State Highway		Water
	Trailhead		RV Dump Station	(9)	County Highway		Trail
	Downhill Ski Area		Restrooms	(200)	Trail Number		River or Stream
	Boat Launch		Handicap Accessible	[1105]	Forest Service Road		Primary Road - Paved
	Bicycle Trail		Hunting	▲	Mountain/Peak		Improved Road - Unpaved
	4WD Road		Campground		Colorado Trail		Unimproved Road - 4WD
	Motorcycle Trail		Towns & Locals		Continental Divide Trail		Forest/Wilderness Boundary

HOW TO CATCH COLORADO FISH
David Rye

If you want to catch fish in Colorado, you must first become familiar with the various species that the state has to offer. There are nine cold water fish, most of which are trout and six warm water fish that you should get to know.

Trout are more difficult to catch than many of their warm water cousins. Trout rely on sight to feed rather than smell techniques that are typical of many warm water fish such as catfish and panfish.

Trolling and casting are common methods to attract fish. Stream and river fishing involves the use of artificial flies and lures that can be carried by the current to fish in as natural a process as possible. Trolling is a common technique used on lakes.

Fish are one of the lowest forms of animal life. They have a relatively small brain for their body size. However, what they may be missing in intelligence, is more than made up for in keen eyesight.

Most fresh water fish feed at three basic times during the day. Morning feeding starts at sunrise and continues until 9 or 10 a.m. Feeding drops off until about noon when a short feeding frenzy will last until about 2 p.m. Late afternoons are the slowest time to fish. Feeding will start up again around sunset and can continue into the late evening.

Brown Trout

Brown trout were imported from Europe into the United States in 1883. They were planted in the streams and tributaries of the Colorado Rockies and have survived ever since.

They are one of the strongest survivors of the trout specie. They can tolerate warm, muddy water that would kill most other trout. Browns prefer slow moving cold water that has lots of large deep holes. Brown trout do most of their feeding at night. They will feed early in the morning but will move to the deep water and pools at sunrise.

Most of their feeding is done on the bottom. Browns are one of the more aggressive trout and will eat just about any aquatic form of life, small swimming birds and mammals.

Spawning season for browns is in the fall. They will congregate in headwater streams. The female will produce from 200 to 600 eggs in 10 to 30 feet of water.

Rainbow Trout

The rainbow trout is one of the scrappiest fish in the trout family, and hence a favorite with fishermen. Rainbow trout were originally a native of the West Coast. The trout was introduced into Colorado in the 1880s and has done extremely well ever since. In fact, about 75% of the trout caught in the state are rainbows.

Rainbows are notorious for being aggressive strikers. They are attracted to artificial flies and bright colored lures. They like lower, warmer waters. Rainbows spawn in the spring.

Brook Trout

Many consider the brook trout to be the prettiest of all the trout. Their body is distinguished by side markings are spattered with red and white spots on a dark green background.

Cutthroat Trout

Cutthroat trout are the only trout know to be native to Colorado. Their name is derived by the fact that they have a splash of red behind the gills.

Cutts, as they are fondly called, are found in the upper stretches of the mountain streams and lakes. They do not adapt well to warm, silty water. If you want to catch one of these fish, you'll have to be prepared to hike into their habitat.

These fish will go after any of the artificial material including flies and lures. If you hook one, chances are it is the first time that they have ever seen what your are using. Cutts move into the headwaters of mountain streams in the spring to spawn.

Mackinaw Lake Trout

The Mackinaw can be found in many of Colorado's deep, cold water lake. It is by far, the largest trout in the Colorado's trout inventory. Mackinaw in excess of 60 pounds have been consistently caught.

Mackinaw are the most difficult trout to catch because they spend most of the year in deep water. When we say deep water, we are talking about depths in excess of 60 feet. They move to the shallow water to feed in the early spring, right after "ice-off" and in the fall to spawn, which is the best time to catch these fish.

Most fish are caught on deep rigged trolling gear. They will also hit salmon eggs that are cast from shore or dropped from a boat. Winter ice fishermen will attach sucker meat to Airplane jigs dropped to 60 plus feet to successfully catch Mackinaw.

Whole dead suckers also work just as well during the spring and summer. Weight the sucker to help get it down near the bottom where you want it.

The next step is to rig the fish so that when you're done, it will be rigged like an artificial plug. This is accomplished by attaching two No. 2 or 4 treble hooks to the front and posterior of the fish. The hooks can be either tied onto the sucker or you can use a needle to thread the line through the sucker and attach the hooks to the end of the line.

Grayling

Grayling are probably the least known trout in the Colorado trout family. When fishermen mention grayling, most think of Canada and Alaska. They can be found only in selected regions of high Colorado mountain lakes and cool streams.

These fish are very fond of insects and most often are caught by fly fishermen. They can also be attracted by the typical small trout lures such as the Kasmasters. Grayling will mature at about 20 inches or 4 pounds. They like to swim in schools, which can add to your fishing pleasure if you find the school. Spawning begins in March and ends in June.

Kokanee Salmon

Kokanee are land locked pacific sockeye salmon. They were introduced into Colorado in the early fifties and inhabit many of the same lakes that are popular with trout fishermen. Kokanee will often be taken while fishing for trout. They will go after all of the popular trout lures and are equally fond of their own salmon eggs and other common trout baits.

These fish like to surface feed during the day. They will move down to deep water at night and move back up to the surface at sunrise. Most kokanee are taken when trolling. Spawning begins in October and runs through December.

How to Catch Colorado Fish

The fish school up in the tributaries that flow out of their home lakes. Colorado allows fishermen to snag kokanee with weighted treble hooks during the spawning run.

Mountain White Fish

Whitefish live in Colorado's faster and larger rivers. They are particularly prevalent in the Yampa and White Rivers where they can be found in the large pools. These fish feed at night and prefer insect and larvae. Spawning begins in the fall.

Bluegill

Bluegills were introduced to "Colorado in the early 1920's. They abound in many of the state's lower lakes and streams and are considered a primary food source for trout and bass. They offer fishermen fast paced fishing action and are excellent eating.

They are particularly active in the early morning hours and late evening. Favorite baits are worms and small dry flies. Bluegill like to feed in shallow water. However, as the water warms up in the later summer season, they will move down to deeper water.

Spawning season begins in the spring and continues until late August. Nests are built in colonies by the male of the specie who also guards over their spouse's nest.

Walleye

Walleye are the largest member of the perch family and can be found in many of Colorado's larger reservoirs. A typical walleye will run anywhere from 2 to l0 pounds.

The name walleye was derived from the large bulging eyes that are a dominant characteristic of this fish. Their eyes are very sensitive to light. As a result, they will move down into deep water as soon as the morning sun hits the water surface.

Walleye feed at night. They will prowl the shoreline in search of minnows, their favorite food. Casting in the dark with artificial or live minnows is the best way to catch these fish. Spawning begins in the early spring.

Perch

Perch are relatively small fish that rarely exceed a pound. They are found in many of Colorado's warm water reservoirs and live in schools. They will spend most of the day in deep water. As evening approaches, they will move into shallow water to feed.

The best time to catch perch is from noon on into the evening. Fish with small flies, lures or natural baits a foot or two off the bottom for best results. Perch spawn in the spring.

Crappie

Crappies were introduced into Colorado waters in the 1880's and prefer the warmer reservoirs. They like to gather in schools around submerged brush and rock areas. During the summer months they will stay in about 8 to 15 of water.

Live minnows with a bobber are one of the most popular ways to fish for Crappie. Fishing for crappie requires sensitive tackle, to be successful. A small spin cast bubble can work better than a standard bobber. The line can slipped through the center of the bubble, and you can add water to the inside of the bubble to improve on casting distances. A light hitting crappie will be less likely to drop the bait if it doesn't feel the initial pull of the bubble.

Catfish

Catfish are native to Colorado and inhabit many of the states warmer reservoirs and rivers. These fish like to feed at night. Using natural baits such as night crawlers, crayfish, chicken livers or scented dough balls catches most catfish.

Catfish can grow in excess of 50 pounds. Most will average between 2 and 5 pounds. Catfish have a keen sense of smell, which is the reason, why they will go after odorized bait.

Catfish move out of the reservoirs and into the spillway canals during Colorado's irrigation season, which starts in the late spring. They like the moving water and find plenty of feed in the run off.

Look for the deeper pools to fish. Cast minnows with enough weight to carry them to the bottom. If the cats are there, you'll hook-up within 15 minutes. If you get no immediate action, move on to the next pool.

Bass

Bass are a member of the sunfish family and enjoy the reputation of being furious fighters when hooked. The two species of bass that are prevalent in Colorado are the large and small mouth bass. Largemouth were introduced into the state in the late 1800's. Smallmouth were introduced in the early 1950's.

Largemouth are larger than their smallmouth cousin. Adults will weigh up to 10 pounds or more. A typical smallmouth will average about 2 pounds.

Bass prefer shallow weed infested lakes. Bass action begins to heat up in late spring, just before the spawn. Bass become very aggressive and hungry during spawning. They can be found cruising the shoreline for food in the early morning and late evening hours. Casting and spin fishing are the best ways to catch a bass.

An important point to remember about bass is that they will adjust to the sun reflections on the water by changing their swim depth. The higher the sun's intensity, the deeper the depth that you will find bass.

Start shallow and work incrementally into deeper water. You are bound to find bass sooner or later. Once you get your first hit mark the depth that you were at. The rest of the bass will be at that same level.

Northern Pike

Next to Minnesota, Colorado is one of the better pike fishing states in the nation. Pike were imported into the state in the mid 1950s to help control a rising sucker population in many lakes. Unfortunately, the pike developed an appetite for trout and left the suckers alone.

A mature pike will weigh anywhere from 3 to 15 pounds. They like shallow water with abundant vegetation. However, they will move into deeper water during extremely warm or cold weather.

The best time to catch a pike is in late spring, right after ice off. Most pike are caught casting big spoons and plugs into the shallow water near weed beds. Attach 6 to 8 inches of steel leader to 10 to 20 pound test line.

If possible, wade into the weeds and cast at different angles out into the open water. Retrieve the plug or spoon just over the top of the weeds. If you get a missed strike, stop reeling for a few seconds. Pike have a tendency to want to continue an attack a second time.

FLY FISHING BASICS
David Rye

Any fish, when hooked by a fly, will offer you some exciting action that can not be duplicated by any other type of fishing. A trout will rarely swallow an artificial fly as he does if caught with natural bait. They are typically hooked lightly through the lip by a relatively small hook. As a result, they must be carefully played until netted.

About 90% of a trouts diet consists of aquatic insects. That is why they are by far the most popular fish to go after with artificial flies. There are four categories of artificial flies. Each requires a different technique to effectively lure a trout onto your line.

Dry Flies

The dry fly as its name suggest, floats on the water. As a result, trout will rise to the surface to attack a dry fly. You literally have a split second of reaction time to set the hook. Dry flies are cast upstream and allowed to float in a natural pattern in and out of suggested trout holding spots. Getting the right cast into or near the right spot requires patience and plenty of practice.

Wet Flies

Wet flies are fished just below the surface. These are fished downstream and slowly retrieved to simulate a swimming insect. There are 4 popular pattern to fish in Colorado. They are the Black Gnat, March Brown, Quill Gordon and Royal Coachman.

Nymphs

Nymphs are fished on the bottom of the stream and in their artificial state, have been designed to simulate insect larvae.

The key to successful nymph fishing is to drift the bug along the bottom as though the current had turned up a rock and washed the nymph into the main stream. That is the action that trout are watching for.

The big difference in fishing with nymphs versus dry or wet flies is that you can't see your lure or the fish when a strike occurs. The only strike indication that you will get will be when your line suddenly stops drifting. At that instant, set the hook.

Streamers

Streamers are designed to simulate wounded minnows and insects that may have fallen into the water by accident such as a grasshopper. Streamers are cast down stream or across the water. Retrieve the line in short jerky motion to imitate a wounded minnow or swimming surface bug.

Tactics And Approach

The presentation of the fly is the most important skill that a fly fisherman can develop. You must learn how to show your artificial fly to a trout in such a manner that it appears real.

If the real flies are quietly floating on the surface, follow that pattern with a dry fly. If the organisms are darting around just below the surface, switch over to wet flys, nymphs or streamers.

Study the water carefully to determine the best approach to reach possible feeding fish. Feeding trout generally hold in one position and take insects that pass through their line of sight.

Casting up and across a stream is one popular approach to reach a trout's feeding lane. The cast is placed above and just to the side of where you believe the trout are feeding. This action avoids casting your line on top of feeding fish which would tend to startle them. The object is to allow the fly and leader only to float past the fish. This technique works best in evenly flowing water without strong currents to pull on the line.

Uneven currents pulling on fly line causes "drag" or movement of the fly across the stream. Drag is not desirable if the natural flies are landing quietly on the surface and your fly is skimming across the surface.

One way to avoid drag in strong currents is to cast your fly into the feeding lane. As soon as the fly settles on the surface, lift the tip of the rod. Allow extra line to slip through the guides to act as surplus line for the current to play with.

Fishermen that are unfamilar with the area they choose to fish should visit a local fly shop or sporting goods store. "Locals" are experts on seasonal hatchs and hot spot fishing areas. They can provide you with the flies, etc., needed to be successful.

Fishing With Artificial Lures

SPIN FISHING
David Rye

Spin fishing is the art of casting line a relatively signifi-cant distance to entice fish to hit a variety of food options including lures and natural baits. It has become one of the more popular ways to fish Colorado waters since spin cast-ing does not require extensive training. You still need the skill of knowing where to fish, and what lure or bait to use.

A visit to the local tackle shop can circumvent this problem. Chances are, the local boys already know what the fish are hitting and will share this information with you.

TROLLING

For boat owners, trolling is a great way to fish. There are four key elements that make up successful trolling; proper trolling speed, type of water fished, equipment used, and most important, the depth of water fished.

Fish are more comfortable and numerous at certain water temperatures. As the sun and weather conditions change during the course of the day, different species of fish will seek different water levels.

Measure the temperature of the water before you set your trolling depth. Change trolling depths on a regular basis until you hit on where the fish are. Some fishermen use fish finders to eliminate the guesswork of locating fish.

LURES

In recent years lures and especially plugs that make noise have become increasingly popular. A number of the professional bass tournament fishermen use them with con-sistent success in attracting fish.

Propeller lures have been around for a long time. They are made up of a plug that has been equipped with a metal pro-peller mounted in the front or in the back. They are designed to make a splashing noise when retrieved.

Regardless of what you use, the idea is to make your lure imitate whatever it was designed to look like. If it is a bait fish, it should act like a wounded minnow. Artificial frogs and crayfish should act like those organisms.

The science of fishing with lures requires some experi-mentation. Some fish will respond to a slow, steady retrieve. At other times, they may respond to a fast, erratic retrieve. Vary your retrieve tactics until you hit on the right combination.

PLUGS

Most plugs have been designed to simulate surface swimming organisms such as frogs, crayfish and even mice. If a plug doesn't attract any hits, you have two basic choices. Either change to another plug or change the action of your favorite lure. Adjusting the diving lip of the plug with pliers can vary plug action. Most plugs are manufac-tured to perform a deep dive or simulate a swimming organism.

If the lip is bent down slightly, you can control the depth of the dive. A diving plug can be changed to a sur-face splasher and popper by bending the lip at a 90-degree angle from the face of the plug. Don't be afraid to try dif-ferent angles until you hit upon the right combination.

JIGS

Jigs are designed to sink to the bottom when cast. The rod is jerked upward to pull the jig about a foot off bottom. The slack line is then taken in while the jig is allowed to return to the bottom. The process is repeated until you get a hit or run out of line. Variations in the retrieve such as quick and slow jerks and retrieves can all add up to getting strikes. The idea is to simulate a frantic bait fish.

Although most jigs do not look like bait fish, they have been used over the years to successfully bring in big fish. If you are fishing with a partner who is also using a jig, try casting both jigs in the same area. Fish tend to be attracted to schools of bait fish. In this case, two jigs retrieved together may entice the fish to move into what they think is a school.

Jigs are available in a wide range of weights, sizes and shapes. The head is typically made of lead with a hook that protrudes out and curves above the head. They can be pur-chased with and without any dressing on the hook. Undressed jigs can be baited with natural baits such as night crawlers, salmon eggs or of pork rinds. The dressed version comes in a variety of options. Most have feathers that extend out from the head and cover the hook.

Dressed jigs come in a variety of colors. The light col-ors such as white and yellow are used to simulate bait fish. The darker colors (reds and greens) can be used to help add contrast to the color of the bottom. If the bottom conditions are a light sandy color, a darker color may stand out better than a light color.

PLASTIC WORMS

Many veteran fishermen consider the plastic worm the deadliest of all the artificial lures. They are particularly potent for taking bass. They come in a variety of colors, sizes and shapes. As shown in the illustration that follows, worm rigs can be as simple as a plastic worm draped over a hook or as elaborate as having spinners and feathers trailing the head.

Before you start fishing, get acquainted with the worm rig that you have selected. Cast it out into some shallow water where you can see your worm. Note that the weight-ed head will take it to the bottom leaving the lighter tail to float and wave naturally in the current.

As you begin a slow retrieve, the leaded head will stay on the bottom and kick up mud giving the appearance that the worm is grubbing or feeding. That is the proper action that you want to simulate.

Now for the cast. You may get a strike as soon as the worm hits the surface or before it reaches the bottom. Strikes in this stage are usually very hard and you should set the hook immediately.

The reverse is usually true when you're fishing along the bottom in the manner previously described. You must learn how to distinguish between a tap that is felt from dragging along the bottom and a legitimate strike.

If you are not sure, allow some line to come freely off your reel. If a fish has your worm in its mouth, the line will start to move away in the direction that the fish has elected to swim. When you feel some tension on the line set the hook.

Fish You are Likely to Catch

Wiper

Channel Catfish

Bluegill

Tiger Muskie

White Crappie

Cutthroat Trout

Largemouth Bass

Rainbow Trout

Smallmouth Bass

Brook Trout

Brown Trout

Walleye

Lake Trout (Mackinaw)

Yellow Perch

Kokanee Salmon

Front Range Index Map

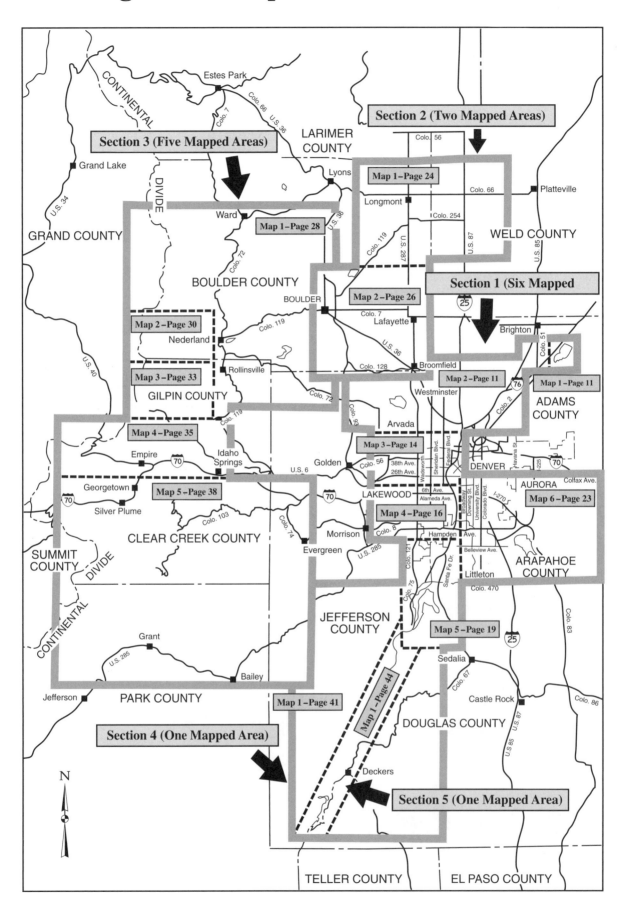

Section 2 (Two Mapped Areas)

Section 3 (Five Mapped Areas)

Section 1 (Six Mapped

Map 1 – Page 24

Map 1 – Page 28

Map 2 – Page 30

Map 3 – Page 33

Map 4 – Page 35

Map 5 – Page 38

Map 2 – Page 26

Map 2 – Page 11

Map 1 – Page 11

Map 3 – Page 14

Map 4 – Page 16

Map 6 – Page 23

Map 5 – Page 19

Map 1 – Page 41

Map 1 – Page 44

Section 4 (One Mapped Area)

Section 5 (One Mapped Area)

CONTINENTAL DIVIDE

GRAND COUNTY

BOULDER COUNTY

LARIMER COUNTY

WELD COUNTY

ADAMS COUNTY

GILPIN COUNTY

CLEAR CREEK COUNTY

SUMMIT COUNTY

CONTINENTAL DIVIDE

PARK COUNTY

JEFFERSON COUNTY

DENVER

AURORA

ARAPAHOE COUNTY

LAKEWOOD

DOUGLAS COUNTY

TELLER COUNTY

EL PASO COUNTY

Estes Park

Grand Lake

Lyons

Ward

Longmont

Platteville

BOULDER

Nederland

Lafayette

Brighton

Rollinsville

Broomfield

Westminster

Arvada

Empire

Idaho Springs

Golden

Georgetown

Silver Plume

Morrison

Evergreen

Grant

Bailey

Jefferson

Sedalia

Castle Rock

Deckers

Littleton

Hampden Ave.

Belleview Ave.

Colfax Ave.

38th Ave.
26th Ave.
6th Ave.
Alameda Ave.

Colo. 7
Colo. 66
U.S. 36
Colo. 56
Colo. 66
Colo. 254
Colo. 119
U.S. 287
U.S. 87
Colo. 51
U.S. 34
U.S. 40
U.S. 36
Colo. 72
Colo. 119
Colo. 7
U.S. 36
Colo. 128
Colo. 72
Colo. 2
Colo. 93
Colo. 56
U.S. 6
Colo. 103
Colo. 74
Colo. 8
U.S. 285
Colo. 121
Colo. 75
Colo. 470
Colo. 67
Colo. 86
U.S. 85 U.S. 87
Colo. 83
Colo. 119
U.S. 285

Sheridan Blvd.
Federal Blvd.
Wadsworth
Broadway
Downing St.
University Blvd.
Colorado Blvd.
Havana St.
Santa Fe Dr.

I-25
I-76
I-70
I-225
I-270

N

8

Front Range Table of Contents

Section 1 Map 1 Barr Lake
1   Barr Lake State Park. 11

Section 1 Map 2 North Metro Area
2   Adams County Fairgrounds Lakes 12
3   Brighton City Park Pond 12
4   Grandview Ponds...............................12
5   Hunter's Glen Lake. 12
5a Loc Amora Pond (Jacob's Pond)........12
6   Broomfield Community Park Ponds ..12
7   Webster Lake......................................12
8   Croke Reservoir (Carlson Res.)..........12
8a Community College Pond 12
8b Westminster City Park Pond 12
8c Water Point and Bellio Ponds (Hyland Ponds)........13
9   Ketner Lake..13
10 Standley Lake 13
11 Pomona Lake. 13
12 Lake Arbor..13
13 Faversham Park Pond 13
14 Camenisch Park Pond 13
15 Bell Roth Park Pond. 13
16 Kiwanis Park Pond 13
17 Rotella Park Pond. 13
18 Engineers Lake...................................14
19 Clear Creek Pond...............................14
20 Twin Lakes Park Ponds 14
21 Arvada Reservoir...............................14

Section 1 Map 3 West Metro Area
22 Lowell Ponds 15
22a Jim Baker Reservoir 15
23 Carl Park Pond...................................15
24 Birdland Lake.....................................15
24a Meadow Park Lake 15
25 Ward Road Pond 15
26 Prospect Park Lakes 15
27 Berkeley Lake 15
28 Rocky Mountain Lake 15
29 Crown Hill Lake 15
30 Sloan Lake 16

Section 1 Map 4 Southwest Metro Area
31 Union Square Ponds...........................16
32 Balsam Park Pond 16
33 Barnum Park Lake 16
34 Garfield Lake......................................16
35 Huston Park Lake...............................17
36 Vanderbilt Park Pond 17
37 Overland Park Pond 17
38 Harvey Park Lake...............................17
39 Bear Creek Ponds...............................17
40 Bear Creek Reservoir 17
41 Soda Lakes 17
42 Main Reservoir (Osner Res.) 17
43 East Reservoir 17
44 Green Gables Park Pond 18
45 Smith Reservoir 18
46 Kendrick Park Reservoir 18
47 Jewell Park Pond 18
48 Cottonwood Park Pond 18
49 Carmody Park Pond 18
49a Harriman Lake Reservoir 18
49b Hine Lake Reservoir 18
49c Blue Heron Pond 18

Section 1 Map 5 South Central Metro Area
50 Centennial Park Lake 20
51 Bowles Grove Pond 20
51a Johnson Reservoir (Clement Park.)....20
52 Lake Geneva 20
52a Progress Park Pond 20
53 Sterne Pond 20
54 Ketring Park Lake (Gallup Lake).... ..20

55 Little's Creek Pond 20
56 Ridgeview Park Pond..........................20
57 South Platte Park Ponds 20
58 Chatfield Reservoir State Park............21
59 Chatfield State Park Ponds.................21

Section 1 Map 6 Southeast Metro Area
60 Washington Park Lakes 23
61 City Park Lake 23
62 Exposition Park Pond 23
63 Garland Park Pond (Lollipop Lake)...23
64 Cherry Creek State Park 23
65 Quincy Reservoir 23
66 Aurora Reservoir 23

Section 2 Map 1 Longmont Area
1   Lagerman Reservoir 25
2   Fairgrounds Lake................................25
3   Golden Ponds.....................................25
4   Loomiller Pond 25
5   Union Reservoir.................................25
6   Barbour Ponds State Park 25
7   Milavec Lake Recreation Area........ ..25

Section 2 Map 2 Boulder/Broomfield Area
8   Boulder Reservoir 26
9   Coot Lake 26
10 Wonderland Lake 27
11 Maxwell Lake 27
12 Walden Ponds 27
13 Sawhill Ponds 27
14 Teller Lake 27
15 Waneka Lake 27
16 Viele Reservoir 27
17 Thunderbird Lake 27
18 Harper Lake..27
19 Stearns Lake 28
20 Boulder Ponds 28

Section 3 Map 1 Mountain Lakes
1   Lake Isabelle 29
2   Long Lake 29
3   Brainard Lake 29
4   Moraine Lake 29
5   Red Rock Lake 29
6   Lefthand Creek Reservoir 29
7   Rainbow Lakes....................................29
8   Barker Reservoir 29
9   Gross Reservoir 29
10 Golden Gate State Park 30
10a Central City Park Ponds 30

Section 3 Map 2 Mountain Lakes
11 Lake Dorothy......................................31
12 Neva Lakes 31
13 Diamond Lake, Upper 31
14 Deep Lake 31
15 Banana Lake 31
16 Diamond Lake 31
17 Storm Lake 31
18 Jasper Lake 31
19 Devil's Thumb Lake 32
20 Skyscraper Reservoir..........................32
21 Woodland Lake 32
22 Bob Lake 32
23 Betty Lake 32
24 King Lake 32
25 Lost Lake 32

Section 3 Map 3 Mountain Lakes
26 Jenny Lake...33
27 Yankee Doodle Lake 33
28 Forest Lakes..33
29 Arapaho Lakes....................................33
30 Crater Lakes 34
31 Clayton Lakes 34

32 Iceberg Lakes......................................34
33 Heart Lake 34
34 Roger Pass Lake 34
35 James Peak Lake 34
35a Little Echo Lake.................................34

Section 3 Map 4 Mountain Lakes
36 Ice Lake 35
37 Steuart Lake..35
38 Reynolds Lake 35
39 Loch Lomond Lake 35
40 Lake Caroline 36
41 Saint Mary's Lake 36
42 Fall River Reservoir 36
43 Slater Lake 36
44 Sherwin Lake 36
45 Chinn's Lake 36
46 Bill Moore Lake 36
47 Byron Lake 37
48 Ethel Lake 37
49 Cone Lake 37
50 Urad Reservoir, Upper........................37
51 Hassel Lake 37

Section 3 Map 5 Mountain Lakes
52 Georgetown Lake 38
53 Clear Lake 38
54 Echo Lake 38
55 Idaho Springs Reservoir 38
56 Chicago Lakes 39
57 Lincoln Lake 39
58 Evergreen Lake 39
59 Roosevelt Lakes...................................39
60 Beartrack Lakes 39
61 Summit Lake 39
62 Abyss Lake 39
63 Frozen Lake 40
64 Square Top Lakes 40
65 Silver Dollar Lake 40
66 Murray Lake 40
67 Shelf Lake 40
68 Gibson Lake...40
69 Pine Valley Ranch Pond 40

Section 4 Map 1 Metro Streams
1   Bear Creek 41
2   Boulder Creek, Middle 41
3   Boulder Creek, North 41
4   Boulder Creek, South 42
5   Clear Creek 42
6   Geneva Creek 42

Section 5 Map 1 South Platte River
1   South Platte River 45
2   South Platte, North Fork 45
3   Strontia Springs Reservoir..................45
4   Cheesman Lake 45

How to Use this Section 10
Appendix 43
Information Phone Numbers 10
Taking care of the catch 37

How to Use Front Range Section

Front Range section contains information for 178 lakes, reservoirs, major streams and rivers near the Boulder/Denver area. Fishing information and location maps have been divided into five sections within the section. Lakes are shown on the map in front of each section by a number. The information for each lake is shown in the text following the map within the section, the map number will proceed the text.

Section 1 - Metro Denver area - (Six maps)
Map 1. Barr Lake.
Map 2. North Metro Denver
Map 3. West Metro Denver
Map 4. Southwest Metro Denver
Map 5. South Central Metro Denver.
Map 6. Southeast Metro Denver.

Section 2 - Longmont/Boulder/Broomfield area - (Two maps)
Map 1. Longmont area.
Map 2. Boulder/Broomfield areas.

Section 3 - Mountain Lakes - (Five maps)
Map 1. Boulder/Nederland area.
Map 2. Eldora area.
Map 3. Tolland/East Portal area.
Map 4. Empire/Alice area.
Map 5. Georgetown/Grant/Idaho Springs area.

Section 4 - Six streams near the Metro Area - (One map)

Section 5 - The South Platte River - (One map)

Fee Information
There are no fees to fish most lakes and reservoirs in this section. Exceptions are: Colorado State Parks, Quincy and Aurora Reservoirs in Aurora, Union Reservoir near Longmont, Milavec Recreation Area near Fredrick, Boulder Reservoir and Arvada Reservoirs. Fishing fees are sometimes waived for walk-in fishermen, this information is noted in the text.

Local lakes and streams provide a good training areas to teach youngsters to fish and sharpen your fishing skills. Both warmwater and coldwater fish are stocked during the summer months.

Phone Numbers Managing Agencies

Adams County Parks & Recreation	(303) 637-8000
Agriculture Ditch and Reservoir Co	(303) 987-2166
Arapaho/Roosevelt National Forest	
Boulder Ranger District	(303) 541-2500
Clear Creek Ranger District	(303) 567-3000
Arvada, City of	(303) 421-2550
Aurora Recreation Administration	(303) 739-6640
Barr Lake State Park	(303) 659-6005
Boulder County Open Space	(303) 441-3950
Boulder (City) Open Space	(303) 441-3440
Broomfield Parks & Recreation	(303) 438-6360
Chatfield Reservoir State Park	(303) 791-7275
Cherry Creek Reservoir State Park	(303) 690-1166
Colorado State Parks	(303) 866-3437
Colorado Division of Wildlife	(303) 297-1192
Denver Parks & Recreation	(303) 964-2500
Denver Water Board	(303) 628-6526
Foothills Metro Park & Recreation	(303) 987-3602
Fredrick, City	(303) 833-2388
Englewood Parks & Recreation	(303) 762-2520
Evergreen Parks & Recreation	(303) 674-0532
Idaho Springs	(303) 567-4421
Jeffco Open Space	(303) 271-5925
Lafayette Parks & Recreation	(303) 665-4206
Lakewood Dept. of Community Res	(303) 987-7800
Littleton Parks & Recreation	(303) 795-3700
Longmont Parks & Forestry	(303) 651-8446
Northglenn Parks	(303) 450-8720
North Jeffco Parks & Recreation	(303) 424-2739
Pike National Forest	
South Platte Ranger District	(303) 275-5610
South Platte Park Ponds (Carson Nature Center)	(303) 730-1022
South Suburban Rec. District	(303) 798-2493
Thornton Parks & Recreation	(303) 255-7831
Westminster Parks & Rec	(303) 430-2400
Wheat Ridge Parks	(303) 422-2790

General Information
General fishing license and fee information

	(303) 291-7533
U.S. Geological Survey map sales.	(303) 202-4700
Fishing Report	(303) 291-7534

Campground reservation and addtional state, federal and city phone numbers on page 42.

1 Barr Lake State Park

Location: North of 128th Ave. between Interstate 76 and Picadilly Road. From I-70 go east on Bromley Lane to Picadilly Road, then south on Picadilly to park entrance. Parking areas are on the east side of lake.
Size: 1,900 acres; 42 feet maximum depth.
Fish: Carp, channel catfish, crappie, largemouth bass, smallmouth bass, rainbow trout (catchable-sized stocked) sucker, yellow perch, wiper and tiger muskie.

Agency: Colorado State Parks.
Comments: Open 5 a.m. to 10 p.m. Motor boats 10 HP or less. No boating in the wildlife refuge. Fee area with free walk-in access. Premier carp and channel catfish fishery. Extreme water level fluctuation. No fishing from dam. May close due to capacity. Boat ramp on east side by parking area. Nature center & trails. Eagle and wildlife viewing area.

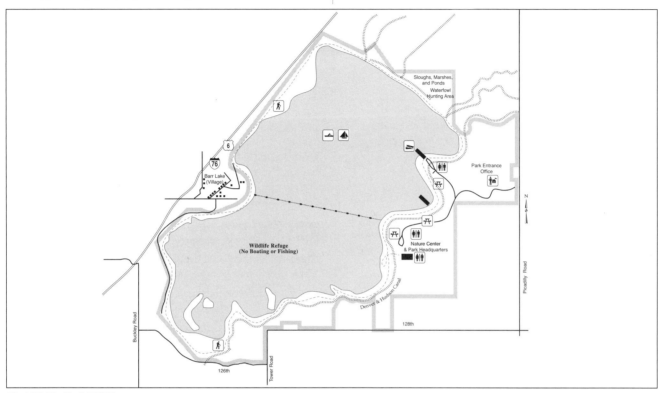

BARR LAKE

SECTION 1 - MAP 1

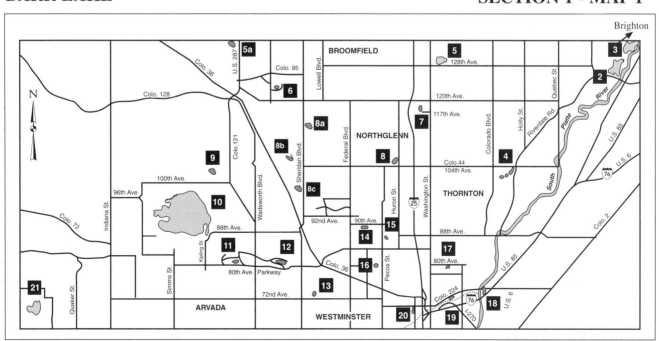

SECTION 1 - MAP 2

2 Adams County Fairground Lakes
Mann Lake

Location: Adams County Regional Park. 9755 Henderson Road. 1 mile west of US 85 on 124th Avenue. Parking area north side of lake.
Size: 50 acres.
Fish: Crappie, largemouth bass, catfish, bluegill, carp.
Agency: Adams County Parks & Community Resources.
Comments: Open 7 a.m. to 11 p.m. Restrooms available, camping in designated sites.

Public Works Lake

Location: Adams County Regional Park. 9755 Henderson Road. 1 mile west of US 85 on 124th Avenue. Parking in campground, handicap accessible.
Size: 20 acres.
Fish: Crappie, largemouth bass, catfish, bluegill carp.
Agency: Adams County Parks & Community Resources.
Comments: Open 7 a.m. to 11 p.m. Restrooms available, camping in designated sites, handicap accessible.

3 Brighton City Park Lake

Location: From highway 85, east on Hwy 7 to 11th Ave., north on 11th Ave. to Baseline Rd. Lake is on the SW corner of 11th and Baseline Rd.
Size: 2.4 acres; maximum depth 16 feet.
Fish: Largemouth bass, bluegill, crappie, yellow perch, channel catfish, and catchable trout. (In Spring.)
Agency: City of Brighton.
Comments: Handicapped accessible fishing pier. No Boats. Fish habitat improvements in pond.

4 Grandview Ponds

Location: Adams County - Off 104th and Riverdale Rd.
Size: 4 ponds; 10 acres total; 8 feet maximum depth.
Agency: Colorado Division of Wildlife.
Fish: Largemouth bass, bluegill, channel catfish, crappie, bullhead, green sunfish, and yellow perch.
Special Regulations: All largemouth bass and smallmouth bass taken must be 15 inches or longer.
Comments: Parking area off 104th Ave.

5 Hunter's Glen Lake

Location: Northeast of the intersection of 128th and Washington. Parking area access from 128th.
Size: 19.8 acres; 5 feet maximum depth (3 feet average).
Fish: Largemouth bass, bluegill, green sunfish, crappie and channel catfish.
Agency: Thornton Department of Parks & Recreation.
Comments: Belly boats allowed.

5a Loc Amora Pond (Jacob's Pond)

Location: From intersection of Hwy 287 and Interstate 36, go north through Broomfield on Hwy 287. Turn west on Miramonte Blvd. and follow to Loc Amora Park, pond is located on south side of park.
Size: 3.0 acres; 8 feet maximum depth.
Fish: Largemouth bass, bluegill, pumpkinseed sunfish, black bullhead, and channel catfish.
Agency: Broomfield Parks and Recreation Department.
Comments: No boats. Handicapped accessible fishing pier accessed off of Rock Creek Rd.

6 Broomfield Community Park Ponds

Location: East of Hwy 287 (Quartz Street), via Midway Blvd. Parking by east pond at Main Street and Community Park Drive.
Size: 2 ponds; 3 acres total; 6 feet maximum depth.
Fish: Largemouth bass, bluegill, bullhead, channel catfish, green sunfish, and yellow perch.
Agency: Broomfield Parks & Recreation.
Comments: Open 5 a.m. to 11 p.m. No boats. Playground and restrooms.

7 Webster Lake

Location: Entrance on E. 117th Ave. west of Washington Street. Parking area on 117th.
Size: 13 acres; 12 feet maximum depth.
Fish: Bluegill, bullhead, channel catfish, crappie, largemouth bass, yellow perch and rainbow trout (catchable size stocked).
Agency: Northglenn Parks & Recreation.
Comments: Open 5 a.m. to 11p.m. No boats. Handicapped accessible fishing pier on the south shore. Playground and restrooms. Extreme water level fluctuation. Hard surface foot trail.

8 Croke Reservoir (Carlson Reservoir)

Location: North of 104th and Huron St.
Size: 16 acres; 10 feet maximum depth.
Fish: Largemouth bass, pumpkinseed sunfish, bluegill, green sunfish and black bullhead.
Agency: Northglenn Parks & Recreation.
Special Regulations: All largemouth and smallmouth bass taken must be 15 inches or larger. Fishing by artificial flies or lures only. No boats or tubing.
Comments: Fishing allowed from April 1 thru Oct. 15. Open 5 a.m. to 11 p.m. north shore closed to fishing.

8a Community College Pond

Location: From intersection of 112th Ave. and Sheridan Blvd., go east on 112th. Park in farthest west parking lot of Front Range Community College. Take foot-trail along path north to lake.
Size: 2.4 acres; 12 feet maximum depth.
Fish: Largemouth bass, bluegill, yellow perch, crappie and channel catfish.
Agency: Westminster Parks and Recreation Department.
Comments: Underwater artificial fish habitat structures (tree bundles, Christmas trees, etc.) placed in lake during construction. Lake is handicapped accessible from the Big Dry Creek recreation trail. No Boats.

8b Westminster City Park Pond

Location: At 104th Ave. and Sheridan Blvd., go north on Sheridan, take first left into Westminster Recreation Facility entrance. Then take first right and follow service road around north side of soccer fields, the lake sits northwest of the recreation center.
Size: 7.4 acres; 14 feet maximum depth.
Fish: Largemouth bass, bluegill, yellow perch, crappie and rainbow trout (catchable size in spring).
Agency: Westminster Parks and Recreation Department.
Comments: Foot-trail around entire lake, handicapped

accessible from cement pavilion area on east side, surrounding picnic areas. No boats. Fish habitat improvements in pond.

8c Water Point and Bellio Ponds (Hyland Ponds)

Location: Turn west onto 100th Ave. from Sheridan Blvd. parking available along street. Walk-in access from foot-trails.
Size: Two lakes: 2.5 acres each; 14 feet maximum depth.
Fish: Largemouth bass, bluegill, green sunfish and channel catfish.
Agency: Westminster Parks and Recreation Department.
Comments: No boats. Handicapped accessible fishing piers. Fish habitat improvements in ponds.

9 Ketner Lake

Location: Off west 100th Ave. and County Side Drive.
Size: 25 acres; 30 feet maximum depth.
Fish: Largemouth bass, crappie, bluegill, green sunfish, yellow perch and bullhead.
Agency: City of Westminster.
Comments: Belly boats allowed for fishing. Ice fishing prohibited.
Special Regulations: All largemouth and smallmouth bass taken must be 15 inches or longer.

10 Standley Lake

Location: W. 88th Ave. and Kipling Street. Parking area is off Kipling. West side of the lake - Eagle nest area, fishing restricted.
Size: 1,210 acres; 80 feet maximum depth.
Fish: Bluegill, carp, channel catfish, green sunfish, large-mouth bass, smallmouth bass, sucker, walleye, yellow perch, wiper and rainbow trout (catchable size stocked).
Agency: South and southwest shore, Jefferson County Open Space. Remaining shore and lake itself, City of Westminster Parks & Recreation.
Comments: Hours as posted, walk-in only spring and fall. All boats over 20 h.p. need Westminster boat permit. Fee area for vehicles at Kipling & W. 88th Ave. Walk-in fishing free. Extreme water fluctuation. Boat ramp on east shore and north shore (dirt boat ramp).No fishing from dam.
Special Regulations: All wipers taken must be 15 inches or longer.

11 Pomona Lake

Location: In Meadow Glen Park. North of W. 80th Ave. and one-quarter mile west of Wadsworth Blvd. Main parking area can be reached via 80th Ave. by going north on Club Crest Drive, and east on W. 81st Place.
Size: 31 acres; 8 feet maximum depth.
Fish: Largemouth bass, yellow perch, bullhead, channel catfish, crappie and green sunfish.
Agency: North Jeffco Parks & Recreation.
Comments: Open dawn to 11 p.m. No boats. Paved trail.

12 Lake Arbor

Location: North of W. 80th Ave. off Pomona Drive or Lamar Street between Wadsworth Blvd. and Sheridan Blvd.
Size: 37 acres; 19 feet maximum depth.
Fish: Bluegill, bullhead, carp, channel catfish, crappie, green sunfish, largemouth bass, pumpkinseed sunfish and sucker. Grass carp stocked to control aquatic plants.
Agency: North Jeffco Parks & Recreation and City of Arvada.
Comments: Open dawn to 11 p.m. Non-motorized boats only. Fishing piers located on the north shore. Artificial fish habitat structures in lake. Playground. Hard surface foot trail.
Special Regulations: All Largemouth and Smallmouth Bass taken must be 15 inches or longer. Bag and possession limits for walleye is 5 fish, 15 inches or longer.

13 Faversham Park Pond

Location: Depew and 73rd Ave., NW off 72nd Ave.
Size: 6 acres; 11 feet maximum depth.
Fish: Bluegill.
Agency: Westminster Parks & Recreation.
Comments: Open sunrise to 11 p.m. No boats. No wading or swimming. Kids 15 years old and under are allowed to fish.

14 Camenisch Park Pond

Location: West of Pecos Street, south of W. 90th Ave. at Fontaine Street. Parking area south of 90th Ave.
Size: 3 acres; 10 feet maximum depth.
Fish: Largemouth bass, pumpkinseed sunfish, sucker, bluegill, bullhead, channel catfish, crappie and green sun-fish.
Agency: Hyland Hills Recreation & Park District.
Comments: Open dawn to 10 p.m. No boats. Playground and restrooms. Hard surface foot trail.

15 Bell Roth Park Pond

Location: On the east side of Pecos Street, 2 blocks north of W. 84th Ave.
Size: 3 acres; 8 feet maximum depth.
Fish: Channel catfish, crappie, green sunfish, sucker, yellow perch, bluegill, bullhead and carp.
Agency: Hyland Hills Recreation & Park District.
Comments: Open dawn to 10 p.m. No boats. Playground.

16 Kiwanis Park Pond

Location: W. 80th Ave. east of Zuni Street. Parking area south of 80th Ave.
Size: 3 acres; 2 feet maximum depth.
Fish: Bullhead and green sunfish.
Agency: Hyland Hills Recreation & Park District.
Comments: Open dawn to half hour after sunset. No boats.

17 Rotella Park Pond

Location: North of E. 78th Ave. between N. Washington Street and N. York Street. Parking north of 78th Ave. or south of Coronado Drive So.
Size: 3 acres; 10 feet maximum depth.
Fish: Bluegill, bullhead, largemouth bass, channel catfish and pumpkinseed sunfish.

Agency: Adams County Park & Recreation.
Comments: Open dawn to dusk. No boats. Extreme water level fluctuation. Playground and restrooms. Hard surface foot trail.

18 Engineers Lake
Location: From I-76 go to Hwy 224. Travel west on Hwy 224. Parking area is south of Hwy 224, just west of the South Platte River. The lake is at the confluence of Clear Creek and the South Platte River. Hard surface foot trail across the river.
Size: 11 acres; 25 feet maximum depth.
Fish: Bullhead.
Agency: Adams County Parks & Recreation.
Comments: Open dawn to dusk. No boats. Walk-in trail and steep shoreline. Picnic shelter.

19 Clear Creek Pond
Location: South of Hwy 224 between Washington Street and York Street. Parking area is south of Hwy 224 and east of Washington Street.
Size: 3 acres; 9 feet maximum depth.
Fish: Bluegill, bullhead, carp, channel catfish, crappie, pumpkinseed sunfish, green sunfish, largemouth bass and yellow perch.
Agency: Adams County Parks & Recreation.
Comments: Open dawn to dusk. No boats. Hard surface trail along side of pond.

20 Twin Lakes Park Ponds
Location: Just west of Broadway on 70th Ave. Parking area south from 70th Ave.
Size: 2 ponds; 7 acres total; 16 feet maximum depth.
Fish: Bullhead, carp, channel catfish, crappie, green sunfish, largemouth bass, sucker and yellow perch.
Agency: Adams County Parks & Recreation.
Comments: Open dawn to dusk. No boats Hard surface foot trail which connects with Clear Creek Trail.

21 Arvada Reservoir
Location: Between Hwy 93 and Indiana on W 66th Ave.
Size: 180 acres; 77 feet maximum depth.
Fish: Rainbow trout (catchable-size stocked), tiger muskie, walleye, largemouth bass, smallmouth bass, yellow perch.
Agency: City of Arvada.
Comments: Arvada permit required; available at Arvada City Hall - Daily passes sold at gate. No ice fishing. Non-motorized boats only. Open sunrise to sunset. Hard surface foot trail.
Special Regulations: Two trout bag limit.

End Section 1 - Map 2

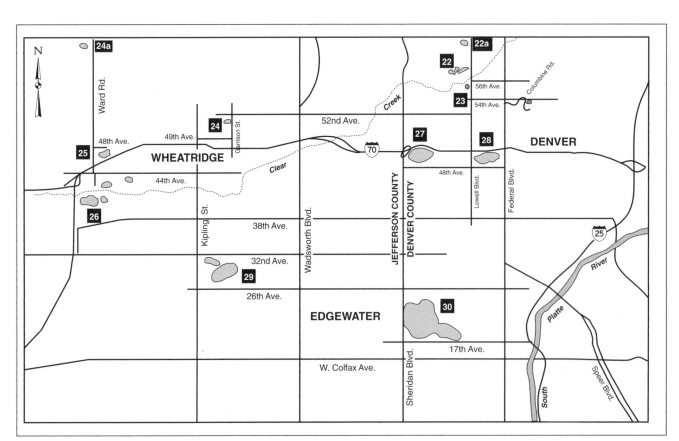

SECTION 1 - MAP 3

22 Lowell Ponds
Location: Adams County, West of Lowell Street on 56th Way.
Size: 3 ponds; 11,2 and 2 acres. Plus Sheets Lake, 5 acres. (Leased from City of Westminster.) Maximum Depth 10 ft.
Fish: Largemouth bass, smallmouth bass, channel catfish, bluegill, crappie and bullhead.
Agency: Colorado Division of Wildlife.
Comments: Belly boats allowed for fishing, except on Sheets Lake. Handicapped accessible fishing pier. Artificial fish habitat structures in ponds.
Special Regulation: All largemouth and small-mouth bass taken must be 15 inches or longer.

22a Jim Baker Reservoir
Location: South of 64th Ave. and Lowell Blvd. intersection on West side of Lowell. Parking area at South-West corner of reservoir, access off of Tennyson St. from 64th Ave.
Size: 80 acres; 30 feet maximum depth.
Fish: Rainbow trout (catchable-size stocked), smallmouth bass, yellow perch, walleye, bluegill and crappie.
Agency: Adams County Parks and Recreation Department.
Comments: Walk-in access along foot trails. No boats.

23 Carl Park Pond
Location: West of Federal Blvd., on W. 54th Ave. at Meade Street. Parking area north of 54th Ave.
Size: 4 acres; 8 feet maximum depth.
Fish: Largemouth bass, bluegill and bullhead.
Agency: Hyland Hills Recreation & Park District.
Comments: Open dawn to 10 p.m. No boats.

24 Birdland Lake (Jack B. Tomlinson Park)
Location: W 51st Ave. and Garrison Street. Parking area west of Garrison at south end of lake.
Size: 3 acres; 10 feet maximum depth.
Fish: Bluegill, channel catfish, green sunfish, largemouth bass, pumpkinseed sunfish and yellow perch.
Agency: North Jeffco Recreation & Park District.
Comments: Open dawn to 11 p.m. Non-motorized boats only. No ice fishing. Playground and hard surface trail.

24a Meadow Park Lake
Location: West of intersection of Ward Rd. and W. 64th Ave. Turn south on Yank Way from 64th Ave., then right to Yank Ct.
Size: 5 acres; 8 feet maximum depth.
Fish: Largemouth bass, bluegill, pumpkinseed sunfish, crappie, yellow perch, black bullhead and common carp.
Agency: City of Arvada.
Comments: No boats.

25 Ward Road Pond
Location: Northeast of the intersection of I-70 and Ward Road. Parking area east of Ward Road and South of W. 48th Ave.
Size: 7 acres; 30 feet maximum depth.
Fish: Largemouth bass, pumpkinseed sunfish, bluegill, bullhead, crappie and green sunfish.
Agency: City of Arvada and Colorado Division of Wildlife.
Comments: Non-motorized boats only. Belly boats allowed. Pond open for fishing only. Good bass fishing.

Restroom. Artificial fish habitat structures in pond.
Special Regulations: 1. Fishing by artificial flies or artificial lures only; 2. All fish caught must be returned to water immediately.

26 Prospect Park Lakes
Location: East of I-70 and south of W. 44th Ave. Parking for Prospect Lake and North Prospect Lake is available south on 44th on Robb Street, next to park headquarters. Parking for West Lake and Bass Lake is available south of 44th on Youngfield Street. Foot trail runs between all the lakes along Clear Creek.
Size: Bass Lake - 3 acres; 13 feet maximum depth.
North Prospect - 16 acres; 26 feet maximum depth.
Prospect Lake - 7 acres; 22 feet maximum depth.
West Lake - 46 acres; 15 feet maximum depth.
Fish: **Bass Lake:** Largemouth bass, bluegill, crappie, green sunfish, and sucker.
North Prospect: (Tabor): Largemouth bass, bluegill, channel catfish, crappie and green sunfish. Artificial fish habitat structures in lake.
Prospect Lake: Largemouth bass, bluegill, channel catfish, crappie and green sunfish.
West Lake: Largemouth bass, pumpkinseed sunfish, sucker, bluegill, bullhead, crappie and green sunfish. Artificial fish habitat structures in lake.
Agency: Wheat Ridge Parks & Recreation.
Comments: Open dawn to dusk except for Prospect Lake, which is open until 10 p.m. No boats on Bass Lake. Non-motorized boats allowed on other lakes with a Wheat Ridge Parks Permit. Prospect Lake has a boat ramp and restrooms. Good bass fishing. Some steep banks. Hard surface trail along Clear Creek.
Special Regulations: 1. All smallmouth and largemouth bass taken must be 15 inches in length or longer; 2. Bass Lake and West Prospect Lake (south of Clear Creek) - fishing by artificial flies or artificial lures only.

27 Berkeley Lake
Location: South of I-70 between Sheridan Blvd. and Tennyson Street. Main entrance is on 46th Ave. with parking. Also access from Tennyson Street.
Size: 40 acres; 12 feet maximum depth.
Fish: Largemouth bass, orange spotted sunfish, sucker, green sunfish, bluegill, bullhead, carp, channel catfish, crappie and rainbow trout (catchable size stocked in spring).
Agency: Denver Parks & Recreation.
Comments: Open 5 a.m. to 11 p.m. No boats. Recreation center, Playground and restrooms on the south side of lake.

26 Rocky Mountain Lake
Location: W. 46th Ave. between Federal Blvd. and Lowell Blvd. Parking areas north of 46th Ave.
Size: 29 acres; 14 feet maximum depth.
Fish: Rainbow trout (catchable size stocked in spring), bluegill, bullhead, carp, channel catfish, crappie, green sunfish, largemouth bass, pumpkinseed sunfish, sucker.
Agency: Denver Parks & Recreation.
Comments: Open 5 a.m. to 11 p.m. No boats. Playground and restrooms. Hard surface foot trail.

27 Crown Hill Lake
Location: Northeast of the intersection of Kipling

Front Range - Section 1 - Map

Street and W. 26th Ave. Parking access is north of 26th Ave. with two parking areas. Hard surface foot trail and bridle path access also from Kipling.
Size: 53 acres; 13 feet maximum depth.
Fish: Largemouth bass, bluegill, sucker, carp, channel catfish, crappie, green sunfish and yellow perch.
Agency: Jeffco Open Space.
Comments: Open one hour prior to dawn, closed one hour past dusk. Restrooms on 26th Ave. side of lake. No boats. Playground. Several artificial fish habitat structures in the lake. No wading or float tubes. Handicapped fishing pier north of parking lot. Wildlife sanctuary.

30 Sloan Lake
Location: East of Sheridan Blvd. between W. 25th Ave. and W 17th Ave. Parking area all around lake.
Size: 174 acres; 9 feet maximum depth.
Fish: Bluegill, bullhead, carp, channel catfish, crappie, green sunfish, orange spotted sunfish, rainbow trout (catchable-size stocked in spring), sucker and yellow perch.
Agency: Denver Parks and Recreation.
Comments: Boating with permit. No fishing from boats. Premier carp fishery. Boat house and boat ramp. Playground and restrooms. Hard surface foot trail around lake.

- -
End Section 1 Map 3

31 Union Square Ponds
Location: South of W. 6th Ave. and West of S. Union St.. Access via W. 2nd Place and S. VanGordon St. The ponds are just west of the Denver Federal Center.
Size: 5 ponds; 8 acres total; 8 feet maximum depth.
Fish: Bluegill, carp, channel catfish, green sunfish and largemouth bass.

Agency: Union Square Development Co. and Lakewood Parks and Recreation.
Comments: No boats.

32 Balsam Park Pond
Location: West of S Wadsworth, south Of W. 1st Ave. at Balsam St.
Size: 1.5 acres; 6 feet maximum depth.
Fish: Bluegill, bullhead, carp, crappie, green sunfish, and sucker.
Agency: Lakewood Department of Community Resources.
Comments: Open dawn to 10:30 p.m. No boats.

33 Barnum Park Lake
Location: West of Federal Blvd. between 6th Ave. and 3rd Ave., with parking access from Hooker St.
Size: 9 acres; 5 feet maximum depth.
Fish: Bluegill, carp, channel catfish and sucker.
Agency: Denver Parks and Recreation.
Comments: Open 5 a.m. to 11 p.m. No boats. Playground, restrooms and recreation center.

34 Garfield Lake
Location: South of W. Mississippi Ave. between S. Federal Blvd. and S. Sheridan Blvd. Access from either S. Lowell Blvd. and Mississippi, or S. Newton St. and W. Arizona (east from S. Osceola St.).
Size: 10 acres; 4 feet maximum depth.
Fish: Largemouth bass, bluegill, carp, channel catfish, crappie, and green sunfish.
Agency: Denver Parks and Recreation.
Comments: Open 5 a.m. to 11 p.m. No boats. Recreation Center, playground and restrooms.

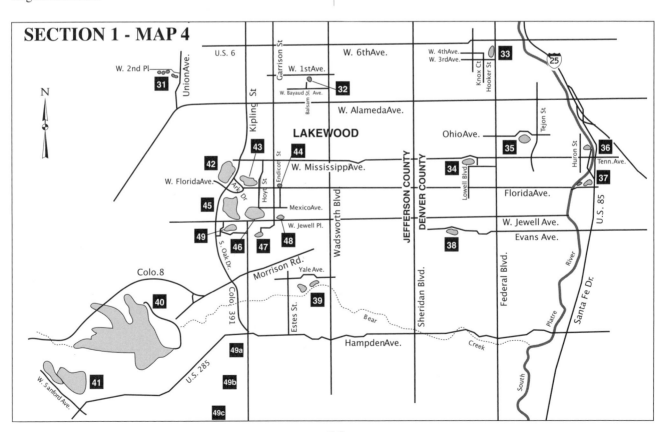

35 Huston Park Lake

Location: East of S. Federal Blvd. about 4 blocks, between W. Ohio Ave. and W. Kentucky Ave. Southeast of the intersection of Ohio and S. Clay St.
Size: 13 acres; 6 feet maximum depth.
Fish: Largemouth bass, sucker, yellow perch, green sunfish, bluegill, bullhead, carp, channel catfish, and crappie.
Agency: Denver Parks and Recreation.
Comments: Open 5 a.m. to 11 p.m. No boats, Recreation Center, playground and restrooms. Hard surface foot trail around lake.

36 Vanderbilt Park Pond

Location: North of W. Tennessee Ave. between S. Santa Fe Drive and S. Huron St. in Vanderbilt Park. Access from W. Mississippi Ave.
Size: 6 acres; 15 feet maximum depth.
Fish: Green sunfish.
Agency: Denver Parks and Recreation.
Comments: Open 5 a.m. to 11 p.m. No boats. Hard surface foot trail.

37 Overland Park Pond

Location: North of W. Florida Ave. between S. Santa Fe Dr. and South Platte River Trail. Parking area is north of Florida.
Size: 1 acre; 7 feet maximum depth.
Fish: Bluegill, carp, largemouth bass, bullhead and crappie.
Agency: Denver Parks and Recreation.
Comments: Open 5 a.m. to 11 p.m. No boats. Fly casting practice pad on south shore. Hard surface foot trail.

38 Harvey Park Lake

Location: Between S Sheridan Blvd. and S. Federal. Just south of W. Evans Ave. and east of S. Tennyson St. Hard surface foot trail across from Evans.
Size: 8.5 acres; 14 feet maximum depth.
Fish: Bluegill, bullhead, carp, channel catfish, crappie, green sunfish, largemouth bass pumpkinseed sunfish, and yellow perch.
Agency: Denver Parks and Recreation.
Comments: Open 5 a.m. to 11 p.m. No boats. Recreation Center. Playground and restrooms.

39 Bear Creek Ponds

Location: West of S Wadsworth and south of Yale Ave. on the east side of S. Estes St. Parking on Estes Street.
Size: 10 acres total; 12 feet maximum depth.
Fish: Bluegill, bullhead, channel catfish, crappie, green sunfish, and largemouth bass.
Agency: Lakewood Department of Community Resources.
Comments: Open 6 a.m. to 10 p.m. No boats. Fishing pier on the west side of the west pond.

40 Bear Creek Reservoir

Location: South of Morrison Rd. (Hwy 8), north of W. Hampden Ave. (US 285), west of S. Kipling St., and east of C-470. The main entrance to the park is on Morrison Rd., with several parking areas on the north side of the reservoir.
Size: 110 acres; 36 feet maximum depth.
Fish: Largemouth bass, smallmouth bass, bluegill, green sunfish, bullhead, rainbow trout, (catchable-size stocked), sucker, tiger muskie, and yellow perch.
Agency: Lakewood Department of Community Resources.
Comments: Open 7 a.m. to 8 p.m. from May to September. Open 7 a.m. to 8 p.m. in October and April. Open 8 a.m. to 6 p.m. from November to March. Boats to 10 hp at wakeless speeds. Boat ramp and picnic shelter on the north side of the reservoir. Fee area $3.00 per car, free walk in access. Ice fishing allowed as posted.
Special Regulations: Tiger muskie; one fish only, 30 inches or longer.

41 Soda Lakes

Location: South of Morrison Road (Hwy 8), north of W. Hampden Ave. (US 285), west of S. Kipling Street, and east of C 4-70. The main entrance to the park is on Morrison Road, with several parking areas on the north side of the reservoir. Also an entrance on Soda Lakes Road, for park and walk access.
Size: Big Soda (South) - 96 acres.
   Little Soda (North) - 44 acres. 40 feet maximum depth.
Fish: Yellow perch, largemouth and smallmouth bass, channel catfish, green sunfish and sucker.
Agency: Lakewood Department of Community Resources.
Comments: Non-motorized boat rental area on Big Soda.

42 Main Reservoir (Osner Reservoir)

Location: West of S. Kipling Street between W. Mississippi Ave. and W. Florida Ave.
Size: 45 acres; 19 feet maximum depth.
Fish: Bluegill, carp, channel catfish, crappie, green sunfish, largemouth bass, pumpkinseed sunfish, rainbow trout (catchable size stocked in spring), smallmouth bass, sucker and yellow perch.
Agency: Lakewood Department of Community Resources.
Comments: Open 6:00 a.m. to 10:00. No boats. Extreme water level fluctuation.

43 East Reservoir

Location: East of Kipling Street between W. Florida Ave. and W. Mississippi Ave. Access from W. Florida via W. Arkansas Drive.
Size: 21 acres; 5 feet maximum depth.
Fish: Bullhead, carp, green sunfish, largemouth bass pumpkinseed sunfish and yellow perch.
Agency: Lakewood Department of Community Resources.
Comments: Open 5 a.m. to 10 p.m.. No boats. Extreme water level fluctuation.

44 Green Gables Park Pond
Location: 1450 Garrison Street. Six blocks north of Jewell on Garrison Street. Parking off Garrison. Hard surface trail around pond.
Size: 0.5 acres; 6 feet maximum depth.
Fish: Bluegill, crappie, green sunfish, largemouth bass and pumpkinseed sunfish.
Agency: Foothills Park Metro. & Recreation District.
Comments: Open 5 a.m. to 10 p.m. No boats, wading or flotation devices.

45 Smith Reservoir
Location: East of S. Kipling Street, north of Jewell Ave. Parking area east of S. Moore Court.
Size: 44 acres; 17 feet maximum depth.
Fish: Bluegill, carp, channel catfish, crappie, green sunfish, largemouth bass, pumpkinseed sunfish, smallmouth bass, sucker and yellow perch.
Agency: Lakewood Department of Community Resources.
Comments: Open 5:00 a.m. to 11:00 p.m. No boats. Extreme water level fluctuation. Two previous state record smallmouth bass caught here.

46 Kendrick Park Reservoir
Location: 9500 W. Jewell Ave. 9 blocks west of Wadsworth on the north side of Jewell. Playground and trail access off South Hoyt Street.
Size: 33 acres; 8 feet maximum depth.
Fish: Bluegill, bullhead, carp, channel catfish, crappie, largemouth bass, pumpkinseed sunfish and yellow perch.
Agency: Foothills Metro. Parks & Recreation District.
Comments: Open dawn to 10:00 p.m. No boats, wading or flotation devices. Fishing pier on southwest shore.

47 Jewell Park Pond
Location: North of W. Jewell Ave. between S. Garrison Street and S. Wadsworth Blvd. Access from S. Dover Way.
Size: 2 acres; 5 feet maximum depth.
Fish: Bluegill, bullhead, carp, channel catfish, crappie, green sunfish and pumpkinseed sunfish.
Agency: Lakewood Department of Community Resources.
Comments: Open dawn to 10:30 p.m. Non-motorized boats only. Fishing pier on the south shore. Hard Surface foot trail.

48 Cottonwood Park Lake
Location: From the Kipling Parkway and W. Jewell Ave., go east on Jewell to S. Oak Street. Then 1 block south on Oak to Park. On Street parking on Oak St. Lake and hard surface trails 75 yards east of Oak St.
Size: 8 acres; 14 feet maximum depth.
Fish: Bluegill, channel catfish, largemouth bass, pumpkinseed sunfish and yellow perch.
Agency: Foothills Metro. Parks & Recreation District.
Comments: Open 5:00 a.m. to 10:00 p.m. No boats, wading or floatation devices.

49 Carmody Park Pond
Location: 2200 South Old Kipling Street. From Kipling Parkway and Jewell head east on Jewell to old Kipling Street. 50 yards east of swimming complex.
Size: .25 acres; 4 feet maximum depth.
Fish: Bluegill, bullhead and largemouth bass.
Agency: Foothills Metro. Park & Recreation District.
Comments: Open 5 a.m. to 10 p.m. No boats, wading or floatation devices.

49a Harriman Lake Reservoir
Location: W. Quincy Ave. and S. Kipling Parkway. Parking off Kipling. Trail to lake.
Size: 70 acres; 18 feet maximum depth.
Fish: Bluegill, green catfish, largemouth bass, crappie, common carp and white sucker.
Agency: Foothills Metro. Park & Recreation District.
Comments: Open 5 a.m. to 10 p.m. No boats, wading or floatation devices.

49b Hine Lake Reservoir
Location: From west Coalmine Road and South Simms Street Head West on Coalmine Road 1/4 mile to S. Van Gordon. Street. Park in ridge at West Meadow Park parking lot. Hard surface foot trail around half the lake.
Size: 50 acres; 15 feet maximum depth.
Fish: Bluegill, largemouth bass, pumpkinseed sunfish, green sunfish and hybrid bluegill.
Agency: Foothills Metro. Park & Recreation District.
Comments: Open 5 a.m. to 10 p.m. No boats, wading or floatation devices. Playground and picnic area.

49c Blue Heron Lake
Location: Go north on S. Simms St. from intersection of W. Bowles Ave. and S. Simms St. turn right on W. Brandt Place follow to T-intersection at S. Quail St. Parking allowed along street.
Size: 8 acres; 12 feet maximum depth.
Fish: Largemouth bass, bluegill, crappie, green sunfish, black bullhead and fathead minnow.
Agency: Foothills Metro. Park and Recreation Department.
Comments: Playground and foot trail around lake. No boats.

End Section 1 Map 4

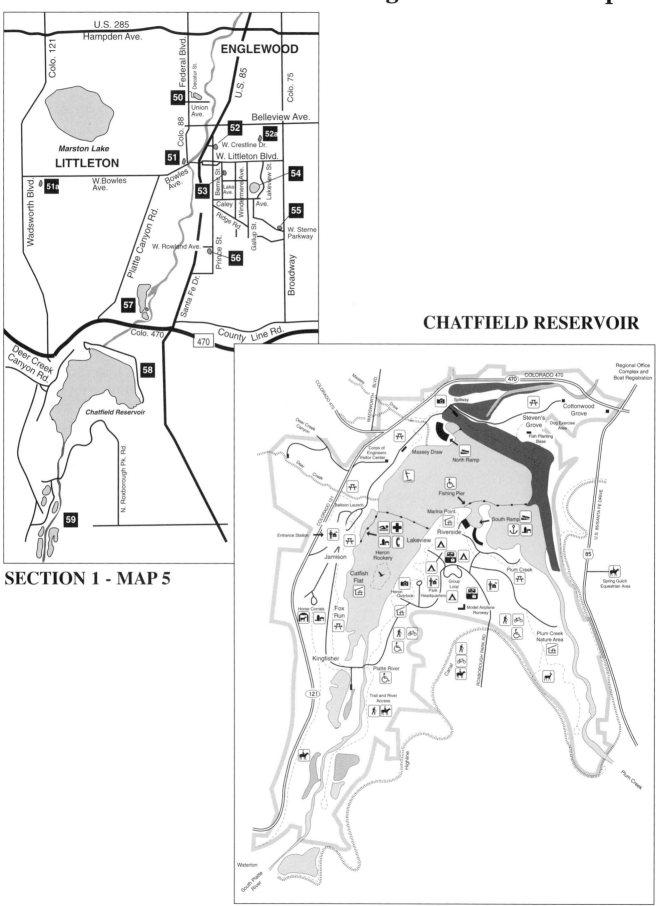

SECTION 1 - MAP 5

CHATFIELD RESERVOIR

Begin Section 1 Map 5

50 Centennial Park Lake
Location: From the intersection of W. Union Ave. and S. Federal Blvd., go north on Federal to Stanford Ave. Turn east on Stanford to S. Decatur Street. Parking area is on the northeast corner of the intersection of Decatur and Stanford. There is a parking area further south of Decatur past the softball field.
Size: 15 acres; 27 feet maximum depth.
Fish: Largemouth and smallmouth bass, pumpkinseed sunfish, rainbow trout (catchable-size stocked), yellow perch, bluegill, channel catfish, sucker, crappie and green sunfish.
Agency: Englewood Parks & Recreation.
Comments: Open dawn to 11 p.m. No boats. Playground and restrooms. Handicapped accessible fishing pier on the west side of the lake. Hard surface foot trail to the pier. Artificial fish habitat structures in lake.

51 Bowles Grove Pond
Location: Northwest of the intersection of S. Federal Blvd. and W. Bowles Ave. Parking west of Federal at north end of the lake.
Size: 2 acres; 6 feet maximum depth.
Fish: Largemouth bass, bluegill, bullhead, carp, crappie, green sunfish, orange spotted sunfish, sucker and yellow perch.
Agency: South Suburban Recreation & Park District.
Comments: Open 6 a.m. to 10 p.m. No boats hard surface foot trail.

52 Johnson Reservoir (Clement Park)
Location: At the corner of W. Bowles Ave. and S. Wadsworth Blvd. Parking available in Clement Park, directly east of lake.
Size: 58.5 acres; 12 feet maximum depth.
Fish: Largemouth bass, bluegill, yellow perch, crappie, smallmouth bass, common carp and some rainbow trout privately stocked from fishing clinic events.
Agency: Foothills Parks and Recreation Department, Jefferson County Open Space.
Comments: Hard surface foot-trail around lake perimeter, cement pavilion areas and no boats.

52 Lake Geneva
Location: South of Crestline Ave. between S. Prince Street and S. Windermere Street. South of the Arapaho County Administration Building.
Size: 1 acre; 12 feet maximum depth.
Fish: Bluegill, crappie, green sunfish, bullhead, carp, channel catfish, sucker and largemouth bass.
Agency: City of Littleton.
Comments: No boats. Fishing is for Handicapped persons, senior citizens only and kids under 15 only.

52a Progress Park Pond
Location: Go east on E. Belleview Ave. from intersection of S. Santa Fe and E. Belleview Ave. Turn south on Hickory St. some parking available along Hickory. Progress Park is immediately southeast of Belleview and Hickory.
Size: 1.0 acres; 10 feet maximum depth.
Fish: Largemouth bass, bluegill, green sunfish, pumpkinseed, yellow perch, black bullhead and channel catfish.
Agency: South Suburban Parks and Recreation District.
Comments: Wetland theme playground nearby, Little Dry Creek trail access and handicapped accessible fishing pier. No boats.

53 Sterne Pond
Location: From the intersection of Littleton Blvd. and S. Bemis Street go south on Bemis. Turn east at W. Aberdeen Ave. At S. Spotswood Street go south to parking area.
Size: 3 acres; 3 feet maximum depth.
Fish: Bluegill, crappie, largemouth bass and yellow perch.
Agency: South Suburban Recreation & Park District.
Comments: Open 6 a.m. to 10 p.m. No boats. Children under 15 years only, are allowed to fish.

54 Ketring Park Lake (Gallup Lake)
Location: West of S. Broadway. From the intersection of Littleton Blvd. and S. Gallup Street, travel south on Gallup to W. Shepperd Ave. Turn east on Shepperd to S. Lakeview Street. Go south on Lakeview to the parking area. Access also from Caley Ave. south of the lake, to Lakeview Street and then north to the parking area.
Size: 15 acres; 9 feet maximum depth.
Fish: Bluegill, carp, channel catfish, crappie, green sunfish and largemouth bass.
Agency: South Suburban Recreation & Park District.
Comments: Open 6 a.m. to 10 p.m. No boats. Artificial fish habitat structures.

55 Little's Creek Pond
Location: From the intersection of Arapaho Road and South Broadway, go south on Broadway to Sterne Parkway. Turn west on Sterne Parkway and the lake will be just north, with access via hard surface foot trail.
Size: 1 acre; 5 feet maximum depth.
Fish: Bluegill, bullhead, carp, sucker, channel catfish, crappie, green sunfish and largemouth bass.
Agency: South Suburban Parks & Recreation District.
Comments: Open 6 a.m. to 10 p.m. No boats.

56 Ridgeview Park Pond
Location: East of Santa Fe Drive and south of Ridge Road. Access from S. Prince Street, S. Costilla Street, W. Rowland, or Houston Warning Circle.
Size: 1.5 acres; 6 feet maximum depth.
Fish: Largemouth bass, bluegill, carp, channel catfish and green sunfish.
Agency: South Suburban Parks & Recreation District.
Comments: Open 6 a.m. to 10 p.m. No boats. Picnic tables.

57 South Platte Park Ponds (Littleton Flood Plain Ponds)
Location: S. Santa Fe Drive and C-470 along South Platte River.

Size: 5 ponds; 80 acres total; 27 feet maximum depth.
Fish: Bluegill, yellow perch, sucker, rainbow trout and largemouth bass.
Agency: City of Littleton and South Suburban Parks & Recreation District.
Comments: No boats. Artificial fish habitat structures in some of the ponds. Check with agencies about access. Nature Center.
Special Regulation: All smallmouth and largemouth bass taken must be 15 inches in length or longer.

58 Chatfield Reservoir State Park (Map Page 13)

Location: In Chatfield Reservoir State Park, between S. Santa Fe Drive (US 85) on the east, and C-470 on the west. From S. Santa Fe go west on County line Road or Titan Road to Roxborough Park Road and go north. Roxborough is the south entrance to the area. From S. Wadsworth go south to C-470 and turn southwest. At Deer Creek Canyon Road turn east, and you will be at the north entrance to the area. There are parking areas all around the reservoir.
Size: 1,100 acres; 50 feet maximum depth.

Fish: Bluegill, brown trout, bullhead, channel catfish, crappie, green sunfish, largemouth bass, rainbow trout (catchable-size stocked) carp, sucker, walleye and yellow perch.
Agency: Colorado State Parks.
Comments: Boating, camping, and ice fishing allowed. No boating in heron rookery from March through October. Boat ramps. Extreme water fluctuation possible. Park pass required, free walk-in access for fishermen. Marina. Boat permit required. Swimming area. May close due to capacity. Handicapped accessible fishing piers by the marina and on the river near Kingfisher Cove. Restrooms. Boat rental available. Heron rookery viewing area. Artificial fish habitat structures in lake. (See map page 13.) Visitors Center.
Special Regulations: Reservoir only - Bag and possession limit for walleye is 4 fish, 18 inches or longer.

59 Chatfield State Park, Ponds

Location: South of Chatfield Reservoir within park boundaries.
Size: 5 ponds; 140 acres total; 34 feet maximum depth.
Fish: Bluegill, bullhead, channel catfish, crappie, green sunfish, largemouth bass, sucker and yellow perch.
Agency: Colorado State Parks.
Comments: No boats except belly boats allowed for fishing. Parks Pass required. Free walk-in access possible from Hwy 75. No motorized access from parking areas. Artificial fish habitat structures in some ponds.

Cherry Creek Reservoir

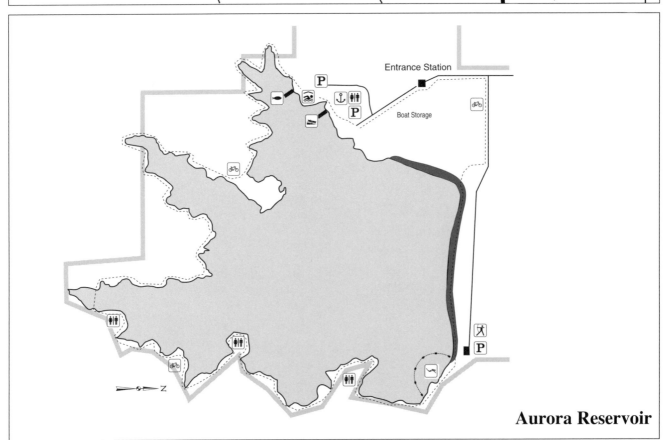

Aurora Reservoir

60 Washington Park Lakes

Location: Northeast of the intersection of S. Downing Street and E. Louisiana Ave. The north lake (Smith Lake) has parking areas while the south lake (Grasmere Lake) has street parking only.

Size: **Smith Lake** - 19 acres; 12 feet maximum depth.
Grasmere Lake - 19 acres; 10 feet maximum depth.
Lily pad Lake - 1 acre; 8 feet maximum depth.

Fish: Smith Lake - Bluegill, bullhead, carp, channel catfish, crappie, gizzard shad, largemouth bass, pumpkinseed sunfish, rainbow trout (catchable size stocked in spring) and yellow perch.
Grasmere Lake - Bluegill, bullhead, carp, channel catfish, green sunfish, largemouth bass, and yellow perch.

Agency: Denver Parks & Recreation.

Comments: Open 5 a.m. to 11 p.m. No boats. Fishing piers at both lakes. Handicapped access to fishing pier on the south shore of Smith Lake. Recreation center, playground and restrooms. Hard surface foot trail.

Special Regulation: Lily Pad Pond is open to anglers 16 years of age or younger for fishing clinics.

61 City Park Lake

Location: North of 17th Ave. and west of Colorado Blvd. Parking area on the northwest side of the lake, between the park and the Denver Zoo.

Size: 25 acres; 8 feet maximum depth.

Fish: Bluegill, bullhead, carp, channel catfish, crappie, gizzard shad, green sunfish, largemouth bass, yellow perch and rainbow trout (catchable size stocked in spring).

Agency: Denver Parks & Recreation.

Comments: Open 5 a.m. to 11 p.m. No private boats. No fishing from rental boats. Restrooms. Hard surface foot trail.

62 Exposition Park Pond

Location: East Havana Street, north of E. Exposition Ave. at S. Moline Street. Foot trail in from Exposition.

Size: 5 acres; 5 feet maximum depth.

Fish: Bluegill, bullhead, carp and sucker.

Agency: Aurora Parks & Open Space.

Comments: Aurora Parks permit required. Open dawn to dusk. No boats. Good bullhead fishing. Extreme water level fluctuation.

63 Garland Park Lake (Lollipop Lake)

Location: Between S. Holly Street and S. Kerney Street north of Cherry Creek Drive North.

Size: 4 acres; 8 feet maximum.

Fish: Largemouth bass, orange spotted sunfish, sucker, yellow perch, bluegill, bullhead, channel catfish, crappie and green sunfish.

Agency: Denver Parks & Recreation.

64 Cherry Creek State Park

Location: I-225 to Parker Road. South on Parker to the east entrance. West entrance is off S. Yosemite Street. There are parking areas all around the reservoir.

Size: 800 acres; 30 feet maximum depth.

Fish: Northern pike, wiper, wiper, tiger muskie, walleye, channel catfish, rainbow trout (catchable size stocked), sucker, yellow perch, bluegill, bullhead, carp, crappie, gizzard shad, green sunfish and largemouth bass. Best time is April and May at night along the dams.

Agency: Colorado State Parks.

Comments: Open 24 hours. Boating, (Rentals available) camping. Fee area. Free walk-in fisherman access. Handicapped accessible fishing pier. State records for walleye. Ice fishing. Boat rentals. Marina. Boat ramps. May close due to capacity. Artificial fish habitat structures in lake. (See map page 15.) Camping.

Special Regulations: Bag and possession limit for walleye is 4 fish, 18 inches or longer.

65 Quincy Reservoir

Location: On E. Quincy Ave., 3 miles east of Parker Road. Parking area is south of Quincy on the northeast side of the reservoir.

Size: 160 acres; 58 feet maximum.

Fish: Brown trout, largemouth bass, rainbow trout (catchable-size stocked), sucker, tiger muskie and yellow perch.

Agency: City of Aurora Parks & Open Space.

Comments: Hours variable. Fee area. Aurora Park Permit required. Capacity is limited to 100 persons. Artificial fish habitat structures in the reservoir. Boat rental available. No boat ramp. No gas motored boats allowed. Waders allowed. Hours; 1/2 hour before sunrise to one hour after sunset. Restrooms, handicapped fishing dock.

Special Regulations: 1.Fishing by artificial flies or artificial lures only; 2. Bag, possession and size limit for trout is 2 fish; 3. All smallmouth and largemouth bass taken must be 15 inches in length or longer; 4. Ice fishing is prohibited; 5.Closed Nov. - Feb.; 6. Evening hours as posted; 7. Tiger muskie must be 40 inches or longer to keep.

66 Aurora Reservoir

Location: From Denver take I-225 to Parker Rd., go south to Quincy Ave., 8 miles east on Quincy to entrance of reservoir.

Size: 820 acres; 110 feet maximum depth.

Fish: Walleye, yellow perch, wiper, channel catfish, rainbow trout, brown trout, smelt, spot-tail shiner, crappie and largemouth bass.

Agency: Aurora Parks & Open Space.

Comments: Handicapped accessible fishing pier and restrooms, hard surface foot trail. Fee area. Ice fishing allowed (Shelters must be portable, have anglers name and address, and be removed nightly). Electric motors only, no gasoline motors allowed. Boat rental available. Open dawn to dusk. Artificial fish habitat structures in lake. Aurora entrance permit required. (See map)

Special Regulation: Two trout limit; All black bass must be 15 inches or longer. Bag and possession limit for walleye is 5 fish 15 inches or longer.

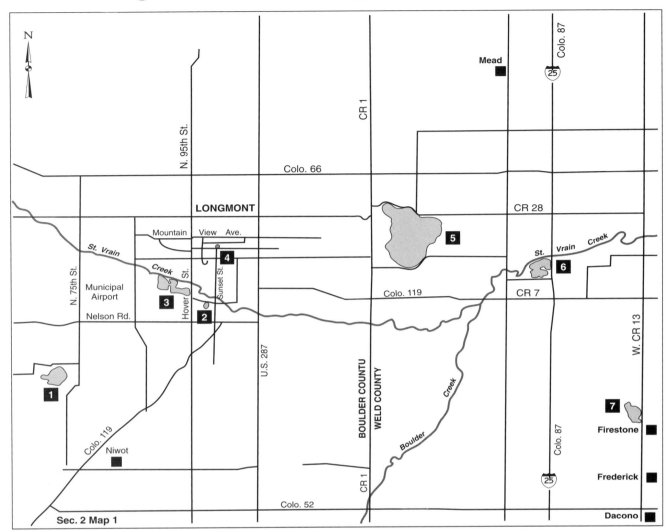

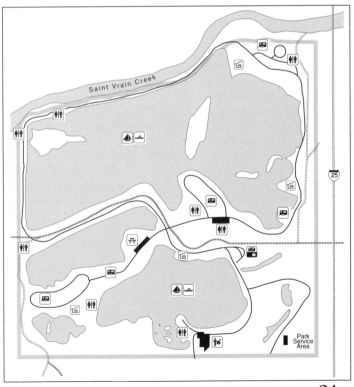

SECTION 2 - MAP 1

St. Vrain State Park

1 Lagerman Reservoir
Location: Boulder County. 4 miles S.W. of Longmont between N 75th and N 63rd St.
Size: 116 acres.
Fish: Largemouth bass, walleye, crappie, bluegill, channel catfish, tiger muskie, bullhead, gizzard shad, fathead minnows and carp.
Agency: Boulder County Parks & Open Space.
Comments: Some boating allowed 7.5 h.p. or less wakeless speed. No swimming. Open dawn to dusk.

2 Fairgrounds Lake
Location: On Hover and Rogers Roads, in Longmont at Boulder County Fairgrounds.
Size: 16 acres.
Fish: Largemouth bass, bluegill and channel catfish.
Agency: Boulder County Parks & Open Space.
Comments: Offshore fishing and belly boats only. No boats. Catch & release only. Open dawn to dusk.

3 Golden Ponds
Location: West of Hover Rd. Located at 2651 Third Avenue.
Fish: Largemouth bass, trout and perch.
Size: 94 acres.
Agency: City of Longmont.
Comments: Outstanding wildlife: deer, beaver and birds. It includes 56 surface acres of water in four ponds. There are 9 picnic shelters, two restrooms facilities and 2.6 miles of trails. Open dawn to dusk.

4 Loomiller Pond
Location: Eleventh and Summer, in Longmont.
Size: 15 acres.

Fish: Trout, catfish and perch.
Agency: City of Longmont.
Comments: Colorado fishing licenses is required. Open dawn to dusk.

5 Union Reservoir
Location: West of I-25 on Colorado 119 to County Line Road 1, north 1 mile, east 1 mile to reservoir.
Size: 700 acres; 30 feet maximum depth.
Fish: Bluegill, crappie, and bass, wiper, trout and catfish.
Agency: City of Longmont. (See map this Page.)
Comments: Fishing pier, camping, restrooms.

6 Barbour Ponds State Park
Location: East of I-25 on Colorado 119, 1 mile north to park entrance.
Size: 130 acres; 6 feet maximum depth.
Fish: Catfish and rainbow trout.
Agency: Colorado State Parks.
Special Restrictions: Small sailing and hand-propelled craft only. Includes air inflated devices if more than one compartment. Swimming prohibited. Closed to vehicle traffic during waterfowl season.
(See map page 18.)

7 Milavec Lake Recreation Area (Firestone Lake).
Location: 2 miles north of Colorado Highway 52 on Weld County Road 13 (Northwest on Fredrick.)
Size: 40 acres.
Fish: Trout (catchable size stocked), carp and crappie.
Agency: City of Fredrick.
Comments: Open one half hour before sunrise to one half hour after sunset. Fee area. No ice fishing. No open fires. No boats or flotation devices.

End Section 2 Map 1

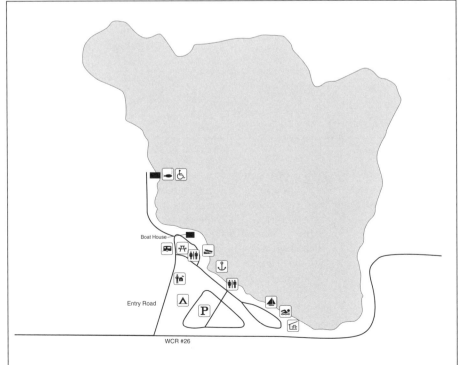

Union Reservoir

Front Range - Section 2 - Map 2

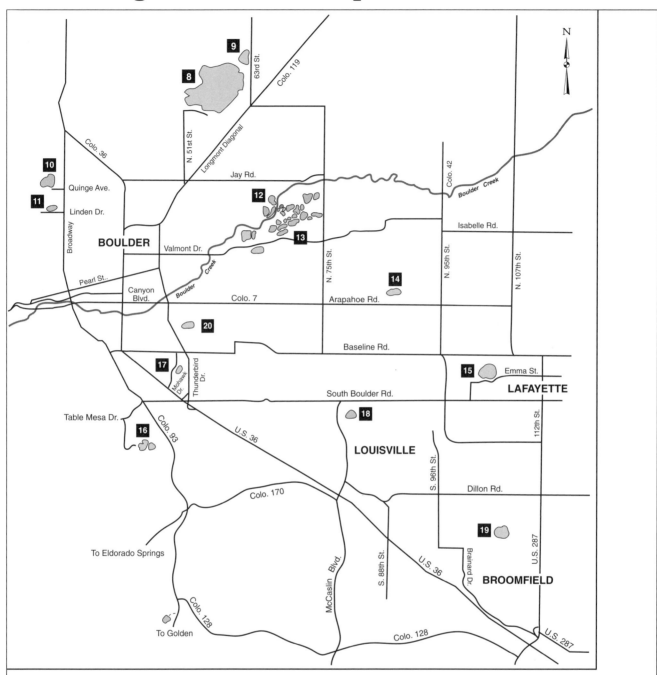

8 Boulder Reservoir

Location: From 28th Street (Hwy 36) go north to the Longmont Diagonal (Hwy 119) and turn northeast. At Jay Road turn west and then north almost immediately onto 51st Street. Access into the reservoir is east from 51st St.
Size: 540 acres; 40 feet maximum depth.
Fish: Walleye, channel catfish, black crappie, bluegill, largemouth bass, yellow perch, rainbow trout (catchable size stocked), carp and sucker.
Agency: Boulder Parks & Recreation Department.
Comments: Open 7 a.m. to dusk. Motorboats with city permit. Non-motorized boats need no permit. Excellent walleye fishery. Fee area but can park outside the area and walk-in free.

9 Coot Lake

Location: One-half mile northeast of Boulder Reservoir parking area. Two miles north of Longmont Diagonal (Hwy 119) on the west side of N. 63rd Street.
Size: 10 acres; 15 feet maximum depth.
Fish: Largemouth bass, crappie, bluegill, sucker, bullhead and smallmouth bass.
Agency: Boulder Parks & Recreation Department.
Comments: Open 7 a.m. to dusk. No boats.

10 Wonderland Lake

Location: N. Broadway to W. Poplar Ave. Turn west on Poplar to Wonderland Hill Road. Go north on Wonderland to the parking area.
Size: 34 acres; 13 feet maximum depth.
Fish: Largemouth bass, crappie, bullhead, yellow perch, carp and bluegill.
Agency: City of Boulder Parks & Open Space.
Comments: Open dawn to dusk. No boats. Walk-in fishing. Artificial fish habitat structures in lake. Dogs must be on hand-held leash. No glass allowed. Swimming and wading prohibited. Fishing only in designated areas.

11 Maxwell Lake

Location: From N. Broadway, one quarter mile west on Linden Ave. Walk in from Linden.
Size: 1.6 acres; 6 feet maximum depth.
Fish: bluegill, largemouth bass, bullhead, channel catfish and sucker.
Agency: Boulder Parks & Recreation Department.
Comments: Open 6 a.m. to 10 p.m. Non-motorized boats only.

12 Walden Ponds

Location: On 75th Street go one-half mile north of Valmont Road, cross the railroad tracks and turn west to the ponds. Immediately north of Sawhill Ponds.
Size: **Picnic Pond (northeast)** - 5.7 acres, 7 feet maximum depth.
  Cottonwood Marsh (middle) - 30.3 acres; 8 feet maximum depth.
  Duck Pond (south) - 6.3 acres; 5.6 feet maximum depth.
  Island Lake and Bass Pond - 10 acres each; 12 feet maximum depth.
Fish: Largemouth bass, crappie, bluegill, carp, bullhead and channel catfish.
Agency: Boulder County Open Space.
Comments: Open dawn to dusk. Picnic Road restricted to handicapped and elderly by Boulder permit only. Permit available at the A-frame office at the park and at county annex located at 2045 13th Street.
Special Regulations: 1. All smallmouth and largemouth bass caught must be returned to the water immediately except in Picnic Pond. 2. Fishing by artificial flies and lures only on all waters except Picnic Pond. Wildlife viewing boardwalk on Cottonwood Marsh Pond.

13 Sawhill Ponds

Location: West of 75th Street between Valmont and Jay Roads. About 2 miles north of Arapaho Road.
Size: 16 ponds; from 1-10 acres; 16 feet maximum depth.
Fish: Largemouth bass, channel catfish, bluegill, crappie, yellow perch, bullhead and sucker.
Agency: Boulder Parks & Recreation Department.
Comments: Open dawn to dusk. No boats. Artificial habitat structures in some ponds.
Special Regulation: 1. All largemouth and smallmouth bass taken must be 15 inches in length or longer (All ponds). 2. Fishing by artificial lures only on all ponds except ponds #1 and #1a (eastern ponds).

14 Teller Lake

Location: Take Arapahoe Road (Hwy 7) west from Lafayette. Drive 1.4 miles west of 95th St. (Hwy 42). At sign for lake, turn north on dirt road for about .5 mile to parking lot. Lake is about .2 mile walk to the east.
Size: 28 acres; 20 feet maximum depth.
Fish: Yellow perch, largemouth bass, bluegill, crappie carp and bullhead.
Agency: City of Boulder Parks & Open Space.
Special Regulations: All largemouth and smallmouth bass taken must be 15 inches or longer.

15 Waneka Lake

Location: Lafayette. West of US 287, north of South Boulder Road. Access to the east entrance is via Hwy 287. At the intersection of Hwy 287 and Emma Street turn west on Emma. Parking area is on the corner of Emma and Caria Ave. The south entrance is via S. Boulder Road. Take S. Boulder Road to Ceres Drive. Turn north on Ceres to Caria Ave. At Caria go east to the parking area.
Size: 55 acres; 19 feet maximum depth.
Fish: Bluegill, carp, crappie largemouth bass, pumpkinseed sunfish and yellow perch.
Agency: Lafayette Parks & Recreation.
Comments: Open 7 a.m. to 10 p.m. Extreme water level fluctuation. Ice fishing. Artificial fish habitat in lake.
Special Regulations: 1. All smallmouth and largemouth bass taken must be 15 inches in length or longer.

16 Viele Reservoir

Location: South of the Table Mesa Shopping Center. From S. Broadway and Table Mesa Drive, go west on Table Mesa to Gillespie Street. Turn south on Gillespie to Harlow Platts Park. The lake is adjacent to the South Boulder Recreation Center.
Size: 6 acres; 15 feet maximum depth.
Fish: Yellow perch, bluegill, largemouth bass, crappie, carp, pumpkinseed sunfish, channel catfish and bullhead.
Agency: Boulder Parks & Recreation.
Comments: Open dawn to dusk. Non-motorized boats only. Hard surface foot trail.

17 Thunderbird Lake

Location: Mohawk and 47th Street.
Size: 2 acres; 10 feet maximum depth.
Fish: Largemouth bass, bluegill, crappie and sunfish.
Agency: Boulder Parks & Recreation.
Comments: Open dawn to dusk. No boats. Hard surface foot trail.

18 Harper Lake

Location: From Denver on U.S. 36 west to the Superior/Louisville exit. North on McCaslin Blvd. 1.5 miles to washington where parking is available.
Size: 31 acres; 39 feet maximum depth.
Fish: Rainbow trout (catchable size stocked), largemouth bass and green sunfish.
Agency: City of Louisville.
Comments: Non-motorized craft only.

19 Sterns Lake

Location: Northwest of Broomfield from Hwy 287 north to Dillon Rd. Dillon west to 104 th, south on 104th to Stearns Lake.
Size: 23.7 acres; 10 feet maximum depth.
Fish: Tiger muskie, channel catfish, largemouth bass, crappie and bluegill.
Agency: Boulder County Parks & Open Space.
Comments: No boats. No wading.
Special Regulations: Tiger muskies must be 30 inches in length. All smallmouth and largemouth bass taken must be 15 inches in length or longer.

20 Boulder Ponds

Location: Go east on S. Boulder Rd from intersection of Interstate 36 and S. Boulder Rd. Turn north on 55th St. to East Boulder Recreation Center. Ponds are south of recreation center.
Size: Two ponds: 1.0 acres each; 8 feet maximum depth.
Fish: Largemouth bass, bluegill, channel catfish and long nose sucker.
Agency: City of Boulder.
Comments: No boats.

End of Section 2

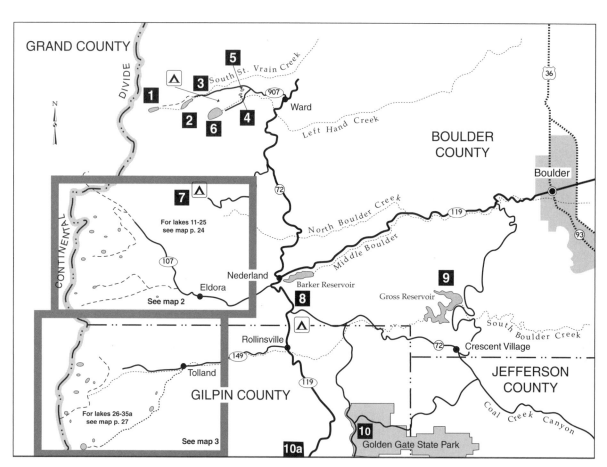

SECTION 3 - MAP 1

Mountain Lakes

The mountain lakes are divided into five maps. On the maps each lake is labeled by number and is accompanied by descriptive text. The descriptions of the mountain lakes include: general location, size and maximum depth, types of fish present, name of managing agency, and comments including USGS topo map, altitude, and any other information specific to the lake.

Mountain fishing near the metro area is often done in the midst of a mixture of national forest and private lands. Lakes, reservoirs, and stretches of stream may be public or private. Anglers are cautioned to respect private property to avoid trespassing. Sometimes a private lake is surrounded by national forest land, but public fishing is not allowed.

Front Range - Section 3 - Map 1

1 Lake Isabelle
Location: Boulder County. Arapaho/Roosevelt National Forest. From Ward, go north one-quarter mile on Hwy 72 to Brainard Lake Road. Go west about 4 miles to Brainard Lake. Drive past Brainard Lake to trailhead. Hike west about one-quarter on Pawnee Pass Trail to Long Lake. Continue west on the trail (along north shore of Long Lake) about 2 miles to Lake Isabelle.
Size: 30 acres; 40 feet maximum depth.
Fish: Rainbow trout.
Agency: USFS-Boulder Ranger District.
Comments: USGS Ward quad; altitude 10,868 feet. In Indian Peaks Wilderness Area. Non-motorized boats only. Fee area. Camping at Pawnee Campground near Brainard Lake by reservation.
Special Regulations: 1. Fishing by artificial flies or artificial lures only; 2. Bag, possession and size limit for trout is 2 fish.

2 Long Lake
Location: Boulder County. Arapaho/Roosevelt National Forest. From Ward, go north one-quarter mile on Hwy 72 to Brainard Lake Road. Go west about 4 miles to Brainard Lake. Drive past Brainard Lake to trailhead. Hike west about 1/4 mile on Pawnee Pass Trail to Long Lake.
Size: 39.5 acres; 22 feet maximum depth.
Fish: Rainbow trout and brook trout.
Agency: USFS-Boulder Ranger District.
Comments: USGS Ward quad; altitude 10,500 feet. Non-motorized boats only. Fee area. Camping at Pawnee Campground near Brainard Lake by reservation.
Special Regulations: 1. Fishing by artificial flies or artificial lures only; 2. Bag and possession limit for trout is 2 fish; 3. Fishing is prohibited in the outlet stream of Long Lake to the bridge at the inlet at Brainard Lake from May 1 through July 15, as posted.

3 Brainard Lake
Location: Boulder County. Arapaho/Roosevelt National Forest. From Ward, go north one-quarter mile on Hwy 72 to Brainard Lake Road. Go west about 4 miles to Brainard Lake.
Size: 15.6 acres; 8 feet maximum depth.
Fish: Rainbow trout (catchable size stocked), brook and brown trout.
Agency: USFS-Boulder County Ranger District.
Comments: USGS Ward quad; altitude 10,350 feet. Non-motorized boats only. Restrooms. Fee area. Camping at Pawnee Campground near Brainard Lake by reservation.

4 Moraine Lake
Location: Boulder County. Arapaho/Roosevelt National Forest. From Ward, go north on Hwy 72 one-quarter mile to Brainard Lake Road. Go west 2 miles past the turnoff for lefthand park. Moraine Lake is on the south beyond Red Rock Lake.
Size: 2.0 acres; 3.5 feet maximum depth.
Fish: Rainbow trout.
Agency: USFS-Boulder Ranger District.
Comments: USGS Ward quad; altitude 10,150 feet. Non-motorized boats only.

5 Red Rock Lake
Location: Boulder County. Arapaho/Roosevelt National Forest. From Ward, go north on Hwy 72 one-quarter mile to Brainard Lake Road. Go west 2 miles past the turnoff for lefthand park. On the south side of the road is a parking area for Red Rock Lake.
Size: 6.5 acres; 3 feet maximum depth.
Fish: Rainbow trout (catchable size stocked).
Agency: USFS-Boulder Ranger District.
Comments: USGS Ward quad; altitude 10,300 Grassy with lily pads. Non-motorized boats only.

6 Lefthand Creek Reservoir
Location: Boulder County. Arapaho/Roosevelt National Forest. From Ward, go north on Hwy 72 one-quarter mile to Brainard Lake Road. Go west 2 miles to Lefthand Park Road. Follow road southwest about 2 miles to the reservoir.
Size: 100 acres; 34 feet maximum depth.
Fish: Rainbow, brook, brown trout and splake.
Agency: USFS-Boulder Ranger District.
Comments: USGS Ward quad; altitude 10,600 feet. Boats allowed, no gasoline motors.

7 Rainbow Lakes
Location: Boulder County. Arapaho/Roosevelt National Forest. From Ward, go south about 3.5 miles on Hwy 72. Turn west on gravel road. (First fork goes to the University of Colorado Camp.) Take south fork about 4 miles to Rainbow Lakes campground and trailhead.
Size: Ten beaver ponds; from 1 to 4 acres; 15 feet maximum depth.
Fish: Brook and rainbow trout.
Agency: USFS-Boulder Ranger District.
Comments: USGS-Ward quad; altitude 10,200 feet. Forest Service campground. Trailhead for Arapaho Glacier Trail. Non-motorized boats only.

8 Barker Reservoir
Location: Boulder County. Arapaho/Roosevelt National Forest.
From Nederland, go one-half mile east along Hwy 119. The reservoir is on Middle Boulder Creek. From Boulder, go 15 miles west along Hwy 119.
Size: 380 acres; 100 feet maximum depth.
Fish: Rainbow trout (catchable size stocked), brook and brown trout, splake and sucker.
Agency: Public Service Company.
Comments: USGS Nederland quad; altitude 8,200 feet. Fluctuation water storage reservoir. No boats or ice fishing.

9 Gross Reservoir
Location: Boulder County. Arapaho/Roosevelt National Forest.
From Boulder, drive west on Baseline Road to Flagstaff Mountain Road. Wind southwest for about 7 miles to Gross Reservoir. From Golden, drive 18 miles north on Hwy 93 to Boulder and turn west on Baseline Road. Follow directions from Boulder. Alternate route from Golden, drive 7 miles north on Hwy 93, then turn west on Hwy 72, Coal Creek Canyon. Drive about 10 miles northwest to Crescent

Village. Drive north about 3 miles to Gross Reservoir. From Nederland, drive about 2.5 miles south on Hwy 119. Turn east on Hwy 72, and drive about 9 miles east to Crescent Village. Turn north and go about 3 miles to Gross Reservoir.

Size: 412 acres; 230 feet maximum depth.

Fish: Rainbow trout (catchable size stocked), brook, brown and lake trout, kokanee salmon and tiger muskie.

Agency: Denver Water Department.

Comments: USGS Tungsten and Eldorado Springs quads; altitude 7,287 feet. Steep banked. No camping, no boating or floating devices. Fires in firepits on north side only. Open 4 a.m. to 9 p.m. Ice fishing at own risk. Water level fluctuation.

Special Regulations: Kokanee snagging permitted September 1 through December 31. West side of reservoir is closed approx. Dec. 1 thru May 15, for critical wildlife habitat.

10 Golden Gate Canyon State Park Lakes

Location: Gilpin and Jefferson Counties. From Golden, drive north 1 mile on Hwy 93 to Golden Gate Canyon Road, then west 14 miles to the park. From Nederland, drive about 8 miles south on Hwy 119 to park entrance. Alternate route from Boulder, drive south on Hwy 93 to Golden Gate Canyon Road, and turn west 14 miles to the park. Also reached from Hwy 119 by turning east about 5 miles north of Black Hawk.

Size: 13 ponds; 15 acres total.

Fish: Rainbow trout (catchable size stocked), brown and brook trout.

Agency: Colorado State Parks.

Comments: USGS Blackhawk quad; altitude 8,230 feet. No fishing in visitor center show pond. Park is a fee area. No boats. Ice fishing allowed on Kriley and Slough Ponds.

10a Central City Park Pond (Dorothy Lee)

Location: Gilpin County. From Highway 199 at Blackhawk go west on Eureka St. through Central City. Take a left onto Gilpin County Road 2. The pond is .5 miles on the left.

Size: 2 acres; 10 feet maximum depth.

Fish: Rainbow Tout (catchable-size stocked).

Agency: Central City.

Comments: USGS Central City quad; altitude 8.940 feet. No boating allowed. Open during daylight hours.

Central City Park Pond (Chase Gulch Res.)

Location: Gilpin County. From Highway 199 at Blackhawk go west on Eureka St. through Central City. Continue to a right to Apex Road (Cty Rd. 3) and follow around to reservoir.

Size: 25 acres; 90 feet maximum depth.

Fish: Various trout species (including catchable-size rainbows).

Agency: Central City. (Call for opening date).

Comments: USGS Central City quad; altitude 8,590 feet. Non-motorized boats only. Open during daylight hours.

End of Section 3 - Map 1

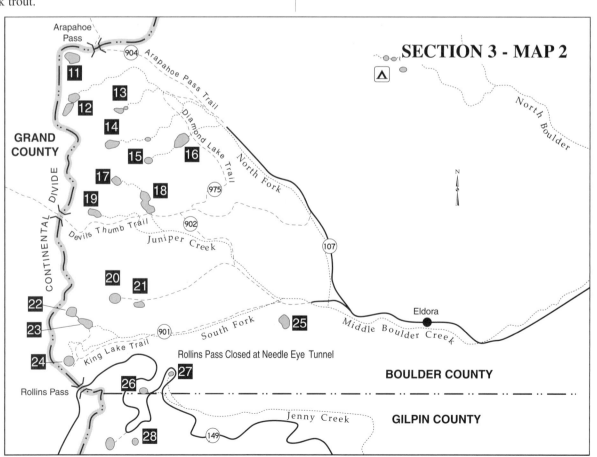

11 Lake Dorothy

Location: Boulder County. Arapaho/Roosevelt National Forest. From Nederland, go one-half mile south on Hwy 72-119. Turn west, go 4 miles to Eldora, continue 1 mile and take the north fork of the road, along the north fork of Middle Boulder Creek. Drive about 4 miles to the Fourth of July Campground. Hike north and northwest on Arapaho Pass Trail for about 3 miles. Lake Dorothy is in open country about one-half mile southwest of the summit.
Size: 16 acres; 100 feet maximum depth.
Fish: Cutthroat trout.
Agency: USFS-Boulder Ranger District.
Comments: USGS Monarch Lake quad; altitude 12,100 feet. Indian Peaks Wilderness Area. Non-motorized boats.

12 Neva Lakes

Location: Boulder County. Arapaho/Roosevelt National Forest. From Nederland, go one-half mile south on Hwy 72-119. Turn west, go 4 miles to Eldora, continue 1 mile and take the north fork of the road, along the north fork of Middle Boulder Creek. Hike north on Arapaho Pass Trail. After one-half mile take the west fork, Diamond Lake Trail. Go northwest about one-half mile where the trail crosses a small stream and then curves southeast. Cut off at the second stream, north fork of Middle Boulder Creek, and follow it cross county for 2 miles. No trail, use topo map advised.
Size: Upper Lake - 8.6 acres; 61 feet maximum depth.
     Lower Lake - 10.0 acres; 49 feet maximum depth.
Fish: Cutthroat trout.
Agency: USFS-Boulder Ranger District.
Comments: USGS Monarch Lake quad; altitude 11,800 feet. Non-motorized boats only. No fish in upper lake.

13 Diamond Lake - Upper

Location: Boulder County. Arapaho/Roosevelt National Forest. From Nederland, go one-half mile south on Hwy 72-119. Turn west, go 4 miles to Eldora, continue 1 mile and take the north fork of the road, along the north of Middle Boulder Creek. Dive about 4 miles to the Fourth of July Trailhead. Hike north on Arapaho Pass Trail. After one-half mile take the west fork, Diamond Lake Trail. Follow trail 904 & 975 to Diamond Lake. Follow obscure trail upstream to Upper Diamond.
Size: 6 acres; 17 feet maximum depth.
Fish: Cutthroat trout.
Agency: USFS - Boulder Ranger District.
Comments: USGS East Portal quad; altitude 11,720 feet. Non-motorized boats only.
Helpful Hints: Try fishing the outlet in areas as soon as the ice goes out in late June or early July for nice sized cutthroat attempting to spawn. Gold or Silver Panther Martin Spinners work extremely well at this time and throughout the summer. Fly fishing with two flies (A dry and wet dropper) off the shoal edges can be productive. Dark colored flies size 16 or smaller seem to work best.

14 Deep Lake

Location: Boulder County. Arapaho/Roosevelt National Forest. From Nederland, go one-half mile south on Hwy 72-119. Turn west, go 4 miles to Eldora, continue 1 mile and take the north fork of the road, along the north fork of Middle Boulder Creek. Drive about 4 miles to the Fourth of July Trailhead. Hike north on Arapaho Pass Trail about 1/4 mile and take the west fork, Diamond Lake Trail. Go northwest about one-half mile. Trail crosses a small stream and then curves southwest. Cut off at the second stream, north fork at Middle Boulder Creek, and follow it cross country about 1/8 mile. Head west at tributary, follow for 3/4 mile.
Size: 4.9 acres; 20 feet maximum depth.
Fish: Cutthroat and rainbow trout.
Agency: USFS - Boulder Ranger District.
Comments: USGS East Portal and Monarch Lake quads. Altitude 11,320 feet. Rough country. Non-motorized boats.

15 Banana Lake

Location: Boulder County. Arapaho/Roosevelt National Forest. From Nederland, go one-half mile south on Hwy 72-119. Turn west, go 4 miles to Eldora, continue one mile and take the north fork of the road, along the north fork Middle Boulder Creek. Drive about 4 miles to the Fourth of July Trailhead. Follow trail 904 and 975 to Diamond Lake, follow obscure trail upstream for one-half mile. Use topo map advised.
Size: 1.5 acres; 13 feet maximum depth.
Fish: Cutthroat trout.
Agency: USFS-Boulder Ranger District.
Comments: USGS East Portal quad; altitude 11,320 feet. No boats.

16 Diamond Lake

Location: Boulder County. Arapaho/Roosevelt National Forest. From Nederland, go one-half mile south on Hwy 72-119. Turn west, go 4 miles to Eldora, continue 1 mile and take the north fork of the road, along the north fork Middle Boulder Creek. Drive about 4 miles to the Fourth of July Trailhead. Follow trail 904 and 975 to lake.
Size: 14 acres; 17 feet maximum depth.
Fish: Brook, cutthroat, lake and rainbow trout.
Agency: USFS-Boulder Ranger District.
Comments: USGS East Portal quad; altitude 10, 920 feet. In Indian Peaks Wilderness area. Non-motorized boats.

17 Storm Lake

Location: Boulder County. Arapaho/Roosevelt National Forest. From Nederland, go one-half mile south on Hwy 72-119. Turn west, and go 4 miles to Eldora, continue 1 mile to the Hessie trailhead. Walk west about 5 miles on trail 902 to Jasper Lake. From north end of Jasper, follow inlet stream one-half mile northwest to Storm Lake.
Size: 7 acres; 22 feet maximum depth.
Fish: Cutthroat trout.
Agency: USFS-Boulder Ranger District.
Comments: USGS East Portal quad; altitude 11,440 feet. Non-motorized boats only.

18 Jasper Lake

Location: Boulder County. Arapaho/Roosevelt National Forest. From Nederland, go one-half mile south on Hwy 72-119. Turn west, and go 4 miles to Eldora, continue one mile to Forest Route 109 to Hessie Trailhead. Walk west about 1.5 miles then take the north fork. Go up the trail one mile, past mine diggings, and take the north fork again. Continue north and west for 2.5 miles to Jasper Lake.
Size: 21 acres; 36 feet maximum depth.
Fish: Brook, brown and cutthroat trout.

Front Range - Section 3 - Map 2

Agency: USFS-Boulder Ranger District.
Comments: USGS Nederland and East Portal quads; altitude 10,814 feet. In Indian Peaks Wilderness area. Non-motorized boats only.

19 Devil's Thumb Lake
Location: Boulder County. Arapaho/Roosevelt National Forest. From Nederland, go one-half mile south on Hwy 72-119. Turn west, go 4 miles to Eldora, continue one mile on Forest Route 109 to Hessie Trailhead. Walk west about 1.5 miles and then take the north fork. Go up the trail one mile, past mine diggings, and take north fork again. Continue north and west for 2.5 miles to Jasper Lake. Follow the trail 902 west for 1 mile to the lake.
Size: 11.5 acres; 37 feet maximum depth.
Fish: Cutthroat trout.
Agency: USFS-Boulder Ranger District.
Comments: USGS East Portal quads; altitude 11,260 feet. In Indian Peaks Wilderness Area. Non-motorized boats.

20 Skyscraper Reservoir
Location: Boulder County. Arapaho/Roosevelt National Forest. From Nederland, go one-half mile south on Hwy 72-119. Turn west, go 4 miles to Eldora. Continue 1 mile on Forest Route 109 to the Hessie Trailhead. Hike west about 1.5 miles then take the north fork. Go up the trail 1 mile, past mine diggings, to the next fork. Go west 2 miles to Woodland Lake. Go a few hundred yards more to Skyscraper Reservoir.
Size: 12.9 acres; 28 feet maximum depth.
Fish: Cutthroat trout.
Agency: USFS-Boulder Ranger District.
Comments: USGS East Portal quads; altitude 11,221 feet. In Indian Peaks Wilderness Area. Non-motorized boats only.

21 Woodland Lake
Location: Boulder County. Arapaho/Roosevelt National Forest. From Nederland, go one-half mile south on Hwy 72-119. Turn west, and go 4 miles to Eldora. Continue 1 mile on Forest Route 109 to the Hessie Trailhead. Hike west about 1.5 miles then take the north fork. Go up the trail 1 mile, past mine diggings, to the next fork. Go west 2 miles to Woodland Lake.
Size: 10 acres; 7 feet maximum depth.
Fish: Cutthroat trout and grayling.
Agency: USFS - Boulder Ranger District.
Comments: USGS East Portal quads; altitude 10,972 feet. In Indian Peaks Wilderness Area. Non-motorized boats only.

22 Bob Lake
Location: Boulder County. Arapaho/Roosevelt National Forest. From Nederland, go one-half mile south on Hwy 72-119. Turn west, and go 4 miles to Eldora. Continue 1 mile on Forest Route 109 to the Hessie Trailhead. Walk 5 miles west on trail 901, then southwest at the fork, following the south fork of Middle Boulder Creek. At intersection with north-south trail go north one-half mile plus, to Betty Lake. From trail along west shore of Betty Lake continue one-eighth mile to Bob Lake. Can also be reached by hiking north from Rollins Pass.
Size: 8.5 acres; 71 feet maximum depth.
Fish: Cutthroat trout.

Agency: USFS - Boulder Ranger District.
Comments: USGS East Portal quad; altitude 11,600 feet. In Indian Peaks Wilderness Area. Non-motorized boats only.

23 Betty Lake
Location: Boulder County. Arapaho/Roosevelt National Forest. From Nederland, go one-half mile south on Hwy 72-119. Turn west, and go 4 miles to Eldora. Continue one mile on Forest Route 109 to Hessie Trailhead. Walk 5 miles west, then southwest at the fork, following the south fork of Middle Boulder Creek. At intersection with north-south trail go north one-half mile plus, to Betty Lake. Can also be reached by hiking north from Rollins Pass. Use East Portal quad.
Size: 8.5 acres; 11 feet maximum depth.
Fish: Cutthroat trout.
Agency: USFS-Boulder Ranger District.
Comments: USGS Nederland and East Portal quads; altitude 11,500 feet. In Indian Peaks Wilderness Area. Non-motorized boats only.

24 King Lake
Location: Boulder County. Arapaho/Roosevelt National Forest. From Nederland, go one-half mile south on Hwy 72-119. Turn west and go 4 miles to Eldora. Continue 1 mile on Forest Route 109 to Hessie trailhead. Walk 6 miles west, then southwest at the fork, following the south fork of Middle Boulder Creek. At intersection with north-south trail go south about one-quarter mile to King Lake. Can also be reached by hiking north one-half mile from Rollins Pass summit. Use East Portal quad.
Size: 11.5 acres; 61 feet maximum depth.
Fish: Cutthroat and rainbow trout.
Agency: USFS-Boulder Ranger District.
Comments: USGS Nederland and East Portal quads; altitude 11,431 feet. In Indian Peaks Wilderness Area. Non-motorized boats only.

25 Lost Lake
Location: Boulder County. Arapaho/Roosevelt National Forest. From Nederland, go one-half mile south on Hwy 72-119. Turn west, and go 4 miles to Eldora. Continue 1 mile on Forest Route 109 to Hessie Trailhead. Hike west on the trail 902 and then southwest at the fork, total distance under 2 miles.
Size: 8.6 acres; 14 feet maximum depth.
Fish: Rainbow and brook trout.
Agency: USFS-Boulder Ranger District.
Comments: USGS Nederland quad; altitude 9,740 feet. Non-motorized boats only.

End Section 3 Map 2

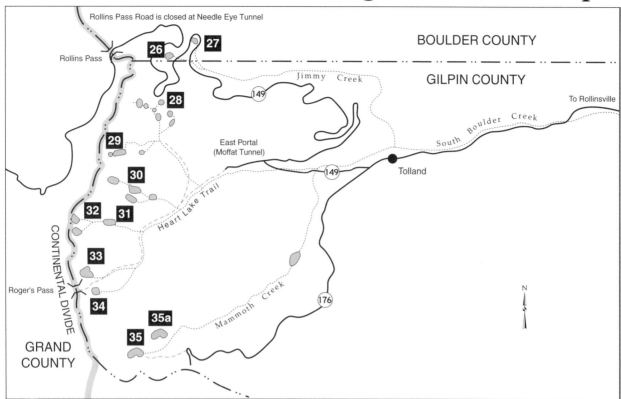

26 Jenny Lake

Location: Boulder County. Arapaho/Roosevelt National Forest. From Rollinsville, drive west about 7 miles on Forest Route 149. Turn north on old railroad grade. (Before East Portal.) Drive about ten miles up Rollins Pass Road (Forest Route 149) to Yankee Doodle Lake. Drive 1 mile further to Jenny Lake.
Size: 4.5 acres; 9 feet maximum depth.
Fish: Brook and rainbow trout (catchable size stocked.) and sucker.
Agency: USFS-Boulder Ranger District.
Comments: USGS East Portal quads; altitude 10,917 feet. Forest Road 149 (Rollins Pass Rd.) is closed at Needle Eye Tunnel. Non-motorized boats only. Check road conditions.

27 Yankee Doodle Lake

Location: Boulder County. Arapaho/Roosevelt National Forest. From Rollinsville, drive west about 7 miles on Forest Route 149. Turn north on old railroad grade. (Before East Portal.) Drive about 10 miles up Rollins Pass Road (Forest Route 149) to Yankee Doodle Lake.
Size: 5.7 acres; 24 feet maximum depth.
Fish: Rainbow (catchable size stocked) and brook trout.
Agency: USFS-Boulder Ranger District.
Comments: USGS East Portal quad; altitude 10,711 feet. Inquire locally about current road conditions. Boats allowed. Forest Road 149 (Rollins Pass Rd.) is closed at Needle Eye Tunnel. Artificial fish habitat structures.

28 Forest Lakes

Location: Boulder County. Arapaho/Roosevelt National Forest. From Rollinsville, drive west about 8 miles on Forest Route 149 to East Portal. Park by tunnel. On the south side of the road walk through the gate. (Gate may be locked). Hike 1 mile southwest on the road, to the intersection with South Boulder Creek Pack Trail. Turn north and go up the trail 1.5 miles. (At 0.5 mile the trail crosses a creek). Where the creeks meet, take the north fork. Hike .5 mile north cross country to the first lake, or another .5 mi. to the second. Can also be reached by hiking south .5 mile from Rollins Pass Road. (FDR 149) south of Jenny Lake.
Size: **Upper** - 4.3 acres; 8.2 feet maximum depth.
    Lower - 2.7 acres; 3.2 feet maximum depth.
Fish: Brook trout.
Agency: USFS - Boulder Ranger District.
Comments: USGS East Portal quad; altitude 10,800 feet. Small forest ponds. Non-motorized boats only.

29 Arapaho Lakes

Location: Gilpin County. Arapaho/Roosevelt National Forest. From Rollinsville, drive about 8 miles on Forest Route 149 to East Portal. Park by tunnel. On the south side of the road walk through the gate (Gate may be locked). Hike one mile southwest on the road, to intersection with South Boulder Creek Trail. Turn north and go up the trail 1.5 miles. (At 0.5 miles the trail crosses a creek.) Where the creeks meet take the west fork. Follow the stream three-quarters of a mile west to the first lake. There are 2 more lakes to the west directly up stream. (After taking the west fork, at about 1/8 a mile a small tributary comes in from the south, there is a small pond about one-half mile up stream.)
Size: **East** - 9.8 acres; 49.2 feet maximum depth.
    Middle - 4 acres; 15 feet maximum depth.
    West - 2.5 acres; 16.4 feet maximum depth.
Fish: Cutthroat and golden trout.
Agency: USFS-Boulder Ranger District.
Comments: USGS East Portal quad; altitude 11,580 feet. Non-motorized boats only.

30 Crater Lakes

Location: Gilpin County. Arapaho/Roosevelt National Forest. From Rollinsville, drive west about 8 miles on Forest Route 149 to East Portal. Park by tunnel. On the south side of the road walk through the gate (Gate may be locked). Hike 1 mile southwest on road, to intersection with South Boulder Creek Trail. Turn south into the clearing. Hike west, upstream for 1/2 mile to the first lake. No trail, use of topo map advised.

Size: **East** - 5.7 acres; 4 feet maximum depth.
           Southeast - 8.6 acres; 29 feet maximum depth.
           Middle - 14.0 acres; 14 feet maximum depth.
           West - 8.5 acres; 58 feet maximum depth.

Fish: Rainbow, brook, brown and cutthroat trout.
Agency: USFS - Boulder Ranger District.
Comments: USGS East Portal quad; altitude 11,000 feet. Non-motorized boats only.
Helpful Hints: The most productive way to fish these four lakes is from a float tube. A tremendous fly ant hatch (size 14-16) occurs in August on the lower three lakes. The best time to fish the upper lake for cutthroat is after the ice melts in late June or early July. At this time cutthroat often cruise the shallow, shoals looking for food and spawning habitat.

31 Clayton Lake

Location: Gilpin County. Arapaho/Roosevelt National Forest. From Rollinsville, drive west about 8 miles on Forest Route 149 to East Portal. Park by tunnel. On the south side of the road walk through gate (Gate may be locked). Hike 1 mile southwest on road, to intersection with South Boulder Creek Trail. Turn south, cross creek, and hike about 1 mile to another creek. Turn west and follow the creek (no trail) for 1/2 mile to Clayton Lake. Use topo map advised. (See Crater Lake)
Size: 5 acres; 4 feet maximum depth.
Fish: Cutthroat trout.
Agency: USFS-Boulder Ranger District.
Comments: USGS East Portal quad; altitude 11,560 feet. Non-motorized boats only.

32 Iceberg Lakes

Location: Gilpin County. Arapaho/Roosevelt National Forest. From Rollinsville, drive west about 8 miles on Forest Route 149 to East Portal. Park by tunnel. On the south side of the road walk through gate (Gate may be locked). Hike 1 mile southwest on road, to intersection with South Boulder Creek Trail. Turn south, cross creek, and hike about one mile to another creek. Turn west and follow the creek (no trail) for 1/2 mile to Clayton Lake. Continue one-half mile west along the creek, then take either fork another 1/2 mile to the lakes.
Size: **North Lake** - 10 acres; 77 feet maximum depth.
           South Lake - 6 acres; 100 feet maximum depth.
Fish: Cutthroat trout.
Agency: USFS-Boulder Ranger District.
Comments: USGS East Portal quad; altitude 11,500 feet. Non-motorized boats only. No fish in south lake.

33 Heart Lake

Location: Gilpin County. Arapaho/Roosevelt National Forest. From Rollinsville, drive west about 8 miles on Forest Route 149 to East Portal. Park by tunnel. On the south side of the road walk through gate (Gate may be locked). Hike 1 mile southwest on road, to intersection with South Boulder Creek Trail. Turn south, cross creek, and hike about 1 mile. Cross another creek and continue south three quarters of a mile, follow the trail west for one-half mile. Trail crosses stream turn off and hike west following stream for one-quarter mile to Heart Lake.
Size: 17 acres; 52 feet maximum depth.
Fish: Cutthroat trout.
Agency: USFS-Boulder Ranger District.
Comments: USGS East Portal quad; altitude 12,218 feet. Trail continues west over Roger Pass. Non-motorized boats only.

35 Rogers Pass Lake

Location: Gilpin County. Arapaho/Roosevelt National Forest. From Rollinsville, drive west about 8 miles on Forest Route 149 to East Portal. Park by tunnel. On the south side of the road walk through gate (Gate may be locked). Hike one mile southwest on road, to intersection with South Boulder Creek Trail. Turn south, cross creek, and hike about 1 mile. Cross another creek and continue south three-quarters of a mile, follow the trail west for one-half a mile. Trail crosses stream. Stay on trail a short distance until Rogers Pass Lake is seen just to the south of the trail. It is before Rogers Pass.
Size: 5.6 acres; 6.5 feet maximum depth.
Fish: Cutthroat trout.
Agency: USFS-Boulder Ranger District.
Comments: USGS Empire quad; altitude 11,200 feet. Non-motorized boats only.

35 James Peak Lake

Location: Gilpin County. Arapaho/Roosevelt National Forest. From Rollinsville, drive west 5.5 miles on Forest Route 149 to Tolland. Turn left on Forest Route 176. Go about 1.5 miles to triple fork. (Left fork goes to Elk park). Take right fork toward Kingston Peak and James Peak, about 4 miles to James Peak trailhead. Hike down the trail, about 1 mile west to James Peak Lake.
Size: 10 acres; 10 feet maximum depth.
Fish: Cutthroat trout.
Agency: USFS-Boulder Ranger District.
Comments: USGS Empire and East Portal quads; altitude 11,100 feet. Non-motorized boats only.

35a Little Echo Lake

Location: Gilpin County, Arapaho/Roosevelt Nat. Forest. From Rollinsville west 5 mi. on Forest Rd 149 to Tolland. South on Forest Rd. 176 about 1.5 mi. to triple fork. (Left fork goes to Elk Park.) Take west fork towards Kingston Peak and James Peak about 4 mi. to James Peak Trailhead. Take trail #804 about 1.5 mi. west to Echo Lake.
Size: 13 acres; 96 feet maximum depth.
Fish: Rainbow and lake trout.
Agency: Central City.
Comments: USGS Empire and East Portal Quads; altitude 11,100 feet. Non-motorized boats only.
Helpful Hints: This lake has naturally sustained lake trout population. Although most of the fish are smaller (Up to 14 inches), a unique angling opportunity exists to catch them on dry flies. Matching a spectacular flying ant hatch (size 14-16) in August while fishing from a float tube can be effective. (Fish often feed in the middle of the lake.)

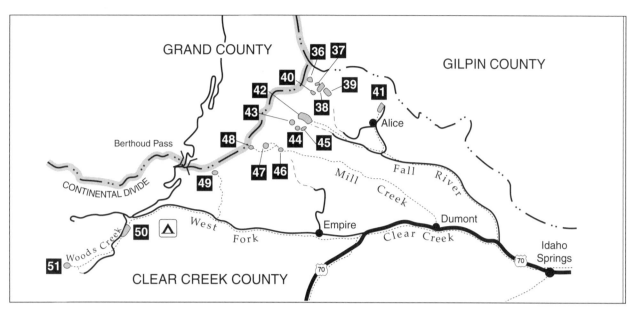

36 Ice Lake

Location: Clear Creek County. Arapaho/Roosevelt National Forest.
West on I-70 about 2 miles past Idaho Springs take exit 238, Fall River Road. Drive north on Fall River Road for 9 miles to the town of Alice. Turn left on Silver Creek then right on Texas Drive past the "Glory Hole Mine". Take first dirt road right after the mine (rough road). Passing by Steuart Lake hike .2 mile to Ohman Lake. Ice Lake is .2 miles past Ohman Lake.
Size: 12 acres; 102 feet maximum depth.
Fish: Cutthroat trout.
Agency: USFS-Clear Creek Ranger District.
Comments: USGS Empire quad; altitude 12,200 feet. Ice stays on very late. Non-motorized boats only.

37 Steuart Lake

Location: Clear Creek County. Arapaho/Roosevelt National Forest. West on I-70 about 2 miles past Idaho Springs take exit 238, Fall River Road. Drive north on Fall River Road for 9 miles to the town of Alice. Turn left on Silver Creek then right on Texas Drive past the "Glory Hole Mine" sign. Take first dirt road after the mine (rough road). Hike around west side of Loch Lomond and uphill next to inlet stream about 1 mile to Reynolds Lake. Turn north and hike around the east side of Reynolds Lake then .1 mile to Steuart Lake.
Size: 7 acres; 15 feet maximum depth.
Fish: Brook and lake trout.
Agency: Agriculture Ditch and Reservoir Company.
Comments: USGS Empire quad; altitude 11,400 feet. No boats.

38 Reynolds Lake

Location: Clear Creek County. Arapaho/Roosevelt National Forest. West on I-70 about 2 miles past Idaho Springs take exit 238, Fall River Road. Drive north on Fall River Road for 9 miles to the town of Alice. Turn left on Silver Creek then right on Texas Drive past the "Glory Hole Mine". Take first dirt road right after the mine (rough road). Hike around west side of Loch Lomond Lake and uphill to next inlet stream about .1 mile to Reynolds Lake.
Size: 3 acres; 28 feet maximum depth.
Fish: Brook trout.
Agency: Agriculture Ditch and Reservoir Company.
Comments: USGS Empire quad; altitude 11,200 feet. Non-motorized boats only.

39 Loch Lomond Lake

Location: Clear Creek County. Arapaho/Roosevelt National Forest. West on I-70 about 2 miles past Idaho Springs take exit 238, Fall River Road. Drive north on Fall River Road for 9 miles to the town of Alice. Turn left on Silver Creek and then right on Texas Drive past the "Glory Hole Mine". Take first dirt road right after the mine (rough road). Loch Lomond Lake is about 3.3 miles from Alice. Note: Roads leading to this lake are rough unimproved dirt and/or gravel. Depending upon road conditions, a 4 wheel drive vehicle may be needed to reach the lake. Persons utilizing 2-wheel drive vehicles may have to park off road and hike to lake.
Size: 23 acres; 76 feet maximum depth.
Fish: Brook, brown and lake trout.
Agency: Agriculture Ditch and Reservoir Company.
Comments: USGS Empire quad; altitude 11,180 feet. Boats allowed.
Special Regulations: The bag and possession limit for lake trout (Makinaw) is one fish, 20 inches or longer.

40 Lake Caroline

Location: Clear Creek County. Arapaho/Roosevelt National Forest. West on I-70 about 2 miles past Idaho Springs . Take exit 238 - Fall River Road. Drive north on Fall River Road to the town of Alice. Turn left on Silver Creek then right on Texas Drive past the "Glory Hole Mine". Take the first dirt road right after the Glory Hole Mine (rough road) and drive to Loch Lomond. Hike west cross county for one-half mile to Lake Caroline.
Note: Roads leading to this lake are rough unimproved dirt and/or gravel. Depending upon road conditions , a 4-wheel drive vehicle may be needed to reach the lake. Persons utilizing 2-wheel drive vehicles may have to park off road and hike to lake.
Size: 8.6 acres; 58 feet maximum depth.
Fish: Cutthroat trout.
Agency: USFS-Clear Creek Ranger District.
Comments: USGS Empire quad; altitude 11,840 feet. Non-motorized boats only.

41 Saint Mary's Lake

Location: Clear Creek County. Arapaho/Roosevelt National Forest. West on I-70 about 2 miles past Idaho Springs take exit 238 - Fall River Road. Drive 10 miles on Fall River Road (past the town of Alice) to St. Mary's Glacier Lodge. Park and hike northwest about one-quarter mile up an old road to Saint Mary's Lake.
Size: 7.2 acres; 21 feet maximum depth.
Fish: Brook trout.
Agency: USFS-Clear Creek Ranger District.
Comments: USGS Empire quad; altitude 10, 710 feet. Non-motorized boats only.

42 Fall River Reservoir

Location: Clear Creek County. Arapaho/Roosevelt National Forest. West on I-70 about 2 miles past Idaho Springs take exit 238 - Fall River Road. Drive north on Fall River Road for 7.3 miles, where the main road turns uphill, take the narrow dirt road which follows the Fall River. Follow this road for 2.3 miles to the "Y" in the road. Take right fork for 2 miles to reservoir.
Note: Roads leading to this lake are rough unimproved dirt and/or gravel. Depending upon road conditions, a 4-wheel drive vehicle may be needed to reach the lake. Persons utilizing 2-wheel drive vehicles may have to park and walk to the lake.
Size: 17 acres; 80 feet maximum depth.
Fish: Rainbow and cutthroat trout.
Agency: Agriculture Ditch and Reservoir Company.
Comments: USGS Empire quad; altitude 10,880 feet. Non-motorized boats only.

43 Slater Lake

Location: Clear Creek County. Arapaho/Roosevelt National Forest. West on I-70 about 2 miles past Idaho Springs take exit 238 - Fall River Road. Drive north on Fall River Road for 7.3 miles, where the main road turns uphill, take the narrow dirt road which follows the Fall River. Follow this road for 2.3 miles to "Y" in the road. Take left fork (rough road) 1.2 miles to Chinn's Lake. Stay on left side of dam and go .1 mile to Sherwin Lake. Then from the northwest side of Sherwin Lake follow the stream and hike one-quarter mile to the lake.
Note: Roads leading to this lake are rough unimproved dirt and/or gravel. Depending upon road conditions, a 4-wheel drive vehicle may be needed to reach the lake. Persons utilizing 2-wheel drive vehicles may have to park and walk to the lake.
Size: 7.2 acres; 4.5 feet maximum depth.
Fish: Cutthroat trout.
Agency: USFS - Clear Creek Ranger District.
Comments: USGS Empire quad; altitude 11,440 feet. Non-motorized boats only.

44 Sherwin Lake

Location: Clear Creek County. Arapaho/Roosevelt National Forest. West on I-70 about 2 miles past Idaho Springs take exit 238 - Fall River Road. Drive north on Fall River Road for 7.3 miles, where the main road turns uphill, take the narrow dirt road which follows the Fall River. Follow this road for 2.3 miles to "Y" in the road. Take left fork (rough road) 1.2 miles to Chinn's Lake. Stay on left side of dam and go .1 mile to Lake.
Note: Roads leading to this lake are rough unimproved dirt and/or gravel. Depending upon road conditions, a 4-wheel drive vehicle may be needed to reach the lake. Persons utilizing 2-wheel drive vehicles may have to park and walk to the lake.
Size: 8.6 acres; 21 feet maximum depth.
Fish: Brook, rainbow, cutthroat trout and splake.
Agency: USFS - Clear Creek Ranger District.
Comments: USGS Empire quad; altitude 11,090 feet. Non-motorized boats only.
Special Regulations: Bag and possession limit for splake is 2 fish, 16 inches or longer. Artificial flies and lures only.

45 Chinn's Lake

Location: Clear Creek County. Arapaho/Roosevelt National Forest. West on I-70 about 2 miles past Idaho Springs take exit 238 - Fall River Road. Drive north on Fall River Road for 7.3 miles, where the main road turns uphill, take the narrow dirt road which follows the Fall River. Follow this road for 2.3 miles to "Y" in the road. Take left fork (rough road) 1.2 miles to Chinn's Lake.
Note: Roads leading to this lake are rough unimproved dirt and/or gravel. Depending upon road conditions, a 4-wheel drive vehicle may be needed to reach the lake. Persons utilizing 2-wheel drive vehicles may have to park and walk to the lake.
Size: 10 acres; 30 feet maximum depth.
Fish: Rainbow trout and splake.
Agency: USFS - Clear Creek Ranger District.
Comments: USGS Empire quad; altitude 11,000 feet. Non-motorized boats only.

46 Bill Moore Lake

Location: Clear Creek County. Arapaho/Roosevelt National Forest. From Empire, drive north on Empire Creek Road to the abandoned Conqueror Mine. Hike north and northwest on the winding 4WD road. Total distance is about 6 miles to Bill Moore Lake from Empire.
Size: 7 acres; 3 feet maximum depth.

Fish: Cutthroat trout.
Agency: USFS - Clear Creek Ranger District.
Comments: USGS Empire quad; altitude 11,280 feet. Non-motorized boats only.

47 Byron Lake

Location: Clear Creek County. Arapaho/Roosevelt National Forest. From Empire, drive north on Empire Creek Road to the abandoned Conqueror Mine. Hike north and northwest on the winding 4WD road. Total distance is about 6 miles to Bill Moore Lake from Empire. From the northwest side of Bill Moore Lake, follow the inlet stream and take the north fork and hike 1 mile (no trail) following the stream to Byron Lake. No trail, use topo map advised.
Size: 2.8 acres; 9 feet maximum depth.
Fish: Cutthroat trout.
Agency: USFS - Clear Creek Ranger District.
Comments: USGS Empire quad; altitude 12,100 feet. Non-motorized boats only.

48 Ethel Lake

Location: Clear Creek County. Arapaho/Roosevelt National Forest. From Empire, drive north on Empire Creek Road to the abandoned Conqueror Mine. Hike north and northwest on the winding 4WD road. Total distance is about 6 miles to Bill Moore Lake from Empire. From the northwest side of Bill Moore Lake, follow the inlet stream and take the south fork and hike west 1.2 miles following the stream to Ethel Lake. No trail, use of topo map advised.
Size: 5 acres; 65 feet maximum depth.
Fish: Cutthroat trout.
Agency: USFS - Clear Creek Ranger District.
Comments: USGS Empire quad; altitude 12,560 feet. Non-motorized boats only.

49 Cone Lake

Location: Clear Creek County. Arapaho/Roosevelt National Forest. From Empire, drive west on US40. Follow the highway to the summit of Berthoud Pass. Hike 2 miles east on trail to Cone Lake.
Size: 3 acres; 8 feet maximum depth.
Fish: Cutthroat trout.
Agency: USFS - Clear Creek Ranger District.
Comments: USGS Berthoud Pass quad; altitude 11,600 feet. Steep hiking. Non-motorized boats only.

50 Urad Reservoir - Upper

Location: Clear Creek County. Arapaho/Roosevelt National Forest. From Empire go about 7 miles west on US 40 to Big Ben Picnic Ground. Go a short distance and turn south, drive 2 miles on dirt road to Urad Reservoir.
Size: 31 acres; 48 feet maximum depth.
Fish: Brook, rainbow (catchable size stocked) and brown trout.
Agency: Amax, Inc.
Comments: USGS Gray's Peak quad; altitude 10,720 feet. Mizpaw Campground is 1.5 miles up US 40 from Big Ben. No boats allowed.

51 Hassell Lake

Location: Clear Creek County. Arapaho/Roosevelt National Forest. From Empire go about 7 miles west on US 40 to Big Ben Picnic Ground. Go west from hairpin turn onto Henderson Mine road. Go a short distance and turn south, drive 2 miles on dirt road to Urad Reservoir. Hike one-half mile northwest from the reservoir along tributary stream to Hassell Lake.
Size: 8.6 acres; 7 feet maximum depth.
Fish: Brook trout.
Agency: USFS - Clear Creek Ranger District.
Comments: USGS Gray's Peak quad; altitude 11,360 feet. Mizpaw Campground is 1.5 miles up US 40 from Big Ben. Non-motorized boats only.

Taking care of the catch
Nebraska Game & Fish

Fresh fish is extremely perishable. Any fish left in the hot sun can spoil in less than an hour. Regardless of how you are going to prepare your fish, your fish needs taken care of from the minute you catch the fish until it reaches the cook. Consider catch and release if you are not prepared to care for the catch.

It is best if the fish is killed immediately, cleaned and placed on ice. If you can not clean the fish immediately keep it cool and clean it within a few hours. This will reduce the chance of spoilage in warm weather and improve the table quality of the catch.

The following methods can be used to freeze the fish:
• **Freezer wrapping:** Package meat sized packages. You can use heavy duty aluminum foil, plastic freezer proof wrap or plastic bags. It is important with any of these wrappings to remove all the air and seal tightly.

• **Glazing:** This is achieved by dipping frozen fish in ice water and letting it freeze between coating. Do this until you have a good coat of ice over the entire fish.
• **Block freezing:** Simply freeze the fish in a solid block of ice.

• **Label and date your packages:** Fish properly wrapped will keep for 3-6 months and retain its good flavor and quality. Thawing fish in the refrigerator, keeping it covered, is the best method for preparing the catch for the frying pan or broiler. However, fish also can be thawed with cold running water or using a microwave oven. Taking steps to protect your catch will reward you with a dinner well worth the time and effort.

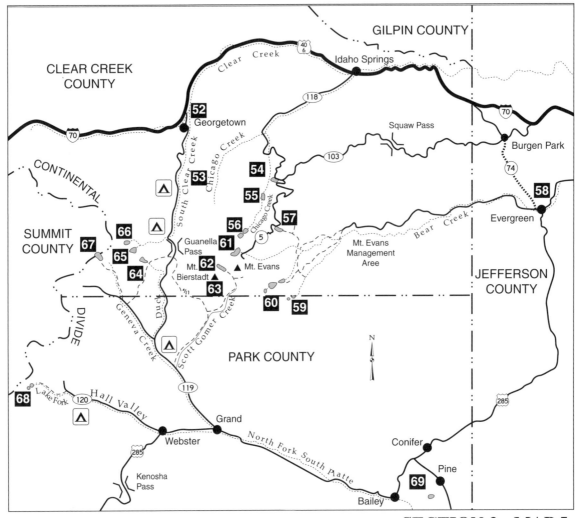

SECTION 3 - MAP 5

52 Georgetown Lake

Location: Clear Creek County. Arapaho/Roosevelt National Forest. From Idaho Springs, continue west on I-70 to Georgetown exit. Go south to first stop sign, turn east and drive to the lake.
Size: 54.3 acres; 11 feet maximum depth.
Fish: Rainbow trout (catchable sized stocked), brown, cutthroat and brook trout.
Agency: City of Georgetown.
Comments: USGS Georgetown quad; altitude 8,460 feet. Clear Lake Campground is 4 miles south on Guanella Pass Road. Non-motorized boats only. Handicapped accessible fishing pier. Bighorn sheep viewing. Ice fishing.

53 Clear Lake

Location: Clear Creek County. Arapaho/Roosevelt National Forest. From Georgetown, drive south on Guanella Pass Road about 4 miles. Clear Lake is just east of the road.
Size: 24 acres; 98 feet maximum depth.
Fish: Rainbow (catchable size stocked), brook trout and sucker.
Agency: Public Service Company.

Comments: USGS Idaho Springs quad; altitude 9,873 feet. Clear Lake campground is about 1 mile south of the lake. No boats.

54 Echo Lake

Location: Clear Creek County. Arapaho/Roosevelt National Forest. From Idaho Springs drive south 12 miles on Hwy 103. Lake is south of the highway just west of Mt. Evans Road.
Size: 18.2 acres; 7 feet maximum depth.
Fish: Rainbow trout (catchable size stocked).
Agency: Denver Parks & Recreation.
Comments: USGS Idaho Springs quad; altitude 10,720 feet. West Chicago Creek Campground is 8 miles west (Reservations suggested). No boats.

55 Idaho Springs Reservoir

Location: Clear Creek County. Arapaho/Roosevelt National Forest. From Idaho Springs, drive south on Hwy 103 about 8 miles (past the Chicago Forks Picnic Grounds) to Chicago Creek Road drive south 1.5 miles and then hike 1.5 miles south on road to reservoir.
Size: 20 acres; 30 feet maximum depth.
Fish: Brook, rainbow, cutthroat trout and sucker.

Agency: City of Idaho Springs.
Comments: USGS Idaho Springs quad; altitude 10,600 feet. West Chicago Creek Campground is 8 miles west (Reservations suggested). No boats.

56 Chicago Lakes

Location: Clear Creek County. Arapaho/Roosevelt National Forest. From Idaho Springs, drive south on Hwy 103 about 8 miles (past the Chicago Forks Picnic Grounds) to Chicago Creek Road drive south 1.5 miles and then hike 1.5 miles south on road to Idaho Springs Reservoir. Hike around the west side of the reservoir and follow the creek upstream. Go 2 miles south to Chicago Lakes. Alternate route from Idaho Springs, drive 12 miles south on Hwy 103 to Echo Lake. Hike west on Chicago Reservoir trail to Chicago Creek road, then continue as above.
Size: Upper Lake - 10 acres; 41 feet maximum depth.
 Lower Lake - 26 acres; 74 feet maximum depth.
Fish: Cutthroat and rainbow trout.
Agency: USFS - Clear Creek Ranger District.
Comments: USGS Idaho Springs and Mt. Evans quads; altitude 11,620 feet. Camping at West Chicago Creek Campground (Reservations suggested). Non-motorized boats only. Located in Mount Evans Wilderness.

57 Lincoln Lake

Location: Clear Creek County. Arapaho/Roosevelt National Forest. From Idaho Springs, drive 12 miles south on Hwy 103 to Echo Lake. Hike 1 mile east on Beaverdam Trail #46. Turn south and hike over 3 miles to next fork. Turn west and hike over one-half mile on Trail #45 to Lincoln Lake.
Size: 12.8 acres; 61 feet maximum depth.
Fish: Brook, Lake trout and sucker.
Agency: USFS - Clear Creek Ranger District.
Comments: USGS Harris Park quad; altitude 11,620 feet. Very difficult hike. Lies some 900 vertical feet directly below Mt. Evans road, 3.5 miles south of Echo Lake junction. Non-motorized boats only.

58 Evergreen Lake

Location: Jefferson County. From Denver, go west on I-70 to Evergreen Parkway exit. Go south on Hwy 74 to Evergreen. The lake is south on Hwy 74 and upper Bear Creek Road.
Size: 42 acres; 22 feet maximum depth.
Fish: Brown and rainbow trout (catchable size stocked), sucker, tiger muskie and splake.
Agency: City of Evergreen Park & Recreation District.
Comments: USGS Evergreen quad; altitude 7,072 feet. Boating by evergreen permit only - No power boats. Open late may. Hours 5 a.m. to 10 p.m. for fishing only. Handicapped accessible fishing pier and marsh viewing boardwalk. Parking available above and below dam.

59 Roosevelt Lakes

Location: Park County. Arapaho/Roosevelt National Forest. From Denver, drive south on US 285. Near the top of Crow Hill, 3 miles north of Bailey, turn northwest on Forest Route 100. Drive about 9 miles to Deer Creek Campground, the end of the road. Hike north 4 miles on Tanglewood Creek Trail #636 to Roosevelt Lakes. From Evergreen, drive about 6 miles west on upper Bear Creek Road. Take the west fork after Brookvale, and continue west for 2 miles. Take the south fork, go 2 miles and take the north fork. Continue west for 4 miles to Camp Rock Trailhead. Hike about 4.5 miles southwest on Beartrack Lakes Trail #43, to Beartrack Lakes. From here hike one mile southeast on trail #78 to Roosevelt Lakes.
Size: 2 lakes; 6 acres total; 22 feet maximum depth.
Fish: Cutthroat, rainbow and brook trout.
Agency: USFS - Clear Creek Ranger District.
Comments: USGS Harris Park quad; altitude 10,400 feet. Located in Mount Evans Wilderness. Non-motorized boats only.

60 Beartrack Lakes

Location: Clear Creek County. Arapaho/Roosevelt National Forest. From Denver, go west on I-70 to Evergreen Parkway exit. Go south on Hwy 74 to Evergreen. From Evergreen drive about 6 miles west on Upper Bear Creek Road. Take the west fork after Brookvale, and continue west for 2 miles. Take the south fork, go 2 miles then take the north fork. Continue west for 4 miles to Camp Rock Trailhead. Hike about 4.5 miles southwest on Beartrack Lakes Trail #43, to the lakes.
Size: Upper Lake - 5 acres; 25 feet maximum depth.
 Lower Lake - 11 acres; 28 feet maximum depth.
Fish: Brook and cutthroat trout.
Agency: USFS - Clear Creek Ranger District.
Comments: USGS Harris Park quad; altitude 10,500 feet. Camping at Beartrack Lakes and Echo Lake Campground. Follow trail signs. Dogs must be on 6 foot leash in elk management area. Located in Mount Evans Wilderness. Non-motorized boats only.

61 Summit Lake

Location: Clear Creek County. Arapaho/Roosevelt National Forest. From Idaho Springs, drive 12 miles south on Hwy 103 to Echo Lake. East of the Lake turn south on Mt. Evans road, Hwy 5. Drive 9 miles, the lake is just west of the road.
Size: 32.8 acres; 70 feet maximum depth.
Fish: Rainbow and cutthroat trout.
Agency: Denver Parks & Recreation.
Comments: USGS Mt. Evans quad; altitude 12,900 feet. Roadside fishery. Non-motorized boats only. Open 5 a.m. to 11 p.m.

62 Abyss Lake

Location: Clear Creek County. Pike National Forest. From Grant, drive north on Guanella Pass Road (Forest Route 118) to Burning Bear Campground. Hike 3.5 miles northeast on Scott Gomer Creek Trail to Lake Fork Trail #602. (Just past Deer Creek Trail #603.) Hike northeast 3 miles on Lake Fork Trail to Abyss Lake. From Georgetown, drive south on Guanella Pass Road. Drive about 6 miles from the summit of the pass to Burning Bear Campground and continue as above. Abyss Lake is between Mt. Evans and Mt. Bierstadt.
Size: 18 acres; 50 feet maximum depth.
Fish: Rainbow and cutthroat trout.

Agency: USFS - South Platte Ranger District.
Comments: USGS Mt. Evans quad; altitude 12,640 feet. Frozen over until mid-June or later. Harsh environment. Camping at Burning Bear and Geneva Park Campgrounds. Non-motorized boats only. Located in Mount Evans Wilderness.

63 Frozen Lake
Location: Clear Creek County. Pike National Forest. From Grant, drive north on Guanella Pass Road (Forest Route 118) to Burning Bear Campground. Hike 3.5 miles northeast on Scott Gomer Creek Trail to Lake Fork Trail, past 2 trails going east, and continue 1 mile north on Scott Gomer. Follow the creek north where the trail heads west. Hike 2 miles upstream to Frozen Lake. Rugged terrain, use of topo map advised. From Georgetown, drive south on Guanella Pass Road. Drive about 6 miles south from the summit of the pass to Burning Bear Campground. Continue as above.
Size: 7 acres; 33 feet maximum depth.
Fish: Cutthroat trout.
Agency: USFS - South Platte Ranger District.
Comments: USGS Mt. Evans quad; altitude 12,960 feet. Harsh environment. Lake is frozen over until mid-June or later. Mt. Bierstadt, 14,060 feet, looms over the lake. Camping at Burning Bear and Geneva Park Campgrounds. No boats. Located in Mount Evans Wilderness.

64 Square Top Lakes
Location: Clear Creek County. Arapaho/Roosevelt National Forest. From Georgetown, drive south on Guanella Pass Road to the summit of the pass. Hike 2 miles west on the trail to Square Top Lakes.
Size: 2 lakes; 10 acres each.
Fish: Cutthroat trout.
Agency: USFS - Clear Creek Ranger District.
Comments: USGS Mt. Evans quad; altitude 12,160 feet. Guanella Pass and Clear Lake Campgrounds nearby on the south fork of Clear Creek. Non-motorized boats only.

65 Silver Dollar Lake
Location: Clear Creek County. Arapaho/Roosevelt National Forest. From Georgetown, go 7 miles south on Guanella Pass Road to Guanella Pass Campground. Just pass the campground take the west fork. Drive one mile to Naylor Lake (which is private). Hike west along the south side of Taylor Lake to a trail along the creek. Hike one-half mile west along the west fork of the trail to Silver Dollar Lake. From Grant, drive north on Forest Route 118, Guanella Pass Road, over the pass to Guanella Pass Campground. Continue from campground as in above directions.
Size: 18.6 acres; 73 feet maximum depth.
Fish: Cutthroat trout.
Agency: USFS - Clear Creek Ranger District
Comments: USGS Mt. Evans and Montezuma quads; altitude 11,950 feet. Non-motorized boats only.

66 Murray Lake
Location: Clear Creek County. Arapaho/Roosevelt National Forest. From Georgetown, go 7 miles south on Guanella Pass Road to Guanella Pass Campground. Just pass the campground take the west fork. Drive one mile to Naylor Lake (which is private). Hike west along the south side of Naylor Lake, to a trail along the creek. Hike 1 mile northwest on the north fork of the trail to Murray Lake.
Size: 11.4 acres; 38 feet maximum depth.
Fish: Cutthroat trout.
Agency: USFS - Clear Creek Ranger District.
Comments: USGS Mt. Evans and Montezuma quads; altitude 12,080 feet. Non-motorized boats only.

67 Shelf Lake
Location: Clear Creek County. Pike National Forest. From Grant, drive north on Guanella Pass Road, Forest Route 118, to Duck Creek Picnic Ground. Take the west fork of the road. Drive 3 miles northwest up Geneva Creek Road, Forest Route 119, to Smelter Gulch. Hike 3 miles up the trail to Shelf Lake.
Size: 9.5 acres; 40 feet maximum depth.
Fish: Cutthroat trout.
Agency: USFS - South Platte Ranger District.
Comments: USGS Montezuma quad; altitude 12,000 feet. Harsh environment. Lake is frozen over until mid-June or later. Mt. Bierstadt, 14,060 feet, looms over the lake. Camping at Burning Bear and Geneva Creek Campgrounds. Non-motorized boats only.

68 Gibson Lake
Location: Park County. Pike National Forest. From Denver, drive south on US 285 and turn north on Webster. Drive 7 miles northwest on Hall Valley Road, Forest Route 120, to trailhead at Gibson Lake Trail Picnic Ground. Hike 2.5 miles south and then west on Gibson Lake Trail #633.
Size: 3 acres; 23 feet maximum depth.
Fish: Brook trout.
Agency: USFS - South Platte Ranger District.
Comments: USGS Jefferson quad; 11,500 feet. Hall Valley Campground near trailhead. Non-motorized boats only.

69 Pine Valley Ranch Pond
Location: Access via U. S. Highway 285 south to Pine Junction, turn south (left) at Pine Junction onto Colo. 126 and follow southeast 5.6 miles to the turn-off for Pine Valley Ranch Park (Jefferson County Open Space) - before the town of Pine. Follow this road west approximately 1 miles to the Visitors Center parking lot. Cross the North Fork of the South Platte River via the foot bridge and follow the trail to the pond. Access to the North Fork of the South Platte River and many hiking trails.
Size: 8 acres; 10 feet maximum depth.
Fish: Rainbow (catchable-size stocked), brown trout and sucker.
Agency: Jefferson County Open Space.
Comments: Excellent access to many hiking trails and picnic area. Visitors center and restrooms located near parking lot. Handicapped-accessible stream and pond piers.
Special Regulations: Four trout bag and possession limit in the park (stream and pond combined); children under 16 without a license - 2 trout bag and possession limit in the park (stream and pond combined).

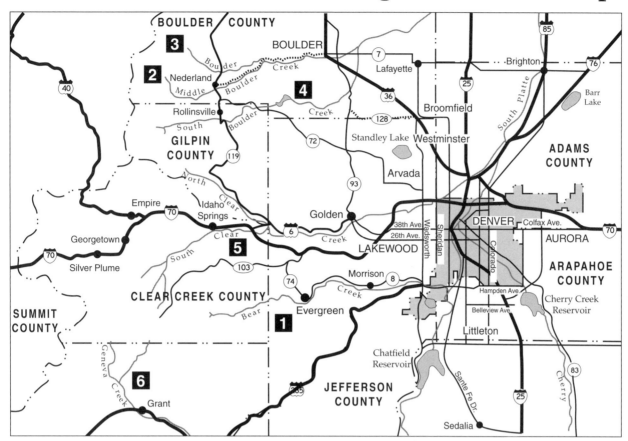

SECTION 4 - MAP 1

Metro Streams

1 Bear Creek

Location: Clear Creek and Jefferson counties. Headwaters on Mt. Evans, flows easterly through the Denver Metro area to the South Platte River.

Fish: Rainbow, brown, cutthroat and brook trout.

Nearby Lakes: Lincoln Lakes, Beartrack Lakes, Evergreen Lake and Bear Creek Reservoir.

Comments: Headwaters are in Arapaho National Forest with the upper reaches accessible only by foot or horseback from Mt. Evans Road. or along the Creek west of Evergreen. Some private property in developed areas. East of Morrison the creek often runs through public green belt areas.

2 Boulder Creek-Middle

Location: Boulder County. Flows easterly from the Continental Divide west of Nederland (Hwy 72) to Barker Reservoir into Boulder Canyon (Hwy 119) to merge with north Boulder Creek to form Boulder Creek which flows through Boulder.

Fish: Rainbow, brown cutthroat and brook trout.

Nearby Lakes: King Lake, Skyscraper Reservoir, Devil's Thumb Lake, Jasper Lake, Diamond Lake, Lake Dorothy, Banana Lake, Upper Diamond Lake, Lost Lake, Betty Lake, Bob Lake, Woodland Lake, Storm Lake, and Glacier Lake.

Comments: Headwaters in Roosevelt National Forest are open to the public. Major portions of stream are private and posted. Upper reaches of the south fork of Middle Boulder Creek are in the Indian Peaks Wilderness Area and are accessible by foot or horseback only. The forks join 1.5 miles west of Eldora at Hessie east of Barker Reservoir Hwy 119 is adjacent to the creek in Boulder Canyon. Fishing possible in the city of Boulder.

Special Regulations: From Upper end of Ebin Fine Park to 55th Street, fishing is by artificial flies or lures only. All fish caught must be returned to the water immediately (Catch and release only).

3 Boulder Creek-North

Location: Boulder County. Flows southwesterly from its headwaters in the lakes at the foot of Arapaho Glacier northwest of Nederland along the Continental Divide.

Fish: Rainbow, cutthroat and brook trout.

Nearby Lakes: Rainbow Lakes.

Comments: The creek and associated lakes are on a mixture of public and private property in Arapaho/Roosevelt National Forest. Best fishing in the area is at Rainbow Lakes where there is Rainbow Lakes Campground and trailhead for going to the Glacier.

4 Boulder Creek-South

Location: Gilpin and Boulder Counties. Flows easterly from the Continental Divide west of Rollinsville (Hwy 72) to Gross Reservoir, Eldorado Canyon State Park, and through Boulder.

Fish: Rainbow, brook, cutthroat and brown trout.

Nearby Lakes: James Peak Lake, Roger's Pass Lake, Heart Lake, Iceberg Lakes, Clayton Lake, Crater Lake, Arapaho Lakes, Forest Lakes, Gross Reservoir, Jenny Lake, and Yankee Doodle Lake.

Comments: Headwaters in Roosevelt National Forest are open to the public. Sections of the stream are on posted private property, portions are channeled west of Rollinsville. Between Pine Cliffe an Eldorado Canyon State Park terrain is extremely rugged and access is difficult. Below the park, 8 miles southeast of Boulder, a mile-long stretch of the stream on the Walker Ranch is open to public fishing. Take Flagstaff Drive from Boulder parking area and hike one mile to the creek.

5 Clear Creek

Location: Clear Creek and Jefferson Counties. Flows easterly from the Continental Divide near the Eisenhower Tunnel along I-70 at the foot of Loveland Pass and into the Denver Metro area. The most fishable portions are adjacent to highways and frontage roads. There is some private property.

Fish: Rainbow, brook, cutthroat and brown trout.

Nearby Lakes: Silver Dollar Lake, Murray Lake, Georgetown Lake, Hassel Lake, Ethel Lake, Bill Moore Lake, Chinn's Lake, Sherwin Lake, Slater Lake, Fall River Reservoir, Reynolds Lake, Steuart Lake, Loch Lomond Lake, Lake Caroline, Ice Lake, St. Mary's Lake, Prospect Park Lakes, Summit Lake, Idaho Springs Reservoir, Echo Lake.

Comments: Headwaters are in Arapaho/Roosevelt National Forest. Streams tributary to Clear Creek (including Chicago Creek, the South Fork of Clear Creek, and the headwaters reaches of the North and West Forks of Clear Creek) support populations of rainbow, brook and cutthroat trout.

6 Geneva Creek

Location: Park and Clear Creek counties. Flows southerly into the north fork of the South Platte River at Grant on US 285.

Fish: Rainbow, brown, cutthroat and brook trout.

Nearby Lakes: Shelf Lake, Square Top Lakes, Abyss Lakes, and Frozen Lake.

Comments: Headwaters to Scott Gomer Creek in Pike National Forest have insignificant fish populations. Below the falls at Burning Bear Campground is intermittent public and private land. Tributary streams have small brook trout. Camping is at Burning Bear and Geneva Park Campgrounds and underdeveloped sites upstream from Guanella Pass junction. Good road parallels most of the stream.

RECREATION INFORMATION PHONE NUMBERS FOR STATE, FEDERAL AND OTHER AGENCIES

APAPAHO/ROOSEVELT NATIONAL FOREST
BOULDER RANGER DISTRICT ....(303) 541-2500
CANYON LAKES RIVER DISTRICT ...(970) 295-6600
CLEAR CREEK RANGER DISTRICT ....(303) 567-3000
PAWNEE RANGER DISTRICT ....(970) 346-5000
SULPHUR RANGER DISTRICT ....(970) 887-4100

GRAND MESA NATIONAL FOREST
COLLBRAN RANGER DISTRICT ....(970) 487-3534
GRAND JUNCTION RANGER DIST......(970) 242-8211

GUNNISON NATIONAL FOREST
CEBOLLA RANGER DISTRICT ....(970) 641-0471
PAONIA RANGER DISTRICT ....(970) 527-4131
GUNNISON RANGER DISTRICT ....(970) 641-0471

PIKE NATIONAL FOREST
PIKES PEAK RANGER DISTRICT ....(719) 636-1602
SOUTH PARK RANGER DISTRICT ......(719) 836-2031
SOUTH PLATTE RANGER DISTRICT ....(303) 275-5610

RIO GRANDE/SAN JUAN NATIONAL FOREST
CONEJOS PEAK RANGER DISTRICT ....(719) 274-8971
DIVIDE RANGER DISTRICT (Creede) ....(719) 658-2556
DIVIDE RANGER DIST. (Del Norte) ......(719) 657-3321
SAGUACHE RANGER DISTRICT ....(719) 655-2547

ROUTT NATIONAL FOREST
HAHNS PEAK/BEAR EARS RANGER ....(970) 879-1870
THE PARKS RANGER DISTRICT ....(970) 723-8204
YAMPA RANGER DISTRICT ....(970) 638-4516

SAN ISABEL NATIONAL FOREST
LEADVILLE RANGER DISTRICT ....(719) 486-0749
SALIDA RANGER DISTRICT ....(719) 539-3591
SAN CARLOS RANGER DISTRICT ......(719) 269-8500

SAN JUAN/RIO GRANDE NATIONAL FOREST
COLUMBINE EAST RANGER ....(970) 884-2512
COLUMBINE WEST RANGER ....(970) 884-2512
MANCOS/DOLORES RANGER DIST.....(970) 882-7296

PAGOSA RANGER DISTRICT ....(970) 264-2268
UNCOMPAHGRE NATIONAL FOREST
GRAND JUNCTION RANGER DISTRICT ..(970) 242-8211
NORWOOD RANGER DISTRICT ....(970) 327-4261
OURAY RANGER DISTRICT ....(970) 240-5300

WHITE RIVER NATIONAL FOREST
ASPEN RANGER DISTRICT ....(970) 925-3445
BLANCO RANGER DISTRICT ....(970) 878-4039
DILLON RANGER DISTRICT ....(970) 468-5400
EAGLE RANGER DISTRICT ....(970) 328-6388
HOLY CROSS RANGER DISTRICT .....(970) 827-5715
RIFLE RANGER DISTRICT ....(970) 625-2371
SOPRIS RANGER DISTRICT ....(970) 963-2266

REGIONAL FOREST SERVICE OFFICE
LAKEWOOD COLORADO ....(303) 275-5350

BUREAU OF LAND MANAGEMENT
GRAND JUNCTION FIELD OFFICE ......(970) 244-3000
GUNNISON FIELD OFFICE ....(970) 641-0471
GLENWOOD SPRINGS FIELD OFFICE ...(970) 947-2800
LITTLE SNAKE FIELD OFFICE ....(970) 826-4441
SAN JUAN FIELD OFFICE ....(970) 385-1207
SAN LUIS FIELD OFFICE ....(719) 589-4975
UNCOMPAHGRE BASIN FLD. OFC......(970) 240-5300
BOULDER MTN. PARKS ....(303) 441-3408

CITY OF LAKEWOOD
BEAR CREEK LAKE PARK ....(303) 697-6159

CITY OF RIFLE
RIFLE MOUNTAIN PARK ....(970) 625-2121

CITY OF TRINIDAD
MONUMENT LAKE RESORT ....(719) 868-2226

COLORADO DIVISION OF WILDLIFE
DOW HEADQUARTERS, DENVER ......(303) 297-1192
NE REGION, DENVER ....(970) 291-7227
NW REGION, GRAND JUNCTION ......(970) 255-6100
SE REGION, COLORADO SPRINGS ....(719) 227-5200
SW REGION, DURANGO ....(970) 247-0855

COLORADO STATE PARKS
HEADQUARTERS, DENVER ....(303) 866-3437
HIGH PLAINS REGION OFFICE, DEN. ...(303) 866-3437
ROCKY MTN SVC CTR, COLO. SPRINGS .(719) 227-5250
ROCKY MTN REGION, CLIFTON ....(970) 434-6862
parksinfo@state.co.us

U.S. FISH AND WILDLIFE SERVICE
BROWNS PARK NTL WILDLIFE REFUGE (970) 365-3613
HINSDALE COUNTY
COUNTY OFFICE, LAKE CITY ....(970) 944-2225
LARIMER COUNTY PARKS & OPEN LAND
PARKS OFFICE, FORT COLLINS ......(970) 679-4570
LONGMONT CITY PARKS DEPARTMENT
UNION RESERVOIR PARK OFFICE ......(303) 772-1265
NATIONAL PARKS SERVICE
BLACK CANYON OF THE GUNNISON ...(970) 641-2337
COLORADO NATIONAL MONUMENT ...(970) 858-3617
CURECANTI NATIONAL REC. AREA ....(970) 641-2337
DINOSAUR NATIONAL MONUMENT ....(970) 374-3000
GREAT SAND DUNES NAT. PARK ......(719) 378-6300
MESA VERDE NATIONAL PARK ....(970) 529-4465
ROCKY MOUNTAIN NATIONAL PARK ...(970) 586-1206

US GEOL. SURVEY MAP SALES (800) HELP MAP ....
....(303) 202-4657
CAMPING RESERVATIONS:
NATIONAL FOREST SERVICE   (8:00am/5:00pm)
....(877) 444-6777
STATE PARKS
(From outside Metro Denver Area) ....(800) 678-2267
(From inside Metro Denver Area) ....(303) 470-1144
Note: Reservation period for State Parks, April through September.
NATIONAL PARKS SERVICE ....(800) 365-2267
(Rocky Mountain National Park)

Front Range Alphabetical Listing

Lake Name	Page
Abyss Lake	39
Arapaho Lakes	33
Arvada Reservoir	14
Aurora Reservoir	23
Balsam Park Pond	16
Banana Lake	31
Barker Reservoir.	29
Barnum Park Lake.	16
Barr Lake State Park	11
Bear Creek Ponds	17
Bear Creek Reservoir	17
Beartrack Lakes.	39
Bell Roth Park Pond	13
Berkeley Lake	15
Betty Lake	32
Bill Moore Lake	36
Birdland Lake	15
Blue Heron Lake	18
Bob Lake	32
Boulder Ponds	28
Boulder Reservoir	26
Bowles Grove Pond	20
Brainard Lake	29
Brighton City Park Lake	12
Broomfield Community Park Ponds	12
Byron Lake	37
Camenisch Park Pond.	13
Carl Park Pond	15
Carmody Park Pond	18
Centennial Park Lake	20
Central City Park Ponds	30
Chatfield Reservoir State Park	21
Chatfield State Park Ponds	21
Cherry Creek State Park.	23
Chicago Lakes.	39
Chinn's Lake	36
City Park Lake.	23
Clayton Lake	34
Clear Creek Pond	14
Clear Lake	38
Community College Pond	12
Cone Lake	37
Coot Lake	26
Cottonwood Park Lake	18
Crater Lakes.	34
Croke Reservoir	12
Crown Hill Lake	15
Deep Lake	31
Devil's Thumb Lake	32
Diamond Lake	31
Diamond Lake, Upper.	31
East Reservoir	17
Echo Lake	38
Engineers Lake	14
Ethel Lake	37
Evergreen Lake	39
Exposition Park Pond	23
Fairgrounds Lake	25
Fall River Reservoir	36
Faversham Park Pond	13
Forest Lakes	33
Frozen Lake	40
Garfield Lake	16
Garland Park Pond (Lollipop Lake)	23
Georgetown Lake.	38
Gibson Lake	40
Golden Gate Canyon State Park	30
Golden Ponds.	25
Grandview Ponds	12
Green Gables Park Pond	18
Gross Reservoir	29
Harper Lake.	27
Harriman Lake Reservoir	18
Harvey Park Lake	17
Hassel Lake.	37
Heart Lake.	34
Hine Lake Reservoir	18
Hunter's Glen Lake	12
Huston Park Lake	17
Ice Lake	35
Iceberg Lakes	34
Idaho Springs Reservoir	38
James Peak Lake.	34
Jasper Lake	31
Jenny Lake	33
Jewell Park Pond.	18
Jim Baker Reservoir	15
Johnson Reservoir (Clement Park)	20
Kendrick Park Reservoir	18
Ketner Lake	13
Ketring Park Pond (Gallup Lake)	20
King Lake	32
Kiwanis Park Pond	13
Lagerman Reservoir	25
Lake Arbor	13
Lake Caroline	36
Lake Dorothy	31
Lake Geneva	20
Lake Isabelle	29
Lefthand Creek Reservoir	29
Lincoln Lake	39
Little's Creek Pond	20
Little Echo Lake	34
Loc Amora Pond (Jacobs Pond)	12
Loch Lomond Lake	35
Long Lake	29
Loomiller Pond	25
Lost Lake.	32
Lowell Ponds.	15
Main Reservoir	17
Mann Lake (Adams Co. Fairgrounds)	12
Maxwell Lake	27
Meadow Park Lake	15
Milavec Lake Recreation Area	25
Moraine Lake	29
Murray Lake	40
Neva Lakes	31
Overland Park Pond	17
Pine Valley Ranch Pond	40
Pomona Lake.	13
Progress Park Pond	20
Prospect Park Lakes	15
Public Works Lake (Adams Co. Fair.)	12
Quincy Reservoir	23
Rainbow Lakes	29
Red Rock Lake	29
Reynolds Lake.	35
Ridgeview Park Pond	20
Rocky Mountain Lake.	15
Rogers Pass Lake	34
Roosevelt Lakes.	39
Rotella Park Pond	13
Saint Mary's Lake.	36
Sawhill Ponds.	27
Shelf Lake	40
Sherwin Lake	36
Silver Dollar Lake	40
Skyscraper Reservoir	32
Slater Lake.	36
Sloan Lake.	16
Smith Reservoir.	18
Soda Lakes.	17
South Platte Park Ponds	20
Square Top Lakes	40
St. Vrain State Park	25
Standley Lake	13
Stearns Lake.	28
Sterne Pond.	20
Steuart Lake	35
Storm Lake	31
Summit Lake	39
Teller Lake	27
Thunderbird Lake	27
Twin Lakes Park Ponds.	14
Union Reservoir	25
Union Square Ponds.	16
Urad Reservoir, Upper	37
Vanderbilt Park Pond	17
Viele Reservoir	27
Walden Ponds.	27
Waneka Lake.	27
Ward Road Pond	15
Washington Park Lakes.	23
Water Point & Bellio Ponds (Hyland Ponds)	13
Webster Lake.	12
Westminster City Park Pond	12
Wonderland Lake	27
Woodland Lake	32
Yankee Doodle Lake	33

METRO STREAMS

Bear Creek	41
Boulder Creek, Middle	41
Boulder Creek, North	41
Boulder Creek, South	42
Clear Creek	42
Geneva Creek	42

SOUTH PLATTE RIVER

Cheesman Lake.	45
South Platte River	45
South Platte River, North Fork	45
Strontia Springs Reservoir	45

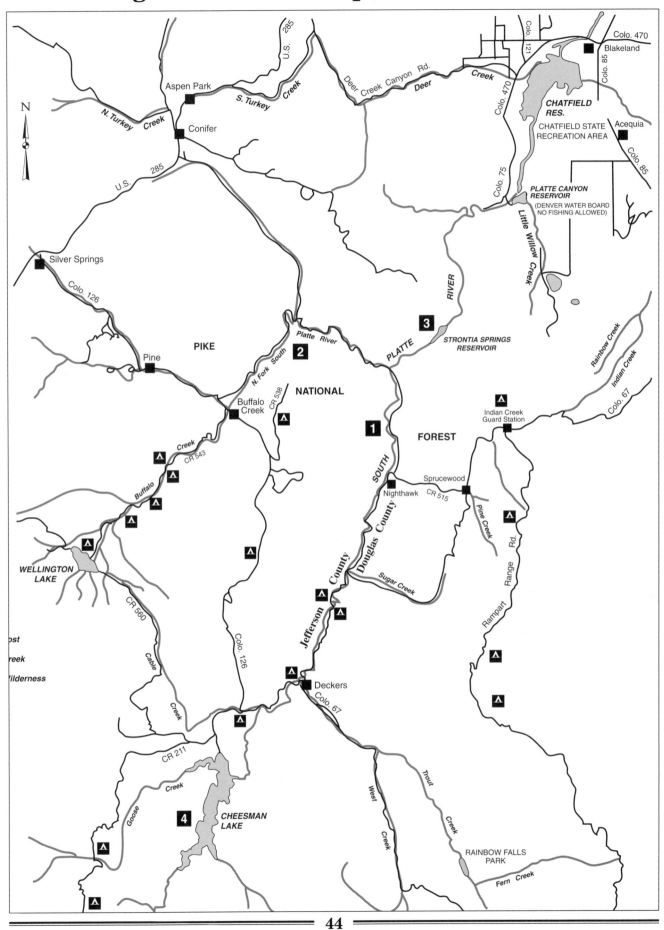

Front Range - Section 5 - Map 1

1 South Platte River

Location: Park, Jefferson, Douglas, and Denver counties. The river enters the area discussed in this guide at Chessman Reservoir - at the juncture of Teller, Douglas, Jefferson, and Park counties about 45 miles Southwest of Denver. Flows northeasterly through Denver.

Fish: Brown, rainbow, and brook trout.

Comments: The South Platte flows through Pike National Forest until it reaches the outskirts of the Denver metro area. In some mountain stretches it is a premier year-round trout stream. Upper portion of the river is accessible via Hwy 67 west from Sedalia, north from Woodland Park, or south from US 285 on Jefferson County roads at Kennedy Gulch, Shaffers Crossing, and Pine Junction. Below Cheesman Lake the river is dammed at Strontia Springs in South Platte River Canyon. The stretch of river through Waterton Canyon (between Strontia Springs and Chatfield) is reached via walk-in access from Kassler Treatment Plant. Below Chatfield, fishing for stocked trout or warm water fish is available on the river through much of the Denver area.

Special Regulations: From Cheesman Dam downstream to the Upper Wigwam property line: 1. Fishing by artificial flies or artificial lures only; 2. All fish caught must be returned to the water immediately (catch & release only). From the lower boundary of the Wigwam Club to Scraggy View Campground: 1. Fishing by artificial flies or artificial lures only; 2. Bag, possession, and size limit four trout is 2 fish, 15 inches or longer. From Scraggy View Picnic Ground downstream to and including Strontia Springs Reservoir; The Bag and possession limit for trout is 2 fish. From Strontia Springs Dam downstream to 300 yards upstream from the Denver Water Board's diversion structure. 1. Fishing by artificial flies or artificial lures (except that only naturally including aquatic nymphs and/or larvae in the South Platte River are permitted as bait); 2. Bag, possession, and size limit for trout is 2 fish, 16 inches or longer.

2 South Platte River - North Fork

Location: Park and Jefferson counties. Flows southeasterly from near Webster and Kenosha passes, along US 285. Most of the river course has been modified by construction and additional water surging in from the Harold G. Roberts Tunnel at Grant. At Bailey, the highway curves north, leaving the river, most of which is on private property until it reaches the South Platte River.

Fish: Rainbow, cutthroat, and brown trout.

Nearby Lakes: Gibson Lake, Abyss Lake, Frozen Lake, Square Top Lakes, Shelf Lake, Beartrack Lake, and Roosevelt Lake.

Comments: Most of the North Fork of the South Platte River is on private land with only limited public fishing opportunity. Public access is greater on segments closer to the North Fork confluence with the South Platte River. Headwaters in Pike National Forest are small, often brushy mountain streams.

Special Regulations: All wipers possessed must be 15 inches or longer.

3 Strontia Springs Reservoir

Location: Jefferson and Douglas counties. From Denver, go south on Hwy 75 (west of Chatfield Recreation Area) to Kassler. Hike 6.2 miles southwest on the road going up along the South Platte River. Rough terrain. From Deckers, go north on Hwy 67 about 12 miles, alongside the South Platte River, where the North Fork meets the South Platte. Park and hike in to the south end of the reservoir.

Size: 118 acres; 212 feet maximum depth.

Fish: Rainbow trout, (catchable size stocked), sucker, tiger muskie, northern pike and kokanee salmon.

Agency: Denver Water Department.

Comments: USGS Platte Canyon quad; altitude 5,900 feet. No ice fishing. Fluctuating reservoir. No boats or floating devices.

Special Regulations: The bag and possession limit for trout is 2 fish.

4 Cheesman Lake

Location: Douglas and Jefferson counties. Pike National Forest. From Denver, drive west on US 285 to Pine Junction. Turn south (to Pine) on County Road 126, drive about 20 miles south to Forest Route 211, and turn west. Go west 1 mile, the road turns south. Go 1.5 miles to the lake. Alternate route from Denver, drive south on US 85 to Sedalia. Turn southwest on Hwy 67, follow 67 through several intersections (4) to Deckers. Drive 3 miles west on County Road 126. Continue west on Forest Route 211 for 1 mile. Road turns south, go 1.5 miles to lake.

Size: 875 acres; 190 feet maximum depth.

Fish: Rainbow, brown and brook trout, northern pike, smallmouth bass, sucker, splake, lake trout, kokanee salmon and yellow perch.

Agency: Denver Water Department.

Comments: USGS- Cheesman Lake quad; altitude 7,425 feet. Shore fishing only. Walk-in from parking area on north end. Restrooms.

Special Regulations: 1. Ice fishing prohibited; 2. Boating and floating devices prohibited. 3. Fishing is prohibited from one-half hour after sunset until one-half hour before sunrise; 4. Fishing is prohibited from the dam, and as posted; (No access on or across dam); 6. Spear fishing equipment is prohibited; 5. Fishing is prohibited January 1, through April 30; 6. Kokanee snagging permitted September 1 through December 31.

Note: In waters open to snagging, all snagged fish, except Kokanee salmon, must be returned to the water immediately.

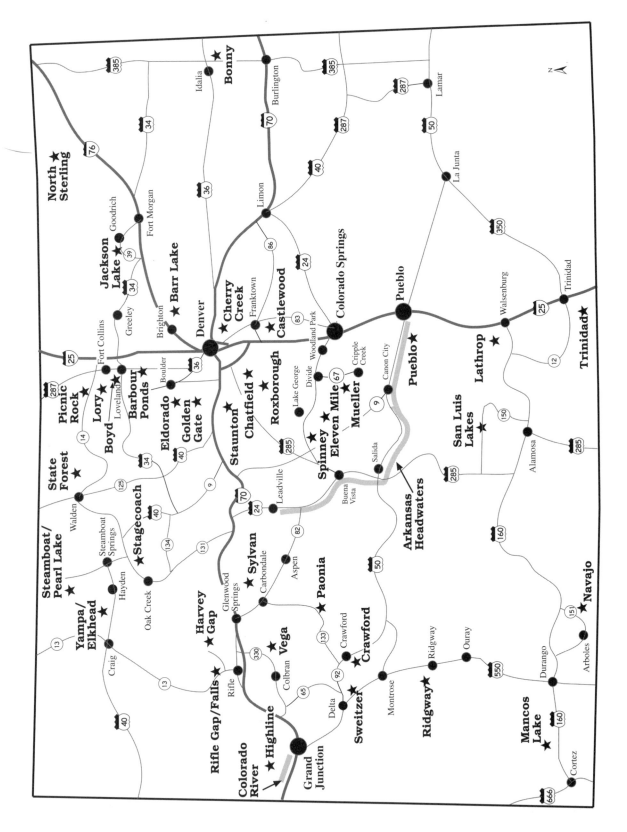

LOCATOR MAP COLORADO STATE PARKS

★ State Park

STATE PARKS TABLE OF CONTENTS

COLORADO STATE PARKS

PARK NAME   PAGE

NORTH REGION

1. BOYD LAKE..............................48
2. ELKHEAD RESERVOIR 49
3. JACKSON LAKE 50
4. NORTH STERLING RESERVOIR..............51
5. STAGECOACH RESERVOIR 52
6. COLORADO STATE FOREST.................53
(Clear Lake, Kelly Lake, Ruby Jewel Lake, North Michigan Reservoir, Ranger Lakes & Michigan River.)
7. STEAMBOAT LAKE/PEARL LAKE.............54
8. YAMPA RIVER 55

SOUTH REGION

9. ARKANSAS RIVER 58
10. BONNY RESERVOIR......................59
11. ELEVEN MILE RESERVOIR 60
12. LATHROP (Horseshoe & Martin) 61
13. PUEBLO RESERVOIR 62
14. SAN LUIS LAKE 63
15. SPINNEY MOUNTAIN RES.................64
16. TRINIDAD RESERVOIR 65

WEST REGION

17. COLORADO RIVER (LOWER) 66
18. CRAWFORD RESERVOIR 67
19. HARVEY GAP RESERVOIR 68
20. HIGHLINE RESERVOIR 69
21. MANCOS (Jackson Gulch Reservoir).....70
23. NAVAJO RESERVOIR 71
24. PAONIA RESERVOIR 72
25. RIDGWAY RESERVOIR 73
26. RIFLE GAP RESERVOIR..................74
27. SYLVAN LAKE..........................75
28. VEGA RESERVOIR......................76

NOTE:

MAPS AND TEXT FOR STATE PARKS LOCATED IN THE FRONT RANGE SECTION:

ST. VRAIN STATE PARK 25
BARR LAKE 11
CHATFIELD 21
CHERRY CREEK 23

STATE PARKS WITH LIMITED FISHING AND NOT INCLUDED IN GUIDE:
ELDORADO, MUELLER, RIFLE FALLS AND SWEITZER STATE PARKS.

GENERAL RULES AND REGULATIONS
STATE PARKS GENERAL INFORMATION

Fees
State Parks require a current parks pass. A daily pass is $3.00-$7.00 per vehicle, annual pass is $55.00 good at all state parks or Aspen Leaf senior citizen pass for Colorado residents age 62 or over is $27.00. Camping fees vary depending on the services and facilities offered. Note: Fees can increase.

Seasons
State Parks weather permitting are open year-round. Most parks attempt to keep some campsite and facilities open during fall and winter months. Day-use areas are generally open from 5 a.m. to 10 p.m. and when they are open campgrounds are open 24 hours a day.

Accessibility
Colorado State Parks strive to make each park as barrier free as possible. Call the State Park for accessibility information for fishing piers and other facilities.

Fishing
To fish the lakes and rivers in the Colorado State Park system you are required to possess a valid Colorado fishing license. Check with the park ranger or the Colorado Division of Wildlife for current bag and possession limits and information on special fishing regulations.

Boating
Boating is permitted at most lakes in the state parks and have good boat ramps. Boating regulations vary from park to park, call the State Park you are going to visit for boating regulations. Water sports may include water-skiing, swimming and personal watercraft; this will irritate some fishermen.

Camping
Most parks have full service campgrounds featuring tables, cooking grills, pads, hookups (water, electric) and dump stations. Newer parks and those near metro areas have showers, laundries, etc. Reservations are a must on holidays, reserve early. See page 42 for phone numbers.

If you are looking for comfort and heavily stocked lakes visit a state park. The many recreation activities in parks attract large numbers of people, especially on weekends and holidays.

BOYD LAKE

Directions: From Denver, take I-25 north to the Loveland exit, U.S. 34. Travel west on U.S. 34 into Loveland to Madison Ave. Travel north on Madison to Larimer Cty. Road 24, then east on Cty. Road 24 to County Road 11C. Take County Road 11C north to the lake entrance.

Fee: Daily pass or annual pass.

Size: 1,700 acres.

Elevation: 4,958 feet.

Maximum Depth: 50 feet.

Facilities: A pavilion at the beach supplies showers, restrooms, first-aid station and food concession. There are picnic sites on the west side of the lake.

Boat Ramp: There is a paved boat ramp north of the swim beach at the inlet and a paved sailboat ramp north of the group picnic area. The Boyd Lake Marina offers boat rentals, mooring services, fuel, and boating and fishing supplies.

Fish: Boyd Lake is popular for its warm-water fishing for bass, catfish, crappie, walleye and perch, but spring walleye fishing is its main attraction. Discover the ridges at the south end of the lake or at the inlet cove when water is flowing in. Some trout caught will weigh 3-5 pounds.

Recreation: Swim beach, boating, fishing, personal watercraft, water skiing, sailing, hunting and camping.

Camping: There are 148 paved, pull-through campsites with picnic tables, fire pits, restrooms and dump station. The sites are located on a grassy knoll dotted with trees near the lake. The sites can accommodate tents, pick-up campers, trailers and motor homes. Three restrooms with showers, playground equipment and horseshoe pits are scattered throughout the campground. Sites 1 through have electrical hookups. Reservations for camping on weekends and holidays are highly recommended. (800) 678-2267.

Information: Park office (970) 669-1739; Handicapped accessible visitors center, restrooms, showers, swimming, trails, fishing and camping; some facilities available with assistance.

Boating is the primary activity on the two-mile-long lake. A 6 lane paved boat ramp with docks is located north of the swim beach at the inlet area and a 2 lane paved ramp is located north of the group picnic area.

The entire lake is open to boating and sailing.

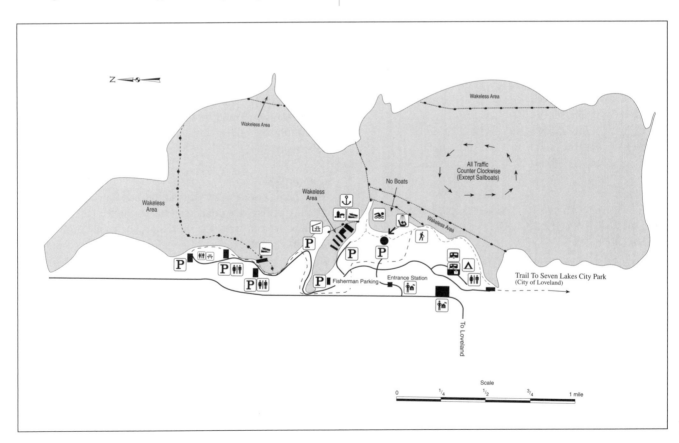

YAMPA RIVER STATE PARK

Directions: From Craig east on Hwy 40 approx. 5 miles to Elkhead turnoff. From Hayden north on County Road 76 to Routt County Road 78.

Fee: Daily Pass or annual pass.

Size: 440 acres.

Elevation: 6,360 feet.

Maximum Depth: 70 feet. Irrigation draws down reservoir during summer months. Watch out for submerged objects.

Facilities; Restrooms and tables. Eleven miles of recreation trails for non-motorized use. This area has been a State Park since 1998 and is continues to be developed.

Boat Ramp: A paved boat ramp is located at Elkhead boat launch area.

Fish: Smallmouth bass, largemouth bass, mackinaw, northern pike, channel catfish, bluegill, green sunfish, black crappie and sucker. Bag and possession limit 2 bass, bass between 12 and 15 inches must immediately be returned to the water. Mackinaw bag and possession limit is one fish, mackinaw between 22 and 34 inches must immediately be returned to the water. Dont overlook fishing in Elkhead Creek above and below the reservoir.

Camping: Two campgrounds vault toilets, tables and grills. Three day maximum stay at any site. No dump station. Located in the north of Routt National Forest the setting is of rolling dry land wheat fields and range land with views of Black Mountain and Bears Ears.

Information:
Yampa River State Park
6185 U.S. 40
Hayden, CO 81639
(970) 276-2061

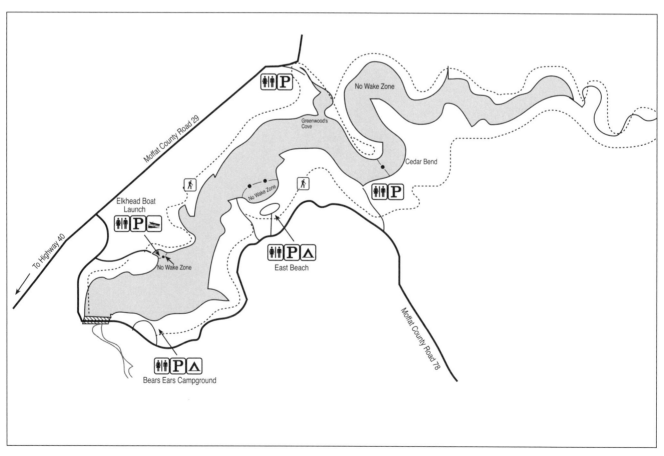

JACKSON LAKE

Directions: From Denver 1-76 northeast to the U.S. 3 interchange. Cty Road 39 north 7 1/4 miles to Goodrich. Travel west on Y5 for 2 1/2 miles to the Jackson Lake State Park

Fee: Daily or annual parks pass.

Size: 2,700 acres.

Elevation: 4,438 feet.

Maximum Depth: 30 feet.

Facilities: Marina, store, showers, toilets, drinking water, picnic tables, and fire pits.

Boatramp: One concrete boat ramp on the west shore with four lanes and a courtesy dock located near the marina. Bait, food, gas, camping supplies, boating and fishing supplies are available at the marina.

Recreation: Fishing, water skiing, personal watercraft, sailing, swimming.

Camping: 262 campsites are available and can accommodate campers, trailers or tents. Campground settings vary from sweeping sandy beaches to stands of stately cottonwoods. Most of the campsites can accommodate campers and trailers as well as tents. There are electrical hookups, showers, toilets and drinking water. A trailer dump station is located near the entrance to the west shore. Reservations are recommended for any weekend.

Fish: Trout, walleye, catfish, perch, crappie and wiper. Fishing is fair to good for all species.

Handicapped accessible showers, restrooms, hunting and fishing. One reserved site at Lakeside Campground, restrooms and picnic tables throughout park. Fishing from boat ramp. Some facilities accessible with assistance.

No boats are allowed in or near the swim beaches and the lake is closed to boating from November through the waterfowl season. Fishermen come here for walleye, wiper, catfish, perch, crappie and trout; but fishing is restricted to designated areas during migratory waterfowl season.

Special Restricions: Place litter in the receptacles provided. Keep your vehicle on designated roads or parking spaces. Keep your pets on a leash six feet long or less. Camp only in designated camping sites and bring no more that the permitted number of vehicles to each site. Report any problems to a park ranger.

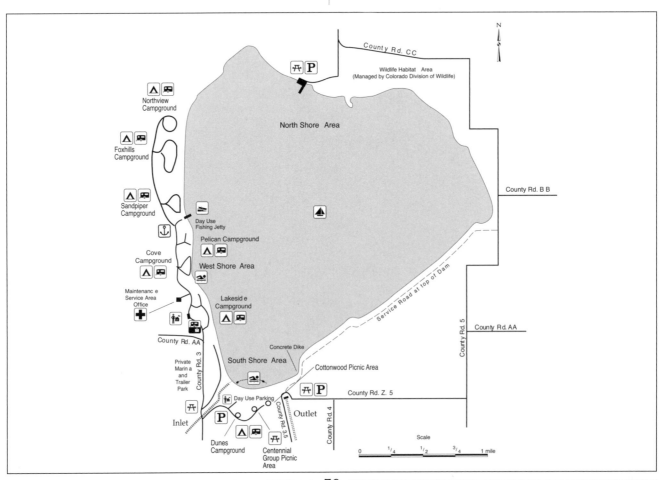

NORTH STERLING

Directions: From Sterling at Highway 14, 8 miles north on 7th Ave. To County Road 46, 2 miles west to County 33, 1 mile north to reservoir.

Fee: Daily or annual park pass.

Size: 3,000 acres.

Elevation: 4,069 feet.

Facilities: Restrooms, picnic tables. Dump station, marina, picnic pavilion, boat ramps and swim beach.

Boatramp: 3 ramps located along the east side of reservoir near County Road 33.

Fish: Walleye, crappie, perch, bass, bluegill, catfish and wiper. The reservoir is regarded as one of the top warm water fisheries in the state, particularly for walleye and wiper. The reservoir is open to fishing year round. The area is closed to boating on November 1, through the end of water fowl hunting season. The water level fluctuates during the irrigation season. Boaters are warned to be alert for submerged hazards.

Recreation: Fishing, water skiing, personal watercraft, sailing, hunting.

Camping: Campgrounds at North Sterling Reservoir can accomodate recreational vehicles, trailers or tents. Electrical hookups are avilable at Elks Campground A centrally located camper services building offers showers, flush toilets, and laundry. An RV dump station is located at Elks Campground. It is illegal and a health hazard to dump waste water and sewage, including dishwater, anywhere else.

Information: Park office (970) 522-3657. Handicapped accessible visitors center, showers, restrooms, hunting, picnic tables, camping and fishing; some facilities accessible with assistance.

Boaters: Private property lies underneath and adjacent to much of the reservoir. Please camp in designated areas only.

North Sterling Park is open daily, year-round. During the winter months, the park offers camping, hunting, ice fishing.

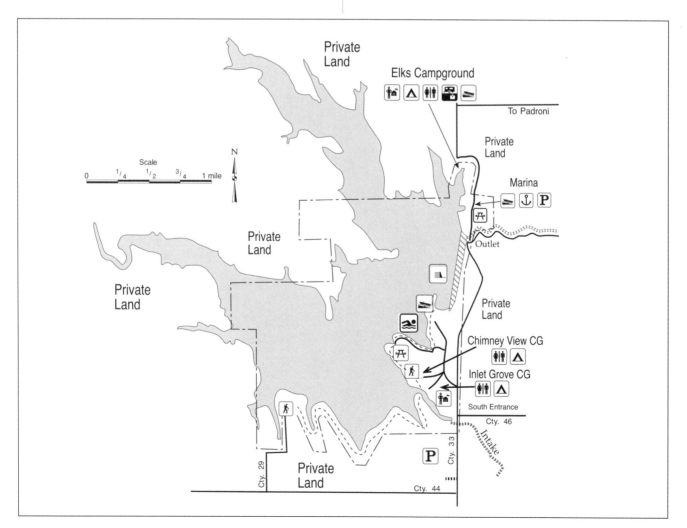

STATE PARKS NORTH REGION

STAGECOACH

Directions: From Denver, take I-70 west to Silverthorne exit, Colorado 9. Travel north on Colorado 9 to Kremmling. North of Kremmling, travel west on Colorado 134 across Gore Pass to Toponas. Take Colorado 131 north out of Toponas through Phippsburg. Turn right on County Road 14 at the Stagecoach Reservoir State Park Area sign.

Fee: Daily or annual park pass.

Size: 700 surface acres, 886 park acres.

Elevation: 7,210 feet.

Maximum Depth: 145 feet.

Facilities: Marina, dump station, boat rentals.

Boat Ramp: A boat ramp is located at the marina near Pinnacle Campground and at the Morrison Cove area.

Fish: Northern pike, kokanee, tasmanian rainbows, cutthroats, white fish, brook, and brown trout. For bank fishing, the best areas are at the north shore of the park around the Keystone picnic area or on County Road 18 below the self-service area.

Recreation: Fishing, water skiing, swimming, personal water craft, boating.

Camping: There are four campgrounds with 92 campsites with running water, flush toilets and dump site facilities; 65 sites have electrical hookups. Camper service area showers and drive-through campsites are offered. The reservoir, which feeds off the Yampa River, has four major coves.

Information: Park office (970) 736-2436.
Handicapped accessible showers, restrooms, picnic tables, camping and fishing. Some facilities accessible with assistance.

The three mile long Stagecoach Reservoir offers many types of recreational opportunities. Mild summer temperatures make for pleasant camping, picnicking, fishing, boating, and swimming.

Visit the Stagecoach Fishing Report at:
http://parks.state.co.us/stagecoach/fishreport.

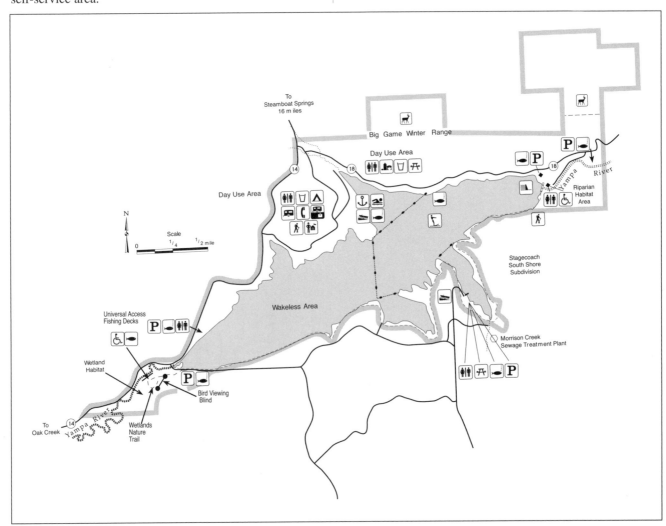

STATE FOREST

Directions: From Fort Collins on U.S. Highway 14 travel west up Poudre Canyon and over Cameron Pass. There are three entrances onto the forest on the west side of Cameron Pass, **Lake Agnes, Ranger Lakes, and North Michigan.** To reach the park office drive 8 miles west of Cameron Pass. The Moose Visitors Center is located on Hwy 14, 1 mile east of Gould Colorado.

Fee: A Colorado vehicle parks pass and a camping fee if applicable.

Size: The park, covers approximately 70,000 acres.

Elevation: Ranges from 8500 to 12,500 feet, visitors may need time to acclimate.

Boatramp: Boating on **North Michigan Reservoir** is allowed at wakeless speeds. There are two boat ramps, one on the north and one on the east side of the reservoir.

Fish: Native brook, rainbow, German brown and California golden trout. The high mountain lakes are **Clear Lake, American Lake, Kelly Lake, Ruby Jewel Lake and Lake Agnes.** **Lake Agnes** is noted for moderate-sized cutthroat, but several 7-8 pound fish are caught each year. This area also includes **North Michigan Reservoir.** All high-county lakes and are restricted to flies and lures. A great number of small feeder streams, **North Michigan Reservoir and Ranger Lakes** in the area are not restricted. The best fishing generally is in the early morning or late afternoon near the drop-offs on all lakes.

Ranger Lakes:

Size: The lower lake, 4.3 surface acres; the upper lake, 8.5 surface acres. No boating of any kind is allowed on Ranger Lakes.

Elevation: 9,243 feet.

Facilities: Camping facilities are toilets, drinking water, picnic tables, fire grates and RV dump station.

Fish: Stocked rainbow trout, but you can expect to hook a brown or brook trout on occasion.

Camping: Camping facilities are toilets, drinking water, picnic tables and fire grates.

Recreation: Fishing, hunting, camping, hiking, backpacking, horseback riding, wildlife viewing, moose viewing, four-wheel drive and OHV riding.

Camping: The State Forest offers four developed campgrounds, **Crags and Ranger Lakes** can be accessed from Highway 14, while **North Michigan Reservoir** and Bockman are accessed from County Road 41. These campgrounds combined offer 158 sites with picnic tables and grills with water available in all campgrounds. The State Park also offers dispersed camping in the areas North of Ruby Jewel Road and south of the Bockman campground. Minimum impact camping techniques are requested. Stop at the park office to learn more about these areas. No. Michigan Campground, Site #207 located near the lake with handicapped accessible restrooms; Bockman Campground has 3 handicapped accessible restrooms; Ranger Lakes Campground has one handicapped accessible space.

Information: Park office (970) 723-8366 9 a.m. to 4:30 p.m.

USGS 7 1/2' Quads, Gould, Clark Peak, Richthofen.

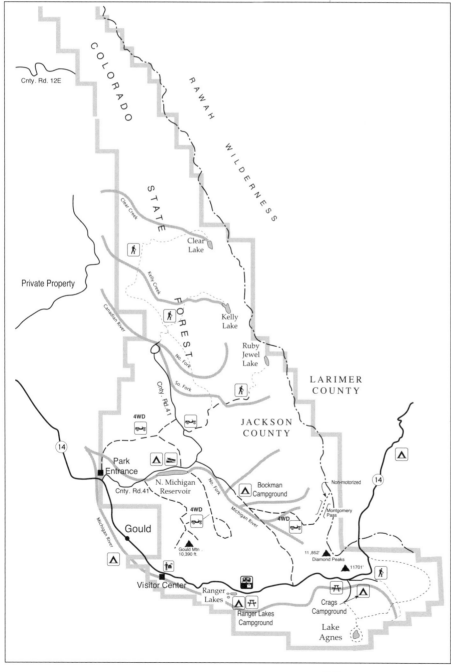

STATE PARKS NORTH REGION

STEAMBOAT/PEARL

Directions: From Steamboat Springs north on County Road 129 (Elk River Road).

Fee: Parks pass and camping fee.

Size: 1,053 acres (Pearl Lake - 190 acres).

Elevation: 8,000 feet.

Facilities: All services with a dump station, boat rentals.

Boat Ramp: Three ramps located on the north side of reservoir. Sage Flats, Placer Cove and Dutch Hill and at the marina.

Fish: Rainbow, brown and cutthroat trout. Shore or boat fishing in the coves or at the inlets produce 10 to 17 inch trout. Pearl Lake contains cutthroat trout and artificial lures are only to be used. Two fish limit 18" or greater at Pearl Lake.

Recreation: All water sports, fishing, picnicking.

Camping: Sunrise Vista, Dutch Hill and Pearl Lake camp-grounds have a total of 222 campsites, which can accommodate tents and campers or trailers. There are some pull through sites in each campground. Only one unit per site is allowed.

Information: Park office (970) 879-3922.

Handicapped accessible: Steamboat; Visitor center, restrooms, swimming, hunting, picnic tables, camping and fishing. Pearl; Restrooms, picnic tables, camping and fishing; Some facilities accessible with assistance.

Steamboat Lake State Park, also includes Pearl Lake. Steamboat Lake is a man made lake that was completed in 1967 and filled in 1968. Pearl Lake, quite small compared to Steamboat, was completed in 1962.

Steamboat Lake State Park is famed for water sports, fishing and winter sports. Anglers will be pleased to note that coves at Steamboat Lake are well known for good-sized trout. Pearl Lake is known for cutthroat. Only fly and lure fishing is permitted here. Placer Cove is the spot for ice fishing.

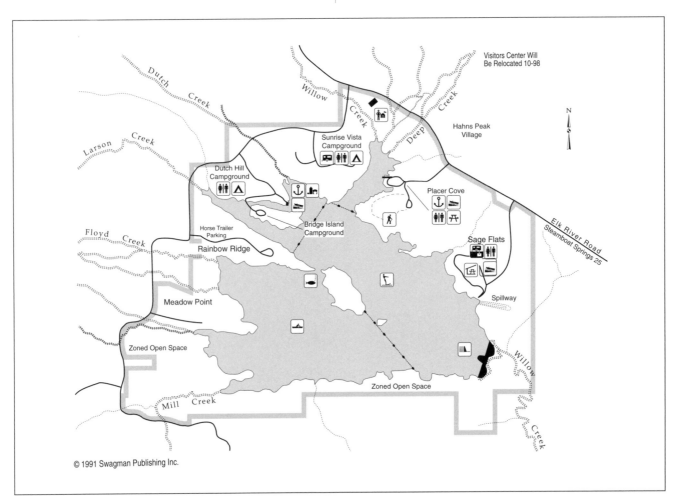

© 1991 Swagman Publishing Inc.

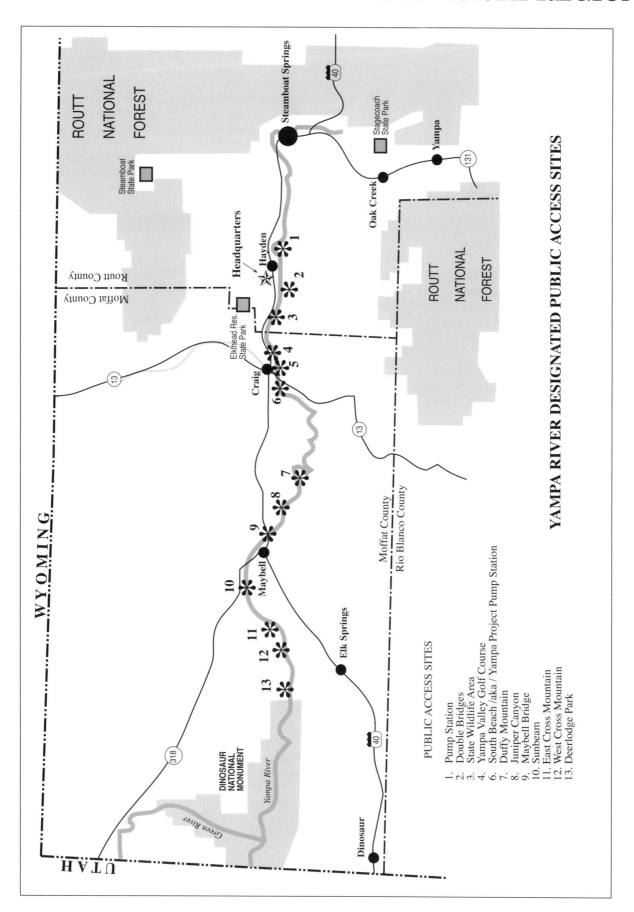

YAMPA RIVER DESIGNATED PUBLIC ACCESS SITES

PUBLIC ACCESS SITES

1. Pump Station
2. Double Bridges
3. State Wildlife Area
4. Yampa Valley Golf Course
6. South Beach /aka / Yampa Project Pump Station
7. Duffy Mountain
8. Juniper Canyon
9. Maybell Bridge
10. Sunbeam
11. East Cross Mountain
12. West Cross Mountain
13. Deerlodge Park

YAMPA RIVER

Directions: West of Steamboat Springs on Highway 40.

Fee: Daily or annual parks pass.

Recreation: Rafting, fishing.

Camping: Elkhead State Park. See text.

Fish: Trout, northern pike, whitefish, western water catfish. Upper Headwaters in Routt National Forest offers brown, brook and rainbow trout averaging 10 inches. West of Steamboat Springs the river widens with deep holes and fast water. Between Craig and Hayden expect big northern pike and whitefish up to 2 pounds. In the slow muddy waters to the west fair to good catfish.

State Parks Headquarters

State Parks will be housed at the new headquarters and campground, located approximately two miles west of Hayden. Here there is a Visitors Center/Outdoor Recreation Facility, a camper services building, nature trails including observation decks, and a group picnic area and 50 overnight units.

Information:

Yampa River Legacy Project,
6185 U.S. 40 Hayden, CO 81639.
(970) 276-2061.

Public River Access Sites

All sites require Parks Pass unless otherwise indicated.

1. Public Service Company (Site #1) located approximately five miles east of Hayden off U.S. Highway 40 on the north side of the highway. The Public Service Company water intake structure is located adjacent to the site. The access road runs parallel to Highway 40 and between the highway and the river. It is imperative that the public doesn't trespass on the PSCO intake structure property. No overnight camping allowed.

2. Double Bridges (Site #2) located approximately 1.75 miles west of Hayden off U.S. Highway 40 on the south side of the highway. The site has limited parking space and a tight turning radius. This site is not recommended for large rigs. No overnight camping allowed.

3. D.O.W. State Wildlife Area (Site #3) located midway between Hayden and Craig is a small metal railroad building that bears the name "Dorsey".
This is the turn which is south of U.S. Highway 40 that accesses the Yampa River. This site has no improvements and is managed by the Colorado Division of Wildlife. There are no pass requirements at this site. No overnight camping is allowed.

4. Yampa Valley Golf Course (Site #4) located south of Craig off Colorado Highway 394. The turnoff for highway 394 is on U.S. Highway 40 at Ranney Street in the middle of Craig, follow the signs to the airport which is located next to the golf course. The best river access is past the signed golf course entrance as well as the airport. There is a paved road heading northeast that will end up behind the maintenance shop of the golf course. A short gravel road paralleling the golf course accesses the Yampa River at a large gravel bar. This site has no improvements and is owned by the City of Craig and Moffat County. There are passes required at this site. No overnight camping allowed.

5. Moffat County's Loudy Simpson Park (Site #6) located off Colorado State Highway 344 south of Craig at the developed ball field complex. This site has a developed boat launch/parking area on the river and is managed and owned by Moffat County. There are no passes required at this site. Overnight camping allowed with permission from the City of Craig.

6. South Beach Yampa AKA Yampa Project Pump Station (Site #6) located off Colorado State Highway 13 bridge south of Craig. This site is approximately 4 miles south of Craig indicated by a large upper graveled pull off area. The access road down to the large parking lot belongs to Tri-State and Trapper Mining Inc. and is utilized for hauling gravel. It is recommended that all recreational users park in the large gravel parking lot to the west of the pump station where the vault toilet is located. The water intake channel is open to fishing but canoe or boat launching is prohibited at the intake channel. There is a boat ramp to the west of the parking area where canoes and boats can be launched or taken out. The wooded area northeast of the pump station is open to foot traffic only. Camping is allowed for 2 consecutive nights only.

7. Duffy Mountain (Site #7) located 32 miles down river from South Beach and approximately 30 miles southwest of Craig. To reach Duffy Mountain River Access, take U.S. Highway 40 west out Craig for approximately 19 miles to Moffat County Road 17 which runs south approximately 6.5 miles to Government Bridge where the road crosses the Yampa River. Parking at on or adjacent to the bridge is prohibited and river access at the bridge is not allowed. From Government Bridge, it is approximately 3.7 miles on County Road 17 to BLM Road 1593 on the left hand (north) site immediately before the cattle guard. This is an unimproved BLM road which becomes impassable when wet it's approximately 1 mile to the river site (staying left at all intersections). The site is improved with boat ramp, vault toilet, parking and overnight camping availability.

8. Juniper Canyon (Site #8) located 12 miles down river from Duffy Mountain Access Site To reach Juniper Canyon River Access Site, take U.S. Highway 40 west out of Craig for approximately 20 miles to Moffat County Road 53. Which runs south approximately 3.6 miles to Moffat County Road 74 (at which point the Yampa River is clearly visible). Turn right (west) at the intersection of Moffat County Roads 53 mid 74 and go, 8 miles to the river access site. The site is improved with boat ramp, vault toilets, parking and overnight camping availability.

CAUTION:
There is a diversion down river in Juniper Canyon and is not recommended for open canoes because of the Class III rapids. There are also smaller rapids below the diversion through the canyon.

9. Maybell Bridge (Site #9) located 28 miles west of Craig on Highway 40. When travelling west on Highway 40, the site is located south of the Highway and east of the river. The site is improved with boat ramp, vault toilet and parking and overnight camping availability. The town of Maybell 3 miles further west on Highway 40.

10. Sunbeam (Site #10) located approximately 7 miles northwest of Maybell. Take U.S. Highway 40 out of Maybell (less then a mile) to the intersection of Moffat County Road 318. It is 6 miles along Moffat County Road 318 to the intersection of Moffat County Road 23 here 318 crosses the Yampa River. It is approximately 1 mile on Moffat County Road 23 to the access site. This site will have minimal improvements and no facilities but a boat ramp and tables do exist.

11. East Cross Mountain (Site #11) located approximately 18 miles southwest of Maybell. Take U.S. Highway 40 west out of Maybell for approximately 13.6 miles to the intersection of Moffat County Road 85. Take Moffat County Road 15 north for approximately 2.4 miles to BLM Road 1551, which you will follow for approximately 1.5 miles to a Y in the road at which point the left branch is taken for 1 mile to the river access site. Be sure not to turn off of BLM 1551, just follow it straight ahead. This site sits in a beautiful ravine, with picturesque sights of Cross Mountain and the surrounding area. Boat ramp, vault toilets, hardened campsites, tables, firepits and parking are provided.

12. West Cross Mountain (Site #12) located at the west end of Cross Mountain Canyon and at the east end Dinosaur National Monument. Both sites are under management by the National Park Service.

At Deerlodge Park (Site #13) ALL BOATERS must secure a permit to float on the Yampa River from Deerlodge Park through Dinosaur National Monument.

ARKANSAS RIVER

Directions: South from Denver on I-25 to Colorado Springs, then southwest on Colorado 115 to Canon City. At Canon City, follow U.S. 50 west along the river to Salida.

Fee: Daily or Annual Pass

Elevation: Ranges from 7,900 feet at Pueblo Reservoir to 8,875 feet at Clear Creek Reservoir.

Boatramp: Boating access points from Nathrop to Parkdale.

Fish: Trout, primarily rainbow and brown. The section of the river from Salida to Nathrop is known primarily for rainbow. While the best area for brown trout is from Salida to Parkdale, the area from the town of Howard to the stockyard bridge is known for larger rainbow trout. Fishing access is clearly marked on the river. Two sections, one just below Nathrop and between Texas Creek and Parkdale, are designated wild trout waters. Most of the river is open for bait as well as artificial lures. From Badger Creek (at the railroad trestle) to the stockyard bridge below Salida (a 7 1/2 mile stretch) and the Mugford Lease just north of Salida, artificial lures only. Check DOW regulations for bag limits and other restrictions.

Recreation: Fishing, rafting.

Camping: Five Points, Hecla Junction, Rincon and Ruby Mountain. Restrooms, picnic tables, fishing access and parking.

Information: Pike and San Isabel National Forests, Pueblo (719) 553-1404. Arkansas Headwaters Recreation Area, Salida, (719) 539-7289

Handicapped accessible restrooms, visitors center, picnic tables, fishing, camping and trails. Lone Pine Recreation site offers a fishing trail. Some facilities available with assistance.

Buena Vista to Salida; This stretch offers fine fishing, as well as camping and picnicking. **Ruby Canyon**; the northern gateway, provides access to the 6,600 acre Browns Canyon Wilderness Study Area. Below Browns Canyon, the valley widens again and the river calms down. This stretch, called the **Big Bend,** offers prime trout fishing, and numerous Division of Wildlife easements give fishermen river access on private land. (Please observe posted rules when using fishing easements). **Salida to Vallie Bridge**; Just below Salida the river flows into Bighorn Sheep Canyon. As the river flows into the Upper Arkansas Canyon, it veers slightly southeast, with the Sangre de Cristo's to the south and west. Anglers especially enjoy this segment as it slows into a series of still, deep pools, rock banks and gravel bars. In addition to public land access along the river, the Division of Wildlife offers a fishing easement just downstream from Howard, on the river's east side. (Please obey posted rules.) **Vallie Bridge to Parkdale**; A few miles below Vallie Bridge, the river enters the Lower Arkansas River Canyon, also called the "Grand Canyon of the Arkansas." The river drops more sharply in this segment. Rapids with names like Maytag, Lose-Your-Lunch, Three Rocks and Sharks Tooth make this prime territory for whitewater rafting. Anglers can take advantage of groups of large rocks placed in the river on public lands from Coaldale to Parkdale. These rocks are part of a successful trout habitat improvement project, providing resting places where trout congregate to take breathers from fast currents. Public river access is available at several pull-offs and recreation sites.

BONNY

Directions: Take I-70 east from Denver to the Burlington exit. Travel north out of Burlington on U.S. 385 for 23 miles. Take County Road 2 or 3 east 1-1/2 miles to the Bonny Reservoir State Park.

Fee: Daily pass or annual pass.

Size: 1,900 - Lake surface acres; 1,300 acres - Park land.

Elevation: 3,670 feet.

Maximum Depth: 37 feet.

Facilities: Marina, picnic tables, swim beach and a group picnic site with covered pavilion, water, electricity, restrooms, horseshoe pits and cooking facilities

Boat Ramp: Boat ramps are located at North Cove Campground and at the Marina Complex, near Wagon Wheel Campground

Fish: Bonny Reservoir has a thriving population of wall-eye, northern pike, freshwater drum, white bass, largemouth and smallmouth bass, crappie, bluegill and channel catfish and is, therefore, one of Colorado's finest warm water fishing spots. A fish cleaning station is located near Wagon Wheel Campground. Bonny Marina has boat rentals, private docks, fishing tackle, food and gas.

Recreation: Swimming, boating, water skiing, personal watercraft, sailing.

Camping: Four campgrounds with 190 sites. Sites within each campground can accommodate tents, motor homes or trailers. Foster Grove Campground has flush toilets, showers, vault toilets, water hydrants and 13 electric sites. North Cove Campground has vault toilets, a boat ramp and water hydrants. East Beach Campground has vault toilets and water hydrants. Wagon Wheel Campground, the least primitive of the four, all campsites have electrical hookups, flush toilets, vault toilets, showers, laundry, water hydrants, telephone and within walking distance - a boat ramp. Wagon Wheel offers drinking water year-round with at least one free flowing water hydrant in each loop. Holding tank dump stations are conveniently located near Wagon Wheel and Foster Grove Campgrounds. It is illegal to dump waste and sewage anywhere else.

Information: Park Office (970) 354-7306.

All campgrounds and many day-use areas including the marina offer facilities for persons with disabilities. Every campground has accessible restrooms, drinking water and parking. Wagon Wheel Campground also has accessible showers and laundry facilities. Campsites, including accessible campsites are available for reservations, see page 42.

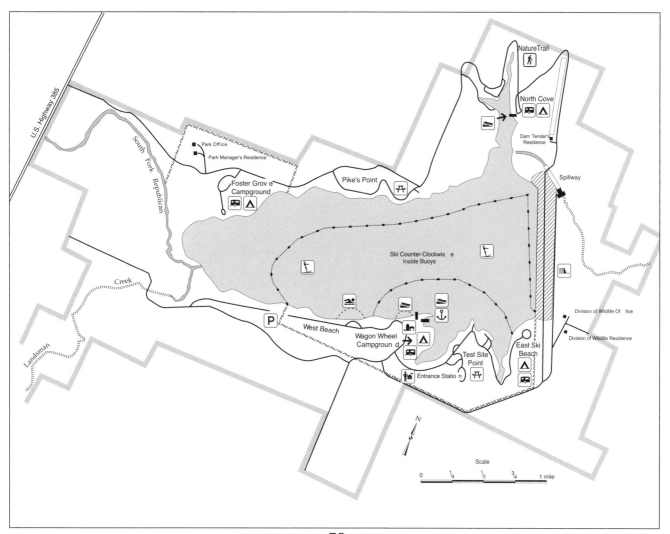

STATE PARKS SOUTH REGION

ELEVEN MILE

Directions: From Denver, travel south on I-25 to Colorado Springs, then west on U.S. 24 to the town of Lake George. One quarter mile west of Lake George turn left and follow the paved road 10 miles to Eleven Mile State Park.

Fee: Daily or annual park pass.

Size: 3,400 acres.

Elevation: 8,600 feet.

Maximum Depth: 117 feet.

Facilities: Picnic tables, fire pits, grills, freshwater pumps, vault toilets and dump stations. A camper services building is located here. Showers, laundry and RV dump station.

Boat Ramp: Boat ramps at North Shore and Witchers Cove, seven total lanes with courtesy docks.

Fish: Anglers have taken some of the largest fish in the state from Eleven Mile's waters. Brown and rainbow trout, mackinaw, kokanee and northern pike abound. Fishing is prohibited in the restricted area at the dam, but is permitted anywhere else on the reservoir. Bow fishing for carp is permitted year round. Rainbow, Snake River cutthroat and brown trout. Pike and kokanee are also available.

Recreation: Fishing, boating - No water contact sports. Hiking trails.

Camping: 350 campsites can accommodate tents, pickup campers and trailers. 25 primitive campsites are located in the back country area at the east end of the reservoir. Holding tank dump stations are located at the entrances to North Shore and Witchers Cove. Some sites have electrical hookups.

Information: Park office (719) 748-3401. Web site coloradoparks.org.
Facilities for the handicapped include reserved parking spaces, and picnic tables, showers, fishing and campgrounds that have been adapted for their use; some facilities accessible with assistance.

Boaters (particularly sailors) find their skills fully tested by the tricky winds and fast rising storms that can occur here. Storms can develop quickly at Eleven Mile bringing sudden strong winds and high waves that can be hazardous to small craft. Underwater hazards are frequently found in the reservoir and not all can be marked. Boaters need to be especially careful when within 150 feet of any shoreline. In addition to the Colorado boating statutes and regulations, boaters must observe the following special regulations: (1) Boat docks are for loading and unloading only; mooring at or fishing from the docks is prohibited and a five minute use limit is enforced. (2) The reservoir is closed to boating 1/2 hour after sunset through 1/2 hour before sunrise. (3) All islands are closed to public use.
All water contact sports are prohibited.

LATHROP
Horseshoe & Martin Reservoirs

Directions: Take I-25 south from Denver to Walsenburg. Go three miles west of Walsenburg on Highway 160. The state park is on the north side of the highway.

Fee: Daily or annual park pass.

Size: Martin Lake - 206 surface acres; Horseshoe Lake - 176 surface acres.

Elevation: 6,410 feet.

Maximum Depth: Horseshoe - 25 feet; Martin 27 feet.

Facilities: Dump stations and water pumps are available throughout both campgrounds. 9 hole golf course.

Boat Ramp: Concrete ramps on the north and south side of Horseshoe. Ramp located on the south side of Martin. Horseshoe Lake is wakeless boating only.

Fish: Rainbow trout, channel catfish, bass, walleye, bluegill, crappie and tiger muskies. Tiger muskies in Horseshoe must be 30" or longer, limit 1 fish.

Recreation: Boating, sailing, personal watercraft, golf, water sports, hiking and bird watching.

Camping: There are two campgrounds - Yucca and Pinion campgrounds. Lathrop State Park has 98 campsites and a group camping area. The campgrounds will accommodate motor homes, trailers and tents. Shower and laundry facilities. Lathrop State Park lies on a high plains grassland, dotted with pinion and juniper typical of southeast Colorado.

Information: Park office (719) 738-2376.
Handicapped accessible visitor center, restrooms, swimming, picnic tables, camping and fishing. Some facilities accessible with assistance.

SPECIAL RESTRICTIONS: Pets must be on a leash not longer than 6 feet and clean up after them or leave them at home. No pets on beach. Keep vehicles on roads or parking lot. Do not cut trees or gather dead wood for fires. Camp only in designated areas. Hunting is allowed only on the west end of the park, small game and water fowl only, short guns only. Hunting is restricted to the period of time after Labor Day, and before Memorial Day.

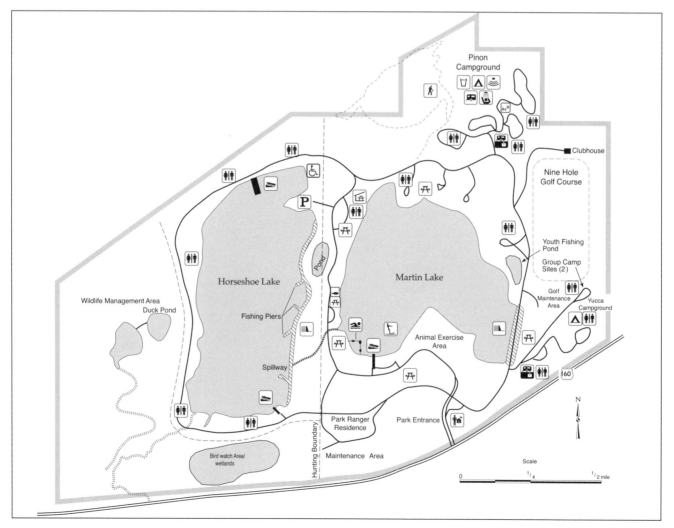

STATE PARKS SOUTH REGION

PUEBLO

Directions: From I-25 west on U.S. 50 from Pueblo follow signs to reservoir.

Fee: Daily or annual park pass.

Size: 4,000 acres.

Elevation: 4,880 feet.

Maximum Depth: 135 feet.

Boatramp: Two ramps; North shore marina and south shore marina.

Recreation: All water sports, bike trail, interpretive trail, picnicking, swimming.

Camping: Lake Pueblo's 401 campsites accommodate tents, pickup campers, motor homes and trailers. Arkansas Point, Prairie Ridge and Yucca Flats campgrounds feature modern toilets, showers, laundry facilities and electricity. Juniper Breaks and Kettle Creek offer primitive facilities with vault restrooms and no running water. Group campgrounds are also available. Dump stations are located in the campgrounds. All campers must register at campground entrance before taking a site. Reservations suggested March 15, through October 15.

Fish: Fishing is the main attraction at Pueblo. Many anglers make this their home base. Both bank and boat fishing are productive. Rainbow trout dominate the fishing action here. Black crappie run a close second, followed by walleye, small mouth bass, bluegill, channel cat, sunfish, largemouth bass and yellow perch and wipers. People who wish to fish at night may stay on the water if their boat is equipped with running lights and a proper anchor.

There are a marinas on the south shore and north shores. Both marinas offer boat slips, boat rentals, food and fuel.

There is plenty of space for open boating and water skiing. Floating debris and changing shorelines are a constant hazard. Boaters should keep a sharp watch for shallow areas and floating or partially submerged objects. Swimming is only permitted at the swim beach in Rock Canyon, lifeguards are on duty.

Information: Park Office (719) 561-9320.

Handicapped accessible campsites in each campground near accessible restrooms. There is a fishing pond in Rock Canyon directly below the dam designed especially to accommodate disabled persons. It has a pier and a paved trail that surrounds the pond. Accessible visitors center, showers, restrooms, swimming, picnic tables, trails, camping and fishing. Some facilities accessible with assistance.

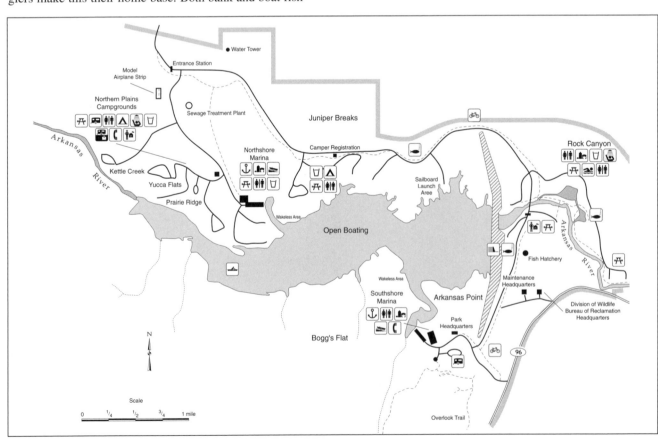

STATE PARKS SOUTH REGION

SAN LUIS

Directions: From Alamosa, north on Highway 17, 14 miles through Mosca. Then east on 6 mile Lane (Sand Dunes Hwy.) approx. 8 miles to park entrance.

Fee: Daily or annual pass.

Size: 890 acres.

Elevation: 7,519 feet.

Maximum Depth: 10 feet.

Facilities: Restrooms, bathhouse, laundry, dump station, water.

Boat Ramp: Concrete ramp near park entrance

Fish: Shallow reservoir rated excellent for rainbow trout all year-round. Check for size bag and possession limits.

Recreation: Boating, fishing, wind surfing, picnicking, hiking, biking, fishing, hunting, swimming and waterskiing.

Camping: The Mosca campground is located in the low sand dunes just west of San Luis Lake. Campsites have electrical hook-ups, sheltered tables, and fire grates. The campground can accommodate motorhomes, trailers and tents. A bathhouse with modern restrooms, hot showers and laundry facilities is located in the campground. There are no individual sewer hookups, but a dump station is available. All campsites offer panoramic view of the lake, and Sangre de Cristo Mountains. For information about group camping contact the park office.

Information: Park office (719) 378-2020.

Handicapped accessible camp site, showers, picnic tables, fishing and restrooms; Some facilities accessible with assistance

Nestled in the heart of the largest worlds alpine valley, the shadow of the spectacular Sangre de Cristo Mountains, near the edge of the world famous Great Sand Dunes National Monument lies the San Luis Lakes State Park. The natural lakes and wetlands of this valley oasis provide excellent fishing and boating in an outstanding setting. Surrounded by eight of Colorado's awesome fourteeners, the scenic splendor of snow-capped peaks, crystal air and broad vistas delight the eye in all directions.

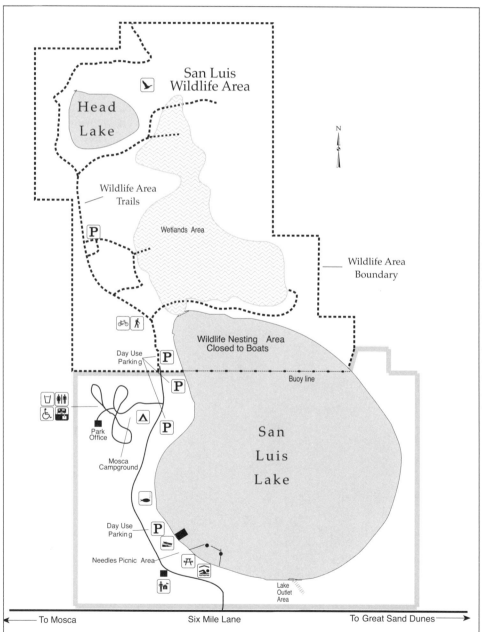

SPINNEY MOUNTAIN

Directions: From Denver, travel south on I-25 to Colorado Springs. Travel west 55 miles from Colorado Springs on Colorado 24, over Wilkerson Pass. Turn left on Park County Road 23 and travel approx. 2 miles, then turn right on County Road 59. Travel 11 miles to the park entrance.
Fee: Daily or annual parks pass.
Size: 2,520 acres.
Elevation: 8,687 feet.
Maximum Depth: 55 feet.
Facilities: Restrooms, fire rings, picnic tables, water hydrant.
Boat Ramp: One 3 lane concrete ramp at the north picnic area and a 2 lane ramp at the south picnic area.
Fish: Cutthroat, rainbow and brown trout and northern pike. Because Spinney is Gold Medal water, only artificial flies and lures may be used. Early fishing at Spinney is best in shallow water, mainly because the shallow water areas will be the warmest. Generally, the north shoreline will get warmer first because of the southern exposure and wind protection. Fishermen may keep only one trout, which must be twenty inches or longer. Ten pike any size.
Recreation: Fishing, boating, wind surfing, hunting, picnicking, wildlife observation.
Camping: No overnight camping is allowed at Spinney. A 350 site campground is available at Eleven Mile State Park, 7 miles the east of Spinney.
Information: Park office (719) 748-3401

Handicapped accessible restrooms, picnic tables and fishing. Some facilities accessible with assistance.
Restrictions:
1. Ice fishing prohibited; reservoir closed to public use from ice-up to ice-off.
2. Fishing and boating are prohibited from a half hour after sunset to a half hour before sunrise.
3. Fishing is prohibited immediately below the dam.
4. Overnight camping is prohibited.
5. Open fires are permitted only in the grate facilities in the picnic areas.
6. Boat launching facilities are provided at the north picnic area and south picnic area.
7. Vehicle use is restricted to designated roads only.
8. Pets must be leashed.
9. Colorado Parks Pass required to enter.
10. Restrictive fishing regulations in force. Check Division of Wildlife regulation brochure.
11. Gates open one half hour before sunrise and close one hour after sunset.
12. Water-skiing and swimming are prohibited.

The area is for day-use only, and its season lasts from ice-up to ice-off. As early as late March to early December.

A high plateau reservoir in South Park, Spinney is set in an open, windswept region. It's shadeless, open and known for constant weather changes during the course of the day.

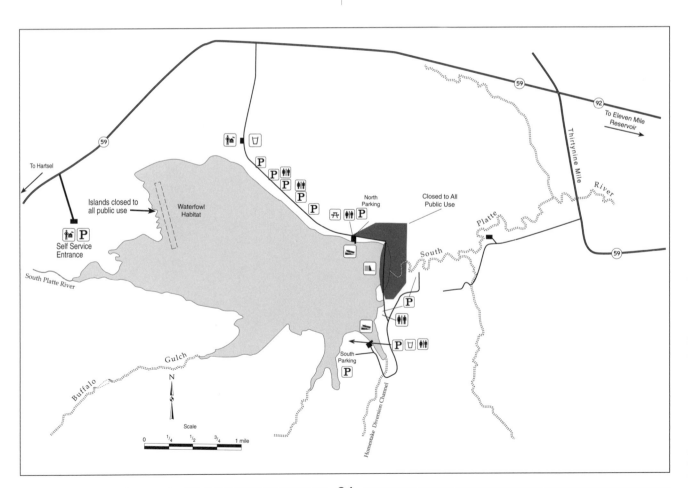

TRINIDAD

Directions: Three miles west of Trinidad on Colorado Highway 12.
Fee: Daily or annual park pass.
Size: 800 acres.
Elevation: 6,276 feet.
Maximum Depth:
Facilities: Full service state park with a dump station
Boat Ramp: One ramp located on the north side near the dam.
Fish: Rainbow and brown trout, largemouth bass, channel catfish, walleye, crappie, bluegill and wipers. Trinidad Lake is rated good for bass and trout fishing. Check current regulations for size and bag limits. The water level can vary, be careful of submerged hazards. Fishing is permitted anywhere on the lake except in the boat launching and docking area. There is a boat ramp on the north end of the lake for access to boaters, fishermen and water skiers. All boats must observe wakeless speeds around the boat launch area, within 150 feet of shore fishermen, and as buoyed. Boaters are warned to be especially alert to submerge hazards. As the water level drops, land outcroppings appear, especially just west of the launching area and along the south shore.
Recreation: Boating, fishing, personal water craft, hunting, no swimming
Camping: 62 sites can accommodate recreation vehicles, trailers, or tents. Modern facilities include water hydrants, coin operated laundry, electrical hookups, showers and flush toilets. Campsites can be reserved in advanced. Campers can stay a maximum of 14 days in any 45 day period. A holding tank dump station is located near the campground. Picnicking is permitted throughout the park. A visitor center is located near the campground that offers drive up service, displays and a book sales area.

Information: Park office (719) 846-6951.

The Carpios Ridge Campground and the picnic area have reserved parking spaces and campsites adapted for handicapped persons. Restrooms, showers, picnic tables, trails, camping, fishing and drinking fountains are also accessible. Some facilities accessible with assistance. Interpretive campfire programs are offered every Friday, Saturday and holiday evenings Memorial Day through Labor Day.

Trinidad Lake, close to the state line in southern Colorado, lies in the Purgatories River valley. This 2,300 acre park, with its 800 acre lake, serves as a destination area or as a camp from which to explore points of scenic and historic interest in southern Colorado. It is an area of unique beauty and ahs been a stopping point for travelers since the early Indian days. Archaeological finds in and around the park are reminders of that early history. These include teepee rings in the Carpios Ridge Picnic Area and the mountain branch of the Santa Fe Trail that is now on of Trinidad's main thoroughfares.

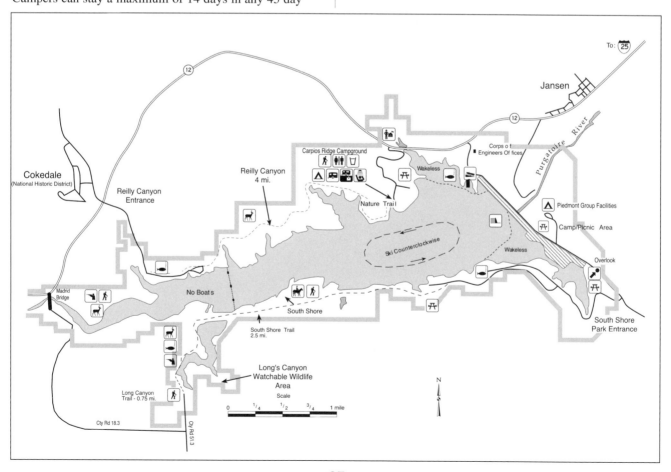

STATE PARKS WEST REGION

COLORADO RIVER

Directions: Grand Junction, along Colorado River east to Island Acres State Park.

Fee: Camping, day or annual pass. There is no fee for hikers and bicyclists at Corn and Connected Lakes.

Elevation: 5000 feet.

Facilities: Restrooms, water.

Boatramp: Corn and Connected Lakes are launching sites for boaters and rafters to the Colorado River.

Fish: Cold water and warm water fishing.

Recreation: Fishing, bicycling, hiking, boating, rafting, swimming.

Camping: 34 sites at Island Acres., restrooms, water, picnic tables, dump station.

Information: **Corn Lake**; Day use area located at 32 Road and the Colorado River. Corn Lake provides a launching site for boaters and rafters to the Colorado River. Trails provide access to the Colorado River and Corn Lake for fishing and are used by hikers and bicyclists. The park also offers picnic sites and restrooms accessible to the physically challenged. There is no charge for bicycle or pedestrian access to the park.

Connected Lakes: Day use area, accessed by travelling north on Dike road off State Highway 340. Connected Lakes provides a net work of trails traversing a series of reclaimed gravel pits giving visitors a wide variety of recreational opportunities including fishing, picnicking, hiking and bird watching. There is no charge for bicycle or pedestrian access to the park.

Island Acres: Located at exit 47 on I-70 in DeBeque Canyon. The Island Acres section is the only area of Colorado River State Park offering camping. The park is open year round for camping and day-use activities with the day-use closing at 10:00 p.m. The park is a convenient and attractive place to fish, swim, camp, picnic and or hike along the Colorado River or near any of the lakes in the park.

Facilities for the Physically Challenged: The Corn Lake and Connected Lakes sections provide accessible picnic areas, parking areas, and restrooms. The Island Acres section provides accessible parking areas, restrooms and campsites. Corn Lake and Island Acres provide a wheelchair accessible concrete fishing pier, and Connected Lakes has four sheltered, accessible fishing sites.

Information: Park Headquarters: (970) 434-3388.

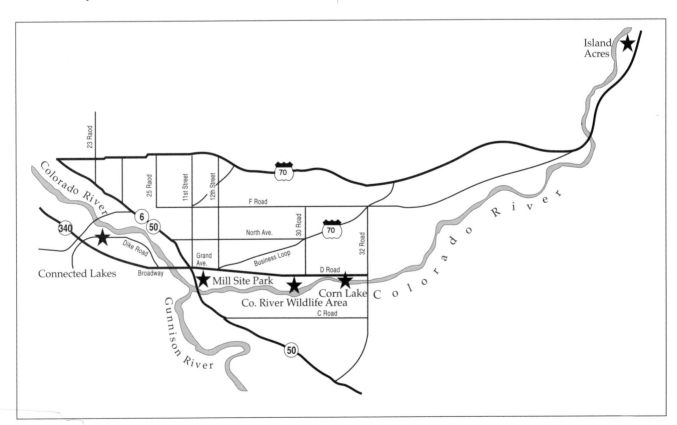

CRAWFORD

Directions: From Delta east on Colorado highway 92, 20 miles to Hotchkiss, continue on C-92 to Crawford. Crawford State Park is one mile south of Crawford on C-92.

Fee: Daily or annual park pass.

Size: 400 surface acres.

Elevation: 6,600 feet.

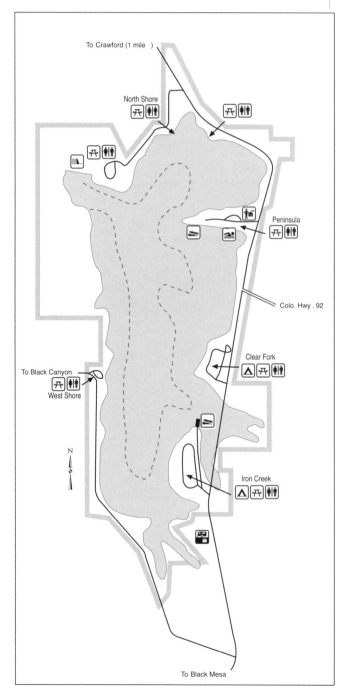

Maximum Depth: 120 feet.

Facilities: Dump station, restrooms, picnic tables

Boatramp: A boat ramp is located on the east side of the reservoir past the ranger station and north end of Iron Creek Campround.

Fish: Yellow perch, northern pike, largemouth bass, channel catfish, rainbow trout and black crappie.

Recreation: Boating, sailing personal watercraft, scuba diving, swimming, picnicking, interpretive programs, bird watching, ice fishing, cross country skiing and tubing.

Camping: Two campgrounds. One class B campground with water and electric hookups at each site, flush toilets, hot showers. Half sites are pull-throughs that can accomodate rigs up to 70 feet, 7 handicap sites. The other campground is a class C with water at key locations, no electic hookups, tents, sites, one flush toilet with showers, and one vault toilet. Two handicap spaces are avilable here.

Information: Park office (970) 921-5721.
e-mail - park.crawford@state.co.us
Handicapped accessible restrooms, swimming, picnic tables, fishing and camping. Some facilities available with assistance.

Crawford State Park offers its visitors camping, fishing, water sports, hunting and numerous other leisure time activities in scenic mountainous terrain. The area around the park is almost exclusively cattle country. The park's 6,600 ft. elevation guarantees visitors a mild climate at any season.

The famous and spectacular Black Canyon of the Gunnison is only 11 miles from the park. Nearer landmarks visible from Crawford State Park are Needle Rock, Castle Rock and Cathedral Peak.

Within the boundaries of Crawford State Park are 734 acres, 334 land acres and the 400 acre reservoir, which was built in 1963 by the US Bureau of Reclamation.

HARVEY GAP

Directions: From Rifle, north 3 miles on Colorado 13 to Colorado 325. Northeast on Colorado 325. You'll pass Rifle Gap Reservoir in route to Harvey Gap Reservoir State Park. From Silt north on County Road 237 approx. 5 miles to reservoir.

Fee: Daily or annual park pass.

Size: 160 surface acres.

Elevation: 6400 feet.

Facilities: Restrooms.

Boat Ramp: A concrete ramp is available on the east side at the main entrance. Boating is restricted to 20 horsepower motors or less.

Fish: Harvey Gap Reservoir is one of the best fisheries in western Colorado. It features rainbow and brown trout, large and smallmouth bass, channel catfish, crappie and northern pike.

Recreation: Fishing.

Camping: No camping is available at the reservoir, it's a day-use area only.

Harvey Gap Reservoir features cottonwood trees along the shoreline. It is in a typical high-plains setting backgrounded by the Grand Hogback mountain range.

Camping is available at Rifle Gap Reservoir. 46 campsites. Reservations are advised throughout the summer. Campsites offer dump station, vault toilets, water, picnic tables, fire pits and grills.

Information: Park office (970) 625-1607.

Handicapped accessible restrooms, swimming, picnic tables, and fishing. Some facilities accessible with assistance.

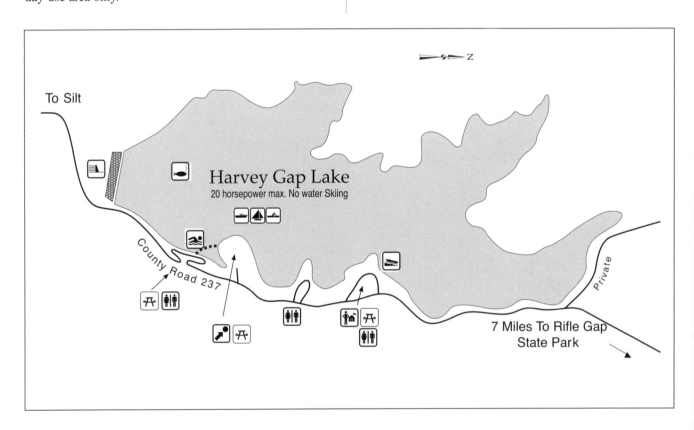

HIGHLINE

Directions: West of Fruita on I-70 use exit 15, north on Highway 139 approximately 8 miles to Q.00 road, west 2 miles, north 1 mile to reservoir.

Fee: Daily or annual pass.

Size: Highline 160 acres, Mack Mesa 30 acres.

Elevation: 4,697 feet.

Facilities: Restrooms, dump station, water.

Boatramps: Concrete boat ramps are located on both sides of Highline Reservoir.

Fish: Mack Mesa Lake is noted for its fine early season trout fishing. Mack Mesa Lake provides good fishing and solitude away from motorized boats. Only hand or electric powered boats are allowed. Highline Lake has good warm-water fishing, especially for catfish and crappie, largemouth bass and bluegill.

Recreation: Fishing, swimming, water skiing, boating, picnicking, hiking, biking and hunting.

Camping: Highline State Park offers 25 grassy campsites that can accommodate both tents and RV's. Showers are available. A holding tank dump station is located in the campground.

Handicapped accessible: A fishing jetty with wheelchair stops is located on the southwest side of Mack Mesa Lake and is designed specifically to accommodate persons with disabilities. The swim area is located 50-75 yards from the parking lot and is accessible with assistance. The beach house, toilet facilities are all accessible. One handicap-accessible campsite is available. Campsites are level with graveled pads and lawn, and a concrete walkway is accessible along the lake shore.

More than 150 species of birds have been observed at Highline State Park, and migrating ducks and geese winter a Highline Lake. Birds such as the great blue heron, white pelican, snowy egret, whooping crane, golden eagle and bald eagle are seen in the park. Many small animals make their home at Highline, and natural areas within the park allow visitors and school groups to observe animals in their natural habitats.

Information: Park office (970) 858-7208.

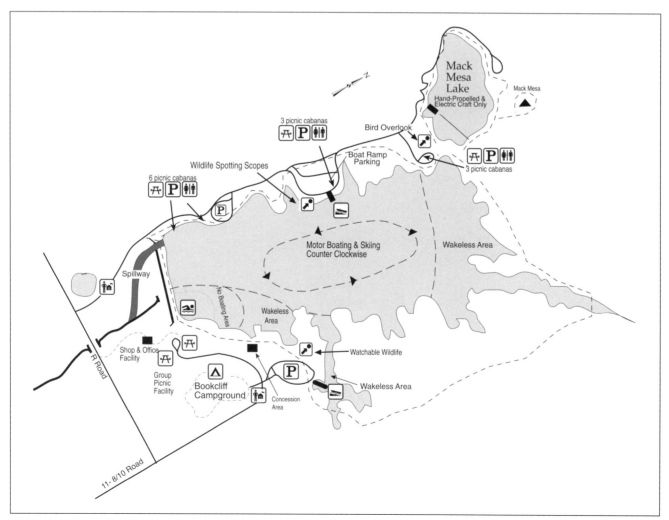

MANCOS STATE PARK

Directions: Located 5 miles northwest of Mancos on Highway 185, just north of Mesa Verde National Park.

Fee: Daily or annual Pass.

Size: 216 surface acres.

Elevation: 7,800 feet.

Facilities: Boatramp, dump station.

Fish: Jackson Gulch Reservoir is located on the Mancos River drainage system and rated good for stocked rainbow and catfish. Year round fishing; ice fishing during winter months. Wakeless boating.

Recreation: Boating, hiking, sail boating.

Camping: Mancos State Park has 34 campsites, most located on the south side of reservoir in mature ponderosa pines forest. There are vault toilets and drinking water but no electrical hookups. A dump station is located at the exit leaving the campground. On the north side of reservoir there are nine campsites primarily for tent campers. Restrooms but no drinking water is available.

Information:
Park office: (970) 553-7065

Scenic Mancos State Park is located 12 miles from Mesa Verde National Park in southwest Colorado. Mancos State Park is surrounded by the majestic San Juan mountain range.

Jackson Gulch Resrvoir (Mancos)
Boats Must Operate at Wakeless Speed

NAVAJO

Directions: From Pagosa Springs west on U.S. 160 to Colorado 151, south on Colorado 151 to the reservoir.

Fee: Daily or Annual pass.

Size: 15,610 surface acres when the reservoir is full.

Elevation: 6,110 feet.

Maximum Depth:100 feet (400 feet at dam).

Facilities: Marina, dump station, air field.

Boatramps: Two in New Mexico. A third in Colorado, San Juan Marina at Arboles.

Fish: Warm and cold water species, with largemouth and smallmouth bass, northern pike, channel catfish, rainbow, brown trout and kokanee salmon. Maintained almost entirely by New Mexico. Two major arms, Los Pinos River and San Juan River. Two major arms within short Colorado stretch, Piedra and San Juan rivers. Several productive side canyons in New Mexico. Access roads off Highway 151 and county road 500 to Pagosa Junction give access to good fishing spots on the Piedra and San Juan Rivers. Fishing condition reports are available at the visitor center. Visitors planning to fish in New Mexico's waters as well as Colorado's must have fishing licenses from both states.

Recreation: Boating, sailing, personal watercraft, and other water sports

Camping: 70 campsites, showers and flush toilets. Many sites have pull throughs, all can accommodate tents, trailers, or pickup campers.There is a dump station, picnic area with tables and grills in the campground.

Information: Park office (970) 883-2208.
Handicapped accessible visitor center, picnic tables and fishing. Some facilities accessible with assistance. Navajo Reservoir, on the southwest border of Colorado, is the main attraction of Navajo State Park. The reservoir is 35 miles long, extends well into New Mexico and is in an area that is unpolluted and sparsely populated. Navajo Dam, located in New Mexico, was constructed on the San Juan River by the U.S. Bureau of Reclamation in 1962.

The park's 5,000 acres offer a challenge to the angler and unlimited pleasure to the boater and water-skier. Navajo boasts Colorado's largest boat ramp - 80 ft. wide and a quarter mile long. A marina is open March through November to provide gas, boat repairs, food service and groceries. Slip and buoy rental is available, as well as fishing and skiing gear and boat rentals.

Boaters are subject either to Colorado boating statutes and regulations or to New Mexico laws, depending on which side of the state line they are on. The two states agreement honor current boat registrations, and boat registrations are available at the visitors center.

There is a good recreational airstrip with a 3,150 ft. N/S dirt runway, 75 ft. wide. It is listed in the FAA Airport Master Record and is frequently used by flying clubs and fly-in campers. Tie downs for nine aircraft are provided. No landing fee.

Waterfowl, shorebirds, birds of prey including the bald eagle and songbirds such a waxwings, thrushes and meadow larks inhabit the area along with game birds like dove, grouse and wild turkey. Beaver, mink, fox, deer, elk, and rabbits may be seen, and in the remote areas, coyotes, bobcat and mountain lion.

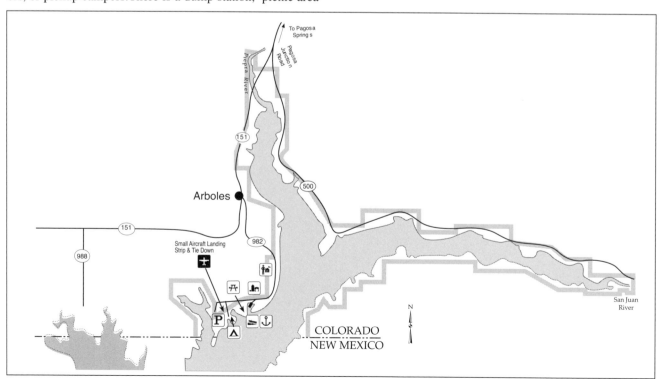

PAONIA

Directions: 16 miles east of Paonia on Colorado 133.

Fee: Daily or annual park pass

Size: 334 acres of water, 1572 acres of land.

Elevation: 6,500 feet.

Maximum Depth: 120 feet.

Facilities: Restrooms, picnic tables, fire grills. No handi-capped facilities.

Boatramp: Ramp is located on the east side of reservoir.

Fish: Northern pike in reservoir, trout in river below dam. Best season for pike in July and August. Best season for trout is spring and fall.

Recreation: Boating sailing, water skiing, personal water-craft, scuba diving, picnicking, hiking, wildlife watching.

Camping: Two primitive campgrounds, 16 campsites, tables, grills and pads. No drinking water. See page 42 for reservations.

Information: At Crawford State Park (970) 921-5721, FAX (970) 921-3636, e-mail crawford.park@state.co.us.

Located in the bottom of Muddy Creek Canyon the park is a picturesque "Scandinavian Fjord" in western Colorado. The campgrounds have lots of shade trees.

The best times to visit is from early June until mid-August (When the water is drawn down too low to launch a boat) and in the fall. Surrounded by steep forested hill sides, the scenery is spectacular, especially in the fall when the colors change! A landmark visible from the campsites is West Beckwith Peak to the south. A landmark visible from the reservoir is the Raggeds Peak Range to the northeast.

The park adjoins U.S. Forest land on the southeast and west and BLM land along the forest service access road on the east.

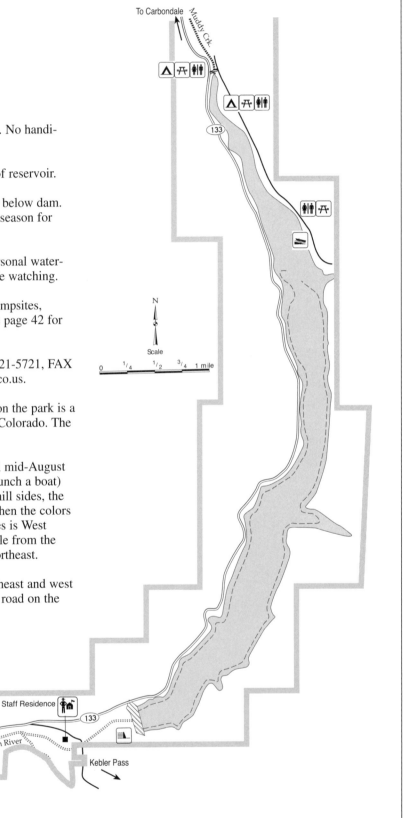

RIDGWAY

Directions: From Montrose 20 miles south on US highway 550 to approximately 4 miles north of the town Ridgway. Parking located on west side of highway.

Fee: Daily or annual pass.

Size: 1000 acres.

Elevation: 6,880 feet.

Maximum Depth: 200 feet.

Facilities: Restrooms, dump station, water, electric hookups, showers.

Boatramp: Four lane concrete ramp.

Fish: Rainbow trout are stocked annually by the Division of Wildlife. Brown trout, which inhabited the Uncompahgre River prior to construction of the dam, are also in the reservoir. Ridgway has a full-service marina with boat and slip rentals.

Recreation: Fishing, boating, camping, swimming, sailing, surf boarding, hunting.

Camping: Dakota Terrace Campgroundis part of the 300 acre Dutch Charlie recreation area and is within walking distance of the lake and swim beach. The campround has RV electrical hookups, water and showers are nearby.

For those who enjoy camping but don't have a tent or motor home the park has three yurts in the A-loop of Dakota Terraces Campground, sites 10, 12, and 14. Call for fee information.

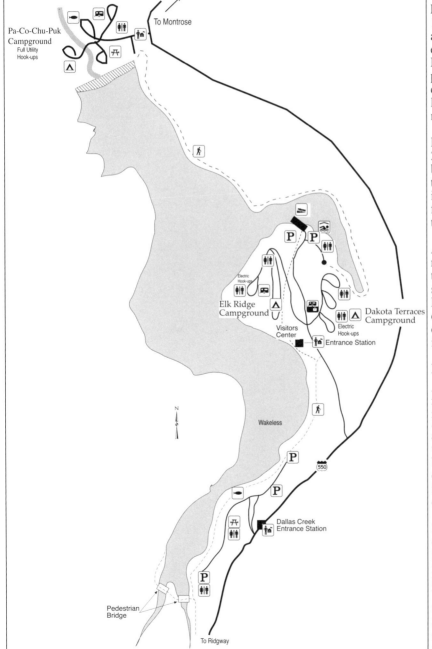

Elk Ridge Campground sites 80 through 187, is also part of Dutch Charlie recreation area. Located in a pinion-juniper forest with panoramic views of the San Juan Mountains. the campground is the most popular in the park. Elk Ridge has electrical hookups, water hydrants, flush toilets, lavatory and shower facilities are located nearby. Ten walk-in tent areas.

Pa-Co-Chu-Puk Campground with sites 200 through 295. Pa-Co-Chu-Puk lies just below the reservoir dam and each site feature full individual utility hookups, including water, sewer and electricity. Addition fees are charge for these luxuries. Walk-in tent sites are available.

A camper's services building with modern restrooms, hot showers and laundry facilities is also on the premises. There are no sewer hookups but there is a dump station. Please use this facility. It is illegal to dump any waste or sewage, including dishwater, anywhere except into the holding tank.

Information: Park office (970) 626-5822.

Facilities for the physically challenged: More than 90 percent of the facilities at Ridgway State Park are accessible to disabled people. For example, the park has a wheelchair walkway leading to the swim beach and tables and grills are constructed on cement high-use pads. For specific information on accessibility call the park office.

Hiking/Nature Trails: Four miles of developed trails wind through the park connecting the various facilities. The trails range from a moderate walk to challenging hikes.

Wildlife and Hunting: Winter is the best time for wildlife watching at Ridgway State Park. Deer, elk, small mammals, eagles, waterfowl, raptors and song birds can often be spotted by visitors.

RIFLE GAP

Directions: From Rifle north on Hwy 13 to Hwy 325, 7 miles north on Colorado Highway 325.
Fee: Daily or annual state park pass.
Size: 360 acres.
Elevation: 6000 feet.
Maximum Depth: 87 feet.
Facilities: Full service state park with a dump station.
Boatramp: Ramp located on north side of reservoir near Pinon Campground.
Fish: Rainbow, brown trout, walleye, perch and small-mouth, largemouth bass. All smallmouth and largemouth bass between 12 and 15 inches must be returned to the water immediately.
Recreation: Fishing, water-skiing personal watercraft, swimming.
Camping: 47 campsites that can accommodate tents, small trailers and campers. There are some pull through sites for larger units. Campground users must have a camping permit, in addition to a parks pass.
Information: Park office (970) 625-1607.

Rifle Gap Reservoir is in northwestern Colorado near Rifle. Although separated by a few miles, Rifle Gap Reservoir and Rifle Falls are two popular state parks. The 360 surface acre reservoir and the falls with its mysterious caves and unique triple waterfall are unified by their beauty and superb recreational opportunities. Rifle Gap's clean, clear waters afford some of the best scuba diving, boating, swimming, water-skiing and wind surfing in Colorado. Golfers can pursue their sport here, a 18 hole golf course is located next to the area.

Sandstone and shale cliffs frame the reservoir. Shore vegetation is pinon, juniper, grasses and sagebrush. The area around Rifle Gap and Falls is rich in history.

For campers there are 47 sites at Rifle Gap, 20 sites (13 with electricity) at Rifle Falls that can accommodate tents, trailers and pickup campers. There are some pull-through sites and a dump station.

Water skiing is popular, as well as swimming and scuba diving. In cold weather there is ice fishing.

Many small mammals ranging from beaver, chipmunks and rabbits to weasels and bobcats live around the area. Blue heron, several kinds of hummingbirds and a wide variety of ducks and other waterfowl are found here. These wild creatures might easily be seen when taking the self-guided nature trail. The trail complete with interpretive view stations, leads walkers above and over Rifle Falls.

Handicapped accessible restrooms, swimming, hunting, picnic tables, camping and fishing. Some facilities at Rifle Gap accessible with assistance.

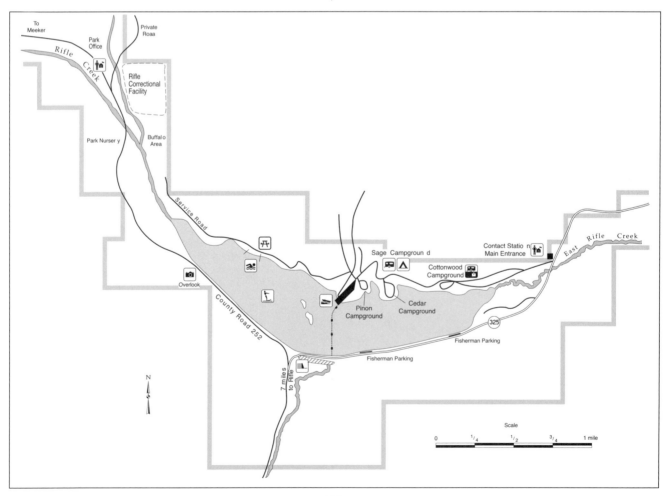

SYLVAN LAKE

Directions: 16 miles south of Eagle on Brush Creek Road.

Fee: Annual Pass/Permit.

Size: 40 acres.

Elevation: 8500 Feet.

Facilities: Water, restrooms.

Boatramp: One ramp located near Fisherman's Paradise Campground.

Recreation: Boating, only non-motorized boats and electric motors are allowed on lake. Hunting

Camping: Sylvan Lake has 50 campsites, 30 at Elk Run Campground and 20 at Fisherman's Paradise Campground. Sites can accommodate tents, trailers and campers, there is a RV dump station and a shower building. There are some pull-through sites for larger units. Campers must have camping permit. There are also 9 cabins for rent.

Fishing: Stocked with brook and rainbow trout.

Information: Park office (970) 328-2021.
Sylvan Lake State Park is one of the most beautiful get-aways in the state with some of the best year-round trout fishing anywhere.

Nestled in the heart of the majestic Rocky Mountains, it is surrounded by the White River National Forest. The visitor enjoys a spectacular 360 degree panoramic view of the alpine scenery --- One of Colorado's best kept secrets.

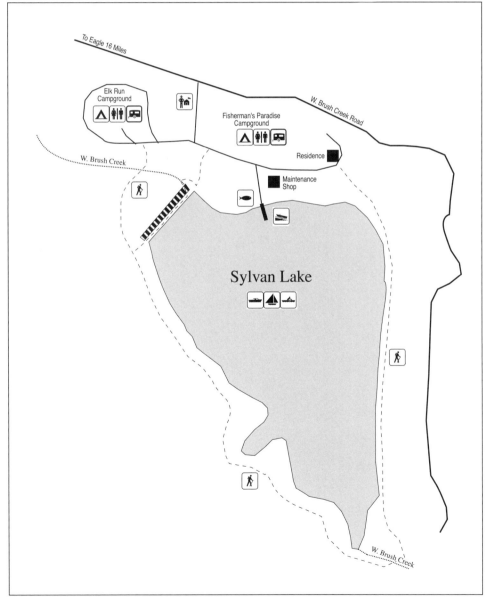

Sylvan Lake is a haven for campers, boaters, picnickers, photographers and hikers. The park is used as a base camp for hunters during the big game hunting season.

VEGA

Directions: Located 12 miles east of Collbran on Mesa County Road 330.
Fee: Daily or annual park pass.
Size: 900 acres.
Elevation: 7,960 feet.
Maximum Depth: 94 feet.
Facilities: Restrooms, picnic tables.
Boatramp: Two boat ramps on the north side of reservoir.
Fish: Few lakes can surpass Vega as a trout fishery. Rainbow weighing five pounds have been caught here. One-and-a-half pound fish are common.
Recreation: Fishing, boating, water skiing, wind surfing, personal watercraft. Cold weather enthusiasts come to Vega for ice fishing, ice skating, snowmobiling, cross country skiing and snow play.
Camping: There are 110 individual and group campsites in the park that can accommodate both tents and campers. Marmot Flats (the group campsite) is on the west end of the lake and Aspen Grove Campground is on the southeast end of the lake. All sites may be reserved in advance by calling for reservations. Sites not reserved are available on a first come, first serve basis. A holding tank dump station is located in the Oak Point Campground. There are many individual picnic sites and the park has one group picnic shelter that accommodates 100 to 200 people.
Information: Park office (970) 487-3407.

Handicapped accessible restrooms, picnic tables, camping and fishing. Some facilities accessible with assistance.

Vega Reservoir is in west central Colorado, south of Highway 330. The lake is fed by Plateau Creek and by a diversion off Leon Creek during the spring runoff. The Primary use of the lake is for irrigation, so fluctuation in water level occurs. The Spanish word "vega" means meadow. Cattle grazed here from the late 1880's until 1962 when the 900 surface acre reservoir was completed by the Bureau of Reclamation.

What was once meadow is now a playground for boaters, water skiers, fishermen and other outdoor recreation enthusiasts. Cattle drives still pass through the area in spring and fall and visitors could be fortunate enough to see one. Vega is already well known as a winter sports area. Warm weather visitors can expect sub-alpine beauty and mild temperatures characteristic of its 8,000 foot altitude.

Water skiing is allowed in an area marked by buoys. Water skiing season usually begins in late June and ends by mid-August depending on water level.

Deer, elk, beaver and many kinds of waterfowl frequent the area. Weasel, rabbits, chipmunks, hawks, blue grouse and the elusive wild turkey are also found here, as well as coyotes and bobcats.
Special Restrictions: Operate vehicles only on designated roads and parking lots. Build campfires only in the fire rings or grills that are provided. Place litter and trash in the receptacles provided. Keep all pets on a leash no more than six feet long.

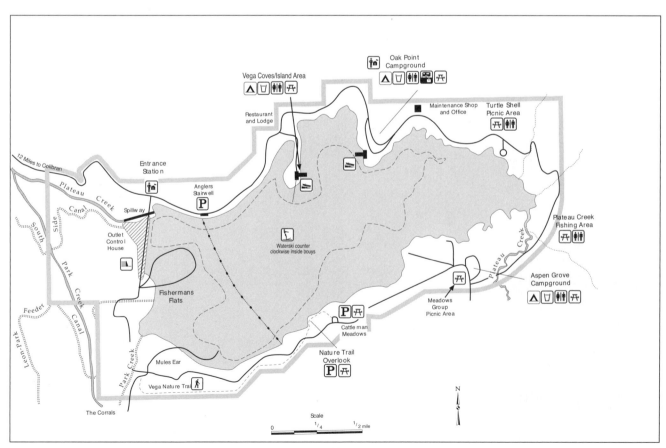

STATE TRUST LANDS

1a.	Blue Lake	80
2a.	Tiger Lily Creek (Arkansas River)	80
3a.	Bakerville (Clear Creek	80
3b.	Golden Watershed (Beaver Brook Creek)	80
4a.	La Jara Reservoir	80
4b.	Vincente Canyon (La Jara Creek)	80
5a.	Squaw Creek	80
5b.	Whiskey Creek	80
6a.	Badger Creek	80
6b.	Grape Creek	80
6c.	Cottonwood Ridge (Cottonwood Creek)	81
7a.	Fraser Canyon (Fraser River)	81
8a.	Black Sage Pass (No Name Creek)	81
8b.	Tomichi Dome (Hot Springs Reservoir	81
9a.	East Delaney Butte Lake	81
9b.	Elk Mountain (Canadian River)	81
9c.	Rabbit Ears (Grizzly Creek)	81
9d.	Three Sisters (Muddy Creek)	81
9e.	Johnny Moore Mountain (Michigan River)	81
9f.	North Platte River	81
10a.	Poudre River (Seaman Res., No. Fork Poudre)	81
10b.	LaGarde Creek	81
11a.	Boston Flats (Yampa River)	82
11b.	Maybell (Yampa River)	82
11c.	Big Hole Gulch (Little Snake River)	82
11d.	Oxbow (Little Snake River)	82
12a.	Antero Reservoir	82
12b.	High Creek	82
12c.	63 Ranch (South Platte River)	82
13a.	Dry Creek	82
14a.	King Creek	82
15a.	Daley Gulch (Agate, Brush & Tominchi Creeks)	82
15b.	Marshall Pass (Marshall & Indian Creeks)	82
15c.	Los Pinos Creek	82

STATE TRUST LANDS were given to the state by the federal government when Colorado was granted statehood in 1876. Revenues from rents, royalties and land sales go to benefit the K-12 public schools and several other smaller trusts. The trust lands total nearly 3 million surface acres and 4 million acres of subsurface mineral rights. Since the trust lands are managed to generate revenue for public schools and to preserve long term productivity and value, the lands are not all open for public use.

Most of the state trust lands are leased to private parties and access is controlled by those lessees. In 1992 the State Land Board adopted a multi-use access policy, which means certain properties may be open to the public for wildlife related recreation.

The State Land Board and the Division of Wildlife have agreed to select about 500,000 acres of trust lands with the best wildlife values to be opened for public use over a 10 year period. The Division will pay for this opportunity, using hunting and fishing license fees. The Land Board will use that money to help finance public schools in Colorado.

In future years the Division of Wildlife may elect not to lease all of the properties shown in this guide. If you are not certain these properties are open to public access, call first.

State Trust Lands Locator Map

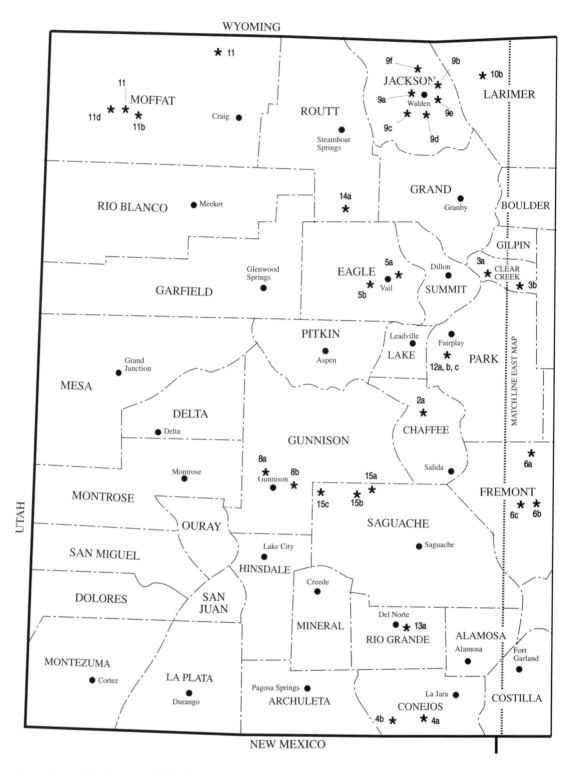

Properties are listed in numerical and alphabetical order.

4. CONEJOS COUNTY
a. LA JARA RESERVOIR - 28/C-2

Page number   Map coordinates

Location of property in *Pierson's Colorado Road Atlas* (ISBN 1-928721-04-4)

Explanation

★ = Approximate State Trust property location.
4a

4 = County in text.
a = Alpha order of listed property.

State Trust Lands Locator Map

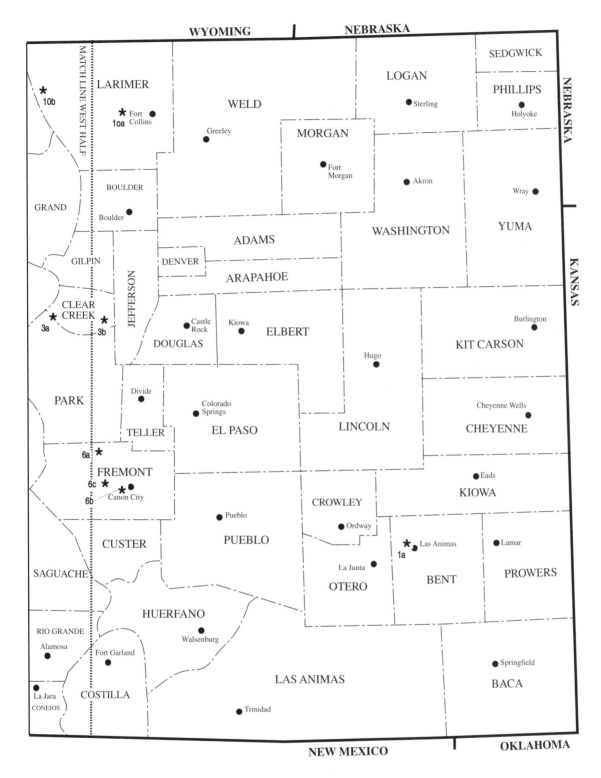

Generalized Location of State Trust Land Fishing Properties

The Colorado Division of Wildlife (DOW) leases the described properties from the State Land Board. Public access to the properties is periodically reviewed, check with the DOW before visiting a State Trust property.

Detailed individual maps of a State Trust Land property can be purchased from the DOW for a small fee.

State Trust Land - Fishing

STATE TRUST LANDS were given to the state by the federal government when Colorado was granted statehood in 1876. Revenues from rents, royalties and land sales go to benefit the K-12 public schools and several other smaller trusts. The trust lands total over 3 million surface acres and 4 million acres of subsurface mineral rights. Since the trust lands are managed to generate revenue for public schools and to preserve long term productivity and value, the lands are not all open for public use.

Most of the state trust lands are leased to private parties and access is controlled by those lessees. In 1992 the State Land Board adopted a multi-use access policy, which means certain properties may be open to the public for wildlife related recreation. This arrangement is periodically reviewed and is subject to change. Properties listed are current through 1999 -- Call DOW if you are uncertain of property status.

The State Land Board and the Division of Wildlife have agreed to select about 500,000 acres of trust lands with the best wildlife values to be opened for public use over a 10 year period. The Division will pay for this opportunity, using hunting and fishing license fees. The Land Board will use that money to help finance public schools in Colorado.

Wildlife Recreation Properties open for hunting (Through 1999) are listed by county. Unless otherwise indicated, these properties are open Sept. 1 to Feb. 28 of each year. The properties are numbered first by county, then with lower case letters with-in each county.

26/A-3 = Pierson Graphics Colorado Road Atlas Page Number and Map Coordinates

1. BENT COUNTY

a. BLUE LAKE - 26/A-3
From Las Animas, take Hwy. 194 west to Cty. Rd. 10, north 11 miles then west 2-1/2 miles on Cty. Rd. TT to eastern property boundary.
ACRES: 14,059.
OPEN: Year-round for fishing only. Sept. 1-Feb. 28 for hunting.
HUNTING: Antelope, deer, waterfowl, upland game.
FISHING: Warm-water lake.
ACCESS: There are several parking lots: (1) at end of Cty. Rd. TT; (2) at bridge on southeast corner; (3) at south end of property. Islands closed to public access from May 15-Aug. 31. Vehicles allowed on designated roads only. Camping allowed as posted.

2. CHAFFEE COUNTY

a. TIGER LILY CREEK - 23/2-B
From Buena Vista go north on Hwy 24 for 12 miles. Property is located on east side of Hwy 24.
ACRES: 398.
OPEN: Sept. 1-Feb. 28 for hunting. Otherwise year-round for fishing and watchable wildlife.
HUNTING: Bighorn sheep. deer, elk.
FISHING: **Arkansas River.**
ACCESS: Direct from Hwy. 24. Also across twin bridges and then south on old Cty. Rd. Foot access only.

3. CLEAR CREEK COUNTY

a. BAKERVILLE - 14/B-1
From Georgetown, take I-70 west 5 miles. Section 16 is about 1 .25 mile east of the Bakerville exit. Majority of tract is north of I-70.
ACRES: 320.
OPEN: Sept. 1-Feb. 28 for hunting. Otherwise, year-round for fishing and watching wildlife only.
HUNTING: Bighorn sheep, elk, mule deer, mountain lions, black bears, blue grouse, ptarmigan, cottontail rabbits and snowshoe hares.
FISHING: **Clear Creek**, cold-water stream.
ACCESS: Vehicle access off I-70 right of way only. Foot access only.

b. GOLDEN WATERSHED - 15/A-1
From Denver take I-70 west to Evergreen Parkway then south to Bergen Park. Go west on Hwy. 103 to Golden Watershed (about 4 miles).
ACRES: 480.
OPEN: Sept. 1-May 31 for hunting. Year-round for fishing and watching wildlife only.
HUNTING: Mule deer, elk, black bears, mountain lions, blue grouse, cottontails, snowshoe hares, turkeys.
FISHING: **Beaver Brook**, cold-water stream.
ACCESS: Access on property limited to two parking lots (Hwy. 103 and Old Squaw Pass Road and Witter Gulch). Access by foot or horseback to tract (1-2 miles).

4. CONEJOS COUNTY

a. LA JARA RESERVOIR - 29/3-B
From La Jara go west on Hwy. 15, 10.5 miles to USFS Rd. 240, then go about 23 miles to property.
ACRES: 32,913.
OPEN: Year-round for fishing only. Sept. 1 - Feb. 28 for hunting.
HUNTING: Deer, elk, antelope, bighorn sheep, black bear, mtn. lion, small game.
FISHING: Lake, three cold-water streams. Timber activity may be present.

b. VINCENTE CANYON - 29/3-B
From Monte Vista, go 21 miles south on Hwy 15 to Capulin. Travel 10 miles southwest on dump road (Cty. Rd. 8) from Capulin to north end of property.
ACRES: 640.
OPEN: Aug.15-May 31 for hunting. Year-round for fishing and watching wildlife.
HUNTING: Bighorn sheep, deer, elk, antelope, mtn lions, black bears, small game.
FISHING: **La Jara Creek.**
ACCESS: On north end from the Cty. Rd. along La Jara Creek.

5. EAGLE COUNTY

a. SQUAW CREEK - 13/1-A
From Vail, take I-70 west to Exit 163 (Edwards), go south to stoplight, turn west on Hwy. 6, go 2 miles to road and bridge over Eagle River. Tract continues 1 mile west from here.
ACRES: 272.
OPEN: Year-round for fishing only.
HUNTING: This property is closed to hunting and discharge of firearms.
FISHING: Cold-water stream.
ACCESS: Road and bridge over Eagle River: parking area and access point. Squaw Creek Rd. and Hwy. 6, parking area and access point. Walk-in access only.

b. WHISKEY CREEK - 13/1-B
From Vail, go west on I-70, take Exit 171, go 1/2 mile west. Property south of I-70.
ACRES: 602.
OPEN: Sept. 1-Feb. 28. Otherwise year-round for fishing.
HUNTING: Deer, elk, black bears, blue grouse, rabbits, coyotes.
ACCESS: Parking available at USFS office at Meadow Mountain (off I-70 Exit 171, 1/4 mile east). Timber activity may be present.

6. FREMONT COUNTY

a. BADGER CREEK (partially in Park County) - 23/2-B
From Cotopaxi, go 21 miles north on Cty. Rd. 12, then west 1 mile on BLM road. Or, from Hartsel, go south on Hwy. 9 to Park Cty. Rd. 53. Follow Cty. Rd. 53, 22 miles to property.
ACRES: 6,032.
OPEN: Year-round for fishing only; Sept. 1-Feb. 28 for all other uses.
HUNTING: Mule deer, elk, bighorn sheep.
FISHING: Cold-water stream.
ACCESS: Timber activity may be present.

b. GRAPE CREEK - 24/3-A
From Canon City at Hwy. 50 and First Street, go south on First Street, 1 mile to Fremont Cty. Rd. 3. West on Cty. Rd. 3, 5.2 miles to Temple Canyon City Park. South 1/2 mile through park to northeast corner of property. Continue through property along Grape Creek and 1.7 miles along Grape Creek through BLM to Pine Gulch. Walk west up Pine Gulch 1.2 miles to property.
ACRES: 1,280.
OPEN: Sept. 1-May 31 for hunting. Year-round for watching wildlife and fishing only. Fishing as posted on Grape Creek.
HUNTING: Deer, elk, bighorn sheep, mountain lions, bears, rabbits, turkeys.
FISHING: Cold-water stream.
ACCESS: Foot or horseback only. No vehicle access on property.

c. COTTONWOOD RIDGE - 23/3-C
From Canon City go west on Hwy. 50 for 12 miles to Hwy. 9. Turn north on Hwy. 9 and go 6 miles. Turn west at Gate, go .8 mile to property.
ACRES: 640.
OPEN: Sept. 1-May 31 for hunting. Otherwise year-round for fishing.
HUNTING: Deer, lion, bear, rabbit.
FISHING: **Cottonwood Creek.**

7. GRAND COUNTY
a. FRASER CANYON - 10/3-A
From Tabernash, go east to Cty. Rd. 84 to fork. Go left at fork 1/2 mile north to Strawberry access road. Left 1.5 miles to property.
ACRES: 320.
OPEN: Sept. 1-Feb. 28 for hunting. Year-round for fishing only.
HUNTING: Deer, elk, bears, small game.
FISHING: **Frazer River,** cold-water stream.
ACCESS: No motorized vehicles off designated roads. Foot access only. Timber activity may be present.

8. GUNNISON COUNTY
a. BLACK SAGE PASS - 23/3-A
From Gunnison at Hwy. 50 and USFS Rd. 243 (Marshall Pass Rd.), go north on Hwy. 50, 1 mile to USFS Rd. 888. Travel north on USFS Rd. 888 for 5.5 miles to south boundary.
ACRES: 415.
OPEN: Year-round for fishing only. Sept. 1-Feb. 28 for hunting.
HUNTING: Mule deer, elk, black bears, mountain lions, blue grouse, rabbits.
FISHING: In small section of **No Name Creek.**
ACCESS: Access by foot or horseback only.

b. TOMICHI DOME - 23/3-A
From Gunnison, at Hwys. 50 and 135 go 17 miles east on Hwy. 50 to BLM Rd. 3095 (Waunita Hot Springs Rd.). Turn north on BLM Rd. 3095 and go 4 miles to west boundary of property.
ACRES: 640.
OPEN: Sept. 1-Feb. 28 for hunting and watching wildlife. Year-round for fishing only.
HUNTING: Mule deer, elk, antelope, black bears, mountain lions, grouse, rabbits.
FISHING: **Hot Springs Reservoir.**
ACCESS: Enter property just southwest of Hot Springs Reservoir. Camping allowed as posted.

9. JACKSON COUNTY
a. EAST DELANEY BUTTE LAKE - 5/2-B
From Walden go 1.2 miles west on Hwy. 14 to Cty. Rd. 12W, then 5.3 miles west to Cty. Rd. 18, then 4.5 miles west to Cty. Rd. 5, 1 mile north to entrance of Delaney Butte Lakes State Wildlife Area.
ACRES: 640.
OPEN: Year-round for fishing only. Sept. 1- Feb. 28 for hunting.
HUNTING: Small game.
FISHING: Cold-water lake.
ACCESS: Foot access only.
RESTRICTIONS: Camping and campfires limited to existing state wildlife area campground next to East Delaney Butte Lake.

b. ELK MOUNTAIN - 6/2-A
From Walden, take 5th Street east, which turns into Cty. Rd.12E, then go 12 miles east, then take Cty. Rd. 12F about 2.5 miles northeast to the parking lot at the end of the road. Access is only from this parking lot and State Forest land.
ACRES: 2,840.
OPEN: Year-round for fishing only. Sept. 1-Feb. 28 for hunting.
HUNTING: Deer, elk, blue grouse, rabbits, coyotes.
FISHING: **Canadian River,** cold-water stream.
ACCESS: All roads off Cty. Rds. 12E and 12F are closed.

c. RABBIT EARS - 5/4-A
From Walden, go southwest toward Muddy Pass on Hwy. 14 for 29 miles to one parking lot, or go 1.5 miles more to another parking lot.
ACRES: 4,948.
OPEN: Year-round for fishing only. Sept. 1- Feb. 28 for hunting.
HUNTING: Deer, elk, blue grouse, rabbits.
FISHING: **Grizzly Creek,** cold-water stream.

ACCESS: Foot and horseback traffic only. Timber activity may be present.

d. THREE SISTERS - 6/2-A
From Walden. take 5th Street east, which turns into Cty. Rd. 12E, go 12 miles east, then take Cty. Rd. 12F for 2.5 miles to parking lot. Access to the property only from parking lot and Colorado State Forest.
ACRES: 1,523.
OPEN: Year-round for fishing only. Sept. 1-Feb. 28 for hunting.
HUNTING: Deer, elk, blue grouse, rabbits, coyotes.
FISHING: **Muddy Creek,** cold-water stream.
ACCESS: All roads off Cty. Rds. 12E and 12F closed. Access also from State Forest to east.

e. JOHNNY MOORE MOUNTAIN - 5/2-C
From Walden, take 5th Street east, which turns into Cty. Rd. 12E; go 6 miles east to Cty. Rd. 23. Go south 3 miles until you reach BLM land. Numerous two-track roads lead to western boundary of property. Or, from Walden, take Hwy. 14 east 12 miles; go north on Cty. Rd. 30 one mile.
ACRES: 7,671.
OPEN: Sept. 1-Feb. 28 for hunting and watching wildlife. Year-round for fishing only as posted on southern portion of property.
HUNTING: Elk, moose, blue grouse, cottontail rabbits, coyotes.
FISHING: In **Michigan River** and along Meadow Creek Reservoir dam as posted. ACCESS: Parking lot west of the dam and a parking lot 1/4 mile north of the dam. Foot or horseback only. Motor vehicles prohibited.

f. NORTH PLATTE - 5/2-B
From Walden, go 1.2 miles west on Hwy. 14 to Cty. Rd. 12. Then head west 5.3 miles to Cty. Rd. 18, and go 2 miles on Cty. Rd. 18 to Cty. Rd. 9. Go about 1 mile and access property to the west from BLM land for hunting. For fishing, instead of turning off on Cty. Rd. 8, stay on Cty. Rd. 18 for 1/4 mile further to bridge over North Platte River. The fishing part of lease is on river above bridge.
ACRES: 152.
OPEN: Year-round for fishing only. Sept. I-Feb. 28 for hunting.
HUNTING: Antelope, rabbits, coyotes, sage grouse.
FISHING: **North Platte River.**

10. LARIMER COUNTY
a. POUDRE RIVER - 7/2-C
From Fort Collins, go northwest on Hwy. 287 to Ted's Place, then go west on Hwy. 14 for 1.7 miles to DOW lands. These lands are north of DOW lands along Hwy. 14, about 1.5 miles to where Hwy. 14 turns north. These lands are east of Hwy. 14 another 1.7 miles. To get to Section 36 take Hwy. 287 NW to Ted's Place. Continue past Ted's 3 miles. Section is on W side of hwy. Property closed east of Hwy. 287.
ACRES: 3,517.
OPEN: Sept. 1-Feb. 28 for hunting and watching wildlife. Year-round for fishing only.
HUNTING: Deer, small game.
FISHING: Cold-water stream (**Poudre River, North Fork of the Poudre and Seaman Reservoir).** Dam and caretaker residence closed to public as posted. Boats prohibited, but float tubes allowed.
ACCESS: Access through private property if permission is obtained first. Written permission from agricultural lessee or his agent required March 1 to Aug. 31. Foot or horseback only.

b. LaGARDE CREEK - 6/1-A
From Fort Collins, take Hwy. 14, 50 miles west. Take Laramie River Road (LCR 103) north 28 miles to Hohnholz Lakes. Go west 15 miles on USFS Road 200, then south on Road 143 and then east on Road 207 to property.
ACRES: 640.
OPEN: Sept. 1-Feb. 28 for hunting. Year-round for fishing only.
HUNTING: Elk, deer, bear.
FISHING: **LaGarde Creek** for brooks and browns.
ACCESS: Foot and horseback only. Timber activity may be present.

State Trust Land - Fishing

11. MOFFAT COUNTY

a. BOSTON FLATS - 1 /2-C
From Maybell, go northwest 3.5 miles on Hwy. 318. On north side of Hwy. 318.
ACRES: 104.
OPEN: Year-round for fishing **Yampa River** and watching wildlife only. Sept. 1- Feb. 28 for hunting.
HUNTING: Big game, small game.
ACCESS: From Hwy. 318, walk-in only. Adequate area for parking between highway and property.

b. MAYBELL - 1 /2-C
From Maybell, go 1.5 miles north on Moffat Cty. Rd. 19. Tract east and west of Cty. Rd. 19, north of Yampa River.
ACRES: 9,208.
OPEN: Year-round for fishing and watching wildlife only. Sept. 1-Feb. 28 for hunting.
HUNTING: Deer, elk, small game.
FISHING: **Yampa River.** Cold-water stream.
ACCESS: Moffat Cty. Rd. 19 bisects the Maybell tract from north and south and provides primary access. Walk-in access across Spring Creek at west side of property and from Hwy. 40. Motor vehicles limited to roads posted. All other roads closed to motor vehicles; open to foot and horseback only. Camping in designated areas.

c. BIG HOLE GULCH - 2 /1-A
From Craig, go 40 miles north on Hwy. 13. Take Cty. Rd. 4 west 15 miles to property.
ACRES: 1,847.
OPEN: Aug. 15-Feb 28 for hunting. Year-round for fishing **Little Snake River.**
HUNTING: Antelope, deer, elk, small game.
ACCESS: Motorized traffic limited to Cty. Rd. 4 unless otherwise designated.
RESTRICTIONS: No camping or campfires.

d. OXBOW - 1 2-B
From Maybell travel 17 miles northwest on Hwy. 318 to parking lot on south side.
ACRES: 640.
OPEN: Aug. 15-Feb. 28 for hunting. Otherwise year-round for fishing and watchable wildlife as posted.
HUNTING: Deer, elk, antelope, waterfowl, dove, rabbits, prairie dogs.
FISHING: In the Oxbow water area only off of the **Little Snake River.**
ACCESS: From parking lot on south side of Hwy 318. Foot or horseback only. Seasonal Youth Mentor Property as posted. Call DOW office in Craig for information, (970) 824-3046.

12. PARK COUNTY

a. ANTERO - 23/2-B
From Fairplay, go south on Hwy. 285 for 16.5 miles.
ACRES: 11,453.
OPEN: Aug. 15-Feb. 28 for hunting. Year-round for fishing only.
HUNTING: Big game, small game, waterfowl.
ACCESS: Hwy. 285, next to Antero State Wildlife Area. North of Antero Jct. on Hwy. 24, 9 miles to **Antero Reservoir** Road, then west 1-3/4 miles to northwest corner of property. Or, 4.5 miles north of Antero Jct. on Hwy. 285. the west on unmarked USFS #433, 1/2 mile to north boundary. Timber activity may be present.

b. HIGH CREEK - 23/1-B
From Fairplay, go 7 miles south on Hwy. 285. There is a road on the east side of Hwy. 285. Go .5 miles east to a road going south. Go .25 miles.
ACRES: 1,121.
OPEN: Aug. 15-Feb. 28 for hunting. Year-round for fishing only.
HUNTING: Antelope. waterfowl.

c. 63 RANCH - 23/1-B
From Fairplay, go south on Hwy. 285, 14-1/2 miles to 63 Ranch parking lot on east side of highway.
ACRES: 1,635.

OPEN: Aug. 15-Feb. 28 for hunting. Year-round for fishing **South Platte River.**
HUNTING: Antelope, deer, elk, waterfowl.

14. RIO GRANDE COUNTY

a. DRY CREEK - 29/3-B
Section 16: From Monte Vista take Hwy. 15 south 2 miles to #2 South Rd. Go 3 miles west to property. Section 36: From Monte Vista, take Hwy. 15 south 2 miles to #2 South Rd. Go west 9.5 miles to property.
ACRES: 1,280.
OPEN: Aug. 15-May 31 for hunting. Tract 2 only open year-round for fishing.
HUNTING: Elk, deer, antelope, cottontail rabbit, coyote, bobcat, mountain lion, fur bearers. Safety zone along east side of Tract 1.
FISHING: In **Rock Creek** on Tract 2 only.
ACCESS: Vehicle access limited to existing roads.
RESTRICTIONS: Camping and campfires prohibited.

15. ROUTT COUNTY

a. KING CREEK - 2/4-C
From Toponas. go l/2 mile south on Hwy. 131 and turn west on Cty. Rd. 5 about 3 miles, then go south on Cty. Rd. 5A for 1 mile to property.
ACRES: 640.
OPEN: Year-round for fishing only. Sept. 1-Feb. 28 for hunting.
HUNTING: Big game, small game.
FISHING: Cold-water stream fishing.
ACCESS: Foot and horseback access from BLM land.

16. SAGUACHE COUNTY

a. DALEY GULCH (partially in Gunnison County) - 23/3-A
From Sargents at USFS Rd. 243 and Hwy. 50, go north 3/4 mile and turn left into property.
ACRES: 644.
OPEN: Year-round for fishing only. Sept. 1 Feb. 28 for hunting.
HUNTING: Mule deer, elk, black bears, mountain lions, blue grouse, rabbits.
FISHING: **Agate Creek, Brush Creek, Tomichi Creek.**
ACCESS: Enter the Daley Gulch property at gravel pit on west side of Hwy. 50 across from state highway barn. Vehicle access on existing USFS Rd. 8192 is allowed. Vehicles not allowed off USFS Rd. 8192, except in designated camping or parking areas. All other access by foot or horseback only.
RESTRICTIONS: Camping in designated areas only.

b. MARSHALL PASS - 23/3-A
From Sargents at Hwy. 50 and USFS Rd. 243 (Marshall Pass Rd.), go east on USFS Rd. 243 for 4.5 miles to property.
ACRES: 659.
OPEN: Year-round for fishing only. Sept. 1-Feb. 28 for hunting.
HUNTING: Mule deer, elk, black bears, mountain lions, blue grouse, rabbits.
FISHING: **Marshall and Indian Creeks.**
ACCESS: Access by vehicle on Indian Creek Rd. only. Foot and horseback everywhere else. Parking provided at Indian Creek. Parking and camping allowed at designated site on Indian Creek.

c. LOS PINOS CREEK - 22/C-4
From Gunnison, on Hwy. 50, go 8 miles to Hwy. 114. Go southeast on Hwy. 114, 20 miles. Turn right on Cty. Rd. NN56. Travel SE about 7.5 miles to USFS Road 787.2A. Go east 2 miles to south access of property.
ACRES: 320.
OPEN: Aug. 15-Feb. 28 for hunting and fishing.
HUNTING: Antelope, elk, deer, bighorn sheep, small game.
FISHING: Coldwater stream.
ACCESS: No motor vehicles off established roads.

State Wildlife Areas Table of Contents

State Wildlife Area   **Page**

1. Adams County
a. Barr Lake 86

2. Alamosa County
a. San Luis Lakes 86

3. Archuleta County
a. Echo Canyon Reservoir 86

4. Baca County
a. Turks Pond 86
b. Two Buttes Reservoir 86

5. Bent County
a. Adobe Creek Reservoir 86
b. John Martin Reservoir 86

6. Chaffee County
a. Clear Creek Reservoir 86
b. Arkansas River 86
c. Franz Lake 86
d. Granite 86
e. Mount Ouray 86
f. Mount Shavano 86
g. Sands Lake 86

7. Clear County
a. Mount Evans 86

8. Conejos County
a. Hot Creek 86
b. LaJara Reservoir 86
c. LaJara 86
d. Sego Springs 86
e. Conejos River 87
f. Terrace Reservoir 87
g. Trujillo Meadows 87

9. Costilla County
a. Smith Reservoir 87
b. Mountain Home Reservoir 87
c. Sanchez Reservoir 87

10. Crowley County
a. Lake Henry 87
b. Meredith Reservoir 87
c. Olney Reservoir 87
d. Ordway Reservoir 87

11. Custer County
a. Middle Taylor Creek 87
b. DeWeese Reservoir 87

12. Delta County
a. Escalante 87
b. Roeber 87

13. Dolores County
a. Fish Creek 87
b. Lone Cone 87
c. Lone Dome 87
d. Groundhog Reservoir 87

14. Eagle County
a. Basalt 87
b. Radium 88
c. Gypsum Ponds 88
d. Eagle River 88

15. El Paso County
a. Ramah Reservoir 88
b. Monument Lake 88

16. Fremont County
a. Beaver Creek 88
b. Brush Hollow 88

17. Garfield County
a. Hunt 88
b. Carbondale 88
c. Rifle Falls SFU 88
d. West Bank 88

18. Grand County
a. Hot Sulphur Springs 88

19. Gunnison County
a. Cimarron 88
b. Gunnison 88
c. Gunnison River 88
d. Viking Valley 88
e. Beaver Lake 88
f. Lake Irwin 88
g. Pitkin SFU 89
h. Roaring Judy SFU 89
i. Spring Creek Reservoir 89
j. Taylor River 89

20. Hinsdale County
a. Brown Lakes 89
b. Cebolla 89
c. Williams Creek Reservoir 89
d. Lake Fork of the Gunnison 89
e. Rito Hondo Reservoir 89
f. Road Canyon Reservoir 89

21. Huerfano County
a. Huerfano 89
b. Wahotoya 89

22. Jackson County
a. Cowdrey Lake 89
b. Delaney Butte Lakes 89
c. Diamond J 89
d. Lake John 89
e. Richards 89
f. Brownlee 89
g. Irvine 89
h. Manville 90
i. Murphy 90
j. Odd Fellows 90
k. Seymore Lake 90
l. Verner 90

23. Kiowa County
a. Queens 90

24. Kit Carson
a. Flagler Reservoir 90

25. La Plata County
a. Durango 90
b. Haviland Lake 90
c. Partorius Reservoir 90

26. Larimer County
a. Big Thompson Ponds 90
b. Bliss 90
c. Boedecker Reservoir 90
d. Cherokee Park 90
e. Dowdy Lake 90
f. Frank 91
g. Hohnholtz Lakes 91
h. Lonetree Reservoir 91
i. Parvin Lake 91
j. Poudre River 91
k. Simpson Ponds 91
l. West Lake 91
m. Douglas Reservoir 91
n. Lon Hagler 91
o. North Fork 91
p. Poudre River 91
q. Watson Lake 91
r. Wellington Res. #4, Smith Lake 91

27. Las Animas County
a. Bosque Del Oso 91
b. Lake Dorothey 91
c. North Lake-North Fork 92

28. Lincoln County
a. Hugo 92
b. Karval Reservoir 92

29. Logan County
a. Jumbo Reservoir 92
b. Prewitt Reservoir 92
c. Red Lion 92

30. Mesa County
a. Horse Thief Canyon 92
b. Walker 92
c. West Lake 92
d. Jerry Creek Lakes 92

31. Mineral County
a. Coller 92
b. Alberta Park Reservoir 92
c. Big Meadows Reservoir 92
d. Creede 92

32. Moffat County
a. Browns Park 92

33. Montezuma County
a. Joe Moore Reservoir 92
b. Narraguinnep Reservoir 92
c. Puett Reservoir 93
d. Summit Reservoir 93

e. Totten Reservoir 93
f. Dolores River 93

34. Montrose County
a. Chipeta Lakes 93

35. Morgan County
a. Brush 93
b. Jackson Lake 93

36. Otero County
a. Holbrook Reservoir 93
b. Melon Valley 93
c. Rocky Ford 93
d. Timpas Creek 93

37. Park County
a. Antero Reservoir 93
b. 63 Ranch 93
c. Spinney Mountain 93
d. Tarryall Reservoir 93
e. Teter 93
f. Tomahawk 93
g. Alma 93
h. Badger Basin 93
i. Buffalo Peaks 93
j. Knight-Imler 93

38. Prowers County
a. Arkansas River 94
b. Mike Higbee 94
c. Thurston Reservoir 94

39. Pueblo County
a. Pueblo Reservoir 94
b. Runyon/Fountain Lakes 94

40. Rio Blanco County
a. Meeker Pasture 94
b. Oak Ridge 94
c. Rio Blanco Lake 94

41. Rio Grande County
a. Rio Grande 94
b. Beaver Creek Reservoir 94
c. Home Lake 94

42. Routt County
a. Indian Run 94
b. Rock Creek 94
c. Service Creek 94
d. Yampa River 94
e. Christina 94
f. Finger Rock 94

43. Saguache County
a. Cochetopa 94
b. Dome Lakes 94

44. San Juan County
a. Andrews Lake 94

45. San Miguel County
a. Miramonte Reservoir 95
b. San Miguel 95
c. Woods Lake 95

46. Summit County
a. Blue River 95

47. Teller County
a. Dome Rock 95
b. Rosemont Reservoir 95
c. Skaguay Reservoir & Beaver Creek 95

48. Weld County
a. Banner Lakes 95
b. Seeley Reservoir 95

49. Yuma County
a. Sandsage 95
b. South Republican 95
c. Stalker Lake 95

State Wildlife Areas Locator Map

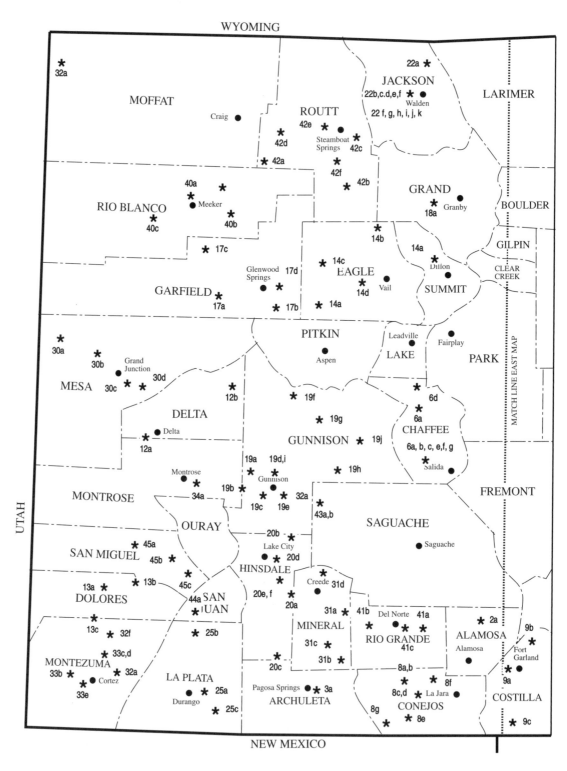

WYOMING

32a

MOFFAT

Craig

22a

JACKSON
22b,c,d,e,f
Walden
22 f, g, h, i, j, k

LARIMER

ROUTT
42e
42d
Steamboat
Springs 42c
42a
42f
42b

GRAND
18a Granby

BOULDER

RIO BLANCO
40a
Meeker
40c
40b

17c

GARFIELD
Glenwood 17d
Springs
17a
17b

14b

14c
EAGLE
14d Vail
14a

14a
Dillon

SUMMIT

GILPIN
CLEAR
CREEK

30a
30b
Grand
Junction
MESA 30c 30d

12b

PITKIN
Aspen

Leadville
Fairplay
LAKE

PARK

6d
6a
CHAFFEE
6a, b, c, e,f, g
Salida

MATCH LINE EAST MAP

DELTA
Delta
12a

19a 19d,i
Montrose
34a 19b Gunnison
19c 19e
32a

19f

19g

GUNNISON 19j

43a,b

19h

FREMONT

MONTROSE

SAN MIGUEL 45a
45b
45c
DOLORES 13a 13b
44a SAN
JUAN

13c 32f
33c,d
MONTEZUMA 32a
33b Cortez
33e

OURAY
20b
Lake City
20d

HINSDALE
Creede 31d
20e, f
20a

31a 41b
MINERAL
31c
31b
20c

25b

LA PLATA
25a
Durango
25c

Pagosa Springs 3a
ARCHULETA

SAGUACHE
Saguache

Del Norte 41a
RIO GRANDE
41c
8a,b

8c,d La Jara
8g CONEJOS 8f
8e

2a
ALAMOSA
Alamosa
9a
COSTILLA
9b
Fort
Garland
9c

NEW MEXICO

Explanation

= 4a

★   Approximate State Wildlife Area location.

4 = County in text.
a = Order of SWA property

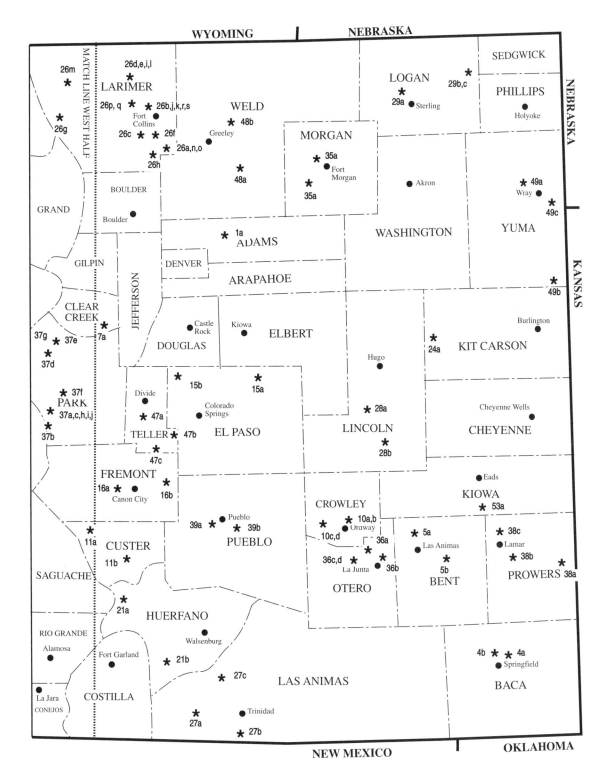

Generalized Location of State Wildlife Areas Fishing Properties

The Colorado Division of Wildlife (DOW) owns and managesthese properties. Public access to the properties is periodically reviewed, check with the DOW before visiting a State Wildlife Area.

State Wildlife Areas - Fishing

1. ADAMS COUNTY

1a. BARR LAKE NATURE CENTER - Adams County - 12/3A
(SEE FRONT RANGE SECTION)
From Denver, go NE on I-76 to Bromley Ln., then 1 mile E to Picadilly Rd., then 1/2 mile S to entrance.1,660 surface acres, So. Platte drainage, 5,095' el.
FISHING: Blue catfish, largemouth bass, channel catfish, flathead catfish, rainbow trout, walleye and wiper, sacramento perch, suckers, yellow perch.
FACILITIES: rest room, drinking water.
RESTRICTIONS: Camping prohibited. Park pass is required.

2. ALAMOSA COUNTY

2a. SAN LUIS LAKES SWA - Alamosa County - 29/2C
(SEE STATE PARKS SECTION)
From Alamosa, go 13 miles N on Hwy. 17 to Sand Dunes Monument Rd:, then 8 miles E to access road, then 1/4 mile N to property. 925 surface acres, Rio Grande drainage, 7,520' el.
FISHING: Rainbow trout.
FACILITIES: boat ramp, parking areas.
RESTRICTIONS: a. Boating prohibited north of buoy line.
b. Access prohibited north of buoy line and east-west fence line Feb. 15 - July 15.
c. Camping prohibited north of buoy line and east-west fence line.

3. ARCHULETA COUNTY

3a. ECHO CANYON RESERVOIR SWA - Archuleta County - 28/4-C
From Pagosa Springs, go 4 miles S on Hwy. 84 to property. 211 acres.118 surface acres, San Juan drainage, 7,200' el.
FISHING: Rainbow trout, channel catfish.
FACILITIES: rest room, boat ramp.
RESTRICTIONS: a. Camping prohibited. b. Fires prohibited.

4. BACA COUNTY

4a. TURK'S POND SWA - Baca County - 32/3-C
From Springfield, go 2 miles N on Hwy. 287 to Cty. Rd. HH, then 14 miles E to Cty. Rd. 39, then 3 1/2 miles N to property. 200 acres, 25 surface acres, Akansas drainage, 3,970' el.
FISHING: Bluegill, channel catfish,black crappie, largemouth bass, saugeye, wipers, bullhead, grass carp.
RESTRICTIONS:
a. Boating prohibited except craft propelled by hand, wind or electric motor.
b. Camping prohibited.
c. Public access prohibited near pond and administrative building except to retrieve downed waterfowl from the opening day of waterfowl season through last day of February.

4b. TWO BUTTES RESERVOIR SWA - Baca & Prowers Counties - 32/2-B
From Springfield, go 18 miles N on Hwy. 287 to Cty. Rd. B.5, then 3 miles E to reservoir. NOTE: Due to drought, reservoir may be low or dry. Check locally for status. 6,793 acres. 1700 surface acres, Arkansas drainage, 4000' el.
FISHING: Channel catfish, bluegill, largemouth bass, bullhead, wipers, carp, grass carp.
FACILITIES: trailer dump station, rest rooms, drinking water, boat ramps.
RESTRICTIONS:
a. Boating prohibited in Two Buttes Ponds below dam except craft propelled by hand, wind or electric motor.
b. Public access prohibited except to retrieve downed waterfowl Nov. 1 through the last day of waterfowl season.

5. BENT COUNTY

5a. ADOBE CREEK RESERVOIR SWA - Bent & Kiowa Counties - 26/4-A
From Las Animas, go 20 miles N on Cty. Rd. 10 to property. 1,200 surface acres, Arkansas drainage, 4,238' el.
FISHING: Largemouth & smallmouth bass, channel catfish, blue catfish, walleye, saugeye, tiger muskie, crappie, perch,wiper, bullhead, white bass,bluegill, northern pike, carp.
FACILITIES: rest rooms, boat ramps.
RESTRICTIONS: Public access prohibited except to retrieve downed waterfowl Nov. 1 through the last day of waterfowl season.

5b. JOHN MARTIN RESERVOIR SWA - Bent County - 26/4-A
From Las Animas, go 20 miles E on Hwy. 50 to Hasty, 2 miles S of Hasty to reservoir. 22,325 acres, 3,000 surface acres, Arkansas drainage, 3,800' el.
FISHING: Wiper, largemouth bass, flathead catfish, channel catfish, blue catfish, striped bass, saugeye, walleye, crappie, bluegill, yellow perch, carp.
FACILITIES: rest rooms, boat ramps. Camping, Corps of Engineers 1-719-336-3476).
RESTRICTIONS:
a. Public access prohibited except to retrieve downed waterfowl Nov. 1 through the last day of waterfowl season.

6. CHAFFEE COUNTY

6a. CLEAR CREEK RESERVOIR SWA - Chaffee County - 23/1-B
From Buena Vista, go 13 miles N on Hwy. 24 to Cty. Rd. 390, then 1/2 mile W to reservoir. 500 acres. 407 surface acres, Arkansas drainage, 8,875' el.
FISHING: Kokanee salmon, rainbow trout, brown trout, cutthroat.
FACILITIES: Boat ramp, rest room.
RESTRICTIONS: Fishing is prohibited from the dam, spillway, outlet structures and downstream to U.S. 24.

6b. ARKANSAS RIVER SWA - Chaffee County - 23/3-B
From Poncha Springs, 4 miles N on Hwy 285, 1/8 mile E on Cty. Rd 165. Parking area at W end.
From Salida, NW on Hwy 291 3 1/2 mi., 3/4 mile S on Cty Rd 150, 1/2 mi SW on Cty Rd 166 to N bank of Arkansas River. Parking on E side of road. 27 ac.
FISHING: coldwater stream, Arkansas River (Note: fishing access may not be on both sides of river; check for signs.) Rainbow & brown trout, cutthroat.

6c. FRANZ LAKE - Chaffee County - SWA 23/3-B
From Salida, go 3/4 mile NW on Hwy 291 to Cty Rd 154, then 3/4 mile W to property. Property is SW of Mt. Shavano Hatchery. 10 surface acres, Arkansas drainage, 7,130' el.
FISHING: Rainbow, brown trout, cutthroat.
FACILTIES: rest rooms, handicapped fishing pier.
RESTRICTIONS: Camping prohibited.

6d. GRANITE SWA - Chaffee County - 23/1-B
17 Miles N of Buena Vista on US 24 to designated parking alongside highway. Access from Chaffee Lake county line downstream to 1/4 mile below Granite Bridge. Fishing access only.
FISHING: Arkansas River. Brown,rainbow trout, cutthroat.
RESTRICTIONS: Camping and fires prohibited.

6e. MOUNT OURAY SFU - Chaffee County - 23/3-B
From Salida, 1/2 mile NW on Hwy 291, 1/2 mile W on Cty Rd 154, 1 1/4 miles NW on Cty Rd 160. 231 acres.
FISHING: Arkansas River (access may not be on both sides of river; check for signs). Rainbow, brown trout, cutthroat.

6f. MOUNT SHAVANO - Chaffee County - SFU 23/3-B
From Salida, go 1/2 mile NW on Hwy 291 to Cty Rd 154, then 1/2 mile W to unit. 186 acres.
FISHING: Arkansas River, brown, rainbow trout, cutthroat. Franz Lake, Sands Lake, rainbow trout, cutthroat.
FACITLITES: rest room, drinking water.
RESTRICTIONS: a. Fishing prohibited except in Sands Lake, Franz Lake and Arkansas River.

6g. SANDS LAKE SWA - Chaffee County - 23/3-B
From Salida, go 1/2 mile NW on Hwy 291. Property on E side of Hwy, opposite Mt. Shavano Hatchery. 6 surface acres, Arkansas drainage, 6,980' el.
FISHING: Rainbow trout, cutthroat.
RESTRICTIONS: Camping prohibited.

7. CLEAR CREEK COUNTY

7a. MOUNT EVANS SWA - Clear Creek County - 15/1-A
From Denver, take I-70 W to Evergreen Parkway exit, go 6 miles S on Hwy.74 to Evergreen Lake, take a right turn on Upper Bear Creek Rd., 6.5 miles to Cty. Rd. 480, go right on Cty. Rd. 480, 3 miles to property. 3,438 ac.
FISHING: Bear Creek, coldwater stream.
RESTRICTIONS:
a. Camping limited to 5 days in any 45-day period except during big game seasons in designated campgrounds.
b. Dogs prohibited except for hunting or when on a leash.
c. Public prohibited Jan. 1 - June 14.

8. CONEJOS COUNTY

8a. HOT CREEK SWA - Conejos County - 29/3-B
From Monte Vista, go 20 miles S on Hwy. 15 to access road, then 5 miles W to property. 3,494 acres.
FISHING: coldwater stream.
RESTRICTIONS: a. Vehicles prohibited Dec.1 - April 30.

8b. LA JARA RESERVOIR SWA - Conejos County - 29/3-B
From Monte Vista, go 20 miles S on Hwy. 15 to access road, then 10 miles W to reservoir. 1,375 surface acres, Rio Grande drainage, 9,698' el.
FISHING: Brook and rainbow trout.
FACILITIES: rest room, drinking water, boat ramp.

8c. LA JARA SWA - Conejos County - 29/4-B
From Capulin, go 11 miles SW on D Road to property. 2,808 acres.
FISHING: La Jara Creek, cold water stream.
RESTRICTIONS: a. Vehicles prohibited Dec. 1 - April 30.

8d. SEGO SPRINGS SWA - Conejos County - 29/4-C
From Manassa, go 3 miles E on Hwy. 142 to access road, then 1/2 mile N to property. 640 acres.
FISHING: North Branch Conejos River, brown, rainbow trout, cutthroat.
RESTRICTIONS: a. Fires prohibited. b. Public prohibited Feb. 15 - July 15.

8e. CONEJOS RIVER SWA - Conejos Co. (Fishing Easements) - 29/4-B
From Antonito, go 15 miles W on Hwy 17 to Conejos Ranch. Fishing Easements are intermittent for next 16 miles and are signed.
FISHING: Rainbow trout, cutthroat.
RESTRICTIONS:
a. Camping is prohibited.
b. Public access prohibited except for fishing.

8f. TERRACE RESERVOIR SWA - Conejos County - 29/3-B
From Monte Vista, go 12 miles S on Hwy 15 to USFS Rd. 250, then 9 miles W to reservoir. 144 ac, 8526' el.
FISHING: Rainbow trout, cutthroat.

8g. TRUJILLO MEADOWS SWA - Conejos County - 29/4-B
From Antonito, go 36 mi. W on Hwy 17 to FS Rd. 118, then 4 mi. N to reservoir.70 acres, Rio Grande drainage, 10,000' el.
FISHING: **Trujillo Meadows Reservoir.** Brown trout, cutthroat.
FACITLITES: rest room (USFS), drinking water.
RESTRICTIONS: Boating prohibited if it creates a whitewater wake.

9. COSTILLA COUNTY
9a. SMITH RESERVOIR SWA - Costilla County - 29/3-C
From Blanca, go 1/2 mi. W on Hwy. 160 to Airport Rd., then 4 mi. S to reservoir. 700 surface acres, Rio Grande drainage, 7,720' el.
FISHING: Rainbow trout, cutthroat.
FACILITIES: trailer dump station, rest room, boat ramp.
RESTRICTIONS:
a. Fishing prohibited Nov. 1 through the last day of waterfowl season except within 200 yards of dam.
b. Public prohibited Feb.15-July 15 on north and east shores.
c. Vehicles prohibited within 50 feet of water.

9b. MOUNTAIN HOME RESERVOIR SWA - Costilla County - 30/3-A
From Ft. Garland, go 2 1/2 miles E on Hwy 160 to Trinchera Ranch Rd., then 2 miles S to Icehouse Rd., then 1 mile W to N entrance or continue 1 mile S to S entrance. 631 surface acres, Rio Grande drainage, 8.145' el.
FISHING: Rainbow, brook trout, cutthroat.
RECREATION: wildlife observation.
FACITLITES: rest room, boat ramp.

9c. SANCHEZ RESERVOIR SWA - Costilla County - 30/4-A
From San Luis, go 3 miles E on Hwy 152 to Hwy 242, then 5.2 miles S to property. 4,571 surface acres, Rio Grande drainage, 8,317' el.
FISHING: Walleye, northern pike, yellow perch.
FACILITIES: rest room, boat ramp.
RESTRICTIONS: a. Camping prohibited in the boat ramp parking area.
b. Public access prohibited except for fishing.

10. CROWLEY COUNTY
10a. LAKE HENRY SWA - Crowley County - 25/4-C
From Ordway, go 3 miles E on Hwy. 96 to Cty. Rd. 20, then 1 mile N to property. 1,350 acres. 1,120 surface acres, Arkansas drainage, 4,370' el.
FISHING: Channel catfish, walleye, wiper, crappie, bluegill, largemouth bass, bullhead and carp.
FACILITIES: boat ramps. campsite, rest room.
RESTRICTIONS: No public use allowed off designated roads (private property) and beyond high water mark.

10b. MEREDITH RESERVOIR SWA - Crowley County - 25/4-C
From Ordway, go 3 miles E on Cty. Rd. G to Cty. Rd. 21, turn right into property. 3,220 surface acres, 15 feet deep, Arkansas drainage, 4,254 el.
FISHING: Channel catfish, tiger muskie, walleye, wiper, bluegill, blue catfish.
FACILITIES: rest rooms, boat ramps.
RESTRICTIONS:
a.Public access prohibited except to retrieve downed waterfowl Nov. 1 through the last day of waterfowl season.
b. Access is at boat ramp area only. Land surrounding reservoir is otherwise private property.

10c. OLNEY RESERVOIR SWA - Crowley County - 25/4-B
From Olney Springs, go 1 mile NW on Cty Rd 7 to reservoir. 8 acres. 6 surface acres, Arkansas drainage, 4,329' el.
FISHING: Largemouth bass, bluegill, channel catfish, perch.
FACILITIES: rest room.
RESTRICTIONS: Discharge of firearms prohibited.

10d. ORDWAY RESERVOIR SWA - Crowley County - 25/4-B
From Ordway, go 2 miles N on Hwy 71 to reservoir (W side of Hwy). 12 ac. 20 surface acres, Arkansas drainage, 4,340' el.
FISHING: Rainbow trout, bluegill, wiper, largemouth bass, channel catfish, perch.
FACILITIES: rest rooms, camping.
RESTRICTIONS: Discharging firearms prohibited.

11. CUSTER COUNTY
11a. MIDDLE TAYLOR CREEK SWA - Custer County - 29/1-C
From Westcliffe, go 8 miles W on Hermit Lakes Rd. to property. 486 acres. Arkansas drainage.
FISHING: Brown, brook trout.
FACILITIES: rest rooms, picnic tables.

11b. DE WEESE RESERVOIR SWA - Custer County - 30/1-A
From Westcliffe, NW on Hwy 69 for 5 miles, turn N on Copper Gluch Rd 1.5 miles to Access Rd. 780 acres, 240 surface acres, Arkansas drainage, 7,665'el.
FISHING: Cutthroat, rainbow, browns, brookies. Warmwater fishing for smallmouth bass. Coldwater fishing in **Grape Creek** for cutthroat, rainbow, browns, brookies.
FACILITIES: rest rooms, boat ramp, drinking water, dump station, campground.

12. DELTA COUNTY
12a. ESCALANTE SWA - Delta, Mesa & Montrose Counties - 21/2-C
WATERWHEEL TRACT: From Delta, go 12 miles NW on Hwy. 50 to Escalante Canyon turnoff, then 3 miles SW into Escalante Canyon, then 3/4 mile upstream on the S side of Gunnison River (this is a primitive road).
GUNNISON RIVER TRACT: From Delta, go 12 miles NW on Hwy. 50 to Escalante Canyon Rd., then 3 miles SW to the Gunnison River, then 3/4 mile upstream on the S side of Gunnison River (this is a primitive road). 5,019 total acres, all tracts.
FISHING: **Gunnison River**, Rainbow, brown trout.
RESTRICTIONS: a. Public access prohibited on Hamilton and Lower Roubideau tracts March 15-July 31.

12b. ROEBER SWA - Delta County - 22/2-A
From Paonia, go 1 mile S on 4100 Rd. (Onarga Ave.), turn left on N80 Lane go, 2 miles to 4200 Dr., turn right, go 1 mile to parking lot. 6 surface acres, Gunnison drainage, 6,960'el.
FISHING: **Roeber Reservoir**, cutthroat.
RESTRICTIONS: a. Camping prohibited.   b. Dogs prohibited.
c. Fires prohibited. d. Access prohibited from last day of big game season to April 30. e. Access prohibited except to hunt or fish.

13. DOLORES COUNTY
13a. FISH CREEK SWA - Dolores County - 27/2-B
From Dolores, go 12 miles N on Hwy. 145 to USFS Rd. 535, then 12 miles N to Fish Creek access road, then 1-1/2 miles N to property. 309 acres.
FISHING: coldwater stream.
RESTRICTIONS: Camping prohibited except in deer and elk seasons.

13b. LONE CONE SWA - Dolores County - 27/2-B
From Norwood, go 1-1/2 miles E on Hwy. 145 to USFS Rd. 610, then 24 miles S to property. 5,030 acres.
FISHING: **Morrison Creek**, coldwater stream.
FACILITIES: two horse corrals, domestic well water, campsites.

13c. LONE DOME SWA - Dolores & Montezuma Counties - 27/2-A
From Cortez, go 21 miles N on Hwy. 666 to Cty. Rd. DD, then 1 mile E to Cty. Rd. 16, then 3 miles N to access road, then 1-1/2 miles E to Bradfield Bridge. 775 acres.
FISHING: **Dolores River**. Rainbow, brown trout, cutthroat.
FACILITIES: USFS campgrounds.
RESTRICTIONS: Parking overnight prohibited except in designated areas.

13d. GROUNDHOG RESERVOIR SWA - Dolores County - 27/2-B
From Dolores, go 25 miles N on USFS Rd. 526 to USFS Rd. 533, then 5 miles NE to reservoir. 667 surface acres, Dolores drainage, 8,720' el.
FISHING: Rainbow, brown, brook trout, cutthroat.
FACILITIES: campsites, drinking water, rest room, boat ramp.
RESTRICTIONS: Boating prohibited if it creates a whitewater wake.

14. EAGLE COUNTY
14a. BASALT SWA - Eagle & Pitkin Counties - GMU 47/444
BASALT UNIT: From Basalt, go 3.2 miles E on USFS Rd. 105 (Fryingpan Rd.) to signs, then N to unit. 2,577 acres.
CHRISTINE UNIT: From Basalt, go 1/2 mile W on Hwy. 82 to dirt access road, then N to unit. 2,230 acres. 3 surface acres, Colorado drainage, 6,590' el.
WATSON DIVIDE UNIT: From Basalt, go 6 miles S on Hwy. 82 to unit.
FISHING: **Christine Lake:** Rainbow, brown trout. **Fryingpan River:** Rainbow, brown trout, cutthroat.
FACILITIES: shooting range.
RESTRICTIONS: a. Boating prohibited on **Christine Lake.**
b. Camping prohibited within 1/4 mile of the **Fryingpan River.**
c. Camping allowed during regular and late big game seasons, plus 3 days before and 3 days after those seasons. Except for Christine Lake and rifle range, public use prohibited from three days after the regular and late big game hunting seasons until April 15.
d. Fires prohibited. e. Water activities prohibited on Christine Lake.

State Wildlife Areas - Fishing

14b. RADIUM SWA - Eagle, Grand & Routt Counties - 9/3-A
From Kremmling, go 2 1/2 miles S on Hwy. 9 to Cty .Rd. 1 (also known as Trough Rd. to State Bridge), then 12 miles SW to property. 12,188 /4,426 ac.
FISHING: **Colorado River.** Rainbow, brown trout.
FACILITIES: rest room.
RESTRICTIONS: hunting prohibited in designated safety zone.

14c. GYPSUM PONDS SWA - Eagle County - 4/2-C
I-70 to the Gypsum exit, take the S side frontage rd. of I-70 E to parking area. 90 acres. 10 surface acres, Colorado drainage, 6,410' el.
FISHING: **Eagle River.** Rainbow trout. **Gypsum ponds:** rainbow trout and cutthroat.
FACILITIES: parking area.
RESTRICTIONS: a. Camping prohibited. b. Fires prohibited. c. Boat launching and takeouts prohibited on the river. d. Dogs prohibited.

14d. EAGLE RIVER (Fishing Leases) 4/2-C
From Eagle, go 1 mile E on Hwy 6, continuing for 5 miles E upstream.
FISHING: Rainbow trout.
RECREATION: non-motorized boating, wildlife observation.
RESTRICTIONS: a. Camping prohibited. b. Fires prohibited. c. Public access prohibited except for fishing. d. Dogs prohibited. e. Public access limited to designated points.

15. EL PASO COUNTY

15a. RAMAH RESERVOIR SWA - El Paso County - 25/1-A
From Ramah, go 4 miles W on Hwy. 24 to reservoir. 4,426 acres, 170 surface acres, Arkansas drainage, 6,100' el. Reservoir water level is often very low.
FISHING: Bluegill, channel catfish, northern pike, walleye, crappie, black bass, rainbow trout.
FACILITIES: boat ramp.
RESTRICTIONS: a. Boating prohibited Nov. 1 through the last day of waterfowl season except for craft propelled by hand, wind or electric motor.
b. Camping prohibited.
c. Fires prohibited.
d. Water contact activities prohibited.

15b. MONUMENT LAKE SWA - El Paso County - 24/1-B
From Monument, W of I-25 on Cty Rd 105, W on 3rd St., W on 2nd St. at Post Office, cross railroad tracks to Mitchell to entrance. Fishing access only. 40 surface acres, Arkansas drainage, 6,960' el.
FISHING: Rainbow trout, cutthroat, channel catfish, largemouth bass, crappie.
FACILITIES: rest rooms.
RESTRICTIONS:
a. Camping prohibited.
b. Fires prohibited.
c. Boating prohibited except hand-propelled craft.
d. Swimming prohibited.

16. FREMONT COUNTY

16a. BEAVER CREEK SWA (Skaguay Res.) - Fremont County - 24/4-A
From Canon City, go 8 miles E on Hwy. 50 to Hwy. 67, then 9 miles N to Cty. Rd. 132 to property. Alternate Route: From Skagway Dam, down-stream 12 miles on trail. 2,120 acres.
FISHING: **Beaver Creek:** Rainbow, brook trout.
Skaguay Reservoir: (see Teller County) 84 surface acre. Rainbow, brook trout, northern pike.

16b. BRUSH HOLLOW SWA - Fremont County - 24/3-A
From Penrose, 1.5 miles N on Hwy 115, to Cty Rd 123, go 2 miles N to property. 461 acres, 186 surface acres, Arkansas drainage, 5,500' el.
FISHING: **Brush Hollow Reservoir:** Walleye, bluegill, crappie, channel catfish, rainbow trout.
FACILITIES: rest rooms, shelters, boat ramp.
RESTRICTIONS:
a. Smallmouth, largemouth and spotted bass must be 15 inches or longer.
b. Boating prohibited if it creates a whitewater wake.
c. Camping prohibited. d. Fires prohibited.

17. GARFIELD COUNTY

17a. HUNT SWA (lease) - Garfield County - 4/2-A
From Rifle go 2 miles E to Mamm Creek exit, take frontage road W 1 mile to property.
FISHING: **Colorado River**. Rainbow, brown trout.
RECREATION: wildlife observation.
RESTRICTIONS: a. Camping prohibited. b. Fires prohibited. c. Vehicles prohibited. d. Non-motorized boating.

17b. CARBONDALE SWA (Roaring Fork River) - Garfield Co. - 4/3-B
In Carbondale on the Roaring Fork River.
FISHING: Rainbow, brown trout, white fish.
RESTRICTIONS: a. Camping prohibited. b. Fires prohibited.

c. From upper Woody Creek bridge to the Colorado River:
1. Artificial flies or lures only. 2. Minimum size limit for trout is 16 inches.

17c. RIFLE FALLS SFU - Garfield County - 4/2-A
From Rifle, go 15 miles N on Hwy 325 to property. 600 acres. Colorado drainage.
FISHING: Rainbow trout, cutthroat.
RESTRICTIONS: a. Fishing prohibited except in **East Rifle Creek.**
b. Dogs prohibited. c. Fires prohibited.
d. Camping prohibited except when authorized by hatchery manager.

17d. WEST BANK SWA - Garfield County - 4/2-B
From Glenwood Springs S on Hwy 82, turn right at mile 5 on Cty Rd. 154.
FISHING: **Roaring Fork River.** Rainbow, brown trout, white fish.
RESTRICTIONS: a. Camping prohibited. b. Fires prohibited.

18. GRAND COUNTY

18a. HOT SULPHUR SPRINGS SWA - Grand County - 9/2-C
PAUL F. GILBERT FISHING AREA: From Hot Sulphur Springs, go 3 miles W on Hwy. 40 to the W end of Colorado River bridge, then S to area.
LONE BUCK UNIT: From Hot Sulphur Springs, go 3 1/2 miles W on Hwy. 40 to unit (S side of Hwy). 1,173 total acres, all units.
FISHING: **Colorado River**. Rainbow, brown trout, white fish.
FACILITIES: rest room, rifle range, campsites.
RESTRICTIONS: a. Camping prohibited except in Beaver Creek Unit & Lone Buck Campgrounds.
BREEZE UNIT: About 15 miles W of Granby on Hwy. 40 past the town of Parshall, 1/2 mile to property. Look for mile marker 196. Turn left 1/4 mile past marker for parking or continue W 3/4 mile for additional parking. Unit is about 11-1/2 miles W of Kremmling.
RESTRICTIONS: a. **On Colorado and Williams Fork Rivers,** artificial flies and lures only. All trout must be returned to the water immediately.
b. Camping prohibited. c. Fires prohibited.
KEMP UNIT: From Granby, about 14.5 miles W on Hwy. 40, turn left on Grand County Road 3 and drive over Colorado River bridge. Turn right on second road or go another 1/2 mile and turn right for parking. Unit is about 12 miles east of Kremmling.
RESTRICTIONS: a. On **Colorado and Williams Fork Rivers**, artificial flies and lures only. All trout must be returned to the water immediately.
b. Camping prohibited. c. Fires prohibited.

19. GUNNISON COUNTY

19a. CIMARRON SWA - Gunnison & Montrose Counties - 22/4-A
From Montrose, go 23 miles E on Hwy. 50 to Little Cimarron Rd., then 2 miles S to access road, then 1-1/2 miles SW to property. 6,161 acres. Gunnison drainage.
FISHING: **Cimarron River**. Rainbow, brook trout, cutthroat.
RESTRICTIONS: a. Camping prohibited. b. Fires prohibited.
c. Parking in established parking areas only.

19b. GUNNISON SWA - Gunnison County - 22/3-B
From Gunnison, go 6 miles W on Hwy. 50 to property. 2,800 acres.
FISHING: **Gunnison River.** Brown, rainbow trout.
RESTRICTIONS: Public access prohibited Dec. 1 - March 31.

19c. GUNNISON RIVER SWA (Van Tuyl & Redden) - 22/3-C
From Gunnison go N on Hwy. l35 to Cty. Rd. 13. Turn left and go 1/4 mile to where the road jogs left and becomes Gunnison city street of Tincup. Travel W 3 city blocks to Palisade city park. Parking on N side of park. Area accessed by foot 1/2 mile W of parking lot.
FISHING: **Gunnison River.** Brown, rainbow trout.
FACILITIES: parking area.

19d. VIKING VALLEY SWA - Gunnison and Saguache Counties - 22/3-C
From Gunnison go E 16 miles on Hwy. 50 to Doyleville. Turn S on Cty. Rd. 3090, go 1 mile to fork in road, turn right on Cty. Rd. 3077, travel 2 miles to property.
FISHING: **Razor Creek**. Brook, brown, rainbow trout.
RESTRICTIONS: Public access prohibited except if authorized by landowner.

19e. BEAVER LAKE SWA (Marble) - Gunnison County - 22/2-B
From Marble, go 1/4 mile E on Cty Rd 3 to property. 41 acres. 25 surface acres, Gunnison drainage, 7,956' el.
FISHING: **Crystal River.** Brook, rainbow trout, cutthroart. **Beaver Lake:** Rainbow, brook trout.
RESTRICTIONS: a. Boating prohibited except for hand-propelled craft.
b. Camping prohibited. c. Fires prohibited. d. Vehicles prohibited on dam.

19f. LAKE IRWIN SWA - Gunnison County - 22/2-B
From Gunnison, go north to Ohio Creek Road (730) to Kebler Pass Road (12), continue north to USFS Rd. 826, 1.5 miles to lake. 30 surface acres, Gunnison drainage, 10,323' el.
ACCESS: limited to summer travel, usually July to October.
FISHING: Rainbow trout, cutthroat.

FACILITIES: campsites, drinking water, rest rooms.

19g. PITKIN SFU 22/3-C
From Gunnison, go 14 miles E on Hwy 50 to Quartz Creek Rd, go 14 miles E to Parlin and turn N to Pitkin. Unit is in Pitkin. 48 acres.
FISHING: Rainbow, brook trout.
RESTRICTIONS: a. Fishing prohibited except in **Quartz Creek**.
b. Dogs prohibited.

19h. ROARING JUDY SFU - Gunnison County - 22/3-C
From Gunnison, go 15 miles NW on the East River to property. 778 acres.
FISHING: **East River:** Rainbow, brown trout, pond fishing.
FACILITIES: rest room.
RESTRICTIONS: a. Fishing prohibited except in the **East River and retention ponds.** Retention ponds closed Oct 1 - Dec. 15. b. Fishing prohibited from sunset to sunrise. c. Camping prohibited. d. Fires prohibited.

19i. SPRING CREEK RESERVOIR SWA - Gunnison Co. - 22/2-C
From Gunnison go N on Hwy 135 to Almont. Turn right on Cty Rd 742, travel 6 miles to Spring Creek. Turn left on Spring Creek Rd. and go 14 miles to reservoir. 86.9 surface acres, Gunnison drainage, 9,915' el.
ACCESS: limited to summer travel, usually July-October.
FISHING: Rainbow, brook trout, cutthroat.
FACILITIES: campsites, drinking water, rest rooms, boat ramp.

19j. TAYLOR RIVER SWA - Gunnison County - 22/2-C
From Gunnison , go 10 miles N on Hwy 135 to USFS Rd. 742 (Taylor River Rd.) then 18 miles E to base of Taylor Reservoir.
FISHING: Rainbow, brown trout.
RESTRICTIONS: a. From 325 yards below Taylor Dam downstream to upper boundary of Cockrell private property (approximately 0.4 miles):
1. Artificial flies or lures only. 2. All fish must be returned to the water immediately.
b. Public access and fishing prohibited from top of Taylor Dam to 325 yards downstream. c. Camping prohibited. d. Fires prohibited.
e. Parking prohibited except in designated areas.

20. HINSDALE COUNTY
20a. BROWN LAKES SWA - Hinsdale County - 28/2-B
From Creede, go 25 miles W on Hwy. 149 to USFS Rd. 515 (Hermit Lakes Rd.), then 1-1/2 miles W to property. 520 acres, 180 surface acres, Rio Grande drainage, 9,840' el.
FISHING: Rainbow, brook, brown trout, cutthroat.
FACILITIES: rest room, boat ramp.
RESTRICTIONS: Camping prohibited.

20b. CEBOLLA SWA - Hinsdale County - 28/1-B
From Powderhorn, go 14.7 miles S on Cty. Rd. 27 (Cebolla Creek Road) to property. 1,429 acres.
FISHING: **Cebolla Creek:** Brook, rainbow trout, cutthroat.

20c. WILLIAMS CREEK RESERVOIR SWA - Hinsdale County - 28/3-B
From Pagosa Springs, go 3 miles W on Hwy. 160 to USFS Rd. 631, then 30 miles N to reservoir. 508 acres, 343 surface acres, San Juan drainage, 8,241' el.
FISHING: Rainbow, brook trout, cutthroat, kokanee.
FACILITIES: rest room, drinking water, boat ramp, campgrounds.

20d. Lake Fork of the Gunnison River SWA (Fishing Easements) 28/1-B
From Lake City, go 5 3/8 miles N on Hwy 149 to S end of easement.
FISHING: Rainbow, brook, brown trout, cutthroat.
Lake Fork of the Gunnison River SWA
a. From the headwaters downstream to waterfall at Sherman:
1. Fishing by artificial flies and lures only.
2. All cutthroat trout must be returned to the water immediately.
b. From inlet of Lake San Cristobal upstream to first bridge crossing:
1. Artifical flies only.
c. From High Bridge Gulch downstream to BLM boundary below Gate CG and from Cherry Creek to upper Red Bridge CG boundary.
1. Artifical flies or lures only.
2. Bag and possession limit for brown trout is 2 fish, 16 inches or longer.
3. All rainbows must be returned to the water immediately.
d. From Argenta Falls downstream to Blue Mesa Reservoir.
1. Snagging kokanee salmon permitted Sept. 1 - Dec. 31.

20e. RITO HONDO RESERVOIR SWA - Hinsdale County - 28/2-B
From Creede, go 35 miles W on Hwy 149 to USFS RD 513, then 2 miles NW to the fork, take right fork 200 yards N to reservoir. 41 surface acres, Rio Grande drainage, 10,280'el.
FISHING: Brook, rainbow trout.
FACILITIES: rest room, campgrounds (USFS).
RESTRICTIONS: Boating prohibited except craft propelled by hand, wind or electric motors.

20f. ROAD CANYON RESERVOIR SWA - Hinsdale County - 28/2-B
From Creede, go 25 miles W on Hwy 149 to USFS Rd. 520, then 4 miles W

to reservoir. 140 surface acres, Rio Grande drainage, 9,275' el.
FISHING: Rainbow, brook trout.
FACILITIES: rest room (USFS), drinking water, boat ramp.
RESTRICTIONS: a. Boating prohibited if it creates a whitewater wake.
b. Camping prohibited.

21. HUERFANO COUNTY
21a. HUERFANO SWA - Huerfano County - 30/2-A
From Gardener, go 13 miles W on Cty. Rd. 580. 544 acres. 7,600' el.
FISHING: **Huerfano River, Sheep Creek**: rainbow, brook, brown, cutthroat trout.
FACILITIES: rest rooms, picnic tables.

21b. WAHATOYA SWA - Huerfano County - 30/3-B
From LaVeta, go 1 mile E on Bear Creek Rd. to property. 203 acres. 28 surface acres, Arkansas drainage, 7,110' el.
FISHING: **Wahatoya Lake Reservoir:** Rainbow, brown trout, cutthroat, splake.
FACILITIES: rest rooms.
RESTRICTIONS: a. Artificial flies or lures only. b. Ice fishing prohibited.
c. Boating prohibited except craft propelled by hand or wind.
d. Camping prohibited.

22. JACKSON COUNTY
22a. COWDREY LAKE SWA - Jackson County - 5/1-B
From Cowdrey, go 2 miles S on Hwy. 125 to property. Alternate Route: From Walden, go 7 1/2 miles N on Hwy. 125. Area entrance W side of road. 280 acres land, 80 acres water, North Platte drainage, 7,940' el.
FISHING: Rainbow, brown trout.
FACILITIES: rest room, boat ramp.
RESTRICTIONS: a. Boating prohibited if it creates a whitewater wake.

22b. DELANEY BUTTE LAKES SWA - Jackson County - 5/2-B
From Walden, go 1/2 mile W on Hwy. 14 to Cty. Rd. 12, then go 5.3 miles W to Cty. Rd. 18. Go 4.5 miles W on Cty. Rd. 18 to Cty. Rd. 5, then 1/2 mile N to property. 2,132 acres. 420 acres water three lakes **North:** 163.5 surface acres, **South:** 150 surface acres, **East:** 67 surface acres. North Platte drainage, 8,145' el.
FISHING: **North:** Gold Medal water. Rainbow, brown trout. Artificial lures and artificial flies only. All brown trout caught between 14 & 18 inches in length must be returned to the water immediately. **South:** Rainbow, brook, brown trout, cutthroat. **East:** Rainbow, snake river cutthroat and brook trout. Fishing by artificial flies or artificial lures only.
FACILITIES: rest room, boat ramp, shade shelters.
RESTRICTIONS: All Lakes:
a. Boating prohibited if it creates a whitewater wake.
b. Bag and possission limit for trout is 2 fish.

22c. DIAMOND J SWA (Michigan & Illinois Rivers) - Jackson Co - 5/2-B
From Walden, go N on Hwy. 125. Parking areas are located 1, 2, and 4 miles N of Walden. 3,129 acres land, 9 miles Michigan River, 1 mile of Illinois River.
FISHING: Brook, rainbow trout.
FACILITIES: City-owned camping.

22d. LAKE JOHN SWA - Jackson County - 5/2-B
From Walden, go 1/2 mile W on Hwy. 14 to Cty. Rd. 12, then 8 miles W to Cty. Rd. 7, then 7 miles N to property. 565 surface acres, 282 land acres, North Platte drainage, 8,048' el.
FISHING: Rainbow, brown, brook trout, cutthroat.
FACILITIES: Private campground and electrical hook-ups, trailer dump station, rest room, boat ramp, shade shelters, picnic tables.
RESTRICTIONS: a. Camping prohibited except in established areas.

22e. RICHARDS SWA - Jackson County - 5/2-B
From Walden, go 1/2 mile W on Hwy. 14 to Cty. Rd. 12W, then 13.7 miles W to property. 3,817 land acres, 6 miles of river.
FISHING: **No. Fork North Platte River:** Rainbow, brown trout.
RESTRICTIONS: a. Camping prohibited.
b. Fishing is by artificial flies or artificial lures only.
c. Bag and possession limit for trout is 2 fish.

22f. BROWNLEE SWA - Jackson County - 5/2-C
From Walden, go 1/2 mile W on Colo. Hwy 14 to Cty Rd 12, then 5.1 miles NW to Cty Rd 18, then 1/2 mile W to area access roads. 1.14 miles of river.
FISHING: **North Platte River:** Brown and rainbow trout.
RESTRICTIONS a. Artificial flies and lures only.
b. Bag and possession limit for trout is 2 fish.

22g. IRVINE SWA - Jackson County - 5/2-B
From Walden, go 1/2 mile W on Hwy 14 to Cty Rd 12, take Rd 12, 5.1 miles W to Cty Rd l8, take Rd. 18, 4.5 miles W to Cty W. Rd 5, 1.5 miles SW to Cty Rd 22, take Rd. 22, 2.5 miles to property. 0.7 miles of river.
FISHING: **Roaring Fork River, Raspberry Creek, Norris Creek:** Rainbow

State Wildlife Areas - Fishing

trout, cutthroat.

RESTRICTIONS: a. **Raspberry Creek, Norris Creek and Roaring Fork River** on the Irvine SWA, artificial flies or artificial lures only. Bag and possession limit for trout is 2 fish. b. Camping prohibited.

22h. MANVILLE SWA - Jackson County -5/2-B
From Walden, go 1/2 mile W on Hwy 14 to Cty Rd. 12W, take Rd 12W 5 miles W to Cty Rd 18, take Rd 18 4 1/2 miles SW to Cty Rd 5, take Rd 5 1/8 miles S to property. Approx. 4.4 miles of river. 8,000' el.
FISHING: **Roaring Fork River:** Rainbow, brown, brook, cutthroat trout.
RESTRICTIONS: a. Artificial flies or artificial lures only on the **Roaring Fork River**. Bag and possession limit for trout is 2 fish. b. Fishing prohibited on North Platte River. c. Hunting prohibited.

22i. MURPHY SWA - Jackson County - 5/2-C
From Walden, go 1 mile E on Cty Rd 12 to property. 6 miles of river.
FISHING: **Michigan River:** Rainbow, brown, cutthroat trout.

22j. ODD FELLOWS SWA - Jackson County -5/2-B
From Walden, go 1/2 mile W on Hwy 14 to Cty Rd. 12, then 5.1 miles W on Cty Rd 12 to Cty Rd 18, then 4.5 miles W on Cty Rd 18 to Cty Rd 5, then 1.5 miles SW on Cty Rd 5 to Cty Rd 22, then 2.5 miles on Cty Rd. 22 to property. Access also at Irvine SWA .7 mile of river.
FISHING: **Roaring Fork River:** Rainbow brown, brook trout.
RESTRICTIONS: a. Artificial flies or lures only. b.Bag and possession limit for trout is 2 fish. c. Camping prohibited.

22k. SEYMOR LAKE SWA - Jackson County - 5/4-B
From Walden, go 14 miles SW on Hwy 14 to Cty Rd. 28, then 1 mile S to Cty Rd 11, then 3 miles S to Cty Rd 288, then 1/2 mile W to property. 81 water acres, North Platte drainage, 8,360' el.
FISHING: **Seymore Reservoir:** Rainbow trout.
FACILITIES: rest room, boat ramp.
RESTRICTIONS: a. Boating prohibited if it creates a whitewater wake.

22l. VERNER SWA - Jackson County - 5/2-B
From Walden, go 1/2 mile W on Hwy 14 to Cty Rd 12, then 5.1 miles W to Cty Rd 18, then 1/2 mile W to access road.
FISHING: **North Platte River:** (1 mile) brown and rainbow trout.
RESTRICTIONS: a. Artificial flies or lures only. b. Bag and possession limit for trout is 2 fish.

23. KIOWA COUNTY

23a. QUEENS SWA - Kiowa County - 26/3-B
LOWER QUEENS: From Eads, go 15 miles S on Hwy. 287 to Cty. Rd. C, then 3 1/2 miles E to Upper Queens, follow access road S 2 miles to property. NOTE: Due to drought, reservoir may be low or dry. Check locally for status. Arkansas drainage.
UPPER QUEENS: From Eads, go 15 miles S on Hwy. 287 to Cty. Rd. C, then 3 1/2 miles E to property. NOTE: Due to drought, reservoir may be low or dry. Check locally for status.
NEE GRONDA: From Eads, go 15 miles S on Hwy. 287 to Cty. Rd. C, then 1 mile W to property. 3,490 surface acres.
NEE SO PAH: No public access.
NEE NOSHE: From Eads, go 11 miles S on Hwy. 287 to Kiowa County Boat Ramp Access Rd., then 1/4 mile E to public boat ramp. 4,426 total acres, all properties. 3,700 surface acres.
FISHING: Tiger muskie, walleye, saugeye, wiper, white bass, largemouth & smallmouth bass, northern pike, channel catfish, blue catfish, crappie, bluegill, bullhead, carp, drum.
FACILITIES: rest rooms, boat ramps.
RESTRICTIONS: a. Boating prohibited in Lower Queens if it creates a whitewater wake from the opening day of waterfowl season to Dec. 1.
b. Boating prohibited if it creates a whitewater wake in channel between Upper Queens and Lower Queens.
c. Public access prohibited in Lower Queens except to retrieve downed waterfowl Dec. 1 through the last day of waterfowl season.
d. Public prohibited in Upper Queens (including the channel), Nee Gronda, Nee Noshe, and Nee So Pah except to retrieve downed waterfowl Nov. 1 through the last day of waterfowl season.

24. KIT CARSON

24a. FLAGLER RESERVOIR SWA - Kit Carson County - 20/3-A
From Flagler, go 5 miles E on Rd. 4 to reservoir. 400 acres, 156 surface acres, Republican drainage, 4,707' el.
FISHING: Walleye, bluegill, wiper, channel catfish, black crappie, yellow perch, largemouth bass, northern pike, tiger muskie.
FACILITIES: rest rooms, boat ramps.
RESTRICTIONS: a. Boating prohibited during waterfowl seasons except craft propelled by hand, wind or electric motors.
b. Boating prohibited if it creates a whitewater wake. c. Waterskiing permitted Sundays and Mondays, June 1 - Aug. 31.

25. LA PLATA COUNTY

25a. DURANGO SRU - La Plata County - 27/3-C
In Durango, on the **Las Animas River.** 14 acres.
FISHING: coldwater stream.
FACILITIES: rest room, drinking water.
RESTRICTIONS: a. Fishing prohibited except in retention ponds.
b. Dogs prohibited.

25b. HAVILAND LAKE SWA - La Plata County - 28/3-A
From Durango, go 18 miles N on Hwy 550 to USFS Rd 671, then 1/2 mile E to property. 208 acres, 22 surface acres, San Juan drainage, 8,106' el.
FISHING: Rainbow trout, cutthroat.
FACILITIES: campgrounds, rest room, drinking water, gravel boat ramp.
RESTRICTIONS: a. Boating prohibited except craft propelled by hand or electric motor.

25c. PASTORIUS RESERVOIR SWA - La Plata County - 28/4-A
From Durango, go 8 miles E on Hwy 160 to Hwy 172, then 2 miles S to Cty Rd 302, then 1 mile S to Cty Rd 304, then 1/2 mile W to reservoir. 85 acres, 53 surface acres, San Juan drainage, 6,860' el.
FISHING: Rainbow trout, northern pike, bluegill, yellow perch, channel catfish, largemouth bass.
FACILITIES: rest room, boat ramp.
RESTRICTIONS: a. Smallmouth and largemouth bass must be 15 inches or longer. b. Camping prohibited c. Fires prohibited.
d. Boating prohibited except craft propelled by hand or electric motor.

26. LARIMER COUNTY

26a. BIG THOMPSON PONDS SWA - Larimer County - 7/4-C
From Loveland, go 5 miles E on Hwy. 402 to I-25 Frontage Rd., then 3/4 mile N to interstate underpass, left through underpass, then 1/4 mile N to property. 51 acres, total 20.65 surface acres, South Platte drainage, 4,850' el.
FISHING: channel catfish, bluegill, largemouth, smallmouth bass.
FACILITIES: rest room.
RESTRICTIONS: a. Boating prohibited except for belly boats used for fishing. b. Camping prohibited. c. Fires prohibited. d. Smallmouth and largemouth bass must be 15 inches or longer.

26b. BLISS SWA - Larimer County - 6/2-B
From Laporte, go 5 miles N on Hwy. 287 to Hwy. 14, then 41 miles W to property. 352 acres.
FISHING: **Poudre River:** 6 miles of river. Rainbow, brown, cutthroat trout, white fish.
FACILITIES: rest room.
RESTRICTIONS: a. boat launchings and takeouts prohibited.

26c. BOEDECKER RESERVOIR SWA - Larimer County - 7/4-B
From Loveland, go 2 miles W on First St. to Cty. Rd. 21, then 1/2 mile S to reservoir. 308 acres surface water, South Platte drainage. 6,062' el.
FISHING: Walleye, yellow perch, crappie, largemouth bass, channel catfish, bluegill, carp, bullhead.
FACILITIES: boat ramp.
RESTRICTIONS: a. Boating prohibited if it creates a white water wake.
b. Camping prohibited. c. Fires prohibited. d. Boating prohibited from boats Nov. 1 to end of waterfowl season.

26d. CHEROKEE PARK SWA - Larimer County - 7/2-A
LONE PINE UNIT: From Ft. Collins, go 20 miles N on Hwy. 287 to Red Feather Lakes Rd., then 8 miles W to unit. 6,880 acres.
UPPER UNIT: From Ft. Collins, go 22 miles N on Hwy. 287 to Cherokee Pk. Rd. 80C, then 22 miles W to unit. 4,960 acres.
MIDDLE UNIT: From Ft. Collins, go 22 miles N on Hwy. 287 to Cherokee Pk. Rd. 80C, then 10 miles W to unit. 4,481 acres.
LOWER UNIT: From Ft. Collins, go 22 miles N on Hwy. 287 to Cherokee Pk. Rd. 80C, then 6 miles W to unit. 2,701 acres.
FISHING: **North Fork Poudre River, Lone Pine Creek, Rabbit Creek, Sheep Creek:** Rainbow, brown, cutthroat trout. On the North Fork of Poudre River from Bull Creek (above Halligan Res.) upstream to Divide Creek Fishng is by artificial flies and lures only. All fish caught must be returned to water immediately.
FACILITIES: rest rooms.
RESTRICTIONS: a. Public access prohibited in upper unit during deer and elk seasons except for deer and elk hunters.
b. Vehicles prohibited in upper unit from the day after Labor Day through the day before Memorial Day, except during deer and elk hunting seasons.
c. Vehicles prohibited in middle unit from the day after Labor Day through the day before Memorial Day.

26e. DOWDY LAKE SWA- Larimer County - 6/2-C
From the town of Red Feather Lakes, go 1 mile NE on USFS Access Rd to property. 120 surface acres, South Platte drainage, 8,135' el.
FISHING: Rainbow, brown, brook trout, cutthroat.

FACILITIES: rest room, boat ramp, campgrounds (USFS).
RESTRICTIONS: a. Boating prohibited if it creates a whitewater wake.

26f. FRANK SWA - Larimer & Weld Counties - 7/4-C
From I-25 at the Windsor exit, go 2.3 miles E on Hwy. 392 to Cty. Rd. 13, then 1/2 mile S to property. 640 acres, 4,800' el.
FISHING: **Frank easement ponds :** Smallmouth & largemouth bass, channel catfish.
RESTRICTIONS: a. Fires prohibited. b. Camping prohibited.
c. Boating prohibited if it creates a whitewater wake d. Smallmouth & largemouth bass must be 15 inches or longer.

26g. HOHNHOLZ LAKES SWA - Larimer County - 6/1-A
From Hwy. 14 at upper end of Poudre Canyon, go 30 miles N on Laramie River Rd (Cty. Rd. 103) to entrance. 80 acres of water, 1 mile of river. Total 24 surface acres, 8 acres each lake, North Platte drainage, 7,880' el.
FISHING: **Laramie River:** Brown trout. Artificial Flies and lures only. Bag and possession limit for trout is 2 fish. **Hohnholz Lakes:** Rainbow, brook, brown trout, cutthroat. Brown trout. Artificial Flies and lures only. Bag and possession limit for trout is 4 fish. Private property surrounds stream and lake. Punlic access is limited to 20 feet above high water.
FACILITIES: rest room.
RESTRICTIONS: a.Boating prohibited except craft propelled by hand, wind or electric motor.
b. Camping prohibited except in Laramie River camping area.
c. Public access prohibited on Grace Creek Road Dec. 1 - Aug. 15.

26h. LONETREE RESERVOIR SWA - Larimer County - 11/1-B
From Campion, go 3 1/2 miles W on Cty. Rd. 14W to Lonetree Dr., then 1 mile S on access road to reservoir. 502 surface acres, South Platte drainage, 5,131' el.
FISHING: Rainbow,channel catfish, crappie, wiper, smallmouth and largemouth bass, perch, walleye.
FACILITIES: rest rooms, boat ramps, shade shelters.
RESTRICTIONS: a. Boating prohibited if it creates a whitewater wake.
b. Fishing prohibited from boats Nov. 1 through the last day of waterfowl season. c. Fishing prohibited in outlet canal. d. Smallmouth and largemouth bass must be 15 inches or longer. Bag and possession limit for wipers is 10 fish, 15 inches or longer, limit for walleye is 5 fish, 15 inches or longer.
e. Camping prohibited. f. Fires prohibited.
g. Public access prohibited in heron nesting closure area.

26i. PARVIN LAKE SWA - Larimer County - 6/2-C
From town of Red Feather Lakes, go 2 miles E on Red Feather Lakes Rd. to property. 62 surface acres, 180 land acres, South Platte drainage, 8,200' el.
FISHING: Rainbow, brown trout.
FACILITIES: rest room.
RESTRICTIONS: a. Artificial flies or lures only. b. Bag and possession limits posted at check station. c. Fishing in the inlet (Lone Pine Creek) prohibited from lake upstream to Red Feather Lakes Rd. d. Fishing prohibited 10 p.m. to 4 a.m. May 1 Oct. 31. e.Boating prohibited except for belly boats for fishing. f. Fishermen must enter on foot through gate at check station and must check in and out at the check station when open.

26j. POUDRE RIVER SWA - Larimer County - 7/3-B
From Laporte, go 5 miles N on Hwy. 287 to Hwy. 14, then 1.5 miles W to property. 395 acres.
FISHING: Rainbow, brown trout, cutthroat, white fish.
FACILITIES: rest room, raft take-out.
RESTRICTIONS: a. Camping prohibited.

26k. SIMPSON PONDS SWA - Larimer County - 7/4-C
From I-25 at take Hwy. 402 exit (#255), go 2 miles W on Hwy. 402 to Cty. Rd. 9E, then 1/2 mile N to property. 44 acres.
FISHING: channel catfish, bluegill, largemouth, smallmouth bass.
RESTRICTIONS: a. Boating prohibited except belly boats for fishing.
b. Camping prohibited. c. Fires prohibited.

26l. WEST LAKE SWA - Larimer County - 6/2-C
From the town of Red Feather Lakes, go 1 mile E on Red Feather Lakes Rd to property. 38 surface acres, South Platte drainage, 8,246' el.
FISHING: Rainbow, brown trout.
FACILITIES: campground (USFS), rest room, drinking water.
RESTRICTIONS: a. Boating prohibited except craft propelled by hand, wind or electric motor.

26m. DOUGLAS RESERVOIR SWA - Larimer County - 7/2-B
From Wellington exit on I-25, go 5.5 miles W, S and W on Hwy 1 to Cty Rd 15, 1 mile N on Cty Rd 15 to Cty Rd 60, then 1/4 mile W to LaVina Drive. North on LaVina Drive to lake.
From Ft. Collins at Hwy 287 and Hwy 1, take Hwy 1 N 4 miles to Waverly cutoff (Cty Rd 15), N on Cty Rd 15 to Cty Rd 60. Then 1/4 mile W to LaVina Drive, N to lake. 565 surface acres, South Platte drainage, 5,150' el.

FISHING: Walleye, wiper, rainbow trout, black crappie, channel catfish, yellow perch, largemouth bass.
RESTRICTIONS: a. Bag and possession limit for trout is 4 fish. b. Fires prohibited. c. Boating prohibited if it creates a whitewater wake.
d. Camping prohibited. e. From one hour after sunset until one hour before sunrise, public access prohibited except fishing. f. Reservoir dam, inlet and outlet are closed to motor vehicles and all activities except fishing as posted.

26n. LON HAGLER SWA - Larimer County - 7/4-B
From Campion, go 3 1/4 miles W on Cty Rd. 14W to Cty Rd 21S, then 1 1/2 miles N to property. 181 land acres. 200 surface acres, South Platte drainage, 5,152' el.
FISHING: **Lon Hagler Reservoir:** Rainbow trout, channel catfish, tiger muskie, largemouth bass.
FACILITIES: rest room, boat ramp, camping areas.
RESTRICTIONS: a. Smallmouth and largemouth bass must be 15 inches or longer. b. Fishing prohibited in inlet structure and annex pond.
c. USE PERMIT REQUIRED: Annual or daily use permit required.
d. Boating prohibited if it creates a whitewater wake.
e. Camping prohibited except in designated areas. f. Fires prohibited.

26o. NORTH FORK SWA - Larimer County - 7/4-A
From Drake, go 1/4 mile W on Devil's Gulch Rd. to property.
FISHING: **North Fork Big Thompson River:** Rainbow, brown trout.
RESTRICTIONS: a. Public access prohibited except for fishing.

26p. POUDRE RIVER SFU - Larimer County - 6/2-B
From Laporte, go 5 miles N on Hwy 287 to Hwy 14, then 38 miles W to property. 460 acres.
FISHING: **Poudre River:**Rainbow, brown trout, cutthroat, white fish. coldwater lake.
FACILITIES: rest room.
RESTRICTIONS: a. Camping prohibited. b. Dogs prohibited.
c. Boat launching and takeouts prohibited.

26q. WATSON LAKE SWA - Larimer County - 7/3-B
From Ft. Collins, go 7 miles NW on Hwy 287 to Rist Canyon Rd. (Cty Rd 52E), 1 mile W to property. 139 acres, youth only fishing pond, 40 surface acres, South Platte drainage, 5,160' el.
FISHING: **Poudre River**: Rainbow, brown trout, cutthroat, white fish.
Watson Lake: Rainbow, brown, brook trout.
FACILITIES: rest rooms, nature trails.
RESTRICTIONS: a. Ice fishing prohibited. b. Boating prohibited except belly boats. c. Access prohibited on northwest side. d. Parking prohibited on South Dam. e. Use or possession of live minnows prohibited. f. Camping prohibited.

26r. WELLINGTON RESERVOIR #4 - Larimer County - SWA 7/2-C
SMITH LAKE - 30 surface acres.
From I-25 at the Wellington exit, go 3 miles W on Hwy 1 to Cty Rd 7, 1.4 miles N to Cty Rd 66, 2 miles W to property. 105 acres, 103 surface acres, South Platte drainage, 5,228' el.
FISHING: Rainbow trout, channel catfish, largemouth bass,yellow perch, walleye, crappie, tiger muskie, carp, bullhead.
FACILITIES: rest rooms, boat ramps.
RESTRICTIONS: a. Boating is prohibited in a manner that creates a whitewater wake. b. Camping prohibited. c. Fires prohibited. d. Sail and surfboards and prohibited on Wellington #4.

27. LAS ANIMAS COUNTY

27a. BOSQUE DEL OSO SWA - Las Animas County - 30/4-B
From Trinidad, take Exit 14A off I-25. Go west on Hwy. 12 approx. 21 miles to Weston and look for access direction signs between Weston and Stonewall. Property on south side of highway. 30,000 acres.
FISHING: **Purgatorie River:** Rainbow, some brown and brookies.
RESTRICTIONS: a. Campfires prohibited except in designated areas and in fire containment structures provided by the DOW.
b. Parking allowed only in designated areas.
c. Leaving unattended food or garbage prohibited unless it is being stored in bear-resistant manner or container.
d. Public prohibited Dec.1 through March 31except for big game hunters.

27b. LAKE DOROTHEY SWA - Las Animas County - 31/4-A
From Raton New Mexico, go 7 miles NE on NM Hwys. 72 & 526, N up Sugarite Canyon 5 miles to property. 4,804 acres, 4 surface acres, Arkansas drainage, 7,600' el.
FISHING: Rainbow trout, cutthroat. Coldwater stream.
FACILITIES: rest room.
RESTRICTIONS: a. Including **Lake Dorothey, Schwachheihm Creek** and all drainage's into lake, artificial flies or lures only.
b. Camping prohibited within 200 yards of Lake Dorothey or 100 feet of a stream except in designated areas.
c. Access by foot or horseback only from established parking areas.

State Wildlife Areas - Fishing

27c. NORTH LAKE-NORTH FORK SWA - Las Animas County - 30/3-B
From Trinidad, go 35 miles NW on Hwy 12 to property. 840 acres.104 surface acres, Arkansas drainage, 8,583' el.
FISHING: **North Fork Purgatorie River:** Rainbow, brown, brook, cutthroat trout. **North Lake:** Rainbow, brown, cutthroat trout, kokanee, splake.
FACILITIES: rest rooms, boat ramp with parking area.
RESTRICTIONS: a. Artificial flies or lures only.
b. Boating prohibited except craft propelled by hand, wind or electric motor.
c. Camping prohibited. d. Fires prohibited.

28. LINCOLN COUNTY
28a. HUGO SWA - Lincoln County - 25/2-C
KINNEY LAKE TRACT: From Hugo, go 14 miles S on Cty. Rd. 109 to Cty. Rd. 2G, then 2.5 miles E to Cty. Rd. 2J, then 1 mile E to tract. 320 acres. 7 surface acres, Arkansas drainage, 5,070' el.
FISHING: Yellow perch, crappie, channel cat, bluegill, bullhead, carp, largemouthbass, sunfish, rainbow trout.
RESTRICTIONS: a. Boating prohibited except for craft propelled by hand, wind or electric motor. b. Fires prohibited.
CLINGINGSMITH TRACT: From Hugo, go 14 miles S on Cty. Rd. 109, 2 1/4 miles E on Cty. Rd. 2G to tract. 2,240 acres. Fishing in 4 **Clingingsmith Ponds** (10 acres total).
FISHING: Rainbow, bluegill, channel catfish, largemouth & smallmouth bass, crappie, carp, bullhead, sunfish.
FACILITIES: rest rooms.
RESTRICTIONS: a. Boating prohibited.

28b. KARVAL RESERVOIR SWA - Lincoln County - 25/2-C
From Hwys. 94 and 109, go S 10 miles on Hwy. 109 to property. 235 acres, 24 surface acres, Arkansas drainage, 5,000' el.
FISHING: Rainbow, hybrid bluegill, channel catfish, largemouth bass, black crappie, yellow perch, wiper, grass carp.
FACILITIES: rest room (closed in winter), shade shelters.
RESTRICTIONS: a. Boating prohibited except craft propelled by hand, wind or electric motor. b. Open fires prohibited.

29. LOGAN COUNTY
29a. JUMBO RESERVOIR SWA - Logan & Sedgwick Counties - 18/1-B
From I-76 at the Red Lion exit (#155), go 3 miles N to Hwy. 138, then 1 mile NE to Cty. Rd. 95, then 2 miles N to reservoir. 1,703 acres, 1570 surface acres, South Platte drainage, 3,705' el.
FISHING: Yellow perch, walleye, channel fish, gizzard shad, walleye, black crappie, wiper, largemouth bass, carp, bullhead, occasional northern pike. Stripped bass & white bass hybrids bass in possession must be 15" in length or longer. Crappie in possession must be 10" or longer. Walleye in possession must be 15" or longer.
FACILITIES: rest rooms, drinking water, boat ramp.
RESTRICTIONS: a. Annual or daily use fee permit required.
b. Boating prohibited Oct. 1 through last day of waterfowl season. Except, hand-propelled craft may be used to set and pick up decoys and retrieve downed waterfowl. c. Number of vehicles limited to 250.
e. Special restrictions during waterfowl season, check with DOW.

29b. PREWITT RESERVOIR SWA - Logan & Washington Co. - 17/2-C
From I-76 and Merino exit, go 1 mile N to Hwy. 6, then 3.3 miles NE to reservoir. 2,924 acres, 2,431 surface acres, South Platte drainage, 4,100' el.
FISHING: Channel catfish, walleye, wiper, crappie, yellow perch.
FACILITIES: rest room, boat ramp.
RESTRICTIONS: a. Annual or daily use permit required.
b. Boating prohibited from Oct. 1 through the last day of waterfowl season. Craft propelled by hand may be used to set and pick up decoys and retrieve downed waterfowl. c. Boating prohibited if it creates a whitewater wake.
d. Fires prohibited as posted. e. Number of vehicles limited to 250.
f. Glass beverage containers prohibited.g. Hunting prohibited from floating devices. h. Camping and fires are prohibited as posted.

29c. RED LION SWA - Logan County - 18/1-B
From I-76 at the Red Lion exit (#155), go 3 miles N to Hwy. 138, then 1 mile NE to Cty. Rd. 95, then 1/4 mile N to property. 1,297 acres.
FISHING: **Jumbo Reservoir:** Yellow perch, walleye, channel fish, gizzard shad, walleye, black crappie, wiper, largemouth bass, carp, bullhead, occasional northern pike. Smallmouth and bigmouth bass in possession must be 15" in length or longer. Crappie in possession must be 10" or longer.
RESTRICTIONS: a. Boating prohibited. Craft propelled by hand may be used to set and pick up decoys and retrieve downed waterfowl.
b. Camping prohibited. c. Fires prohibited. d Public prohibited except as posted. e. Special restrictions during waterfowl season, check with DOW.
f. Annual or daily use fee permit required.

30. MESA COUNTY
30a. HORSE THIEF CANYON SWA - Mesa County - 21/1-A
I-70 W to Fruita exit, from Fruita exit take Hwy. 340 S 1 mile to property sign, take access road 4 miles to property.
FISHING: **Colorado River:** Rainbow, brown trout.
RESTRICTIONS: a. Camping prohibited except in self-contained units.
b. Fires prohibited on Skippers Island.

30b. WALKER SWA - Mesa County - 21/1-B
From Grand Junction, go 2 miles W on Hwy 6 & 50, turn S on River Rd, 1/2 mile on River Rd. turn S on gravel access road. 351 acres.
FISHING: **Lower Colorado River:** Rainbow, brown trout.
FACILITIES: rest room.
RESTRICTIONS: a. Fishing prohibited Oct 1 - Feb. 28.
b. Access prohibited 1/2 hour after sunset to 1/2 hour before sunrise.
c. Discharging firearms or bows prohibited. Bows permitted for bowfishing.
d. Fires prohibited. e. Hunting prohibited. g. Dogs prohibited.

30c. WEST LAKE SWA - Mesa County - 21/1-B
In Grand Junction, at 711 Independent Ave.(in front of DOW Service Center).
FISHING: Rainbow trout.
FACILITIES: rest room.
RESTRICTIONS: a. Boating prohibited. b. Public access prohibited 9 p.m. to 7 a.m. c. Water contact activities prohibited.

30d. JERRY CREEK LAKES SWA - Mesa County - 21/1-C
Couple miles W of Molina off Hwy 330. Walk-in access only, a 1.5 miles from the parking lot.
FISHING: Largemouth bass, bluegill.
a. Fishing by artificial flies and lures only.
b. All fish must be returned to the water immediately.
c. Hunting prohibited. d. Camping prohibited. e. Fires prohibited.
f. Boating, floating, swimming and wading prohibited.
g. Ice fishing on and all public access to the frozen surface of the lakes is prohibited. h. Pets and domestic animals prohibited.
i. Motorized and non-motorized vehicles prohibited.

31. MINERAL COUNTY
31a. COLLER SWA - Mineral & Rio Grande Counties - GMU 28/2-C
From South Fork, go 4 1/2 miles W on Hwy. 149 to property. 579 acres.
FISHING: **Rio Grande River:** Rainbow, brown trout.
FACILITIES: rest room, drinking water.
RESTRICTIONS: a. Camping prohibited. b. Parking overnight prohibited.

31b. ALBERTA PARK RESERVOIR SWA - Mineral County - 28/3-C
From South Fork, go 18 miles W on Hwy 160 to Wolf Creek Ski Area, drive through parking lot, then continue 1.7 miles on FS RD. 391 to reservoir. 240 acres, 40 surface acres, Rio Grande drainage, 10,203' el.
FISHING: Rainbow, brook trout.
FACILITIES: primitive boat ramp.

31c. BIG MEADOWS SWA - Mineral County - 28/3-C
From South Fork, go 11 miles W on Hwy 160 to USFS Rd. 410, then 2 miles W to reservoir. 114 surface acres, Rio Grande drainage, 9,200' el.
FISHING: **Big Meadows Reservoir:** Rainbow, brook trout.
FACILITIES: campgrounds (USFS), rest room, drinking water, boat ramp.

31d. CREEDE SWA - Mineral County - 28/2-C
From Creede, go 1.2 miles E on Hwy 149 to undesignated road (no sign), then 1/2 mile S to the Rio Grande.
FISHING: **Rio Grande River:** Rainbow, brown trout.

32.. MOFFAT COUNTY
32a. BROWNS PARK SWA - Moffat County - 1/1-A
COLD SPRING MOUNTAIN UNIT: From Maybell, go 41 miles NW on Hwy. 318 to Cty. Rd. l0, then 17 miles N to Cty. Rd. 72, then 9 miles W to the fork. Take left fork 4 miles to unit.
WIGGINS UNIT: From Maybell, go 41 miles NW on Hwy. 318 to Cty. Rd. 10, then 17 miles N to Cty. Rd. 72, then 15 miles W to unit.
BEAVER CREEK UNIT: From Maybell, go 59 miles NW on Hwy. 318, unit is on north side of Hwy. 318. 2,226 acres, all units.
FISHING: **Green River:** Rainbow trout.

33. MONTEZUMA COUNTY
33a. JOE MOORE RESERVOIR SWA - Montezuma County - 27/3-B
From Mancos, go 5 miles NE on Hwy. 184 to Cty .Rd. 40, then 4 miles N to reservoir. 120 acres, 35 surface acres, San Juan drainage, 7,690' el.
FISHING: Rainbow, brown trout, largemouth bass.
FACILITIES: rest room, boat ramp.

33b. NARRAGUINNEP RESERVOIR SWA - Montezuma County - 27/3-B
From Cortez, go 11 miles NW on Hwy. 666 to Hwy. 184, then 2 mi. E to reservoir. 386 surface acres, Colorado River drainage, 7,050' el.
FISHING: Rainbow trout, perch, crappie, northern pike, bluegill, channel catfish, some walleye.

FACILITIES: rest room, boat ramp.
RESTRICTIONS: camping prohibited.

33c. PUETT RESERVOIR SWA - Montezuma County - 27/3-B
From Mancos, go 10 miles NW on Hwy. 184 to Cty. Rd. 33, then 1 mile S to access trail, then 1-1/2 miles E (sometimes 4-WD) to reservoir. 150 surface acres, Dolores River drainage, 7,260' el.
FISHING: Northern pike, walleye, rainbow trout.
RECREATION: Picnicking, wildlife observation.

33d. SUMMIT RESERVOIR SWA - Montezuma County - 27/3-B
From Mancos, go 9 miles NW on Hwy. 184 to property. 351 surface acres, Dolores River drainage, 7,388' el.
FISHING: Rainbow trout, channel catfish, northern pike, walleye, crappie.
FACILITIES: rest room, boat ramp.
RESTRICTIONS: Smallmouth and largemouth bass must be 15 inches or longer.

33e. TOTTEN RESERVOIR SWA - Montezuma County - 27/3-B
From Cortez, go 3 1/2 mi. E on Hwy. 160 to Cty. Rd. 29. then 1 mi. N to reservoir. 204 surface acres, Dolores River drainage, 6,158' el.
FISHING: Channel catfish, largemouth bass, northern pike, walleye.
FACILITIES: rest room, boat ramp.
RESTRICTIONS: a. Boating prohibited if it creates a whitewater wake.
b. Camping prohibited.   c. Fires prohibited.
d. Public access prohibited along north shore March 1 - May 31.

33f. DOLORES RIVER SWA - Montezuma County - 27/3-B
From Dolores, go 5 miles NE on Hwy 145 to property. 980 acres.
FISHING: Rainbow, brown trout, cutthroat.
RECREATION: wildlife observation.
RESTRICTIONS: a. Camping prohibited. b. Fires prohibited.

34. MONTROSE COUNTY
34a CHIPETA LAKES SWA - Montrose County - 21/3-C
From Montrose, go 3 miles S on Hwy 550 to Chipeta Dr., then 1/2 mile N to property. 12 acres, 8.5 surface acres, Gunnison drainage, 5,900' el.
FISHING: Rainbow trout.
RESTRICTIONS: a. Camping is prohibited. b. Fires prohibited.

35. MORGAN COUNTY
35a. BRUSH SWA - Morgan County - 17/3-C
From Brush, go 2 1/2 miles N on Hwy. 71 to Cty. Rd. 28, then 1 mile N to property. 588 acres.
FISHING: **Chartier Ponds:** Smallmouth & largemouth bass, crappie, bluegill.
RESTRICTIONS: a. Smallmouth & largemouth bass must be 15 inches or longer. b. Camping prohibited. c. Fires prohibited.
d. Public access prohibited 9 p.m. to 3 a.m. daily except with night hunting permit.

35b. JACKSON LAKE SWA - Morgan County - 17/2-B
(SEE STATE PARKS SECTION)
From I-76 at the Hwy. 39 exit, go 7.4 miles N on Hwy. 39 to Hwy. 144, then 1 mile NE to Cty. Rd. 5, then 3.8 miles N to Cty. Rd. CC, then 1 mile W to Cty. Rd. 4, then 1/4 mile S to property. 394 land acres, 2,967 surface acres, South Platte drainage, 4,438' el.
FISHING: Rainbow trout, walleye, wiper, black crappie. Fishing is prohibited from Nov. 1 through the last day of regular waterfowl season. Ice fishing prohibited except in designated ares.
RESTRICTIONS: a. Camping prohibited.   b. Fires prohibited.

36. OTERO COUNTY
36a. HOLBROOK RESERVOIR SWA - Otero County - 31/1-C
From Swink, go 3 miles N on Cty. Rd. 24.5 to Cty. Rd. FF, then 1/2 mile E to reservoir. 670 acres. 400 surface acres, Arkansas drainage, 4,150' el.
FISHING: Largemouth bass, channel catfish, saugeye, tiger muskie, walleye, wiper, rainbow trout, crappie, bluegill, yellow perch, green sunfish, bullhead and carp.
FACILITIES: rest rooms, boat ramps, handicap fishing pier.

36b. MELON VALLEY SWA - Otero County - 31/1-C
West of Rocky Ford and1 mile E of Hwy. 71 between Arkansas River and Fort Lyon Canal. 350 acres.
FISHING: **Arkansas River:** Rainbow, brown trout, cutthroat.

36c. ROCKY FORD SWA - Otero County - 31/1-B
From Rocky Ford, go 2 miles NE on Hwy. 266, cross river bridge, turn E on Cty. Rd. 80.5. 550 acres. Go 1-1/4 mi. further E to McClelland tract. 662 acres.
FISHING: **Arkansas River:** Rainbow, brown trout, cutthroat.
FACILITIES: rest rooms.
RESTRICTIONS: a. Fires prohibited.

36d. TIMPAS CREEK SWA (including Otero Pond) - Otero Co. - 31/1-B
From Rocky Ford, go 4 miles S on Hwy. 71 to Hwy. l0, then 2 miles E across Timpas Creek Bridge, then 1 mile S on Cty. Rd. 21, then 1 mile W on Cty. Rd. Z to property. 141 acres, 2.0 surface acres, Arkansas drainage, 4,200' el.
FISHING: **Timpas Creek:** Sunfish, bullhead, channel catfish, **Otero Pond:**

Bluegill, channel catfish, largemouth bass.
RESTRICTIONS: Fires prohibited.

37. PARK COUNTY
37a. ANTERO RESERVOIR SWA - Park County - 23/2-C
From Hartsel, go 5 miles SW on Hwy. 24 to reservoir. 5,000 acres, 4,102 surface acres, South Platte drainage, 8,940' el.
FISHING: Rainbow, brown trout, cutthroat, splake.
FACILITIES: rest rooms, boat ramp.
RESTRICTIONS: a. Boating prohibited 9 p.m. to 4 a.m.
b. Public access prohibited on west face of dam, along south and west shoreline, and on the island, except for waterfowl hunting.

37b. 63 RANCH SWA - Park County - 23/2-B
From Fairplay, 15 miles S on Hwy. 285 or 5.5 miles N of Antero Junction on Hwy. 285. 1,200 acres.
FISHING: **South Fork South Platte River:** Rainbow, brown, cutthroat trout.
Antero Reservoir: Rainbow, brown, cutthroat trout, splake.
RESTRICTIONS: a. Camping and fires prohibited.

37c. SPINNEY MOUNTAIN SWA - Park County - 23/2-C
(SEE STATE PARKS SECTION)
From Hartsel, go 3 miles S on Cty. Rd. 59 to property. 3,000 acres.
FISHING: **South Platte River:** Rainbow, brown trout, cutthroat, northern pike.
RESTRICTIONS: Special regulations apply - Call first.
a. Camping prohibited. b. Fires prohibited.

37d. TARRYALL RESERVOIR SWA - Park County - 14/4-B
From Jefferson, go 15 miles SE on Cty. Rd. 79 to reservoir. 886 acres. 175 surface acres, South Platte drainage, 8,860' el.
FISHING: **Tarryall Reservoir:** Rainbow, brown trout, kokanee. **Tarryall Creek:** Brown, brook trout.
FACILITIES: rest room, drinking water, boat ramp, fishing jettys.
RESTRICTIONS: Public access prohibited from dam, spillway and outlet structures.

37e. TETER SWA - Park County - 14/3-B
From Jefferson, 2 mi. west on Hwy. 285 and then 2 mi. north on Cty. Rd. 950 acres. 9,500' el.
FISHING: **Michigan Creek:** Rainbow, brown, cutthroat trout.
RESTRICTIONS: a. Camping prohibited. b. Fires prohibited.

37f. TOMAHAWK SWA - Park County -23/1-B
From Hartsel, go 5 miles N on Hwy. 9, then 1/2 mile to parking area. Alternate route: From Fairplay, go 10 miles S on Hwy. 9, then 1/2 mile to parking area. 3,400 acres, 9,000' el.
FISHING: **Middle Fork South Platte River:** Rainbow, brown, cutthroat trout.
RESTRICTIONS: a. Camping and fires prohibited.

37g. ALMA SWA - Park County - 23/1-B
From Alma, go 1 1/2 mi. N on Hwy 9 to Cty Rd 4, then 1/4 mi. NW to property.
FISHING: **Middle Fork South Platte:** Rainbow, brown, cutthroat.
FACILITIES: rest rooms, campsites.

37h. BADGER BASIN SWA - Park County - 23/1-B
From Hartsel immediately E and W along Hwy 24, directly N of Hartsel; and immediately N and S along Hwy 9.
FISHING: 22 miles of fishing access along the **South Fork and Middle Fork of the South Platte and Four Mile Creek:** Rainbow, brown, brook, cutthroat trout, northern pike.
RESTRICTIONS: a. Camping prohibited. b. Fires prohibited.
c Parking prohibited except in designated areas.   d. Public access allowed only from designated parking areas and prohibited beyond the fenced and posted easement.   e. Artificial flies or lures only.
f. All trout 12-20 inches must be returned to the water immediately.
g. Bag and possession limit for trout is 2 fish, no more than 1 can be longer than 20 inches.

37i. BUFFALO PEAKS SWA - Park County - 23/1-B
From Hartsel, 1 mile W and 7 miles N on Hwy 9 to Garo Park. Private road E of Garo Park. Area borders Tomahawk SWA on N. 3,400 total acres in both SWA's.
FISHING: 4 miles fishing access. **Middle Fork South Platte:** Rainbow, brown trout, cutthroat.
RESTRICTIONS: a. Artificial flies or lures only. b. All trout 12-20 inches must be returned to the water immediately.
c. Bag and possession limit for trout is 2 fish, no more than 1 can be longer than 20 inches.

37j. KNIGHT-IMLER SWA - Park County - 23/1-B
From Fairplay, go 10 miles S on Hwy 285 to property.
FISHING: **Fourmile Creek:** Rainbow, brown trout, cutthroat.
RESTRICTIONS:

State Wildlife Areas - Fishing

a. Camping prohibited.
b. Fires prohibited.
c. Public access prohibited beyond 25 feet from centerline of stream.

38. PROWERS COUNTY

38a. ARKANSAS RIVER SWA - Prowers County - 32/1-C
From Holly, go 4 miles E on Hwy. 50 to Cty. Rd. 39, then 3/4 mile S, across canal, then 1/2 mile W to property. 98 acres, 3,350' el.
FISHING: Rainbow, brown, cutthroat trout, channel catfish.

38b. MIKE HIGBEE SWA - Prowers County - 32/1-B
From Lamar, go 4 miles E on Hwy. 50 to property. 876 acres.
FISHING: **Arkansas River/Clay Creek**, Bullhead, channel catfish and sunfish.**Property ponds:** Sunfish, bullheads.

38c. THURSTON RESERVOIR SWA - Prowers County - 32/1-B
From Lamar, go 9 miles N on Hwy. 196 to Cty. Rd. TT, then 1 mile W to Cty. Rd. 7, then 1/4 mile N to reservoir. 173 surface acres, Arkansas drainage, 3,797' el.
FISHING: Tiger muskie, channel catfish, largemouth bass, crappie,walleye, saugeye, wiper, drum, sunfish.
FACILITIES: boat ramps, rest room. (Camping.)
RESTRICTIONS: a. Boating prohibited if it creates a whitewater wake Nov. 1 through the last day of waterfowl season.

39. PUEBLO COUNTY

39a. PUEBLO RESERVOIR SWA - Pueblo County - 24/4-B
(SEE STATE PARKS SECTION)
From Pueblo, go 7 miles W on Hwy. 96 to reservoir. 4,100 acres, 3,000 surface acres, Arkansas drainage, 4,880' el.
FISHING: **Pueblo Reservoir:** Rainbow trout, walleye, wiper, flathead catfish, blue catfish, channel catfish, smallmouth & largemouth bass, crappie, bluegill, northern pike, perch, some brown trout. **Arkansas River:** Rainbow, brown, cutthroat trout.
FACILITIES: rest room, nature trail, boat ramps.
RESTRICTIONS: a. Camping prohibited. b. Fires prohibited.

39b. RUNYON/FOUNTAIN LAKES SWA - Pueblo County - 24/4-B
From Pueblo, go S on I-25 to exit 98-A, then S on Santa Fe to Runyon Field, then E on Runyon Field Rd. for 1/2 mile to property. 40 acres, 20 surface acres, Arkansas River drainage, 4,700' el.
FISHING: Rainbow trout,walleye, bluegill, channel catfish, largemouth & smallmouth bass, carp, yellow perch, black crappie.
FACILITIES: rest rooms, nature trail, handicapped fishing dock.
RESTRICTIONS: a. Ice fishing prohibited. b. Boating prohibited.
c. Camping prohibited. d. Fires prohibited.
e. Public prohibited sunset to sunrise except for fishing.

40. RIO BLANCO COUNTY

40a. MEEKER PASTURE SWA - Rio Blanco County - 1/3-C
From Meeker, go 1-1/2 miles N on Hwy. 13 to Cty. Rd. 8, then 2 miles E to property. 48 acres.
FISHING: **White River:** Rainbow, brook, brown trout, cutthroat, whitefish.

40b. OAK RIDGE SWA - Rio Blanco County - 2/4-A
BELAIRE UNIT: From Meeker, go 21 miles E on Cty. Rd. 8 to Cty. Rd. 17 (Buford/Newcastle Rd.), then 1-1/2 miles S to unit.
LAKE AVERY UNIT: From Meeker, go 1-1/2 miles N on Hwy. 13 to Cty. Rd. 8, then 19 miles E to unit.
SLEEPY CAT PONDS UNIT: From Meeker, go 16 miles E on Cty. Rd. 8 to unit.
SLEEPY CAT FISHING EASEMENT: 9,325 total acres, all units.
FISHING: **White River:** Rainbow, brown, brook trout, cutthroat, whitefish.
FACILITIES: campsites, rest room, drinking water, boat ramp.
RESTRICTIONS: a. Public access prohibited on **Sleepy Cat Ponds** Unit and Sleepy Cat fishing easement except for fishing.
b. Camping prohibited except in designated areas.
c. Public access prohibited Dec.1-July 15.

40c. RIO BLANCO LAKE SWA - Rio Blanco County - 1/3-C
From Meeker, go 20 miles W on Hwy. 64 to property. 383 acres.
FISHING: **Rio Blanco Lake:** Rainbow, largemouth, smallmouth bass, crappie, perch, northern pike, channel catfish, bullhead. **White River:** Rainbow, brown, brook trout, cutthroat, whitefish.
FACILITIES: rest room, boat ramp. (Camping.)
(Piceance SWA)
From Meeker, go 20 miles W on Hwy. 64 to Cty. Rd. 5 (Piceance Creek Rd.), then 7 miles S to Dry Fork turn-off, follow signs to station (3 miles).
FISHING: **Rio Blanco Lake:** Rainbow, largemouth, smallmouth bass, crappie, perch, northern pike, channel catfish, bullhead.
FACILITIES: rest room, drinking water.

41. RIO GRANDE COUNTY

41a. RIO GRANDE SWA - Rio Grande County - 29/3-B

(Del Norte fishing easements)
From Monte Vista, go 3 miles E on Sherman Ave. to property. 935 acres.
FISHING: **Rio Grande River:** Rainbow, brown trout.
FACILITIES: rest room, parking areas.
RESTRICTIONS: a. Camping prohibited except in parking areas with toilet facilities. b. Fires prohibited. c. Public access prohibited Feb. 15 - July 15.

41b. BEAVER CREEK RESERVOIR SWA - Rio Grande County -29/2-A
From South Fork, go 2 miles SW on Hwy 160 to USFS Rd 360 (Beaver Creek Rd.), then 6 miles S to reservoir. 113.9 surface acres, Rio Grande drainage, 8,850' el.
FISHING: Rainbow, brown, brook trout, kokanee.
FACILITIES: campgrounds, rest room, drinking water, boat ramps.
RESTRICTIONS: a. Snagging kokanee permitted Oct. 1 - Dec 31.
b. Discharging firearms prohibited. c. Open fires prohibited on ice.
d. Boating prohibited if it creates a whitewater wake.

41c. HOME LAKE SWA - Rio Grande County - 29/3-B
From Monte Vista, go 1 1/2 miles E on Sherman Ave to property. 67 surface acres, Rio Grande drainage, 7,624' el.
FISHING: Rainbow trout, northern pike, channel catfish.
RESTRICTIONS: a. Boating prohibited except craft propelled by hand, wind, electric motor, or motorboats as provided in B and C below.
b. Motorboats up to 10 horsepower may be used at anytime.
c. Motorboats greater than and including 10 horsepower may be used only 10 a.m. to 4 p.m.

42. ROUTT COUNTY

42a. INDIAN RUN SWA - Routt County - 2/3-B
From Hamilton, go 12 miles SE on Hwy. 317 to Cty. Rd. 67, then 6 miles S to property. 2,039 acres.
FISHING: **Beaver Creek**: Brook trout. (Camping.)

42b. ROCK CREEK SWA - Routt County - 9/2-A
From Kremmling, go 6 miles N on Hwy. 40 to Hwy. 134, then 12 miles W over Gore Pass to USFS Rd. 206, then 2 1/2 miles SW to property.
FISHING: coldwater stream. (Camping.)

42c. SERVICE CREEK SWA - Routt County - 2/3-C
From Steamboat Springs, go 4 1/2 miles S on Hwy. 131 to Cty. Rd. 18, then 7 miles SE to property.
FISHING: coldwater stream.
FACILITIES: rest room.
RESTRICTIONS: Camping prohibited except 3 days before the beginning of regular big game seasons through 3 days after the end of regular big game seasons.

42d. YAMPA RIVER SWA - Routt County - 2/2-B
From Craig, go 7 miles E on Hwy. 40 to property.
Alternate: From Hayden, go 6 miles W on Hwy 40. Area is S of Hwy. 863 acres.
FISHING: **Yampa River:** Northern pike.
RESTRICTIONS: a. Camping prohibited. h. Fires prohibited.

42e. CHRISTINA SWA - Routt County - 2/2-C
(Elk River Fishing Easement)
From Steamboat Springs, go 7 miles N on Cty Rd 129 (Elk River Rd.) to property.
FISHING: **Fryingpan River:** Rainbow trout.
RESTRICTIONS: a. Camping prohibited. b. Fires prohibited.

42f. FINGER ROCK SFU - Routt County - 2/3-C
From Yampa, go 3 miles S on Hwy 131 to unit. 20 acres.
FISHING: coldwater pond fishing.
RESTRICTIONS: a. Fishing prohibited except in **retention ponds.**
b. Fishing prohibited sunset to sunrise. c. Camping prohibited.
d. Dogs prohibited. e. Fires prohibited.

43. SAGUACHE COUNTY

43a. COCHETOPA SWA (Coleman) - Saguache County - 22/4-C
From Gunnison, go 8 miles E on Hwy. 50 to Hwy. 114, then 20 miles S to Cochetopa Creek.
FISHING: **Cochetopa Creek:** Rainbow, brown, brook trout.
RESTRICTIONS: a. Camping prohibited. b. Dogs prohibited.
c. Fires prohibited. d. Foot access only from established parking areas.

43b. DOME LAKES SWA - Saguache County - 22/4-C
From Gunnison, go 8 miles E on Hwy. 50 to Hwy. 114, then 22 miles SE to property. 239 acres, 75 surface acres, Gunnison drainage, 9,017' el,
FISHING: **Dome Lakes:** Rainbow, brook trout. **Cochetopa Creek:** Rainbow, brown, brook trout.
FACILITIES: rest room, drinking water.

44. SAN JUAN COUNTY

44a. ANDREWS LAKE SWA - San Juan County - 28/2-A
From Durango, go 39 mi. N on Hwy 550 to access road, then 1/2 mi. E to property. 10 surface acres, San Juan drainage, 10,745' el.
FISHING: Rainbow, brook trout.

FACILITIES: rest rooms (USFS), trailhead, parking, overlook.

45. SAN MIGUEL

45a. MIRAMONTE RESERVOIR SWA - San Miguel County - 27/1-B
From Norwood, go 1-1/2 miles E on Hwy. 145 to USFS Rd. 610 (Dolores-Norwood Rd.), then 17 miles S to reservoir. 831 acres, 420 surface acres, Dolores drainage, 7,700' el.
FISHING: Rainbow trout.
FACILITIES: trailer dump station, rest rooms, drinking water, boat ramps, shelters, well with potable water.
RESTRICTIONS: a. Camping prohibited except in designated areas.

45b. SAN MIGUEL SWA - San Miguel County - 27/1-C
(Applebaugh fishing easement)
From Placerville, go 3/4 mile S on Hwy 145 to property.
FISHING: **San Miguel River:** Rainbow, brown trout.

45c. WOODS LAKE SWA - San Miguel County - 27/2-C
From Telluride, go 13 miles W on Hwy 145 to USFS Rd 618 in Fall Creek, then 9 miles S to property. 160 acres, 19.8 surface acres, Dolores drainage, 9,423' el.
FISHING: **Woods Lake:** Rainbow, brook trout, occasional brown trout, cutthroat.
FACILITIES: rest room.
RESTRICTIONS: a. Artificial flies or lures only. b. Camping prohibited.
c. Boats prohibited except if propelled by hand, wind or electricity.

46. SUMMIT COUNTY

46a. BLUE RIVER SWA - Summit County - 13/1-C
Blue River Unit: From Silverthorne, go 17 miles N on Hwy 9 to unit. 82 ac.
Eagle's Nest Unit: From Silverthorne, go 9 miles N on Hwy 9 to unit. 29 ac.
Sutton Unit: From Silverthorne, go 7 miles N on Hwy 9 to unit.
FISHING: Rainbow, brown trout.
RESTRICTIONS: a. Camping prohibited. b. Discharging firearms or bows prohibited. c. Fires prohibited. d. Firewood cutting prohibited. e. Vehicle parking overnight prohibited.

47. TELLER COUNTY

47a. DOME ROCK SWA - Teller County - 24/2-A
From Divide, go 5 miles S on Hwy. 67 to intersection at Rainbow Valley, then 3/4 mi. on right fork to access road on right (North Ranch is Mueller State Park).
FISHING: **Four Mile Creek:** Rainbow, brown, brook trout.
RESTRICTIONS: a. Camping prohibited. b. Dogs prohibited.
c. Fires prohibited.

47b. ROSEMONT RESERVOIR - Teller County - SWA 24/2-B
From Divide, go 15 miles S on Hwy to Gold Camp Rd. near Victor, then 20 miles E to reservoir. 20 surface acres, Arkansas drainage, 9,640' el.
FISHING: Rainbow, brook, brown, cutthroat, lake trout, splake.
FACILITIES: rest rooms.
RESTRICTIONS: a. Artificial flies or lures only. b. Ice fishing prohibited.
c. Fishing prohibited 9 p.m. until 5 a.m. d. Boating prohibited.
e. Camping prohibited. f. Dogs prohibited. g. Fires prohibited.
h. Access prohibited except by foot from established parking areas.
i. Access prohibited Nov 1 - May 10.
j. Access prohibited near dam, caretaker's house and north side of reservoir.
k. Picnicking prohibited. l. Water contact activities prohibited.

47c. SKAGUAY RESERVOIR SWA - Teller County - 24/2-A & BEAVER CREEK
From Victor, go 1/2 mile E on Cty Rd 67 to Cty Rd 441, then 6 1/2 miles E to reservoir. 174 acres, 114 surface acres, Arkansas drainage, 8,880' el.
FISHING: **Skaguay:** Rainbow, brook, mackinaw (lake) trout, northern pike.
Beaver Creek: Rainbow, brown and brookies.
FACILITIES: rest rooms, boat ramps.
RESTRICTIONS:
a. Boating prohibited if it creates a whitewater wake.

48. WELD COUNTY

48a. BANNER LAKES SWA - Weld County - 12/2-B
From Hudson, go 4 miles E on Hwy. 52 to property. 934 acres.
FISHING: Sunfish, bass, crapie, catfish.
FACILITIES: rest rooms.
RESTRICTIONS: a. Boating prohibited except for hand-propelled craft and belly boats. b. Camping prohibited. d. Fires prohibited.
e. Public access prohibited from the first day of the regular waterfowl season to the first day of pheasant season except Saturdays, Sundays, Mondays and legal holidays. f. Public access prohibited north of Hwy. 52 April 1 - July 15.

48b. SEELEY RESERVOIR SWA - Weld County - 8/4-A
From Greeley, go 3 miles N on 35th Ave to reservoir. 118 surface acres, South Platte drainage. 4,700' el.
FISHING: Smallmouth/largemouth bass, crappie, yellow perch, walleye, bluegill, channel catfish, rainbow stocked occasionally.
FACILITIES: rest room, boat ramp.
RESTRICTIONS: a. Fishing prohibited except along west shore or from boats 1/2 hour after sunset until 1/2 hour before sunrise.
b. Smallmouth and largemouth bass must be 15 inches or longer.
c. Access prohibited 1 hour after sunset to 1 hour before sunrise except for fishing. d. Camping prohibited. e. Fires prohibited.

49. YUMA COUNTY

49a. SANDSAGE SWA - Yuma County - GMU 132
From Wray, go 4 1/2 miles W on Hwy. 34 to Cty. Rd. 35, then 1/4 mile W to Cty. Rd. CC, then 1/2 mile S to property.
FISHING: **North Fork Republican River:** Rainbow trout.
RESTRICTIONS: a. Camping prohibited. b. Fires prohibited.

49b. SOUTH REPUBLICAN SWA - Yuma County - 20/2-C (SEE STATE PARKS SECTION - BONNY)
From Burlington, go 21 miles N on Hwy. 385 to Cty. Rd. 1, then 3 miles E, 2 miles N and 2 miles E to property. 13,140 acres, 1,924 surface acres, Republican drainage, 3,670' el.
FISHING: Walleye, wiper, channel catfish, largemouth bass, yellow perch, bullhead, carp, bluegill, white bass, a few northern pike, crappie.
FACILITIES: campsites, trailer dump station, rest rooms, drinking water, boat ramps, picnic area with barbecue pit.
RESTRICTIONS: a. Seining prohibited in Bonny Reservoir stilling basin and down-stream Oct. 1-Jan. 31. b. Boating is prohibited from 1/2 hour after sunset to 1/2 hour before sunrise from March 15 to April 15.

49c. STALKER LAKE SWA - Yuma County - 20/1-C
From Wray, go 2 miles W on Hwy. 34 to Cty. Rd. FF, then 1-1/2 miles N to access road, then 1/2 mile west to property. 75 acres, 26 surface acres, Republican drainage, 3,566' el.
FISHING: Rainbow trout, channel catfish, bluegill, largemouth bass, tiger muskie.
FACILITIES: rest room, boat ramp, picnic shelters, tables, playground.
RESTRICTIONS: a. Boating prohibited except if propelled by hand, wind or electricity. b. Camping prohibited. c. Fires prohibited.

Colorado National Forests Index Map

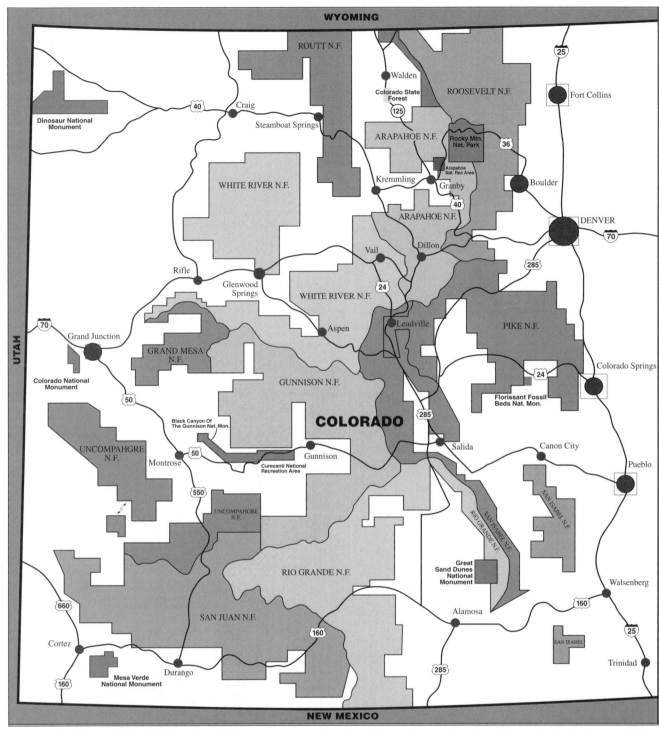

Ten National Forests are located in Colorado and attract over 32 million visitors annually. Eighty percent of all Colorado recreation occurs within their boundaries, fishing is one of the main attractions. Natural beauty, wildlife and the outdoor recreation of national forests and wilderness areas within their boundaries are the fisherman's dream.

Stream, river and high lake fishing in these forests and especially in the wilderness can be physically demanding. Elevations over 10,000 feet are common; weather conditions change from warm sunshine to snow within hours, especially in the spring. Streams and lakes in the higher elevations can be iced over or impossible to reach, keep this in mind while planning your trips.

Good physical condition and being acclimated are a must for extended backpacking trips to high lakes. High lakes can be temperamental but also can provide excellent fly fishing, magnificent settings and peace of mind. Trail information to high lakes in this guide has sometimes been determined by scaling from maps of the area, confirm the distance and difficulty by contacting the Forest Service or from a trails guide.

In this guide each National Forest is shown in alphabetical order. Physical features such as the Continental Divide generally separate National Forests. Each Forest is divided into Ranger District. Ranger Districts are the primary managers within the National Forest; their phone numbers are listed on page 42.

Colorado National Forests Table of Contents

Arapaho/Roosevelt National Forest ....Page 98
Located west of the Boulder/Fort Collins area in north central Colorado near the high populations of Front Range communities, and areas of nationally known significance. Arapaho/Roosevelt National Forests rank among the top national forests for year round recreation use. Camping, hiking, mountain biking, fishing, hunting, skiing and other winter sports and driving for pleasure are popular activities.

Grand Mesa National Forest.........................Page 124
The Grand Mesa National Forest offers excellent fishing, hiking, camping and other winter and summer recreation opportunities. Some 300 stream fed lakes, sixteen developed campgrounds and four picnic grounds are open from early July when the snow melts until late September. Excellent fishing, hiking and camping can be enjoyed along this byway. The 300 hundred lakes scattered across the Grand Mesa provide superb opportunities for anglers. Golden aspen shimmering in the fall provide an unequaled panoramic view.

Gunnison National Forest ....Page 150
Located north and east of Gunnison in central Colorado the present Forest includes 1.7 million acres of public land within the boundary. Outstanding mountain scenery can be found in the Forest during any season of the year. Fishing is good throughout the year. Deer and elk make the Forest a popular hunter's haven during the fall season.

Pike National Forest ....Page 170
East of South Park in Park County are the popular fishing and camping areas of Lost Park, Tarryall Creek, and Eleven Mile Canyon. Most of the Pike National Forest in this area remains undeveloped allowing the visitor to enjoy his recreation experience in a near natural environment.

Rio Grande National Forest ....Page 178
Variety is the word describing the outdoor recreation opportunities of the Rio Grande National Forest. From the rugged and jagged peaks of the Sangre de Cristos to the forested table lands and glacial canyons of the San Juans, the outdoor enthusiast can choose an activity suited to the day or the season.

High lakes and tumbling streams beckon the fisherman while big game and other wildlife lure the hunter or nature photographer. Hiking, backpacking, and camping amid spectacular scenery await the visitor to the Weminuche, La Garita, or South San Juan Wilderness. The trail along the Continental Divide, or the rugged Sangre de Cristo back-country is equally exciting and challenging.

Routt National Forest ....Page 193
The Continental Divide and spectacular peaks of the 160,560 acre Mt. Zirkel Wilderness split the major watersheds of the National Forest. On the East, the North Park region is drained by the North Platte River, a tributary of the Missouri and Mississippi and on the west, the Yampa River flows to the Green River and Colorado River. On the southeast corner of the Forest the 47,140 acre Sarvis Creek Wilderness Area was created in 1993. Elevations are high, ranging from 7,000 feet in the irrigated valley's to 13,000 feet along the Divide. Heavy winter snows are common and frost may occur anytime during the short summer season.

San Isabel National Forest ....Page 204
Located south of Leadville in central Colorado San Isabel National Forest includes over one million acres of beautiful scenery with snowcapped mountains, wildflowers, autumn colors, mountain lakes and clear blue skies to enjoy. Fishing in the Arkansas River, Turquoise Lake, Twin Lakes the many streams and high lakes is rated good for most cold water species. Almost 800 miles of trails, nineteen peaks over 14,000 feet, scenic byways, numerous roads amid highways, campgrounds and picnic areas provide challenges and opportunities for everyone. All this is yours to enjoy.

San Juan National Forest 216
The San Juan National Forest is located north of Durango in southwestern Colorado on the western slope of the Continental Divide. It covers an area from east to west of more than 120 miles and from north to south more than 60 miles, encompassing an area of 1,869,931 acres. Fishing for trout in high mountain lakes, swift streams, or reservoirs such as McPhee, Vallecito, Lemon and Williams Creek Lake offer the angler many challenges. Hunters stalk mule deer, elk, bear, bighorn sheep, mountain lion, grouse, turkey and ducks.

Uncompahgre National Forest 229
The Uncompahgre National Forest includes the Uncompahgre Plateau that rises to about 10,000 feet with its sides cut by gorges. The San Juan Mountain Range with four peaks over 14,000 feet and another 100 peaks over 13,000 feet in elevation, and the Uncompahgre, Mount Sneffels, and Lizard Head Wilderness areas. The 4.2 mile Bear Creek National Recreation Trail traverses along steep narrow rocky ledges. Some of the best 4-wheel drive opportunities on primitive mining roads are located in these areas. Ouray is well known as the "Jeep Capital of the World" and the "Switzerland of America".

White River National Forest 234
White River National Forest provides quality recreation experiences for visitors from around the world. Hundreds miles of trails, provide challenges and opportunities for everyone. Hiking, mountain biking, fishing, horseback riding, 4 wheel and ATV drives. Numerous campgrounds and picnic sites are scattered through the Forest. Fishing for trout in high mountain lakes, swift streams, or reservoirs such as Trappers Lake, Ruedi Reservoir offer the angler many challenges, all this is yours to enjoy.

Arapaho National Recreation Area 99
The Arapaho National Recreation Area covers over 36,000 acres and contains five major lakes, often referred as "the Great Lakes of Colorado." Boating and fishing are primary activities, with many developed campgrounds, picnic areas, and hiking trails available for public recreation and enjoyment.

Rocky Mountain National Park 100
The snow-mantled peaks of Rocky Mountain National Park rise above verdant subalpine valleys and glistening lakes. One third of the park is above tree line, and here alpine tundra predominates a major reason these peaks and valleys have been set aside as a national park.

In the mountain streams and lakes of Rocky Mountain National Park are four species of trout: German brown, rainbow, brook and cutthroat. These cold waters may not produce large fish, but you will enjoy the superb mountain scenery as you fish.

Remember, you must have a valid Colorado fishing license. Use of live bait is prohibited except under certain special conditions. Review the special fishing regulations at park headquarters or at the nearest park ranger station before you fish. Fishing is not permitted in Bear Lake at any time. Other lakes and streams in the park are under restrictions to protect the Colorado River greenback cutthroat that is being reintroduced to its native habitat. Check with a ranger for details.

Curecanti National Recreation Area 165
Twenty mile long Blue Mesa is the largest body of water in Colorado. Several arms of the lake reach into beautiful side canyons and offer boaters secluded campsites and many areas to explore, while three broad basins surrounded by open mesa country provide large areas for sailing and windsurfing. Fishing is the number one sport on Blue Mesa Lake, anglers have the opportunity to catch rainbow, brown, and lake trout, and kokanee salmon. Hunting is allowed in season and Colorado state laws are enforced.

Arapaho/Roosevelt National Forest Index

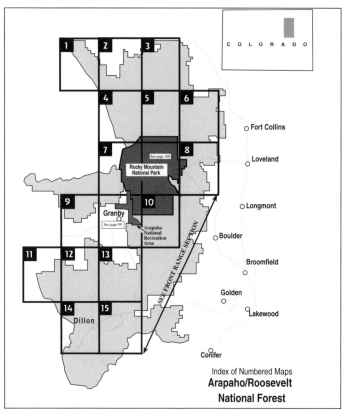

Index of Numbered Maps
**Arapaho/Roosevelt
National Forest**

COLORADO

Arapaho National Recreation Area **99**
Rocky Mountain National Park **100**
MAP 1
1. Boswell Creek 106
2. Johnson Creek 106
3. Fish Creek 106
4. Pole Creek 106
5. Stuck Creek 106
6. Grace Creek 106
MAP 2
1. Hohnholtz State Wildlife Area........................107
2. LaGarde Creek 107
3. McIntyre Creek 107
4. Drink Creek 107
5. Stub Creek 107
6. Link Creek 107
7. Nunn Creek 107
8. Deadman Creek 107
9. Sand Creek...107
MAP 3
1. Sheep Creek 109
2. Beaver Creek 109
3. Panhandle Creek 109
4. George Creek 109
5. Cornelius Creek 109
6. Creedmore Lakes 109
7. Elkhorn Creek 109
8. Bellaire Lake 109
9. West Lake 109
10. Dowdy Lake..109
11. Parvin Lake 109
12. Cache le Poudre River, N. Fk........................109
13. Lone Pine Creek 109
14. Lone Pine Creek, S. Fork 109
15. Lone Pine Creek, N. Fork 109
MAP 4
Rawah Wilderness
1. Twin Lakes...111
2. Iceberg Lake...111
3. Sugarbowl Lake ....
4. McIntyre Lake 111
5. Rainbow Lakes...111
6. Rawah Lakes 111
7. Sandbar Lakes 111

8. Camp Lakes, Lower 111
9. Camp Lakes, Upper 111
10. Bench Lake 111
11. Rock Hole Lake 111
12. Twin Crater Lakes 111
13. Cary Lake 111
14. Island Lake 111
15. Timber Lake 111
16. Hang Lake 111
17. Blue Lake 111
18. Rawah Creek 111
19. West Branch, North Fork 111
20. West Branch Creek..111
Map 4 other
21. Chambers Lake 111
22. Lost Lake 111
23. Laramie Lake 111
24. Twin Lakes East 111
25. Barnes Meadow Reservoir..............................111
26. Joe Wright Reservoir 111
27. Zimmerman Lake 111
28. Trap Lake 111
29. Trap Creek 111
30. Corral Creek 111
31. Long Draw Reservoir.....................................111
32. Peterson Lake 111
33. Bliss State Wildlife Area 111
MAP 5
1. Sheep Creek, Black Hollow Creek 112
2. Beaver Creek, Little..112
3. Timberline Lake 112
4. Browns Lake 112
5. Comanche Reservoir 112
6. Beaver Creek 112
7. Emmaline Lake 112
8. Pennock Creek 112
MAP 6
1. Cache le Poudre River 113
2. Poudre River SWA 113
3. Cache le Poudre River, S. Fk. 113
4. Buckhorn Creek 113
MAP 7
1. Bowen Lake, Blue Lake 114

2. Lost Lake 114
3. Supply Creek 114
MAP 8
1. Lake Estes 115
2. Big Thompson River 115
MAP 9
1. Willow Creek 116
2. Cabin Creek 116
3. Beaver Creek 116
4 Williams Fork Reservoir...................................116
MAP 10
Indian Peaks Wilderness
1. Watanga Lake 118
2. Stone Lakes 118
3. Grouse Creek 118
4. Crawford Lake 118
5. Long Lake 118
6. Pika Lake 118
7. Gilbralter Lake 118
8. Envy Lake 118
9. Red Deer Lake 118
10. Island Lake 118
11. Gourd Lake 118
12. Buchanan Creek 118
13. Coney Lakes 118
14. Blue Lake 118
15. Mitchell Lake 118
16. Crater Lake 118
17. Long Lake 118
18. Lake Isabelle 118
19. Arapaho Creek 118
20. Columbine Lake 118
21. Lake Dorothy 118
22. Banana Lake 118
Map 10 other
23. Monarch Lake 118
24. Brainard Lake 118
MAP 11
Eagles Nest Wilderness
1. Cataract Lake, Lower.......................................119
2. Cataract Lake, Upper.......................................119
3. Tipperary Lake 119
4. Eaglesmere Lakes 119
5. Surprise Lake 119
6. Dora Lake 119
7. Cliff Lake 119
8. Mirror Lake 119
9. Flapjack Lake 119
Map 11 other
10. Green Mountain Reservoir 119
11. Mahan Lake 119
MAP 12
1. Blue River SWA 120
MAP 13
1. Frazer River 121
2. St. Louis Creek 121
3. St. Louis Lake 121
4. Clear Creek, West Fork 121
MAP 14
1. Slate Lakes 122
2. Boulder Lakes, Boulder Creek 122
3.,4 Peeble and South Rock Creeks 122
5. Deluge Lake 122
6. Gore Lakes 122
7. Lost Lake 122
8. Wheeler Lakes 122
9. Blue River 122
10. Dillon Reservoir..122
11. Ten Mile Creek 122
12. Copper Mountain Pond 122
13. Black Lakes 122
MAP 15
1. Hassel Lake 123
2. Woods Lake 123
3. Clear Creek 123
4. Chihuahua Lake 123
5. Grays Lake 123
6. Keystone, Deer, Peru Creeks, Snake River 123

Arapaho National Recreation Area/Grand Lake

Directions: From Denver, take I-70 west to U.S. 40. North on U.S. 40 through to the town of Granby. On the west side of Granby, turn north at the Lake Granby sign onto U.S. 34 north.
Fee: Camping fees.
Size: Grand Lake - 506 acres; Lake Granby - 7,256 acres; Monarch Lake - 147 acres; Shadow Mountain - 1,400 acres; Willow Creek Reservoir - 750 acres; Meadow Creek Reservoir.
Elevation: 8,367 feet.
Maximum Depth: Grand Lake - 226 feet; Lake Granby - 221 feet; Monarch Lake - 30 feet; Shadow Mountain - 24 feet
Facilities: Dump stations at Stillwater and Green Ridge Campgrounds, toilets, picnic tables and fire grates. Beginning Memorial Day weekend and through the summer, running water also is available.
Boat Ramps: Boat ramps are at the Stillwater Campground, Sunset Point, Arapaho Bay Campground, Green Ridge Campground, Willow Creek Campground, and Hilltop picnic area. Some ramps are concrete. Marinas with fee ramps are located around some of the lake.
Fish: **Lake Granby**: Rainbow, brown and lake trout and kokanee salmon. Rainbow and brown trout fishing is best for shore using typical baits such as salmon eggs, Power Bait and nightcrawlers on the bottom. Lures such as Kastmasters, Panther Martins, Rooster Tails and Blue Fox also produce good action trolled or fished from shore. Lake trout are caught trolling or jigging, Rapala lures or using whole suckers at depths of 50-60 feet. As the water warms, the lake trout will tend to move to shallow water for a short time before moving back to deeper depths. Kokanee can be caught trolling with a single hook lures in fluorescent colors.
Willow Creek Reservoir: Rainbow and brook trout. This reservoir can produce excellent stocker rainbow with larger ones being taken occasionally. The best fishing is from shore in early mornings and late evenings on pink Power Bait, rigged just off the bottom, as well as salmon eggs, marshmallows or corn. Fair to good results are generally reported from slow trolling with flashers or

Pop Gear. Wakeless speeds only. No restrictions on boat or motor size.
Shadow Mountain: Best for rainbow and brown through July, kokanee later in the summer. Can become weedy in the summer and tough to fish. Use typical baits and lures.
Grand Lake: Considered one of the best lake trout fisheries in the state with fish caught weighing 20 pounds or more. Rainbow, brown and kokanee are also present. Rainbow fishing is best in the spring. Wet flies and lures are good for brown and rainbow. Sucker meat for mackinaw.
Recreation: Fishing, boating, sailing, hiking.
Camping: 348 campsites in four campgrounds and two group campsites are available. Stillwater campground has 148 sites, Arapaho Bay Campground 84 sites, Greenridge 81 sites, and Willow Creek has 35 sites. Unreserved sites are available on a first-come, first-serve basis. Reservations can be made for Stillwater, Arapaho Bay and Green Ridge Campgrounds.
Information: USDA Forest Service (970) 887-4100.

The Arapaho National Recreation Area (NRA) is located in Grand County in the upper reaches of the Colorado River Valley. It was established by Congress on October 11, 1978, and is administered by the Forest Service, U.S. Department of Agriculture. Most of the area was formerly part of Shadow Mountain NRA administered by the National Park Service.

The Arapaho NRA covers over 36,000 acres and contains the major lakes: Lake Granby, Shadow Mountain Lake, Monarch Lake, Willow Creek Reservoir, and Meadow Creek Reservoir. Grand Lake, the largest natural lake in Colorado, is located outside the NRA, northeast of Shadow Mountain Lake.

The three largest lakes in the NRA (Shadow Mountain, Lake Granby and Willow Creek Reservoir) lie in the glacier sculpted valleys of the upper Colorado River. Most of the rolling terrain is composed of glacial debris and outwash. Many of the islands in the lakes are actually the tops of moraines, which are deposits of sand, gravel, and rock left by melting glaciers.

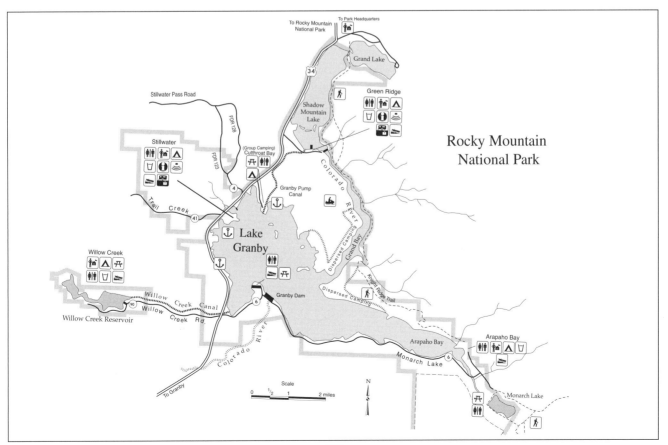

Rocky Mountain National Park

The park is located west of Estes Park and north of Granby, Colorado. State Highway 34 runs through the middle of the park. Fishing is a part of the historic use of this magnificent park. Early stocking practices in the park included non-native species of trout in the lakes and streams that lacked them.

In more recent years, the Park Service has mounted a campaign to remove the non-native trout and to restock the area with native greenback cutthroat and Colorado River cutthroat. Trout populations are maintained through natural reproductions with the exception of stocking practices to restore the native species. As a result, the Park offers a wide variety of quality fishing in a unique natural setting.

The Park is open to fishing all year. There are only 45 lakes of the 156 lakes that have reproducing populations of fish. Supplemental stocking is done only to restore native species.

Protected areas are set up to help the restoration process and are well marked. Possession limits vary by species from year to year depending upon the success of the restoration process. Current information flyers can be obtained at any of the Park's entry points.

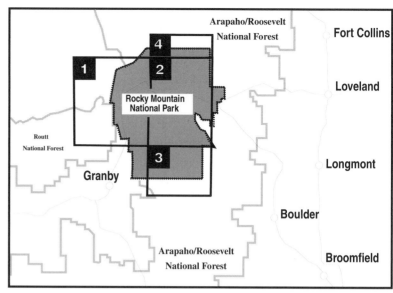

Mapped Areas
Rocky Mountain National Park

TABLE OF CONTENTS

MAP 1 - PAGE 101

NAME	MAP COORDINATES
Big Dutch Creek	B-1
Lake of the Clouds	B-1
North Fork Colorado River	B-2
Cache la Poudre River	C-1
Cascade Creek	C-1
Chapin Creek	C-1
Hague Creek	C-1
Poudre Lake	C-1
Willow Creek	C-1
Gorge Lakes	C-2
(Rock Lake, Little Rock Lake, Arrowhead Lake, Donut Lake)	
Hatnach Lake	C-2
Onahu Creek	C-2
Timber Creek	C-2
Timber Lake	C-2
North Inlet Creek	C-3
Tonahutu Creek	C-3

MAP 2 - PAGE 102

Loomis Lake	A-2
Spruce Lake	A-2
Dream Lake	A-3
Fern Creek	A-3
Fern Lake	A-3
Lake Nanita (Outlet Closed)	A-3
Lake Nokini	A-3
Odessa Lake	A-3
Pettingell Lake	A-3
Sky Pond	A-3
Crystal Lake	B-1
Fall River	B-1
Fay Lakes	B-1
Jewel Lake	B-1
Lawn Lake	B-1
Ypsilon Lake	B-1
Big Thompson River	B-2
Black Lake	B-3
Chasm Lake	B-3
Emerald Lake	B-3

Glacier Creek	B-3
Lake of Glass	B-3
Lake Haiyaha	B-3
Mills Lake	B-3
Peacock Pool	B-3
Solitude Lake	B-3
Sprague Lake	B-3

MAP 3 - PAGE 104

East Inlet Creek	A-1
Fifth Lake	A-1
Fourth Lake	A-1
Lake Adams	A-1
Lake Verna	A-1
Lone Pine Lake	A-1
Spirit Lake	A-1
Box Lake	B-1
Cony Creek	B-1
Hutcheson Lakes	B-1
Ouzel Creek	B-1
Ouzel Lake	B-1
Pear Reservoir	B-1
Roaring Fork of Cabin Creek	B-1
Sandbeach Lake	B-1
Thunder Lake	B-1
North St. Vrain Creek	B-1

MAP 4 - PAGE 104

Lake Husted, Lost Lake,
No. Fork Big Thompson River

CLOSED WATERS

Bear Lake, inlet and outlet streams as posted.
Bench Lake and Ptarmigan Creek.
Hidden Valley Beaver Ponds.
(Closed April 1 -- July 31)
Hidden Valley Creek east of ponds.
(Closed April 1 -- July 31)
Hunters Creek above Wild Basin Ranger Station.
Lake Nanita Outlet downstream 100 yards.
South Fork Poudre River above Pingree Park.
West Creek above West Creek Falls.

CATCH AND RELEASE WATERS

Adams Lake**
Big Crystal Lake*
Cony Creek*
Fern Lake and Creek*
Fifth Lake**
Hidden Valley Beaver Ponds and Hidden Valley Creek (Open 8-1/3/31)*
Lake Husted*
Lake Louis*
Lawn Lake*
Lily Lake*
Loomis Lake*
Lost Lake*
Hutcheson Lake, Lower *
Hutcheson Lake, Mid*
Hutcheson Lake, Upper*
No. Fork of the Big Thompson above Lost Falls*
Odessa Lake*
Ouzel Lake and Creek*
Paradise Creek drainage**
Pear Lake and Creek*
Roaring River*
Sandbeach Lake and Creek*
Spruce Lake*
Timber Lake and Creek**

* Greenback Cutthroat Trout
** Colorado River Cutthroat

NOTE:
You must have a valid Colorado fishing license. Only artificial lures or flies with one (single, double or treble) hook with a common shank maybe used. Possession limits vary with species. You must be able to identify each species of fish taken.

CLOSED WATERS, REGULATIONS AND POSSESION LIMITS CHANGE -- CHECK REGULATIONS AT PARK HEADQUARTERS!

Rocky Mountain National Park

Map 1

Big Dutch Creek (B-1) Access from Milner Pass, 7 mile hike. Cutthroat trout.

Lake of the Clouds (11,400'; 3 ac; B-1) Above timberline at the headwaters of Hitchens Gulch on Big Dutch Creek. Cutthroat. 6.5 mile hike from Milner Pass.

North Fork of Colorado River (B-2) Flows for approximately 13 miles in the park and 5 miles on private land before entering Shadow Mountain Reservoir. A medium-size, brushy stream with rainbow, brown and brook, many beaver ponds.

Cache la Poudre River (C-1) Flows from Poudre Lake at Milner Pass on Trail Ridge Road. Park along road and hike down to the stream for good brook trout fishing. A rough hike back up to the road.

Cascade Creek, Chapin Creek and Hague Creek, Willow Creek (C-1) Good streams for brook trout and some cutthroat for a mile or so up from the Cache le Poudre River.

Poudre Lake (10,700'; 14 ac; C-1) Good for brook trout.

Gorge Lakes (C-2) Located above timberline and are very difficult to reach. Experienced hikers and good weather conditions a must. Access from Milner Pass parking area on Trail Ridge Road. All have cutthroat.

Rock Lake and Little Rock Lake (10,300'; 1 ac;), Arrowhead Lake (11,200'; 43 ac;) and Donut Lake (11,520'; 5 ac;)

Haynach Lake (C-2) Cutthroat and brook. Access from Tonahutu Trail.

Onahu Creek (C-2) Brook trout to 10 inches. Difficult hike from trailhead on Hwy 34, 6 miles north of Grand Lake.

Timber Creek (C-2) Rated good for Colorado River cutthroat.

Timber Lake (10,900'; 10 ac; C-2) Colorado River cutthroat.

North Inlet (C-3) North Inlet contains brook trout below Cascade Falls and cutthroat above the falls. Rated fair to good.

Tonahutu Creek (C-3) Fishing in Tonahutu Creek rated good for small brook below Granite Falls and cutthroat above the falls. Access from trailhead on Hwy 34.

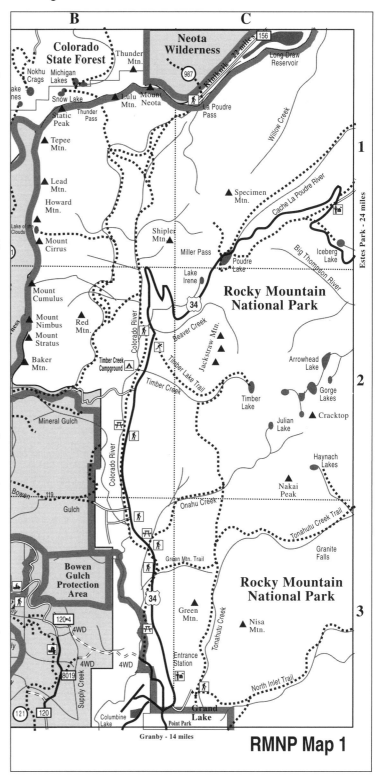

RMNP Map 1

Text Explanation

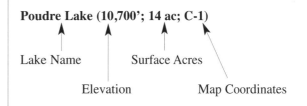

Poudre Lake (10,700'; 14 ac; C-1)

Lake Name   Surface Acres

Elevation   Map Coordinates

Rocky Mountain National Park

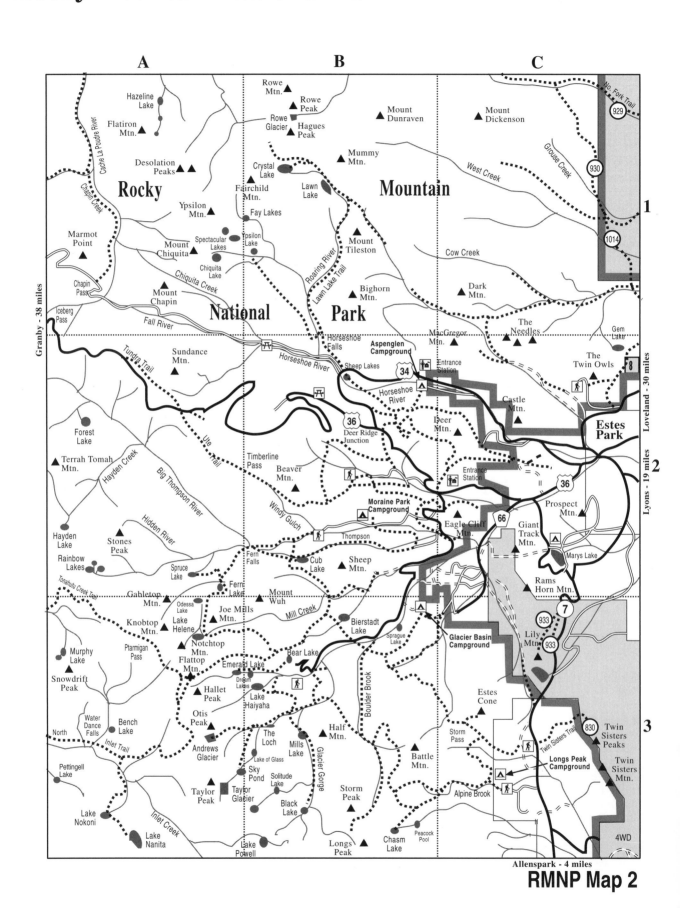

RMNP Map 2

Allenspark - 4 miles

Rocky Mountain National Park: Map 2

Loomis Lake (10,200'; 3 ac; A-2) Rainbow and brook. Rated poor to fair. Strenuous hike.

Spruce Lake (9,640'; 4 ac; A-2) Rainbow and brook. Rated poor to fair.

Dream Lake (9,840'; 6 ac; A-3) Cutthroat and brook. Southwest of Bear Lake. Rated poor.

Fern Creek (A-3) Cutthroat.

Fern Lake (A-3) Cutthroat.

Lake Nanita (10,800'; 34 ac; A-3) Cutthroat. Deep lake with lots of pressure. Note outlet restrictions. Three and one half miles above falls.

Lake Nokoni (10,800'; 25 ac; A-3) Cutthroat. Deep lake with lots of pressure. Twelve miles above the falls.

Odessa Lake (A-3) Cutthroat.

Pettingell Lake (A-3) Cutthroat and brook. 0.5 mile northwest of Lake Nokini.

Sky Pond (11,000'; 11 ac; A-3) Lakes are rated good for Cutthroat and brook. Steep 3.5 mile climb from Trailhead. Two miles further up and approximately half mile apart are The Loch; Glass Lake; Sky Pond.

Crystal Lake (11,480'; 25 ac; B-1) Rated poor to good for cutthroat.

Fall River (B-1) Rated fair for cutthroat.

Fay Lakes (11,100'; 1 to 5 ac; B-1) Three Fay Lakes. Greenback cutthroat.

Jewel Lake (10,230'; 3 ac; B-1) Cutthroat. Approximately one mile upstream from Glacier Falls.

Lawn Lake (10,987'; 20 ac; B-1) Rated good for Cutthroat. Head of Roaring River.

Ypsilon Lake (10,520'; 7 ac; B-1) Rated good for cutthroat. Tough 3-mile hike.

Big Thompson River (B-2) Rated fair for cutthroat, brook and brown trout. Access from Beaver Meadows entrance.
Black Lake (11,000'; 9 ac; B-3) Fair to good for brook and cutthroat. Rocky trail.

Chasm Lake (11,800'; 19 ac; B-3) Rated fair for cutthroat. Deep with rocky shoreline. Take Longs Peak Trail to a fork in the trail about 2.5 miles below the boulder field. Follow signage to Chasm Lake. It is 0.75 mile to Peacock Pool.

Emerald Lake (10,200'; 7 ac; B-3) Rated poor for cutthroat. A mile up the trail from Dream Lake.

Glacier Creek (B-3) Cutthroat.

Lake of Glass (B-3) Cutthroat and brook. Located 0.5 mile southeast of Sky Pond.

Lake Haiyaha (10,200'; 6 ac; B-3) Rated poor for cutthroat.

Mills Lake (10,000'; 16 ac; B-3) Rated poor for rainbow and cutthroat. A mile upstream from Glacier Falls.

Peacock Pool (11,360 ft; 4 ac B-3) Brook and cutthroat to 9 inches.

Solitude Lake (B-3) Cutthroat and Brook.

Sprague Lake (8,720'; 3 ac; B-3) Rated good for brook. Shallow lake. Ice Fishing.

NOTE:
An overview map of Rocky Mountain National Park can be obtained from the National Parks Service.
SUPERINTENDENT
ROCKY MOUNTAIN NATIONAL PARK
ESTES PARK, CO 80517
PHONE (970) 586-1206

Rocky Mountain National Park

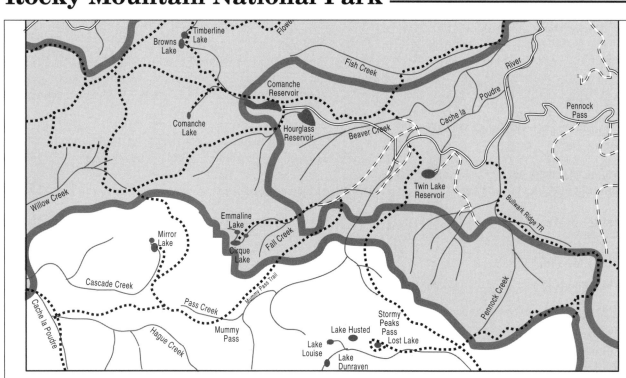

RMNP Map 4

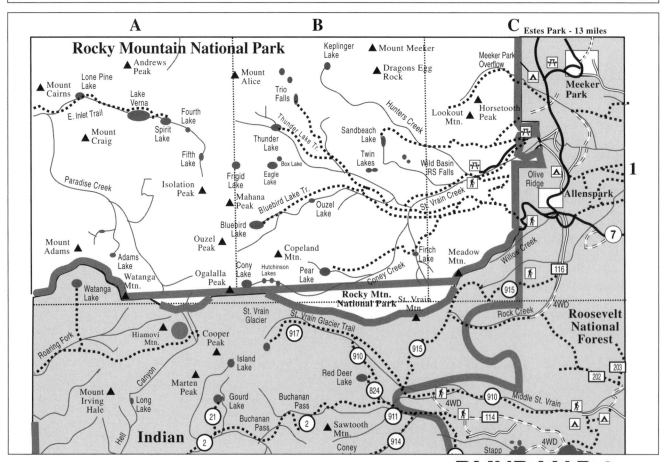

RMNP MAP 3

Rocky Mountain National Park Map 3

East Inlet Creek (A-1) Brook for 5.5 miles below Lone Pine Lake.

Fifth Lake (11,020'; 7 ac; A-1) Cutthroat to 12 inches.

Fourth Lake (10,400'; 7 ac; A-1) Brook. A short walk from Spirit Lake.

Lake Adams (11,200'; 5 ac; A-1) Cutthroat. Tough 7 mile hike from East Inlet.

Lake Verna (10,200'; 33 ac; A-1) Rated fair for brook. Long and narrow.

Lone Pine Lake (10,240'; 8 ac; A-1) Small brook. Lots of pressure.

Spirit Lake (10,240'; 8 ac; A-1) Rated fair for brook.

Cony Creek (B-1) Rated good for rainbow and cutthroat.

Hutcheson Lakes (10,200'; 0.5 to 3 ac; B-1) Rated good for cutthroat. South of Pear Reservoir.

Box Lake (B-1) Rainbow and brook. Located 1 mile south of Thunder Lake.

North St. Vrain Creek (B-1) Brook and brown, rainbow and cutthroat. Access is via the Wild Basin Campground.

Ouzel Creek (B-1) Greenback cutthroat.

Ouzel Lake (10,010'; 6.4 ac;B-1) Greenback cutthroat.

Pear Reservoir (10,582'; 7 ac; B-1) Rated fair for cutthroat. Rocky shoreline.

Roaring Fork of Cabin Creek (B-1) Rated fair for cutthroat and brook.

Sandbeach Lake (10,283'; 16.5 ac; B-1) Rated fair for rainbow and cutthroat. Located 6 miles west of the park boundary. Tough hike.

Thunder Lake (10,600'; 17 ac; B-1) Rated fair for rainbow. Located 7.5 miles west of Wild Basin Campground.

Rocky Mountain National Park Map 4

Lake Husted (11,000'; 1 ac;) Rated good for brook trout. West of Lost Lake 1.0 mile.

Lost Lake (10,500'; 9 ac;) Rated fair for brook and cutthroat.

North Fork Big Thompson River. Brook and cutthroat From Glen Haven travel northeast 1.75 miles to parking lot. From the parking lot at the end of Dunraven Rd, it is 2.5 miles to the park boundary. Fast stream with beaver ponds.

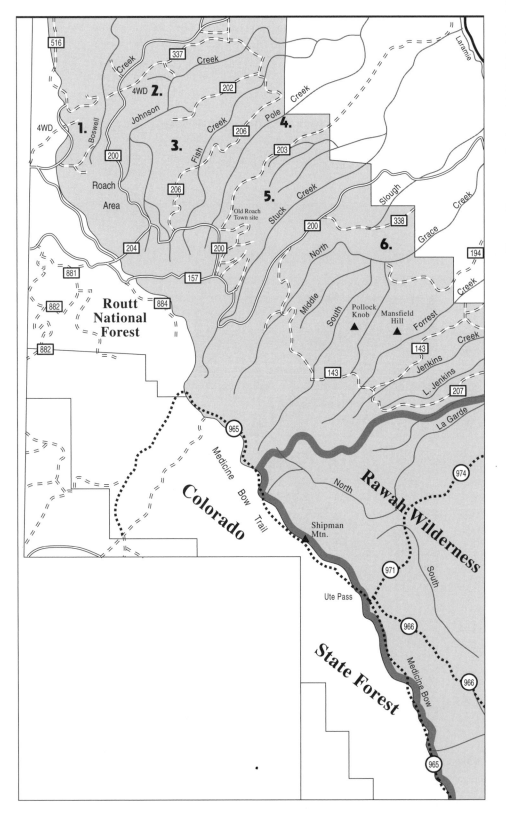

In the northwest corner of Arapaho/Roosevelt National Forest are several streams that empty into the Laramie River. These streams can be reached from Honholtz Lakes SWA on FDR 200. West from Hwy 103 past Honholtz Lakes to the forest boundary is approx. 6 miles.

1. Boswell Creek; Rated good for brook. From forest boundary follow FDR 200 for approx. 16 miles. Parts of road are 4WD.

2. Johnson Creek; Rated fair for brook and brown. From forest boundary follow FDR 200 for approx. 15 miles. Parts of road are 4WD.

3. Fish Creek; Rated excellent for brook. From forest boundary follow FDR 200 for approx. 10 miles to FDR 206 , south to where road crosses creek. Parts of road are 4WD. Some beaver ponds.

4. Pole Creek; Rated excellent for brook. From forest boundary follow FDR 200 for approx. 7.5 miles to FDR 203, follow FDR 203 north to creek and beaver ponds. Parts of road are 4WD.

5. Stuck Creek; Rated poor for small brook. Creek passes near Old Roach town site. Some beaver ponds.

6. Grace Creek; Rated poor for brook and small brown. To reach upper drainage Three miles west of forest boundary on FDR 200 turn south on FDR 143. Some beaver ponds.

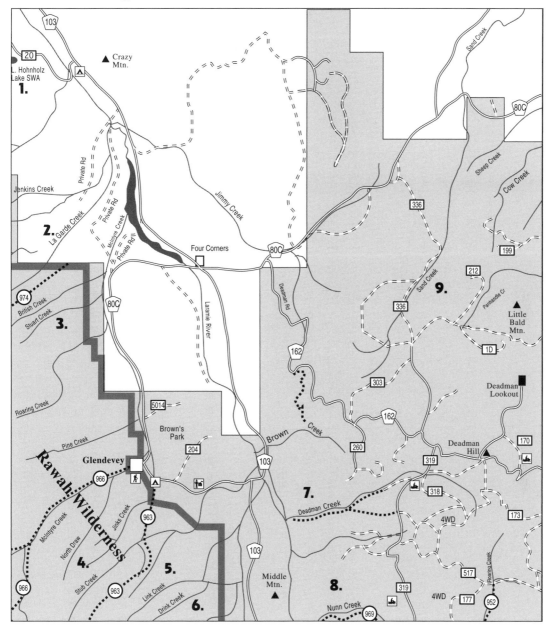

1. Hohnholz State Wildlife Area; Rated good for rainbow, brown and cutthroat. See page 91 for DOW information.

2. LaGarde Creek; Lower section is rated poor. Upper section and north and south forks are rated fair for brook. FDT 974 and FDT 966 (Link McIntyre) at Glendevey near Browns Park Campground lead to north and south forks and upper section of creek. Some beaver ponds. Upper section in Rawah Wilderness.

3. McIntyre Creek; Rated poor for brook. FDT 966 (Link McIntyre) at Glendevey near Browns Park Campground follows McIntyre Creek into Rawah Wilderness.

4, 5, 6. Drink, Stub and Link Creeks: Rated good for brook. From Browns Park Campground use FDT 963 into

Rawah Wilderness. Small fast streams.

7, 8. Nunn and Deadman Creeks; Rated good for brook. From Four Corners east on County road 80C 1.5 miles, south on county road 162 (Deadman Road) approx. 10 miles to FDR 319. South 2 miles to Deadman Creek, 5 miles to Nunn Creek. Nunn Creek parallels FDT 969 down to Hwy 103. Small fast streams. Lower sections of Deadman and Nunn Creeks on private property.

9. Sand Creek; Rated fair for brook and brown. From Four Corners east on County road 80C 1.5 miles, south on County Road 162 (Deadman Road) approx. 5 miles to FDR 303. East on FDR 303 to upper section. Several beaver ponds on creek.

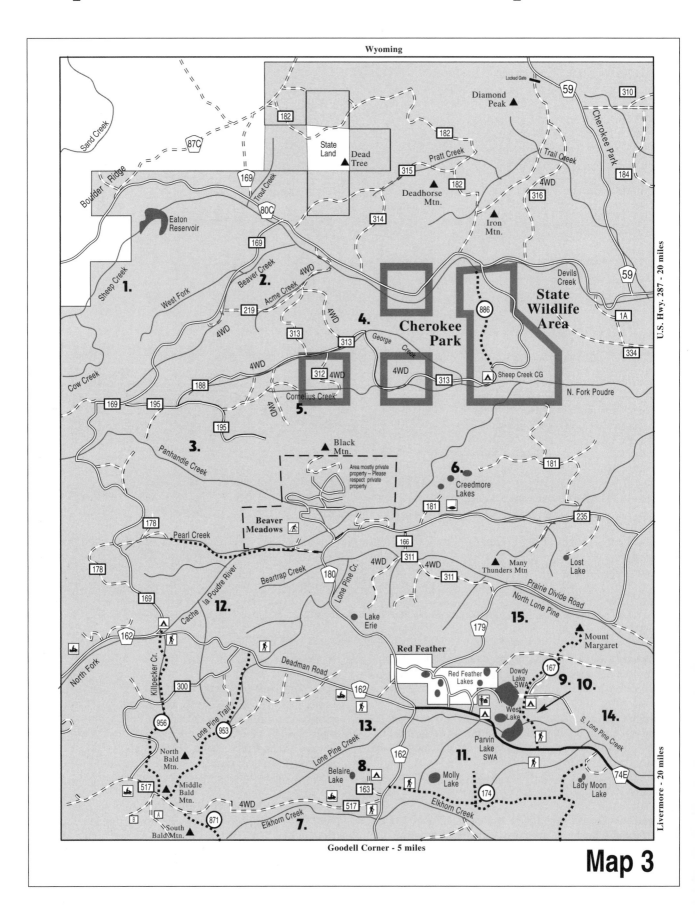

Wyoming

Locked Gate

Diamond Peak ▲

59
310

182

Sand Creek

87C

Boulder Ridge

Trout Creek

182

315

Pratt Creek

Deadhorse Mtn.

182

4WD

316

184

169

80C

314

Iron Mtn. ▲

59

State Land
Dead Tree ▲

Eaton Reservoir

169

Devils Creek

1A

886

State Wildlife Area

334

169

Sheep Creek

1.

West Fork

Beaver Creek

2.

Acme Creek

4WD

4.

Cherokee Park

Sheep Creek CG

N. Fork Poudre

219

4WD

313

George Creek

Cow Creek

313

4WD

4WD

313

188

312 4WD

169 195

Cornelius Creek

5.

195

Black Mtn. ▲

Area mostly private property -- Please respect private property

6.

Creedmore Lakes

181

3.

Panhandle Creek

181

235

178

Beaver Meadows

166

Lost Lake

Pearl Creek

311

4WD

Many Thunders Mtn ▲

178

Beartrap Creek

180

311

4WD

Prairie Divide Road

North Lone Pine

169

Cache la Poudre River

12.

Lone Pine Cr.

Lake Erie

179

15.

162

North Fork

Killpecker Cr.

Mount Margaret ▲

300

Lone Pine Trail

953

Deadman Road

162

Red Feather

Red Feather Lakes

Dowdy Lake SWA

167

9. 10.

956

13.

West Lake

S. Lone Pine Creek

14.

North Bald Mtn. ▲

Lone Pine Creek

Parvin Lake SWA

517

Middle Bald Mtn. ▲

Belaire Lake

8.

162

11.

Molly Lake

174

74E

Lady Moon Lake

B A

871

4WD

163

517

South Bald Mtn. ▲

Elkhorn Creek

7.

Elkhorn Creek

U.S. Hwy. 287 - 20 miles

Livermore - 20 miles

1. Sheep Creek; Rated fair for brook. From Eaton Reservoir (Closed to public) east Hwy 80C parallels the stream. Intermittent private/public ownership (Check forest service map) Stream flows into Cherokee Park State Wildlife Area. (See page 90 for DOW information.) Small stream with some beaver ponds.

2. Beaver Creek; Rated fair for brook. From Hwy 80C south on FDR 169. Road parallels stream. Intermittent private/public ownership (Check forest service map). Small stream with some beaver ponds.

3. Panhandle Creek; Rated fair for brook. To access upper section from Red Feather Lakes take Deadmans Road 8 miles to North Fork Poudre Campground. North on FDR 169. Check forest service map for access. Small fast stream.

4., 5. George and Cornelius Creeks; Rated good for cutthroat, brown and rainbow. See page 90 for DOW information on Cherokee Park SWA. South from Hwy 80C at Sheep Creek Road to Sheep Creek Camping area in Cherokee Park SWA. West on 4 WD road FDR 313. Catch and release, artificial lures and flies only.

6. Creedmore Lakes (8,300 ft; all three less than 10 ac); Rated good for brook and brown. Northeast of Beaver Meadows Area on County Road 180 approx. 2 miles to FDR 181, north 1 mile to lakes.

7. Elkhorn Creek; Rated fair for brook and brown. From Red Feather south on County Road 162, 2 miles to FDR 517. (Bald Mountain Trailhead). 4WD road or trail follows creek west. Only the upper end is open to fishing.

8. Bellaire Lake (8,600 ft; 11 ac); Rated good for rainbow. Two miles south from Red Feather on County Road 162 then west .5 mile. It is a put-and-take lake with Bellaire Campground located on south side lake.

9. West Lake (8,200 ft; 25 ac); Rated fair rainbow and brown. West Lake Campground on south shore; See page 91 for DOW information.

10. Dowdy Lake (8,133 ft; 115 ac); Rated good for rainbow, brook, brown and cutthroat. Dowdy Lake Campground on south shore. See page 91 for DOW information.

11. Parvin Lake (8,130 ft; 63 ac); Rated good for rainbow and brown. See page 91 for DOW information.

12. North Fork Cache Ia Poudre River; Rated good for brook and rainbow. The upper section can be reached from Red Feather on County Road 162 west to North Fork Poudre Campground. Much of lower section is posted. Narrow fast stream, catch and release, artificial lures and flies.

13. Lone Pine Creek; Rated good rainbow and brown.

County Road 162 south of Red Feather crosses creek just south of town. Check forest service map for public access. Creek flows southeast from Bald Mountain area. Much of lower section is posted.

14. South Fork of Lone Pine; Rated good for rainbow and brown. Short section of open stream near Parvin Lake. Much of stream is posted. Check forest service map for public access.

15. The North Fork of Lone Pine Creek; Rated good for rainbow and brown. Much of stream is posted. Check forest service map for public access.

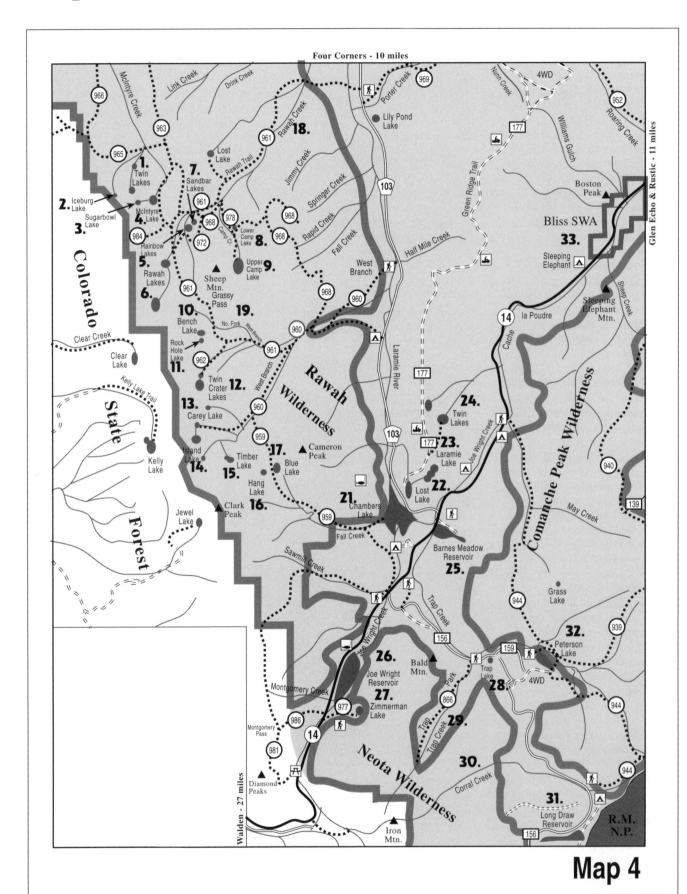

Map 4

Rawah Wilderness

Lake Numbers 1 through 18 are high lakes located in the Rawah Wilderness Area near the Continental Divide. There are 4 main access points to lakes: From Hwy 103 at Chambers Lake, FDT 959. Four miles north on Hwy 103 (Near Tunnel Campground) West Branch Trailhead, FDT 960; Four miles further north on Hwy 103 to Rawah Trailhead, FDT 961; Four miles further north on Hwy 103 to Stub Creek Road, west 2 miles to Browns Park Campground and Link McIntyre Trailhead, FDT 966. Map 4 scale is approx. 1/2 inch = 1 mile this will aid in determining distance to selected lake. Rawah Wilderness lakes are above 10,000 feet in elevation, this and heavy pressure contribute to unpredictable fishing. Most lakes contain cutthroat and brook; some are stocked with rainbow.

1. Twin Lakes (Upper, 10,600 ft; 9 ac) (Lower, 10,500 ft; 5 ac) Both are rated good for brook.

2. Iceberg Lake (11,100 ft; 6 ac); Rated good for brook.

3. Sugarbowl Lake (10,790ft; 8 ac); Rated fair for brook.

4. McIntyre Lake (10,200 ft; 14 ac); Rated fair for brook.

5. Rainbow Lakes (10,836 ft; 6 ac); Rated fair for brook and rainbow.

6. Rawah Lakes (#1 10,700 ft; 8 ac), (#2 10,750 ft; 8 ac) (#3 10,8590 ft; 25 ac) (#4 10,400 ft; 31 ac); Rated good for rainbow, brook and cutthroat.

7. Sandbar Lakes (Upper, 10,690 ft; 9 ac) (Middle, 10,600 ft; 1 ac), (Lower, 10,600 ft; 4 ac); Rated good for brook.

8. Lower Camp Lake (10,510 ft; 13 ac); Rated good for brook.

9. Upper Camp Lake (10,720 ft; 41 ac); Rated good for brook and cutthroat.

10. Bench Lake (10,950 ft; 6 ac); Rated good for cutthroat.

11. Rock Hole Lake (11,200 ft; 6 ac); Rated good for cutthroat.

12. Twin Crater Lakes (11,045 ft; 7 and 17 ac); Rated good for cutthroat.

13. Cary Lake 11,044ft; 6 ac); Rated fair for brook and cutthroat.

14. Island Lake (10,900 ft; 15 ac); Rated fair for brook and cutthroat.

15. Timber Lake (10,900; 10 ac); Rated fair for rainbow and cutthroat.

16. Hang Lake (11,160 ft; 4 ac); Rated good for cutthroat.

17. Blue Lake (10,720ft; 16 ac); Rated fair for cutthroat, rainbow and brook.

18. Rawah Creek; Rated Rated good for brook. From Rawah Trailhead at Hwy 103 FDT 961 follows stream to headwaters.

19. North Fork West Branch; Rated good for brook. FDT 960 to FDT 961 parallels stream from junction with West Branch Creek.

20 West Branch Creek; Rated good for brook. FDT 960 parallels stream from West Branch Trailhead at Hwy 103.

21. Chambers Lake (9,164 ft; 350 ac); Rated fair for rainbow, brown and kokanee. Located on Hwy 14 approx. 42 miles west of Fort Collins. Boatramp and campground.

22. Lost Lake (9,290 ft; 25.7 ac); Rated good for stocked rainbow. North of Chambers Lake on Hwy 103.

23. Laramie Lake (9,300 ft; 15 ac); Rated poor for rainbow. One mile north of Chambers Lake.

24. Twin Lakes East (9,450 ft; 21 ac),(West 15 ac); Rated fair for stocked rainbow. North from Lost Lake on FDR 177.

25. Barnes Meadow Reservoir (9,153 ft; 113 ac); Rated fair for rainbow and cutthroat. East of Chambers Lake on Hwy 14.

26. Joe Wright Reservoir (10,184 ft; 163 ac); Rated good for cutthroat and grayling. South of Chambers Lake 3 miles on Hwy 14. Special fishing regulations apply. Artificial flies and lures only.

27. Zimmerman Lake (10,495 ft; 11 ac); Grayling and cutthroat. On Hwy 14 south of Chambers Lake 5 miles, east on FDT 977 1/2 mile to lake.

28. Trap Lake (9960 ft; 13 ac); Rated fair for rainbow, cutthroat and brook. South of Chamber Lake 2 miles to Box Canyon Road. East on Box Canyon Road (FDR 156) 3 miles to lake. Special restrictions apply.

29. Trap Creek; Rated poor for cutthroat. From Trap Lake south on FDT 866 to headwaters.

30. Corral Creek; Rated poor for cutthroat. Corral Creek crosses FDR 156 near Long Draw Campground. Small stream with undergrowth.

31. Long Draw Reservoir (10,100 ft; 242 ac); Rated poor for cutthroat. From Hwy 14 east on FDR 156 approx. 8 miles. Long Draw Campground north of reservoir.

32. Peterson Lake (9,100 ft; 41 ac); Rated poor for cutthroat. From Hwy 14 to Trap Lake on FDR 156. East on FDR 159 to lake. No boats.

33. Bliss State Wildlife Area; Rated good for rainbow, brown, cutthroat, and white fish. Six miles of Poudre.See page 90 for DOW information.

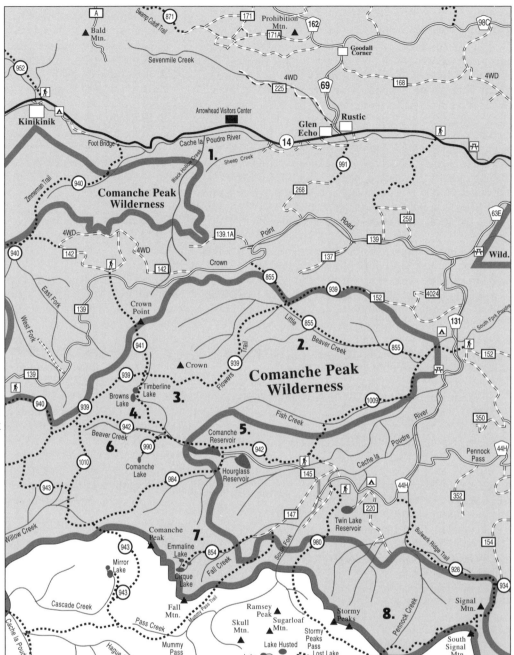

1. Sheep Creek,. Black Hollow Creek; Cutthroat. Enter Poudre near visitors center on Hwy 14. Special restrictions enforce. Check for access and regulation.

2. Little Beaver Creek; Rated poor for brown. South of Hwy 14 on Hwy 131 approx. 6 miles to Fish Creek Trailhead. Take trail 1 mile to FDT 855. Trail follows creek into wilderness.

3. Timberline Lake (10,500 ft; 4 ac); Rated poor for brook. Can be reach on the west from Browns Lake Trailhead (FDT 941) on FDR 139. From the east from Beaver Creek Trialhead (FDT 941) at Tom Bennett Campground.

4. Browns Lake (10,520 ft; 19 ac); Rated good for brook and cutthroat. Can be reach on the west from Browns Lake Trailhead (FDT 941) on FDR 139. Four mile hike.

5. Comanche Reservoir (9,400 ft; 20 ac); Rated fair for brook. From just south of Tom Bennett Campground take FDR 145 west to reservoir.

6. Beaver Creek; Rated fair for brook and cutthroat. Lower section is public land interspersed with private property. Above Comanche Reservoir Beaver Creek follows FDT 942 into Comanche Peak Wilderness.

7. Emmaline Lake (11,000 ft; 6 ac); Rated fair for cutthroat. From Tom Bennett Campground follow FDR 147 (4WD) south to roads end. Hike 3 miles on FDT 854 to reach lake. Nearby Cirque Lake may be barren. Fall Creek follows trail is rated fair for brown.

8. Pennock Creek; Rated fair for cutthroat and brown. Two mile east of Tom Bennett Campground on Hwy 13 to FDT 928. Trail follows creek to wilderness boundary.

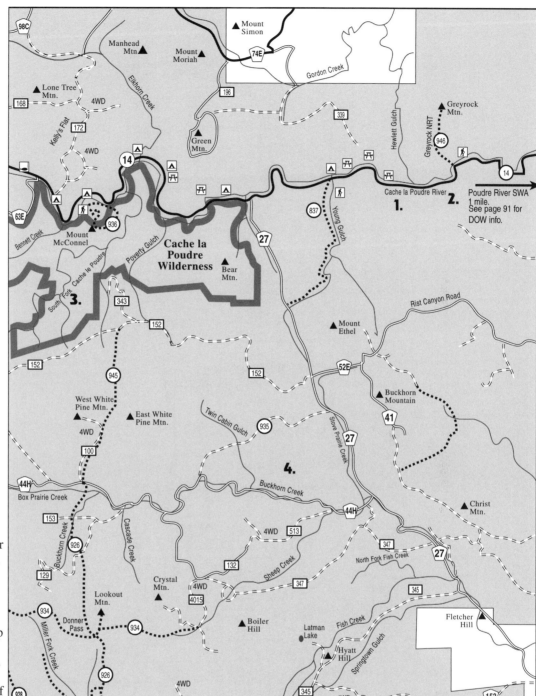

1. Cache le Poudre River; Rated good for rainbow, brown and a few cutthroat. The headwaters of the Poudre start in lakes that surround Chambers Lake. (Map 4) and parallels Hwy 14 to forest boundary. The Poudre is shown on maps 4, 5, and 6 of this section. Most of the river is open and accessible to the public. The river has been designated a wild and scenic river.
Stretches of the river are restricted to artificial flies and lures only.

2. Poudre River State Wildlife Area; Rated good for rainbow, brown, cutthroat and white fish. See page 91 for DOW information.

3. South Fork Cache la Podre River; Rated good for brown and rainbow. Appro. 8 miles east of Rustic on Hwy 14 the South Fork enters the Poudre River. The lower South is in the Cache le Poudre Wilderness, no designated trail follows the river into the wilderness. The upper section (Map 5) can be accessed FDR 131 (62E) north from just west of Kelly Flats Campground on Hwy 14. Upper section intermittent public/private property.

4. Buckhorn Creek; rated fair for brook. South of Hwy 14 on Hwy 27 approx. 10 miles to FDR 44H. Road parallels stream. Intermittent public/private property.

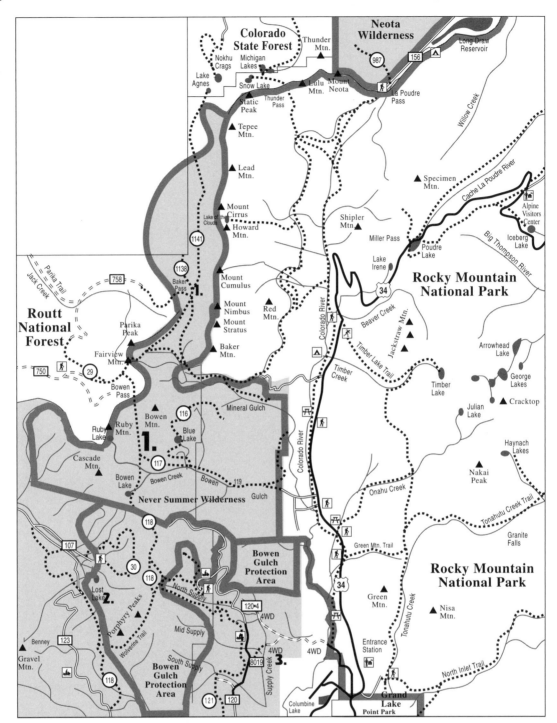

1. Bowen Lake (11,000 ft; 10 ac) Blue Lake (10,650 ft; 5 ac); Both are rated fair for cutthroat. West from Granby on Hwy 50, 3 miles to Hwy 125. North on Hwy 125 approx. 20 miles to FDR 107/123 (Stillwater Pass Road). East on FDR 107 approx. 5 miles to fork, left at fork (FDR 107), east 1.5 miles to Lost Lake Trailhead. (FDT 30). FDT 30 east 2 miles to FDT 118, north on FDT 118 (Wolverine Trail) to Bowen and Blue Lakes, they are located near the Continental Divide in Never Summer Wilderness. From Bowen Lake **Bowen Creek** follows FDT 117 into Rocky Mountain National Park. Small fast stream with under brush.

2. Lost Lake: (9,662 ft; 5 ac); Rated fair for cutthroat. West from Granby on Hwy 50 3 miles to Hwy 125. North on Hwy 125 approx. 20 miles to FDR 107/123 (Stillwater Pass Road). East on FDR 107 approx. 5 miles to fork, left at fork (FDR 107), east 1.5 miles to Lost Lake Trailhead 0.5 mile to lake.

3. Supply Creek; Rated poor for brook. FDR 120 north from Arapaho National Recreation Area crosses Supply Creek and three branches of Supply Creek.

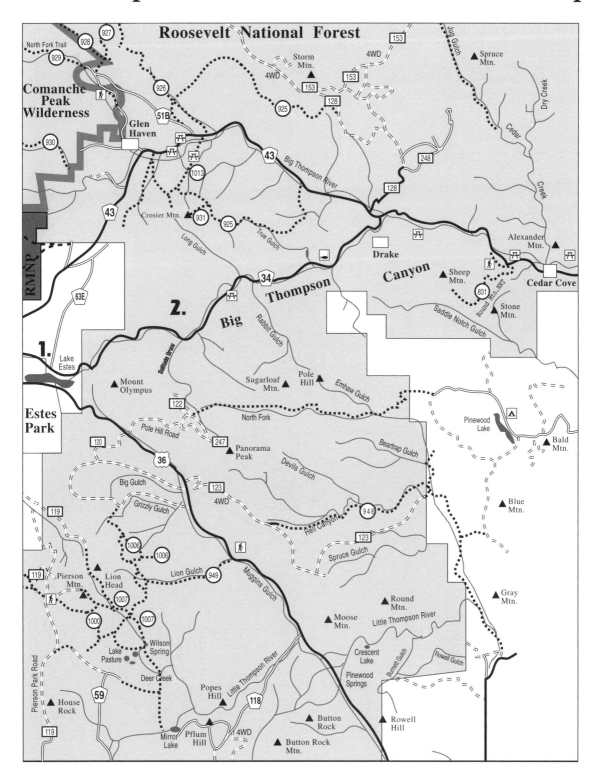

1. Lake Estes (7,475 ft; 185 ac); and St. Marys Lake (8,050 ft; 42 ac); Rated fair for stocked rainbow. Both lakes are near Estes Park. Both are heavily fished lakes with some restrictions.

2. Big Thompson River; Rated fair for rainbow and brown. Follows Hwy 34 through Big Thompson Canyon. Intermittent public and private land to Narrows Park, lower section is posted. Some restrictions apply.

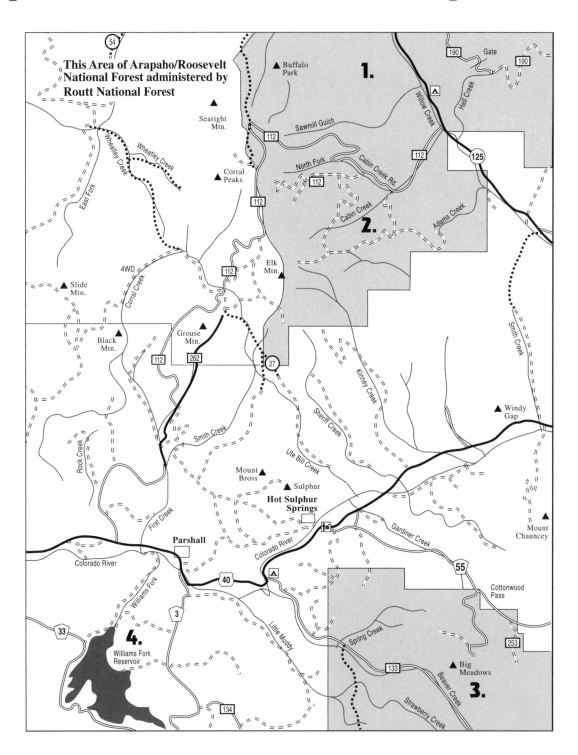

1. Willow Creek; Rated fair for rainbow and brook. From Hwy 50 at Windy Gap north on Hwy 125 11 miles to forest boundary. Willow Creek follows stream.

2. Cabin Creek; Rated fair for rainbow and brook. From Hwy 50 at Windy Gap north on Hwy 125 for approx. 12 miles to FDR 112. East on FDR 112. Road follows creek.

3. Beaver Creek; Rated fair for brook. From Hwy 40 southeast on FDR 133 (Beaver Creek Road). Road parallels stream.

4. Williams Fork Reservoir (7, 811 ft; 1,810 ac); Rated good for rainbow, kokanee, northern pike. East of Kremmling on Hwy 40 6 miles, south on FDR 33 6 miles to reservoir. Campground and boatramps. Managed by the Denver Water Board.

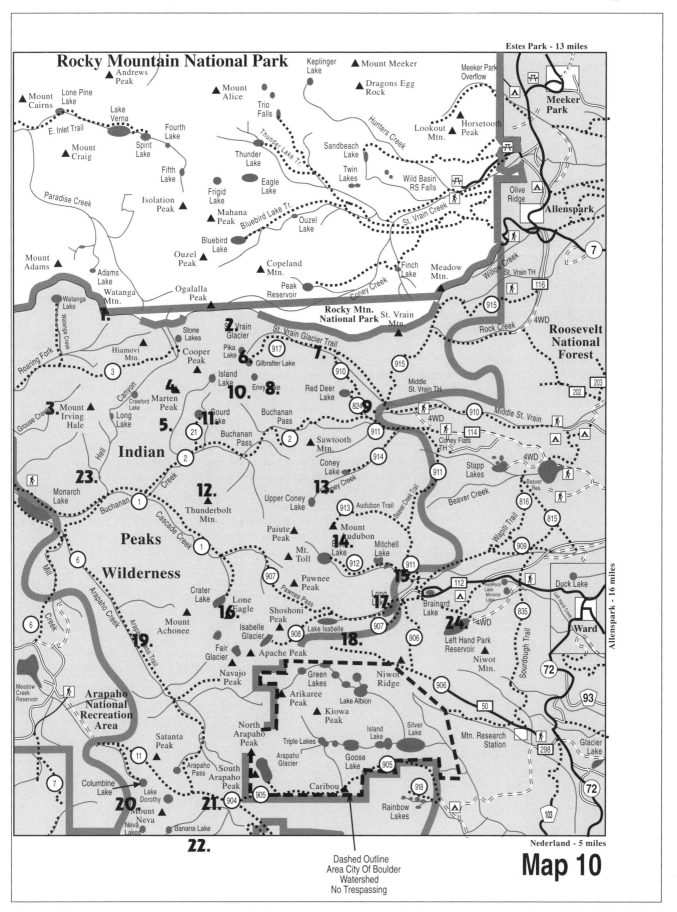

Map 10

Indian Peaks Wilderness

Numbers 1 through 22 are high lakes and streams located in the Indian Peaks Wilderness Area located south of Rocky Mountain National Park. The main access points for Indian Peaks on the east are Brainard Lake west of Ward, Middle St.Vrain Trailhead west of Peaceful Valley and on the south on Fourth of July Trailhead west of Nederland. On the west Arapaho Bay and Monarch Lake Trailheads on the southeast arm of Lake Granby. Junco Lake Trailhead east of Meadow Creek reservoir.

Map scale is approx. 1/2 inch = 1 mile this will aid in determining distance to selected lake. Indian Peaks Wilderness lakes are above 10,000 feet in elevation, this and heavy pressure contribute to unpredictable fishing. Most lakes contain cutthroat and brook, some are stocked with rainbow. Be certain of your physical condition before hiking to high lakes. Wilderness areas steep climbs and high elevation require that you be in good physical condition.

1. Watanga Lake (10,800 ft; 3 ac); Rated good for cutthroat. Steep trail follows Watanga Creek from FDT 3 (Roaring Fork Trail).

2. Stone Lakes (10,683 ft; 7 ac) Upper (10,750 ft; 8 ac); Rated good for cutthroat. Upper end of FDT 3 (Roaring Fork Trail).

3. Grouse Creek; Rated poor for cutthroat.

4., 5. Crawford Lake (10,110 ft; 7 ac), Long Lake (9,950 ft; 6 ac); Rated fair for cutthroat and rainbow. From Monarch Lake take FDT 1 east to Hells Creek. Follow Hells Creek up rough steep trail up to Crawford and Long Lakes.

6. Pika Lake (11,140 ft; 2 ac); Rated fair for cutthroat. From Middle St. Vrain Trailhead take FDT 917 west to lake.

7. Gilbralter Lake; Rated fair for cutthroat. From Middle St. Vrain Trailhead take FDT 917 west to lake.

8. Envy Lake; Rated fair for cutthroat. From Middle St. Vrain Trailhead take FDT 917 west to lake.

9. Red Deer Lake (10,700 ft; 16 ac); Rated fair for brook, rainbow and cutthroat. From Coney Flats Trailhead west on FDT 911 to lake.

10., 11. Island Lake (11,500 ft; 16 ac), Gourd Lake (10, 850 ft; 15 ac); Rated fair for cutthroat. From FDT 2 north on FDT 21. Steep rough trail.

12. Buchanan Creek; Rated fair for cutthroat. Follows FDT 1 from Monarch Lake to junction with FDT 2. FDT 2 follows stream.

13. Coney Lake (10,600 ft; 9ac), Coney Lake, Upper (10,940 ft;10 ac); Rated good for cutthroat. From Coney Flats Trailhead west on FDT 914 to lakes.

14. Blue Lake (11,320 ft; 16 ac); Rated fair cutthroat. From Brainard Lake take FDT 912 to lake.

15. Mitchell Lake, (10,700 ft; 4ac); Upper Mitchell Lake (10,800 ft; 14 ac); Rated fair for brook and cutthroat. From Brainard Lake take FDT 912 to lake.

16. Crater Lake (10,400 ft; 10 ac); Rated fair for brook and cutthroat. Follow cascade creek up on FDT 1.

17. Long Lake (10,500 ft; 45 ac); Rated fair to good for rainbow and cutthroat. Short hike up from Brainard Lake. Artificial flies and lures only. Bag and possession limit two fish.

18. Lake Isabelle (10,852 ft; 30 ac); Rated fair to good for rainbow and cutthroat. Short hike up from Long Lake. Artificial flies and lures only. Bag and possession limit two fish.

19. Arapaho Creek; (Rated fair for brook, rainbow and cutthroat. From Monarch Lake FDT follows stream.

20. Columbine Lake (11,000 ft; 6 ac); Rated fair for cutthroat) From Meadow Creek Reservoir in Arapaho National Recreation Area take trail southeast to lake.

21. Lake Dorothy (12,100 ft; 16 ac); Rated good for cutthroat. From Junco Lake Trailhead (FDT 11) east to lake or Forth of July Trailhead (FDT 904) west to lake.

22. Banana Lake (11,320 ft; 2ac); Rated good for cutthroat. From Junco Lake Trailhead (FDT 11) east to lake or Forth of July Trailhead (FDT 904) west to lake.

23. Monarch Lake; Rated fair for brook. See Arapaho National Recreation Area page 99.

24. Brainard Lake (10,350 ft; 15 ac); Rated fair for stocked rainbow, brown and brook. West from Ward on FDR 112. Lots of pressure because of easy access and nearby trailheads.

Eaglesnest Widerness Area
Map Numbers 1 through 9 are high lakes and located in the Eagles Nest Wilderness Area located in Summit County. The main access point on the north is Cataract Creek Trailhead south of Green Mountain Reservoir on FDR 1725 (203).

Most Eagles Wilderness lakes are above 10,000 feet in elevation, this and heavy pressure contribute to unpredictable fishing.

Be certain of your physical condition before hiking to high lakes. Wilderness areas steep climbs and high elevation require that you be in good physical condition. Mount Powell and Piney Peak 7 1/2 minute USGS topographic quads cover map 11.

1. Lower Cataract Lake (8,630 ft; 60 ac); Rated good for brook, brown, cutthroat. Located near trailhead. **Cataract Creek** is rated good for brook and cutthroat.

2. Upper Cataract Lake (10,700 ft; 40 ac); Rated good for cutthroat. From Cataract Creek Trailhead use FDT 61 to FDT 60 (Gore Range Trail) to the junction of FDT 63, follow trail to lake.

3. Tipperary Lake (9,750 ft; 10 ac); Rated fair for rainbow. From Cataract Creek Trailhead use FDT 61 to FDT 60 (Gore Range Trail) to lake.

4. Eaglesmere Lakes, Upper (10,700 ft; 40 ac), Lower (8,650 ft; 55 ac); Rated fair for brook, brown and cutthroat. From Cataract Creek Trailhead use FDT 61 to FDT 60 (Gore Range Trail) to lake.

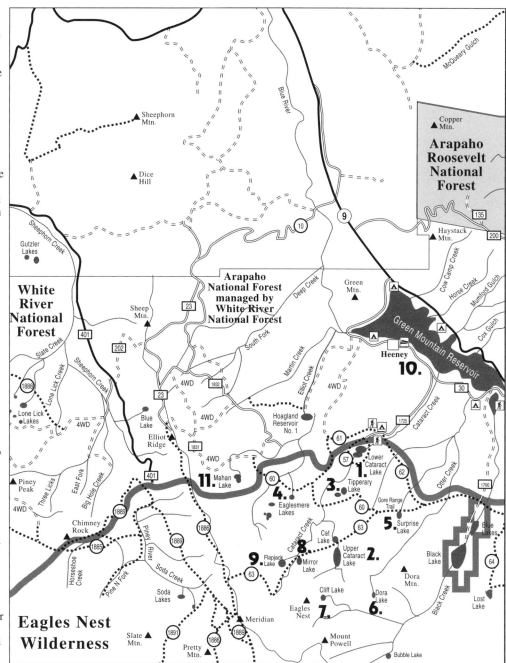

5. Surprise Lake (10,100 ft; 8 ac); Rated fair for brook and cutthroat. From Cataract Creek Trailhead use FDT 62 (Surprise Trail) to lake.

6. Dora Lake (12,225 ft; 12 ac); Rated good for cutthroat. From Cataract Creek Trailhead use FDT 62 (Surprise Trail) to FDT 63 to Upper Cataract Lake. No designated trail and difficult to reach.

7. Cliff Lake (10,740 ft; 3 ac); Rated fair for cutthroat. From Cataract Creek Trailhead use FDT 61 to FDT 60 (Gore Range Trail) to the junction of FDT 63, follow trail to lake. No designated trail to lake.

8. Mirror Lake (10,550 ft; 5 ac); Rated poor for cutthroat. One mile west of Upper Cataract Lake on FDT 63.

9. Flapjack Lakes (10,750 ft; 3 lakes 3, 2, & 10ac); Rated fair for cutthroat. .5 mile from Mirror Lake.

10. Green Mountain Reservoir (8,000 ft; 2,215 ac); Rated good for rainbow, brown and kokanee. From Dillon exit on I-70 north on Highway 9 to reservoir. Boat ramps and six campgrounds. The land surrounding reservoir is treeless.

11. Mahan Lake (10,814 ft; 8.2 ac); Rated fair for stocked brook. North from Green Mountain Reservoir to Spring Creek Road (10) Follow road to reservoir.

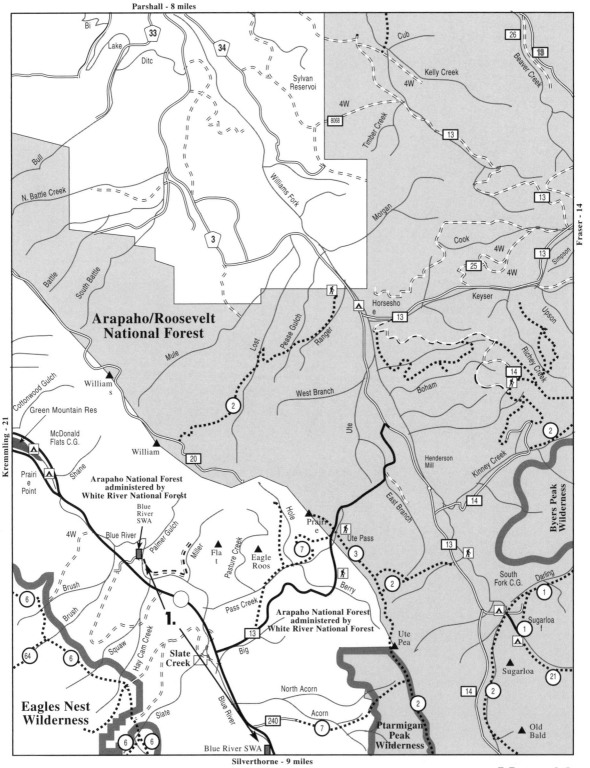

Map 12

1. **Blue River SWA;** Rated good for rainbow and brown. Three Units; **1.** Blue River 17 miles north of Silverthorne on Hwy 9. **2.** Eaglesnest Unit 9 miles north of Silverthorne on Hwy 9. **3.** Sutton Unit 7 miles miles north of Silverthorne on Hwy 9. See page 95 for DOW information.

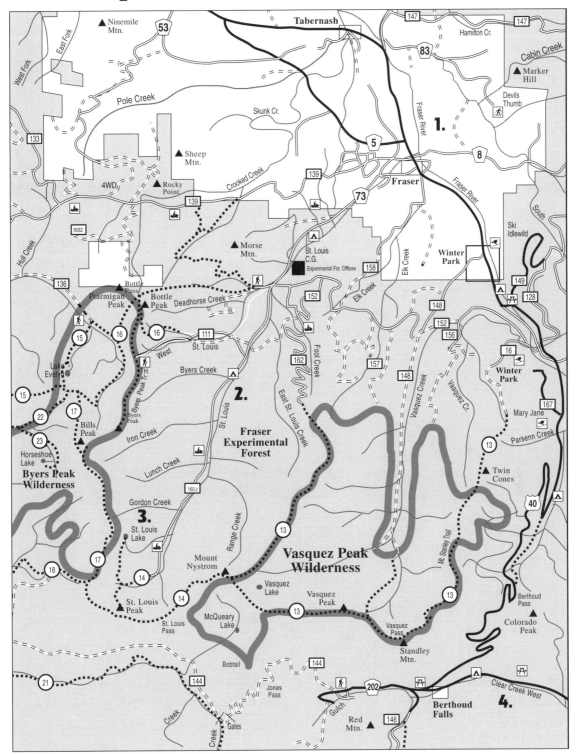

1. Frazer River; Rated good for brown and rainbow. River parallels Hwy 40. River runs through mostly private property.

2. St. Louis Creek; Rated good for cutthroat and rainbow. South on Hwy 73 to forest boundary, continue on FDR 1602 which parallels stream.

3. St. Louis Lake (11,531 ft; 3.2 ac); Rated fair for cutthroat. Follow FDR 1602 to end of road. Use FDT 14 to reach lake.

4. West Fork Clear Creek; Rated poor for brook. Follows Hwy 40 from Berthoud Falls.

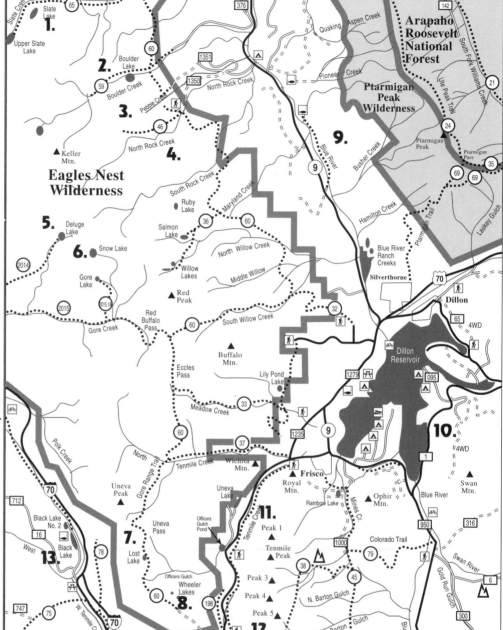

1. Slate Lakes (9,800 ft; 20 ac) (Upper 11,000 ft; 15 ac); Rated good for rainbow, brook and cutthroat. West from FDT 60 on FDT 65. Trail follows Slate Creek up to Lake.

2. Boulder Lakes (5 stocked lakes. El. 10,984 to 11,900 ft; 1.4 to 14 ac) and Boulder Creek; Rated fair for cutthroat and brook. West from FDR 376 to FDT 59. Trail follows creek.

3. , 4. Peeble Creek, North and South Rock Creeks; Rated fair for brook. From Blue River Campground west on FDR 1351 (4WD in part) to trailhead.

5. Deluge Lake (11,740 ft; 5.0 ac) Rated fair for cutthroat. Six mile east of Vail off I-70 at Gore Creek Campground. Take FDT 2014 east to lake.

6. Gore Lakes (11,975 ft; 3.0 ac); Rated fair for cutthroat. Six mile east of Vail off I-70 at Gore Creek Campground. That FDT 2015 that follows Gore Creek to FDT 2015-1A north to lake.

7. Lost Lake (11,600 ft; 2 ac); Rated fair for cutthroat and brook. From I-70 at Copper Mountain take FDT 60 (Gore Range Trail) approx. 3 miles to lake.

8. Wheeler Lakes (11,050 ft; 6.0 ac); Rated fair for cutthroat. From I-70 at Copper Mountain take FDT 60 (Gore Range Trail) approx. 2 miles to lake.

9. Blue River; Rated fair for brown, rainbow and cutthroat. River parallels Hwy 9 from above Breckenridge to Green Mountain Reservoir. Gold Medal Waters, artificial flies and lures only. Intermittent private and public ownership. Three State Wildlife Areas on Blue River north of Silverthorne.

10. Dillon Reservoir (9,000 ft; 3200 ac); Rated fair for brown, rainbow and kokanee. Located south of the town Dillon. Campgrounds, boatramps and full service marinas.

11. Ten Mile Creek; Rated fair for stocked rainbow. Stream flows down from Vail Pass following I-70 and parallels paved trail to Frisco.

12. Copper Mountain Pond (9,670 ft; 6 ac); Rated fair for stocked brook. I-70 and Copper Mountain.

13. Black Lakes (Upper 10,470 ft; 15 ac, Lower 10,400 ft; 12.5 ac); Rated fair for stocked rainbow. Near Vail Pass on I-70.

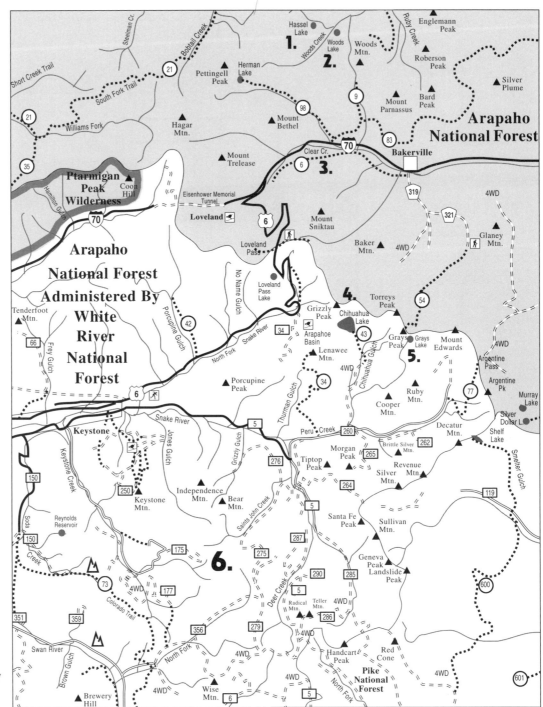

1. Hassel Lake (11,400 ft; 9 ac); Rated fair for brook and rainbow. From Empire west on Hwy 40 six miles to Big Bend south on FDR 146 to Woods Lake. Short hike to lake.

2. Woods Lake (10,700 ft; 31 ac); Rated fair for rainbow and brook. From Empire west on Hwy 40 six miles to Big Bend south on FDR 146 to Woods Lake. The lake is part of Henderson Mine property.

3. Clear Creek; Rated fair for rainbow. Follows I-70 down from Eisenhower/Johnson Tunnels.

4. Chihuahua Lake (12,200 ft; 10 ac); Rated fair for cutthroat. From FDR 260 north on 4WD road 4 miles to FDT

43 approx. 1.5 mile hike to lake.

5. Grays Lake (12,500 ft; 2 ac); Rated poor for brook and cutthroat. From Bakersville south on FDR 321 approx. 3 miles to Grays Peak Trailhead. Take FDT 54 to end of trail. Refer to 7 1/2 minute USGS topographic map Grays Peak.

6. Keystone Creek, Deer Creek, Peru Creek, Snake River and the other drainage in the area are rated poor for brook and rainbow. Pollution, development and posted areas adversely influence the fishing. Check with a "local" for fishing information.

Grand Mesa

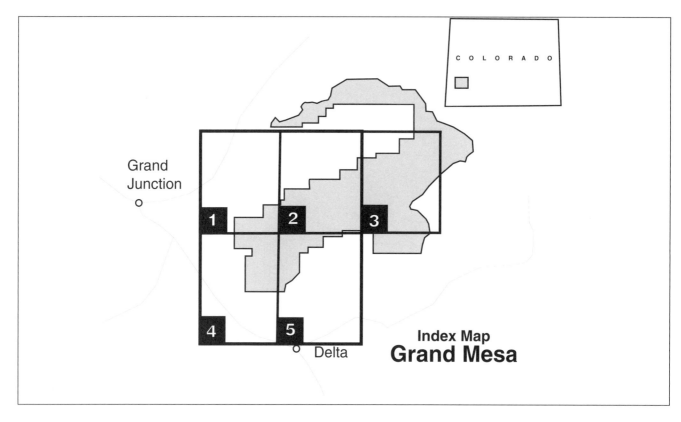

Grand Junction

Delta

Index Map
Grand Mesa

COLORADO

FISHING THE GRAND MESA
COLORADO DIVISON OF WILDLIFE

Spanish explorers named the Grand Mesa "Mesa Grande," which means large table. While not officially recognized as such, the Grand Mesa is regionally known as the World's Largest Flat Top Mountain.

The Grand Mesa is in fact a very large, flat-topped mountain of volcanic origin whose summit area covers some 800 square miles. The Grand Mesa averages 10,000 feet in elevation and towers 6,000 feet above the surrounding Colorado and Gunnison River valleys.

In addition to its geological notoriety, the Grand Mesa is well known for its numerous natural lakes. In all, some 300 lakes and reservoirs lie on the benches and top of the Grand Mesa. Of these, roughly a third provide the aquatic habitat needed to sustain trout populations on a year-round basis.

Volcanic activity produced lava whose flows formed the massive Y-shaped basalt cap with the tail to the east. Pleistocene glaciers caused a weathering process known as "slumping" whereby lava blocks from the margin of the Grand Mesa's cap slid down the mountainside to produce broad landslide benches.

It is these slim benches, primarily along the tail of the Y-shaped cap, which have been dammed to create reservoirs. The reservoirs on these benches of the Grand Mesa hold and grow the trout so eagerly sought by anglers.

The Grand Mesa offers fishing opportunities for seven species of trout including rainbows, Colorado River cut-

throat, Snake River cutthroat, brown, and brook trout, as well as splake (hybrid between lake and brook trout), and Arctic grayling. This fishing guide lists 100 lakes and 25 streams, which are monitored or managed by the Colorado Division of Wildlife.

Almost all of the lakes and streams listed lie between 8,000 and 11,000 feet in elevation. Keep in mind your physical abilities as you recreate at these elevations. This altitude combined with strenuous activity can aggravate or trigger health problems.

The climate at these elevations can change drastically as storms come and go. Near freezing temperatures, even in the middle of the summer, can result following a small thunderstorm in Colorado's high country. Be prepared by taking a jacket along, even if you are only going to fish the other side of the lake.

Nowhere else in Colorado boasts so many diverse trout fishing options situated so closely together. These options include various combinations of trout species in the different lakes, along with access ranging from roads suitable for four-wheel drive or motor homes, to trails accessible by foot and horseback only. All of these opportunities are located within an hour drive of the conveniences offered by the larger towns of Grand Junction and Delta and all of the smaller towns in between.

Welcome to the Grand Mesa! We hope that you find the time to enjoy the many recreational opportunities that can be part of your fishing trip in this incredibly scenic part of western Colorado.

MAP 1

KANNAH CREEK BASIN AREA...................147

MAP 2

NAME   PAGE
MESA LAKES AREA
Jumbo Reservoir 127
Sunset Lake 127
Beaver Lake 127
Glacier Springs Lake 127
Mesa Lake 127
Mesa Lake, South 127
Lost Lake 127
Waterdog Reservoir 127
Mesa Creek 127

BULL BASIN AREA
Griffith Lake #1 128
Griffith Lake, Middle 128
Bull Creek Reservoir #1 128
Bull Creek Reservoir #2 128
Bull Creek Reservoir #5 128
Bull Creek 128

ISLAND LAKE AREA
Island Lake 129
Little Gem Reservoir 129
Rim Rock Lake 129

WARD LAKE AREA
Carp Lake 129
Ward Lake 129
Alexander Lake 129
Hotel Twin Lake 130
Baron Lake 130
Deep Slough Reservoir 130
Sheep Slough Reservoir (Sheep Lake) 130
Ward Creek Reservoir 130
Ward Creek 130

EGGLESTON LAKE AREA
Eggleston Lake 131
Reed Reservoir 131
Kiser Slough Reservoir 131
Youngs Creek Reservoir #1 131
Youngs Creek Reservoir #2 131
Youngs Creek Reservoir #3 131
Pedro Reservoir 132
Kiser Creek 132
Little Grouse Reservoir 132
Stell Lake 132
Kiser Creek 132
Youngs Creek 132

CRAG CREST TRAIL AREA
Forrest Lake 123
Eggleston Lake, Upper (Little) 133
Buffs Lake 133

TRICKLE PARK AREA
Military Park Reservoir 133
Stell Lake, East 133
Park Reservoir 133
Vela Reservoir 134
Elk Park Reservoir 134
Knox Reservoir 134
Trout Lake 134

COTTONWOOD LAKES AREA
Silver Lake 134
Forty-Acre Lake 134
Neversweat Reservoir 134
Kitson Reservoir 135
Cottonwood Reservoir #1 135
Cottonwood Reservoir #4 135
Lily Lake 135
Decamp Feservoir 135
Big Meadows Reservoir 135
Cottonwood Reservoir #5 135
Cottonwood Creek 135

BONHAM RESERVOIR AREA
Bonham Reservoir 136
Big Creek Reservoir #1 136
Atkinson Reservoir 136
Atkiinson Creek 136
Big Creek 136

MAP 3

BONITA RESERVOIR AREA
Cedar Mesa Reservoir 139
Bonita Reservoir 139
Trio Reservoir 139
Bonita Creek 139

WEIR & JOHNSON RESERVOR AREA
Twin Lake #1 140
Twin Lake #2 140
Sackett Reservoir 140
Weir and Johnson Reservoir 140
Leon Peak Reservoir (Sissie Lake) 140
Finney Cut Lake #1 140
Finney Cut Lake #2 140
Cole Reservoir #1 141
The Pecks Reservoir #1 141
The Pecks Reservoir #2 141

LEON CREEK AREA
Rock Lake 141
Youngs Lake 141
Kenney Creek Res. (Kendall Res.) 141
Lost Lake 142
Kenney Creek 142
Monument Reservoir #1 142
Colby Horse Park Reservoir 142
Leon Lake 142
Lanning Lake 142
Hunter Reservoir 142
Leon Creek 143
Leon Creek, East 143
Leon Creek, Middle 143
Marcott Creek 143
Monument Creek 143
Park Creek 143

LEROUX CREEK AREA
Doughty Reservoir................................144
Hanson Reservoir 144
Dogfish Reservoir 144
Goodenough Reservoir 144
Doughty Creek 144
Leroux Creek, East 144
Leroux Creek, West 144

BUZZARD CREEK AREA
Buzzard Creek 145
Owens Creek 145
Willow Creek 145

MAP 4

KANNAH CREEK BASIN AREA
Carson Lake......................................147
Blue Lake 147
Kanah Creek 147
Sheep Creek......................................147

MAP 5

THE DOUGHSPOONS AREA
Doughspoon Res. #1 (Delta Res. #1) 148
Doughspoon Res. #2 (Delta Res. #2) 148
Dugger Reservoir 148
Morris Reservoir 148
Porter Reservoir #1 & #4 (Little Davies) 148

THE GRANBYS AREA
Granby Reservoir #1 148
Granby Reservoir #2 148
Granby Reservoirs #4, 5,10, 11 149
Granby Reservoir #12 149
Granby Reservoir #7 149
Big Battlement Reservoir 149
Little Battlement Reservoir 149
Clear Lake 149
Dirty George Creek 149

BOATING
Regulations, boatramps and information 137

HOW TO USE THIS SECTION

Grand Mesa area has been divided into five mapped areas. Each mapped area is divided into a named geographical area, (LEON CREEK AREA, etc.). The area is outlined and named on the map. Lakes and streams within each area are located and described in text. (Lost Lake, etc.).

INFORMATION

Fish stocking, catch limits, regulations and boat facilities vary from year to year. Before planning your trip contact a Colorado Division of Wildlife or a Grand Mesa National Forest Office.

It is your responsibilty to understand and obey all state and federal fishing and boating regulations on the Grand Mesa.

Colorado Division of Wildlife:
Grand Junction 970-255-6100
Montrose...........................970-252-6000
Denver 303-297-1192
Grand Mesa National Forest:
Collbran Ranger District ....(970) 487-3534
Grand Junction Ranger District ....(970) 242-8211

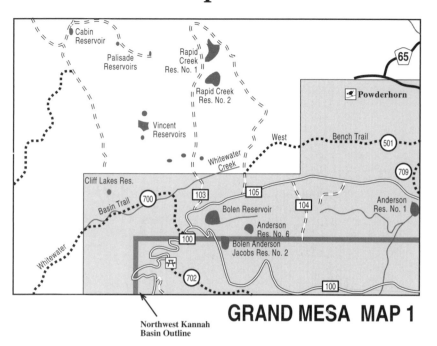

GRAND MESA MAP 1

Northwest Kannah
Basin Outline

Kannah Creek Basin Area is described on page 147

Grand Mesa text in this guide was compiled from "Fishing the Grand Mesa" published by the Colorado Division of Wildlife.

A large scale detailed map of each area in this section are shown in "Fishing the Grand Mesa".

To purchase a copy of "Fishing the Grand Mesa" contact the Colorado Division of Wildlife:
Grand Junction..............970-255-6100
Montrose 970-252-6000
Denver 303-297-1192

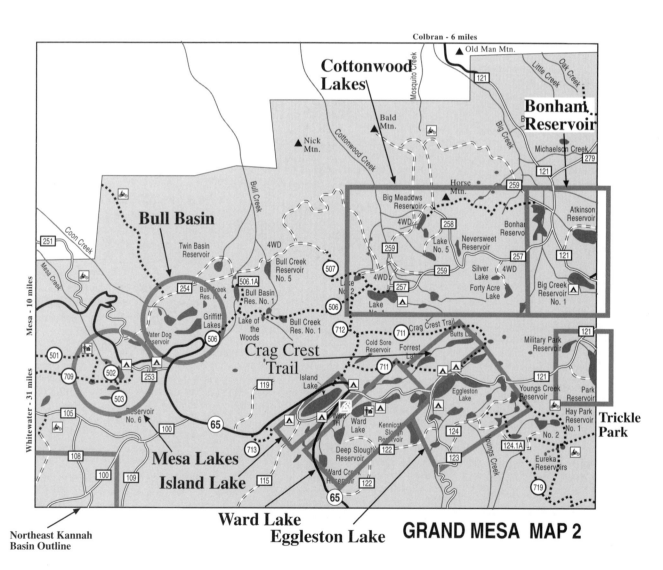

GRAND MESA MAP 2

Northeast Kannah
Basin Outline

Ward Lake
Eggleston Lake

Map 2 - Mesa Lakes Area

MESA LAKES AREA

Convenient access off Highway 65 makes this area a very popular destination spot. From Mesa, travel south on Highway 65 13.6 miles to Jumbo Reservoir. Several developed campgrounds, picnic sites.

The Mesa Lakes area includes eight reservoirs, most of which receive very heavy fishing pressure. This area offers drive-to lakes, stream fishing, a handicap fishing pier on Jumbo Reservoir, and hike-in lakes, Lost and South Mesa, within 1 mile of the campground. The drive-to lakes heavily stocked with catchable rainbow trout occasionally produce lunker specimens. The hike-in lakes, accessed by a very good trail winding through the forest, offer fishing for brook trout.

JUMBO RESERVOIR

Access: From Mesa, travel south on Highway 65 13.6 miles to Jumbo Reservoir. A paved parking area is located right along the highway. To reach the campground turn right just past the lake and then turn at the first right into the campground area.
Size, Depth, and Elevation: 6.8 acres, 6 feet deep, and 9,880 feet.
Fish: Rainbow and brook trout. Catchable rainbow trout are stocked annually, several times throughout the spring and summer.
Agency: U.S. Forest Service.
Comments: This reservoir has a handicap fishing area along the paved parking lot on the east shore. Fishing pressure is heavy due to the easy access and local popularity of this lake. Campgrounds, picnic tables, restrooms, and a small store are available nearby.
Special Regulations: Motorized watercraft of any kind are prohibited.

SUNSET LAKE

Access: Just past Jumbo Reservoir turn right and follow this paved road directly to the lake. To reach the dam take the right fork and follow the road alongside the lake 0.4 mile to the dam.
Size, Depth, and Elevation: 18 acres, 22 feet deep, and 9,790 feet.
Fish: Rainbow, brown and brook trout, and white suckers. Catchable rainbow trout are stocked annually, several times throughout the spring and summer.
Agency: Mesa Lakes Reservoir and Ditch Company.
Comments: Fishing pressure is heavy due to the easy access and local popularity of this lake. Campgrounds, picnic tables, restrooms, and a small store are available nearby.
Special Regulations: None.

BEAVER LAKE

Access: Just past Jumbo Reservoir turn right and follow this paved road directly to Mesa Lakes Lodge. Beaver Lake is directly southeast across the road from the Mesa Lakes Lodge.
Size, Depth, and Elevation: 6.5 acres, 9 feet deep, and 9,820 feet.
Fish: Rainbow, brown, and brook trout. Subcatchable rainbow trout are stocked annually.
Agency: Mesa Creek Reservoir and Canal Company. Colorado Division of Wildlife owns the dam on this reservoir.
Comments: Fishing pressure is heavy due to the easy access and local popularity of this lake. Campgrounds, picnic tables, restrooms, and a small store are available nearby.
Special Regulations: Motorized watercraft of any kind are prohibited.

GLACIER SPRINGS LAKE

Access: Just past Jumbo Reservoir turn right and follow this paved road, passing the Mesa Lakes Lodge, to Sunset Lake. Turn left and travel 0.1 mile, passing Beaver Lake to the Glacier Springs Lake.
Size, Depth, and Elevation: 3 acres, 8 feet deep, and 9,830 feet.
Fish: Rainbow, Colorado River cutthroat, and brook trout. catchable rainbow trout are stocked annually, several times throughout the spring and summer.
Agency: U.S. Forest Service.
Comments: Fishing pressure is heavy due to the easy access and local popularity of this lake. Campgrounds, picnic tables, restrooms, and a small store are available nearby.
Special Regulations: None.

MESA LAKE

Access: Just past Jumbo Reservoir turn right and follow this paved road, passing the Mesa Lakes Lodge, to Sunset Lake. Turn left and travel 0.3 mile to the end of the road to reach the lake.
Size, Depth, and Elevation: 26 acres, 9 feet deep, and 9,840 feet.
Fish: Rainbow and brook trout. Catchable rainbow trout are stocked annually, several times throughout the spring and summer.
Agency: Mesa Creek Reservoir and Canal Company.
Comments: Fishing pressure is heavy due to the easy access and local popularity of this lake. Campgrounds, picnic tables, restrooms, and a small store are available nearby.
Special Regulations: None.

SOUTH MESA LAKE

Access: Just past Jumbo Reservoir turn right and follow this paved road, passing the Mesa Lakes Lodge, to Sunset Lake. Turn left and travel 0.3 mile to the end of the road at Mesa Lake. Walk across the Mesa Lake Dam and follow the marked trail 0.5 mile to South Mesa Lake.
Size, Depth, and Elevation: 10 acres, 18 feet deep, and 10,100 ft.
Fish: Brook trout, stocked as subcatchables.
Agency: Mesa Creek Reservoir and Canal Company.
Comments: This is a natural lake. Fishing pressure is moderate. The trail to the lake is short and easy to walk. No developed campsites exist at this lake. The nearby Mesa Lakes area offers camping, picnicking, restrooms and a small store.
Special Regulations: None.

LOST LAKE (MESA CREEK)

Access: From Mesa, travel south on Highway 65 13.7 miles to the access road just past Jumbo Reservoir. Turn right and follow this paved road, passing the Mesa Lakes Lodge, to Sunset Lake. Turn left and travel 0.3 mile to the end of the road at Mesa Lake. Walk across the Mesa Lake Dam and follow the marked trail, past South Mesa Lake, 1 mile to Lost Lake.
Size, Depth, and Elevation: 3.7 acres, 17 feet deep, and 9,990 feet.
Fish: Brook trout, from wild spawn.
Agency: U.S. Forest Service.
Comments: This is a natural lake. Fishing pressure is light. The trail to the lake is an easy walk over a gradual grade. No developed campsites exist at this lake. The nearby Mesa Lakes area offers camping, picnicking, restrooms and a small store. Please pack out trash.
Special Regulations: None.

WATERDOG RESERVOIR

Access: From Mesa, travel south on Highway 65 13.6 miles to the dirt road taking off to the left. Travel this road 0.3 mile to the fork in the road and turn right. Continue 0.2 mile to Waterdog Reservoir.
Size, Depth, and Elevation: 24 acres, 20 feet deep, and 9,930 feet.
Fish: Rainbow trout, stocked annually as catchables.
Agency: Mesa Creek Reservoir and Canal Company.
Comments: An undeveloped boat ramp is present on the north shore. Fishing pressure is heavy. No developed campsites exist at this reservoir.
Special Regulations: None.

MESA CREEK

Access: Just past Jumbo Reservoir turn right, follow the paved road to Sunset Lake, and turn right at the fork. Travel 0.4 mile along the lake to the dam. Mesa Creek is accessible below the dam. Highway 65 also intersects Mesa Creek approximately 2 miles north of Jumbo Reservoir.
Land Status: Mesa Creek is 11 miles long from Sunset Lake to Plateau Creek. The upper 2.5 miles lie within the National Forest, the lower 8.5 miles are on private land.
Stream Width and Elevation on Public Lands: 8 feet wide and 7,800 to 9,820 feet.
Fish: Rainbow, brown, and brook trout. Occasionally the stream below the Sunset Lake dam is stocked with catchable rainbow trout.
Comments: Mesa Creek below the dam of Sunset Lake has several nice pools and good undercut banks, and receives heavy fishing pressure for about 0.25 mile. Further downstream, fishing is limited by the steepness of the stream, very steep banks, and difficult access.
Special Regulations: None.

Map 2 - Bull Basin Area

BULL BASIN AREA

Situated on a large bench of the Grand Mesa, Bull Creek Basin offers a beautiful backcountry lake setting. Access is limited to four-wheel-drive vehicles, ATV, horseback, or foot travel due to very poor road conditions. No formal campsites exist in the area. Fishing pressure is moderate on all of the lakes.

A complex trail system provides a variety of options for exploring the basin. Continuing east on the rugged Lake of the Woods trail would bring you to Cottonwood Lake #1. Please pack out your trash.

GRIFFITH LAKE #1

Access: From Mesa, travel south on Highway 65 15.6 miles to the large, unpaved turnout on the left side of the road. From this turnout, follow the dirt road (Forest Road #254) 0.5 mile to Griffith Lake #1. A four-wheel-drive vehicle is strongly recommended.
Size, Depth, and Elevation: 45 acres, 31 feet deep, and 10,050 feet.
Fish: Rainbow trout, stocked annually as subcatchables.
Agency: Coon Creek Reservoir Company.
Comments: Fishing pressure is moderate. No developed campsites exist at this lake.
Special Regulations: Fishing by artificial flies and lures only. The bag, possession, and size limit for trout is 2 fish, 16 inches or longer.

MIDDLE GRIFFITH LAKE

Access: From Mesa, travel south on Highway 65 15.6 miles to the large, unpaved turnout on the left side of the road. From this turnout, follow the dirt road (Forest Road #254) 0.5 mile to Griffith Lake #1. Continue 0.6 mile around Griffith #1 to Middle Griffith Lake. A four-wheel-drive vehicle is strongly recommended.
Size, Depth, and Elevation: 45 acres, 47 feet deep, and 10,025 feet.
Fish: Rainbow and brook trout. Subcatchable rainbow trout are stocked annually.
Agency: Coon Creek Reservoir Company.
Comments: Fishing pressure is moderate. No developed campgrounds exist at this lake.
Special Regulations: None.

BULL CREEK RESERVOIR #2

Access: From Mesa, travel south on Highway 65 16.0 miles to the giant hairpin turn in the highway and turn left onto the dirt road (Forest Road #506). Travel 0.3 mile to the parking lot. From the parking area, travel 2.2 miles on the ATV trail (actually the old four-wheel-drive road) to Lake of the Woods, a shallow, marshy pond. Turn right at this pond and continue 0.5 mile to Bull Creek Reservoir #2.
Size, Depth, and Elevation: 10 acres, 10 feet deep, and 10,140 feet.
Fish: Rainbow trout stocked alternate years as subcatchables.
Agency: Bull Creek Reservoir Company.
Comments: Fishing pressure is moderate. The water level fluctuates greatly with irrigation demand. No developed campsites exist at this reservoir. Please pack out trash.
Special Regulations: Fishing by artificial flies and lures only. The bag, possession, and size limit for trout is 2 fish, 16 inches or longer.

BULL CREEK RESERVOIR #1

Access: From Mesa, travel south on Highway 65 16.0 miles to the giant hairpin turn in the highway and turn left onto the dirt road (Forest Road #506). Travel 0.3 mile to the bladed parking lot. From the parking area, travel 2.2 miles on the ATV trail (actually the old four-wheel-drive road) to Lake of the Woods, a shallow, marshy pond. Turn right at this pond and continue 0.6 mile, passing below the dam on Bull Creek Reservoir #2, to Bull Creek #1.
Size, Depth, and Elevation: 10 acres, 12 feet deep, and 10,140 feet.
Fish: Rainbow trout stocked alternate years as subcatchables.
Agency: Bull Creek Reservoir Company.
Comments: Fishing pressure is moderate. The water level fluctuates greatly with irrigation demand. No developed campsites exist at this reservoir. Please pack out trash.
Special Regulations: Fishing by artificial flies and lures only. The bag, possession, and size limit for trout is 2 fish, 16 inches or longer.

BULL CREEK RESERVOIR #5

Access: From Mesa, travel south on Highway 65 13.6 miles to the dirt road (Forest Road #254) taking off to the left. Travel this road 0.3 mile to the fork in the road and turn right. Continue 0.2 mile to Waterdog Reservoir. From Waterdog, continue 5 miles to Bull Creek Reservoir #5. A four-wheel-drive vehicle is strongly recommended.
Size, Depth, and Elevation: 18 acres, 27 feet deep, and 9,640 feet.
Fish: Rainbow and cutthroat trout.
Agency: Bull Creek Reservoir Company.
Comments: Fishing pressure is light. The water level fluctuates greatly with irrigation demand and the reservoir has a history of winterkill. No developed campsites exist at this reservoir. Please pack out trash.
Special Regulations: None.

BULL CREEK

Access: From Mesa, travel south on Highway 65 16.0 miles to the giant hairpin turn in the highway and turn left on the dirt road (Forest Road #254). Travel 0.3 mile to the bladed parking lot. From the parking area, travel 2.5 mile on the ATV trail (actually the old four-wheel-drive road) to the Bull Creek reservoirs. Bull Creek flows from the outlets of Bull Creek reservoirs #1 and #2 and through reservoir #5.
Land Status: Bull Creek is 12.5 miles long from the Bull Creek reservoirs to Plateau Creek. The upper 5.5 miles lie within the National Forest, 0.2 mile crosses BLM land downstream, and the lower 6.8 miles are on private land.
Stream Width and Elevation on Public Lands: 6 feet wide and 7,840 to 10,140 feet. **Fish:** Rainbow trout, which enter the stream from the Bull Creek reservoirs.
Comments: The upper mile of this stream is easily fished and if has several good pools. However, downstream the majority of Bull Creek is steep and brushy, and much of the stream has poor accessibility.
Special Regulations: Bull Creek reservoirs #1 and #2 and the connecting channels require fishing by artificial flies and lures only, and a bag, possession, and size limit for trout of 2 fish 16 inches or longer.

Map 2 - Island Lake & Ward Lake Areas

ISLAND LAKE AREA

Island Lake is the largest lake on the Grand Mesa National Forest. Accessed by Highway 65, the Island Lake area is extremely popular and well developed. Two major campgrounds accommodate large camp trailers and motor homes. Island Lake is "just across the street" from numerous other fishing lakes.

Shore and boat access is easy, and spring and summer fishing activity is heavy. Nearby Little Gem and Rim Rock lakes help absorb this fishing pressure.

Ice fishing, which is becoming more popular, gives anglers their best shot at Island Lake splake.

ISLAND LAKE

Access: From Cedaredge, travel north on Highway 65 17.0 miles to Island Lake. To access the boat ramp travel only 16.0 miles and turn left onto Forest Road #116 (across from Carp Lake) and follow this graveled road along the southern shore. Go 0.3 mile to reach the boat ramp located near the Little Bear Campground.
Size, Depth, and Elevation: 179 acres, 77 feet deep, and 10,290 ft.
Fish: Rainbow trout, brook trout, splake, and white suckers. Catchable rainbow trout are stocked annually, several times throughout the spring and summer. Fingerling splake are stocked periodically. Brook trout and suckers are from wild spawn.
Agency: Surface Creek Ditch and Reservoir Company.
Comments: Island Lake is the largest reservoir on the Grand Mesa National Forest. Fishing pressure is heavy due to the easy access and local popularity of this lake. Campgrounds, picnic tables, restrooms, and a small store are available nearby. This lake is a popular spot for boaters due to the size of the lake and the good boat ramp. Maintained highways offer good winter access for ice fishing.
Special Regulations: None.

LITTLE GEM RESERVOIR

Access: From Cedaredge, travel north on Highway 65 16.0 miles and turn left onto Forest Road #116 (across from Carp Lake) and follow this graveled road along the south shore of Island Lake. Continue 0.7 mile and turn left onto the dirt road (Forest Road 115). Follow this road 0.3 mile to the reservoir.
Size, Depth, and Elevation: 40 acres, 25 feet deep, and 10,020 ft.
Fish: Rainbow trout, brook trout, splake, and white suckers. Subcatchable rainbow trout are stocked annually. Fingerling splake are stocked periodically. Brook trout and suckers are from wild spawn.
Agency: Private permittee.
Comments: Fishing pressure is heavy due to the easy access, close proximity to Island Lake and local popularity of this lake. Campgrounds, picnic tables, restrooms, and a small store are available nearby at Island Lake.
Special Regulations: None.

RIM ROCK LAKE

Access: From Cedaredge, travel north on Highway 65 16.0 miles and turn left onto Forest Road #116 (across from Carp Lake) and follow this graveled road along the south shore of Island Lake. Follow this road 1.5 miles to the far end of the Island Lake Campground loop drive. From here, you can leave your vehicle in the parking area and begin hiking, or you can proceed by four-wheel drive, ATV, or horseback. Follow the four-wheel-drive road 0.6 mile to the road taking off to the left. Proceed on this road 0.4 mile to Rim Rock Lake.
Size, Depth, and Elevation: 13 acres, 20 feet deep, and 10,120 ft.
Fish: Rainbow and cutthroat trout are present. Subcatchable rainbow trout are stocked every other year.

WARD LAKE AREA

The Ward Lake area is readily accessible off Highway 65. This area is well developed with several major campgrounds that accommodate large camp trailers and motor homes, and a lodge/store that offers food, fuel, fishing tackle, and lodging. A U.S. Forest Service information trailer is located at the junction of Highway 65 and Forest Road 121 near Carp Lake.

The numerous lakes in this area are mostly drive-to reservoirs providing fishing in a convenient setting. The larger lakes in this area, Ward, Alexander, Hotel Twin, and Baron, are very popular with fishermen and have boat launching areas. Most of the reservoirs in this area receive several plants of catchable rainbow trout throughout the spring and summer months to help keep pace with the extremely heavy fishing pressure.

CARP LAKE

Access: From Cedaredge, travel north on Highway 65 16.0 miles to Carp Lake, which is immediately adjacent to the highway on the right-hand side. This lake is accessible by road on three sides.
Size, Depth, and Elevation: 12 acres, 30 feet deep, and 10,260 ft.
Fish: Rainbow trout and white suckers. Catchable rainbow trout are stocked annually, several times throughout the spring and summer.
Agency: U.S. Forest Service.
Comments: Fishing pressure is heavy due to easy access and the local popularity of this lake. A campground and restrooms are available on the lake's eastern shore. A Forest Service information trailer is located on the south shore and is usually staffed during the summer months.
Special Regulations: Motorized boats are prohibited.

WARD LAKE

Access: From Cedaredge, travel north on Highway 65 16.0 miles and turn right onto Forest Road 121 (paved), just before reaching Carp Lake. Continue 0.3 mile and turn right into the Ward Lake Campground. Follow the road through the campground to the lower camping area adjacent to the lake. An unimproved boat launching area is located just north of the lake's dam. The lake can also be reached by continuing 0.2 mile past the campground entrance to the Wardway Picnic Area on the right-hand side of the road. The lake is easily accessible at this point.
Size, Depth, and Elevation: 85 acres, 72 feet deep, 10,100 feet.
Fish: Rainbow trout, brook trout, splake, and white suckers. Catchable rainbow trout are stocked annually, several times throughout the spring and summer. Subcatchable splake are stocked periodically. Brook trout and suckers are from wild spawn.
Agency: Surface Creek Ditch and Reservoir Company.
Comments: The boat access area allows the launching of smaller trailered boats, water levels permitting. Fishing pressure is heavy due to the easy access and local popularity of this lake. Two major campgrounds and lodge complete with a small store offer convenient accommodations.

ALEXANDER LAKE

Access: From Cedaredge, travel north on Highway 65 16.0 miles and turn right onto Forest Road #121 (paved), just before reaching Carp Lake. Proceed 1.3 miles to Alexander Lake, on the right-hand side of the road. The lake is situated adjacent to Forest Road #121, which borders the lake's entire northern shore, making for very easy access. A graveled boat ramp, on the lake's western tip, is conveniently located off Forest Road #121.
Size, Depth, and Elevation: 41 acres, 48 feet deep, and 10,130 ft.
Fish: Rainbow and brook trout and white suckers. Catchable rainbow trout are stocked annually, several times throughout the spring and summer. Brook trout and suckers are from wild spawn.

Map 2- Ward Lake Area

Agency: Surface Creek Ditch and Reservoir Company.
Comments: This is a well developed area with easy access. Fishing pressure is heavy. Picnic areas, a lodge with a small store, and restrooms are present at this lake. The improved boat ramp easily accommodates trailered boats.
Special Regulations: None.

HOTEL TWIN LAKE

Access: From Cedaredge, travel north on Highway 65 16.0 miles and turn right onto Forest Road #121 (paved), just before reaching Carp Lake. Proceed 1.5 miles to Hotel Twin Lake, adjacent to Forest Road #121 on the left-hand side. This lake has road access to the eastern and northern shores. An unimproved boat launching area, on the lake's eastern shore, is conveniently located off Forest Road #121.
Size, Depth, and Elevation: 40 acres, 36 feet deep, 10,208 ft.
Fish: Rainbow and brook trout. Catchable rainbow trout are stocked annually, several times throughout the spring and summer. Fingerling brook trout are stocked periodically.
Agency: Surface Creek Ditch and Reservoir Company.
Comments: Fishing pressure is heavy due to the easy access and local popularity of this lake. Several small stores and a gas station provide food, fishing tackle and fuel. The boat access area allows the launching of smaller trailered boats, water levels permitting. Many private cabins surround this lake.
Special Regulations: None.

BARON LAKE

Access: From Cedaredge, travel north on Highway 65 16.0 miles and turn right onto Forest Road #121 (paved), just before reaching Carp Lake. Proceed 2.2 miles to Baron Lake, on the right-hand side of the road. The lake is situated adjacent to Forest Road #121, which borders the lake's entire northern shore, making for very easy access. An unimproved boat launching area, on the lake's northern shore, is conveniently located off Forest Rd #121.
Size, Depth, and Elevation: 100 acres, 38 feet deep, 10,125 feet.
Fish: Rainbow trout and white suckers. Catchable rainbow trout are stocked annually, several times throughout the spring and summer.
Agency: Surface Creek Ditch and Reservoir Company.
Comments: Fishing pressure is heavy due to the easy access and local popularity of this lake. Several small stores and a gas station, providing food, fishing tackle and fuel, are located within 0.5 mile of the lake. The boat access area allows the launching of smaller trailered boats, water levels permitting. Private cabins are located on the lake's northern shore.
Special Regulations: None.

DEEP SLOUGH RESERVOIR

Access: From Cedaredge, travel north on Highway 65 16.0 miles and turn right onto Forest Road #121 (paved), just before reaching Carp Lake. Continue 0.3 mile and turn right into the Ward Lake Campground. Follow the road through the campground to the lower camping area adjacent to the lake. From here, you will drive below the dam on Ward Lake. A four-wheel-drive vehicle with good ground clearance is recommended from this point, or you can hike. Continue for 0.3 mile to Deep Slough Reservoir.
Size, Depth, and Elevation: 48 acres, 15 feet deep, 10,018 feet.
Fish: Rainbow trout and white suckers. Catchable rainbow trout are stocked periodically.
Agency: Surface Creek Ditch and Reservoir Company.
Comments: Fishing pressure is moderate. No developed campsites exist at this reservoir. Please pack out trash. Camping facilities are available nearby at Ward Lake.
Special Regulations: None.

SHEEP SLOUGH RESERVOIR (SHEEP LAKE)

Access: From Cedaredge, travel north on Highway 65 16.0 miles and turn right onto Forest Road #121 (paved), just before reaching Carp Lake. Continue 0.3 mile and turn right into the Ward Lake Campground. Follow the road through the campground to the lower camping area adjacent to the lake. From here, you will drive below the dam on Ward Lake. A four-wheel-drive vehicle with good ground clearance is recommended from this point, or you can hike. Continue for 0.3 mile to Deep Slough Reservoir. From here, hike 0.2 mile directly east to Sheep Slough Reservoir. Sheep Slough Reservoir can also be reached by hiking 0.4 mile across the dam on Ward Lake and following the level footpath.
Size, Depth, and Elevation: 15 acres, 13 feet deep, 10,060 feet.
Fish: Rainbow and cutthroat trout. Neither species has been stocked in recent years.
Agency: Surface Creek Ditch and Reservoir Company.
Comments: Fishing pressure is moderate. No developed campsites exist at this reservoir. Please pack out trash. Camping facilities are available nearby at Ward Lake.
Special Regulations: None.

WARD CREEK RESERVOIR

Access: From Cedaredge. travel north on Highway 65 10.0 miles to Ward Creek Reservoir, which is immediately adjacent to the highway on the right-hand side. There is a parking area and small picnic site next to the highway.
Size, Depth, and Elevation: 26 acres, 28 feet deep, 9,800 feet.
Fish: Rainbow trout, cutthroat trout, and white suckers. Catchable rainbow trout are stocked annually, several times throughout the spring and summer. Cutthroat trout and white suckers are from wild spawn.
Agency: Surface Creek Ditch and Reservoir Company.
Comments: Access is easy and fishing pressure is heavy. No developed campsites exist at this reservoir. A picnic area is available for day use.
Special Regulations: None.

WARD CREEK

Access: From Cedaredge, travel north on Highway 65 14.0 miles to where the highway crosses Ward Creek. The stream can be accessed above or below the highway at this point. The highway parallels Ward Creek for 1.0 mile upstream, which encompasses Ward Creek Reservoir, from this point. Ward Creek can also be accessed between Ward Lake and Deep Slough Reservoir, and downstream of Deep Slough.
Land Status: Ward Creek is 16.8 miles long from Deep Slough Reservoir to Tongue Creek. The upper 8.1 miles are on National Forest; the lower 8.7 miles lie on private land.
Stream Width and Elevation on Public Lands: 9 feet wide and 7,220 to 10,018 feet.
Fish: Rainbow trout, cutthroat trout, and white suckers. All three species enter the stream from the reservoirs on Ward Creek. Fingerling Colorado River cutthroat trout are stocked periodically.
Comments: Fishing pressure is light to moderate. Much of the stream is steep and overgrown with vegetation.
Special Regulations: None.

Map 2 - Eggleston Lake Area

EGGLESTON LAKE AREA

Eggleston, the second largest lake on the Grand Mesa National Forest, and the smaller lakes nearby create another extremely popular destination area for fishermen. Situated in the heart of the Grand Mesa lakes, this area offers excellent recreational opportunities including camping, hiking, boating, fishing, and four-wheeling.

Eggleston Lake has three major campgrounds along its shores that accommodate larger camp trailers and motor homes. The Crag Crest Campground serves as the eastern trailhead to the Crag Crest National Recreation Trail. Eggleston Lake also has a good graveled boat ramp.

The other lakes in the area, accessible by car or four-wheel drive, offer camping in undeveloped settings. Be aware of road and weather conditions before traveling to the outlying lakes.

General Directions for Access:
From Cedaredge, travel north on Highway 65 16.0 miles and turn right onto Forest Road #121 (paved), just before reaching Carp Lake.

EGGLESTON LAKE

Access: From Cedaredge, travel north on Highway 65 16.0 miles and turn right onto Forest Road #121 (paved), just before reaching Carp Lake. Proceed 2.5 miles to the dam on Eggleston Lake. The road forks here and is no longer paved. Forest Road #121 continues to the left, paralleling the northern shore of Eggleston Lake for its entire length. Several access areas to the lake are present along the road. A graveled boat ramp, on the lake's northern shore, is conveniently located off Forest Road #121, just west of the Crag Crest Trail parking lot.
Size, Depth, and Elevation: 164 acres, 52 feet deep, 10,140 feet.
Fish: Rainbow trout and white suckers. Catchable rainbow trout are stocked annually, several times throughout the spring and summer.
Agency: Surface Creek Ditch and Reservoir Company.
Comments: Fishing pressure is heavy due to the easy access and local popularity of this lake. Three major campgrounds are located along the lake's shores. The improved boat ramp easily accommodates trailered boats. Private cabins are located at the western tip of the reservoir.
Special Regulations: None.

REED RESERVOIR

Access: From Cedaredge, travel north on Highway 65 16.0 miles and turn right onto Forest Road #121 (paved), just before reaching Carp Lake. Proceed 2.5 miles to the dam on Eggleston Lake. The road forks here and is no longer paved. Take the right fork onto Forest Road #123 (unpaved) and travel 0.7 mile to Reed Reservoir, located on the left-hand side of the road.
Size, Depth, and Elevation: 23 acres, 14 feet deep, 9,980 feet.
Fish: Rainbow trout and white suckers. Catchable rainbow trout are stocked annually, several times throughout the spring and summer.
Agency: Palmer and Company.
Comments: Fishing pressure is moderate. No developed campsites exist at this reservoir. Please pack out trash. Camping facilities are available 0.5 mile to the north at Kiser Creek Camppound.
Special Regulations: None.

KISER SLOUGH RESERVOIR

Access: From Cedaredge, travel north on Highway 65 16.0 miles and turn right onto Forest Road #121 (paved), just before reaching Carp Lake. Proceed east 2.5 miles to the fork in the road and turn right onto Forest Road #123 (unpaved). Continue 1.2 miles to Kiser Slough Reservoir, on the righthand side of the road.
Size, Depth, and Elevation: 34 acres, 25 feet deep, 9,827 feet.
Fish: Rainbow trout and white suckers. Catchable rainbow trout are stocked annually, several times throughout the spring and summer.
Agency: U.S. Forest Service.
Comments: Fishing pressure is heavy. This reservoir may be completely drained during drier years. No developed campsites exist at this reservoir. Please pack out trash. Camping facilities are available 1.0 mile to the north at Kiser Creek Campground.
Special Regulations: None.

YOUNGS CREEK RESERVOIR #3

Access: From Cedaredge, travel north on Highway 65 16.0 miles and turn right onto Forest Road #121 (paved), just before reaching Carp Lake. Proceed east 2.5 miles to the dam on Eggleston Lake. The road forks here and is no longer paved. Continue left on Forest Road #121 1.5 miles to Youngs Creek Reservoir #3, adjacent to the road on the right-hand side. A graveled boat ramp on the lake's western shore is conveniently located off Forest Rd 121.
Size, Depth, and Elevation: 23 acres, 16 feet deep, 10,200 feet.
Fish: Rainbow trout and white suckers. Catchable rainbow trout are stocked periodically.
Agency: Youngs Creek Ditch and Reservoir Company.
Comments: Fishing pressure is moderate. The improved boat ramp easily accommodates trailered boats. No developed campsites exist at this reservoir. Please pack out trash.
Special Regulations: None.

YOUNGS CREEK RESERVOIR #2

Access: From Cedaredge, travel north on Highway 65 16.0 miles and turn right onto Forest Road #121 (paved), just before reaching Carp Lake. Proceed east 2.5 miles to the dam on Eggleston Lake. The road forks here and is no longer paved. Continue left on Forest Road #121 2.0 miles, and turn right onto the dirt road (Forest Road #124). Continue 0.6 mile to Youngs Creek Reservoir #2. Four-wheel drive is recommended on Forest Road #124 when it is wet.
Size, Depth, and Elevation: 33 acres, 20 feet deep, 10,180 feet.
Fish: Rainbow and brook trout and white suckers. Catchable rainbow trout are stocked annually, several times throughout the spring and summer. Brook trout and suckers are from wild spawn.
Agency: Youngs Creek Ditch and Reservoir Company.
Comments: During the spring, the water level in Youngs Creek reservoirs #1 and #2 may be high enough to inundate the connecting channel between these reservoirs, creating a single lake of 53 acres. Bank access is easy and fishing pressure is moderate. No developed campsites exist at this reservoir. Please pack out trash.
Special Regulations: None.

YOUNGS CREEK RESERVOIR #1

Access: From Cedaredge, travel north on Highway 65 16.0 miles and turn right onto Forest Road #121 (paved), just before reaching Carp Lake. Proceed east 2.5 miles to the dam on Eggleston Lake. The road forks here and is no longer paved. Continue left on Forest Road #121 2.0 miles and turn right onto the dirt road (Forest Road #124). Continue 0.7 mile to Youngs Creek Reservoir #1. Four-wheel drive is recommended on Forest Road #124 when it is wet.
Size, Depth, and Elevation: 17 acres, 16 feet deep, 10,180 feet.
Fish: Rainbow and brook trout, and white suckers. Catchable rainbow trout are stocked annually, several times throughout the spring and summer. Brook trout and suckers are from wild spawn.
Agency: Youngs Creek Ditch and Reservoir Company.
Comments: During the spring, the water level in Youngs Creek reservoirs #1 and #2 may be high enough to inundate the connect-

Map 2 - Eggleston Lake Area

ing channel between these reservoirs creating a single lake of 53 acres. Bank access is easy and fishing pressure is moderate. No developed campsites exist at this reservoir. Please pack out trash.
Special Regulations: None.

PEDRO RESERVOIR

Access: From Cedaredge, travel north on Highway 65 16.0 miles and turn right onto Forest Road #121 (paved), just before reaching Carp Lake. Proceed east 2.5 miles to the dam on Eggleston Lake. The road forks here and is no longer paved. Continue left on Forest Road #121 2.0 miles and turn right onto the dirt road (Forest Road #124). Continue 0.9 mile, passing Youngs Creek reservoirs #1 and #2, to Pedro Reservoir. Four-wheel drive is recommended on Forest Road #124 when it is wet.
Size, Depth, and Elevation: 14 acres, 18 feet deep, 10,080 feet.
Fish: Brook trout, stocked alternate years as subcatchables.
Agency: Palmer and Company.
Comments: Bank access is easy; fishing pressure is light to moderate. No developed campsites exist at this reservoir. Please pack out trash.
Special Regulations: None.

KISER RESERVOIR

Access: From Cedaredge, travel north on Highway 65 16.0 miles and turn right onto Forest Road #121 (paved), just before reaching Carp Lake. Proceed east 2.5 miles to the fork in the road and turn right onto Forest Road #123 (unpaved). Continue 2.1 miles, passing Kiser Slough Reservoir, and turn left onto the dirt road (Forest Road #124). Proceed 0.3 mile to the fork in the road. Take the left fork and continue 0.6 mile directly to Kiser Reservoir, on the right-hand side of the road. Four-wheel drive is recommended on Forest Road #124 when it is wet.
Size, Depth, and Elevation: 14 acres, 9 feet deep, and 10,000 feet.
Fish: Rainbow trout, however, this species has not been stocked in recent years.
Agency: Surface Creek Ditch and Reservoir Company.
Comments: Bank access is easy; fishing pressure is light to moderate. No developed campsites exist at this reservoir. Please pack out trash.
Special Regulations: None.

LITTLE GROUSE RESERVOIR

Access: From Cedaredge, travel north on Highway 65 16.0 miles and turn right onto Forest Road #121 (paved), just before reaching Carp Lake. Proceed east 2.5 miles to the fork in the road and turn right onto Forest Road #123 (unpaved). Continue 2.1 miles, passing Kiser Slough Reservoir, and turn left onto the dirt road (Forest Road #124). Proceed 0.3 mile to the fork in the road. Take the right fork and continue 0.5 mile directly to Little Grouse Reservoir on the left-hand side of the road. Four-wheel drive is recommended on Forest Road #124, when it is wet.
Size, Depth, and Elevation: 2 acres, 13 feet deep, 9,880 feet.
Fish: Cutthroat and brook trout. Neither species has been stocked in recent years.
Agency: Private permittee.
Comments: This is apparently the smallest reservoir on the Grand Mesa that will sustain trout year-round. Bank access is easy; fishing pressure is light to moderate. No developed campsites exist at this reservoir. Please pack out trash.
Special Regulations: None.

STELL LAKE

Access: From Cedaredge, travel north on Highway 65 16.0 miles and turn right onto Forest Road #121 (paved) just before reaching Carp Lake. Proceed east 2.5 miles to the fork in the road. Continue to the left on Forest Road #121 for 5.0 miles and turn

left onto the four-wheel-drive road. Proceed on this road 1.5 miles (you will drive past Military Park Reservoir and East Stell Lake) directly to Stell Lake.
Size, Depth, and Elevation: 7 acres, 20 feet deep, 10,240 feet.
Fish: Rainbow and cutthroat trout. Neither species has been stocked in recent years.
Agency: Private permittee.
Comments: Bank access is easy; fishing pressure is light. No developed campsites exist at this reservoir. Pack out trash.
Special Regulations: None.

KISER CREEK

Access: From Cedaredge, travel north on Highway 65 16.0 miles and turn right onto Forest Road #121 (paved) just before reaching Carp Lake. Proceed 2.5 miles to the dam on Eggleston Lake. Kiser Creek essentially begins here and flows south through Reed and Kiser Slough reservoirs. Kiser Creek is fishable and has fairly good access along Forest Road #123 until it leaves Kiser Slough Reservoir. Below this dam, the stream becomes steep and overgrown with vegetation making streamside access difficult.
Land Status: Kiser Creek is 12.5 miles long from the dam on Eggleston Lake to Ward Creek. The upper 4.7 miles are on National Forest; the lower 7.8 miles lie on private land.
Stream Width and Elevation on Public Lands: 3 feet wide and 7,520 to 10,110 feet.
Fish: Rainbow trout and white suckers enter the stream from the reservoirs on Kiser Creek.
Comments: Kiser Creek is a small shallow stream with few really good pools for trout. The stream is heavily populated with white suckers. Fishing pressure is light.
Special Regulations: None.

YOUNGS CREEK

Access: From Cedaredge, travel north on Highway 65 16.0 miles and turn right onto Forest Road #121 (paved), just before reaching Carp Lake. Proceed east 2.5 miles to the dam on Eggleston Lake. The road forks here and is no longer paved. Continue left on Forest Road #121 1.5 miles to Youngs Creek Reservoir #3, adjacent to the road on the right-hand side. Youngs Creek begins below the dam of Youngs Creek Reservoir #3 and flows south through Youngs Creek reservoirs #2 and #1. A small tributary of Youngs Creek, flowing from the dam on Little Grouse Reservoir, also holds trout. These streams are easily accessible where they intersect Forest Road #124, as well as below the reservoirs. Youngs Creek is fishable and has fairly good access along Forest Road #124 until its confluence with the tributary from Little Grouse Reservoir. Below this confluence, the stream becomes steep and overgrown with vegetation making streamside access difficult.
Land Status: Youngs Creek is 10.7 miles long from the dam on Youngs Creek Reservoir #3 to Kiser Creek. The upper 3.7 miles are on National Forest; the lower 7.0 miles lie on private land.
Stream Width and Elevation on Public Lands: 3 feet wide and 7,520 to 10,165 feet.
Fish: Brook trout and cutthroat trout. Fingerling Colorado River cutthroat are stocked periodically. Brook trout are from wild spawn.
Comments: Youngs Creek is a small shallow stream with some good pools that hold trout. This stream has vegetation that overhangs stretches of undercut banks. Fishing pressure is light.
Special Regulations: None.

Map 2 - Crag Crest Trail & Trickle Park Areas

CRAG CREST TRAIL AREA

The Crag Crest Trail designated as part of the National Recreational Trail system in 1978 highlights this scenic area. Two trailheads, one at the Crag Crest Campground (Eggleston Lake) and the other off Highway 65 across from Island Lake, are shared by the Crag Crest Trail and the lower Crag Crest Loop Trail. The Crag Crest Trail (7 miles long) is reserved for foot travel only while the Loop Trail (4 miles long) is also open to horseback use.

The Loop Trail allows hikers to leave from and return to the same trailhead over a 10-mile-long circular route. Crag Crest, at 11,189 feet in elevation, is referred to as the "backbone of the Grand Mesa." It offers breathtaking vistas of distant mountain ranges and the surrounding valleys.

The three lakes along this trail, Upper Eggleston, Butt and Forrest, offer fishing for cutthroat, rainbow and brook trout. Fishing pressure is light to moderate. Please pack out trash.

FORREST LAKE

Access: From Cedaredge, travel north on Highway 65 16.0 miles and turn right onto Forest Road #121 (paved) just before reaching Carp Lake. Proceed 1.5 miles to Hotel Twin Lake, adjacent to Forest Road #121 on the left-hand side. This lake has road access to the eastern and northern shores. Turn left onto the road on the eastern shore of Hotel Twin and proceed 0.4 mile around the lake. Continue straight (to the right) and travel 0.4 mile directly to Forrest Lake. This last 0.4 mile is over a rough road up a small hill; four-wheel drive is recommended during wet weather.
Size, Depth, and Elevation: 33 acres, 50 feet deep, 10,360 feet.
Fish: Cutthroat, brook, and rainbow trout. Fingerling Snake River cutthroat trout are stocked annually. Fingerling rainbow trout are stocked periodically. Brook trout are from wild spawn.
Agency: Surface Creek Ditch and Reservoir Company.
Comments: Fishing pressure is moderate. The Loop Trail of the Crag Crest Trail intersects the access road just below Forrest Lake. No developed campsites exist at this reservoir.
Special Regulations: None.

UPPER (LITTLE) EGGLESTON LAKE

Access: From Cedaredge, travel north on Highway 65 16.0 miles and turn right onto Forest Road #121 (paved), just before reaching Carp Lake. Proceed 2.5 miles to the dam on Eggleston Lake. The road forks here and is no longer paved. Continue left on Forest Road #121, paralleling the northern shore of Eggleston Lake, to the Crag Crest Campground. Several parking sites are available. The Crag Crest National Recreation Trail begins here and is well marked. Hike 0.4 mile on the Crag Crest Trail to Upper Eggleston Lake, which is adjacent to the trail on the right-hand side.
Size, Depth, and Elevation: 42 acres, 27 feet deep, 10,360 feet.
Fish: Brook and rainbow trout. Brook trout are from wild spawn. Fingerling rainbow trout are stocked annually.
Agency: Surface Creek Ditch and Reservoir Company.
Comments: This is a hike-in-only lake. Fishing pressure is moderate. No developed campsites exist at this reservoir.
Special Regulations: None.

BUTTS LAKE

Access: From Cedaredge, travel north on Highway 65 16.0 miles and turn right onto Forest Road #121 (paved) just before reaching Carp Lake. Proceed 2.5 miles to the dam on Eggleston Lake. The road forks here and is no longer paved. Continue left on Forest Road #121, paralleling the northern shore of Eggleston Lake, to the Crag Crest Campground. Several parking sites are available. The Crag Crest National Recreation Trail begins here and is well marked. Hike 1.0 mile on the Crag Crest Trail, passing Upper Eggleston Lake, to a fork leaving the main trail to the left. Follow this left fork 0.3 mile directly to Butts Lake.
Size, Depth, and Elevation: 23 acres, 50 feet deep, 10,500 feet.
Fish: Snake River cutthroat trout stocked alternate years as fingerlings.
Agency: U.S. Forest Service.
Comments: This is a hike-in-only lake. Fishing pressure is light. No developed campsites exist at this reservoir.
Special Regulations: Motorized boats are prohibited.

TRICKLE PARK AREA

The Trickle Park area offers a good variety of camping and fishing opportunities in the open settings of mountain parks and meadows. This group of reservoirs provides developed and undeveloped campsites, and car or four-wheel-drive access.

Park and Vela reservoirs have smaller campgrounds nearby, and both have good graveled boat ramps for convenient boat access.

If you are looking for a bit more solitude, Military Park and Stell reservoirs are off the beaten path and receive much less fishing. Please pack out trash.

MILITARY PARK RESERVOIR

Access: From Cedaredge, travel north on Highway 65 16.0 miles and turn right onto Forest Road #121 (paved) just before reaching Carp Lake. Proceed east 2.5 miles to the fork in the road. Continue to the left on Forest Road #121 (unpaved) for 5.0 miles and turn left onto the four-wheel-drive road. Proceed on this road 0.1 mile directly to Military Park Reservoir, on the left-hand side of the road.
Size, Depth, and Elevation: 31 acres, 15 feet deep, 10,100 feet.
Fish: Rainbow and cutthroat trout. Catchable rainbow trout are stocked periodically. Cutthroat trout have not been stocked in recent years.
Agency: Private permittee.
Comments: The water level in this reservoir may be very low by midsummer. Fishing pressure is moderate. No developed campsites exist at this reservoir. Please pack out trash.
Special Regulations: None.

EAST STELL LAKE

Access: From Cedaredge, travel north on Highway 65 16.0 miles and turn right onto Forest Road #121 (paved) just before reaching Carp Lake. Proceed east 2.5 miles to the fork in the road. Continue to the left on Forest Road #121 (unpaved) for 5.0 miles and turn left onto the four-wheel drive road. Proceed on this road 1.1 miles, passing Military Park Reservoir, to East Stell Lake, on the left-hand side of the road.
Size, Depth, and Elevation: 3 acres, 33 feet deep, and 10,240 feet.
Fish: Rainbow and cutthroat trout. Neither species has been stocked in recent years.
Agency: U.S. Forest Service.
Comments: Fishing pressure is light. No developed campsites exist at this reservoir.
Special Regulations: None.

PARK RESERVOIR

Access: From Cedaredge, travel north on Highway 65 16.0 miles and turn right onto Forest Road #121 (paved) just before reaching Carp Lake. Proceed east 2.5 miles to the fork in the road. Continue to the left on Forest Road #121 (unpaved) for 5.5 miles and turn right onto Forest Road #125. Proceed 0.5 mile to the reservoir, on the right-hand side of the road.
Size, Depth, and Elevation: 125 acres, 22 feet deep, and 9,928 feet.
Fish: Rainbow, brook and cutthroat trout and white suckers. Catchable rainbow trout are stocked annually several times throughout the spring and summer. Brook and cutthroat trout have not been stocked in recent years.
Agency: Park Reservoir Company.
Comments: A developed, graveled boat ramp is conveniently located off Forest Road #125 on the eastern shore of the reservoir. Bank access is easy and fishing pressure is heavy. A small campground is located a short distance from the lake's eastern shore.
Special Regulations: None.

Map 2 - Trickle Park & Cottonwood Lakes Areas

VELA RESERVOIR

Access: From Cedaredge, travel north on Highway 65 16.0 miles and turn right onto Forest Road #121 (paved) just before reaching Carp Lake. Proceed east 2.5 miles to the fork in the road. Continue to the left on Forest Road #121 (unpaved) for 6.1 miles. Vela Reservoir is adjacent to the right-hand side of the road.

Size, Depth, and Elevation: 23 acres, 23 feet deep, and 10,160 feet.

Fish: Rainbow trout, stocked as catchables several times throughout the spring and summer.

Agency: Private permittee.

Comments: The water level in this reservoir may be very low by midsummer. A good graveled boat ramp on the west shore offers easy access for trailered boats, water levels permitting. Fishing pressure is heavy. The Trickle Park Campground is located adjacent to the boat ramp.

Special Regulations: None.

ELK PARK RESERVOIR

Access: From Cedaredge, travel north on Highway 65 16.0 miles and turn right onto Forest Road #121 (paved) just before reaching Carp Lake. Proceed east 2.5 miles to the fork in the road. Continue to the left on Forest Road #121 (unpaved) for 4.6 miles and turn right into the parking area adjacent to the road. From the parking area, hike, bike, or ride on the old four-wheel-drive road 0.4 mile to Elk Park Reservoir.

Size, Depth, and Elevation: 21 acres, 10 feet deep, and 10,065 feet.

Fish: Brook and rainbow trout stocked as fingerlings. Rainbow trout are stocked every other year. Brook trout are stocked periodically.

Agency: Private permittee.

Comments: Fishing pressure is moderate. No developed campsites exist at this reservoir. Please pack out trash.

Special Regulations: None.

KNOX RESERVOIR

Access: From Cedaredge, travel north on Highway 65 16.0 miles and turn right onto Forest Road #121 (paved) just before reaching Carp Lake. Proceed east 2.5 miles to the fork in the road. Continue to the left on Forest Road #121 (unpaved) for 4.6 miles and turn right into the parking area adjacent to the road. From the parking area, hike, bike, or ride on the old four-wheel-drive road 0.7 mile to the fork in the road. Follow the right fork 0.3 mile to Knox Reservoir.

Size, Depth, and Elevation: 16 acres, 10 feet deep, and 10,000 feet.

Fish: Brook and cutthroat trout, apparently from wild spawn. Neither species has been stocked in recent years.

Agency: Private permittee.

Comments: Fishing pressure is light. No developed campsites exist at this reservoir. Please pack out trash.

Special Regulations: None.

TROUT LAKE

Access: From Cedaredge, travel north on Highway 65 16.0 miles and turn right onto Forest Road #121 (paved) just before reaching Carp Lake. Proceed east 2.5 miles to the fork in the road. Continue to the left on Forest Road #121 (unpaved) for 4.6 miles and turn right into the parking area adjacent to the road. From the parking area, hike, bike, or ride on the old four-wheel-drive road 0.7 mile to the fork in the road. Follow the right fork 0.3 mile to Knox Reservoir. From Knox Reservoir, walk southwest 0.5 mile to Trout Lake.

Size, Depth, and Elevation: 8 acres, 10 feet deep, 10,280 feet.

Fish: Rainbow trout stocked alternate years as subcatchables.

Agency: Private permittee.

Comments: Fishing pressure is light. No developed campsites exist at this reservoir. Please pack out trash.

Special Regulations: Motorized boats are prohibited.

COTTONWOOD LAKES AREA

The Cottonwood Lakes area sits on a large bench to the north of Crag Crest. It offers excellent fishing opportunity in 10 drive-to lakes. Most of the lakes are easily accessible on the recently upgraded roads. Four-wheel drive is recommended for accessing a couple of the outlying lakes.

The lakes and streams in this area also supply water to the two Bureau of Reclamation hydroelectric power plants near Molina.

This area is extremely popular locally and most of the lakes receive heavy fishing pressure. Cottonwood Lake #1, the largest reservoir on the north side of the National Forest, has a graveled boat ramp and a large campground. Small boats and canoes are used by many fishermen to pursue trout in many of these lakes. Numerous informal camping spots are available in this area.

Introductions of Arctic grayling in Kitson Reservoir and splake in Cottonwood Lake #1 diversifies the options for anglers in this outstanding group of lakes.

SILVER LAKE

Access: From Collbran, travel south on Forest Access Road #121 (the first 7.0 miles of this drive is paved) 12.0 miles to the junction of Forest Road #257, at the southern end of Bonham Reservoir, and turn right. Proceed west 1.6 miles and turn left onto the four-wheel-drive road. Continue 0.3 mile to Silver Lake on the right-hand side of the road.

Size, Depth, and Elevation: 12 acres, 20 feet deep, and 10,176 feet.

Fish: Colorado River cutthroat trout stocked alternate years as subcatchables.

Agency: Bureau of Reclamation.

Comments: Bank access is easy and fishing pressure is heavy. No developed campsites exist at this reservoir. Please pack out trash.

Special Regulations: Fishing by artificial flies and lures only. The bag, possession, and size limit for trout is 2 fish, 16 inches or longer.

FORTY-ACRE LAKE

Access: From Collbran, travel south on Forest Access Road #121 (the first 7.0 miles of this drive is paved) 12.0 miles to the junction of Forest Road #257, at the southern end of Bonham Reservoir, and turn right. Proceed west 1.6 miles and turn left onto the four-wheel-drive road. Continue 0.8 mile, passing Silver Lake, to Forty-Acre Lake on the right-hand side of the road.

Size, Depth, and Elevation: 17 acres, 24 feet deep, 10,160 feet.

Fish: Brook trout stocked alternate years as subcatchables.

Agency: Bureau of Reclamation.

Comments: This lake has a reputation for producing large but difficult-to-catch brookies. Fishing pressure is moderate. No developed campsites exist at this reservoir. Please pack out trash.

Special Regulations: None.

NEVERSWEAT RESERVOIR

Access: From Collbran, travel south on Forest Access Road #121 (the first 7.0 miles of this drive is paved) 12.0 miles to the junction of Forest Road #257, at the southern end of Bonham Reservoir, and turn right. Proceed west 3.3 miles (you will pass above Neversweat Reservoir as you drop down the hill) to the fork in the road and turn right onto Forest Road #258. Continue 0.3 mile to Neversweat Reservoir adjacent to the road on the right-hand side.

Size, Depth, and Elevation: 19 acres, 15 feet deep, and 10,070 feet.

Fish: Rainbow and brook trout. Catchable rainbow trout are stocked annually, several times throughout the spring and summer. Subcatchable brook trout are stocked annually.

Agency: Bureau of Reclamation.

Comments: An unimproved boat launching area is usable by those skilled in trailer use, water levels permitting. Fishing pressure is heavy due to easy access and local popularity of this lake. No developed campsites exist at this reservoir, but numerous informal camping spots are available. Please pack out trash.

Special Regulations: None.

KITSON RESERVOIR

Access: From Collbran, travel south on Forest Access Road #121 (the first 7.0 miles of this drive is paved) 12.0 miles to the junction of Forest Road #257, at the southern end of Bonham Reservoir, and turn right. Proceed west 3.3 miles to the fork in the

Map 2 - Cottonwood Lakes Area

road and turn left, continuing on Forest Road #257. Travel 0.6 mile to Kitson Reservoir, on the left-hand side of the road.

Size, Depth, and Elevation: 18 acres, 13 feet deep, and 10,040 feet.

Fish: Rainbow trout, brook trout and Arctic grayling. Catchable rainbow and subcatchable brook trout are stocked annually. Arctic grayling were introduced into this reservoir in 1988.

Agency: Bureau of Reclamation.

Comments: An unimproved boat launching area is usable by those skilled in trailer use, water levels permitting. Bank access is easy and fishing pressure is moderate. No developed campsites exist at this reservoir. Please pack out trash.

Special Regulations: All grayling caught must be returned to the water immediately.

COTTONWOOD RESERVOIR #4

Access: From Collbran, travel south on Forest Access Road #121 (the first 7.0 miles of this drive is paved) 12.0 miles to the junction of Forest Road #257, at the southern end of Bonham Reservoir, and turn right. Proceed west 3.3 miles to the fork in the road and turn left, continuing on Forest Road #257. Travel 1.3 miles, passing Kitson Reservoir, and turn left. Proceed 0.3 mile directly to Cottonwood Reservoir #4.

Size, Depth, and Elevation: 32 acres, 41 feet deep, 10,200 feet.

Fish: Rainbow trout, stocked annually as catchables, several times throughout the spring and summer.

Agency: Bureau of Reclamation.

Comments: An unimproved boat launching area is usable by those skilled in trailer use, water levels permitting. Bank access is easy and fishing pressure is moderate. No developed campsites exist at this reservoir. Please pack out trash.

Special Regulations: None.

COTTONWOOD RESERVOIR #1

Access: From Collbran, travel south on Forest Access Road #121 (the first 7.0 miles of this drive is paved) 12.0 miles to the junction of Forest Road #257, at the southern end of Bonham Reservoir, and turn right. Proceed west 3.3 miles to the fork in the road and turn left, continuing on Forest Road #257. Travel 2.1 miles, passing Kitson Reservoir, to Cottonwood Reservoir #1. The road dead-ends at the dam where large parking areas and access to the boat ramp are located.

Size, Depth, and Elevation: 77 acres, 44 feet deep, 10,065 feet.

Fish: Rainbow trout, cutthroat trout, brook trout, splake, and white suckers. Catchable rainbow trout are stocked annually, several times throughout the spring and summer. Subcatchable Colorado River cutthroat trout are stocked periodically. Subcatchable splake, introduced in 1989, are stocked periodically. Brook trout and white suckers are from wild spawn.

Agency: Bureau of Reclamation.

Comments: Easy bank access, a graveled boat ramp, and a major campground make this lake a very popular destination. These features and the variety of fish present result in heavy fishing pressure.

Special Regulations: None.

LILY LAKE

Access: From Collbran, travel south on Forest Access Road #121 (the first 7.0 miles of this drive is paved) 12.0 miles to the junction of Forest Road #257, at the southern end of Bonham Reservoir, and turn right. Proceed west 3.3 miles to the fork in the road and turn left, continuing on Forest Road #257. Travel 1.3 miles, passing Kitson Reservoir, and turn left. Proceed 0.3 mile directly to Cottonwood Reservoir #4. Hike south across the dam and follow the trail 0.6 mile to Lily Lake.

Size, Depth, and Elevation: 4 acres, 27 feet deep, and 10,220 feet.

Fish: Rainbow and brook trout. Subcatchable rainbow trout are stocked annually. Brook trout are from wild spawn.

Agency: U.S. Forest Service.

Comments: Lily Lake is a natural lake. This is a hike-in-only lake. Fishing pressure is light. No developed campsites exist at this reservoir. Please pack out trash.

Special Regulations: None.

DECAMP RESERVOIR

Access: From Collbran, travel South on Forest Access Road #121 (the first 7.0 miles of this drive is paved) 12.0 miles to the Junction of Forest Road #257, at the southern end of Bonham

Reservoir, and turn right. Proceed west 3.3 miles to the fork in the road and turn left, continuing on Forest Road #257. Travel 1.3 miles, passing Kitson Reservoir, and turn right onto the four-wheel-drive road. Proceed 0.9 mile, bearing left at the fork near the lake, directly to DeCamp Reservoir.

Size, Depth, and Elevation: 9 acres, 11 feet deep, and 9,760 feet.

Fish: Brook trout from wild spawn.

Agency: Bureau of Reclamation.

Comments: While Decamp does not hold large numbers of brook trout, the fish present tend to be larger individuals. Fishing pressure is light. No developed campsites exist at this reservoir. Please pack out trash.

Special Regulations: None.

BIG MEADOWS RESERVOIR

Access: From Collbran, travel south on Forest Access Road #121 (the first 7.0 miles of this drive is paved) 12.0 miles to the Junction of Forest Road #257, at the southern end of Bonham Reservoir, and turn right. Proceed west 3.3 miles (you will pass above Neversweat Reservoir as you drop down the hill) to the fork in the road and turn right onto Forest Road #258. Continue 1.9 miles, passing Neversweat Reservoir, to Big Meadows Reservoir on the left-hand side of the road.

Size, Depth, and Elevation: 40 acres, 24 feet deep, and 9,800 feet.

Fish: Rainbow and brook trout. Fingerling rainbow trout are stocked every other year. Brook trout are from wild spawn.

Agency: Bureau of Reclamation.

Special Regulations: None.

COTTONWOOD RESERVOIR #5

Access: From Collbran, travel south on Forest Access Road #121 (the first 7.0 miles of this drive is paved) 12.0 mile to the junction of Forest Road #257, at the southern end of Bonham Reservoir, and turn right. Proceed west 3.3 miles (you will pass above Neversweat Reservoir as you drop down the hill) to the fork in the road and turn right onto Forest Road #258. Continue 1.1 miles and turn left. Proceed 0.9 mile directly to Cottonwood Reservoir.

Size, Depth, and Elevation: 28 acres, 30 feet deep, and 9,966 feet.

Fish: Cutthroat and brook trout. Subcatchable Colorado River cutthroat trout are stocked every other year. Brook trout are from wild spawn.

Agency: Bureau of Reclamation.

Comments: The cutthroats in this reservoir tend to he large but hard to catch. The road to this lake has been recently upgraded. An unimproved boat launching area is usable by those skilled in trailer use, water levels permitting. bank access is easy and fishing pressure is moderate. No developed campsites exist at this reservoir, but numerous informal camping spots are available. Please pack out trash.

Special Regulations: None.

COTTONWOOD CREEK

Access: From Collbran, travel south on Forest Access Road #121 (the first 7.0 miles of this drive is paved) 12.0 miles to the junction of Forest Road #257, at the southern end of Bonham Reservoir, and turn right. Proceed west 3.3 miles to the fork in the road and turn left, continuing on Forest Road #257. Travel 2.1 miles, passing Kitson Reservoir, to Cottonwood Reservoir #1. The road dead-ends at the dam, park in parking area on the right-hand side of the road. Cottonwood Creek flows from the dam on Cottonwood Lake #1 and is accessible by hiking downstream.

Land Status: Cottonwood Creek is 12.5 miles long from the dam of Cottonwood Lake #1 to Plateau Creek. The upper 4.5 miles lie within the National Forest. The lower 8.0 miles lie on private land. Obtain permission before accessing the stream on private land!

Stream Width and Elevation on Public Lands: 6 feet wide and 7,440 to 10,020 feet.

Fish: Rainbow and brook trout. Fingerling rainbow trout are stocked periodically. Brook trout are from wild spawn.

Comments: Cottonwood Creek is a steep, swift-flowing stream. Some good pools are present, but streamside access is limited in some reaches due to dense vegetation.

Special Regulations: None.

Map 2 - Bonham Reservoir Area

BONHAM RESERVOIR AREA

Bonham Reservoir is a well-known reference point on the Grand Mesa. The signs along the road from Collbran direct recreationists to Bonham Reservoir, which sits at the junction of Forest Roads #121 and #157.

Proceeding south past Bonham Reservoir on Forest Road #121 takes you over the divide of the Grand Mesa to the numerous lakes on the Mesa's southern benches. This divide, just south of Big Creek Reservoir, separates Grand Mesa's north flowing and south-flowing drainage's which feed the Colorado and Gunnison Rivers. Turning west at Forest Road #157 provides access to another 10 reservoirs holding trout.

The reservoirs in this area, and those in the Cottonwood Lakes area, are managed by the Bureau of Reclamation. The Bureau stores and releases water from these reservoirs to generate electricity at their Upper and Lower Molina Power Plants. Bonham Reservoir is essentially operated as a forebay for the Upper Molina Power plant. A large conduit on the west end of the Bonham Reservoir dam collects the water and the Grand Mesa provides the elevation needed to send the water rushing down to the turbines located over 2,000 feet down the mountainside.

Access to Bonham and Big Creek reservoirs is easy; four-wheel drive may be needed to reach Atkinson Reservoir, depending on weather and road conditions. Developed campgrounds at Bonham and Big Creek reservoirs add to the area's popularity. Big Creek, particularly between Big Creek and Bonham reservoirs, helps absorb the heavy fishing pressure that this area receives.

BONHAM RESERVOIR

Access: From Collbran, travel south on Forest Access Road #121 (the first 7.0 miles of this drive is paved) 11.5 miles to Bonham Reservoir. The northern end of the lake can be accessed by turning right (Forest Road 259) and driving through the Bureau of Reclamation facility. Driving to the southern end of the reservoir and turning right onto Forest Road #121 takes you to several parking areas located a short distance from the reservoir.
Size, Depth, and Elevation: 88 acres, 48 feet deep, and 9,755 feet.
Fish: Cutthroat and creel-sized rainbow trout.
Agency: Bureau of Reclamation.
Comments: This area is very popular locally and this lake receives heavy fishing pressure. The campground and the lake's location at the junction of two major Forest Access Roads makes Bonham Reservoir a convenient destination.
Special Regulations: None.

BIG CREEK RESERVOIR #1

Access: From Collbran, travel south on Forest Access Road #121 (the first 7.0 miles of this drive is paved) 13.9 miles, passing Bonham Reservoir, directly to Big Creek Reservoir. Proceed 0.3 mile around the lake and turn right to access the campground and boat ramp.
Size, Depth, and Elevation: 63 acres, 22 feet deep, 10,120 feet.
Fish: Colorado River cutthroat.
Agency: Bureau of Reclamation.
Comments: Colorado River cutthroat fishery.
Special Regulations: Check the fishing season information brochure.

ATKINSON RESERVOIR

Access: From Collbran, travel south on Forest Access Road #121 (the first 7.0 miles of this drive is paved) 12.0 miles to the junction of Forest Road #257 at the southern end of Bonham Reservoir. From here, continue straight on Forest Road #121 0.4 mile and turn left onto the four-wheel-drive road. Proceed 0.6 mile to the reservoir.
Size, Depth, and Elevation: 87 acres, 30 feet deep, and 10,120 feet.
Fish: Rainbow, cutthroat, and brook trout. Subcatchable rainbow trout are stocked annually. Fingerling brook trout are stocked periodically. Cutthroat trout have not been stocked in recent years.
Agency: Bureau of Reclamation.
Comments: This reservoir is susceptible to winterkill. Bank access is easy and fishing pressure is heavy. No developed campsites exist at this reservoir. Please pack out trash.
Special Regulations: None.

ATKINSON CREEK

Access: From Collbran, travel south on Forest Access Road #121 (the first 7.0 miles of this drive is paved) 11.5 miles to the northern access to Bonham Reservoir (Forest Road #259). Atkinson Creek crosses the main road here and flows into Big Creek, just below the dam on Bonham Reservoir. You could also hike up Atkinson Creek from the main road or drive to Atkinson Reservoir and hike downstream below the dam. Atkinson Creek above Atkinson Reservoir is very small.
Land Status: Atkinson Creek 1.5 miles long from the dam of Atkinson Reservoir to Big Creek. Its entire length is within the National Forest.
Stream Width and Elevation on Public Lands: 3 feet wide and 9,680 to 10,090 feet.
Fish: Rainbow, cutthroat, and brook trout enter the stream from Atkinson Reservoir.
Comments: This stream is shallow, but is has some good pools. Streamside access is easy and fishing pressure is moderate.
Special Regulations: None.

BIG CREEK

Access: From Collbran, travel south on Forest Access Road #l21 (the first 7.0 miles of this drive is paved) 11.5 miles and turn right, accessing the northern end of Bonham Reservoir where the road actually crosses the dam. Big Creek flows from the dam of Bonham Reservoir and is fishable, but streamside access soon becomes difficult due to the steepness of the banks. Big Creek can also be accessed between the dam of Big Creek Reservoir and the upper end of Bonham Reservoir. The stream in this area is accessed by hiking. The most popular spot to fish Big Creek is where it crosses Forest Road #257.
Land Status: Big Creek is 14.5 miles long from the dam of Big Creek Reservoir to Plateau Creek. The upper 4.0 miles lie within the National Forest. The lower 8.5 miles lie on private land. Obtain permission before accessing the stream on private land!
Stream Width and Elevation on Public Lands: 8 feet wide and 8,400 to 10,100 feet.
Fish: Cutthroat trout are found above Bonham Reservoir. Cutthroat and brook trout are found below Bonham Reservoir. Both species enter the stream from the reservoirs in Big Creek drainage.
Comments: The stream flows through a rock bed below the Bonham Reservoir dam and is difficult to fish where the stream flows in the steep-sided draw. Dense vegetation in this area can also hamper fishing. Fishing pressure in this area is light. Above Bonham Reservoir the stream flows through a large meadow and has many nice pools. Fishing pressure in this area is moderate.
Special Regulations: None.

Boating on the Grand Mesa

Boaters are welcome on the Grand Mesa! Boats allow Grand Mesa angler's additional opportunities to enjoy some of the greatest trout fishing and scenery to be found in Colorado.

Boaters should keep in mind that most of the Grand Mesa's lakes are relatively small. With the notable exceptions of Vega (900 acres), Island (179 acres), Eggleston (164 acres), Park (125 acres), and Baron (100 acres) reservoirs, most of the Grand Mesa's lakes are less than 100 acres in size. The smallest lake where you could launch a boat is probably Little Grouse Reservoir, which covers only 2 acres. Remember some of the lakes are just too small for motorboats. Except for Vega Reservoir, which combines paved access and boat ramps, the Grand Mesa is not a destination spot for larger powerboats.

What the Grand Mesa does offer is myriad options for boaters with smaller watercraft. Small watercraft that do not require a trailer can be launched at just about any lake on the Grand Mesa that you can drive to. The following will help you plan your fishing trip if you plan to bring a boat.

No Boats

Operating any kind of boat or raft is illegal on Blue Lake, Carson Lake and Colby Horse Park Reservoirs, all within Mesa County.

No Motors

Mesa County:

While boats are permitted on the following lakes, having any kind of motorized watercraft is illegal.

Beaver Lake and Jumbo Reservoir,

Delta County:

Bonita Reservoir, Butts Lake, Carp Lake, Granby Reservoir #7, Sackett Reservoir and Trout Lake.

Boat Access

The following reservoirs have undeveloped, unsurfaced boat launch areas. It is possible for individuals skillful in trailer use to access and launch trailered boats at these launching areas if water levels permit. These areas also provide convenient access points for loading and unloading watercraft and gear. However, if you are trailering a boat to one of these waters, consider the weather and road conditions, and the suitability of your vehicle, trailer, and boat for getting in and getting out of these access points.

Mesa County:

Atkinson Reservoir, Cottonwood Reservoir #4, Cottonwood Reservoir #5, Kitson Reservoir, Neversweat Reservoir and Waterdog Reservoir.

Delta County:

Baron Lake, Hotel Twin Lake, Kiser Slough Reservoir, Sackett Reservoir (no motors), Ward Lake and Wier & Johnson Reservoir.

Developed Boat Ramps

The following reservoirs have developed boat ramps, either well graveled or paved. These boat ramps provide good access for trailered boats, water levels permitting. Again, it is wise to be aware of weather and road conditions before traveling to some of the more remote reservoirs with a trailer in tow.

Mesa County:

Big Creek Reservoir, Cottonwood Reservoir #1 and Vega Reservoir.

Delta County:

Alexander Lake, Eggleston Lake, Island Lake, Park Reservoir, Vela Reservoir and Youngs Creek Reservoir #3.

Map 3 - Grand Mesa

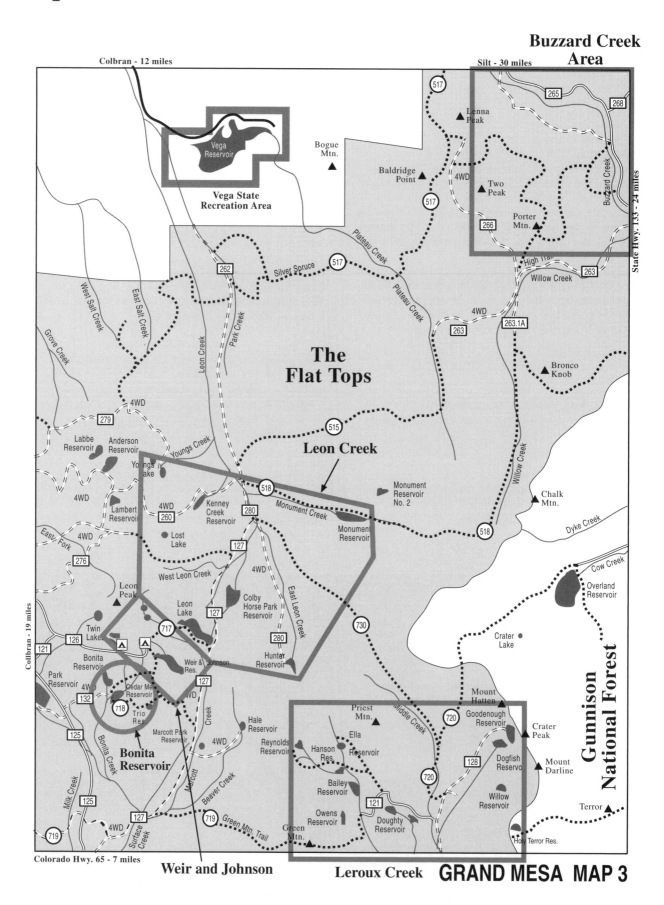

Buzzard Creek Area

Colbran - 12 miles

Silt - 30 miles

Vega Reservoir

Vega State Recreation Area

Bogue Mtn.

▲ Lenna Peak

265

268

517

Baldridge Point ▲

4WD

▲ Two Peak

517

Buzzard Creek

266

Porter Mtn. ▲

State Hwy. 133 - 24 miles

262

Silver Spruce

517

Plateau Creek

High Trail

263

Willow Creek

West Salt Creek

East Salt Creek

Leon Creek

Park Creek

Plateau Creek

4WD

263.1A

Grove Creek

The Flat Tops

263

279

4WD

Leon Creek

515

Bronco Knob ▲

Labbe Reservoir

Anderson Reservoir

Youngs Creek

Youngs Lake

518

Monument Reservoir No. 2

Willow Creek

Chalk Mtn. ▲

4WD

Lambert Reservoir

4WD 260

Kenney Creek Reservoir

280

Monument Creek

Dyke Creek

East Fork

4WD

276

Lost Lake

127

4WD

Monument Reservoir

518

Cow Creek

Overland Reservoir

West Leon Creek

East Leon Creek

Leon Peak ▲

Leon Lake

127

Colby Horse Park Reservoir

280

730

Crater Lake

Collbran - 19 miles

126

717

Hunter Reservoir

Gunnison National Forest

Twin Lakes

121

⛺ ⛺

Bonita Reservoir

Weir & Johnson Res.

127

Mount Hatten ▲

Park Reservoir

4WD 132

Cedar Mesa Reservoir

718

Trio Res.

127

4WD

720

Goodenough Reservoir

Crater Peak ▲

125

Bonita Reservoir

Marcott Park Reservoir

Marcott Creek

4WD

Hale Reservoir

Priest Mtn. ▲

Middle Creek

128

Dogfish Reservoir

Mount Darline ▲

Reynolds Reservoir

Hanson Res.

Ella Reservoir

720

Milk Creek

125

Bonita Creek

Beaver Creek

Bailey Reservoir

121

Willow Reservoir

Terror ▲

127

4WD

719

Green Mtn. Trail

Owens Reservoir

Doughty Reservoir

Holy Terror Res.

719

Surface Creek

Green Mtn. ▲

Colorado Hwy. 65 - 7 miles

Weir and Johnson

Leroux Creek

GRAND MESA MAP 3

Map 3 - Bonita Reservoir

BONITA RESERVOIR AREA

The access to the lakes in this beautiful backcountry setting is limited to four-wheel-drive vehicles only. The challenging four-wheel-drive road winds up and down through the small open meadows in the coniferous forest. This somewhat limited access makes this an excellent location for fishing, hiking and watching wildlife.

The three lakes in this area - Cedar Mesa, Bonita, and Trio reservoirs - are stocked with Snake River cutthroat trout. This cutthroat subspecies is highly prized since it is not as available for widespread stocking as other trout species. Snake River cutthroats have shown excellent growth in Colorado and their performance in these reservoirs should be no exception.

There are no developed campgrounds in this area. Please pack out trash.

CEDAR MESA RESERVOIR

Access: From Cedaredge, travel north on Highway 65 16.0 miles and turn right onto Forest Road #121 (paved) just before reaching Carp Lake. Proceed east 2.5 miles to the fork in the road. Continue to the left on Forest Road #121 (unpaved) for 5.5 miles and turn right onto Forest Road #125. Proceed on Forest Road #125 1.3 miles and turn left onto Forest Road #132, a four-wheel-drive road. Continue 1.3 miles to the dam of Cedar Mesa Reservoir.
Size, Depth, and Elevation: 38 acres, 22 feet deep and 9,960 feet.
Fish: Snake River cutthroat trout stocked alternate years as fingerlings.
Agency: Cedar Mesa Ditch and Reservoir Company.
Comments: Fishing pressure is moderate. No developed campsites exist at this reservoir.
Special Regulations: None.

BONITA RESERVOIR

Access: From Cedaredge, travel north on Highway 65 16.0 miles and turn right onto Forest Road #121 (paved) just before reaching Carp Lake. Proceed east 2.5 miles to the fork in the road. Continue to the left on Forest Road #121 (unpaved) for 5.5 miles and turn right onto Forest Road #125. Proceed on Forest Road #125 1.3 miles and turn left onto Forest Road #132, a four-wheel-drive road. Continue 1.2 miles to the fork in the road and go left, traveling 0.2 mile to the dam of Bonita Reservoir.
Size, Depth, and Elevation: 22 acres, 12 feet deep, and 10,050 feet.
Fish: Snake River and Colorado River cutthroat trout stocked as fingerlings. Snake River cutthroats are stocked every other year. Colorado River cutthroats are stocked periodically.
Agency: U.S. Forest Service.
Comments: Fishing pressure is moderate. No developed campsites exist at this reservoir.
Special Regulations: Motorized boats are prohibited.

TRIO RESERVOIR

Access: From Cedaredge, travel north on Highway 65 16.0 miles and turn right onto Forest Road #121 (paved) just before reaching Carp Lake. Proceed east 2.5 miles to the fork in the road. Continue to the left on Forest Road #121 (unpaved) for 5.5 miles and turn right onto Forest Road #125. Proceed on Forest Road #125 1.3 miles and turn left onto Forest Road #132, a four-wheel-drive road. Continue 1.3 miles to the dam of Cedar Mesa Reservoir. Proceed across the top of the dam 1.2 miles to Trio Reservoir.
Size, Depth, and Elevation: 17 acres, 24 feet deep, 10,200 feet.
Fish: Snake River cutthroat trout stocked alternate years as sub-catchables.
Agency: Private permittee.
Comments: The water level in this reservoir may be very low by midsummer. Fishing pressure is moderate. No developed campsites exist at this reservoir. Please pack out trash.
Special Regulations: None.

BONITA CREEK

Access: From Cedaredge, travel north on Highway 65 16.0 miles and turn right onto Forest Road #121 (paved) just before reaching Carp Lake. Proceed east 2.5 miles to the fork in the road. Continue to the left on Forest Road #121 (unpaved) for 5.5 miles and turn right onto Forest Road #125. Proceed on Forest Road #125 1.3 miles and turn left onto Forest Road #132, a four-wheel-drive road. Continue 1.2 miles to the fork in the road and go left, traveling 0.2 mile to the dam of Bonita Reservoir. Bonita Creek essentially begins here and flows through Cedar Mesa Reservoir. The stream, also accessible below Cedar Mesa Reservoir, parallels Forest Road #125 for 0.5 mile about 1 mile below the dam.
Land Status: Bonita Creek is 3.0 miles long from the dam of Cedar Mesa Reservoir to West Surface Creek. Its entire length is within the National Forest.
Stream Width and Elevation on Public Lands: 4 feet wide and 9,200 to 10,038 feet.
Fish: Colorado River cutthroat trout stocked periodically as fingerlings.
Comments: This small stream supports a good trout population and has numerous small pools. Stream bank vegetation overhangs the channel in many areas.
Special Regulations: None.

Map 3 - Weir & Johnson Reservoir Area

WEIR & JOHNSON RESERVOIR AREA

Commonly mistaken to be two separate lakes, our reference point for this fishing area, Weir and Johnson Reservoir, is actually a single body of water. This area includes not only the the Grand Mesa's highest fishing lakes, but also the Grand Mesa's highest point, Leon Peak.

Leon Peak, at 11,231 feet, is the single best indicator of the divide that separates the drainages and reservoirs on the south side of the Grand Mesa from those on the north side. The streams that flow north and east feed the Colorado River. The streams flowing south and west drain into the Gunnison River, one of the Colorado River's largest tributaries.

This area offers a wide variety of recreational opportunities and receives heavy use. Two developed campgrounds add to the convenience of recreating in this area. Several hike-in-only lakes provide getaways from the popular drive-to lakes. The trails to the outlying lakes are incredibly scenic and offer good opportunities for watching wildlife.

TWIN LAKE #1

Access: From Cedaredge, travel north on Highway 65 16.0 miles and turn right onto Forest Road #121 (paved) just before reaching Carp Lake. Proceed east 2.5 miles to the fork in the road. Continue to the left on Forest Road #121 (unpaved) for 9.0 miles and turn right onto the Weir and Johnson Road (Forest Road #126). Proceed 1.6 miles and turn left onto the dirt road. Travel 0.3 mile to Twin Lake #1.
Size, Depth, and Elevation: 23 acres, 42 feet deep, 10,400 feet.
Fish: Rainbow trout stocked annually as fingerlings.
Agency: Private permittee.
Comments: This area is very popular locally and this lake receives heavy fishing pressure. A developed campground and restrooms are available on south shore.
Special Regulations: None.

TWIN LAKE #2

Access: From Cedaredge, travel north on Highway 65 16.0 miles and turn right onto Forest Road #121 (paved) just before reaching Carp Lake. Proceed east 2.5 miles to the fork in the road. Continue to the left on Forest Road #121 (unpaved) for 9.0 miles and turn right onto the Weir and Johnson Road (Forest Road #126). Proceed 1.6 miles and turn left onto the dirt road. Travel 0.6 mile, passing Twin Lake #1, to Twin Lake #2.
Size, Depth, and Elevation: 21 acres, 23 feet deep, 10,400 feet.
Fish: Rainbow trout stocked annually as fingerlings.
Agency: Private permittee.
Comments: This area is very popular locally and this lake receives heavy fishing pressure. A developed campground and restrooms are available nearby at Twin Lake #1.
Special Regulations: None.

SACKETT RESERVOIR

Access: From Cedaredge, travel north on Highway 65 16.0 miles and turn right onto Forest Road #121 (paved) just before reaching Carp Lake. Proceed east 2.5 miles to the fork in the road. Continue to the left on Forest Road #121 (unpaved) for 9.0 miles and turn right onto the Weir and Johnson Road (Forest Road #126). Proceed 2.8 miles to Sackett Reservoir, located directly west of Weir and Johnson Reservoir.
Size, Depth, and Elevation: 10 acres, 24 feet deep, 10,460 feet.
Fish: Rainbow and brook trout. Subcatchable rainbow trout are stocked annually. Brook trout are from wild spawn.
Agency: Private permittee.
Comments: This area is very popular locally and this lake receives heavy fishing pressure. A developed campground and restrooms are available nearby at the Wier and Johnson Campground. An unimproved boat launching area on the lake's eastern shore is conveniently located right off the road.
Special Regulations: Motorized boats are prohibited.

WEIR AND JOHNSON RESERVOIR

Access: From Cedaredge, travel north on Highway 65 16.0 miles and turn right onto Forest Road #121 (paved) just before reaching Carp Lake. Proceed east 2.5 miles to the fork in the road. Continue to the left on Forest Road #121 (unpaved) for 9.0 miles and turn right onto the Weir and Johnson Road (Forest Road #126). Proceed 2.8 miles directly to Weir And Johnson Reservoir.
Size, Depth, and Elevation: 47 acres, 55 feet deep, 10,480 feet.
Fish: Rainbow and brook trout. Catchable rainbow trout are stocked annually, several times throughout the spring and summer. Brook trout are from wild spawn.
Agency: Private permirtee.
Comments: This area is very popular locally and this lake receives heavy fishing pressure. A developed campground and restrooms are available nearby at the Wier and Johnson Campground. An unimproved boat launching area is usable by those skilled in trailer use, water levels permitting.
Special Regulations: None.

LEON PEAK RESERVOIR (SISSIE LAKE)

Access: From Cedaredge, travel north on Highway 65 16.0 miles and turn right onto Forest Road #121 (paved) just before reaching Carp Lake. Proceed east 2.5 miles to the fork in the road. Continue to the left on Forest Road #121 (unpaved) for 9.0 mile and turn right onto the Weir and Johnson Road (Forest Road #126). Proceed 2.8 miles directly to Weir And Johnson Reservoir. Hike across the dam on Weir and Johnson Reservoir to the fork in the trail and turn left. Proceed 0.5 mile to Leon Peak Reservoir on the left-hand side of the trail.
Size, Depth, and Elevation: 9 acres, 20 feet deep, 10,640 feet.
Fish: Cutthroat trout. Subcatchable Colorado River cutthroat trout are stocked periodically.
Agency: U.S. Forest Service.
Comments: Leon Peak Reservoir is the highest lake on the Grand Mesa managed for trout. This is a hike-in-only lake. Fishing pressure is light. No developed campsites exist at this reservoir. Please pack out trash.
Special Regulations: None.

FINNEY CUT LAKE #1

Access: From Cedaredge, travel north on Highway 65 16.0 miles and turn right onto Forest Road #121 (paved) just before reaching Carp Lake. Proceed east 2.5 miles to the fork in the road. Continue to the left on Forest Road #121 (unpaved) for 9.0 miles and turn right onto the Weir and Johnson Road (Forest Road #126). Proceed 2.8 miles directly to Weir And Johnson Reservoir. Hike across the dam on Weir and Johnson Reservoir to the fork in the trail and turn left. Proceed 1.0 mile, passing Leon Peak Reservoir, to Finney Cut Lake #1 on the right-hand side of the trail.
Size, Depth, and Elevation: 3 acres, 9 feet deep, 10,420 feet.
Fish: Cutthroat trout. Subcatchable Colorado River cutthroat trout are stocked every other year.
Agency: U.S. Forest Service.
Comments: Finney Cut Lake #1 is a natural lake. This is a hike-in-only lake. Fishing pressure is light. No developed campsites exist at this reservoir. Please pack out trash.
Special Regulations: None.

FINNEY CUT LAKE #2

Access: From Cedaredge, travel north on Highway 65 16.0 miles and turn right onto Forest Road #121 (paved) just before reaching Carp Lake. Proceed east 2.5 miles to the fork in the road.

Map 3 - Weir & Johnson Reservoir and Leon Creek Areas

Continue to the left on Forest Road #121 (unpaved) for 9.0 miles and turn right onto the Weir and Johnson Road (Forest Road #126). Proceed 2.8 miles directly to Weir and Johnson Reservoir. Hike across the dam on Weir and Johnson Reservoir to the fork in the trail and turn left. Proceed 1.5 miles, passing Leon Peak Reservoir and Finney Cut Lake #1, directly to Finney Cut Lake 2.
Size, Depth, and Elevation: 9 acres, 36 feet deep, 10,490 feet.
Fish: Cutthroat trout. Subcatchable Colorado River cutthroat trout are stocked every other year.
Agency: U.S. Forest Service.
Comments: This is a hike-in-only lake. Fishing pressure is light. No developed campsites exist at this reservoir.
Special Regulations: None.

COLE RESERVOIR #1

Access: From Cedaredge, travel north on Highway 65 16.0 miles and turn right onto Forest Road #121 (paved) just before reaching Carp Lake. Proceed east 2.5 miles to the fork in the road. Continue to the left on Forest Road #121 (unpaved) for 9.0 miles and turn right onto the Weir and Johnson Road (Forest Road #126). Proceed 2.5 miles and turn right into the parking area at Slide Rock Reservoir. Hike 0.7 mile east around Slide Rock Reservoir (intermittent) to Cole Reservoir #1.
Size, Depth, and Elevation: 8 acres, 52 feet deep, 10,420 feet.
Fish: Rainbow trout stocked periodically as fingerlings.
Agency: Private permittee.
Comments: The water level in this reservoir fluctuates greatly. This is a hike-in-only lake. Fishing pressure is light. No developed campsites exist at this reservoir. Please pack out trash.
Special Regulations: None.

THE PECKS RESERVOIR #1

Access: From Cedaredge, travel north on Highway 65 16.0 miles and turn right onto Forest Road #121 (paved) just before reaching Carp Lake. Proceed east 2.5 miles to the fork in the road. Continue to the left on Forest Road #121 (unpaved) for 9.0 miles and turn right onto the Weir and Johnson Road (Forest Road #126). Proceed 2.5 miles and turn right into the parking area at Slide Rock Reservoir. Hike east 0.8 mile, around Slide Rock Reservoir (intermittent) and past Cole Reservoir #1 to The Pecks Reservoir #1.
Size, Depth, and Elevation: 3 acres, 28 feet deep, 10,520 feet.
Fish: Rainbow and cutthroat trout. Neither species has been stocked in recent years.
Agency: U.S. Forest Service.
Comments: This is a hike-in-only lake. Fishing pressure is light. No developed campsites exist at this reservoir.
Special Regulations: None.

THE PECKS RESERVOIR #2

Access: From Cedaredge, travel north on Highway 65 16.0 miles and turn right onto Forest Road #121 (paved) just before reaching Carp Lake. Proceed east 2.5 miles to the fork in the road. Continue to the left on Forest Road #121 (unpaved) for 9.0 miles and turn right onto the Weir and Johnson Road (Forest Road #126). Proceed 2.5 miles and turn right into the parking area at Slide Rock Reservoir. Hike east 0.8 mile around Slide Rock Reservoir (intermittent) and past Cole Reservoir #1 and The Pecks Reservoir #1 to The Pecks Reservoir #2.
Size, Depth, and Elevation: 4 acres, 17 feet deep, 10,520 feet.
Fish: Rainbow and cutthroat trout. Neither species has been stocked in recent years.
Agency: U.S. Forest Service.
Comments: This is a hike-in-only lake. Fishing pressure is light. No developed campsites exist at this reservoir. Please pack out trash.
Special Regulations: None.

LEON CREEK AREA

Leon Creek is one of the Grand Mesa's larger streams. Three routes can be used to access the Leon Creek drainage, its tributaries, and the reservoirs in its basin. While two-wheel-drive vehicles with adequate clearance will get you into much of this basin when the roads are dry, four-wheel drive is strongly recommended since thunderstorms can make for hazardous travel. Be prepared!

Leon Creek itself is best accessed from Vega Reservoir. Be sure to check land status along this lower stretch of the stream, as much of it is private. Portions of Leon Creek must he accessed by hiking over the ridge west of Forest Road 518.

Streamside access can be challenging due to steep banks and dense brush. Some of the upper stretches of Leon Creek are comparatively flat and more easily accessed, however, these stretches tend to hold fewer fish.

The Leon Creek drainage can also be reached from the Bonham Lake Road (Forest Road 121). Traveling east on Forest Road #260 provides access to Kenney Creek Reservoir, and Youngs, Rock, and Lost lakes. Do not be misled by the well-graveled condition at the beginning of this road, as it eventually turns into a four-wheel-drive road. Sort of "on the other side of the mountain," Marcott Creek is included here as it provides access to the Leon Creek drainage and it receives some of its water from there as well. The Marcott Creek Road, Forest Road #127 provides access to Leon Creek from the south. Marcott Creek receives water via a tunnel from Leon Lake, the area's largest reservoir. Marcott Creek offers excellent fishing for cutthroats. Again, four-wheel drive is recommended.

ROCK LAKE

Access: From Collbran, travel south on Forest Access Road #121 (the first 7.0 miles of this drive is paved) 10.0 miles and turn left onto Forest Road #260. Proceed 1.2 miles and turn left onto Forest Road #279 (this road soon requires four-wheel drive). Proceed 4.5 miles to Rock Lake on the right-hand side of the road.
Size, Depth, and Elevation: 4 acres. 12 feet deep, 10.200 feet.
Fish: Rainbow trout stocked alternate years as subcatchables.
Agency: U.S. Forest Service.
Comments: Fishing pressure is light. No developed campsites exist at this reservoir. Please pack out trash.
Special Regulations: None.

YOUNGS LAKE

Access: From Collbran, travel south on Forest Access Road #121 (the first 7.0 miles of this drive is paved) 10.0 miles and turn left onto Forest Road #260. Proceed 1.2 miles and turn left onto Forest Road #279 (this road soon requires four-wheel drive). Proceed 5.0 miles, passing Rock Lake, to Youngs Lake.
Size, Depth, and Elevation: 10 acres, 6 feet deep, 10,180 feet.
Fish: Brook trout, from wild spawn.
Agency: U.S. Forest Service.
Comments: Youngs Lake is a natural lake. Fishing pressure is light. No developed campsites exist at this reservoir. Please pack out trash.
Special Regulations: None.

KENNEY CREEK RESERVOIR (KENDALL RES.)

Access: From Collbran, travel east on County Road 330 (paved) 14 miles to Vega Reservoir. At the park entrance (kiosk), turn right and proceed 1.0 mile, traveling across the dam, and turn right onto Forest Road #262. Proceed 7.9 miles and turn right onto the four-wheel-drive road. Ford Leon Creek and continue 1.0 mile to Kenney Creek Reservoir on the left-hand side of the road.
Size, Depth, and Elevation: 16 acres, 11 feet deep, and 9,880 feet.

Map 3 - Leon Creek Area

Fish: Rainbow, brook and cutthroat trout. Subcatchable rainbow and brook trout are stocked every other year. Cutthroat trout are from wild spawn.
Agency: Private perniittee.
Comments: Fishing pressure is light. No developed campsites exist at this reservoir. Please pack out trash.
Special Regulations: None.

LOST LAKE (KENNEY CREEK)

Access: From Collbran, travel east on County Road 330 (paved) 14 miles to Vega Reservoir. At the park entrance (kiosk), turn right and proceed 1.0 mile, traveling across the dam, and turn right onto Forest Road #262. Proceed 7.9 miles and turn right onto the four-wheel-drive road. Ford Leon Creek, and continue 2.1 miles, passing Kenney Creek Reservoir, to where the road crosses Kenney Creek. From here, hike up Kenney Creek 0.3 mile directly to Lost Lake.
Size, Depth, and Elevation: 3 acres, 7 feet deep, and 10,300 feet.
Fish: Cutthroat trout. Subcatchable Colorado River cutthroat trout are stocked every other year.
Agency: U.S. Forest Service.
Comments: Lost Lake is natural lake which receives light fishing pressure due to its remoteness. No developed campsites exist at this reservoir. Please pack out trash.
Special Regulations: None.

MONUMENT RESERVOIR #1

Access: From Collbran, travel east on County Road 330 (paved) 14 miles to Vega Reservoir. At the park entrance (kiosk), turn right and proceed 1.0 mile, traveling across the dam, and turn right onto Forest Road #262. Proceed 7.9 miles and turn left. Continue 3.0 miles to Monument Reservoir #1, on the right-hand side of the road.
Size, Depth, and Elevation: 34 acres, 33 feet deep, 10,400 feet.
Fish: Cutthroat trout. Subcatchable Colorado River cutthroat trout are stocked every other year.
Agency: Private permittee.
Comments: Four-wheel drive is not necessary to access this reservoir, but wet roads may limit access. Fishing pressure is light. No developed campsites exist at this reservoir.
Special Regulations: None.

COLBY HORSE PARK RESERVOIR

Access: From Collbran, travel east on County Road 330 (paved) 14 miles to Vega Reservoir. At the park entrance (kiosk), turn right and proceed 1.0 mile, traveling across the dam, and turn right onto Forest Road #262. Proceed 8.8 miles, fording Monument (at Monument Creek, the road becomes four-wheel drive only) and East Leon creeks, to the fork in the road. Proceed on the right fork (Forest Road #127) 2.6 miles, fording West Leon and Middle Leon creeks, and take a sharp left after crossing Middle Leon Creek. Continue 0.4 mile, fording Middle Leon Creek again, directly to Colby Horse Park Reservoir.
Size, Depth, and Elevation: 56 acres, 14 feet deep, 10,000 feet.
Fish: Cutthroat and rainbow trout. Subcatchable Colorado River cutthroat trout are stocked every other year. Rainbow trout have not been stocked in recent years.
Agency: Leon Lake Ditch and Reservoir Company.
Comments: Fishing pressure is moderate. No developed campsites exist at this reservoir. Please pack out trash.
Special Regulations: All boats and rafts are prohibited.

LEON LAKE

Access: Leon Lake can be accessed by several routes. The two routes listed below provide four-wheel drive and hiking alternatives. From Collbran, travel east on County Road 330 (paved) 14 miles to Vega Reservoir. At the park entrance (kiosk), turn right

and proceed 1.0 mile, traveling across the dam, and turn right onto Forest Road #262. Proceed 8.8 miles, fording Monument (at Monument Creek, the road becomes four-wheel drive only) and East Leon creeks, to the fork in the road. Proceed on the right fork (Forest Road #127) 3.0 miles, fording West Leon and Middle Leon creeks, to Leon Lake, on the right-hand side of the road. From Cedaredge, travel north on Highway 65 16.0 miles and turn right onto Forest Road #121 (paved) just before reaching Carp Lake. Proceed east 2.5 miles to the fork in the road. Continue to the left on Forest Road #121 (unpaved) for 9.0 miles and turn right onto the Weir and Johnson Road (Forest Road #126). Proceed 2.8 miles directly to Weir and Johnson Reservoir. Hike across the dam on Weir and Johnson Reservoir to the fork in the trail and turn right. Proceed 1.0 mile to Leon Lake on the left-hand side of the trail.
Size, Depth, and Elevation: 94 acres, 76 feet deep, 10,360 feet.
Fish: Brook trout from wild spawn. Lake provides a good opportunity to take advantage of the Bonus Brook Trout regulation.
Agency: Leon Lake Ditch and Reservoir Company.
Comments: This large reservoir is very popular and receives moderate fishing pressure. No developed campsites exist at this reservoir. Please pack out trash.
Special Regulations: None.

LANNING LAKE

Access: Lanning Lake can be accessed by several routes. The two routes listed below provide four-wheel-drive and hiking alternatives. From Collbran, travel east on County Road 330 (paved) 14 miles to Vega Reservoir. At the park entrance (kiosk), turn right and proceed 1.0 mile, traveling across the dam, and turn right onto Forest Road #262. Proceed 8.8 miles, fording Monument (at Monument Creek, the road becomes four-wheel drive only) and East Leon creeks, to the fork in the road. Proceed on the right fork (Forest Road #127) 3.0 miles, fording West Leon and Middle Leon creeks, to Lanning Lake on the left-hand side of the road. From Cedaredge, travel north on Highway 65 16.0 miles and turn right onto Forest Road #121 (paved), just before reaching Carp Lake. Proceed east 2.5 miles to the fork in the road. Continue to the left on Forest Road #121 (unpaved) for 9.0 miles and turn right onto the Weir and Johnson Road (Forest Road #126). Proceed 2.8 miles directly to Weir and Johnson Reservoir. Hike across the dam on Weir and Johnson Reservoir to the fork in the trail and turn right. Proceed 2.0 mile to the dam of Leon Lake. Lanning Lake is located below the Leon Lake dam just across the road.
Size, Depth, and Elevation: 3 acres, 12 feet deep, 10,310 feet.
Fish: Brook and cutthroat trout from wild spawn.
Agency: U.S. Forest Service.
Comments: Fishing pressure is light. No developed campsites exist at this reservoir. Please pack out trash.
Special Regulations: None.

HUNTER RESERVOIR

Access: From Collbran, travel east on County Road 330 (paved) 14 miles to Vega Reservoir. At the park entrance (kiosk), turn right and proceed 1.0 mile, traveling across the dam, and turn right onto Forest Road #262. Proceed 8.8 miles, fording Monument (at Monument Creek, the road becomes four-wheel drive only) and East Leon creeks, to the fork in the road. Proceed on the left fork (Forest Road #280) 3.5 miles, fording Leon and East Leon creeks, directly to Hunter Reservoir.
Size, Depth, and Elevation: 17 acres, 8 feet deep, and 10,360 feet.
Fish: Cutthroat trout. Subcatchable Colorado River cutthroat trout are stocked periodically.
Agency: U.S. Forest Service.
Comments: The access to this lake may be difficult, but the

Map 3 - Leon Creek Area

scenery is outstanding. Fishing pressure is light. No developed campsites exist at this reservoir. Please pack out trash.
Special Regulations: None.

LEON CREEK

Access: From Collbran, travel east on County Road 330 (paved) 14 miles to Vega Reservoir. At the park entrance (kiosk), turn right and proceed 1.0 mile, traveling across the dam, and turn right onto Forest Road #262. Proceed 1.5 miles to the Grand Mesa National Forest Boundary. From this boundary, upstream for 5.0 miles, the stream must be accessed by hiking up to 0.7 mile over the ridge to the west. About 5 miles south of the National Forest Boundary, Forest Road #262 swings close to Leon Creek and parallels the stream for about 0.7 mile. Streamside access in this area is comparatively easy.
Land Status: Leon Creek is 10.2 miles long from the confluence of Middle Leon and East Leon creeks to Plateau Creek. The lower 2.7 miles are on private land. The upper 7.5 miles lie within the National Forest.
Stream Width and Elevation on Public Lands: 18 feet wide and 8,500 to 9,650 feet.
Fish: Cutthroat, rainbow, and brown trout. Fingerling Colorado River cutthroat trout are stocked periodically. Rainbow and brown trout are from wild spawn.
Comments: This large stream has many good pools, especially farther downstream. In the lower reaches, the stream banks are steep and brushy limiting fishing access in some areas.
Special Regulations: None.

EAST LEON CREEK

Access: From Collbran, travel east on County Road 330 (paved) 14 miles to Vega Reservoir. At the park entrance (kiosk), turn right and proceed 1.0 mile, traveling across the dam, and turn right onto Forest Road #262. Proceed 8.8 miles, fording Monument (at Monument Creek, the road becomes four-wheel drive only) and East Leon creeks, to the fork in the road. Proceed on the left fork (Forest Road #280) 3.5 miles, fording Leon and East Leon creeks, directly to Hunter Reservoir. The road parallels the stream and provides easy access in most areas.
Land Status: East Leon Creek is 3.3 miles long from the dam of Hunter Reservoir to its confluence with Middle Leon Creek. Its entire length is in the National Forest.
Stream Width and Elevation on Public Lands: 5 feet wide and 9,650 to 10,358 feet.
Fish: Colorado River cutthroat stocked periodically as fingerlings.
Comments: The stream flows over a bed of large rocks, but good pools are present. Dense streamside vegetation makes fishing difficult in spots.
Special Regulations: None.

MIDDLE LEON CREEK

Access: From Collbran, travel east on County Road 330 (paved) 14 miles to Vega Reservoir. At the park entrance (kiosk), turn right and proceed 1.0 mile, traveling across the dam, and turn right onto Forest Road #262. Proceed 8.8 miles, fording Monument (at Monument Creek, the road becomes four-wheel drive only) and East Leon creeks, to the fork in the road. Proceed on the right fork (Forest Road #127) 2.6 miles, fording West Leon and Middle Leon creeks, and take a sharp left after crossing Middle Leon Creek. Continue 0.4 mile, fording Middle Leon Creek again, directly to Colby Horse Park Reservoir. Proceeding at the right fork (Forest Road #127) 3.0 miles takes you to Leon Lake. Middle Leon Creek is accessible at the road crossings and below Leon and Colby Horse Park reservoirs.
Land Status: Middle Leon Creek is 3.0 miles long from the dam of Leon Lake to its confluence with East Leon Creek. Its entire length is in the National Forest.

Stream Width and Elevation on Public Lands: 8 feet wide and 9,650 to 10,360 feet.
Fish: Colorado River cutthroat stocked periodically as fingerlings.
Comments: This is a swift-flowing stream, but some good pools are present. Dense streamside vegetation in spots makes fishing difficult.
Special Regulations: None.

MARCOTT CREEK

Access: From Cedaredge, travel north on Highway 65 3.5 miles and turn right on the Surface Creek Road. Proceed 6.0 miles to the Grand Mesa National Forest boundary and turn right on Forest Road #127 (four-wheel drive). Proceed 1.5 miles to where the road crosses Bonita Creek. After crossing Bonita Creek, the road parallels Marcott Creek for 4.5 miles.
Land Status: Marcott Creek is 4.9 miles from Leon Lake to Surface Creek. Its entire length is in the National Forest.
Stream Width and Elevation on Public Lands: 5 feet wide and 8,800 to 10,420 feet.
Fish: Cutthroat and rainbow trout. Fingerling Colorado River cutthroat trout are stocked periodically. Rainbow trout have not been stocked in recent years.
Comments: Marcott Creek is a midsize stream having some good pools. Road into this area is very rough, but stream is easy to fish.
Special Regulations: None.

MONUMENT CREEK

Access: From Collbran, travel east on County Road 330 (paved) 14 miles to Vega Reservoir. At the park entrance (kiosk), turn right and proceed 1.0 mile, traveling across the dam, and turn right onto Forest Road #262. Proceed 7.9 miles and turn left. Monument Creek parallels the road to the south. Continue 3.0 miles to Monument Reservoir #1 on the right-hand side of the road.
Land Status: Monument Creek is 2.3 miles long from the dam of Monument Reservoir to Leon Creek. Its entire length is in the National Forest.
Stream Width and Elevation on Public Lands: 8 feet wide and 9,500 to 10,200 feet.
Fish: Colorado River cutthroat stocked periodically as fingerlings.
Comments: Streamside access is easy. This small stream has good pools and good undercut banks.
Special Regulations: None.

PARK CREEK

Access: From Collbran, travel east on County Road 330 (paved) 14 miles to Vega Reservoir. At the park entrance (kiosk), turn right and proceed 1.0 mile, traveling across the dam, and turn right onto Forest Road #262. Proceed 1.5 miles to the Grand Mesa National Forest Boundary. Park Creek parallels the road on the east side, usually within 200 yards for most of its length.
Land Status: Park Creek is 10 miles long from its headwaters to Plateau Creek. The lower 2.3 miles of the stream lie on private land. After entering the National Forest, another 1.5 miles of the stream lies within private property. The stream is open to public access above and below this private in holding. Be sure to refer to a Grand Mesa National Forest map before fishing this stream. Respect private property.
Stream Width and Elevation on Public Lands: 4 feet wide and 8,260 to 10,560 feet.
Fish: Brook trout from wild spawn.
Comments: Park Creek is a small shallow stream with small pools that hold most of the fish. Dense streamside vegetation makes fishing difficult in some spots.
Special Regulations: None.

Map 3 - Leroux Creek Area

LEROUX CREEK AREA

Leroux Creek is a large drainage whose flows supply much of the water to irrigate the orchards that you pass through on your way to the Grand Mesa from Delta. Actually, it is Leroux Creek's major tributaries, West and East Leroux creeks, and Doughty Creek, which lie within the Grand Mesa National Forest. Leroux Creek itself lies almost entirely on private land.

In addition to the fishing opportunity offered by Leroux Creek's tributary streams, this area also has several small reservoirs that contain good trout populations. The fishing pressure in this area is light to moderate.

Vehicles with good ground clearance are recommended for traveling the roads in this area. Four-wheel drive is strongly recommended if roads are wet. Informal campsites are limited in this area. Please pack out trash.

DOUGHTY RESERVOIR

Access: From Delta, travel east on Highway 92 17.0 miles and turn left onto the Leroux Creek Road. Proceed on this road (It becomes Forest Road #128 at the National Forest Boundary) 18.8 miles to the fork in the road. Turn left here, onto Forest Road #121, and continue 1.0 mile to Doughty Reservoir on the left-hand side of the road.
Size, Depth, and Elevation: 24 acres, 18 feet deep, 9,750 feet.
Fish: Rainbow and cutthroat trout. Fingerling rainbow trout are stocked periodically. Cutthroat trout are from wild spawn.
Agency: Leroux Creek Water Users Association.
Comments: Fishing pressure is moderate due to the area's remoteness. No developed campsites exist at this reservoir.
Special Regulations: None.

HANSON RESERVOIR

Access: From Delta, travel east on Highway 92 17.0 miles and turn left onto the Leroux Creek Road. Proceed on this road (it becomes Forest Road #128 at the National Forest Boundary) 18.8 miles to the fork in the road. Turn left (continuing on Forest Road #121) and proceed 1.5 miles, passing Doughty Reservoir, and turn right onto the four-wheel-drive road. Proceed 0.5 mile directly to Hanson Reservoir.
Size, Depth, and Elevation: 24 acres, 18 feet deep, 9,750 feet.
Fish: Rainbow and cutthroat trout. Neither species has been stocked in recent years.
Agency: Leroux Creek Water Users Association.
Comments: Fishing pressure is light due to the lake's remoteness. No developed campsites. Pack out trash.
Special Regulations: None.

DOGFISH RESERVOIR

Access: From Delta, travel east on Highway 92 17.0 miles and turn left onto the Leroux Creek Road. Proceed on this road (it becomes Forest Road #128 at the National Forest Boundary) 18.8 miles to the fork in the road. Turn right, continuing on Forest Road #128 and proceed 3.0 miles by four-wheel drive to Dogfish Reservoir on the right-hand side of the road.
Size, Depth, and Elevation: 38 acres, 18 feet deep, 10,440 feet.
Fish: Rainbow trout, stocked periodically as fingerlings.
Agency: Leroux Creek Water Users Association.
Comments: Fishing pressure is light due to the lake's remoteness. No developed campsites. Please pack out trash.
Special Regulations: None.

GOODENOUGH RESERVOIR

Access: From Delta, travel east on Highway 92 17.0 miles and turn left onto the Leroux Creek Road. Proceed on this road (it becomes Forest Road #128 at the National Forest Boundary) 18.8 miles to the fork in the road. Turn right, continuing on Forest Road #128, and proceed 3.0 miles by four-wheel drive to Goodenough Reservoir on the left-hand side of the road.
Size, Depth, and Elevation: 54 acres, 12 feet deep, 10,500 feet.
Fish: Rainbow and cutthroat trout. Fingerling rainbow trout are stocked periodically. Cutthroat trout are from wild spawn.
Agency: Leroux Water Users Association.
Comments: Fishing pressure is light due to the lake's remoteness. No developed campsites exist at this reservoir.
Special Regulations: None.

DOUGHTY CREEK

Access: From Delta, travel east on Highway 92 17.0 miles and turn left onto the Leroux Creek Road. Proceed on this road (it becomes Forest Road #128 at the National Forest Boundary) 18.8 miles to the fork in the road. Turn left here onto Forest Road #121 and continue 1.0 mile to Doughty Reservoir on the left-hand side of the road. Doughty Creek flows from the dam.
Land Status: Doughty Creek is 3.0 miles long from the dam of Doughty Reservoir to East Leroux Creek. Its entire length is in the National Forest.
Stream Width and Elevation on Public Lands: 5 feet wide and 8,700 to 9,730 feet.
Fish: Rainbow and brook trout. Rainbow trout enter the stream from Doughty Reservoir. Brook trout are from wild spawn.
Comments: This small stream has many good pools. Dense streamside vegetation overhangs the stream, providing good cover, but it makes fishing difficult in spots.
Special Regulations: None.

EAST LEROUX CREEK

Access: From Delta, travel east on Highway 92 17.0 miles and turn left onto the Leroux Creek Road. Proceed on this road (it becomes Forest Road #128 at the National Forest Boundary) 18.8 miles to the fork in the road. Turn right, continuing on Forest Road #128 and proceed 3.0 miles by four-wheel drive to Dogfish Reservoir on the right-hand side of the road. East Leroux Creek flows from the dam.
Land Status: East Leroux Creek is 6.1 miles long from the dam of Dogfish Reservoir to Leroux Creek. Its entire length it is in the National Forest.
Stream Width and Elevation on Public Lands: 8 feet wide and 8,300 to 10,400 feet.
Fish: Rainbow and cutthroat trout. Rainbow trout enter the stream from Dogfish Reservoir. Cutthroat trout are from wild spawn.
Comments: East Leroux Creek is a larger stream with many good pools. Good streamside cover shades the stream, but it is accessible to anglers in many spots.
Special Regulations: None.

WEST LEROUX CREEK

Access: From Delta, travel east on Highway 92 17.0 miles and turn left onto the Leroux Creek Road. Proceed on this road (it becomes Forest Road #128 at the National Forest Boundary) 18.8 miles to the fork in the road. Turn left (continuing on Forest Road #121) and proceed 2.1 miles, passing Doughty Reservoir (bearing left) to where the road crosses West Leroux Creek.
Land Status: West Leroux Creek is 2.5 miles long from its intersection with Forest Road #121 to Leroux Creek. Its entire length is in the National Forest.
Stream Width and Elevation on Public Lands: 6 feet wide and 8,300 to 9,700 feet.
Fish: Cutthroat and rainbow trout. Fingerling Colorado River cutthroat trout are stocked periodically. Rainbow trout probably access the stream from Doughty Creek.
Comments: This small stream has many good pools. Dense streamside vegetation limits fishing access in some reaches.
Special Regulations: None.

Map 3 - Buzzard Creek Area

BUZZARD CREEK AREA

The Buzzard Creek drainage is a uniquely beautiful area situated in what is commonly referred to as "the back side of the Grand Mesa." The open rolling hills in this area contrast with the forested benches of the Grand Mesa. The area has no lakes, no developed campgrounds, and no services of any kind. Numerous roads off the main access road, Forest Road #265, provide access to the small streams in the area. The road access, generally good when dry, can suddenly turn treacherous following a thunderstorm. Four-wheel drive is recommended, if not required, when traveling off of Forest Road #265.

Since this area lacks lakes and facilities of any kind, fishing pressure is light. The streams are quite small and may carry little water. In fact, it is sometimes surprising to find trout in some of the stream reaches at all. However, these streams do hold trout, and this area may be just what you're looking for if you want to "get away from it all" on your fishing trip. Several hiking trails also exist in this often-overlooked area. The lower reaches of Buzzard Creek lie on private land. Be sure to obtain permission before entering these areas.

BUZZARD CREEK

Access: From Collbran, travel east on County Road 330 (paved) 6.0 miles to the Silt Cutoff/Vega fork. Proceed left on the Silt Cutoff Road 8.0 miles to the Hightower Road (Forest Road #265) and turn right. Proceed 2.0 miles to the Grand Mesa National Forest boundary. Forest Road #265 parallels Buzzard Creek for most of its length on the National Forest up to its headwaters. However, accessing the stream requires a short hike in many areas, and streamside access can be difficult due to steep banks and dense vegetation.
Land Status: Buzzard Creek is 30.5 miles long from Bird to Plateau Creek. The lower 20 miles lie on private land. Obtain permission before fishing in this area. The upper 10.5 miles lies entirely in the National Forest.
Stream Width and Elevation on Public Lands: 10 feet wide and 7,480 to 8,648 feet.
Fish: Rainbow, cutthroat, brook and brown trout, and white suckers and mottled sculpin. Subcatchable rainbow and brook trout are stocked periodically. Fingerling Colorado River cutthroat trout are stocked periodically. Brown trout, white suckers, and mottled sculpin are from wild spawn.
Comments: While this stream appears intermittent and stagnant during periods of low flow, surprisingly, it supports a fairly good trout population. The stream contains large rocks but few good pools. Much of the stream bottom is covered with algae during the summer. Livestock is common along this stream.
Special Regulations: None.

OWENS CREEK

Access: From Collbran, travel east on County Road 330 (paved) 6.0 miles to the Silt Cutoff, Vega fork. Proceed left on the Silt Cutoff Road 8.0 miles to the Hightower Road (Forest Road #265) and turn right. Proceed 8.2 miles and turn left on the Owens Creek Road (Forest Road #268). The lower 2.0 miles of stream is accessible along the road before it enters private property. Owens creek is again accessible upstream where it is crossed by the road, which parallels the stream for about 2.5 miles.
Land Status: Owens Creek runs through private land for about1.5 miles. The remainder of the stream is in the National Forest. Be sure to refer to the Grand Mesa National Forest map before fishing Owens Creek.
Stream Width and Elevation on Public Lands: 3 feet wide and 8,200 to 10,240 feet.
Fish: Rainbow, cutthroat, and brook trout stocked periodically as subcatchables.
Comments: Owens Creek is a small stream that often appears dry at its confluence with Buzzard Creek due to water diversions about 2 miles upstream. Above the private property, the stream is shallow and has few good pools. However, the numerous small beaver ponds hold fish.
Special Regulations: None.

WILLOW CREEK

Access: From Collbran, travel east on County Road 330 (paved) 6.0 miles to the Silt Cutoff/Vega fork. Proceed left on the Silt Cutoff Road 8.0 miles to the Hightower Road (Forest Road #265) and turn right. Proceed 11.0 miles and turn right onto the four-wheel-drive High Trail Road (Forest Road #263). Proceed 0.5 miles to reach the Willow Creek/Buzzard Creek confluence. The road continues to parallel Willow Creek for 4.0 miles up to Wagon Park. The stream is accessible by a short hike off the road for most of its length.
Land Status: Willow Creek is 10.0 miles long from its headwaters to Buzzard Creek. Its entire length is in the National Forest.
Stream Width and Elevation on Public Lands: 4 feet wide and 8,550 to 10,640 feet.
Fish: Brook and cutthroat trout. Fingerling Colorado River cutthroat trout are stocked periodically. Brook trout are from wild spawn.
Comments: In spite of its small size, Willow Creek supports a good trout population. Many small pools and beaver ponds are present. Streamside vegetation provides good cover, but may limit fishing in some reaches.
Special Regulations: None.

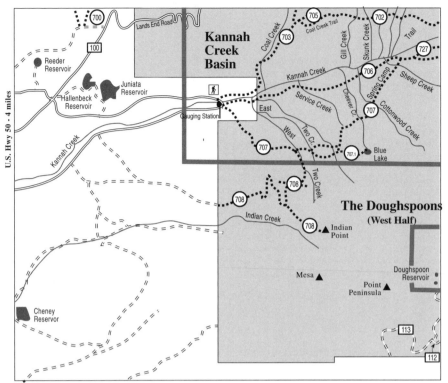

GRAND MESA MAP 4

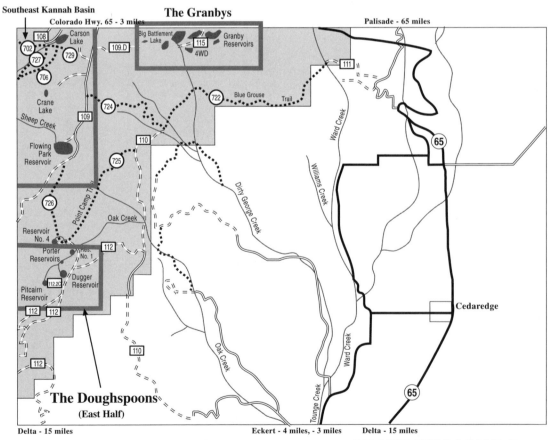

GRAND MESA MAP 5

Map 4 - Kannah Creek Basin Area

KANNAH CREEK BASIN AREA

Kannah Creek is one of the largest streams on the Grand Mesa. The Kannah Creek Basin serves as a municipal watershed for the City of Grand Junction, so please, treat this resource with respect.

An excellent trail system has routes to virtually the entire drainage and provides very scenic fishing access. Kannah Creek can be accessed via several trails; however, the Kannah Creek Trail provides the most direct access. This trail spans 4,000 feet in elevation over 12 miles from the City Intake trailhead at 6,000 feet to the Carson Lake trailhead at 10,000 feet. Remember, the trails throughout the Kannah Creek Basin are good, but can be very steep and rocky in spots.

Getting to the banks of Kannah Creek can be very difficult, if not treacherous in some areas. Dense thickets of oakbrush, many deadfalls, beaver ponds on tributary streams and high, steep banks often force fishermen to follow established game trails to reach the water's edge.

Carson Lake, brimming with brook trout, is a drive-to lake requiring a short hike over level terrain to reach the lake. Blue Lake, containing cutthroat trout, is accessible only by foot or horseback on a good but very steep trail of several miles.

CARSON LAKE

Access: From Mesa, travel south on Highway 65 18.3 miles to the Lands End Road (Forest Access Road #100). Turn right and proceed 3.3 miles to the Carson Lake Road #1082. Turn left and travel 1.4 miles down to the lake.
Size, Depth, and Elevation: 35 acres, 32 feet deep, 10,000 feet.
Fish: Brook trout, from wild spawn. Lake provides a good opportunity to take advantage of the Bonus Brook Trout regulation.
Agency: City of Grand Junction.
Comments: The road down to Carson Lake is steep but well graveled with several switchbacks. A large parking area is available. This area provides access to the lake as well as the Kannah Creek Trail. Fishing pressure is moderate to heavy with easily accessible banks. No established campgrounds exist. Toilets are available at the parking area. Please pack out trash.
Special Regulations: Wading and boating are prohibited. All watercraft, including belly-boats, are prohibited.

BLUE LAKE

Access: From Whitewater, travel 4.0 miles south on Highway 50 and turn left onto the Kannah Creek Road. Follow Lands End Road 2.9 miles to its junction (this forks into three roads) with the Purdy Mesa Road. Turn onto the rightmost road and proceed 6.1 miles to the City Intake Picnic Area. The Kannah Creek Trail (#706) trailhead begins here. About 0.2 mile up the hill, the Spring Camp Trail (#707) takes off to the right. Follow this trail 7.5 miles directly to the lake. Blue Lake could also be accessed from Carson Lake, but most anglers and hikers access it from the City Intake trailhead.
Size, Depth, and Elevation: 8 acres, 24 feet deep, and 9,800 feet.
Fish: Colorado River and Snake River cutthroat trout, stocked as subcatchables or fingerlings.
Agency: U.S. Forest Service.
Comments: The trail to Blue Lake is extremely steep. Blue Lake is a natural lake on Cheever Creek. Fishing pressure is light to moderate. Bank fishing is difficult due to brush and boulders on the shoreline. No developed campsites exist at this reservoir.
Special Regulations: All boats and rafts are prohibited.

KANNAH CREEK

Access: To access Kannah Creek from the City Intake trailhead, travel 4.0 miles south from Whitewater on Highway 50 and turn left onto the Lands End Road. Follow Lands End Road 2.9 miles to its junction (this forks into three roads) with the Purdy Mesa Road. Turn onto the rightmost road and proceed 6.1 miles to the City Intake Picnic Area. The Kannah Creek Trail trailhead begins here. The Kannah Creek Trail (#706) parallels Kannah Creek on

the south side of the basin all the way up to Carson Lake; however, the trail is up to a mile from the creek in some areas. Also, streamside access can be very difficult if not impossible in some areas. From the City Intake, some anglers simply walk up Kannah Creek on the north side using non-designated trails that have become established through years of use.

To access Kannah Creek from Carson Lake, travel 18.3 miles south from Mesa on Highway 65 to the Lands End Road (Forest Access Road #100). Turn right and proceed 3.3 miles to the Carson Lake Road #1082. Turn left and travel 1.4 miles down to the lake. Cross the dam on Carson Lake to reach the Kannah Creek Trail trailhead that begins 0.3 mile from the Carson Lake parking area. Keep in mind that while it is fairly easy hiking down this trail, it is actually very steep and difficult to ascend.

Extremely dense bushes and vegetation border the stream below Carson Lake. Also, the large boulders and rocks that form the numerous pools are very slick and sometimes can be loose. Use, caution when accessing or crossing Kannah Creek.
Land Status: From the City intake upstream, all of Kannah Creek flows through Forest Service land except for the lower mile, which is on private land. About 0.1 mile below the bridge crossing Kannah Creek at the City Intake area, the stream again enters private land.
Stream Width and Elevation on Public Lands: 18 feet wide and 6,000 to 10,520 feet. Above Carson Lake the stream is much smaller and is typically fishable only up to the Flowing Park Road.
Fish: Above Carson Lake, only brook trout, from wild spawn, are present. Below Carson Lake down to the City Intake parking area the stream holds rainbow, brook, cutthroat, and brown trout, all from wild spawn; however, fingerling rainbows are occasionally packed in and stocked in Kannah Creek.
Comments: Depending on where you fish, fishing pressure is light to moderate. The greatest numbers of trout are found further away from either trailhead. Making a day of fishing and hiking into Kannah Creek will generally allow you to reach the more remote reaches and pools. In spite of the fact that this drainage is a municipal watershed, drinking untreated water from the stream or its tributaries is not a good idea. No developed campsites exist in this area. Please make every effort to practice clean camping and sanitation in this area.
Special Regulations: None.

SHEEP CREEK

Access: Sheep Creek is a tributary of Kannah Creek flowing from the southern slopes of the Kannah Creek basin. The stream can be accessed from either the City Intake or Carson Lake trailheads of the Kannah Creek Trail (#706). Both the Kannah Creek and Spring Camp (#707) trails intersect Sheep Creek within 0.5 mile of its confluence with Kannah Creek. While Sheep Creek is closer to Carson Lake than the City Intake, it is probably a toss-up as to which trailhead offers the easiest access.
Land Status: Sheep Creek lies entirely within the National Forest.
Stream Width and Elevation on Public Lands: 9 feet wide and 8,100 to 10,055 feet.
Fish: Cutthroat and brook trout, from wild spawn.
Comments: Sheep Creek offers good pools, an occasional beaver pond, and undercut banks within 0.5 mile of its confluence with Kannah Creek. The fishable portion of this stream is within the lower one mile. Above this, fishing is limited by the steepness of the stream, few pools, and very poor streamside access. Fishing pressure is light. Please pack out trash.
Special Regulations: None.

Maps 4 & 5 - The Doughspoons Area

THE DOUGHSPOONS AREA

These backcountry lakes situated under the southern rim of the Grand Mesa are somewhat difficult to reach. The road to these lakes is long and rough, making four-wheel drive an absolute necessity. This requirement does limit the fishing pressure that these lakes receive.

Several of these reservoirs have a reputation for producing large brook trout. In addition, this secluded area offers excellent opportunities for hiking and watching wildlife. There are no developed camping facilities in this area.

DOUGHSPOON RESERVOIR #2 (DELTA RES. #2)

Access: From Delta, travel north on the airport road (off of Highway 50) 1.3 miles and turn left onto the gravel road. Proceed on this road (it becomes Forest Road #112 at the National Forest Boundary) 16.0 miles to Doughspoon Reservoir #2. It will be very helpful to consult a Forest Service map before traveling to these lakes. 4 wheel drive is necessary for traveling in this area.
Size, Depth, and Elevation: 2 acres, 5 feet deep, and 9,380 feet.
Fish: Rainbow trout and brook trout. Fingerling rainbow trout are stocked every other year. Brook trout are from wild spawn.
Agency: City of Delta.
Comments: In spite of its shallowness, this small reservoir sustains trout. These lakes have a reputation of producing large brook trout. Fishing pressure is light due to the remoteness of these lakes. No developed campsites exist at this reservoir.
Special Regulations: None.

DOUGHSPOON RESERVOIR #1 (DELTA RES. #1)

Access: From Delta, travel north on the airport road (off of Highway 50) 1.3 miles and turn left onto the gravel road. Proceed on this road (it becomes Forest Road #112 at the National Forest Boundary) 16.7 miles, passing Doughspoon #2, to Doughspoon Reservoir #1. It will be very helpful to consult a Forest Service map before traveling to these lakes. Four-wheel drive is necessary for traveling in this area.
Size, Depth, and Elevation: 4 acres, 11 feet deep, and 9,380 feet.
Fish: Rainbow trout and brook trout. Fingerling rainbow trout are stocked every other year. Brook trout are from wild spawn.
Agency: City of Delta.
Comments: These lakes have a reputation of producing large brook trout. Fishing pressure is light due to the remoteness of these lakes. No developed campsites exist at this reservoir.
Special Regulations: None.

DUGGER RESERVOIR

Access: From Eckert, travel west on the pipeline road (Forest Access Road #110) 12.7 miles and turn left onto Forest Road #112. Continue 2.8 miles to the intersection in the road and turn left. Go south 0.3 mile to Dugger Reservoir on the right-hand side of the road. It will be very helpful to consult a Forest Service map before traveling to these lakes. Four-wheel drive is necessary for traveling in this area.
Size, Depth, and Elevation: 17 acres, 15 feet deep, 9,180 feet.
Fish: Rainbow trout stocked alternate years as fingerlings.
Agency: U.S. Forest Service.
Comments: This reservoir is drained periodically. Fishing pressure is moderate due to the remoteness of these lakes. No developed campsites exist at this reservoir. Please pack out trash.
Special Regulations: None.

MORRIS RESERVOIR

Access: From Eckert, travel west on the pipeline road (Forest Access Road #110) 12.7 miles and turn left onto Forest Road #112. Continue 2.8 miles to the intersection in the road and proceed straight 0.3 mile directly to the reservoir. It will be very helpful to consult a Forest Service map before traveling to these lakes. Four-wheel drive is necessary for traveling in this area.
Size, Depth, and Elevation: 3 acres, 14 feet deep, and 9,180 feet.
Fish: Rainbow trout stocked alternate years as subcatchables.
Agency: U.S. Forest Service.
Comments: Fishing pressure is moderate due to the remoteness of these lakes. No developed campsites exist at this reservoir.
Special Regulations: None.

PORTER RESERVOIR #1 (BIG DAVIES RES.)

Access: From Eckert, travel west on the pipeline road (Forest Access Road #110) 12.7 miles and turn left onto Forest Road #112. Continue 2.8 miles to the intersection in the road and turn right. Proceed 0.5 mile to Porter Reservoir #1 adjacent to the road on the left-hand side. It will be very helpful to consult a Forest Service map before traveling to these lakes. Four-wheel drive is necessary for traveling in this area.
Size, Depth, and Elevation: 11 acres, 23 feet deep, 9,100 feet.
Fish: Brook trout stocked alternate years as subcatchables.
Agency: U.S. Forest Service.
Comments: Fishing pressure is moderate due to the remoteness of these lakes. No developed campsites. Pack out trash.
Special Regulations: None.

PORTER RESERVOIR #4 (L1TTLE DAVIES)

Access: From Eckert, travel west on the pipeline road (Forest Access Road #110) 12.7 miles and turn left onto Forest Road #112. Continue 2.8 miles to the intersection in the road and turn right. Proceed 1.0 mile, passing Porter Reservoir #1, directly to Porter Reservoir #4. It will be very helpful to consult a Forest Service map before traveling to these lakes. Four-wheel drive is necessary for traveling in this area.
Size, Depth, and Elevation: 13 acres, 10 feet deep, 9,380 feet.
Fish: Brook trout stocked alternate years as subcatchables.
Agency: U.S. Forest Service.
Comments: Fishing pressure is moderate due to the remoteness of these lakes. No developed campsites exist at this reservoir. Please pack out trash.
Special Regulations: None.

THE GRANBYS AREA

The Granby Reservoir area includes seven of the most productive reservoirs on the Grand Mesa, and one natural lake, Clear Lake. These lakes and one stream offer outstanding fishing in a spectacular backcountry setting. Access is limited to four-wheel drive, ATV, foot, or horseback.

Four-wheel-drive enthusiasts will be challenged by the large rocks, narrow corridors through the timber, and numerous mud holes. It is commonly stated that access to these lakes is so severe that one can walk the road faster than it can be driven.

Fishing pressure at these lakes is moderate due to the severe road conditions. The productivity of these lakes and the limited fishing pressure allow trout to grow to very desirable sizes. Reports of 2- to 5-pound trout from these reservoirs are not uncommon. No developed campsites are available. Please pack out your trash.

GRANBY RESERVOIR #1

Access: From Cedaredge, travel north on Highway 65 16.0 miles and turn left onto Forest Road #116 (across from Carp Lake) and travel the graveled road along the south shore of Island Lake. Follow this road 1.5 miles to the far end of the Island Lake Campground loop drive. From here, you can leave your vehicle in the parking area and begin hiking or you can proceed by four-wheel drive, ATV, or horseback. Travel the four-wheel-drive road (Forest Road #115)1.4 miles and turn left off the main road. Continue 0.4 mile to the reservoir.
Size, Depth, and Elevation: 26 acres, 11 feet deep, 10,080 feet.
Fish: Rainbow trout, stocked alternate years as fingerlings.
Agency: Granby Reservoir and Ditch Company.
Comments: Fishing pressure is moderate. Dense aquatic vegetation in late summer may hinder fishing success. No developed facilities exist at this reservoir. Please pack out trash.
Special Regulations: None.

GRANBY RESERVOIR #2

Access: From Cedaredge, travel north on Highway 65 16.0 miles and turn left onto Forest Road #116 (across from Carp Lake) and travel the graveled road along the south shore of Island Lake. Follow this road 1.5 miles to the far end of the Island Lake Campground loop drive. From here, you can leave your vehicle in the parking area and begin hiking or you can proceed by four-wheel, ATV, or horseback. Travel the four-wheel-drive road

Map 5 - The Granbys Area

(Forest Road #115) 1.4 miles and turn left off the main road. Continue 0.4 mile to Granby Reservoir #1. You'll have to park your four-wheel-drive vehicle here and proceed by foot or horseback. Cross the dam on Granby Reservoir #1 and follow the trail 0.2 mile to Granby Reservoir #2.

Size, Depth, and Elevation: 19 acres, 22 feet deep, 10,060 feet.
Fish: Rainbow trout, stocked alternate years as fingerlings.
Agency: U.S. Forest Service.
Comments: Fishing pressure is moderate. Dense aquatic vegetation in late summer may hinder fishing success. No developed facilities exist at this reservoir. Please pack out trash.
Special Regulations: None.

GRANBY RESERVOIR #4,5,10,11

Access: From Cedaredge, travel north on Highway 65 16.0 miles and turn left onto Forest Road #116 (across from Carp Lake) and travel the graveled road along the south shore of Island Lake. Follow this road 1.5 miles to the far end of the Island Lake Campground loop drive. From here, you can leave your vehicle in the parking area and begin hiking or you can proceed by four-wheel drive, ATV, or horseback. Travel the four-wheel-drive road (Forest Road #115) 3.0 miles directly to the reservoir.
Size, Depth, and Elevation: 74 acres, 32 feet deep, 10.000 feet.
Fish: Rainbow trout, stocked alternate years as fingerlings.
Agency: Granby Ditch and Reservoir Company.
Comments: As the name indicates, a single dam now inundates the basins of four formerly separate reservoirs. Fishing pressure is moderate. No developed facilities exist at this reservoir.
Special Regulations: None.

GRANBY RESERVOIR #12

Access: From Cedaredge, travel north on Highway 65 16.0 miles and turn left onto Forest Road #116 (across from Carp Lake) and travel the graveled road along the south shore of Island Lake. Follow this road 1.5 miles to the far end of the Island Lake Campground loop drive. From here, you can leave your vehicle in the parking area and begin hiking or you can proceed by four-wheel drive, ATV, or horseback. Travel the four-wheel-drive road (Forest Road #115) 3.5 miles, traveling past Granby Reservoir #4, 5, 10, 11, directly to the reservoir.
Size, Depth, and Elevation: 49 acres. 23 feet deep, 10,000 feet.
Fish: Rainbow trout, stocked alternate years as fingerlings.
Agency: Granby Ditch and Reservoir Company.
Comments: Fishing pressure is moderate. No developed facilities exist at this reservoir. Please pack out trash.
Special Regulations: None.

GRANBY RESERVOIR #7

Access: From Cedaredge, travel north on Highway 65 16.0 miles and turn left onto Forest Road #116 (across from Carp Lake) and travel the graveled road along the south shore of Island Lake. Follow this road 1.5 miles to the far end of the Island Lake Campground loop drive. From here, you can leave your vehicle in the parking area and begin hiking or you can proceed by four-wheel drive, ATV, or horseback. Travel the four-wheel-drive road (Forest Road #115) 3.7 miles, traveling past Granby reservoirs #4, 5, 10, 11 and #12, directly to the reservoir.
Size, Depth, and Elevation: 15 acres, 7 feet deep, and 9,920 feet.
Fish: Rainbow trout, stocked alternate years as fingerlings.
Agency: Granby Ditch and Reservoir Company.
Comments: Fishing pressure is moderate. No developed facilities exist at this reservoir. Please pack out trash.
Special Regulations: Motorized boats are prohibited.

BIG BATTLEMENT LAKE

Access: From Cedaredge, travel north on Highway 65 16.0 miles and turn left onto Forest Road #116 (across from Carp Lake) and travel the graveled road along the south shore of Island Lake. Follow this road 1.5 miles to the far end of the Island Lake Campground loop drive. From here, you can leave your vehicle in the parking area and begin hiking or you can proceed by four-wheel drive, ATV, or horseback. Travel the four-wheel-drive road (Forest Road #115) 4.0 miles, traveling past Granby reservoirs #4, 5, 10,11, #12, and #7, directly to the reservoir.
Size, Depth, and Elevation: 42 acres, 45 feet deep, 10,080 feet.

Fish: Rainbow and brook trout. Subcatchable rainbow trout are stocked annually. Brook trout are from wild spawn.
Agency: U.S. Forest Service.
Comments: Fishing pressure is moderate. No developed facilities exist at this reservoir. Please pack out trash.
Special Regulations: None.

LITTLE BATTLEMENT LAKE

Access: From Cedaredge, travel north on Highway 65 16.0 miles and turn left onto Forest Road #116 (across from Carp Lake) and travel the graveled road along the south shore of Island Lake. Follow this road 1.5 miles to the far end of the Island Lake Campground loop drive. Here, you can leave your vehicle in the parking area and begin hiking or you can proceed by four-wheel drive, ATV, or horseback. Travel the four-wheel-drive road (Forest Rd #115) 4.3 miles, traveling past Granby reservoirs #4, 5, 10, 11, #12, and #7, and Big Battlement Lake, directly to the reservoir.
Size, Depth, and Elevation: 16 acres, 22 feet deep, 10,050 feet.
Fish: Rainbow and brook trout. Subcatchable rainbow trout are stocked annually. Brook trout are from wild spawn.
Agency: U.S. Forest Service.
Comments: Fishing pressure is moderate. No developed facilities exist at this reservoir. Please pack out trash.
Special Regulations: None.

CLEAR LAKE

Access: From Cedaredge, travel north on Highway 65 16.0 miles and turn left onto Forest Road #116 (across from Carp Lake) and travel the graveled road along the south shore of Island Lake. Follow this road 1.5 miles to the far end of the Island Lake Campground loop drive. From here, you can leave your vehicle in the parking area and begin hiking or you can proceed by four-wheel drive, ATV, or horseback. Travel the four-wheel-drive road (Forest Road #115) 4.3 miles, traveling past Granby reservoirs #4, 5, 10, 11, #12 and #7 and Big Battlement Lake, to Little Battlement Lake. From here, you must proceed by foot or horseback. Hike around the north shore of Little Battlement Lake and continue 0.8 mile west to Clear Lake.
Size, Depth, and Elevation: 6 acres, 17 feet deep, 10,180 feet.
Fish: Colorado River and Snake River cutthroat trout, stocked as fingerlings. Snake River cutthroats are stocked every other year. Colorado River cutthroats are stocked periodically.
Agency: U.S. Forest Service.
Comments: Clear Lake is a natural lake having no obvious inlet or outlet. This lake lives up to its name by having extremely clear water that allows fishermen to see the trout. It sits in a large boulder field which makes for a rather unique setting. Fishing pressure is light. No developed facilities exist at this reservoir.
Special Regulations: None.

DIRTY GEORGE CREEK

Access: From Cedaredge, travel north on Highway 65 16.0 miles and turn left onto Forest Road #116 (across from Carp Lake) and travel the graveled road along the south shore of Island Lake. Follow this road 1.5 miles to the far end of the Island Lake Campground loop drive. From here, you can leave your vehicle in the parking area and begin hiking or you can proceed by four-wheel drive, ATV, or horseback. Travel the four-wheel-drive road (Forest Road #115) 4.0 miles, traveling past Granby reservoirs #4,5, 10, 11, #12, and #7, directly to Big Battlement Lake. Dirty George Creek flows between Little and Big Battlement lakes, and out of Big Battlement Lake. No roads or designated trails provide access to this stream.
Land Status: Dirty George Creek is 10.4 miles long from the dam of Big Battlement Lake to Tongue Creek. However, only the upper 2.4 miles are in National Forest, 1.3 miles are on BLM, and the lower 6.7 miles lies entirely on private lands.
Stream Width and Elevation on Public Lands: 18 feet wide and 7,220 to 10,040 feet.
Fish: Brook and rainbow trout. Both species escape from Big Battlement Lake and probably produce some fish from wild spawn in the stream.
Comments: The first mile below Big Battlement Lake offers the best fishing. Below here, the stream becomes extremely steep and overgrown with vegetation.

Gunnison National Forest Index Map

Index of Numbered Maps
Gunnison National Forest

MAP 1
1. East Muddy Creek 151

MAP 2
1. Hubbard Creek 151
2. Overland Reservoir.........................151
3. Crater Lake 151

MAP 3
1. Lee Creek 152
2. West Muddy Creek 152
3. Paonia Reservoir 152
4. Coal Creek...................................152
5. Anthracite Creek............................152

MAP 4
1. Anthracite Creek, North, East, Middle
   Ruby Anthracite Creek 153
2. Emerald Lake 153
3. Oh Be Joyful Creek 153
4. Blue Lake 153
5. Peeler Lake 153
6. Washington Creek 153
7. Slate River 153
8. Lake Irwin 153
9. Meridan Lake 153
10. Nicholson Lake 153

MAP 5
1. Taylor Lake 154
2. Brush Creek, West, East, Middle 154
3. Twin Lakes 154
4. Spencer Lake 154
5. Copper Lake 154
6. Maroon Lake 154
7. East River 154

MAP 6
1. Ptarmigan Lake 155
2. Bowman Creek...............................155
3. Pine Creek 155
4. Tellurium Creek 155
5. Italian Creek 155
6. Pot Hole Reservoirs 155
7. Red Mountain Creek 155
8. Mysterious Lake 155
9. Horsethief Lake 155
10. Illinois Creek 155
11. Taylor River 155

MAP 7
1. Illinois Lake 156

MAP 8
1. Smith Fork 156
2. Crawford Reservoir 156

MAP 9
1. Little Gunnison, Cascade Creek,
   Robinson Creek, Cliff Creek, Willow
   Creek 157

MAP 10
1. Lost Lake 159
2. Lost Lake Slough 159
3. Dollar Lake 159
4. Coal Creek 159
5. Green Lake 159
6. Beaver Ponds 159
7. Long Lake, Golden Lake 159
8.. Sheep Lake 159
9. Costo Lake 159
10. Pass Creek, Little Pass Creek..........159
11. Ohio Creek 159
12. Carbon Creek 159
13. Castle Creek 159
14. Mill Creek 159

MAP 11
1. Farris Creek 159
2. Cement Creek................................159

3. Bear Creek 159
4. East River 159
5. Spring Creek.................................159
6. Taylor River 159
7. Roaring Judy Fishing Unit 159

MAP 12
1. Spring Creek Reservoir 162
2. Rocky Brook Creek 162
3. Taylor Reservoir 162
4. Texas Creek 162
5. Willow Creeks 162
6. Lottis Creeks 162
7. Beaver Creek, East 162
8. Henry Lake 162
9. Lamphier Lake, Upper 162
10. Mill Lake 162
11. Crystal Lake 162
12. Boulder Lake 162
13. Fairview Lake...............................162

MAP 13
1. Texas Creek Lakes 163
2. Pass Creek, Cow Creek 163
3. Cow Lake 163
4. Willow Creeks 163
5. Mirror Lake 163
6. Quartz Creek, North 163

MAP 14
1. Dyer Creeks 164
2. Curecanti Creek 164

3. Soap Creek 164

MAP 15
1. Beaver Creek 164
2. Gunnison State Wildlife Area..........164

MAP 16
1. Quartz Creek 166
2. Pitkin State Fish Unit 166
3. Viking Valley State Wildlife Area ..166

MAP 17
1. Quartz Creek, Middle, South 167
2. Tomichi Creek 167
3. Canyon Creek 167
4. Agate Creek 167
5. Marshall Creek 167

MAP 18
1. Los Pinos Creek 168
2. McDonough Reservoir 168

MAP 19
1. Needle Creek 168
2. Needle Creek Reservoir 168
3. Razor Creek 168
4. Dome Lakes 168

MAP 20
1. Baldy Lake 169

MAP 21
1. Cochetopa Creek 169
2. Pauline Creek 169

Curecanti National Recreation Area 165

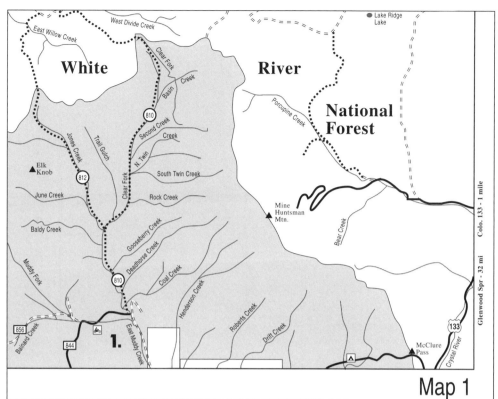

1. East Muddy Creek;
Rated fair for brook, cutthroat
an occasional rainbow.
From Paonia Reservoir north
on East Muddy Creek Road
to Forest Boundary (Approx.
13 mi.).Continue on FDR 285
approx. 2.5 miles to FDR
844, north approx. 2.5 miles
to FDT 810. Access to Clear
Fork Creek, Jones Creek,
East Fork Muddy Creek.
Beaver ponds and mostly
high meadows.
East Muddy Creek is primarily on private property. Refer
to Gunnison Forest map for
open sections of these
streams.

Map 1

1. Hubbard Creek; Rated fair for
brook. North from Paonia on Hwy 133
to Juanita junction, north on FDR 704,
road parallels creek.

**2. Overland Reservoir (10,800 ft;
170 ac);** Rated fair cutthroat, brook
and rainbow. North from Paonia on
Hwy 133 to Juanita junction, north on
FDR 704, approx. 14 miles to FDR
265 West on FDR 265 to FDR 701
(approx. 3 miles), south on approx.
FDR 701 south on approx. 2miles to
FDR 705. Follow road to reservoir.

3. Crater Lake (10,000 ft; 6 ac);
Rated poor for stocked rainbow. North
of Overland Reservoir on FDT 720
approx. 2 miles.

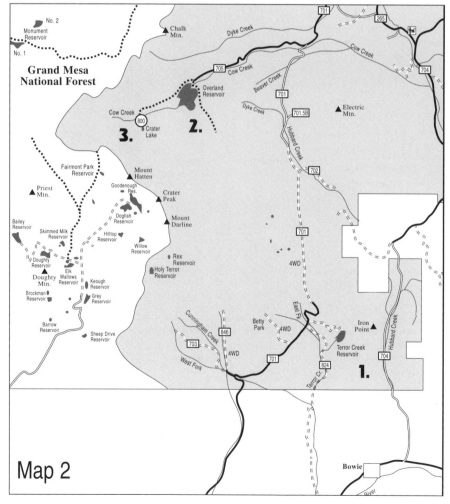

Map 2

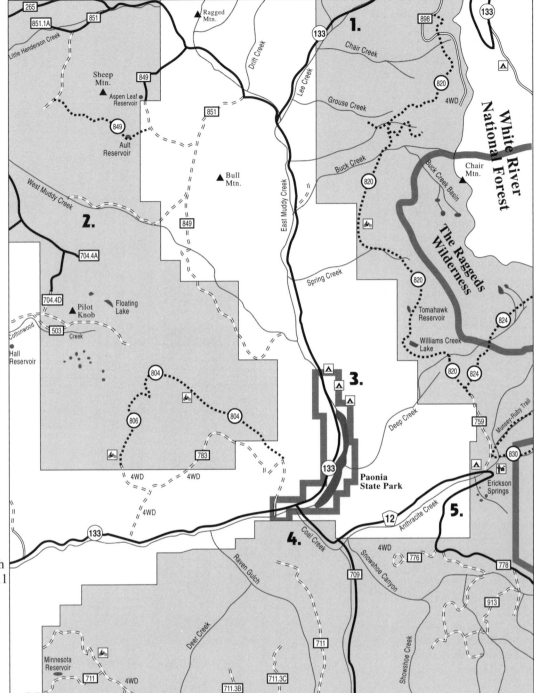

1. Lee Creek; Rated fair for brook. From Paonia Reservoir north on Hwy 133 approx. 11 miles to forest boundary. Hwy 133 follows stream up to McClure Pass. McClure Campground along side creek. Fast small stream.

2. West Muddy Creek; Rated fair for small brook. From Paonia north on Hwy 133 to Juanita junction. North on FDR 704 approx. 10 miles to creek. Beaver ponds and meadows.

3. Paonia Reservoir (6450 ft; 300 ac); is fair fishing in spring and fall for rainbow, some good size northern pike, which respond best in summer.
See State Parks section.

4. Coal Creek; Rated good for rainbow and brook. Follow FDR 709 from Hwy 12. Road parallels creek.

5. Anthracite Creek; Rated fair for rainbow, cutthroat and brook. East from Paonia Reservoir on Hwy 12 to Ericson Springs Campground FDT 830 follows creek into Raggeds Wilderness. A number of beaver ponds.

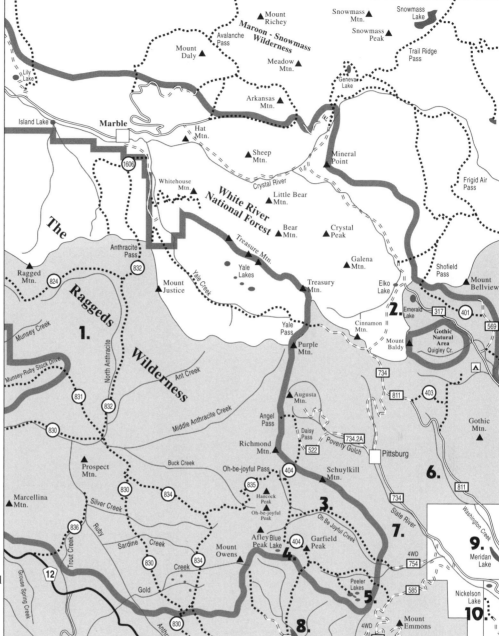

1. North Anthracite Creek, East Anthracite Creek, Ruby Anthracite Creek and Middle Anthracite Creek. Rated fair for cutthroat and brook. East from Paonia Reservoir on Hwy 12 to Ericson Springs Campground FDT 830 follows trail into Raggeds Wilderness. Plenty of beaver ponds.

2. Emerald Lake (10,500 ft; 12 ac); Rated fair for rainbow and cutthroat Located on Schofield Pass, about 4.5 miles above Gothic on rough (FDR 317) road.

3. Oh Be Joyful Creek; Rated fair for small cutthroat and brook. Slate River about 6 miles north of Crested Butte on Slate River Road (FDR 734). Left on 4WD FDR 754 and trail that follows Peeler Creek to Junction with Oh Be Joyful Creek.

4. Blue Lake (11,100 ft; 5 ac); Rated fair for brook. Located in Raggeds Wilderness is reached from Lake Irwin on trail that connects to FDT 404 Approx. 6 miles.

5. Peeler Lake (10,800 ft; 5 ac); Rated fair for small cutthroat and brook. Slate River about 6 miles north of Crested Butte on Slate River Road (FDR 734). Left on 4WD FDR 754 and trail that follows Peeler Creek, 4 miles from the end of the road.

6. Washington Creek; Rated fair for brook trout. Reached on FDR 811 a dirt road 2 miles north Crested Butte. Two miles of fishing in small stream.

7. Slate River; Rated good for small brook and cutthroat. From Crested Butte FDR 734 9 miles to Pittsburg. The river above is mostly open water.

8. Lake Irwin (10,350 ft; 30 ac); Rated good for Rainbow and cutthroat. Located 6 miles west of Crested Butte on County Road 12 to FDR 825. North on FDR 825 approx. 2 miles to Lake. Reservations can be made for Lake Irwin Campground. Hand propelled boats permitted. See page 88 for DOW information.

9. Meridan Lake (9,700 ft; 40 ac); Rated fair for rainbow and Brook trout. Located approx. 4 miles northeast of Crested Butte on FDR 811. Short walk on trail to lake.

10. Nicholson Lake (8,900 ft); Rated fair for brook, a small lake located 3 miles north of Crested Butte on the Slate River Road. (FDR 734)

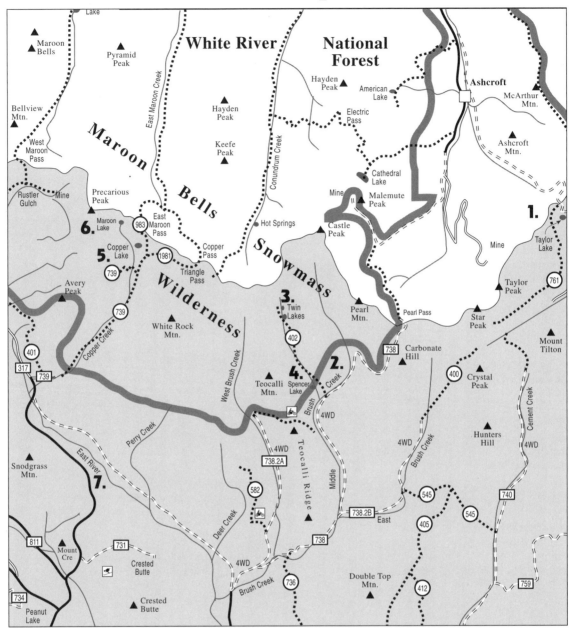

1. Taylor Lake (12,400 ft; 30 ac); Rated good for rainbow and brook. Lots of pressure. From Gunnison 11 miles north to FDR 742. Follow FDR 742 40 miles right on 4WD FDR 761 for approx. 2.5 miles. Near Taylor Pass. No boats permitted. North of Dorchester Campground.

2. Brush Creek, West Brush Creek, East Brush Creek and Middle Brush Creek; Rated fair for cutthroat, brook and rainbow. Located approx. 25 miles north of Gunnison on Colo. 135 to FDR 738. Four miles north on FDR 738 to 4WD FDR 738, road follows creek upstream. Four-wheel-drive roads go up both Middle and East Brush Creeks. Some beaver ponds.

3. Twin Lakes (11,800 ft; lower 3 ac, upper 7 ac); Rated fair for rainbow and cutthroat. Located approx. 25 miles north of Gunnison on Colo. 135 to FDR 738. Four miles north on FDR 738 to 4WD FDR 738, road follows creek upstream. Four-wheel-drive roads go up both Middle and East Brush Creeks. Three mile hike on FDT 402 from Middle Brush Creek Road. Maroon Bells-Snowmass Wilderness.

4. Spencer Lake (10,000 ft; 3 ac); Rated fair for brook. Off trail 0.5 mile up Twin Lake Trail. Difficult to locate.

5. Copper Lake (11,450 ft); Rated fair for cutthroat. Headwaters of Copper Creek, 6 miles from Gothic on FDT 739. Copper Creek is small and fast poor fishing.

6. Maroon Lake (12,500 ft; 5 ac); Rated fair for cutthroat. Located 2 miles north of Copper Lake on marked trail.

7. East River; Rated good for brown, rainbow and brook. North from Almont on Hwy 135 to FDR 738, Northeast on FDR 738 approx. 5 miles to junction, 4WD road on the left follows upper river.

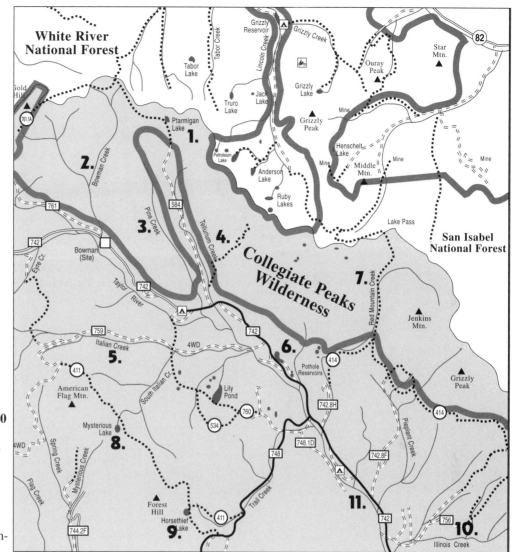

1. Ptarmigan Lake (12,300 ft; 6 ac); Rated good for cutthroat. Follow FDR 584 to end of road. Short steep hike to lake. In Collegiate Peaks Wilderness.

2. Bowman Creek; Rated fair for small cutthroat, rainbow and an occasional brown. Located north of Pothole Lakes on FDR 742. In Collegiate Peaks Wilderness. Small and fast.

3. Pine Creek; Rated fair for cutthroat and brook. Located near Dorchester Campground on FDR 742. Small stream with beaver ponds, 4 miles of stream in Collegiate Peaks Wilderness.

4. Tellurium Creek; Rated fair for cutthroat and an occasional brown. From FDR 742, FDR 584 (4WD) follows stream for 8 miles. Small stream with some beaver ponds.

5. Italian Creek; Rated good for cutthroat and brown. From Pothole Reservoirs west on FDR 759 , 4WD road follows small stream for 5 miles.

6. Pot Hole Reservoirs (9,724 ft 3ac. 5 ac.); Rated good for rainbow. Located 5 miles north of Taylor Reservoir on FDR 742.

7. Red Mountain Creek; Rated fair for small brook. North of Dinner Station Campground on FDR 742 1 mile to FDR

742.8H. Drive north 1.5 miles to FDT 414. Small stream follows trail into Collegiate Peaks Wilderness. Some fishable beaver ponds.

8. Mysterious Lake (10,800; 2 ac); Rated good for small brook. Follow FDT 411 from Horsethief Lake approx. 4 miles.

9. Horsethief Lake (11,250 ft; 3.8 ac); Rated good for small brook. From Gunnison N on Hwy 135 to Almont, 7.2 miles NE on FDR 742, 12.1 miles N on FDR 744 to FDR 748. Approx. 7 miles N to FDT 411. Short hike to lake. Mosca Campground near junction of 742 and 748.

10. Illinois Creek; Rated fair for small brook with an occasional brown. Located 2 miles north of Taylor Reservoir on FDR 742. Five miles of fishing in small stream.

11. Taylor River; Rated fair for rainbow and brown. Follows FDR 742 to headwaters. Stocked from East River to headwaters. Public access for just about the entire upper river with several campgrounds in upper section.

Gunnison National Forest Maps 7 & 8

1. Illinois Lake (10,720 ft; 2 ac); Rated good for cutthroat to 12 inches. Located 2 miles north of Taylor Reservoir on FDR 742. East on FDR 756 to trailhead. 1.5 miles by trail from the end of the road. Heavily fished.

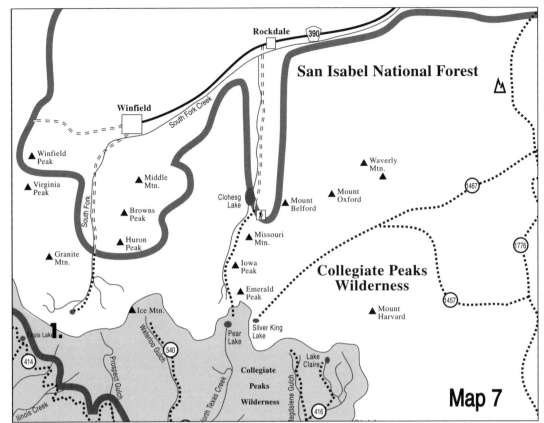

1. Smith Fork, North Smith Fork, South Smith Fork; Rated fair for brook, cutthroat and rainbow. From Crawford travel east to FDR 712. FDR 712 parallels creek to trailhead FDT 860. FDT 860 follows streams into West Elk Wilderness. (See map 10). Lower section of Smith Fork is on private property, approx. 3 miles of open water.

2. Crawford State Park; See State Parks section.

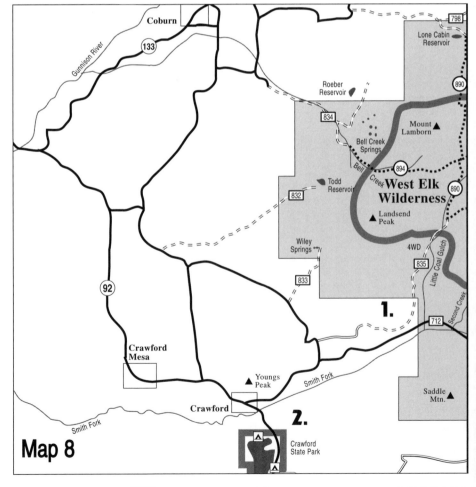

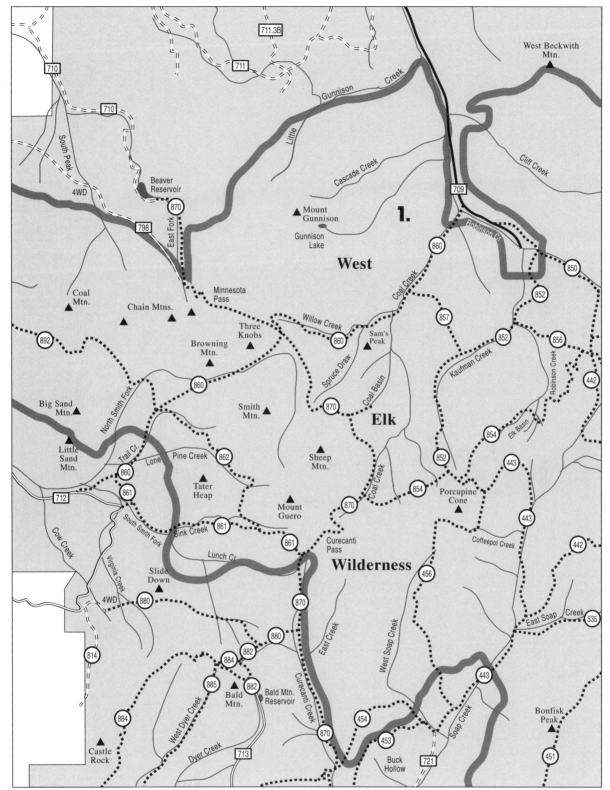

1. Little Gunnison, Cascade, Robinson, Cliff Creek and Willow Creeks; Rated fair for Rainbow and Cutthroat. From Hwy 12 near Paonia Reservoir south on FDR 709 road. Road parallels Coal Creek. Refer to Gunnison Forest map for location of streams along road.

Gunnison National Forest Map 10

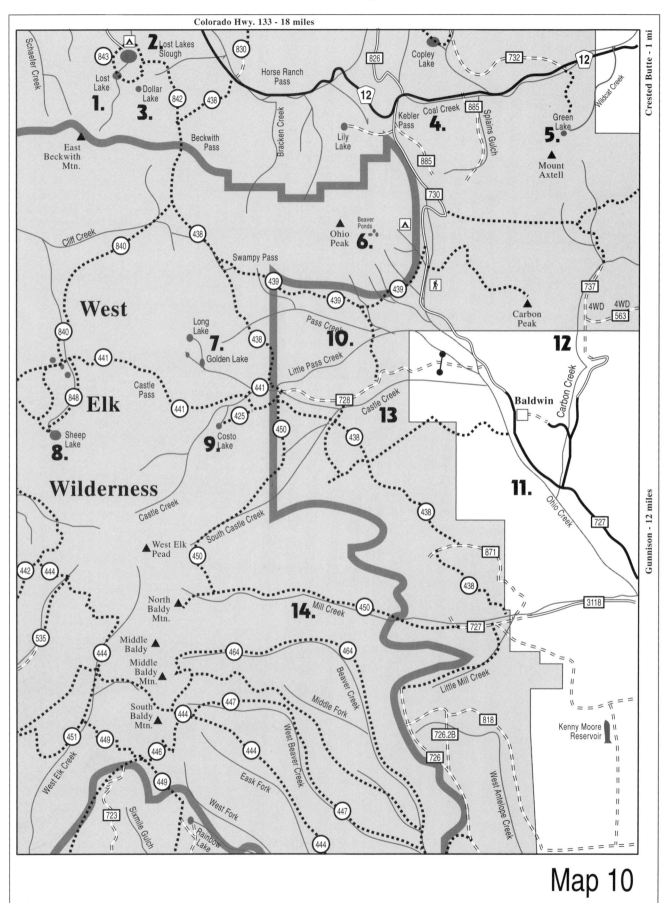

Colorado Hwy. 133 - 18 miles

Crested Butte - 1 mi

Schaefer Creek

843

2. Lost Lakes Slough

830

826

Copley Lake

732

12

Wildcat Creek

Lost Lake

1.

Dollar Lake

3.

842

438

Beckwith Pass

Horse Ranch Pass

12

Kebler Pass

Coal Creek

4.

885

Splains Gulch

Green Lake

5.

East Beckwith Mtn.

Lily Lake

Mount Axtell

Bracken Creek

885

730

Cliff Creek

840

438

Swampy Pass

Beaver Ponds

Ohio Peak

6.

737

4WD

4WD

563

439

439

439

Pass Creek

Carbon Peak

West

840

Long Lake

7.

438

10.

12

441

Golden Lake

Little Pass Creek

Baldwin

848

Elk

Castle Pass

441

441

425

Costo Lake

9.

728

Castle Creek

13.

Carbon Creek

8.

Sheep Lake

450

438

11.

Wilderness

Castle Creek

South Castle Creek

West Elk Pead

450

871

438

Ohio Creek

727

Gunnison - 12 miles

442

444

North Baldy Mtn.

450

Mill Creek

14.

727

3118

535

Middle Baldy

464

464

444

Middle Baldy Mtn.

Beaver Creek

Little Mill Creek

Kenny Moore Reservoir

South Baldy Mtn.

444

447

Middle Fork

818

726.2B

451

449

446

444

726

West Elk Creek

449

Eask Fork

West Beaver Creek

447

West Antelope Creek

723

Sixmile Gulch

West Fork

444

Rainbow Lake

Map 10

MAP 10

1. Lost Lake (9,870 ft; 8 ac); Rated good for 8 to 10-inch brook.

2. Lost Lake Slough (9,625 ft; 53 ac); Rated fair for rainbow and brook. Lost Lake and Dollar lake are reached from Campground by FDT 843. Trailhead FDT 842 from campground leads to West Elk Wilderness.

3. Dollar Lake (10,500 ft; 2 ac); Rated poor for stocked brook. From Crested Butte on Hwy 12 approx. 17 miles to FDR 706. South on FDR 2 miles to Lost Lake Campground.

4. Coal Creek; Rated fair for brown trout. Parallels Hwy 135 west of Crested Butte for several miles.

5. Green Lake (10,560 ft; 5 ac); Rated fair for cutthroat. Travel 3 miles west of Crested Butte on Cty Road 12 to trailhead on left side of road. Approx. 2 mile hike to lake. Wildcat Creek; is rated good for small cutthroat. Only 1 mile of the upper creek in National Forest.

6. Beaver Ponds; Rated fair for brook. From Crested Butte west on Hwy 12 7 miles to FDR 730 (Keebler Pass). South on FDR 730 4 miles to Beaver Ponds picnic grounds. A 0.5 mile hike to ponds.

7. Long Lake (10,080 ft; 3.2 ac); and the Golden Lake (11,040 ft; 8.4 ac); Golden trout. Located northwest of Costo Lake 1 mile cross country off FDT 438.

8. Sheep Lake (10,505 ft; 10 ac); Rated fair for brook and rainbow. From Paonia State Park east on Hwy 12 1.5 miles to FDR 709. Follow FDR 709 southeast to trailhead to West Elk Wilderness. (Approx. 10 miles.) Follow FDT 850 to lake. (Approx. 6 miles).

9. Costo Lake (10,100 ft; 15 ac); Rated fair for small brook. Travel north from Baldwin to Beaver Ponds trailhead. Hike approx. 2 miles to junction, south to Castle Creek trail, approx. 3 miles west to lake. Inside West Elk Wilderness.

10. Pass and Little Pass Creeks; Rated good for brook. Travel north from Baldwin to Beaver Ponds trailhead. Hike approx. 2 miles to junction, follow trail south for 1 mile to Pass Creek. Upper sections in West Elk Wilderness.

11. Ohio Creek; Flows in mainly through private property and is rated poor for rainbow. You must get permission to fish from property owner.

12. Carbon Creek; Rated good for brook in beaver ponds on upper section. Two miles south of Baldwin to Carbon Creek road. North on road to FDR 737(4WD) 1.5 miles to trail that follows stream.

13. Castle Creek; Rated good fishing for small brook in upper portion. Lower section is posted. Travel north from Baldwin to Beaver Ponds trailhead. Hike approx. 2 miles to junction, south approx. two mile to Castle Creek. Upper section in West Elk Wilderness.

14. Mill Creek; Rated poor for brook. Take FDR 727 north from Hwy 135 to BLM road 3118. West on BLM road 3118 (FDR 727) trailhead. FDT 450 parallels Mill Creek into West Elk Wilderness. Only the upper section is not posted.

MAP 11 (See map page 160)

1. Farris Creek; Rated good for brook. Located north of Almont on HWY 135 to FDR 738. North on FDR 738 approx. 3 miles to 4WD road FDR 736 to FDT 736. Lower section is private public access begins at trailhead. Three miles of fishable water, narrow stream.

2. Cement Creek; Rated fair to good for cutthroat, brook and rainbow. From Almont north on Hwy 135 to FDR 740. FDR follows creek for 18 miles. Nine miles of road are 4WD on upper section. Cement Creek Campground located on lower section.

3. Bear Creek; Rated fair for small brook and cutthroat. From Almont north on FDR 742 8 miles, left on Spring Creek Road, approx. 8 miles to FDR 744.21 on left FDT 420 parallels Bear Creek up Deadmans Gulch.

4. East River; Rated fair for brown. At Almont, East River joins Taylor River. Except for a stretch of river near Roaring Judy SFU the lower section is private. Lower section fishing is with artificial lures or flies only. See page 89 for information on Roaring Judy State Fishing Unit.

5. Spring Creek; Rated fair for rainbow and brook. From Almont north on FDR 742 8 miles, left on Spring Creek Road. Public and private ownership interspersed access.

6. Taylor River; Rated good for rainbow and browns. Travel north out of Gunnison on Hwy 135 to the Taylor Canyon Road at Almont. Most of its waters are open to the public and receive heavy pressure. The lower river through the canyon offers fair fishing. See page 89 for Taylor River SWA.

7. Roaring Judy State Fishing Unit; Brown and rainbow. Fishing on East River and in retention pond. See page 89 for DOW information.

Gunnison National Forest Map

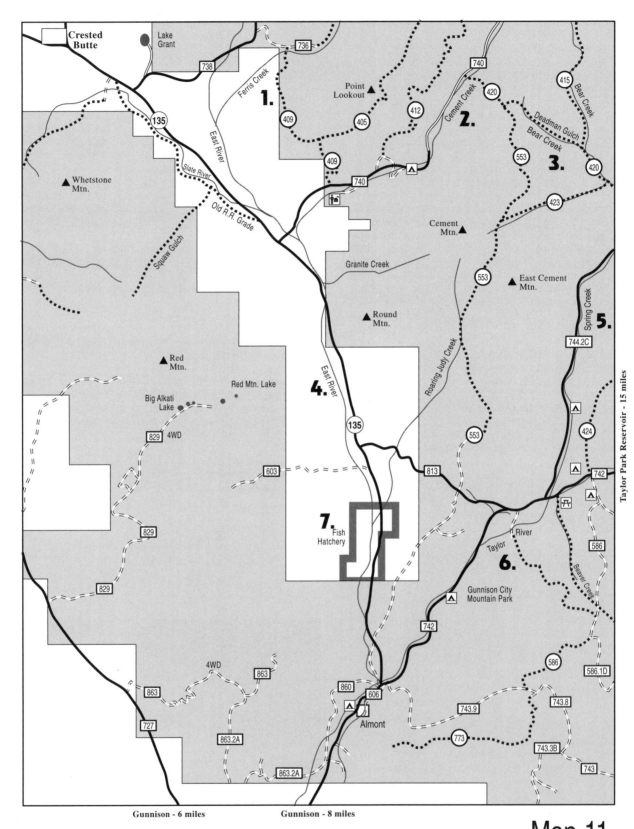

Crested Butte

Lake Grant

738

736

740

415

Bear Creek

Ferris Creek

1.

Point Lookout

409

405

412

420

Cement Creek

2.

Deadman Gulch

Bear Creek

553

3.

420

East River

135

409

740

423

Whetstone Mtn.

Slate River

Old R.R. Grade

Squaw Gulch

Granite Creek

Cement Mtn.

East Cement Mtn.

553

Spring Creek

5.

744.2C

Round Mtn.

Roaring Judy Creek

Red Mtn.

Red Mtn. Lake

East River

4.

553

424

742

Big Alkati Lake

829 4WD

603

135

Taylor Park Reservoir - 15 miles

586

7.
Fish Hatchery

813

Taylor River

6.

Beaver Creek

829

Gunnison City Mountain Park

829

742

586

586.1D

4WD

863

860

606

743.9

743.8

863

773

727

863.2A

Almont

743.3B

743

863.2A

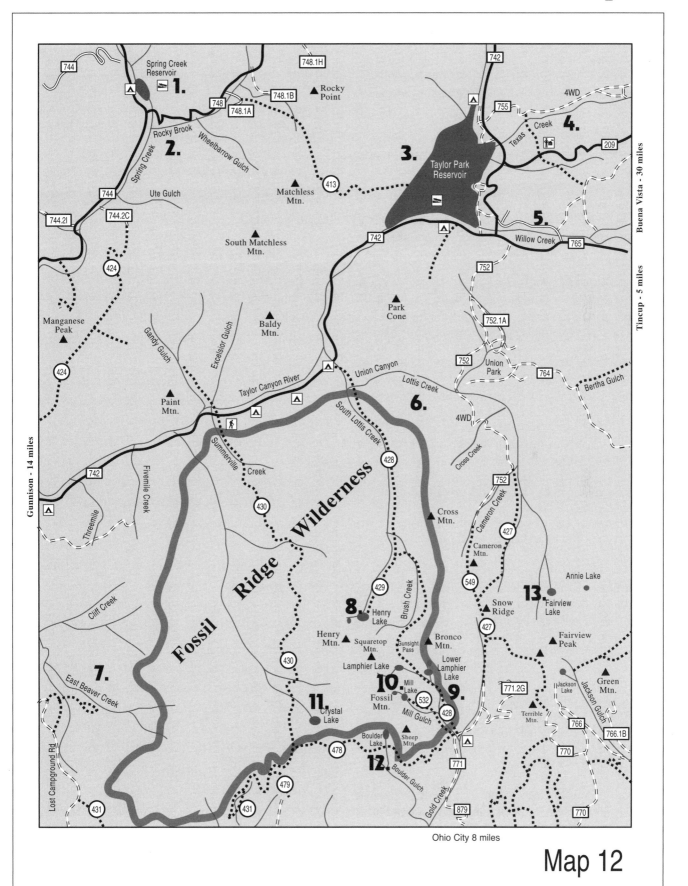

Gunnison - 14 miles

Buena Vista - 30 miles

Tincup - 5 miles

Ohio City 8 miles

Map 12

Gunnison National Forest Map

MAP 12 (See map page 161)

1. Spring Creek Reservoir (9,900 ft; 86.9 ac); Rated fair to good for rainbow, cutthroat and brook. From Almont turn right on FDR 742, 6 miles to Spring Creek. Turn left on Spring Creek Road, go 14 miles to reservoir. See page 89 for DOW information.

2. Rocky Brook Creek; Rated fair for brook trout. Located south of Spring Creek Reservoir parallel to FDR 748. Fast narrow stream.

3. Taylor Reservoir (9,330 ft; 2,000 ac); Rated good for rainbow and brown. From Gunnison north on Hwy 135 10 miles to FDR 742 (Taylor River Road), 18 miles east to reservoir. See page 89 for DOW information.

4. Texas Creek; Rated good for rainbow, cutthroat, brook and brown. Texas Creek begins near Continental Divide in Collegiate Peaks Wilderness. It enters Taylor Park Reservoir at northeast inlet on FDR 742. FDR 755 paralles creek for 16 miles to wilderness boundary. FDT 416 to the headwaters.

5. Willow Creek, West Willow Creek, East Willow Creek; Rated good for brook and brown. From Taylor Park Reservoir FDR 755 follows Willow Creek to Tincup. West Willow Creek follows Cumberland Pass road. East Willow Creek follows Mirror Lake road for 3.5 miles to lake.

6. Lottis Creek, North Lottis Creek and South Lottis Creek; Rated fair for brook. Access from Lottis Creek Campground. 17.4 miles north of Almont on FDR 742. Cameron and Cross Creeks, offer some fishing, but have dense vegetation.

7. East Beaver Creek; Rated fair for brook and an occasional brown. From Gunnison on Hwy 135 north 1 mile to BLM 3109/3110. Follow road approx. 10 miles to forest boundary and FDR 743. Follow mostly 4WD road approx. 5 miles to Brush Creek. Narrow stream with some beaver ponds.

8. Henry Lake (11,700 ft; 13 ac); Rated fair for rainbow and cutthroat. Located 8 miles north of Ohio City on FDR 771. Follow FDT 428 from Gold Creek Campground approx. 7 miles to FDT 429 south on FDT 428 2 miles to lake. Fossil Ridge Wilderness

9. Upper Lamphier Lake (11,700 ft; 4 ac); Both lakes are rated fair for cutthroat. **Lower Lamphier Lake (11,250; 3 ac);** Upper lake is 0.25 mile above Lower Lake. Located 8 miles north of Ohio City on FDR 771. Follow FDT 428 from Gold Creek Campground approx. 2 miles to lakes in Fossil Ridge Wilderness.

10. Mill Lake (11,500 ft; 2 ac); Rated fair for small brook and cutthroat. Located 8 miles north of Ohio City on FDR 771. From Gold Creek Campground approx. 1.5 miles on FDT 532 (Boulder Lake Trail) Fossil Ridge Wilderness.

11. Crystal Lake (11,250 ft; 3 ac); Rated good for cutthroat. Located 1.5 miles northwest of Boulder Lake 0.25 mile from FDT 478 and FDT 430.

12. Boulder Lake (11,100 ft; 20 ac); Rated fair for small brook. Located 8 miles north of Ohio City on FDR 771. Follow FDT 478 southwest from Gold Creek Campground approx. 3 miles.

13. Fairview Lake (11,296 ft; 8.7 ac); Rated fair for cutthroat. West of Taylor Reservoir on FDR to FDR 752. South on FDR 752 (4WD) approx. 10 miles to the intersection of FDT 427. No designated trail to lake. Refer to Fairview Peak USGS 7 1/2' quad.

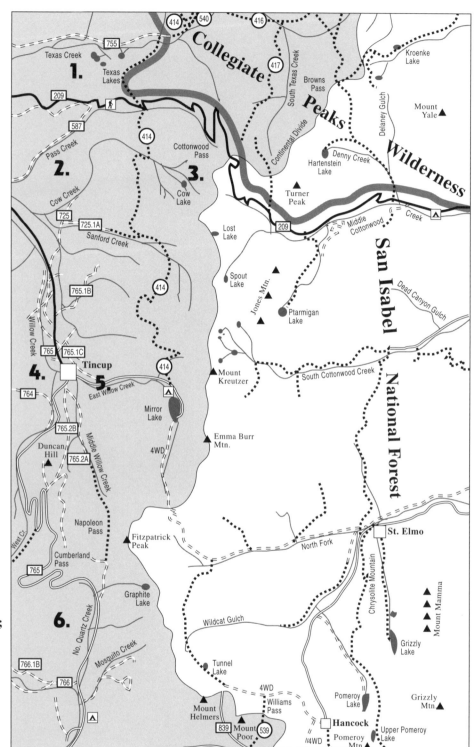

1. Texas Creek Lakes (10,500 ft); Rated good for brook. See Texas Creek on map 12 for directions. Three small lakes. Only the two upper lakes have fish. No boats.

2. Pass Creek and Cow Creek; Rated fair for brook. Located east of Taylor Park Reservoir on FDR 765 approx. 5 miles to FDR 587 to access pass Creek. Further south to FDR 725 to access Cow Creek. Small fast streams with some beaver ponds.

3. Cow Lake (11,400 ft; 6 ac); Rated good for cutthroat. From FDR 209 take FDT 414 south for approx. 3 miles. Located at the headwaters of Cow Creek.

4. Willow Creeks; See text for Map 12.

5. Mirror Lake (11,000 ft; 22 ac); Rated fair for brook and brown. Travel 8 miles southeast of Taylor Park Reservoir on FDR 765 to Tincup. Three miles SE on FDR 267 to lake. Mirror Lake Campground at lake.

6. North Quartz Creek; Rated fair for small brook and rainbow. Located 3 miles east of Pitkin on FSR 765 (Cumberland Pass Road) Quartz Campground located on creek.

Gunnison National Forest Map 14 & 15

1. Dyer Creek, West Dyer Creek, South Dyer Creek; Rated fair for small brook. South from Crawford Reservoir on Hwy 92 approx. 12 miles to FDR 713. East on road to forest boundary, to road on left just inside boundary. Road leads to FDT 884 that follows North Dyer Creek. Check with ranger district about access from this road. Or continue on FDR 713 to Bald Mountain Reservoir. A number of beaver ponds.

2.Curecanti Creek; Rated fair for small brook. West from Lake Fork Campground on Blue Mesa Reservoir on Hwy 92 approx. 10 miles to FDR 720. North on FDR 720, (road parallels creek) approx. 5 miles to FDT 870. Creek and trail continues into West Elk Wilderness

3. Soap Creek; Rated good for rainbow, brook and brown. From Lake Fork Campground on Blue Mesa Reservoir travel west on Hwy 92 1.5 miles to Soap Creek Road. (FDR 721). Soap Creek Road parallels Soap Creek to edge of West Elk Wilderness. Several campground along creek. Fishing at Blue Mesa Reservoir.

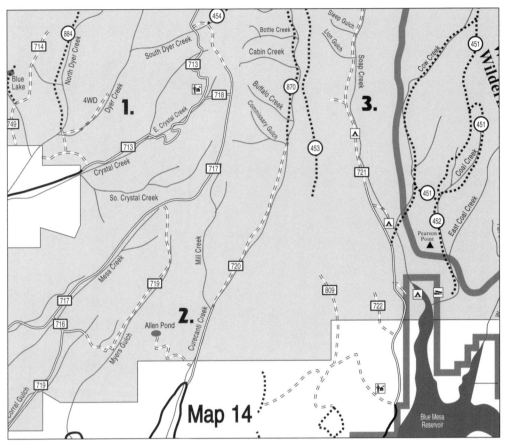

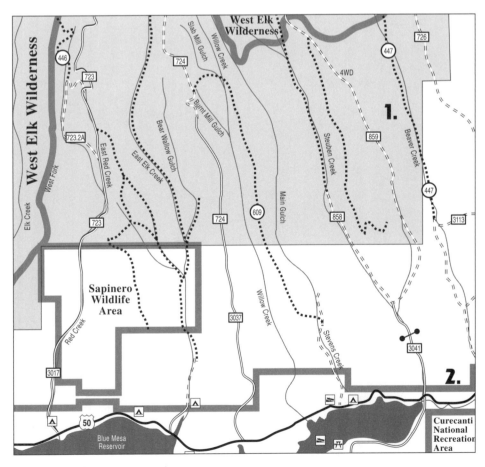

1. Beaver Creek; Rated good for brook and rainbow. Six miles west Gunnison to BLM road 3113 N approx. 1.5 miles to fork in road. Check with BLM for access from this point. From forest boundary FDT 447 follows Beaver Creek to West Elk Wilderness Boundary. Follow Creek up FDT 464 to Headwaters. Lower section is posted to forest boundary. Approx. 10 miles of open water.

2. Gunnison State Wildlife Area; Brown and Rainbow. Gunnison River Fishing. See page 88 for DOW information.

Directions: From Pueblo, go west on U.S. 50 to Gunnison. Blue Mesa Reservoir is 10 miles west of Gunnison on U.S. 50.

Fee: No entrance fee. Camping fees during summer.

Size: Blue Mesa - 9,000 acres - Morrow Point 820 acres.

Elevation: 7,519 feet.

Maximum Depth: 338.5 feet.

Facilities: Most areas offer drinking water and RV sewage dumps. All are accessible to travel trailers.

Boat Ramps: North side; Ponderosa and Stevens Gulch. South side; Elk Creek, Iola and Lake Fork.

Fish: Rainbow trout, kokanee, brown trout and mackinaw. Rainbow trout; the best action from shore is using bait on the bottom such as nightcrawlers or Power Bait. Trolling from a boat using cow bells with a nightcrawler also produces fair to good rainbow action. Kokanee; the best results for snagging is around the dam and up the Lake Fork of the Gunnison. Trolling flashers, with a night crawler or Cherry Bobber. The best areas for trolling have been the East Iola Basin and Soap Creek area by the dam. Brown trout; good results from boat drift fishing and casting flies near the shallow water areas. Mackinaw; the best area is the Sapinero Basin near the Sapinero Island. Jigging three-eights-ounce jigheads trailing a piece of sucker meat.

Recreation: Fishing, boating, personal watercraft, wind surfing, swimming, scuba diving, sailing, water skiing, boat tours.

Camping: Curecanti offers a variety of drive-in, boat-in, and hike-in campgrounds. Facilities range from Elk Creek Campground with showers, marina, restaurant, amphitheater and visitor center, to the remote West Elk Creek Boat-In Campsite located on the secluded West Elk Arm of Blue Mesa Lake.

Major campgrounds; Elk Creek, Lake Fork, Stevens Creek and Cimarron. Full service campgrounds except there are no electrical hookups or laundries. Stevens Creek does not have pull through sites or showers,

Cimarron - No showers. Combined there are 342 sites in the four campgrounds.

Limited Facilities camping; Dry Gulch, Red Creek, Gateview, Ponderosa, East Portal, and East Elk Creek. All have picnic tables, fire grates, vault toilets and water. Ponderosa has a boat ramp and horse corral.

Information: Handicapped accessible facilities are available in the major campgrounds. Park Office, (970) 641-2337.

Special Restrictions: Morrow Point Lake is primarily accessible only by the Pine Creek Trail, and private boats must be hand carried. Pets must be kept under physical control. Dispose of waste water only at proper dump sites. Fishing requires a Colorado License. Boaters should be aware of frequent high winds. Head for shore immediately when winds come up.

Blue Mesa Lake, the focus of water sports, is Colorado's largest lake when filled to capacity. Morrow Point and Crystal Lakes, narrow and deep within the canyon carved out by the Gunnison, suggest fjords. Boat tours offered in season on Morrow Point Lake provide an insight into the ancient sculpting work of time and the river.

Curecanti, named for the Ute Chief Curecanti who once hunted the Colorado territory provides year round water recreation. The area is managed by the National Park service. The main season for camping, boating, fishing, sailing and sightseeing runs from mid-May until mid-October. One million people come to Blue Mesa Lake every year to fish for Kokanee salmon, rainbow, brown, and Mackinaw trout. During May and early June, brown trout give anglers an opportunity to catch some of the largest fish in Blue Mesa Lake. Occasional large Mackinaw are also taken here, but rainbow trout is the mainstay, summer and winter. Trollers find the rainbow and Kokanee holding up well throughout the season, with late June, July, and August best for salmon. October brings spawning runs of Kokanee salmon up the Gunnison River within the recreation area. Hundreds of thousands of rainbow and Kokanee are planted annually in the lake by state and federal wildlife agencies.

Winter offers ice fishing, snowmobiling, cross-country skiing, snowshoeing, and wildlife observation from mid-

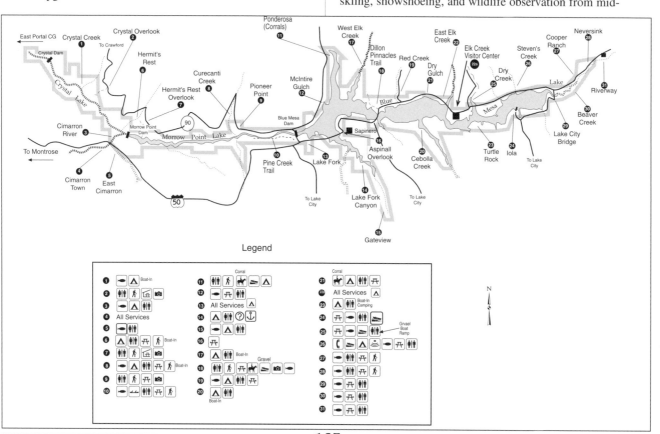

Legend

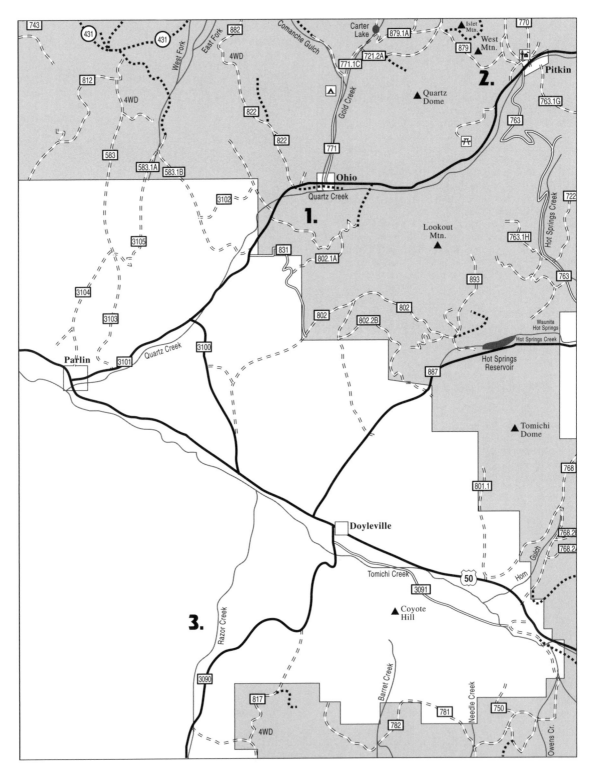

1. Quartz Creek; Rated good for rainbow and brook. Creek parallels Quartz Creek Road FDR 765. Lower section below Pitkin is posted. Some portions of the creek are open to the public near Pitkin. Camping at Gold Creek, Quartz and Middle Quartz Campgrounds.

2. Pitkin State Fish Unit; Rainbow and brook. Fishing on Quartz Creek. See page 89 for DOW information.

3. Viking Valley State Wildlife Area; Brook, brown and rainbow. Fishing on Razor Creek. See page 88 for DOW information.

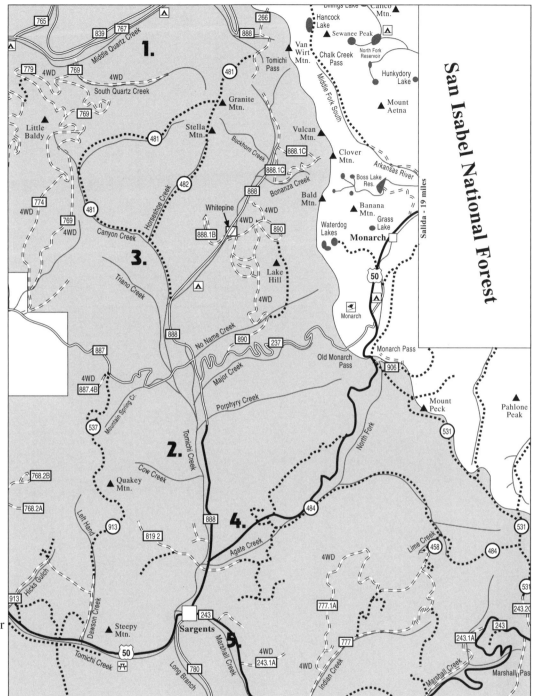

1. Middle Quartz Creek; South Quartz Creek; Rated good for small rainbow and brook. Both creeks are reached from Pitkin, east on FDR 767 approx. 3 miles. Narrow, fast creeks with a few beaver Ponds.

2. Tomichi Creek; Rated good for small brook. Most open water is above White Pine. A short distance above White Pine the road FDR 888 turns to 4WD. Seven Miles north of Sargents is Snowblind Campground. Narrow fast stream with heavy growth.

3. Canyon Creek; Rated good for brook. North of Sargents on FDR 888. Small fast steam with heavy growth.

4. Agate Creek; Rated good for brook and an occasional rainbow. Access is approx. 3.5 miles north of Sargents on Hwy 50 to FDT 484. FDT follows creek to near its headwaters. Approximately 8 miles of open water.

5. Marshall Creek; Rated good for brook, brown and rainbow. From Sargents travel southeast on FDR 243. Road parallels creek to Marshall Pass. Lower section on private property. Upper section provides approx. 6 miles of open water.

Gunnison National Forest Maps 18 & 19

1. Los Pinos Creek; Rated good for brown, brook and cutthroat. Travel 8 miles east of Gunnison on Hwy 50 to Hwy 114. South on Hwy 114 through Cochetopa Canyon to BLM road 3083. South on BLM 3083 for approx. 5 miles to BLM 3084. West on BLM 3084 to forest boundary. From forest boundary use FDR 788 to upper section of creek that is open water. Road parallels creek. Fishing is catch-and-release with artificial lures or flies.

2. McDonough Reservoir (9,420 ft; 54.3 ac); Rated good for rainbow and brook. Located on Los Pinos Creek approx. 4 miles from forest boundary. Boating allowed, no boat ramp.

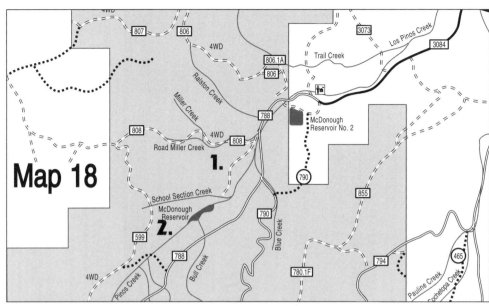

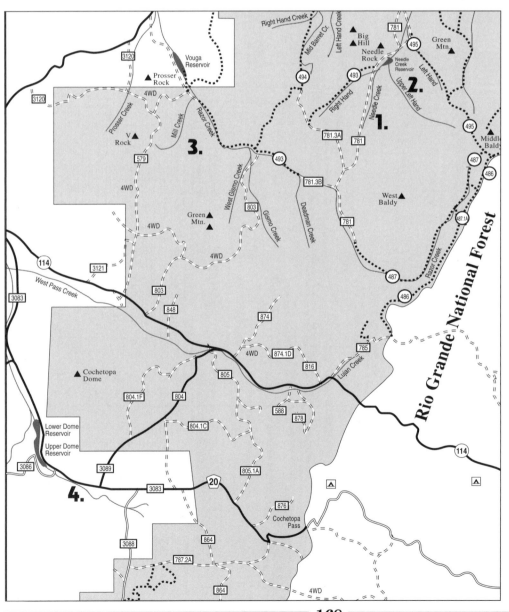

1. Needle Creek; Rated fair fishing for brook in upper section. From Doyleville east on BLM 3091 road for approx. 8 miles to forest boundary. Refer to Gunnison Forest map for directions to reach lake and creek. Approx. 3 miles south.

2. Needle Creek Reservoir (8,800 ft; 6 ac); Rated fair for rainbow and brook. Best fishing in spring and fall.

3. Razor Creek; Rated fair for brook trout. From Needle Creek Reservoir south on a rough road (FDR 781) approx. 5 miles to FDR 781.3B. West one mile to FDT 483. Trail follows creek to forest boundary.

4. Lower and Upper Dome Lakes; See page 95 for DOW information.

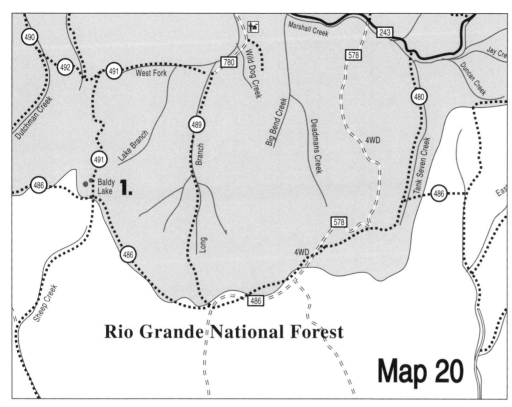

1.Baldy Lake: (11,266 ft; 5.2 ac); Rated good for rainbow. South from Sargents on FDR 780 to Long Branch Station. Continue on rough road another 3 miles to trailhead FDT 491. Follow FDT 491 to lake. (Approx. 6 miles). Lake is near Continental Divide.

1. Cochetopa Creek; Rated fair for rainbow and brown. From Dome Lakes take BLM road 3086 3 miles south to FDR 794. FDR 794 south will cross Pauline Creek on the way to Cochetopa Creek at LaGarita Wilderness. FDT 465 follows Cochetopa Creek into wilderness.

2. Pauline Creek; Rated good for rainbow and brown, See Cochetopa Creek.

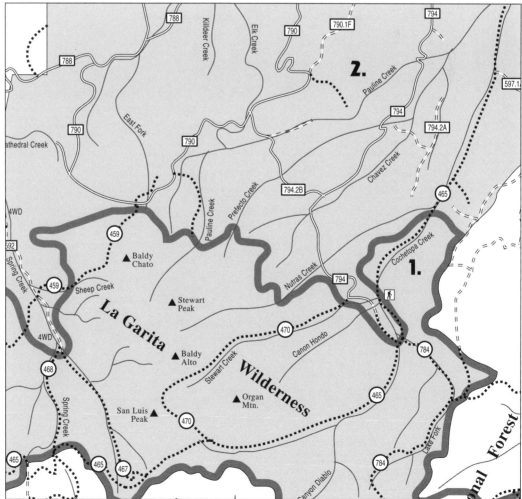

Pike National Forest Index Map

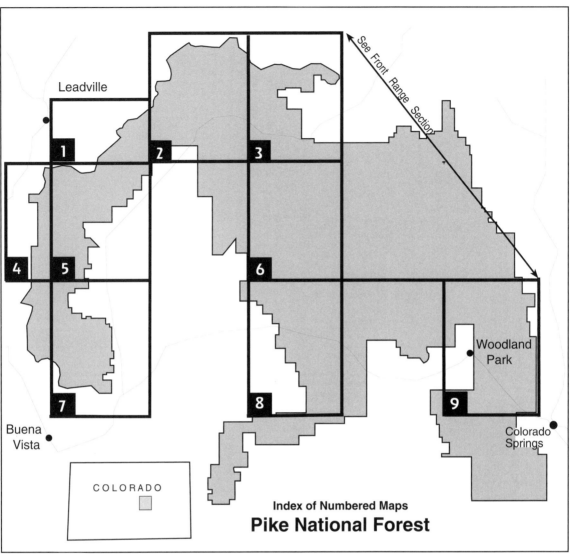

Index of Numbered Maps
Pike National Forest

MAP 1
1. Michigan Lake...........................171
2. Michigan Creek 171
3. French Creek 171

MAP 2
1. Shelf Lake 172
2. Square Top Lakes 172
3. Abyss Lake 172
4. Geneva Creek 172
5.,6.,7. Handcart Gulch, Burning
   Bear Creek, Beaver Creek 172
8. Threemile Creek 172
9. Gibson Lake............................172
10. North Fork South Platte..........172
11. Jefferson Lake 172

MAP 3
1. Mount Evans SWA 173
2. Deer Creek..............................173

MAP 4
1. Wheeler Lakes 173
2. Lake Emma 173
3. Kite Lake 173
4. Cooney, Oliver Twist Lakes 173
5. Twelvemile Lakes 173
6. Ruby Lake 173

MAP 5
1. Montgomery Reservoir 174
2. Alma SWA 174
3. Beaver Creek 174
4. Trout Creek 174
5. Crooked Creek..........................174
6. Mosquito, Buckskin, Pennsylvanian,
   Sacramento Creeks 174
7. Fourmile Creek 174

MAP 6
1. Craig Creek 175
2. Tarryall Reservoir 175

MAP 7
1. Tumbling, Willow, Lynch
   Creeks 176
2. Antero Reservoir 176

MAP 8
1. South Platte River 176

MAP 9
1. Palmer Lake..............................177
2. Manitou Reservoir....................177
3. Monument Lake........................177
4. Rampart Reservoir....................177
5. Nichols Lake 177
6. Stanley Reservoir......................177
7. North Catamount Reservoir
   South Catamount Reservoir
   Crystal Creek Reservoir 177

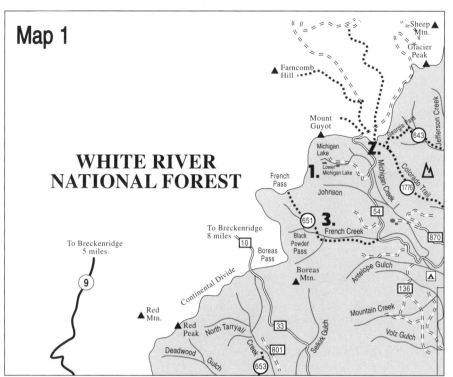

Map 1

WHITE RIVER
NATIONAL FOREST

1. Michigan Lake, Lower (11,222 ft; 3.7 ac); Rated Fair for cutthroat. Northeast of Fairplay on Hwy 285 approx. 14 miles to Hwy 35. North on Hwy 35 3 miles to Hwy 54, north on 54 to Forest boundary. Continue on FDR 54 to lake (Approx. 5 miles form boundary). Road can be rough.

2. Michigan Creek; Rated fair for brook and rainbow. Generally follows FDR 54 up to lake. Public and private property.

3. French Creek; Rated fair for brook. Approx. 2 miles above Michigan Creek Campground, FDT 651 follows creek to headwaters.

Pike National Forest Map 2

1. Shelf Lake (11,790 ft; 9 ac); Rated fair for cutthroat. From Georgetown south on hwy 62 to Guanella Pass. From the pass continue south approx. 8 miles to FDR 119. West on FDR 119 approx. 3 miles to FDT 634 trailhead. Follow trail to lake.

2. Square Top Lakes (Lower 12,046 ft; 8.6 ac, Upper 12,240 ft; 10 ac); Rated Fair for cutthroat. From Georgetown south on Hwy 62 to Guanella Pass. From the pass take FDT 600 west to lake.

3. Abyss Lake (12,650 ft; 18 ac); Rated fair for cutthroat and rainbow. From Hwy 285 take Hwy 62 north to Abyss Lake Trailhead (Approx. 5 miles). Take FDT 602 approx. 8 miles to lake. Located in Mount Evans Wilderness.

4. Geneva Creek; Rated fair for rainbow. Follows FDR 119 from Hwy 62 near Geneva Park Campground.

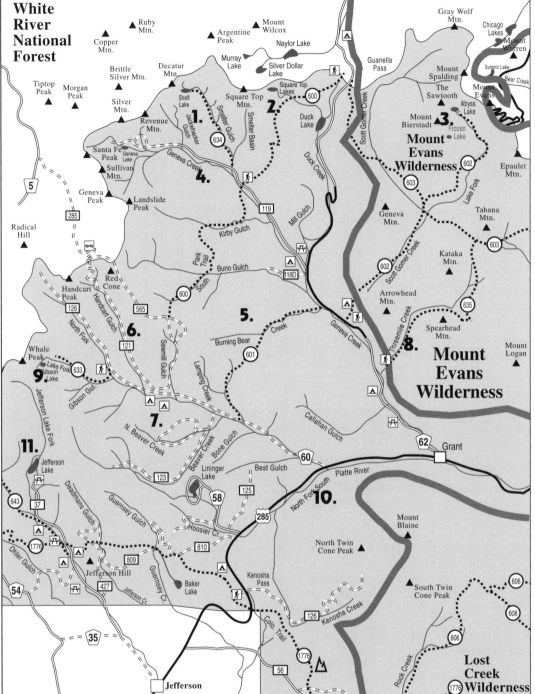

5, 6, 7. Handcart Gulch; Burning Bear Creek; Beaver Creek; Rated poor for brook.

8. Threemile Creek; North from Grant on Hwy 62 approx. 3 miles to Threemile Creek Trailhead. East on FDT 635 into Mount Evans Wilderness.

9. Gibson Lake (11,500 ft; 4 ac); Rated fair for brook. From Hwy 285 take Hall Valley Road (FDR 60) northwest to just above Hall Valley Campground. Take FDT 633 to lake.

10. North Fork So. Platte; From above Roberts Tunnel outlet above Grant is rated poor for rainbow and brook. From Grant to South Platte River it is mostly private. River follows Hwy 285 from Grant to Kenosha Pass.

11. Jefferson Lake (10,687 ft; 145 ac); Rated fair for rainbow and lake trout. From Jefferson & Hwy 285 northwest on Hwy 35 2 miles to FDR 37. North on FDR 37 approx. 5 miles to lake.

1. Mount Evans State Wildlife Area; Rated fair for rainbow. See page 86 for DOW information.

2. Deer Creek; Rated fair for rainbow. From Hwy 285 north on Cty Road 43 to forest boundary. Continue to Rosalie Trailhead (FDT 603). Trail follows stream into Mount Evans Wilderness. Lower section below forest boundary is mostly private.

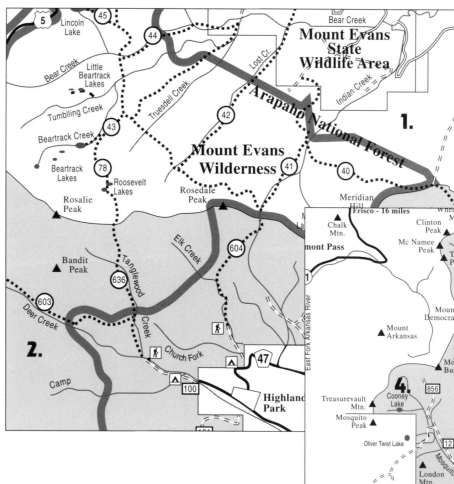

1. Wheeler Lakes (Upper, 12,500 ft; 4 ac) (Lower 12,180 ft; 28 ac); Rated fair for cutthroat. From Montgomery Reservoir follow 4WD road up Middle Fork So. Platte. (FDR 188).

2. Lake Emma (12,600 ft; 9 ac); Rated fair for rainbow. From Alma take Hwy 8 6 miles to Kite Lake Campground. A short hike to lake.

3. Kite Lake (12,000 ft; 6 ac); Rated fair for rainbow. From Alma take Hwy 8 6 miles to Kite Lake Campground. A short hike to lake.

4. Cooney Lake (12,600 ft; 8 ac); Oliver Twist Lake ((12,250 ft; 6 ac); rated fair for cutthroat. From Alma Junction at Hwy 285 west on FDR 12.

Follow FDR 12 to FDR 452, short 4 WD to lake. Continue on Mosquito Pass Road a short distance to Oliver Twist lake.

5. Twelvemile Lakes (Upper, 11,580 ft; 3ac) (Lower,11,180 ft; 8 ac); Rated fair for cutthroat and brook. Five miles south of Fairplay take FDR 20 west approx. 6 miles to FDR 175. FDR 175 south 1 mile to FDR 173, follow 173 to roads end. Short hike to lake on FDT 684.

6. Ruby Lake (11,850 ft; 2 ac); Rated fair for cutthroat. Six miles south of Fairplay take Hwy 5 south to FDR 22. Follow 22 to Weston Pass. Lake is at pass.

Pike National Forest Map 5

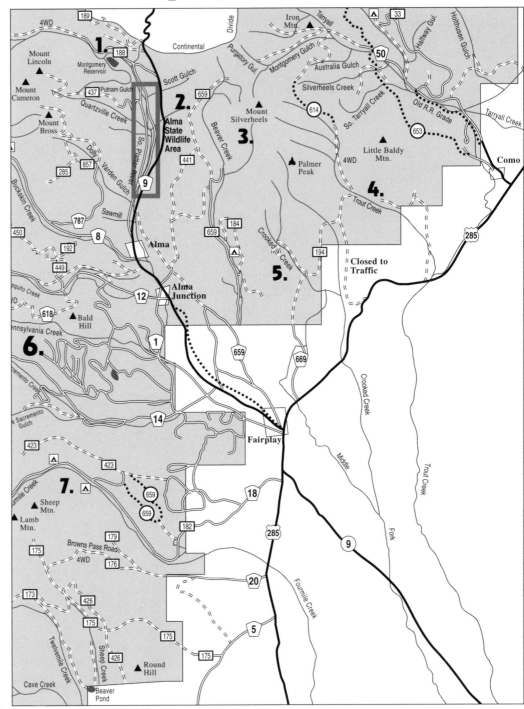

1. Montgomery Reservoir (10,820 ft; 80ac); Rated fair for rainbow. North of Alma off Hwy 9.

2. Alma State Wildlife Area; Rated good for rainbow, brown and cutthroat. See page 93 for DOW information

3. Beaver Creek; Rated fair for cutthroat. North of Fairplay on FDR 659. Road follows stream for 5 miles. Beaver Creek Campground is 5 miles north of Fairplay.

4. Trout Creek; Rated fair for cutthroat. North of Fairplay on Cty Rd. 669 to forest boundary. Follow FDR 194 to stream.

5. Crooked Creek; Rated fair for cutthroat. North of Fairplay on Cty Rd. 669 to forest boundary. Follow FDR 194 to stream.

6. Mosquito, Buckskin, Pennsylvania and Sacramento Creeks have little publc access.

7. Fourmile Creek; Rated fair for brook and rainbow. From Fairplay south on Hwy 285 1 mile to County Road 18, south on 18 to forest boundary. Take FDR 182 the road follows stream.

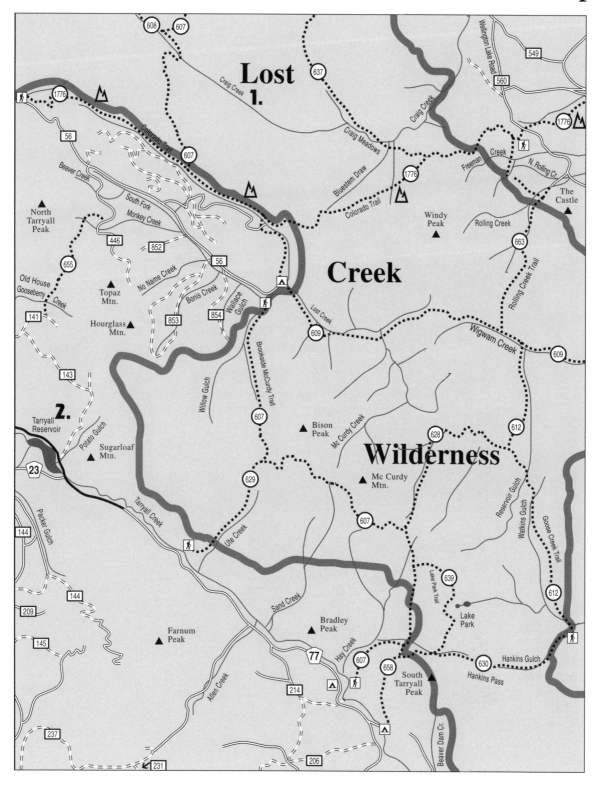

1. Craig Creek; Rated good for small brook. From Glenisle use FDT 607 (Approx. 6 miles) or from Singleton @ Hwy 285 use FDT 606 to Craig Park Trail (FDT 608) trail follows stream. Lost Creek Wilderness.

2. Tarryall Reservoir (8,860 ft; 175 ac); Rated good for rainbow, brown and kokanee. Tarryall Creek below reservoir is mostly on private property. See page 93 for DOW information.

Pike National Forest Maps 7 & 8

1. Tumbling, Willow and Lynch Creeks are small and fast and contain only small brook.

2. Antero Reservoir (7,260 ft; 4,102 ac); Rated good for rainbow, splake, brown and cutthroat. See page 93 for DOW information.

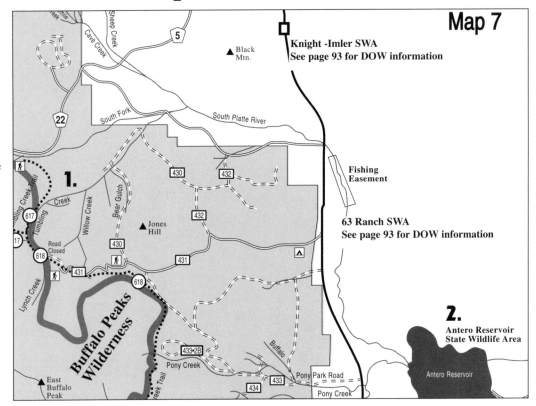

1. South Platte River; Rated excellent between Spinney Mountain and Eleven Mile Reservoirs. Gold Medal waters. Artificial flies and lures only. All fish must be returned to the water immediately. From below Eleven Mile Reservoir (Eleven Mile Canyon) artificial flies and lures only. Limit 2 fish 16" or longer.

See State Parks section for Spinney Mountain and Eleven Mile reservoirs.

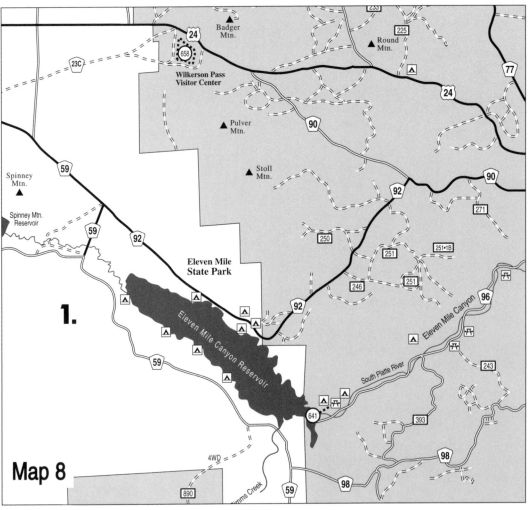

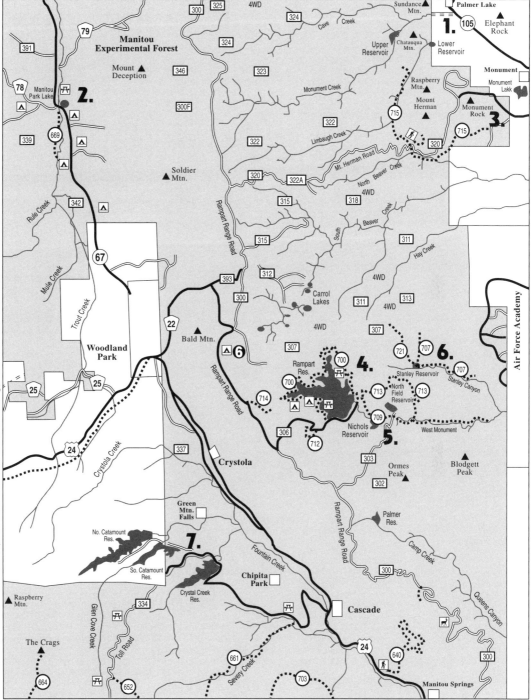

1. Palmer Lake (7,500 ft; 100 ac); Rated fair for rainbow and cutthroat. From Monument northwest 3 miles on Hwy 105 to lake. Fishing piers, no boats. Managed by El Paso County and City of Monument.

2. Manitou Reservoir (7,700 ft; 10 ac); Rated fair for rainbow and cutthroat. North of Woodland Park on Cty Road 67 approx. 6.5 miles.

3. Monument Lake (6,960 ft; 40 ac); Rated fair for rainbow, cutthroat, channel catfish, largemouth bass. Near town of Monument

4. Rampart Reservoir (9,000 ft; 500 ac); Rated fair for mackinaw, rainbow and cutthroat. East of Woodland Park on FDR 22 to Rampart Range Road (FDR 330). South on FDR 300 to Rampart Reservoir Road FDR 306, east to reservoir. Boat ramps, campgrounds and picnic areas.

5. Nichols Lake (11,800 ft; 10 ac); Rated fair for rainbow and cutthroat. Located south east of Rampart Reservoir. Use FDT 709 from dam of Rampart Reservoir south to lake.

6. Stanley Reservoir (8,800 ft; 12 ac); Rated fair for stocked rainbow and cutthroat. West from Air Force Academy on FDT 707 an easy 2 mile hike.

7. North and South Catamount and Crystal Creek Reservoirs (9,335 ft; North 210 ac, South 140 ac, Crystal Creek 136 ac); Rated good for rainbow, cutthroat and brook. From Cascade take Pikes Peak Highway west to lakes.
Managed by Colorado Springs, special fees and restrictions apply. No boat ramps but belly boats are allowed.

Rio Grande National Forest Index Map

TABLE OF CONTENTS

MAP 1
1. Sheep Creek 179
2. Middle Creek, Middle Creek, East,
   Indian Creek 179

MAP 2
1. Kerber Creek, Slaughterhouse Creek,
   Brewery Creek, Elkhorn Creek 179
2. San Luis Creek, Clover Creek, Alder
   Creek, Spring Creek 179

MAP 3
1. Cotton Lake 180
2. Cherry Lake 180
3. Rio Alto Lake 180
4. San Isabel Lake.............................180
5. Crestone Lake 180

MAP 4
1. Pole Creek 181
2. Clear Creek, North, Lost Trail Creek,
   Lost Trail Creek, West 181
3. Heart Lake 181
4. Kitty Creek, Ruby Creek, Big Buck
   Creek...181

MAP 5
1. Continental Reservoir 182
2. Rito Hondo Reservoir......................182
3. Spring Creek, Mesa Creek 182
4. Miners Creek 182
5. Crystal Lake 182
6. Spring Creek Pond 182
7. Black Mountain Lake 182
8. Brown Lakes..................................182
9. Regan Lake 182
10. Road Canyon Reservoir..................182
11. Ghost Lake....................................182

MAP 6
1. Rat Creek, Willow Creek, West 183
2. Machin Lake 183
3. Bellows Creek, Bellows Creek, West,
   Bellows Creek, East 183
4. Rio Grand River 183
5. Deep Creek 183

MAP 7
1. Saguache Creek, South Fork 184
2. Bear Creek, Johns Creek 184
3. California Gulch 184
4. Fork Creek, South, Miners Creek, Cave
   Creek...184

MAP 8
1. Willow Creek Lake..........................185
2. Cottonwood Lakes 185
3. Sand Creek Lakes 185
4. Deadman Lakes 185
5. Little Sand Creek Lake....................185
6. Medano Lake 185

MAP 9
1. Ute Lake, Upper 185
2. Ute lake, West...............................185
3. Ute Lake, Middle 185
4. Ute Lake, Main 185
5. Twin Lakes 185
6. Ute Creek 185
7. Rio Grande Reservoir 185
8. Squaw Lake 185

MAP 10
1. Squaw Creek, Little 186
2. Texas Creek 186
3. Ruby Lakes 186
4. Jumper Lake 186
5. Trout Lake.....................................186
6. Trout Creek, Trout Creek, West, Trout
   Creek, East 186
7. Love Lake 186

Map 11
1. Goose Lake 187
2. Hunters Lake..................................187
3. Shaw Lake 187
4. Big Meadows Reservoir 187
5. Archuletta Lake 187
6. Spruce Lakes 187
7. Goose, Fishers, Ivy, Lime Creeks....187
8. Pass Creek, South Fork, Lake Fork 187

MAP 12
1. Coller SWA (Rio Grande River)......188
2. Alder Creek....................................188
3. Millions Reservoir 188
4. Lost Lake 188
5. Beaver Creek Reservoir 188
6. Park Creek 188

MAP 13
1. Tucker Ponds 189
2. Alberta Park Reservoir 189

MAP 14
1. Snow Lake 189
2. Ranger Lake 189
3. Poage Lake 189
4. Crystal Lakes 189
5. Fuch Reservoir 189
6. Alamosa River 189
7. Lily Pond 189
8. Kerr Lake 189
9. Tobacco Lake 189
10. Lake Ann 189
11. Glacier Lake...................................189
12. Twin Lakes....................................189
13. Bear Lake......................................189
14. Platoro Reservoir, Mix Lake 189
15. Lake Fork Creek 189
16. Conejos River 189
17. Conejos River, Middle, North Fork
    Rito Azul, Adams Fork 189

MAP 15
1. Rock Creek, North Fork, South
   Fork 190
2. San Francisco Lakes 190
3. Spencer Lake 190
4. Big Lake 190
5. Empedrado Lake.............................190
6. La Jara Reservoir 190
7. Terrace Reservoir 190

MAP 16
1. Blue Lake 191
2. South Fork 191
3. Timber Lake 191
4. Green Lake 191
5. Alver Jones Lake 191
6. Trail Lake 191
7. Rio Chama, West Fork 191

MAP 17
1. Lost Lake 192
2. No Name Lake 192
3. Ruybalid Lake.................................192
4. Spectacle Lake................................192
5. Elk, La Manga and So. Elk Creeks 192
6. Sheep Creek 192
7. Red Lake.......................................192
8. Duck Lake.....................................192
9. Rock Lake......................................192
10. Trujillo Meadows Reservoir 192

Salida

2

1

Lake
City

3

Saguache

4 5 6 7

8

9 10 11 12

Del
Norte

South
Fork

Monte Vista

13

14

15

Alamosa

COLORADO

Pagosa
Springs

16

17

Index of numbered Maps

Rio Grande National Forest

1. Sheep Creek; Rated fair for brook. Northwest from Saguache approx. 25 miles to FDR 810. North on FDR 810 3 miles to FDR 999 approx. 3 miles to FDT 770. FDT 770 parallels the creek at this point.

2. Middle Creek, East Middle Creek and Indian Creek; Rated good for brook. Northwest from Saguache on Hwy 114 approx. 10 miles to BLM Road to Middle Creek. North approx. 10 miles to trailhead. From here FDT 766,767 and 768 follow the separate creeks. Below the forest boundary Middle Creek is on private propery.

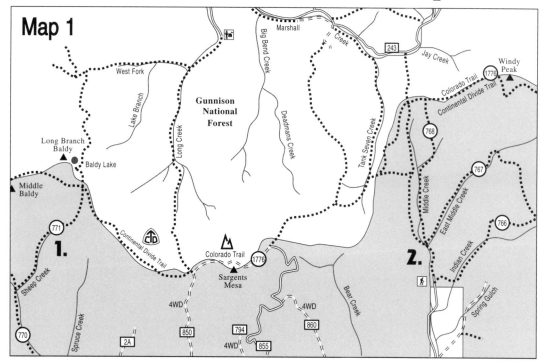

1. Kerber Creek drainage; Slaughterhouse Creek, Brewery Creek and Elkhorn Creek are rated good for small brook. From Bonanza use roads or trails that lead to streams.

2. San Luis Creek drainage; Clover Creek, Alder Creek and Spring Creek. Rated fair for small brook. From Hwy 285 near Alder Take FDT 875, 890 or 876 to reach upper section of streams. (4WD roads). Some beaver ponds on creeks. San Luis Creek is entirely on private property.

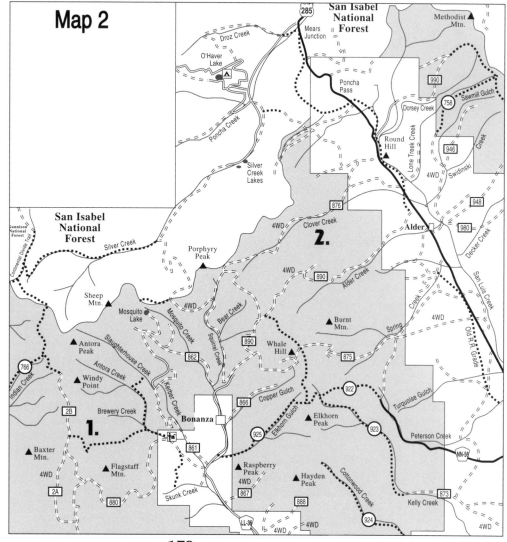

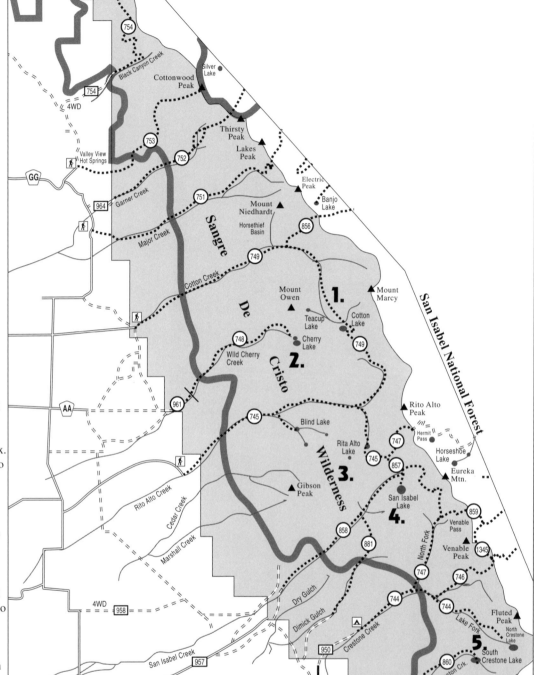

1. Cotton Lake (11,520 ft; 9.9 ac); Rated good for cutthroat. South of Villa Grove 11 miles on Hwy 17 to County Road AA east on AA 5 miles, north 2 miles, east 2 miles to FDT 749.approx. 11 miles to lake. Refer to forest service map for access. San de Cristo Wilderness.

2. Cherry Lake (11,769 ft; 9.9 ac); Rated good for cutthroat. South of Villa Grove 11 miles on Hwy 17 to County Road AA east on AA 8 miles to trailhead FDT 748. Approx. 4.6 miles to lake. Refer to forest service map for access. San de Cristo Wilderness.

3. Rito Alto Lake (11,240 ft; 4 ac); Rated good for cutthroat. South of Villa Grove 11 miles on Hwy 17 to County Road AA east on AA 5 miles, south 2.5 miles, east 4 miles to FDT 745 trailhead. Approx. 7 miles to lake. Refer to forest service map for access. San Isabel Lake is one mile south. San de Cristo Wilderness.

4. San Isabel Lake (11,600 ft; 5.9 ac); Rated good for cutthroat. From Moffat east on Crestone Road 7 miles, to FDR 957, northeast 5 miles to 4WD road 1 mile to trailhead. Approx 4.5 miles on FDT 858 to lake. Refer to forest service map for access. San de Cristo Wilderness.

5. Crestone Lakes (North 11,560 ft; 31.6 ac, South 11,780 ft; 8.9 ac); Rated good for cutthroat and brook. Refer to forest service map for access. North Crestone; North from Crestone on FDR 950 2 miles to North Crestone Creek Campground and trailhead. Approx. 6 miles on FDT 744 to lake. South Crestone; East from Crestone on FDR 949 2 miles to trailhead. Approx. 3.3 miles on FDT 860 to lake. San de Cristo Wilderness.

6. Streams in this area are small fast and brushy. Some are rated fair for brook and cutthroat.

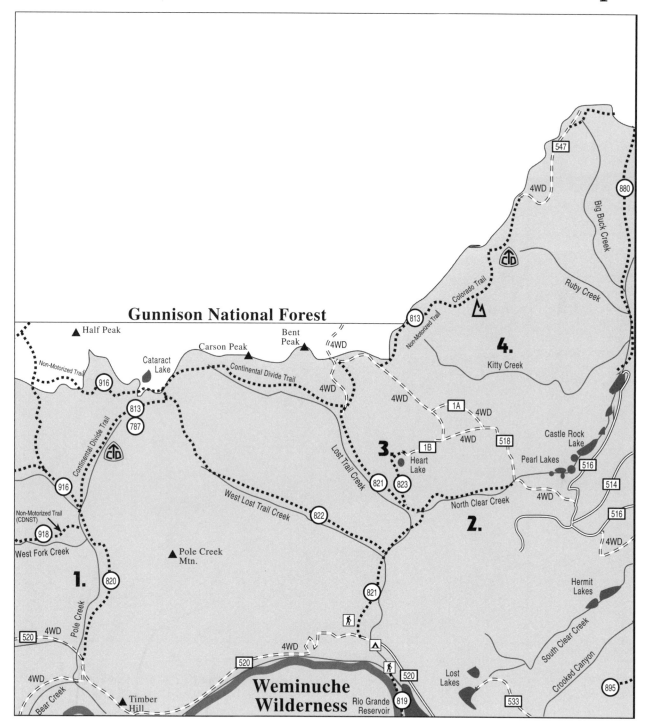

1. Pole Creek; Rated good for cutthroat. West of Rio Grande Reservoir at Lost Trail Campground on FDR 520 (4WD) 8 miles to trail. (Road may be closed). Pole Creek parallels trail FDT 820.

2. North Clear Creek, W. Lost Trail Creek and Lost Trail Creek; Rated fair for brook, cutthroat and stocked rainbow in North Clear Creek. West of Rio Grande Reservoir at Lost Trail Campground take FDT 821 to streams.

3. Heart Lake (10,550 ft; 16.8 ac); Rated good for brook. West of Rio Grande Reservoir at Lost Trail Campground take FDT 821 3. 5 miles to FDT 823, continue1 mile to lake.

4. Kitty Creek, Ruby Creek and Big Buck Creek; Rated good for rainbow and cutthroat. From west end of Continental Reservoir FDT 880 leads to lower sections of streams. All have beaver ponds.

1. Continental Reservoir (10,300 ft; 50 ac); Rated fair for brook, cutthroat and rainbow. Approx. 32 miles west of Creede on Hwy 149 to FDR 513. North on FDR 513 3.5 miles to Rito Hondo, 5 miles to Continental Reservoir.

2. Rito Hondo Reservoir (10,280 ft; 41 ac); Rated good for brook and rainbow. Boat ramp but no motorized boats.

3. Spring Creek and Mesa Creek; Rated fair for small brook, cutthroat and rainbow. Some beaver ponds on Spring Creek. Spring Creek parallels Hwy 149. No designated trail to access Mesa Creek.

4. Miners Creek; Rated good for cutthroat and brook. From Creede south on Hwy 149 approx. 3 miles to FDR 507, north on FDR 507 3 miles to end of road. Take FDT 803 a 7 mile trail to near the Continental Divide.

5. Crystal Lake (11,560 ft; 3 ac); Rated fair for cutthroat. From Creede south on Hwy 149 approx. 3 miles to FDR 507, north on FDR 507, north approx. 2 miles to road on left, .5 mile to FDT 804. FDT 804 west approx. 7 miles to lake.

6. Spring Creek Pond (9,200 ft; 7.9 ac); Rated fair for stocked rainbow. From Creede west on Hwy 149 approx. 25 miles to pond. Next to highway on west side.

7. Black Mountain Lake (11,200 ft; 5.9 ac); Rated fair for cutthroat. Southwest from Brown Lakes SWA on FDR 516 (Trouble Hill Road) approx. 5 miles to FDR 514. Northeast on FDR 514 approx. 3 miles to lake.

8. Brown Lakes State Wildlife Area (9,840 ft; 180 ac); Rated good for rainbow, brook, cutthroat and brown. See page 89 for DOW information.

9. Regan Lake (10,041 ft; 80 ac); Rated fair for rainbow and cutthroat. From Creede on Hwy 149 approx. 24 miles to FDR 520. West on FDR 520 approx 3.5 miles to Bristol View, take FDR 521 (4WD) approx. 5 miles to lake.

10. Road Canyon Reservoir (9,275 ft; 140 ac); Rated fair for rainbow and cutthroat. From Creede on Hwy 149 approx. 24 miles to FDR 520. West on FDR 520 approx. 5 miles to reservoir. Boat ramp.

11. Ghost Lake (9,400 ft; 2.5 ac); Rated poor for cutthroat. From Creede on Hwy 149 approx.12 miles to FDR 509. West on FDR 509 approx. 4 miles, the last 3 miles of road is 4WD. Near Santa Maria Pass

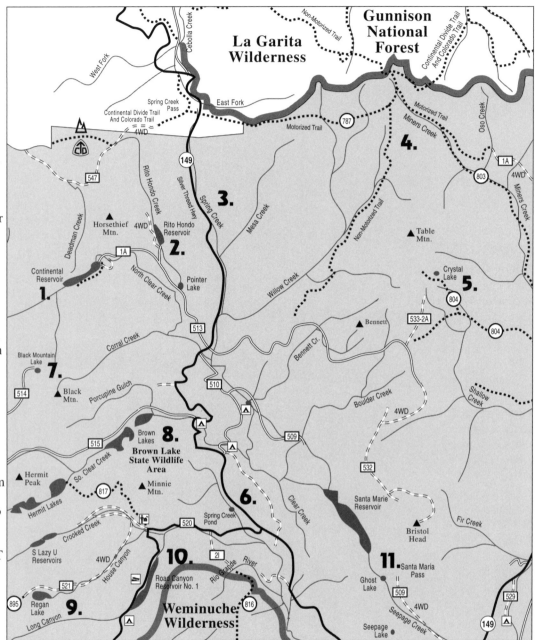

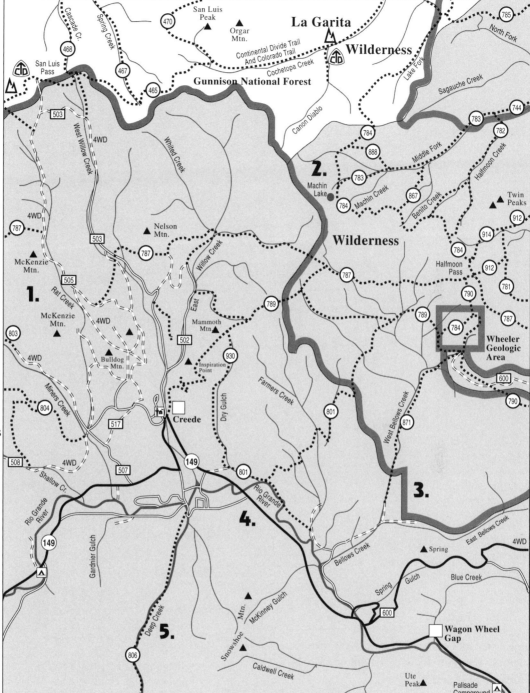

1. Rat Creek, West Willow Creek; Rated fair for brook. Lower section of W. Willow Creek on private property. Access from just north and west of Creede.

2. Machin Lake (12,560 ft; 11.4 ac); Rated fair for cutthroat. Located 6 miles southwest of Stone Cellar Campground (Map 4) on FDR 744 (4WD) to La Garita Wilderness Boundary. Continue on FDT 783 approx 8 miles to lake. **Middle Saguache Creek;** Rated Good for cutthroat and brook. Parallels trail and road.

3. Bellows Creek, West Bellows Creek and East Bellows Creek; Bellows Creek is on private property. West Bellows Creek in to La Garita Wilderness is rated good for brook and brown. East Bellows Creek is rated good for brook. Southeast of Creede on Hwy 149 approx. 8 miles to bridge crossing Rio Grande River. Northwest on Bellows Creek Road approx. 4 miles to end of road. Last section of road can require 4WD. FDT 871 follows West Bellows Creek. There is no designated trail for East bellows Creek located to the east.

4. Rio Grande River; Rated good for cutthroat, brown and rainbow. Marshall Park Campground is a put in point for rafters. From Wagon Wheel Gap to along Hwy 149 there is a 4 mile stretch of National Forest access. Palisade Campground southeast of Wagon Wheel Gap is another put in site. Most of the Rio Grande River flows through private property. Review Forest service map and contact a Ranger District before fishing the river, special fishing and boating regulations apply.

5. Deep Creek; Rated good for brook. Three miles south of Creede to FDT 806. Trail follows stream to headwaters for approx. 7 miles. Fast small stream.

Rio Grande National Forest Map 7

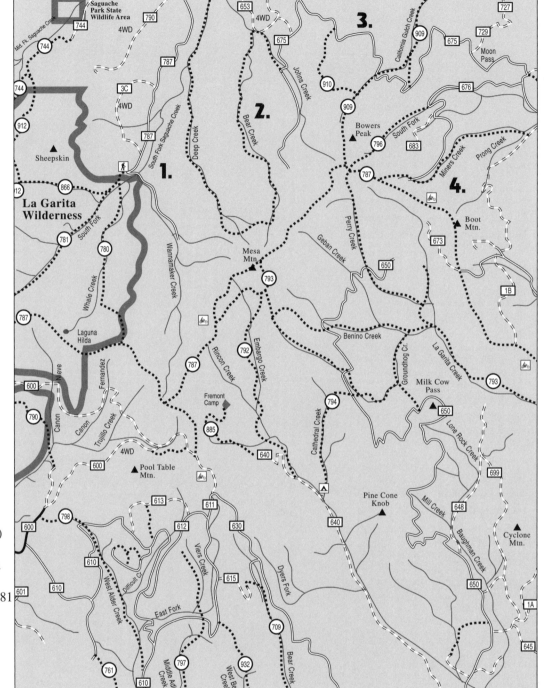

1. South Fork Saguache Creek; From Stone Cellar Campground (Map 4) south on FDR 787 approx. 7 miles to La Garita Wilderness Boundary and FDT 781 trailhead. The road generally follows stream. The trail follows the stream approx. 4 miles into wilderness. A gated road continues up Wannamaker Creek to the east for a short distance, check with forest service about access. South Fork and Wannamaker are small streams with undergrowth.

2. Bear Creek and Johns Creek; Rated good for small brook. Southeast of Stone Cellar Campground (Map 4) approx. 3 miles to streams. Check Forest Service map for access. Some beaver ponds.

3. California Gulch; Rated good for small brook. Stream flows into Saguache Creek from the south near forest boundary. Any number of roads will you guide to the stream. Check Forest Service map for routes.

4. South Fork Creek, Miners Creek and Cave Creek; Rated good for small brook. Northwest of La Garita on County Road 690 approx. 8 miles to FDR 675, 2 miles west to Poso Campground. FDR 675 follows South Fork Creek northwest. Streams have some beaver ponds. Cave Creek to the south is similar to these streams and can be reached from Poso campground on FDR 673. Refer to Forest Service map.

1. Willow Creek Lake (11,564 ft; 19.8 ac); Rated fair for cutthroat. East of Moffat on Crestone Road to Crestone approx. 12 miles. East of Crestone 1.5 miles to 4WD road, .75 miles to trailhead. Approx. 4 miles on FDT 865 to lake.

2. Cottonwood Lakes (12,310 ft; 3 ac, South 11,800; 2 ac); Rated fair for stocked rainbow and cutthroat. Cottonwood Lakes, Sand Creek Lakes, Little Sand Creek Lake and Deadman Lake are accessed from Cottonwood on the Baca Grant. Cottonwood is southeast of Crestone. To access trails stop in Cottonwood and obtain permission and directions at administrative and maintenance building, permission must be given. Refer to Forest Service map. Distance and trail conditions vary.

3. Sand Creek Lakes (Lower 11,471 ft; 62.8 ac, Upper 11,745 ft 42.8 ac); Rated good for rainbow and cutthroat.

4. Deadman Lakes (Lower 11,780 ft; 2.5 ac, Upper 11,704 ft; 13.8 ac); Rated good for brook and cutthroat. No designated trail to lakes.

5. Little Sand Creek Lake (1,998 ft; 12.6 ac); Rated good for rainbow and cutthroat.

6. Medano Lake (11,680 ft; 2.7 ac); Rated fair for cutthroat and small brook. From Great Sand Dunes National Monument on Hwy 150 to Pinyon Flats Campground. Continue on FDR 235 (4WD) north and east to approx. 10 miles to just below Medano Pass. Northwest on FDT 887 4 miles to lake. Medano Creek follows road and is rated poor for small brook. Fast small stream.

7. NOTE: South of the Sixmile Lane Road and Hwy 150 approx. 2 miles is Zapata Creek Trailhead. Zapata Creek Trail (FDT 852) follows Zapata Creek to several high lakes. Zapata Creek and Zapata Lakes are known to have fair fishing for cutthroat. Refer to Forest Service map for directions.

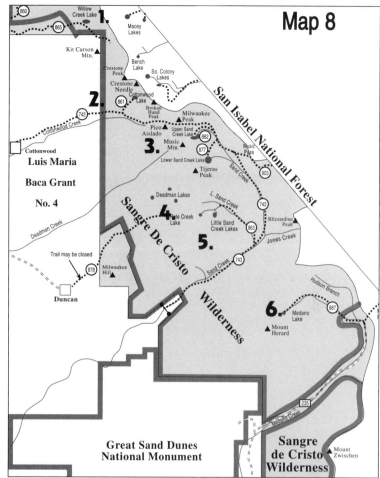

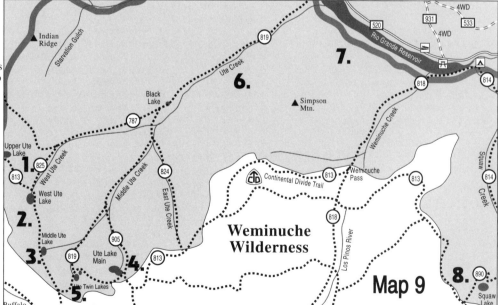

MAP 9

1. Ute Lake, Upper (12,326 ft; 4.7 ac); Rated fair for cutthroat. Approx. 7 miles up on FDT 819 take FDT 787 west to FDT 825 an additional 5 miles to West Lake. Continue east on 813 to Upper Lake. Weminuche Wilderness

2. Ute Lake, West (11,801 ft; 16 ac); Rated fair for cutthroat and rainbow. Approx.7 miles up on FDT 819 take FDT 787 west to FDT 825 an additional 5 miles. Weminuche Wilderness.

3. Ute Lake, Middle (11,949 ft; 11.4 ac); Rated fair to poor for cutthroat. Can be reached from Twin Lakes or West Lake. Weminuche Wilderness

4. Ute Lake, Main (11,847 ft; 32.1 ac); Rated good for cutthroat. Approx.10 miles up on FDT 819 take FDT 905 east to lake west to FDT 825. Weminuche Wilderness.

5. Twin Lakes (Ute) (lower 11,792 ft; 4.7 ac, upper11,792 ft; 15.8 ac); Rated fair for cutthroat and rainbow. From west end of Rio Grande Reservoir take FDT 819 12.1 miles to Twin lakes. Weminuche Wilderness. Early in the spring and summer expect high water crossings.

6. Ute Creek and branches; Rated fair for brook and cutthroat. FDT 819 follows Ute Creek to Middle, west and east Branches (See Map). Weminuche Wilderness.

7. Rio Grande Reservoir (9,449 ft; 1,120 ac); Rated good for rainbow, brown and cutthroat. From Creede 20 miles west on Hwy 149 to FDR 520. On FDR 520 approx. 13 miles to reservoir. Boat ramps, campgrounds and picnic areas. Weminuche Creek from the south is rated good for cutthroat FDT 818 follows stream. Squaw Creek enters reservoir near outlet of reservoir. Rated good for brook and brown. FDT 814 follows stream. Weminuche Wilderness.

8. Squaw Lake (11,632 ft; 16.8 ac); Rated fair for brook. Located near the Continental Divide Trail on FDT 890. Refer to Forest Service map for best route to reach lake.

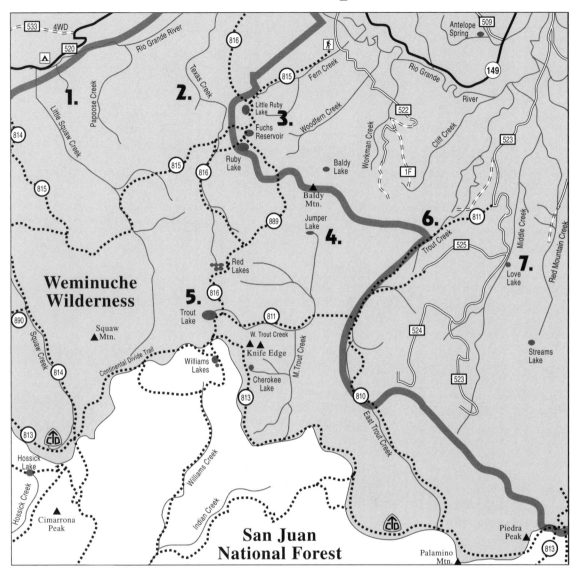

1. Little Squaw Creek; Rated good for cutthroat. From Thirty Mile Campground at Rio Grande Reservoir take FDT 814 2 miles to FDT 815, FDT east approx. 7 miles to upper section of stream. No designated trail from River Hill Campground and Rio Grande River. Weminuche Wilderness.

2. Texas Creek; Rated good for brook, brown and rainbow. From Creede approx. 18 miles to FDR 522. Turn left and cross over Rio Grande River, approx. 1 mile to Fern Creek Trailhead (FDT 815). Forest Service maps do not show Texas Creek Trail, (FDT 816) in lower section of creek. FDT 816 is described as a difficult 12.9 mile hike along Texas Creek. FDT 815 follows Fern Creek to FDT 816 on upper section of Texas Creek. Weminuche Wilderness.

3. Ruby Lake, Little (11,250 ft; 17.8 ac), Ruby Lake, Big (11,290 ft; 29.6 ac); Rated fair for rainbow and brook. From Creede approx. 18 miles to FDR 522. Turn left and cross over Rio Grande River, approx. 1 mile to Fern Creek Trailhead. Aprox. 3.5 miles to lakes.

4. Jumper Lake (11,577 ft; 8.4 ac); Rated fair for cutthroat. From Ruby lakes on FDT 899. There is no designated trail to lake from FDT 899. Refer to USGS topographic map.

5. Trout Lake (11,685 ft; 23.7 ac); Rated fair for cutthroat. From Creede west on Hwy 149 approx. 7 miles to Marshall Park campground and FDR 523. South on FDR 523 approx 9 miles to FDT 811, west on trail approx. 6 miles to lake. Weminuche Wilderness.

6. Trout Creek, West Trout Creek and East Trout Creek; Rated good for cutthroat and rainbow. From Creede west on Hwy 149 approx. 7 miles to Marshall Park campground and FDR 523. South on FDR 523 approx. 8 miles to FDT 811. Road and trail follows stream. Refer to map.

7. Love Lake (10,00 ft; 5 ac); Rated fair for stocked brook and rainbow. From Creede west on Hwy 149 approx. 7 miles to Marshall Park campground and FDR 523. South on FDR 523 approx.10 miles to lake.

1. Goose Lake (12,000 ft; 26.7 ac); Rated fair for cutthroat. From Spar City on FDR 528 east 4 miles to North Lime Trailhead, FDT 806. South on FDT 806 to FDT 805, continue on FDT 805 to lake. Approx. 9 mile hike into Weminuche Wilderness.

2. Hunters Lake (11,383 ft; 10 ac); Rated fair for cutthroat and brook. From Del Norte go 27. 5 miles west on Hwy 160 to FDR 410, west 2 miles to Big Meadows Reservoir. Continue on FDR 410 approx. 7.5 miles to trail on the left that is a short hike to lake. Lake Fork Creek parallels FDT 835 to lake and is rated good for brook.

3. Shaw Lake (9,860 ft; 70 ac); Rated fair rainbow and cutthroat. From Del Norte go 27. 5 miles west on Hwy 160 to FDR 410, west 2 miles to Big Meadows Reservoir, 2 miles north to lake.

4. Big Meadows Reservoir (9,200 ft; 113.9 ac); Rated good for small rainbow, brook and a few cutthroat. From Del Norte go 27. 5 miles west on Hwy 160 to FDR 410, west 2 miles to reservoir. Campground and boat ramp for small craft.

5. Archuletta Lake (11,720 ft; 4 ac); Rated fair for cutthroat and brook. From Del Norte go 27. 5 miles west on Hwy 160 to FDR 410, west 2 miles to Big Meadows Reservoir. Take FDT 839 west approx. 5 miles to lake.

6. Spruce Lakes (Lower 11,100 ft; 19.8 ac, Upper 11,120 ft; 19.8 ac); Rated fair for cutthroat. From Del Norte go 27. 5 miles west on Hwy 160 to FDR 410, west 2 miles to Big Meadows Reservoir. Take FDT 839 to junction of FDT 750, approx. 4 miles

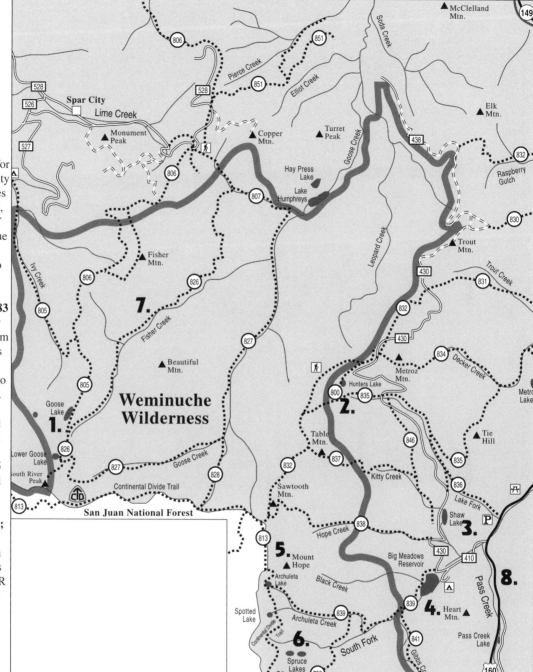

from trailhead go west to lakes. No designated trails to lakes from FDT 839.

7. Goose Creek, Fisher Creek, Ivy Creek and Lime Creek; Creeks are rated fair to poor for small brook and cutthroat. Lower section of Goose Creek flows through private property. Hay Press Lake and Lake Humpreys are private.

8. South Fork, Lake Fork and Pass Creeks; Rated fair to good for rainbow, brook and cutthroat. Lower section of South Fork has intermittent public and private property. From town of South Fork HWY 160 parallels South Fork and Pass Creeks.

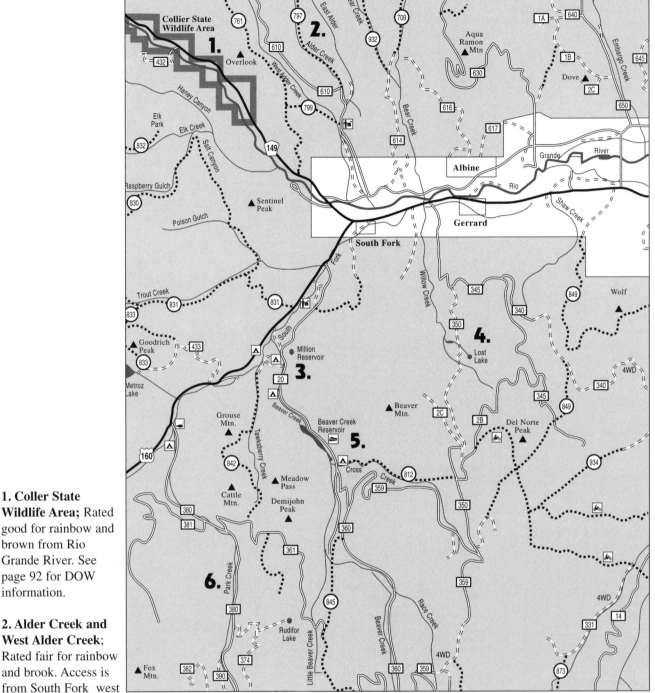

1. Coller State Wildlife Area; Rated good for rainbow and brown from Rio Grande River. See page 92 for DOW information.

2. Alder Creek and West Alder Creek; Rated fair for rainbow and brook. Access is from South Fork west 1.5 miles to access road. East 1.5 miles on access road to FDR 610, this road follows past private property to un-posted water.

3. Millions Reservoir (8,460 ft; 3.7 ac); Rated fair for rainbow. From South Fork 1.5 miles to FDR 20, (FDR 360), approx. 2.5 miles to lake.

4. Lost Lake (10,120 ft; 1 ac); Rated fair for stocked cut-throat. From South Fork 2 miles east on Hwy 160 to FDR 345. South on FDR 345 approx. 2.5 miles to FDR 350 continue south 2 mile to just west of lake.

5. Beaver Creek Reservoir (8,850 ft; 113.9 ac); Rated good for cutthroat, rainbow, kokanee and brown. From South Fork 1.5 miles to FDR 20, (FDR 360), approx. 7 miles to lake. Cross Creek Campground at reservoir. Boat ramp for small craft. Beaver Creek is posted for approx. 2 miles before it enters reservoir this creek and its tributaries are rated fair to poor for brook.

6. Park Creek; Rated good for rainbow, cutthroat and browns. From Park Creek Campground on Hwy 160 east on FDR 380, road parallels creek. Heavy pressure.

MAP 13

1. Tucker Park Ponds (9,640 ft; 9.9 ac); Rated fair for stocked rainbow. At Tucker Ponds Campground approx 3 miles northeast of Wolf Creek Pass on Hwy 160.

2. Alberta Park Reservoir (10,203 ft; 40 ac); Rated fair for brook and rainbow. North of Wolf Creek pass approx. 1.5 miles to FDR 391, east to reservoir

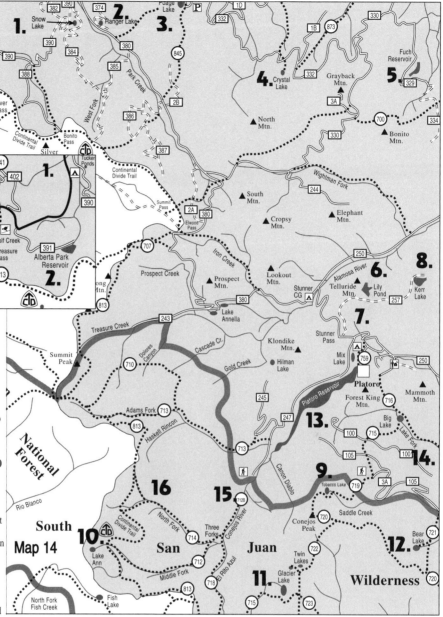

1. Snow Lake (10,320 ft; 1.2 ac); Rated fair for cutthroat. From Hwy 160 and Tucker Ponds Campground (Map 13) east on FDR 390. Reaching Snow and Ranger Lakes from this road can become confusing check Forest Service map.

2. Ranger Lake (9,600 ft; 3 ac); Rated good for stocked rainbow. See Snow Lake.

3. Poage Lake (11,065 ft; 28.9 ac); Rated good for rainbow and cutthroat. From South Fork on Hwy 160 1 mile to FDR 20 (360). South on FDR 360 approx. 16 miles to reservoir.

4. Crystal Lakes (Lower 11,220 ft; 11.4 ac, Upper 11,540 ft; 20 ac); Rated good for cutthroat and brook. Two mile east of Poage Reservoir take FDR 332 east for approx. 3.5 miles to lake.

5. Fuch Reservoir; Rated fair for stocked rainbow (has not have been stocked in recent years); From Del Norte south on County Road 14 (FDR 329) approx. 20 mile to lake. Can be reached from Crystal Lake. Call Forest Service before trip.

6. Alamosa River; Rated good for brook, cutthroat and rainbow above Stunner Campground. This includes Treasure and Prospect Creeks. Below Stunner Campground river is rated fair for brook and rainbow. Beyond Map 15 the river is mostly on private property. South of Monte Vista 12 miles on Hwy 15 to FDR 250 West on FDR 250 9 miles west to Terrace Reservoir. FDR 250 follows river to Stunner Campground.

7. Lily Pond (10,940 ft; 24 ac); Rated fair for stocked cutthroat, may winter kill. North of Platoro Reservoir on FDR 250 and 257 approx. 3 miles. Some of road 4WD.

8. Kerr Lake (11,380 ft; 39.5 ac); Rated good for cutthroat. North of Platoro Reservoir on FDR 250 and 257 approx. 5 miles. Some of road 4WD. Artificial flies and lures only. Boats allowed, no motors.

9. Tobacco Lake (12,280 ft; 12.8 ac); Rated fair for cutthroat and rainbow. From FDR 250 southeast of Platoro Reservoir approx. 8 miles to FDR 105. From Tobacco Lake Saddle Creek is the wilderness northern boundary. Fast small stream with under brush, rated good for cutthroat.

10. Lake Ann (11,910 ft; 15.6 ac); Rated fair cutthroat. From south end of Platoro Reservoir at wilderness boundary. Take FDT 712 approx. 6 miles to lake.

11. Glacier Lake (11,960 ft; 21.2 ac); Rated fair for rainbow. From trailhead just west of FDR 105 and 250. Take FDT 721, 2 miles to Bear Lake, 6 miles to FDT 722, 2 miles to Twin Lakes, 3 miles to Glacier Lake.

12. Twin Lakes (Lower 11,710 ft; 3 ac, Upper 11,740 ft; 2 ac); Rated fair for rainbow. See Glacier Lake.

13. Bear Lake (11,520 ft; 18.3 ac); Rated fair for cutthroat and rainbow. See Glacier Lake.

14. Platoro Reservoir (9970 ft; 700 ac); Rated good for brown, rainbow and kokanee. South of Monte Vista 12 miles on Hwy 15 to FDR 250 West on FDR 250 9 miles west to Terrace Reservoir. Continue on FDR 250 approx. 21 miles to reservoir. Boat ramp and campground. Mix Lake (21.7 ac) at the north end of reservoir (25 ac) has restrictions.

15. Lake Fork Creek; Rated good for cutthroat. Catch and release, artificial flies and lures only. From south of Lake Fork Campground at FDR 250. Use FDT 716 for approx. 4 mile hike to lake.

16. Conejos River; Rated good for rainbow and brown. From Antonito west on Hwy 17 13 miles to forest boundary. Hwy 17 follows river approx.10 miles to FDR 250. FDR 250 follows river to Platoro Reservoir. Thirty miles of high quality wild trout fishing. Although much of river flows through private land access is provided through cooperative efforts of Forest Service and property owners. Open areas are well marked. Some areas have restrictions.

17. Middle Conejos River, North Fork Conejos, Rito Azul and Adams Fork; Rated good for rainbow, cutthroat and brown. Located in San Juan Wilderness all but Adams Fork can be reached from FDT 712. Adams Fork can be reached from FDT 713. Both trailheads are on the south end of Platoro Reservoir.

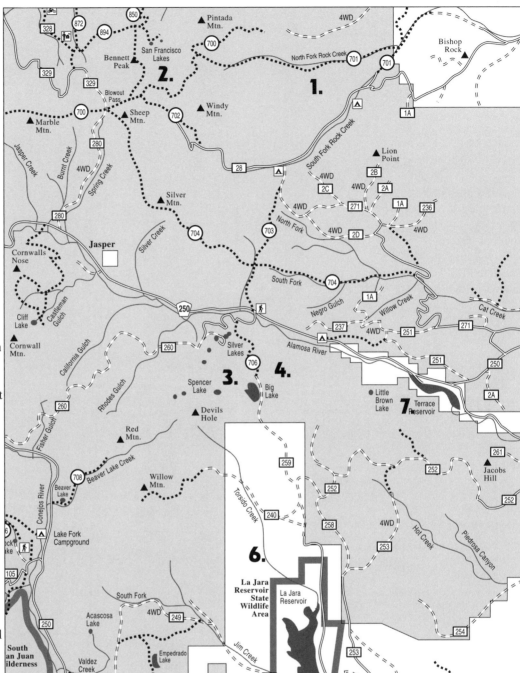

1. North and South Forks Rock Creek; Rated fair for rainbow. From Monte Vista south on Hwy 15 2 miles, west on Rock Creek Road (FDR 28) to forest boundary. At boundary use FDR 28 for South Fork or FDT 701 for North Fork.

2. San Francisco Lakes (Lake 11.900 ft; 5 ac, Lower, E. 11,900 ft; 5.7 ac, Upper, W. 11,980 ft; 4.2 ac); Rated fair for cutthroat. South of Del Norte on FDR13 approx. 10 miles to Middle Fork trailhead. South on Trail approx. 5.5 miles to lakes.

3. Spencer Lake (9,820 ft; 11.4 ac); Rated fair for stocked rainbow. West of Terrace Reservoir 4 miles on FDR 250 to trailhead. Take FDT 706 south approx. 4 miles. No designated trail to lake from trail, consult topographic map.

4. Big Lake (10,060 ft; 73.4 ac); Rainbow. East of Spencer Lake 1mile. Access is an area on the northwest corner of the lake only. No designated trail to lake.

5. Empedrado Lake (10,990 ft; 36.8 ac); Rated fair for stocked cutthroat. Southeast of Platoro Reservoir on FDR 250 approx. 11 miles to FDT 717. Take FDT 717 approx. 2

miles to 4WD road, north on road 1.5 miles , east on trail approx.1 mile to lake.

6. La Jara Reservoir State Wildlife Area; (9,698 ft; 1,375 ac); Rated fair for brook and rainbow. Boat ramp. See page 86 for DOW information.

7. Terrace Reservoir State Wildlife Area (8,526 ft; 144 ac); Cutthroat and rainbow. The reservoir has not been stocked in recent years and is subject to draw down. See page 87 for DOW information.

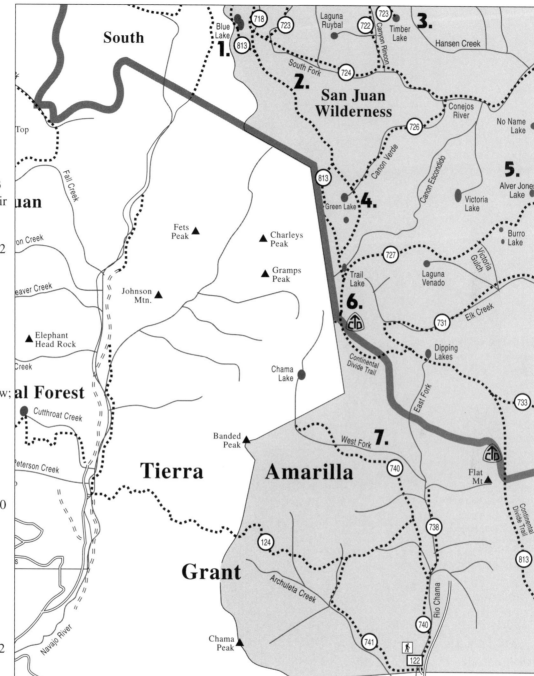

1. Blue Lake (11,463 ft; 49.4 ac); Rated fair for brook and brown. South of Platoro Reservoir on FDT 712 2 mile to FDT 718, south 3 miles to lake.

2. South Fork, rated good for rainbow, brook and cutthroat; Canon Rincon, rated poor; Canon Verde, rated good for rainbow; Conejos River rated good for rainbow, brook and cutthroat; Hansen Creek, rated good for cutthroat. Southeast of Platoro Reservoir on FDR 250 approx.14 miles to trailhead FDT 724. FDT 724 will access these streams.

3. Timber Lake (11,322 ft; 11,9 ac); South of Platoro Reservoir on FDT 712 2 mile to FDT 718, south 3 miles to FDT 723, continue approx. 5 miles to lake.

4. Green Lake (11,550 ft; 15 ac); Rated good for cutthroat and rainbow. Southeast of Platoro Reservoir on FDR 250 approx.14 miles to trailhead FDT 724. Take FDT 724 west approx. 4 miles to FDT 726, continue approx. 4 miles to lake.

5. Alver Jones Lake (11,180 ft; 16.1 ac); Rated fair for cutthroat. Southeast of Platoro Reservoir on FDR 250 approx.18 miles to trailhead FDT 855. Take FDT 855 west approx. 3 miles to FDT 727, continue approx. 1 mile to lake.

6. Trail Lake (11,987 ft; 29.6 ac); Rated fair for rainbow Southeast of Platoro Reservoir on FDR 250 approx. 14 miles to trailhead FDT 724. Take FDT 724 west approx. 4 miles to FDT 726, continue approx. 4 miles to Green Lake. South approx. 3 miles to lake.

7. West Fork Rio Chama; Rate fair for rainbow and cutthroat. On FDR 121 12 miles to forest boundary. From here FDT 740 follows stream.

Rio Grande National Forest Map 17

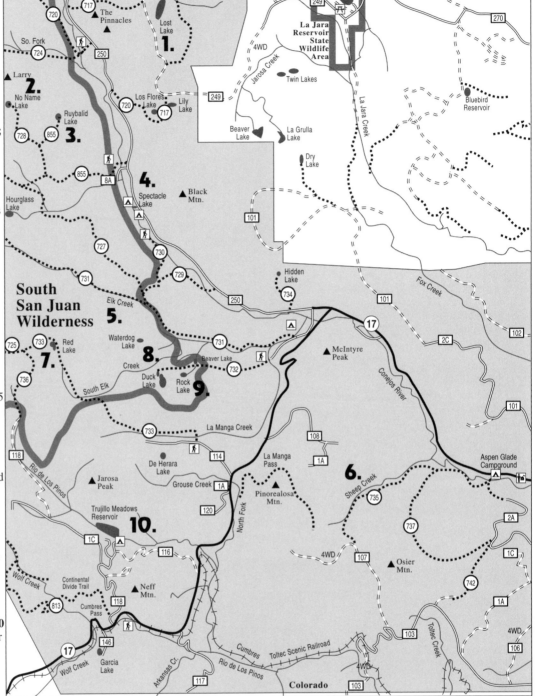

1. Lost Lake (10,580 ft; 28.2 ac); Rated fair for cutthroat. Southeast of Platoro Reservoir on FDR 250 approx. 11 miles to FDT 717. Take FDT 717 approx. 2 miles to 4WD road, north on road 1.5 miles, east on trail approx.1 mile to Empedrado Lake. Lost Lake is 1 mile south.

2. No Name Lake (11,360 ft; 39.5 ac); Rated fair for cutthroat. Southeast of Platoro Reservoir on FDR 250 approx.18 miles to trailhead FDT 855. Take FDT 855 west approx 3.5 miles to FDT 728, north 2 miles to lake. South San Juan Wilderness.

3. Ruybalid Lake (11,200 ft; 6.9 ac); Rated fair for rainbow and brook. Southeast of Platoro Reservoir on FDR 250 approx.18 miles to trailhead FDT 855. Take FDT 855 west approx 4.5 miles to lake. South San Juan Wilderness.

4. Spectacle Lake (8,780 ft; 4.2 ac); Rated fair for stocked rainbow. From Antonito on Hwy 17 west approx. 30 miles to lake. Catch and release.

5. Elk Creek, South Elk Creek, La Manga Creek; Rated fair for small brook. West of Antonito on Hwy 17 approx. 23 miles to Elk Creek Campground. FDT 731 to Elk Creek and South Elk Creek. Further south from FDR 114, west on FDT 733 to reach upper La Manga Creek.

6. Sheep Creek; Rated fair for cutthroat. From Aspen Glade Campground take FDT 735.

7. Red Lake (11,520 ft; 21.2 ac); Rated fair for rainbow and cutthroat. West of Antonito on Hwy 17 approx. 29 miles to FDR 114, west 1.5 miles to trailhead. Take FDT 733 approx. 7 miles to lake. South San Juan Wilderness.

8. Duck Lake (10,080 ft; 3.5 ac); Rated good for brook. From Antonito on Hwy 17 west approx. 23 miles to Elk Creek Campground. Southeast 1.5 miles to Trailhead, take FDT 732 west 3.5 miles to lake. South San Juan Wilderness.

9. Rock Lake (9,600 ft; 7.2 ac); Rated fair for cutthroat. See Duck Lake. South San Juan Wilderness.

10. Trujillo Meadows Reservoir (10,020 ft; 69.2 ac); Rated fair for rainbow, cutthroat and brown. West of Antonito on Hwy 17 approx. 36 miles, north on FDR 118, 2.5 miles north to FDR 118.1B, bear left, .3 mile to reservoir. Boat ramp, no wake boating and campground. Rio de Los Pinos feeds the reservoir the upper portion can be accessed 4WD FDR 118 to wilderness boundary.

ROUTT TABLE OF CONTENTS

MAP 1
1. Freeman Reservoir.........................194
2. Sawmill Creek 194

MAP 2
1. Little Snake and Middle Fork 194
2. Torso, Armstrong, Grizzly and
   Slater Creeks 194

MAP 3
1. Whiskey Creek and Silver City
   Creek 195
2. King Solomon Creek, Box and
   Little Red Park Creek, Smith
   and Independence Creeks 195
3. Encampment River, West Fork
   Encampment River,
   South Fork Hog Park Creek 195
4. Manazanares Lake 195
5. West Fork Lake 195
6. Sanchez Lakes 195
7. Trail Creek, No. Fork Elk River,
   Lost Dog and English Creeks 195
8. Hinman Creek and Scott Run 195
9. Steamboat/Pearl State Park 195
10. Hahns Peak Lake 195

MAP 4
1. Big Creek Lakes 196
2. Lake Eileen 196
3. Seven Lakes.................................196
4. Gem Lake 196
5. Lake Diana...................................196
6. Forester, Goose, Shaffer, Ute
   and Box Creeks 196
7. Blue Lake.....................................196
8. Peggy Lake 196
9. Twin Lakes 196
10. Ute Lake 196
11. Bear Lakes 196
12. Bighorn Lakes 196
13. Beaver Lake 196
14. Three Island Lake 196
15. Mica Lake 196
16. Slide Lake 196

MAP 5
1. Elk River 197
2. Burn Creek....................................197
3. Big Creek......................................197
4. Mad Creek, North, South and
   Middle Forks 197
5. Margaret, Edward, Snowstorm
   and Fish Hawk Lakes 197
6. Soda and Spring Creeks 197

MAP 6
1. Lake Katherine 198
2. North Lake....................................198
3. Ptarmigan Lake Dome Lake,
   Wolverine Lake, Pristine Lake 198
4. Roxy Ann Lakes 198
5. Big Creek Lake 198
6. Lake of the Crags, Luna and
   Elbert Lakes..................................198

7. Mirror and Rosa Lakes 198
8. Porcupine Lake 198
9. Slide Lakes 198
10. Ceanothuse Lake and Rainbow
    Lakes 198
11. Agua Fria Lake 198
12. Round Mountain Lake.................198
13. Albert, Victoria, Martha, Summit,
    Shoestring, Jonah, Whale Lakes ..198
14. Tiago Lake and Teal Lakes,
    Burns Reservoir. 198
15. Sawmill Lakes 198
16. Stambaugh Reservoir, Hidden Lakes
   198
17. Dinosaur Lake 198
18. Chedsey Creek, Newcomb
    Creek and Whalen Creeks 198

MAP 7
1. Fish Creek Reservoir....................199
2. Long, Percy, Round, Elmo
   Lakes 199
3. Lost Lake 199
4. Dumont Lake................................199
5. Harrison, Green, Service and
   Walton Creeks 199

MAP 8
1. Slack-Weiss Reservoir, Kathleen,
   Kidney Lakes, Two Ledge
   Reservoir, Long, Alder,
   Disappointment, Deep, Willow,
   Cliff, Bundy, Beaver, Finger and
   Brook Lakes...................................200
2. Seymore Reservoir 200

MAP 9
1. Beaver Creek
   (Indian Run SWA).........................200
2. Beaver Flat Tops Ponds................200
3. Vaughn Lake 200

4. South Fork Williams Fork,
   Pine Creek, Indian Run, Beaver
   Creek 200

MAP 10
1. Shaffer Reservoir, Dunkley &
   Dubeau Reservoir,
   Seller-Crowell Reservoir 201
2. Chapman Reservoir 201
3. Crosho Reservoir, Allen Basin
   Reservoir 201
4. Haley Reservoir 201
5. Sheriff Reservoir, Oat, Crater,
   Wheat, Sand Lakes 202
6. Killarney Reservoir, Chatfield
   Reservoir 202
7. Heart Lake 202
8. Yamcolo Reservoir, Bear Lake 202
9. Stillwater Reservoir......................202
10. Gardner Park Reservoir...............202
11. Lost Lakes, Deep, Dines, Long
    and Round Lakes..........................202
12. Causeway Lakes 202
13. Rainbow, Skillet and
    Mosquito Lakes 202
14. Rainbow Slide Mandall Lake,
    Black Mandall Lake, Twin
    Mandall Lake, Mud Mandall
    Lake, Smith Lake 202
15. Spring Lake 202

MAP 11
1. Red Dirt Reservoir........................203
2. Rock Creek SWA...........................203
3. Rock Creek 203

Index of Numbered Maps
Routt National Forest

Routt National Forest Maps 1 & 2

1. Freeman Reservoir (8,800 ft; 16.6 ac); Rated fair cutthroat. for From Craig north on Hwy 13 for 13 miles to FDR 112(CR 11). East on FDR 112 8 miles to lake. Campground and picnic near lake, no motor propelled water craft.

2. Sawmill Creek; Rated fair for brook. From Craig north on Hwy 13 approx. 13 miles miles to FDR 27 (110), east 14 miles to Sawmill Creek Campground.

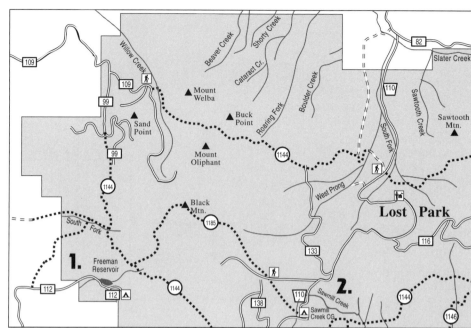

Map 1

1. Little Snake, Middle Fork; Rated poor for rainbow. North of Steamboat State Park on FDR 129 approx. 16 miles to near forest boundary. Stream generally parallels road north .25 mile.

2. Torso Creek, Armstrong Creek and Grizzly Creek; Rated poor for stocked brook. **Slater Creek;** Rated fair for stocked rainbow. West of Steamboat State Park on FDR 42 approx. 10 miles to FDR 150 (A section of this road is 4WD). Area can be reached from Hayden, north on County Road 80 (FDR 150).

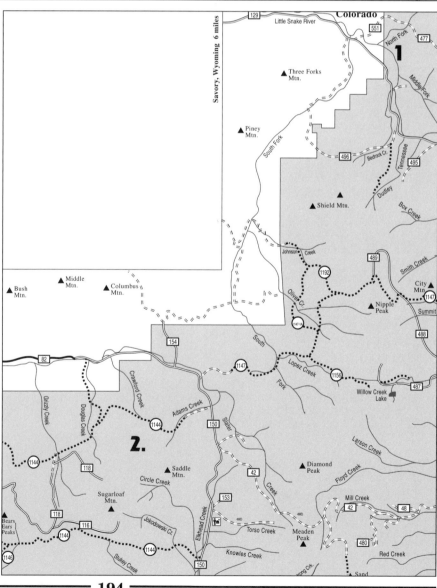

Map 2

1. Whiskey Creek and Silver City Creek; Rated good for brook. North of Steamboat State Park on FDR 129 to FDR 550 to Whiskey Creek, east off FDR 550 on 500 to Silver City Creek.

2. King Solomon Creek, Box Creek, Summit Creek, Little Red Park, Smith Creek and Independence Creek; Rated good for brook. North of Steamboat State Park on FDR 129.

3. Encampment River, West Fork Encampment River and South Fork of Hog Park Creek; Rated god for cutthroat and brook. Upper sections of streams are in Mount Zirkel Wilderness and are reached from the west from FDR 500. From the north on FDR 80 approx. 20 miles west of Pearl.

4. Manazanares Lake (9,238 ft; 4.2 ac); Rated good for brook and cutthroat. Mount Zirkel Wilderness. North of Steamboat State Park on FDR 129 to FDR 550, north on FDR 550 to FDR 500, east on FDR 550 to FDR 520. Approx. 1 mile east to FDT 1204, take FDT 1204 approx. 5 miles to lake.

5. West Fork Lake (9,305 ft; 13 ac); Rated good for brook and cutthroat. Mount Zirkel Wilderness. North of Steamboat State Park on FDR 129 to FDR 550, north on FDR 550 to FDR 500, east on FDR 550 to FDR 520. Approx. 1 mile east to FDT 1204, take FDT 1204 approx. 5 miles to FDT 1204.2A cutoff to FDT 1153 an addition 3 miles to lake.

6. Sanchez Lakes (Lower 10,440 ft; 4.6 ac, Upper 10,640 ft; 2.8 ac); Rated fair for rainbow and cutthroat. Mount Zirkel Wilderness. Near the Continental Divide there is no designated trail to lakes. Southeast of West Fork Lake 2 miles, refer to Forest Service and topographic maps.

7. Trail Creek, North Fork Elk River, Lost Dog Creek and English Creek; Rated good for brook and rainbow. North from Clark on FDR 400 approx.10 miles to Seedhouse Campground.

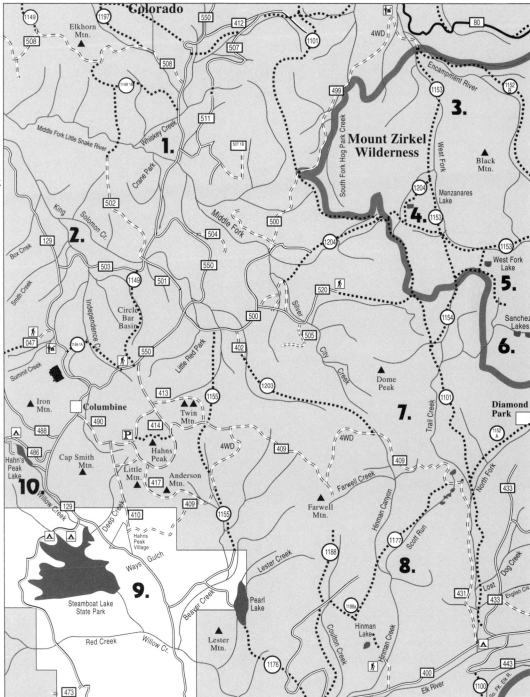

FDR 431 follows stream north.

8. Hinman Creek and Scott Run; Rated good for brook. North from Clark on FDR 400 approx.10 miles to Seedhouse Campground. FDR 431 north to reach upper sections. Lower sections can be reached from FDT 1177 located approx. 8 miles east of Clark on FDR 400.

9. Steamboat/Pearl Lake State Park; Rated good for cutthroat, brook and rainbow. See state parks section.

10. Hahns Peak Lake (8,387 ft; 40 ac); Rated fair for cutthroat and rainbow. Four miles north of Steamboat State Park. Campground north of lake.

Routt National Forest Map 4

1. Big Creek Lakes (Lower 8,997 ft; 350.7 ac, Upper 9,009 ft; 101.2 ac); Rated good for Brown, rainbow, tiger muskie, mackinaw. Upper; rainbow and brook. **South Fork of Big Creek** below lakes is rated good for brook and rainbow. From Pearl on FDR 600 southwest parallels creek to lakes. Campground and Seven Lakes trailhead near lakes.

2. Lake Eileen (10,207 ft; 3.9 ac); Rated fair for cutthroat. From Big Creek Lakes south on FDT 1125 approx. 6 miles to Lake Eileen and 7 miles to Seven Lakes. Mount Zirkel Wilderness.

3. Seven Lakes (10,733 ft; 14 ac); Rated fair for cutthroat. Mount Zirkel Wilderness.

4. Gem Lake (10,160 ft; 6.9 ac); Rated good for brook. From Big Creek Lakes on FDT 1125 approx. 9 miles to FDT 1152. South on FDT 1152 1.5 miles to FDT 1152.2A, west 1.5 miles to lake. Mount Zirkel Wilderness.

5. Lake Diana (10,268 ft; 9.2 ac); Rated fair for cutthroat. North from Clark on FDR 400 approx.10 miles to Seedhouse Campground. FDR 431 north 6 miles to Diamond Park and trailhead. East approx. 3 miles on FDT 1152.

6. Forester Creek, Goose Creek, Shafer Creek, Ute Creek, and Bear Creek; Rated fair for brook and cutthroat. Streams can be reached from FDT 1126, trailhead is located on FDR 640 northwest of Delaney Buttes. (See map 6 for trailhead.) Streams enter North Fork North Platte River from the west.

7. Blue Lake (9,815 ft; 21.4 ac); Rated fair for cutthroat and brook. Mount Zirkel Wilderness. West from Walden on County Road 12W 12 miles to FDR 640. West on FDR 640 approx. 6 miles to FDT 1126 trailhead. North approx. 7 miles to FDT 1178, west 2 miles to lake.

8. Peggy Lake (11,165 ft; 9.8 ac); Rated fair for cutthroat and brook. Mount Zirkel Wilderness. From Blue Lake west 1 mile, no designated trail to lake.

9. Twin Lakes (Lower 9,865 ft; 4.3, Upper 9,990 ft; 5.7 ac); Rated fair for cutthroat and brook. Mount Zirkel Wilderness. From FDT 1126 trailhead. North approx. 6 miles to FDT 1148, west 2 miles to lake.

10. Ute Lake (9,752 ft; 5.6 ac); Rated fair for cutthroat and brook. Mount Zirkel Wilderness. From trailhead approx. 4 miles north on FDT 1126 approx. 4 miles to FDT 1128, west 1.5 miles. No designated trail to lake.

11. Bear Lakes (North 10,330 ft; 10.1 ac, Upper 10,984 ft; 5.7 ac); Rated poor for cutthroat and brown. Mount Zirkel Wilderness. From FDT 1126 trailhead. North approx. 1 mile to FDT 1180, west 4 miles to lake.

12. Bighorn Lakes (10,106 ft; 13.8, Upper 10,200 ft; 4 ac); Rated fair for cutthroat. Mount Zirkel Wilderness. West of FDT 1126 trailhead .5 mile to FDT 1129. Three miles west on FDT 1129/1040 to lake.

13. Beaver Lake (10,360 ft; 7 ac); Rated good for brook. Mount Zirkel Wilderness. East of Clark approx. 10 miles to Seedhouse Campground. East on FDT 1163 approx. 4 miles to Three Island Lake, 6.5 miles to Beaver Lake.

14. Three Island Lake (9,878 ft; 23.2 ac); Rated good for brook. **Three Island Creek;** is rated good for brook. Mount Zirkel Wilderness.

15. Mica Lake (10,28 ft; 5.5 ac); Rated fair for cutthroat. Mount Zirkel Wilderness. From Seedhouse Campground east on Middle Fork Road approx. 3 miles to Slavonia. East on FDT 1161 1.5 miles to FDT 1162, north on FDT 1162 2.5 miles to Mica Lake. Slide Lakes are northeast of Mica Lake 1.5 miles, no designated trail to Slide Lakes.

16. Slide Lakes (10,400 ft; 5.2 ac, #2 10,500 ft; 2.1 ac, #3 10,700 ft; 4.8 ac); Rated fair for cutthroat. Mount Zirkel Wilderness. See Mica Lake.

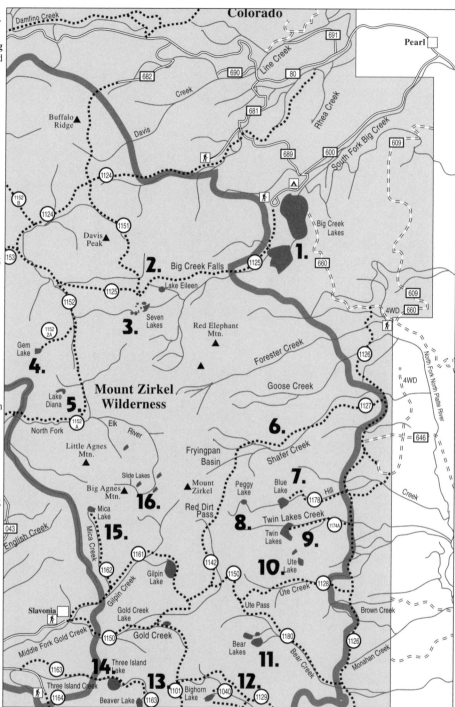

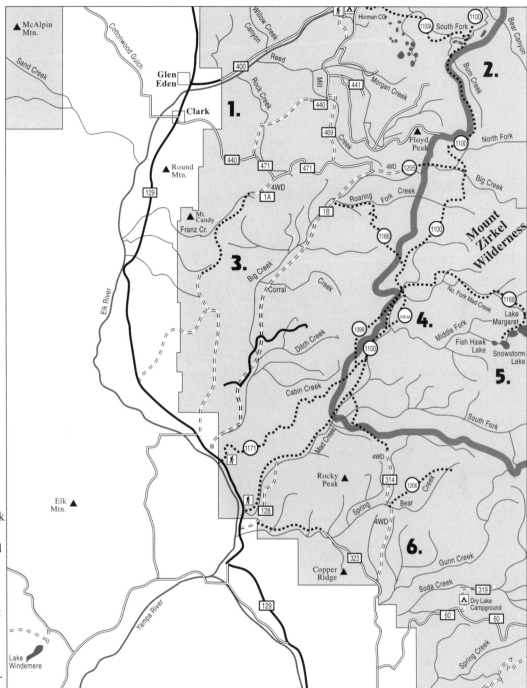

1. Elk River; Rated good for rainbow, brook and whitefish. From Clark on FDR 400 road follows river. Lower section flows through private property and is posted. Refer to Forest Service map.

2. Burn Creek; Rated good for brook and cutthroat. From Hinman Campground east on FDT 1100A approx. 4 miles to FDT 110, trail parallels stream.

3. Big Creek; Rated good for brook and cutthroat. From Hinman Campground south FDR 440 to FDR 441, continue approx. 6 miles a total of 6 miles to end of road. From Clark west on FDR 440 to to FDR 471, continue to stream. Refer to Forest Service map. Lower section flows through private property and is posted.

4. Mad Creek, North Fork, Middle Fork, South Fork; Rated good for brook. From Steamboat Springs on County Road 129 approx. 7.5 miles to Mad Creek Trailhead (FDT 1100). FDT 1100 parallels creek.

5. Lake Margaret, Lake Edward, Snowstorm Lake and Fish Hawk Lake (9700 ft; 9987 ft); Rated fair for rainbow. (Chain of lakes.)
See 7 1/2' Floyd Peak topographic map.

6. Soda Creek and Spring Creek; Rated fair for rainbow and brook. From Steamboat Springs 4 miles north to Dry Creek Campground. Both creeks can be reached from the campground.

1. Lake Katherine (9,859 ft; 23 ac); Rated fair for brook and cutthroat. From Delaney Buttes SWA, north on Hwy 5 1.5 miles, west on Hwy 12 approx. 9 miles to trailhead. West 2 miles on FDT 1129, south .25 mile on FDT 1157 to lake. Mount Zirkel Wilderness.

2. North Lake (10,313 ft; 5.5 ac); Rated good for brook. From Seedhouse Campground (Map 3) east on FDR 443 approx. 5 miles to trailhead. Take FDT 1164 approx. 4.5 miles to lake. Mount Zirkel Wilderness.

3. Ptarmigan Lake (10,699 ft; 7.3 ac); Cutthroat. **Dome Lake (10,060 ft; 14.7 ac);** Cutthroat. **Wolverine Lake (10,284 ft; 7.3 ac);** Rainbow and cutthroat. **Pristine Lake (10,040 ft; 9.7 ac);** Rated good for brook.. Mount Zirkel Wilderness. From Seedhouse Campground (Map 3) east on FDR 443 approx. 5 miles to trailhead. Take FDT 1164 approx. 5.2 miles to FDT 1101. South on FDT 1101 approx. 3 miles. Lakes are west of trail, no designated trail to lakes. Mount Zirkel Wilderness.

4. Roxy Ann Lakes (10,204 ft; 63 ac, Upper 10,400 ft; 4.3 ac); Rate fair for cutthroat, rainbow, and brook. South from Delaney Buttes Lakes south on Hwy 5 2.5 miles to Hwy 22, west approx. 7 miles to trailhead. Take FDT 1130 6.5 miles to FDT 1179, east 1.5 miles to lake.

5. Big Creek Lake (10,620 ft; 8.2 ac); Rated fair for cutthroat. See Lake of the Crags, etc.

6. Lake of the Crags (10,850 ft; 4.8 ac); Luna Lake (10,482 ft; 38.6 ac); Elbert Lake (10,800 ft; 11 ac); Cutthroat. From Steamboat Springs on County Road 129 approx. 7.5 miles to Mad Creek Trailhead (FDT 1100). North on FDT 1100 approx. 5 miles to FDT 1168, east on FDT 1168 approx. 6 miles. Big Creek Lake is north on FDT 1184 2miles.

7. Mirror Lake (10,040 ft; 6.4 ac); Rosa Lake (10,000 ft; 5.7 ac); Rated fair for cutthroat. Steamboat Springs on County Road 129 approx. 7.5 miles to Mad Creek Trailhead (FDT 1100). FDT 1100 North on FDT 1100 approx. 5 miles to FDT 1168, east on FDT 1168 approx. 4 miles.

8. Porcupine Lake (9,880 ft; 4.2 ac); Rated fair for rainbow. South of Elbert Lake 1 mile. No designated trail.

9. Slide Lakes (#1 9,890 ft; 3.7 ac, #2 10,500 ft; 2.1 ac, #3 10,700 ft; 4.8 ac, #4 11,500 ft; 4.2 ac); Rated fair for cutthroat. Delaney Buttes Lakes south on Hwy 5 2.5 miles to Hwy 22, west approx. 7 miles to trailhead. Take FDT 1130 5 miles to lake.

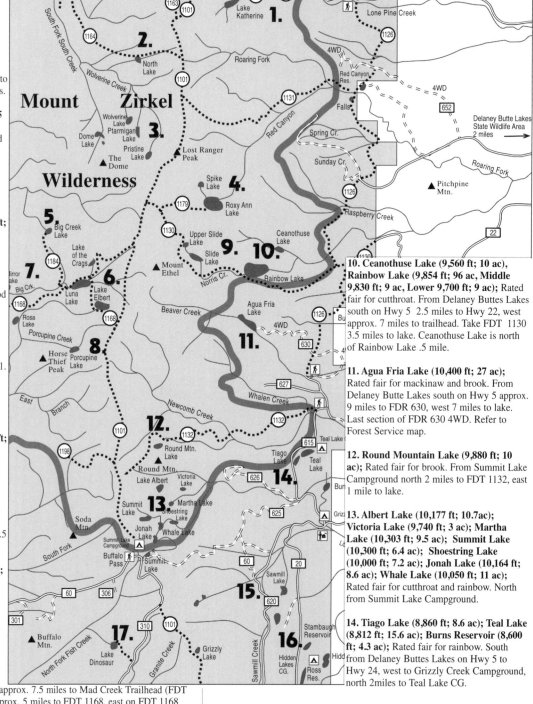

10. Ceanothuse Lake (9,560 ft; 10 ac), Rainbow Lake (9,854 ft; 96 ac, Middle 9,830 ft; 9 ac, Lower 9,700 ft; 9 ac); Rated fair for cutthroat. From Delaney Buttes Lakes south on Hwy 5 2.5 miles to Hwy 22, west approx. 7 miles to trailhead. Take FDT 1130 3.5 miles to lake. Ceanothuse Lake is north of Rainbow Lake .5 mile.

11. Agua Fria Lake (10,400 ft; 27 ac); Rated fair for mackinaw and brook. From Delaney Butte Lakes south on Hwy 5 approx. 9 miles to FDR 630, west 7 miles to lake. Last section of FDR 630 4WD. Refer to Forest Service map.

12. Round Mountain Lake (9,880 ft; 10 ac); Rated fair for brook. From Summit Lake Campground north 2 miles to FDT 1132, east 1 mile to lake.

13. Albert Lake (10,177 ft; 10.7ac); Victoria Lake (9,740 ft; 3 ac); Martha Lake (10,303 ft; 9.5 ac); Summit Lake (10,300 ft; 6.4 ac); Shoestring Lake (10,000 ft; 7.2 ac); Jonah Lake (10,164 ft; 8.6 ac); Whale Lake (10,050 ft; 11 ac); Rated fair for cutthroat and rainbow. North from Summit Lake Campground.

14. Tiago Lake (8,860 ft; 8.6 ac); Teal Lake (8,812 ft; 15.6 ac); Burns Reservoir (8,600 ft; 4.3 ac); Rated fair for rainbow. South from Delaney Buttes Lakes on Hwy 5 to Hwy 24, west to Grizzly Creek Campground, north 2miles to Teal Lake CG.

15. Sawmill Lakes (Lower 8,900 ft; 12.8 ac, Upper 8,980 ft; 12.8 ac); Rated poor for brook.. South from Grizzly Creek Campground on FDR 20 approx. 2 miles.

16. Stambaugh Reservoir (8,880 ft; 10 ac); Rated good for rainbow. **Hidden Lakes (8,855 ft; 10 ac);** Rated fair rainbow, cutthroat. Near Hidden Lakes Campground.

17. Dinosaur Lake (10,182 ft; 9 ac); Rated fair for cutthroat and brook. South from Summit Lake Campground approx. 2.5 miles on FDR 311. Granite Campground is 1 mile further south.

18. Streams in this area contain rainbow, brook and cutthroat. **Chedsey Creek, Newcomb Creek and Whalen Creeks** on the east offer the best fishing.

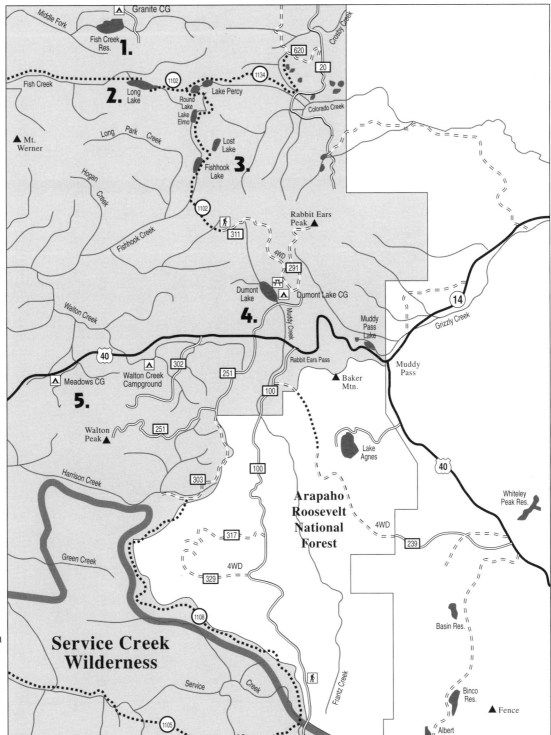

1. Fish Creek Reservoir (9,858 ft; 78.6 ac); Rated fair for brook. From Steamboat Springson FDR 60 Buffalo Pass, south on FDR 310 to Granite Campground and lake.

2. Long Lake (9,850 ft; 30 ac);
East of Steamboat Springs to FDT 1102 (Fish Creek Falls trail) east approx. 5 miles to Long Lake. To the east are **Percy Lake (10,034 ft; 17 ac); Round Lake (10,060 ft; 16 ac); Elmo Lake (10,0338 ft; 10 ac);** All are rated good for brook.

3. Lost Lake (9,920 ft; 15 ac); Fishhook Lake (9,877 ft; 16 ac); Rated fair for brook. South from Elmo Lake on FDT 110 .75 mile.

4. Dumont Lake (9,508 ft; 35 ac); Rated fair for brook. North from Kremmling on US 40 approx. 35 miles to FDR 315, 1.5 miles north to campground and lake.

5. Harrison Creek, Green Creek, Service Creek, Walton Creek and other streams in the area are rated good to fair for brook.

Routt National Forest Maps 8 & 9

1. South of Walden on Hwy 14 approx. 30 miles to County Road 11, south on County Road 11 approx. 9 miles to FDR 700 and Forest boundary. For the next 6 miles are a series of lakes and ponds. From north to south along road; **Slack-Weiss Reservoir (8,970 ft; 14.8 ac); Kathleen Lake (9,500 ft; 2.5 ac); Kidney Lake (9,018 ft; 4.3 ac); Two Ledge Reservoir (9,740 ft; 5.7 ac); Long Lake (9,343 ft; 3 ac); Alder Lake (9,500 ft; 3 ac); Disappointment Lake (9,700 ft; 1.5 ac); Deep Lake (9,540 ft; 1 ac); Willow Lake (9,146 ft; 4 ac); Cliff Lake (9,790 ft; 4.5 ac); Bundy Lake (9,840 ft; 3 ac); Beaver Lake (9,400 ft; 4.5 ac); Finger Lake (9,400 ft; 5.7 ac); Brook Lake (9,600 ft; 2.5 ac);** Lakes are rated good for brook. **Grassy Run; Arapahoe Creek; Middle Fork Arapahoe Creek; East Fork Arapahoe Creek;** Rated good for brook and some rainbow.

2. Seymore Reservoir State Wildlife Area; Rated good for rainbow. See page 90 for DOW information.

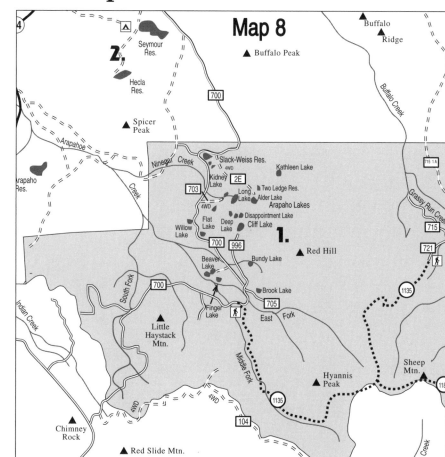

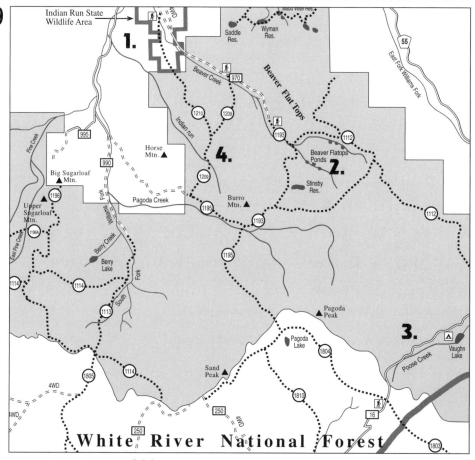

1. Indian Run State Wildlife Area; Rated good for brook. See page 94 for DOW information.

2. Beaver Flat Tops Ponds; (9,320 ft; 40 ac); Rated good for brook. From Indian Run State Wildlife Area southeast on FDR 970 (4WD) approx. 6 miles to trailhead FDT 1193. Follow trail and Beaver Creek to ponds.

3. Vaughn Lake (9,390 ft; 36 ac); Rated fair for rainbow. From Buford north on FDR 8/16 approx. 27 miles to lake. Campground at lake.

4. South Fork Williams Fork; Pine Creeks; Indian Run; Beaver Creek; Rated fair for brook and rainbow. Tributaries of South Fork that are small, fast with beaver ponds.

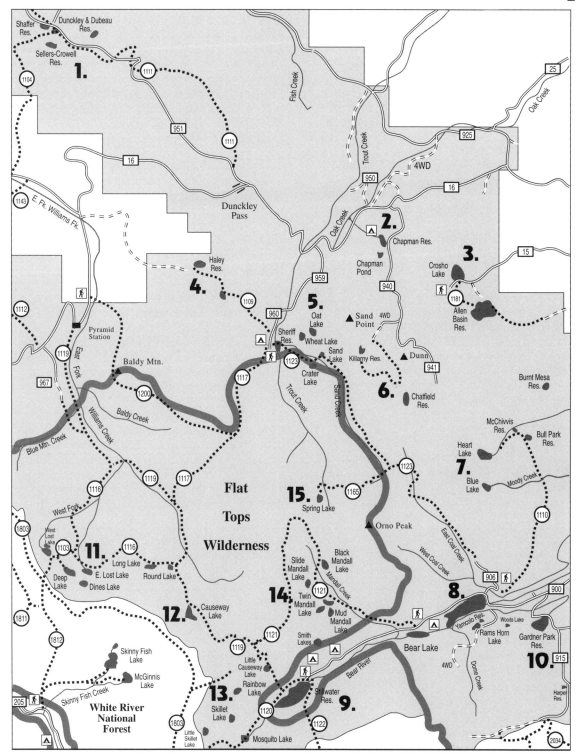

1. Shaffer Reservoir (8,830 ft; 5 ac); Rainbow. **Dunckley & Dubeau Reservoir 8,950 ft; 3.3 ac);** Rainbow. **Seller-Crowell (8,950 ft; 5 ac);** Rated good for cutthroat. From Oak Creek on FDR 25 southwest 10.5 miles to FDR 16, west 2.5 miles to 6 miles west to FDR 951. (FDR 951is just east of Dunckley Pass.) North on FDR 951, 7 miles.

2. Chapman Reservoir (9,280 ft; 25 ac); Rated good for rainbow. From Oak creek southwest on FDR 25 10.5 miles to FDR 940, south 1 mile to lake. Campground at lake.

3. Crosho Reservoir (8,900 ft; 56 ac); Rated good for cutthroat, grayling and rainbow. From Yampa 4 miles west on County Road 17 to County Road 15, west 5 miles to lake. **Allen Basin Reservoir (8,680 ft; 60 ac);** Rated good for rainbow and brook is 1 mile south.

4. Haley Reservoir (8,788 ft; 12.8 ac); Rated fair for brook. West of Dunckley Pass approx. 6 miles to road on the left side, south 3 miles to lake.

Continued on page 202

Continued from Page 201

5. Sheriff Reservoir (9,723 ft; 40 ac); Rainbow. **Oat lake (10,150 ft; 2 ac);** Cutthroat and brook. **Crater Lake (10,150 ft;1 ac);** Brook. **Wheat Lake (9,930 ft; 2 ac);** Cutthroat. **Sand Lake (10,192; 2 ac);** Cutthroat. Lake in this group are rated fair to good. Campground at Sheriff Reservoir. South of Chapman Reservoir 5 miles on FDR 959.

6. Killarney Reservoir (10,943 ft; 19.2 ac); Chatfield Reservoir (10,480 ft; 13.2 ac); Rated good for cutthroat. South of Chapman Reservoir on FDR 940 3 miles, last section is 4WD. No designated trail to Chatfield Reservoir.

7. Heart Lake (9,947 ft; 48 ac); Rated fair for rainbow. From Yamcolo Reservoir take FDT 1110 north approx. 6 miles to lake.

8. Yamcolo Reservoir (9,680 ft; 175 ac); Rated good for rainbow, brown, brook and whitefish. From Yampa 12 miles southwest on County Road 7/FDR 900 to reservoir. Bear Lake Campground and trailhead located on southwest end of reservoir. Southeast of reservoir is **Bear Lake (9,720 ft; 46.7 ac);** Rated fair for brook and rainbow.

9. Stillwater Reservoir (10,255 ft; 88 ac); Rated good for rainbow, brook and cutthroat. West of Yamcolo Reservoir on FDR 900 5 miles. Boat ramp.

10. Gardner Park Reservoir (9,630 ft; 47 ac); Rated fair for rainbow and brown. From Yampa southwest on County Road 7 approx. 7 miles to FDR 900. Follow FDR 900 3 miles to FDR 910, south on FDR 910 2 miles.

FLAT TOPS WILDERNESS

11. Lost Lake, West (10,296 ft; 18.2 ac); Cutthroat. **Lost Lake, East (10,300 ft; 13.8 ac)**; Cutthroat and rainbow. **Deep Lake (10,270 ft; 23 ac);** Rainbow and brook. **Dines Lake (10,342 ft; 3 ac);** Cutthroat. **Long Lake (10,464 ft; 21.6 ac);** Cutthroat and brook. **Round Lake (10,350 ft; 8.3 ac);** Cutthroat. From Buford north on FDR 8 18.5 miles to FDR 205, east approx. 3.5 miles to Picket Pin Trailhead, north on FDT 1811 approx. 3.5 miles to lakes.

12. Causeway Lakes (10,420 ft; 4.8 ac, Little 10,740 ft; 15 ac); Rated good for cutthroat and brook. From Stillwater Reservoir northwest on FDT 1119 one and four miles.

13. Rainbow Lake (10,764 ft; 8 ac); Cutthroat. **Skillet Lake (10,710 ft; 7.5 ac);** Brook. **Mosquito Lake (10,620 ft; 10 ac)**; Brook. Lakes in this area are rated fair to good. South west of Stillwater Reservoir.

14. Rainbow Slide Mandall Lake (10,670 ft 12 ac); Cutthroat. **Black Mandall Lake (10,820 ft; 9 ac);** Rainbow. **Twin Mandall Lake (Upper 10,550 ft; 7.5 ac);** Cutthroat. **Mud Mandall Lake (10,550 ft; 2 ac);** Brook. **Smith Lake (10,550 ft; 5 ac);** Cutthroat and brook. Lakes in this area are rated good.

15. Spring Lake (10,080 ft; 3 ac); Rated fair for rainbow. From trailhead north of Yamcolo Reservoir on FDR 906. Take FDT 1123 north to FDT 1165 west on FDT to lake, approx. 6.5 miles. Refer to topographic map to locate lake.

16. Streams in this area are rated good to fair for brook and rainbow.

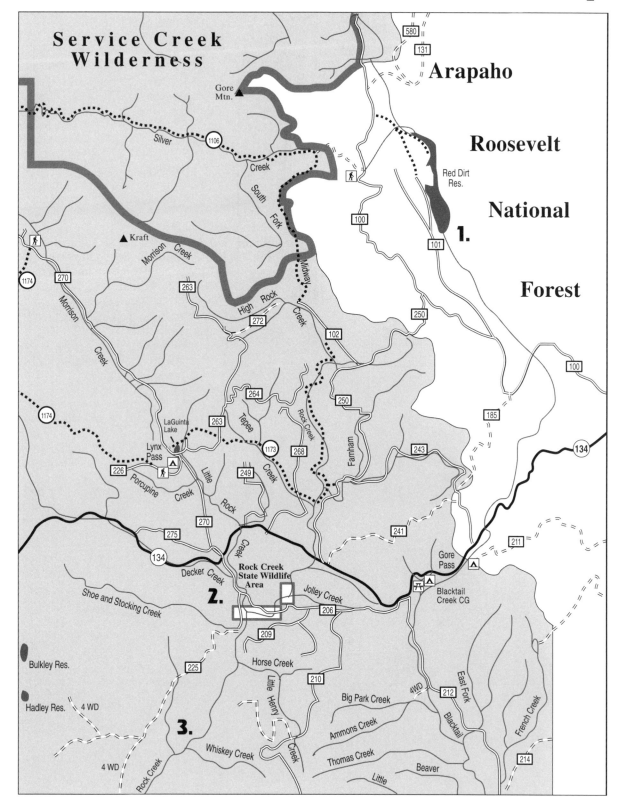

1. Red Dirt Reservoir (9,055 ft; 30 ac); Rated fair for rainbow and brook. From Kremmling northwest on Hwy 40 6 miles to Hwy 134, 5 miles west to FDR 100, northwest on FDR 100 5 miles to FDR 101, 4 miles to reservoir.

2. Rock Creek State Wildlife Area; Rated good for rainbow and brook. See page 94 for DOW information.

3. Rock Creek: Rated good for rainbow and brook. Other streams in the area are rated fair for brook and rainbow.

San Isabel National Forest Index Map

MAP 1
1. Slide Lake 205
2. West Tenneesee Lakes, Deckers
   Lake 205
3. St. Kevin, Galena, Bear Lakes 205
4. Timberline Lake 205
5. Hagerman Lake 205
6. Lake Fork and Glacier Creek........205
7. Turquoise Lake 205

MAP 2
1. Buckeye Lake............................205
2. Arkansas River, East Fork 205

MAP 3
1. Windsor Lake, Three Lakes,
   Native Lake, Swamp Lake,
   Hidden Lakes and Rock
   Creek 206
2. Halfmoon Lakes 206
3. Emerald Lake 206
4. Blue Lake 206
5. Divide Lake 206
6. Hollenbeck Ponds 206
7. Sayers Gulch 206
8. Crystal Lake 206
9. Willis Lake 206

MAP 4
1. Crystal Lakes 207
2. Union Creek, Spring Creek and
   Twobit Creek 207
3. Mount Elbert Forebay 207
4. Twin Lakes 207
5. Clear Creek Reservoir 207

MAP 5
1. Alan Lake..............................208
2. Harrison Flats 208
3. Lake Ann 208
4. Lost Lake 208
5. Ptarmigan Lake 208
6. Clear Creek, North Fork and
   South Fork.............................208

MAP 6
1. Silver King Lake, Pine Creek 209
2. Rainbow Lake 209
3. Frenchman, Fourmile Creeks 209
4. Bear Lake and Anglemeyer
   Lake 209
5. Kroenke Lake..........................209
6. Hartenstien Lake 209
7. Cottonwood Creek, Middle and
   South 209
8. Cottonwood Lake.......................209

MAP 7
1. Chalk Lake 210
2. Grizzly Lake..........................210
3. Pomeroy Lakes.........................210
4. Rosedale Lake 210
5. Baldwin Lake 210
6. Browns Creek, Browns Creek,
   Little 210
7. Hancock Lakes 210
8. North Fork Reservoir 210
9. Hunkydory Lakes.......................210
10. Boss Lake Reservoir 210
11. Hunt Lake 210
12. Waterdog Lakes 210
13. Grass Lake 210
14. Arkansas River, South, Foose
    Creek, Green Creek 210

MAP 8
1. Pass Creek Lake 211
2. Liitle Cochetopa 211
3. O'Haver Lake 211
4. Poncha Creek, Starvation
   Creek and Silver Creek 211

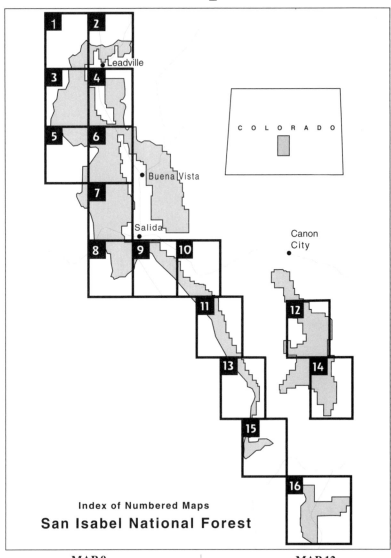

Index of Numbered Maps

San Isabel National Forest

MAP 9
1. Hunts Lake 211
2. West Creek Lake 211
3. Stout Creek Lakes 211
4. Bushnell Lakes 211
5. Bear Creek, Howard Creek and
   Spring Creek...............................211

MAP 10
1. Hayden Creek................................212
2. Rainbow Lake 212
3. Balman Reservoir...........................212

MAP 11
1. Silver Lake 212
2. Brush Creek Lakes 212
3. Banjo Lake 212
4. Lake of the Clouds 212
5. Horseshoe Lake 212
6. Eureka Lake 212
7. Hermit Lake 212
8. Goodwin Lakes 212
9. Venable Lakes 212
10. Comanche Lake 212
11. Dry Lakes 212
12. Horn Lakes 212
13. South Branch Creek, Brush Creeks,
    Greenleaf Creek, Texas Creek, Swift
    Creek, Goodwin Creek, Middle
    Taylor Creek and Venable
    Creek 212

MAP 12
1. North Hardscrabble Creek, South
   Hardscrabble Creek,
   Ophir Creek 213

MAP 13
1. Macey Lakes, Dry Lake...............213
2. North Colony Lakes.....................213
3. South Colony Lakes.....................213

MAP 14
1. Lake Isabel 214
2. Saint Charles River, Little Saint
   Charles Creek............................214
3. Blue Lakes 214

MAP 15
1. Huerfano SWA, Huerfano River ..214
2. Lost Lake 214
3. Lily Lakes 214
4. Strawberry Creek 214

MAP 16
1. Bear Lakes 215
2. Blue Lake 215
3. Wolf Lake 215
4. North Lake SWA, North Lake and
   North Fork Purgatorie River 215

1. Slide Lake (11,725 ft; 35.6 ac); Stocked cutthroat. North from Leadville on Hwy 24 approx. 8 miles to FDR 145. West on 145 (4WD) to Lake. Refer to Forest Service Map.

2. West Tennessee Lakes (Lower 11,775 ft; 4 ac, 11,800 ft; 18.8 ac); Rated good for cutthroat and brook. **Deckers Lake (11,350 ft; 14 ac);** Rated fair for stocked cutthroat. North from Leadville on Hwy 24 approx. 8 miles to FDR 131 (4WD). West to trailheads. Holy Cross Wilderness. Refer to Forest Service Map.

3. St. Kevin Lake (11,850 ft; 4.2 ac); Stocked cutthroat. **Galena Lake (11,150 ft; 1.8 ac);** Stocked cutthroat **Bear Lake (11,050 ft; 12.3 ac);** Rated fair for rainbow. From north side of Turquoise Lake and Hwy 9 take FDR 107 approx. 3 miles north to trailhead. Follow Bear Creek to Lakes.

4. Timberline Lake (10,950 ft; 62 ac); Closed to fishing. Reintroduction of Greenback cutthroat fingerlings in 2000, it will be several years for the fish to reach catchable size.

5. Hagerman Lake (11,400 ft; 4.2 ac); Rated fair cutthroat. Southwest of Turquoise Lake on County Road 4. Refer to Forest Service map.

6. Lake Fork and Glacier Creek; Rated good for cutthroat. Special regulations may apply.

7. Turquoise Lake (9,869 ft; 1,650 ac); Rated fair for rainbow, brown, cutthroat and mackinaw. West of Leadville on Hwy 9. Campgrounds, boat ramps and picnic areas.

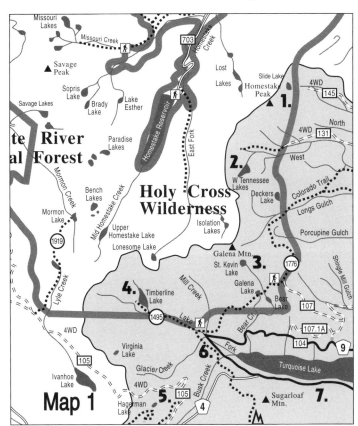

Map 1

Map 2

1. Buckeye Lake (11,900 ft; 1.7 ac); Rated fair for cutthroat.

2. East Fork Arkansas River; Rated fair for cutthroat, brown and rainbow. South of Fremont Pass on Hwy 91. Approx. 5 miles of upper section is open to public.

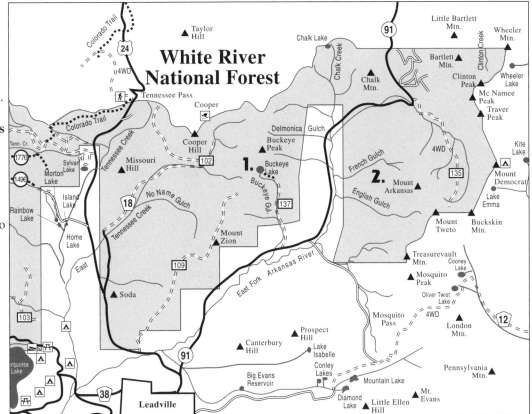

San Isabel National Forest Map 3

1. Windsor Lake (11,625 ft; 43 ac); Three Lakes (Lower 11,950 ft; 6.6 ac); Native Lake (11,200 ft; 5.5 ac); Swamp Lakes (10,850 ft; 7.5 ac); Hidden Lakes (11,350 ft; 2.4 ac); Rock Creek; Rated good for greenback cutthroat. Catch and release. Artificial flies and lures only.

2. Halfmoon Lakes (11,900 ft; 6 ac); Rated fair for cutthroat and brook. South of Leadville on Hwy 24 3 miles to Malta, west .75 mile to FDR 110. South on FDR 110 6 miles to Elbert Creek Campground, from here hike or drive two miles to FDT 1485 up North Halfmoon Creek. Approx. 3 miles to lakes. **Halfmoon Creeks;** Rated good rainbow and cutthroat.

3. Emerald Lake (10,00 ft; 6 ac); Rated good for rainbow. Located near Elbert Creek Campground.

4. Blue Lake (12,495 ft; 23.4 ac); Rated good for cutthroat. From Hwy 82 on east side Independence Pass north on FDT 1483. No designated trail to lake. Refer to USGS topographic map.

5. Divide Lake (12,378 ft; 3.2 ac); Rated fair for cutthroat. From Hwy 82 on east side Independence Pass.

6. Hollenbeck Ponds (9,450 ft; 5 ac); Rated fair for cutthroat, bluegill and largemouth bass. From Elbert Creek CG on the north or from Twin Lakes on the south on Mount Elbert Trail.

7. Sayers Gulch; Rated fair cutthroat. West of Twin Lakes on Hwy 82 7 miles to FDR 391, follow South Fork up to Sayers Gulch. (4WD).

8. Crystal Lake (9,400 ft; 6.7 ac); Rated fair for rainbow. South of Twin Lakes on Colorado Trail (FDT 1776) approx. 2 miles to Willis Gulch Trail. Continue south on trail approx. 4 miles tp Willis and Crystal lakes.

9. Willis Lake (11,800 ft; 22.3 ac); Rated fair for cutthroat. See Crystal Lake.

206

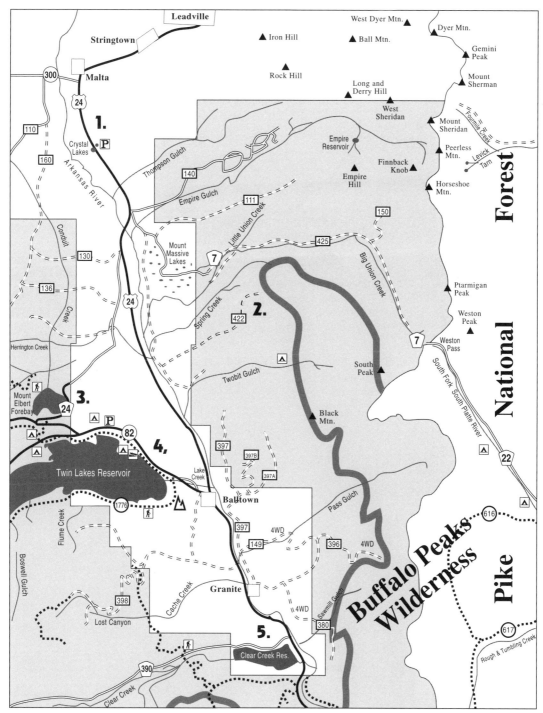

1. Crystal Lake (9,400 ft; 6.7 ac); Rated fair for rainbow. Catch and release, artificial flies and lures only.

2. Union Creeks, Spring Creek and Twobit Creek; rated fair for cutthroat. From Leadville 8 miles south on Hwy 24 to County Road 7 East to Union Creek. Refer to Forest Service map.

3. Mount Elbert Forebay (9,500 ft; 200 ac); Rated good for rainbow and cutthroat. Located 1 mile north of Twin lakes.

4. Twin Lakes Reservoir (9,200 ft; 1,700 ac); Rated good for rainbow cutthroat and mackinaw. From Leadville 17 miles south on Hwy 24 to reservoir.

5. Clear Creek Reservoir (8,875 ft; 407 ac); Rated good for rainbow, kokanee, brown and cutthroat. From Leadville 22 miles south on Hwy 24 to reservoir.

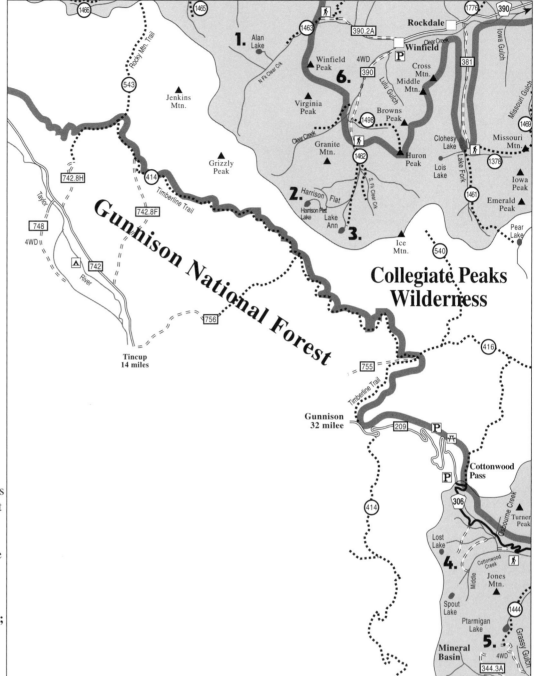

1. Alan Lake (12,100 ft; 2.3 ac); Rated fair for cutthroat and brook. West of Rockdale on FDR 390.2A approx. 3 miles to trailhead. Southwest on FDT 1463 1.5 miles. No designated trail to lake. Collegiate Peaks Wilderness.

2. Harrison Flats Lake (11,909 ft; 5 ac); Rated fair cutthroat. South from Rockdale on FDR 390 (4WD) approx. 3 miles to FDT 1462, approx. 2.5 miles to Lake Ann. No designated trail to lake. Collegiate Peaks Wilderness.

3. Lake Ann (11,800 ft; 18.6 ac); Rated good for cutthroat and brook. See Harrison Flats Lake.

4. Lost Lake (11,880 ft; 4 ac); Rated fair for cutthroat. Southeast of Cottonwood Pass approx. 2 miles to closed road. Southwest 1 mile on road. No designated trail to lake, refer to Forest Service map.

5. Ptarmigan Lake (12,147 ft; 27.9 ac); Rated fair for cutthroat. Southeast of Cottonwood Pass approx. 3 miles to closed road. Southwest 1 mile on road. Southwest 1 mile on road. No designated trail to lake, refer to Forest Service map.

6. Clear Creek, North Fork, South Fork; Rated fair for brook and cutthroat.

1. Silver King Lake (12,640 ft; 16.2 ac); Pine Creek; Rated good for cutthroat. South from Leadville on Hwy 24 approx. 24 miles to FDT 1467. West on FDT 1467 to FDT 1374, continue to follow Pine Creek on FDT 1374 to Lake, approx. 11 miles.

2. Rainbow Lake (11,650 ft; 5 ac); Rated fair for cutthroat. South from Leadville on Hwy 24 approx. 24 miles to FDT 1467. West on FDT 1467 to FDT 1776, south approx. 2 miles. No designated trail to lake.

3. Frenchman Creek; Stocked cutthroat and **Fourmile Creek;** Stocked rainbow. From river side on Hwy 24 Frencman Creek parallels FDR 386, Fourmile Creek is east of Riverside.

4. Bear Lake (12,377 ft; 18.5 ac); Anglemeyer Lake (11,338 ft; 1.5 ac); Rated fair for cutthroat. From Buena Vista west on FDR 365 approx. miles to FDT 1449. West on FDT 1449 approx. 3 miles to Anglemeyer Lake, and 5 miles to Bear Lake.

5. Kroenke Lake (11,600 ft; 24 ac); Rated fair for cutthroat. From Buena Vista west on FDR 365 approx. 6 miles to FDT 1449. West on FDT 1449 approx. 2 miles to FDT 1448, approx. 2 miles west to lake.

6. Hartenstien Lake (11,432 ft; 15 ac); Cutthroat. West of Buena Vista approx. 14 miles to FDT 1442, north approx. 2 miles to FDT 1443, west .75 mile to lake.

7. Cottonwood Creek, Cottonwood Creek, Middle, Cottonwood Creek, South; Rated fair for cutthroat and brook. From Buena Vista west to Forest boundary. Cottonwood Creek parallels road.

8. Cottonwood Lake (9,552 ft 43 ac); Rated good for rainbow and cutthroat. From Buena Vista west on 306 8 miles to FDR 344. South on FDR 344, 3 miles to lake. Campground, boat ramp, and picnic areas.

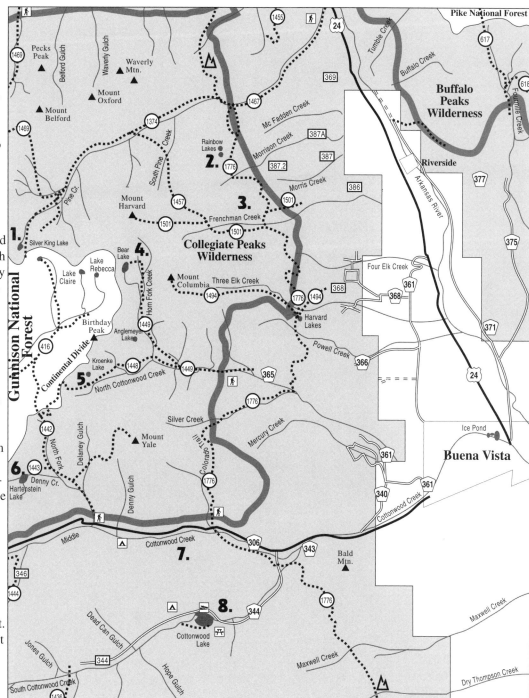

San Isabel National Forest Map 7

1. Chalk Lake (8,800 ft; 3 ac); Rated fair for stocked rainbow. Chalk Creek has intermittent public fishing access. West of Mount Princeton Hot Spring on Hwy 162.

2. Grizzly Lake (11,202 ft; 36.3 ac); Rated fair for brook. Grizzly Creek; From St. Elmo south on FDR 296 (4WD) approx. 3 miles to lake. Road parallels creek.

3. Pomeroy Lakes (Lower 12,035 ft; 35 ac, Upper 12,300 ft; 37 ac); Rated fair for cutthroat. From St Elmo south on FDR 295 approx. 3 miles to FDR 297 (4WD), east on FDR 297 approx. 3 miles. Short easy hike to upper lake.

4. Rosedale Lake (12,093 ft; 3 ac); Rated fair for cutthroat. From Grizzly Lake continue to follow Grizzly Creek south 2 miles to lake.

5. Baldwin Lake (Upper 12,100 ft; 21 ac); Rated good for cutthroat. From Alpine south on FDR 277 (4WD) approx. 5 miles to lake. Road parallels Baldwin Creek rated fair for brook.

6. Browns Creek; Little Browns Creek; Rated fair for rainbow, brook and brown. West from Nathrop approx. 9 miles to FDT 1429 trailhead. Refer to map.

7. Hancock Lakes (Lower 11,615 ft; 23 ac, Upper 11,675 ft; 7 ac); Rated fair for cutthroat. South from Hancock on FDR 295 .5 mile to FDT 1422, short hike to lake.

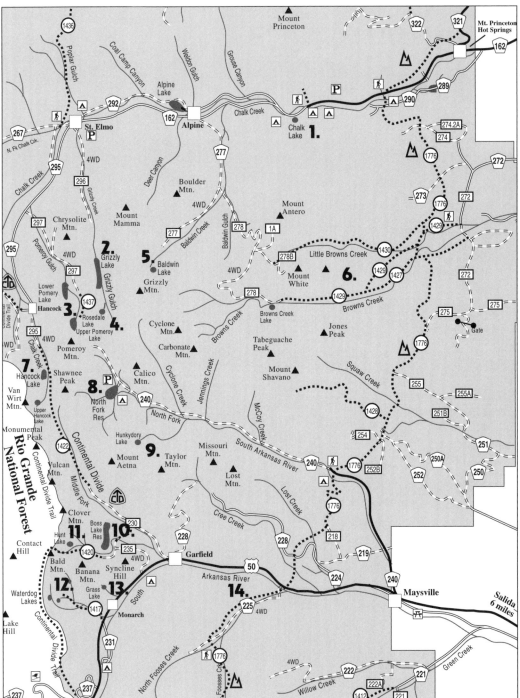

8. North Fork Reservoir (11,420 ft; 20 ac); Rated fair for cutthroat and rainbow, North Fork Arkansas River parallels FDR 240 to lake. From Maysville north on FDR 240 approx. 12 miles to lake.

9. Hunkydory Lakes (11.860 ft; 5 ac, Upper 12,040 ft; 5 ac); Rated fair cutthroat and brook. From Maysville north on FDR 240 approx. 8 miles. No designated trail to lake.

10. Boss Lake Reservoir (10,872 ft; 32 ac); Rated fair for brook and cutthroat. Has not been stocked recently. One mile west of Garfield to FDR 235 (4WD) north approx. 1 mile to lake.

11. Hunt Lake (11,500 ft; 6 ac); Rated fair for cutthroat. One mile west of Boss Lake on FDT 1420.

12. Waterdog Lakes (11,475 ft; 15 ac); Rated fair cutthroat and brook. West of Monarch on FDT 1417 approx. 2 miles.

13. Grass Lake (11,500 ft; 6.1 ac); Rated fair cutthroat and brook. Northwest of Monarch approx. .75 mile, no designated trail to lake.

14. Arkansas River, South.; Foose Creeks; Green Creek; Rated good for rainbow, cutthroat and brook. Intermittent public access. West of Maysville on Hwy 50.

1. Pass Creek Lake (9,240 ft; 14.8 ac); Rated fair for rainbow and brook. Pass Creek is rated poor for brook. From Poncha Springs west on Hwy 50 2 miles to FDR 210, south 1.5 miles to FDR 212, approx. 4 miles south to end of road. Take FDT 1411 approx. 4 miles to lake. Trial parallels creek.

2. Little Cochetopa Creek; Rated good for cutthroat. From Poncha Springs west on Hwy 50 2 miles to FDR 210, south approx. 4 miles to public access. Stream follows 4WD road and FDT 1409.

3. O'Haver Lake (9,160 ft; 14.4 ac); Rated good for rainbow and cutthroat. Handicap fishing pier. Heavy pressure. From Poncha Springs south on Hwy 285 approx. 5 miles to Mears Junction and FDR 200. Southwest on FDR 200 approx. 5 miles to lake.

4. Poncha Creek: Starvation Creek; Silver Creek; (Silver Creek has intermittent public access.) Rated fair for brook and cutthroat. Other small streams in area have offer similar fishing. From Poncha Springs south on Hwy 285 approx. 5 miles to Mears Junction and FDR 200. Southwest on FDR 200 approx. 3 miles to FDR 201, road and FDT 1407 parallels stream.

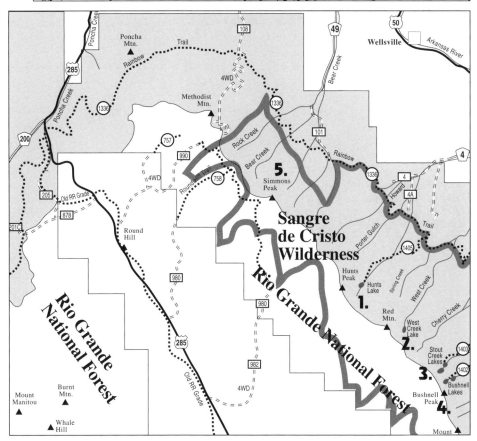

Map 8

Map 9

1. Hunts Lake (11,320 ft; 3.5 ac); Rated good for cutthroat. From Salida southeast on Hwy 50 approx. 18 miles to County Road 6 at Coaldale. West on CR 6 5 miles to Hayden Creek Campground. Northwest on FDT 1336 (Rainbow Trail), access to all lakes from this trail. Hunts Lake 9 miles to FDT 1405, No designated trial to West Creek Lake, Stout Creek Lakes 5 miles to FDT 1403, Bushnell Lakes 3 miles to FDT 1402.

2. West Creek Lake (11,675 ft; 8.3 ac); Rated good for cutthroat. See Hunts Lake.

3. Stout Creek Lakes (#3 11,850 ft; 12.3 ac, Lower 11720 ft; 19.5 ac, Upper 11,800 ft; 12.3 ac); Rated good for cutthroat. See Hunts Lake.

4. Bushnell Lakes (Lower 11,120 ft; 4 ac, Upper 11,900 ft; 8.5 ac); Rated good for cutthroat. See Hunts Lake.

5. Bear Creek; Howard Creek; Spring Creek; Rated poor for cutthroat. Public access in upper sections in national forest and in wilderness area. Rainbow Trail (FDT 1336) crosses streams. Refer to Forest Service map.

San Isabel National Forest Maps 10 &

1. Silver Lake (11,950 ft; 5.2 ac); Rated fair to poor for cutthroat. From Hillsdale at Hwy 50 west on FDR 198 approx. 10 miles, short hike to lake.

2. Brush Creek Lakes (Lower 11,400 ft; 45.6 ac, Upper 11,560 ft; 44.6 ac); Rated good for cutthroat and brook. From Hillsdale at Hwy 50 west on FDR 198 west 2 miles to FDR 332, south to trailhead. Approx. 4 miles to lake on FDT 1356. Refer to Forest Service map.

3. Banjo Lake (12,350 ft; 5.4 ac); Rated good for cutthroat. Southwest from Brush Creek lakes 1 mile to FDT 1352, east approx.3.5 mile to lake.

4. Lake of the Clouds (Lower 11,480 ft; 10.5 ac, Middle 11,560 ac, Upper 11,640 13.4 ac); Rated good for cutthroat. West of Westcliffe on County Road 160 approx. 7 miles. Refer to Forest Service map. Take FDT 1349 approx. 4 miles to lake.

5. Horseshoe Lake (11,960 ft; 18.1 ac); Rated good for cutthroat. West from Westcliffe on County Road 160 six miles to FDR 160, south on FDR 160 (4WD) approx. 5 miles to Horseshoe and Hermit Lakes

6. Eureka Lake (11,960 ft; 18.1 ac); Rated good for cutthroat. Lake is .25 mile southwest of Hermit Lake.

1. Hayden Creek; Rated fair for rainbow. From Coaldale Hayden Creek parallels County Road 6 and FDR 6. Public access to upper section only. Campground near Rainbow Trail.

2. Rainbow Lake (10,400 ft; 10.7 ac); From Hillside and Hwy 50 west approx. 6 miles on FDR 198 to lake. Lake Creek Campground east of lakes.

3. Balman Reservoir (9,440 ft; 5 ac); From Hillside and Hwy 50 west approx. 5 miles on FDR 198 to lake.

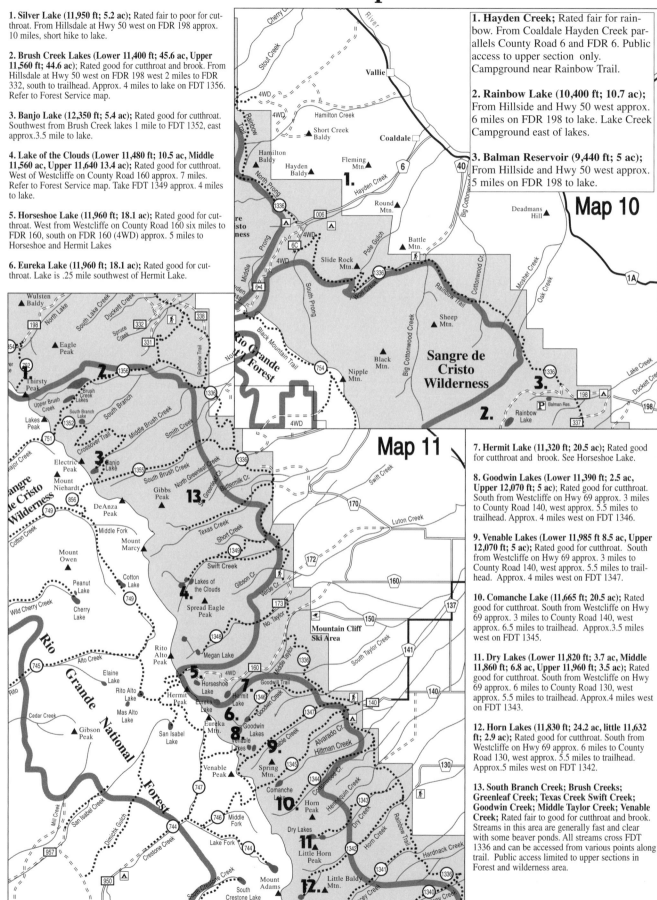

Map 10

Map 11

7. Hermit Lake (11,320 ft; 20.5 ac); Rated good for cutthroat and brook. See Horseshoe Lake.

8. Goodwin Lakes (Lower 11,390 ft; 2.5 ac, Upper 12,070 ft; 5 ac); Rated good for cutthroat. South from Westcliffe on Hwy 69 approx. 3 miles to County Road 140, west approx. 5.5 miles to trailhead. Approx. 4 miles west on FDT 1346.

9. Venable Lakes (Lower 11,985 ft 8.5 ac, Upper 12,070 ft; 5 ac); Rated good for cutthroat. South from Westcliffe on Hwy 69 approx. 3 miles to County Road 140, west approx. 5.5 miles to trailhead. Approx. 4 miles west on FDT 1347.

10. Comanche Lake (11,665 ft; 20.5 ac); Rated good for cutthroat. South from Westcliffe on Hwy 69 approx. 3 miles to County Road 140, west approx. 6.5 miles to trailhead. Approx.3.5 miles west on FDT 1345.

11. Dry Lakes (Lower 11,820 ft; 3.7 ac, Middle 11,860 ft; 6.8 ac, Upper 11,960 ft; 3.5 ac); Rated good for cutthroat. South from Westcliffe on Hwy 69 approx. 6 miles to County Road 130, west approx. 5.5 miles to trailhead. Approx.4 miles west on FDT 1343.

12. Horn Lakes (11,830 ft; 24.2 ac, little 11,632 ft; 2.9 ac); Rated good for cutthroat. South from Westcliffe on Hwy 69 approx. 6 miles to County Road 130, west approx. 5.5 miles to trailhead. Approx.5 miles west on FDT 1342.

13. South Branch Creek; Brush Creeks; Greenleaf Creek; Texas Creek Swift Creek; Goodwin Creek; Middle Taylor Creek; Venable Creek; Rated fair to good for cutthroat and brook. Streams in this area are generally fast and clear with some beaver ponds. All streams cross FDT 1336 and can be accessed from various points along trail. Public access limited to upper sections in Forest and wilderness area.

Map 13

1. Macey Lakes (Lower 11,506 ft; 8.8 ac, South 11,643 ft; 6.9 ac, West 11,865 ft; 12.5 ac); Rated good for cutthroat. South from Westcliffe on Hwy 69 approx. 6 miles to County Road 130, west approx. 5.5 miles to trailhead. South on FDT 1336 approx. 2 miles to FDT 1341. Approx. 4 miles west on FDT 1341.

2. North Colony Lakes (#1 11,511 ft; 5.3 ac, #2 11,750 ft; 5 ac, #3 11,730 ft; 5.4 ac; #4 11,600 ft; 2 ac; #5 12,485 ft; 5.4 ac); Rated good for cutthroat and rainbow. South from Westcliffe on Hwy 69 approx. 6 miles to County Road 130, west approx. 5.5 miles to trailhead. South on FDT 1336 approx. 4 miles to FDT 1340. Approx. 3 miles west on FDT 1341.

3. South Colony Lakes (Lower 11,660 ft; 6 ac, Upper 12,030 ft; 16.3 ac); Rated good for cutthroat and rainbow. South from Westcliffe on Hwy 69 4.5 miles to County Road 119, south on County Road 199 5.5 miles to County Road 120, west 1 mile road becomes 4WD road. Approx 5.5 miles southwest on 4WD road to trailhead. West on FDT 1339 1.5 miles to lake.

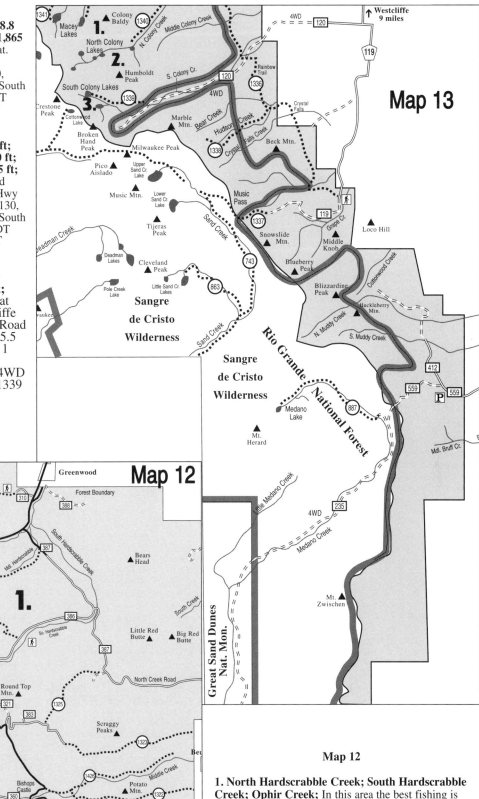

Map 12

1. North Hardscrabble Creek; South Hardscrabble Creek; Ophir Creek; In this area the best fishing is in these streams. Brook and rainbow trout have been stocked and the streams are rated fair to good. This area is 25 miles southwest of Pueblo with good roads to streams. Approx. four miles of North Hardscrabble Creek and four miles of South Hardscrabble Creek has public access. Intermittent public access to Ophir Creek. Refer to Forest Service map.

San Isabel National Forest Maps 14

1. Lake Isabel Recreation Area; (8,800 ft; 40 ac); Rated fair for rainbow. From Rye on Hwy 165 northwest 10 miles to lake Campground, picnic area handicap accessible.

2. Saint Charles River; Little Saint Charles Creek; Rated fair for brook and rainbow. Inlet and below Lake Isabel.

3. Blue Lakes (Lower 11,280 ft; 1.2 ac, Middle 11,320 ft; 4 ac, Upper11,360 ft; 2.7 ac); Rated fair for rainbow.   From near Ophir Creek Campground and Hwy 165 southwest on FDR 360 6 miles to FDR 369, southeast 15 miles to lakes.

Map 14

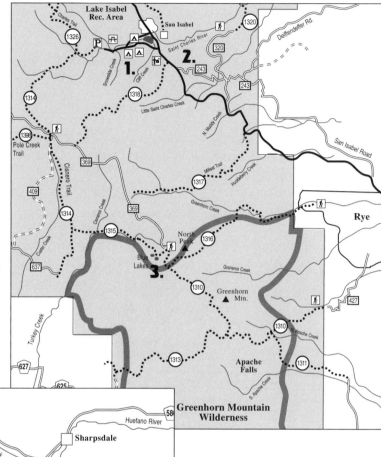

Map 15

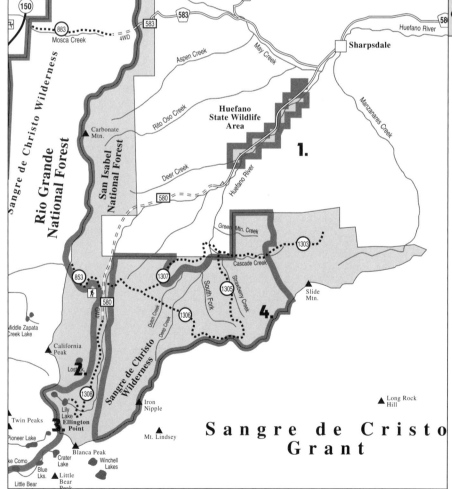

1. Huerfano SWA; Huerfano River; Rated good for rainbow, brook, cutthroat and brown. See page 89 for DO information.

2. Lost Lake (12,265 ft; 3.2 ac); Rated fair for cutthroat. See Lily Lakes.

3. Lily Lakes (Lower 12,350 ft; 7.3 ac, Upper 12,630 ft; 4 ac); Rated fair for cutthroat. Twenty two miles southwest of Gardner, (Last several mile 4WD) to FDT 1308. Approx. 4 miles south on FDT 1308.

4. Strawberry Creek; Rated good for cutthroat. Southwest of Gardner approx. 20 miles to FDT 1306. East on FDT 1306 approx. 6 miles to upper section of stream. Catch and release, artificial flies and lures.

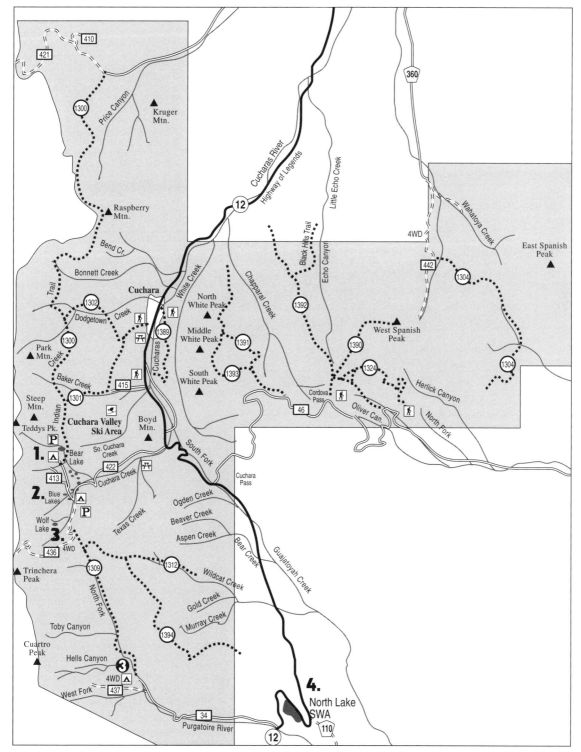

1. Bear Lakes (10,500 ft; 2.5 ac, Lower 10,460 ft; 3ac); Rated fair for stocked rainbow. From La Veta south on Hwy 12 12 miles to Cucharas, continue 4 miles to FDR 422, west 3 miles to Blue lake, 4 miles to Bear Lakes. Wolf Lake is 1 mile south of Blue Lake.

2. Blue Lake (10,400 ft; 1 ac); Rated fair for stocked rainbow and cutthroat. See Bear Lakes.

3. Wolf Lake (11,100 ft; 0.5 ac); Rated fair for stocked rainbow. See Bear lakes.

4. North Lake State Wildlife Area, North Lake and North Fork Purgatorie River; Rated good for rainbow, brown, brook and cutthroat, North lake also contains kokanee and splake. See page 92 for DOW information.

San Juan National Forest Index Map

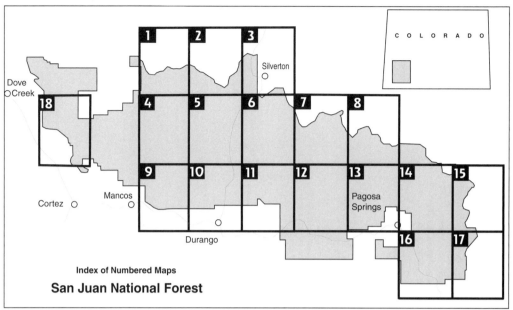

Index of Numbered Maps
San Juan National Forest

TABLE OF CONTENTS

MAP 1
1. Woods Lake State Wildlife Area, Fall Creek.....................217
2. Fish Creek State Wildlife Area 217
3. Fish Creek, Fish Creek, Little, Willow Creek 217
4. Navajo Lake.....................217
5. Cold Creek, Kilpacker Creek, Meadow Creek, Coal Creek 217

MAP 2
1. Columbine Lake.....................217
2. Crystal Lake 217
3. Clear Lake, Island Lake, Ice Lake, Little Ice Lake, Fuller Lake.....................217
4. Dolores River, Slate Creek, Lizard Head Creek, Snow Creek, Spur Creek, Coke Oven Creek 217

MAP 3
1. Bullion King Lake 218
2. Highland Mary Lake, Big, Highland Mary Lake Little 218
3. Verde Lakes Big/Upper Verde Lakes Little/Lower.....................218

MAP 4
1. West Dolores River 218
2. Stoner Creek, Priest Gulch Creek, Bear Creek and Taylor Creek 218
3. McJunkin Creek, Scotch Creek, Ryman Creek, Roaring Forks Creek, Bear Creek 218
4. Dolores River.....................218

MAP 5
1. Bolam Pass Lake 220
2. Potato Lake 220
3. Haviland Lake, Electra Lake 220
4. Forbay Reservoir (Lake) 220
5. Hermosa Creek 220
6. Hermosa Creek, East Fork.....................220
7. Cascade Creek 220

MAP 6
1. Molas Lake, Big, Little Molas Lake, Andrews Lake 221
2. Henderson Lake 221
3. Lost Lake 221

4. Eldorado Lake, Big, Eldorado Lake, Little ..221
5. White Dome Lake 221
6. Vallecito Lake 221
7. Garfield Lake, Lower, Garfield Lake, Upper 221
8. Vestal Lake.....................221
9. Trinity Peaks Lake 221
10. Twilight Lake Lower, Twilight Lake,North, Twilight Lake South,Twilight Lake Upper ..221
11. Ruby Lake Lower, Ruby Lake Upper 221
12. Chopper Lake.....................221
13. Leviathan Lake, Lower, Leviathan Lake, South, Leviathan Lake, North 221
14. Webb Lake 221
15. Pearl Lake 221
16. Emerald Lake 221
17. Jewell Lake 221
18. Hazel Lake, Hazel Lake Lower 221
19. Columbine Lake.....................221
20. Irving Lake.....................221
21. Hidden Lake.....................221
22. Lost Lake 221
23. Grizzly Gulch Lake, Lower, Grizzly Gulch Lake, Upper 221
24. Lillie Lake, Castilleja Lake, Marie Lake, City Resevoir 221
25. Elk Creek, Tenmile Creek, Noname Creek, Needle Creek 221

MAP 7
1. Annie Lake.....................222
2. Betty Lake 222
3. Rock Lake 222
4. Flint Lake, Big, Flint Lake, Little 222
5. Moon Lake.....................222
6. Half Moon Lake.....................222
7. Elk Lake 222
8. Granite Lake, Lower 222
9. Divide Lake, Divide Lake Pothole 222
10. Dollar Lake 222
11. Emerald Lake, Big, Emerald Lake, Little 222
12. Los Pinos River 222

MAP 8
1. Williams Lake, Williams & Indian Creeks ..223
2. Hossick Lake 223
3. Piedra River, East Fork, Deadman Creek 223
4. Williams Creek Reservoir 223

MAP 9
1. Turkey Creek, Chicken Creek 224
2. Mancos River, West, Mancos River, Middle, Mancos River, East 224
3. LaPlata River 224

MAP 10
1. Junction Creek 224
2. Clear Creek, Hermosa Creek 224

MAP 11
1. Lemon Reservoir 225
2. Vallecito Reservoir.....................225
3. Vallecito Creek.....................225

MAP 12
1. Los Pinos River 225
2. Jacobs Ladder Lake 225
3. Piedra River 225

MAP 13
1. Turkey Creek Lake 226
2. Fourmile Lake Lower, Fourmile Lake Upper 226
3. Piedra River, East & Middle Forks, Williams Creek, Pagosa Creek, Plumtaw Creek..........226

MAP 14
1. Borns Lake, Hatcher Lakes 226
2. San Juan River, West Fork.....................226
3. San Juan river, East Fork 226
4. Quartz Lake 226

MAP 15
1. Crater Lake 227
2. Fish Lake 227

MAP 16
1. Echo Canyon Reservoir State Wildlife Area 227
2. Buckles Lake 227
3. Harris Lake 227
4. Table Lake 227

MAP 17
1. Opal Lake.....................228
2. Price Lakes.....................228

MAP 18
1. Lone Dome State Wildlife Area, Dolores River 228
2. McPhee Reservoir 228
3. Narraquinnep Reservoir State Wildlife Area 228

1. Woods Lake State Wildlife Area; Woods Lake and Fall Creek; Rated good for rainbow and brook. Artificial flies and lures only. See DOW information page 95.

2. Fish Creek State Wildlife Area; Rated good for rainbow and brook. See DOW information on page 87.

3. Fish Creek; Little Fish Creek; Willow Creek; Rated fair for rainbow and cutthroat. Little Fish and Willow Creeks are narrow with beaver ponds. Fish Creek is 15 to 20 feet wide with numerous beaver ponds.

4. Navajo Lake (11,154 ft; 10.9 ac); Rated good for brook. Artificial flies and lures only.

5. Cold Creek, Kilpacker Creek; Meadow Creek; Coal Creek; Rated fair for cutthroat and rainbow. **West Fork Dolores River;** Rated good for rainbow brown and cutthroat. Intermittent public access.

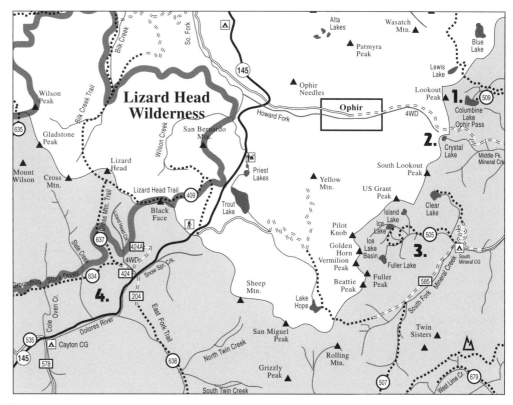

Map 2

1. Columbine Lake (12,685 ft; 21.7 ac); Rated good for brook. From Durango north on Hwy 550 57 miles to FDR 679, west on road 1 mile to FDT 509. A difficult 5 mile hike to lake.

2. Crystal Lake (12,055 ft; 2ac); Rated good for brook and cutthroat. East from Ophir on 4 WD road approx. 3 miles to lake.

3. Clear Lake (12,000 ft; 41.5 ac); Island Lake (12,398 ft; 4.9 ac); Ice Lake (12,260 ft; 14.8ac); Little Ice Lake (12,600 ft; 1 ac); Fuller Lake (12,588 ft; 19.8ac); Rated good for brook and cutthroat. From Durango north on Hwy 550 50 miles to FDR 585, west approx. 4 miles on road 1 mile to South Mineral Campground. Lakes can be reached from campground.

4. Dolores River; Lizard Head Creek; Snow Creek; Spur Creek; Slate Creek; Coke Oven Creek; Dolores River is stocked with rainbow, brown and cutthroat, other streams are rated fair for cutthroat and brook. Northeast of Rico on Hwy 145, road parallels river.

1. Bullion King Lake (12,570 ft; 3.0 ac); Rated fair for rainbow. Mineral Creek has been stocked with brook and cutthroat. From Silverton north on Hwy 550 approx. 9 miles to 4WD road, west approx. 2 miles to lake.

2. Highland Mary Lakes (Big 12,089 ft; 46.4 ac, Little 12,099 ft; 11.6 ac); Rated fair for rainbow, cutthroat and brook. From Silverton south east approx. 9 miles, refer to map for best route.

3. Verde Lakes Little/Lower (12,160 ft; 9.1 ac, Big/Upper 12,165 ft; 10.9 ac); Rated fair for rainbow, cutthroat and brook. From Silverton south east approx. 9 miles, refer to map for best route.

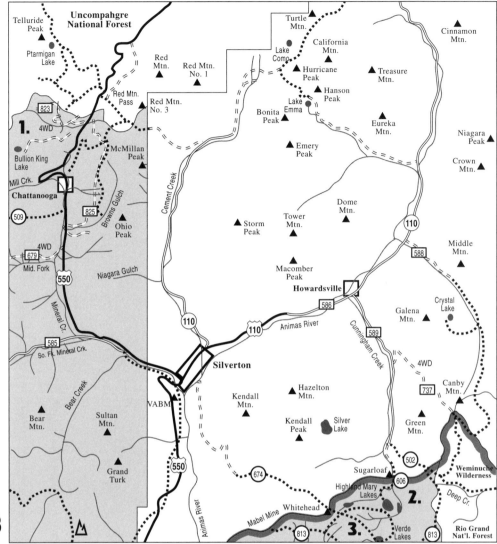

Map 3

MAP 4

1. West Dolores River; Upper section is rated fair for rainbow, brown and cutthroat, limited public access.

2. Stoner Creek; Rated fair for cutthroat. From Hwy 145 private property blocks access for the first 2 miles of FDT 625 that parallels stream. Access stream from FDT 624 at Emerson Campground on FDR 535. Check with ranger district for alternate access routes. Other small streams in the areas **Priest Gulch Creek, Bear Creek and Taylor Creek** are rated fair for brook and cuthroat.

3. McJunkin Creek; Scotch Creek; Ryman Creek; Roaring Forks Creek; Bear Creek; Rated fair for brook and cutthroat. Small streams that enter Dolores River from the southeast. Refer to map for access from Hwy 145.

4. Dolores River; Rated fair for rainbow, brown and cutthroat. Dolores River has limited public access from Dolores to several miles below Rico. Above Rico the river is in the national forest. River parallels Hwy 145.

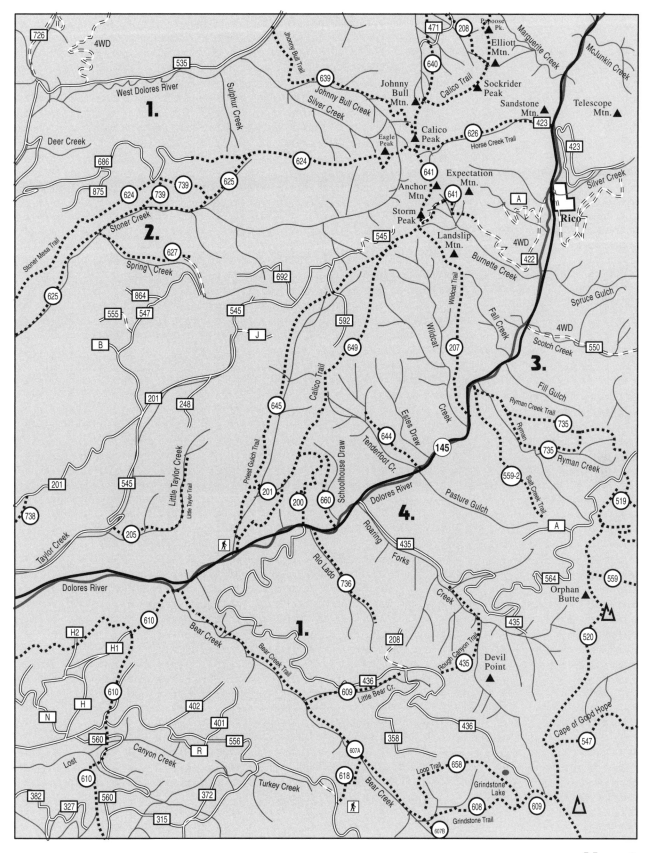

Map 4

219

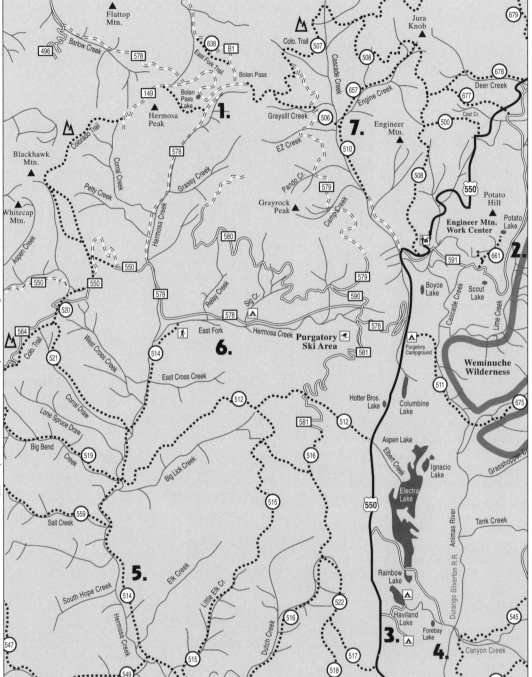

1. Bolam Pass Lake (11,093 ft; 3.5 ac); Rated fair for brook. Six miles north of Rico on Hwy 145 to Cayton Campground. Southeast on FDR 578 approx. 9 miles to lake.

2. Potato Lake (9,800 ft; 20 ac); Rated fair for brook and rainbow. North of Durango approx. 30 miles to FDR 591. East on FDR 591 approx. 2 miles to FDT 661, north on trail approx. 1.25 miles to lake.

3. Haviland Lake State Wildlife Area (8,106 ft; 22 ac); Rated fair for rainbow and cutthroat. **Electra Lake (8,320 ft; 816 ac);** North of Durango approx. 18 miles to access road. East to Electra Lake, Forebay Lake and Haviland Lake. Electra Lake is privately owned. Gravel boat ramp, non motorized craft, campground. See page 90 for DOW information.

4. Forbay Reservoir (Lake) (8,300 ft; 2.5 ac); Fated fair for brook. See Haviland Lake.

5. Hermosa Creek; Rated fair for brook and rainbow. From Hermosa on Hwy 550 west on FDR 576 approx. 5 miles to FDT 514, continue on FDT 514, trail follows creek for approx. 15 miles to FDR 578. FDR 578 follows creek to headwaters. Small stream.

6. East Fork Hermosa Creek; Rated fair for cutthroat and brook. East Fork parallels FDR 578 west from near Purgatory Ski Area.

7. Cascade Creek; Rated fair for cutthroat, brook and rainbow. From Cascade Campground 2 miles north on FDR 550 to Cascade Summer Home Group Road, road and FDT 510 parallels creek.

1. Molas Lake, Little 10,906 ft; 6.9 ac); Andrews Lake (10,745 ft; 8 ac); Rated good for rainbow and brook. South from Silverton approx. 6 miles on Hwy 550 near, Molas Pass.

2. Henderson Lake (9,970 ft; 14.8 ac); Rated fair for rainbow and brook. Canyon Creek; Rated fair for brook. A small fast stream. From Trimble and Hwy 550 east 1 mile to FDR 682, north approx. 17 miles to lake. No designated trail to Canyon Creek.

Weminuche Wilderness
Several trials access the wilderness, trails number 504, 529 on the east and 623 on the west are the main trails. Estimate distances from map, scale is approx. 1/2 inch = 1 mile. Foot traffic is heavy in this area and climbs to lakes can be difficult.

3. Lost Lake (12,182 ft; 12.8 ac); Rated fair for rainbow and brook. South of Silverton approx. 4 miles to FDT 813. Follow FDT 813 approx. 4 miles to lake.

4. Eldorado Lakes (Big 12,503 ft;14.1 ac, Little 12,506 ft 2.2 ac); Rated fair for rainbow. From Molas Pass east on FDT 503 approx.10 miles.

5. White Dome Lake (12,560 ft; 6.9 ac); Rated fair for cutthroat and rainbow. Located south of Eldorado Lake .5 mile.

6. Vallecito Lake (12,010 ft; 13.8 ac); Rated good for cutthroat.

7. Garfield Lakes (Lower 11,510 ft; 14.8 ac, Upper 12,300 ft; 11.4 ac); Rated fair for rainbow.

8. Vestal Lake (12,260 ft; 5.7 ac); Rated fair for brook, cutthroat and rainbow.

9. Trinity Peaks Lake (12,396 ft; 8.4 ac); Rated fair for rainbow.

10. Twilight Lakes Lower (11,570 4.2 ac, North 12,050 ft; 3.5 ac, South 11,700 ft; 3.5 ac, Upper 11,880 ft 4.2 ac); Rated fair for rainbow and brook.

11. Ruby Lake Lower (10,820 ft; 12.8 ac, Upper 12,600 ft; 2 ac); Rated good for rainbow.

12. Chopper Lake (12,620 ft; 4 ac); Rated fair for cutthroat.

13. Leviathan Lakes (Lower 11,550 ft; 1.5 ac, South 11,978 ft; 9 ac, North 12,460 ft; 8 ac); Rated fair for cutthroat.

14. Webb Lake (10,942 ft; 5.9 ac); Rated fair for rainbow and cutthroat.

15. Pear Lake (11,579 ft; 6.9 ac); Rated fair for cutthroat and rainbow.

16. Emerald Lake (11,276 ft; 11.4 ac); Rated fair for cutthroat and rainbow.

17. Jewell Lake (Ruby Lake) (11,910' ft; 1 ac); Rated fair for cutthroat and rainbow.

18. Hazel Lake (12,435 ft; 21 ac, Lower 12,430 ft; 3 ac); Rated fair for cutthroat.

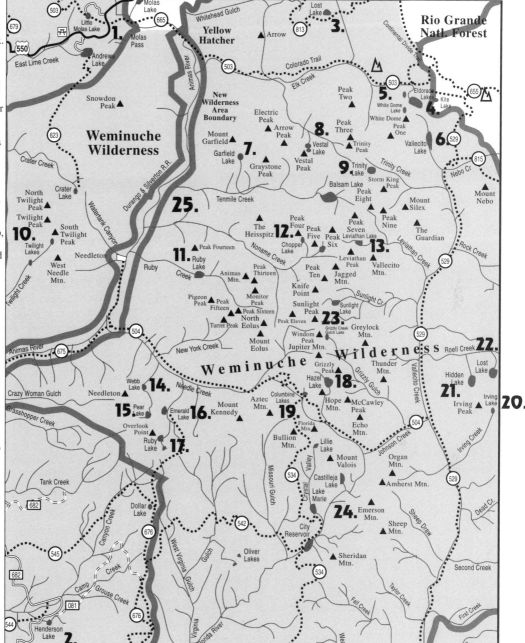

19. Columbine Lake (12,370 ft; 3.7 ac); Rated fair for cutthroat and brook.

20. Irving Lake (11,662 ft; 7.9 ac); Rated fair for cutthroat.

21. Hidden Lake (11,940 ft; 16.8 ac); Rated fair for cutthroat and rainbow.

22. Lost Lake (11,839 ft; 18.8 ac); Rated fair for cutthroat and rainbow.

23. Grizzly Gulch Lakes (Lower 12,235 ft; 5.9 ac, Upper 13,100 ft; 8.9 ac); Rated fair for cutthroat.

24. Lillie Lake (12,550 ft; 5.7 ac); Castilleja Lakes (12,200 ft; 9.8 ac, East 12,100 ft 5.9 ac); Marie Lake (11,555 ft; 9.9 ac); City Reservoir (10,917 ft; 39.5 ac); Rated good for cutthroat.

25. Elk Creek; Rated good for rainbow and brook in lower section. **Tenmile Creek;** Rated good for rainbow in upper section some beaver ponds. **Noname Creek;** Rated good for rainbow. **Needle Creek;** From D & R. G. Railroad Needleton Station, FDT 504 parallels stream. A number of small streams offer good to fair fishing for brook and cutthroat on the Vallecito Drainage.

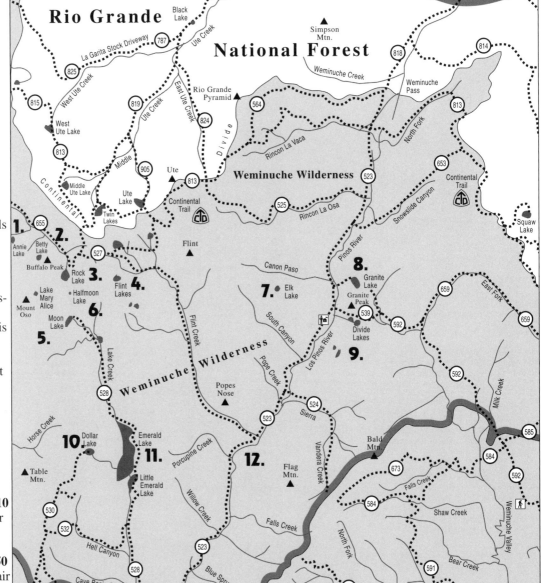

Weminuche Wilderness

Main connecting trails are FDT 523, FDT 528, FDT 539, FDT 524, FDT 592 and FDT 525. Refer to map for estimated distance. The main trail (FDT 523) trailhead is located approx. 4 miles north of Vallecito Reservoir at Pine River Campground.

1. Annie Lake (12,200 ft; 5.9 ac); Rated fair for cutthroat.

2. Betty Lake (12,210 ft; 8.2 ac); Rated fair for cutthroat.

3. Rock Lake (11,850 ft; 30.9 ac); Rated fair for cutthroat.

4. Flint Lake (Little 11,870 ft; 9.6 ac, Big 11,650 ft 38 ac); Rated good for cutthroat.

5. Moon Lake (11,653 ft; 14.8 ac); Rated fair for small rainbow, brook and cutthroat.

6. Half Moon Lake (13,200 ft; 3 ac); Rated fair for small rainbow, brook and cutthroat.

7. Elk Lake (11,470 ft; 7 ac); Rated fair for cutthroat and rainbow.

8. Granite Lake (Lower 10,280 ft; 32 ac); Rated fair for cutthroat and rainbow.

9. Divide Lakes (9,950 ft; 11 ac, Pothole (9,850 ft; 4.9 ac); Rated fair for cutthroat and rainbow.

10. Dollar Lake (11,560 ft; 3 ac); Rated fair for cutthroat.

11. Emerald Lakes (Big 10,023 ft; 275.7 ac, Little10,000 ft; 9.9 ac); Rated good for rainbow-cutthroat hybrid. Artificial flies and lures only. Bag and possession limit is two fish 14 inches or less. Lake Creek also contains hybrid fish, same regulations apply.

12. Los Pinos River; Rated good for brown, brook and rainbow. Small stream tributaries that are rated good for cutthroat include Rincon La Vaca, Rincon La Osa, North Fork, Snowslide Creek, Canon Paso, and Sierra Vandera Creek.

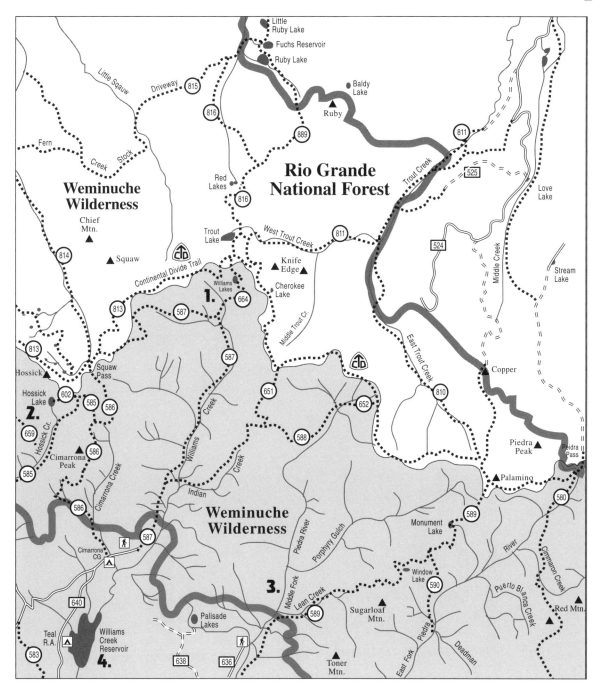

1. Williams Lake (11,695 ft; 12.8 ac); Rated fair for cutthroat. From Pagosa Springs 2 miles west on Hwy 160, north on FDR 631 22 miles, north on FDR 640 5 miles. Trail FDT 587 follows Williams Creek up to lake, approx. 7 miles. Weminuche Wilderness. **Williams Creek;** Rated good for rainbow and cutthroat. **Indian Creek;** rated good for cutthroat.

2. Hossick Lake (11, 886 ft; 1 ac); Rated fair for cutthroat. From Pagosa Springs 2 miles west on Hwy 160, north on FDR 631 22 miles, north on FDR 640 5 miles to Cimmarrona Campground. A 7 mile hike on FDT 586 to lake.

3. Piedra River, East Fork; Rated fair for cutthroat. From Pagosa Springs 2 miles west on Hwy 160, north on FDR 631 22 miles, north on FDR 640, east on FDR 636 7 miles to trailhead. No designated trail to lower section. Take FDT 589 approx.6 miles to FDT 590, southeast on FDT 590 approx. 2 miles to stream. **Deadman Creek** offers fair fishing for brook and cutthroat.

4. Williams Creek Reservoir (8,241 ft; 343 ac); Rated good for rainbow, brook, cutthroat and kokanee. See page 89 for DOW information.

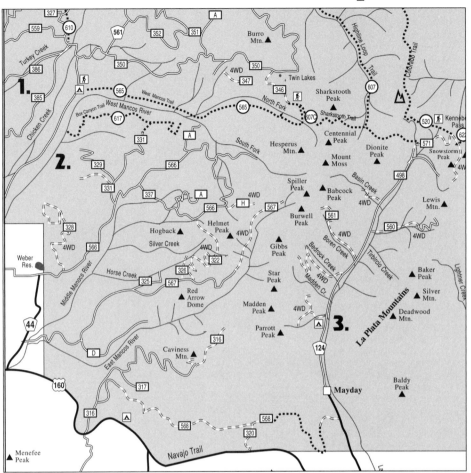

1. Turkey Creek; Rated fair for brook and cutthroat. Intermittent public access. **Chicken Creek;** Rated fair for rainbow.

2. Mancos River West, Mancos River, Middle, Mancos River, East; Rated fair for brook, rainbow and cutthroat. East of Mancos approx. 2.5 mile to FDR 44 north to access this area.

3. LaPlata River; Upper section rated fair for rainbow and brook. Intermittent public access, lower section is privately owned. FDR 124 parallels river north from Hesperus

Map 9

Map 10

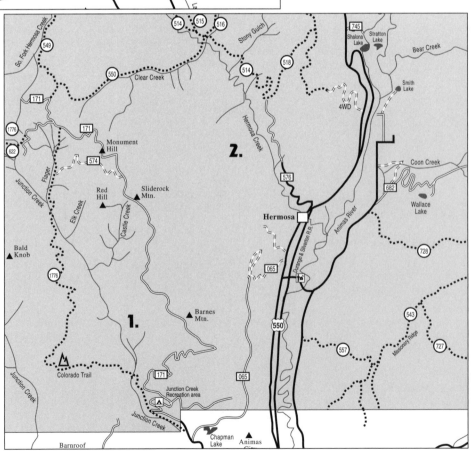

1. Junction Creek; Rated fair for cutthroat and brook. Northwest of Durango on County Road 204 to Junction Creek Recreation Area. No designated trail.

2. Clear Creek; Hermosa Creek; From Main Street in Durango turn west on 25 th Street until it becomes Junction Creek Road. Follow road approx. 22 miles to trailhead. FDT 550 parallels creek. Trail intersects FDT 514 which follows Hermosa Creek. Animas River has no public access in this area.

1. Lemon Reservoir (8,148 ft; 622 ac); Rated good for rainbow and brook. North from Bayfield on County Road 501 to County Road 240, north on FDR 243 to reservoir. Approx. 14 miles. Campground, boat ramp and picnic areas.

2. Vallecito Reservoir (7,664 ft; 2,718 ac); Rated good for rainbow, cutthroat, northern pike and brown. North from Bayfield on County Road 501 approx. 11 miles to reservoir. Boat ramps, campgrounds and picnic areas.

3. Vallecito Creek. Rated fair rainbow, brook and cutthroat, kokanee. Above Vallecito Reservoir to Vallecito Campground stream is on private property. Above campground stream is in Weminuche Wilderness and is paralleled by FDT 529.

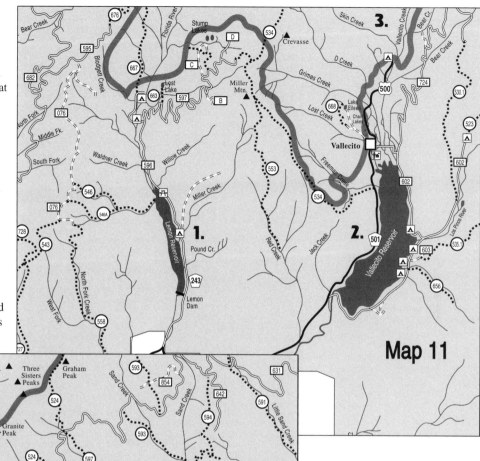

Map 11

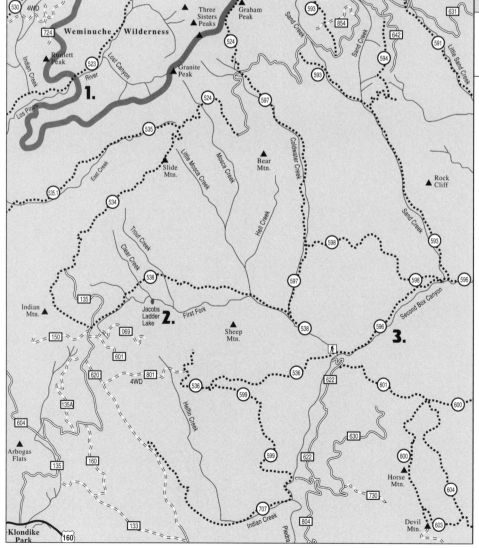

Map 12

1. Los Pinos River; Rated good for brown, rainbow and brook. Trailhead to Weminuche Wilderness is at Pine River Campground approx. 4 miles north of Vallecito Reservoir on FDR 602. FDT 523 follows stream in wilderness. No public access below the wilderness boundary.

2. Jacobs Ladder Lake (8,640 ft; 12 ac); Rated fair for brook. Located on First Fork Piedra River. First Fork Trailhead is located at the end of First Fork Road (FDR 804/622). First Fork Trail (FDT 538) follows First Fork for several miles, no designated trail from this point to lake. First Fork is rated fair for cutthroat.

3. Piedra River; Rated good for rainbow, brown. From Piedra on Hwy 160 north First Fork Road follows river to First Fork Trailhead. FDT 596 follows river northeast through Second Box Canyon to Piedra and FDR 631.

San Juan National Forest Maps 13 & 14

1. Turkey Creek Lake (11,800 ft; 22.7 ac); Rated good for brook. North from Pagosa Springs on County Road 400 to Forest Boundary, continue north on FDR 645 to end of road and trailhead, a distance of approx. 13 miles. Take FDT 579 approx. 5 miles to FDT 569, north approx. 2.5 miles to lake. Weminuche Wilderness.

2. Fourmile Lakes (Lower 11,185 ft; 12 ac, Upper 11,675 ft; 9 ac); Rated good for cutthroat. North from Pagosa Springs on County Road 400 to Forest Boundary, continue north on FDR 645 to end of road and trailhead, a distance of approx. 13 miles. Take FDT 579 approx. 6.5 miles to lake. Fourmile Creek; Rated fair for brook. Generally follows road and trail to lakes. Lower section has little public access. Weminuche Wilderness.

3. Piedra River, East Fork; Piedra River, Middle Fork; Williams Creek; Pagosa Creek; Plumtaw Creek. Rated good for cutthroat and brook. East Fork has intermittent public access up to wilderness boundary. From Pagosa Springs 2 miles west to County Road 600/FDR 631, north approx. 15 miles to Piedra Ranger Station and access to streams.

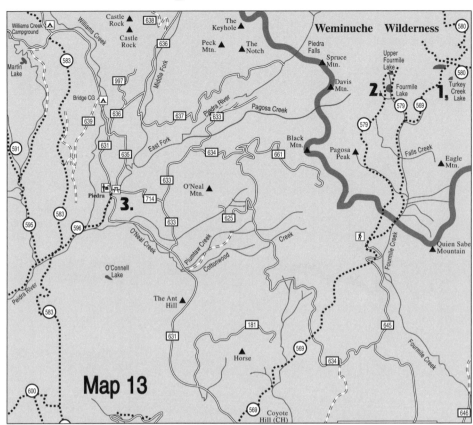

Map 14

1. Hatcher Lakes (8,400 ft; 7 ac); Borns Lake (8,365 ft; 15 ac); Rated poor for brook and rainbow. Located north and at West Fork Campground.

2. West Fork San Juan River; Rated good for rainbow and brook. North on Hwy 160 to FDR 648 west 1.5 miles to West Fork Campground. FDT 561 follows stream into wilderness.

3. East Fork San Juan River; Rated good for rainbow and brook. North on Hwy 160 to East Fork Campground, FDR 667 parallels stream. East Fork has approx. 5 miles of public access above East Fork Campground. San Juan River has no public access in this area.

4. Quartz Lake (11,600 ft; 6.9 ac); Rated good for cutthroat. From Pagosa Springs East on FDR 662 approx. 8 miles to FDR 665 continue east approx. 7 miles to FDT 572. Take FDT 572 northeast approx. 3 miles to FDT 568 approx. 1.5 miles to lake.

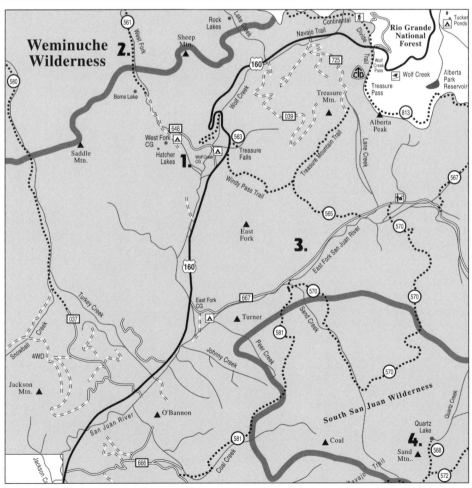

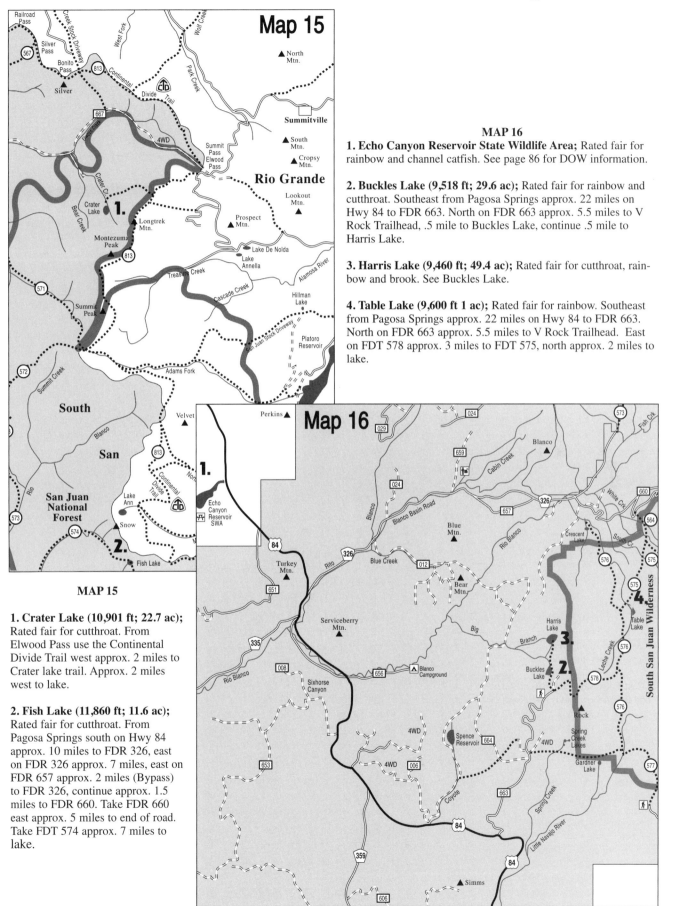

Map 15

North Mtn.

Summitville

South Mtn.

Cropsy Mtn.

Rio Grande

Lookout Mtn.

Prospect Mtn.

Lake De Nolda

Lake Annella

Alamosa River

Hillman Lake

Platoro Reservoir

Crater Lake

Longtrek Mtn.

Montezuma Peak

Treasure Creek

Cascade Creek

San Juan Stock Driveway

Summit Peak

Adams Fork

South

San

San Juan National Forest

Velvet

Lake Ann

Snow

Fish Lake

MAP 16

1. Echo Canyon Reservoir State Wildlife Area; Rated fair for rainbow and channel catfish. See page 86 for DOW information.

2. Buckles Lake (9,518 ft; 29.6 ac); Rated fair for rainbow and cutthroat. Southeast from Pagosa Springs approx. 22 miles on Hwy 84 to FDR 663. North on FDR 663 approx. 5.5 miles to V Rock Trailhead, .5 mile to Buckles Lake, continue .5 mile to Harris Lake.

3. Harris Lake (9,460 ft; 49.4 ac); Rated fair for cutthroat, rainbow and brook. See Buckles Lake.

4. Table Lake (9,600 ft 1 ac); Rated fair for rainbow. Southeast from Pagosa Springs approx. 22 miles on Hwy 84 to FDR 663. North on FDR 663 approx. 5.5 miles to V Rock Trailhead. East on FDT 578 approx. 3 miles to FDT 575, north approx. 2 miles to lake.

Map 16

Perkins

Echo Canyon Reservoir SWA

Blanco

Cabin Creek

White Crk

Blanco

Blanco Basin Road

Crescent Lake

Blue Mtn.

Rio Blanco

South Cr

Turkey Mtn.

Rito

Blue Creek

Bear Mtn.

Harris Lake

Serviceberry Mtn.

Big Branch

Leche Creek

Table Lake

Buckles Lake

Blanco Campground

Sixhorse Canyon

Rio Blanco

Spence Reservoir

V Rock

Spring Creek Lakes

Gardner Lake

Coyote

Spring Creek

Little Navajo River

Simms

South San Juan Wilderness

MAP 15

1. Crater Lake (10,901 ft; 22.7 ac); Rated fair for cutthroat. From Elwood Pass use the Continental Divide Trail west approx. 2 miles to Crater lake trail. Approx. 2 miles west to lake.

2. Fish Lake (11,860 ft; 11.6 ac); Rated fair for cutthroat. From Pagosa Springs south on Hwy 84 approx. 10 miles to FDR 326, east on FDR 326 approx. 7 miles, east on FDR 657 approx. 2 miles (Bypass) to FDR 326, continue approx. 1.5 miles to FDR 660. Take FDR 660 east approx. 5 miles to end of road. Take FDT 574 approx. 7 miles to lake.

San Juan National Forest Maps 17 & 18

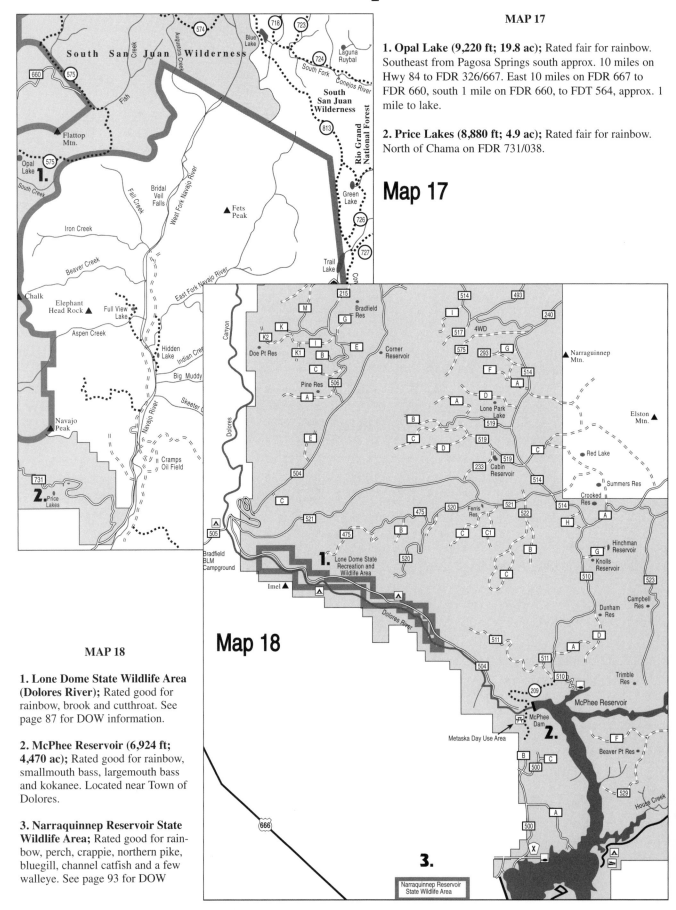

MAP 17

1. Opal Lake (9,220 ft; 19.8 ac); Rated fair for rainbow. Southeast from Pagosa Springs south approx. 10 miles on Hwy 84 to FDR 326/667. East 10 miles on FDR 667 to FDR 660, south 1 mile on FDR 660, to FDT 564, approx. 1 mile to lake.

2. Price Lakes (8,880 ft; 4.9 ac); Rated fair for rainbow. North of Chama on FDR 731/038.

Map 17

Map 18

MAP 18

1. Lone Dome State Wildlife Area (Dolores River); Rated good for rainbow, brook and cutthroat. See page 87 for DOW information.

2. McPhee Reservoir (6,924 ft; 4,470 ac); Rated good for rainbow, smallmouth bass, largemouth bass and kokanee. Located near Town of Dolores.

3. Narraquinnep Reservoir State Wildlife Area; Rated good for rainbow, perch, crappie, northern pike, bluegill, channel catfish and a few walleye. See page 93 for DOW

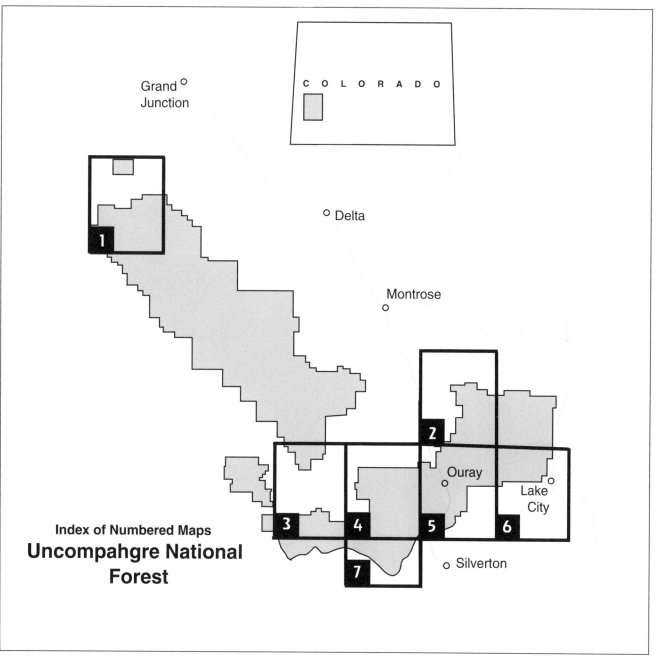

TABLE OF CONTENTS

MAP 1
1. Fruita Reservoirs.............................230
2 Big Creek Reservoir......................230
3. Costo Reservoir 230

MAP 2
1. Fish Creek Reservoirs (2)..............230
2. Beaver Lake 230
3. Hampton Lakes 230
4. Clear, Aspen, Rowdy Lakes 230
5. Silverjack Reservoir 230
6. Cimarron River, West Fork, East
   Fork, Little Cimarron River 230

MAP 3
1. Woods Lake SWA.........................231

MAP 4
1. Blue Lakes (3) 231
2. Wrights Lake 231
3. Silver Lake 231
4. Alta Lakes..................................231
5. San Miguel River 231

MAP 5
1. Uncompahgre River 232
2. Cow Creek 232
3. Canyon Creek 232
4. Ptarmigan Lake............................232

MAP 6
1. Larson Lake 233
2. Crystal Lake 233
3. Hay Lake....................................233
4. Thompson Lake 233
5. San Cristabol Lake 233
6. Cooper Lake 233
7. Henson Creek 233
8. Lake Fork Gunnison River............233

MAP 7
1. Trout Lake 233
2. Hope Lake 233

Uncompahgre National Forest Maps 1 & 2

1. Fruita Reservoirs (# 9,160 ft; 11 ac, #2 8,820 ft; 16 ac, #3 8,980 ft; 5.5 ac); Stocked rainbow. Southwest of Grand Junction to Glade Park, south on County Road 16.5 to FDR 400 to isolated part of Grand Mesa National Forest.

2. Big Creek Reservoir (8,240 ft; 35 ac); Rated fair to good for rainbow, cutthroat and brown. South from Grand Junction to Unaweep Canyon on Hwy 141 to Divide Road (FDR 402), southwest approx. 12 miles to FDR 403, west on road for approx. 7 miles to Reservoir.

3. Costo Reservoir (9,500 ft; 96.8 ac); Rated fair for rainbow and cutthroat. South from Grand Junction to Unaweep Canyon on Hwy 141 to Divide Road (FDR 402), southwest approx. 12 miles to FDR 403, west on road for approx. 4 miles to reservoir.

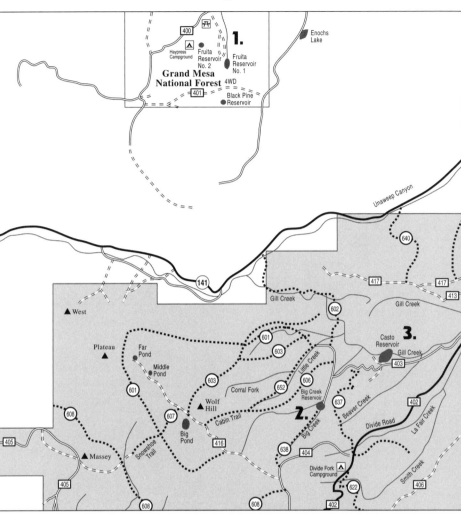

Map 1

1. Fish Creek Reservoirs (Big 9,420 ft; 64.2 ac, Little 9,330 ft; 29.6 ac); rainbow. From Montrose 20 miles east on Hwy 50 to County Road 69 (FDR 863), south 22 miles to lakes. Lakes in this area are rated fair to poor.

2. Beaver Lake (8,740 ft; 9.9 ac); Rainbow.

3. Hampton Lakes (9,660 ft; 9.9 ac); Rated good for rainbow, brook and cutthroat.

4. Clear Lake (9,100 ft; 3 ac); Aspen Lake (8,820 ft; 3 ac); Rowdy Lake (8,800 ft; 10 ac); Rainbow.

5. Silverjack Reservoir (8,900 ft; 318 ac); Rainbow. Irrigation reservoir that can draw down in late summer.

6. Cimarron River; West Fork; Middle Fork; East Fork; Little Cimarron Rivers; Rated fair for stocked rainbow.

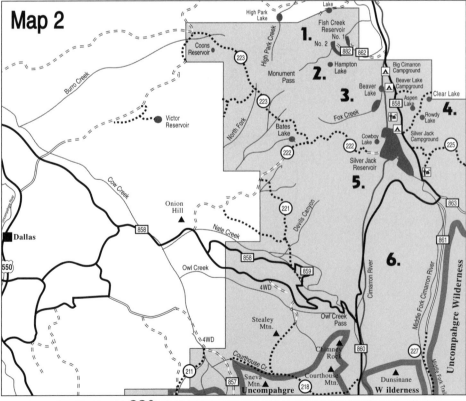

Map 2

1. Woods Lake State Wildlife Area (9,423 ft; 19.8 ac); Rated good for rainbow and brook. See page 95 for DOW information.

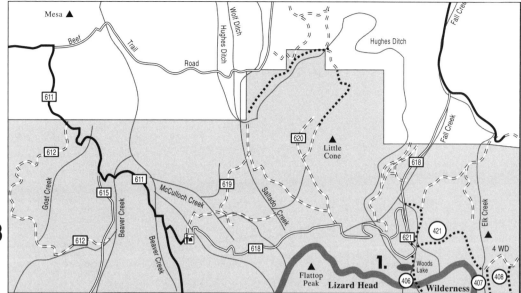

Map 3

Map 4

1. Blue Lakes (Lower 10,980 ft; 12.4 ac, Middle 11,500 ft; 5 ac, Upper 11,740 ft; 9.3 ac); Stocked cutthroat and rainbow. From Ouray south on Hwy 361 approx. 6 miles to FDR 853.1B, west on 4WD road approx. 5 miles to where road ends. Take FDT 201 a short distance to Wrights Lake, approx. 3 miles to Blue Lakes

2. Wrights Lake (12,203 ft; 1.5 ac); Stocked cutthroat. See Blue Lakes for directions.

3. Silver Lake (11,788 ft; 4 ac); Stocked cutthroat. Southeast of Telluride west of Bridal Veil Creek Road (Locked gate).

4. Alta Lakes (Lower 11,216 ft; 9.9 ac); Rated fair for brook and rainbow. From Telluride on Hwy 145 approx. 10 miles south to FDR 632, east approx. 6 miles to lake.

5. San Miguel River; Rated fair to poor for rainbow. Limited public access in this area.

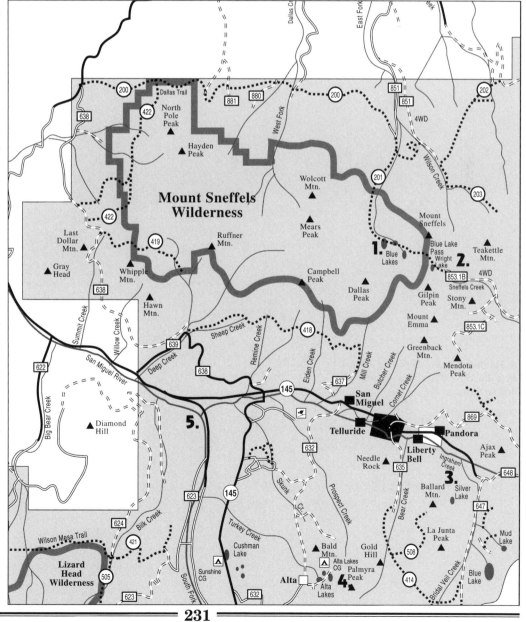

Uncompahgre National Forest Map 5

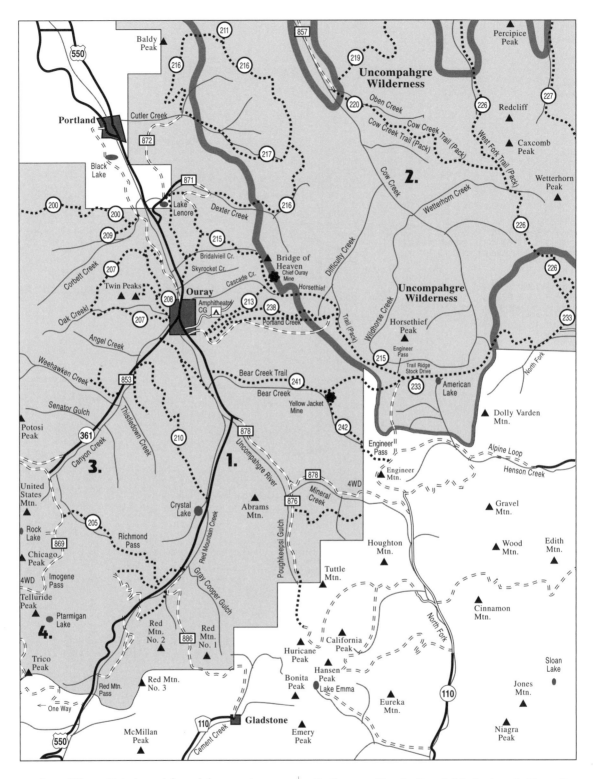

1. Uncompahgre River; Rated good for rainbow, cutthroat, brook and kokanee. Parallels Hwy 550 and FDR 878. Limited public access.

2. Cow Creek; Rated fair to good for cutthroat. From Ridgway east on county road to FDR 857 at forest boundary to end of road, approx. 14 miles. No designated trial.

3. Canyon Creek; Rated fair for brook. From Ouray south, creek parallels FDR 853. Fast and clear.

4. Ptarmigan Lake (12,939 ft; 4.9 ac); Stocked cutthroat. South from Red Mountain Pass approx. 3 miles on Hwy 550, 2 miles west, no designated trial.

1. Larson Lake (11,160 ft; 4 ac); Rated fair for rainbow and brook. North of Lake City north to cemetery road. Take FDT 236 approx. 6 miles to lake.

2. Crystal Lake (11,760 ft; 18 ac); Rated good for brook and rainbow. North of Lake City north to cemetery road. Take FDT 235 approx. 5 miles to lake.

3. Hay Lake (11,000 ft; 2.5 ac); Stocked brook. Take FDT 235 approx. 3 miles to lake.

4. Thompson Lake (9,920 ft; 4.3 ac); Rated fair for cutthroat, rainbow and brook. Take FDT 235 approx. 1.5 miles to lake.

5. San Cristabol Lake (8,995 ft; 346 ac); Rated fair for brook, rainbow and mackinaw. From Lake City south approx. 3.5 miles to Alpine Loop Byway, south 2 miles to lake. Campground, boat ramp, heavy pressure.

6. Cooper Lake (12,750 ft; 9.6 ac); Rated good for cutthroat. North from Whitecross on Alpine Loop Byway on Cooper Creek Trail approx. 3 miles. No designated trail to lake. **Cooper Creek** is rated good for brook.

7. Henson Creek; Rated fair for brook and rainbow. From Lake City Henson Creek Road parallels creek. Lower section in narrow canyon.

8. Lake Fork Gunnison River; North Fork from Lake City north is mostly private, intermittent public access from Lake San Cristabol west to headwaters. Upper section is difficult to access, narrow canyon.

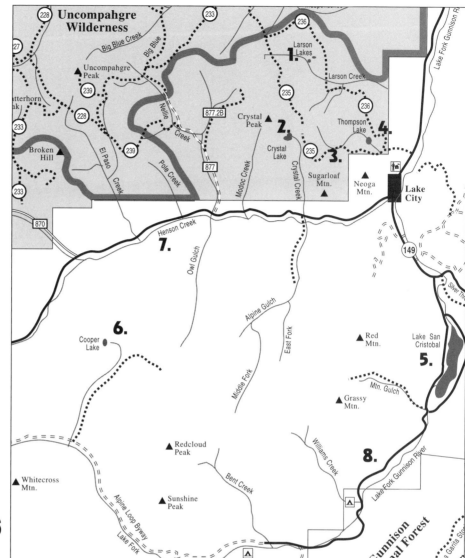

Map 6

Map 7

1. Trout Lake (9,714 ft; 126.5 ac); Rated fair rainbow, brook and cutthroat. From Telluride west on Hwy 145 4 miles, south approx. 12 miles to lake. Heavy pressure.

2. Hope Lake (11,900 ft; 36.6 ac); Stocked cutthroat. Southeast from Trout Lake on FDR 627 approx. 3 miles to FDT 410, take FDT 410 approx. 2.5 miles to lake.

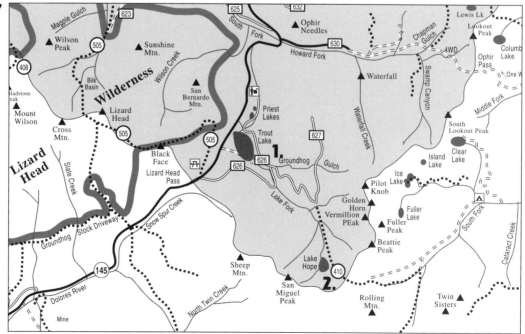

White River National Forest Index Map

TABLE OF CONTENTS

MAP 1
1. Aldrich Lakes 235

MAP 2
1. Pagoda Lake 235
2. White River, North Fork 235
3. Sable Lake 235
4. Mirror Lake and Shamrock Lake 235
5. Anderson Lake 235
6. Lake of the Woods 235
7. Boulder Lake and Doris Lake 235
8. Johnson Lake.................................235

MAP 3
1. Elk Lake, McGinnis Lake and Skinny
   Fish Lakes 236

MAP 4
1. Sleepycat Ponds, Oakridge SWA 236
2. Miller Creek, Miller Creek, Middle,
   Miller Creek, East 236

MAP 5
1. Avery Lake (Big Beaver Reservoir) 237
2. Bailey Lake and Swede Lake 237
3. Peltier Lake 237
4. Gilley Lake 237
5. Cliff Lakes and Meadow Creek Lake ...237

MAP 6
1. Guthrie Lakes, Shallow Lake, Rainbow Lake 238
2. Big Fish Lake, Gwendolyn Lake 238
3. Slide Lake, Pine Isle Lake, Ruby Lake..............238
4. Marvine Lakes, Murphy Lake, Frosty Lake, Mary
   Loch Lake, Trail Lake, Ned Wilson Lake 238
5. Lost Solar Lakes, Windy Point Lake 238
6. Crater Lake, Blair Lake, Shadow Lake, Jet Lake,
   Mahaffey Lake, Cliff Lakes, Meadow
   Creek Lake 238
7. Elks Lakes, Limestone Lake 238
8. Heart Lake, Supply basin Reservoir,
   Bison Lake, Deep Lake 238

MAP 7
1. Coffin Lake, Trappers Lake, Little Trappers
   Lake, Little Trappers Creek. 239
2. Edge Lake, Keener Lake, Bailey Lakes 239
3. Sunnyside Lakes 239
4. Wall Lake 239
5. Surprise Lake 239
6. Deer Lake 239
7. Island Lakes 239
8. Muskrat, Mud Lakes, ...239
9. Solitary Lake 239
10. McMillan Lake 239
11. Mackinaw Lake, Crescent Lake, Emerald Lake 239
12. Shingle Peak Lake 239
13. Shepard Lake, Rim Lake...................239
14. Buck Lake 239
15. Sweetwater Lake 239

MAP 8
1. Lone Licks Lake, Beaver Dam Lake 240
2. Walter Lake 240
3. Lava Lake 240
4. Three Licks Lake...........................240
5. Lily Lake 240
6. Soda Lake 240

MAP 9
1. Deep Creek 241
2. Colorado River (Glenwood Canyon) 241

MAP 10
1. Adams Lake 241
2. White Owl Lake 241
3. Grizzly Lake, Monument Lake 241
4. Quartzite Lake 241
5. Palmer Lake 241
6. Blue Lake 241
7. Yellow Lake 241
8. Grizzly Creek 241
9. Canyon Creek, Canyon Creek, East 241

MAP 11
1. Beaver Lake 242
2. Turquoise Lakes 242
3. Middle Lake 242
4. Slide Lake 242
5. Thomas Lake 242
6. Waterdog Lakes, Olsen Lake 242

MAP 12
1. Piney Lake, Piney River 243

2. Lost Lake.................................243
3. Crater Lake 243
4. Long Lake (Upper Piney Lake) 243
5. Booth Lake 243
6. Pitkin Lake 243
7. Booth Creek, Bighorn Creek, Pitkin Creek 243
8. Gore Creek 243
9. Eagle River 243
10. Grouse Lake 243
11. Buffalo Lake 243
12. Cross Creek 243

MAP 13
1. Rollins Reservoir..........................244
2. South Mamm Peak Lake 244

MAP 14
1. Park Lake Reservoir 244
2. Thompson Creeks 244

MAP 15
1. Dinkle Lake, West Sopris Creek 245
2. Thomas Lakes 245

MAP 16
1. Sourdough Lakes 246
2. Shingle Lake 246
3. Sugarloaf Lake, Rim Lake 246
4. Red Lake 246
5. LEDE Reservoir 246
6. Lost Lake.................................246
7. Ruedi Reservoir 246
8. Fryingpan River 246

MAP 17
1. Nolan Lakes 247
2. New York Lake 247
3. Big Pine Lake, Gold Dust Lakes 247
4. Horseshoe Lake, Big Lake, Big Spruce Lake......247
5. Mystic Island Lake, Lake Charles 247
6. Eagle Lake, Halfmoon Lake, Fairview Lake 247
7. Cross Lakes 247
8. Blodgett Lake, Harvey Lake, Treasure
   Vault Lake, Missouri Lakes, Nancy Lake..........247
9. Sherry Lake, Strawberry Lake 247
10. Tellurium Lake 247
11. Lake Josephine 247
12. Savage Lake 247
13. Mormon Lake 247
14. Lyle Lake 247
15. Sylvan Lake State Park 247
16. Leeman Lakes 247
17. Diemer Lake 247
18. Sellar Lake 247
19. Chapman Reservoir, South Fk. Fryingpan River 247
20. Chapman Lake 247
21. Nast Lake 247
22. Ivanhoe Lake 247

MAP 18
1. Lake Patricia 248
2. Cross Creek, East 248

3. Tuhare Lakes 248
4. Seven Sisters Lakes 248
5. Lake Constantine..........................248
6. Whitney Lakes 248
7. Hunky Dory Lake, Cleveland Lakes..............248
8. Mulhall Lakes 248
9. Fancy Lake 248
10. Sopris Lake, Brady Lakes 248
11. Esther Lake 248
12. Lost Lakes 248
13. Paradise Lakes.............................248
14. Bench Lakes 248
15. Homestake Lake, Upper 248
16. Isolation Lakes 248
17. Lonesome Lake 248
18. Homestake Reservoir.....................248
19. Eagle River, South Fork 248

MAP 19
1. Williams Lake 249
2. Hardscrabble Lake 249
3. Capitol Lake 249
4. Avalanche Lake 249
5. Moon Lake 249
6. Pierre Lakes 249
7. Snowmass Lake 249
8. Siberia Lake, Little Gem Lake 249
9. Snowfield Lake 249
10. Beaver Lake 249
11. Lizard Lake 249
12. Yule Lakes.................................249

MAP 20
1. Willow Lake 250
2. Maroon Lake 250
3. Crater Lake 250
4. American Lake 250
5. Cathedral Lake 250

MAP 21
1. Sawyer Lake, Hunter Creek 251
2. Granite Lakes 251
3. Fryingpan Lakes 251
4. Deadman Lake 251
5. Lost Man Lake 251
6. Terrells Lake 251
7. Scott Lake 251
8. Independence Lake 251
9. Linkins Lake 251
10. Weller Lake 251
11. Tabor Lake 251
12. Truro Lake, Jack Lake...................251
13. Grizzly Lake 251
14. Lost Man Reservoir.....................251
15. Grizzly Reservoir 251
16. Petroleum Lake, Anderson Lake, Lincoln Creek 251
17. Roaring Fork River 251

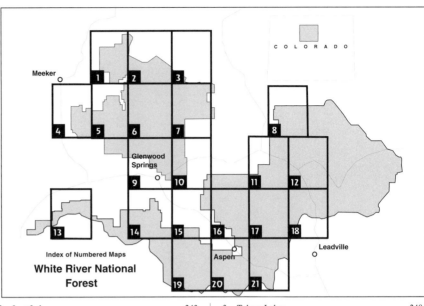

White River National
Forest

1. Aldrich Lakes #1 (7,440 ft; 50.7 ac); #2 (7,505 ft; 13.5 ac); #3 (7,555 ft; 5 ac); Rated fair for mackinaw, brook, cutthroat and rainbow. From Meeker 2.5 miles northeast on Hwy 13 to Hwy 15, northeast approx. 15 miles, turn right on (CR 51) FDR 252, 2 miles to lakes.

Map 2

1. Pagoda Lake (10,313 ft; 15 ac); Rated good for rainbow, cutthroat, brook trout. From Meeker take Hwy 13 east 1 mile to County Road 8, east on CR 8 37.2 miles to trailhead. Six miles to Pagoda Lake on motorized trail FDT 1810. (Presently allowed ATV and motorcycle.)

2. North Fork White River; Rated fair for cutthroat. Intermittent public access. Snell Creek; Rated fair for brook in upper section. See Pagoda Lake for directions.

3. Sable Lake (9,882 ft; 7 ac); Rated fair for stocked rainbow and cutthroat. Aprrox. 2.5 miles west of Shamrock Lake on FDT 1820.

4. Mirror Lake (10,010 ft; 17 ac); Shamrock Lake (9,820 ft; 4 ac); Rated good for brook. From Meeker 1 mile east on Hwy 13 to County Road 8, east 39 miles to Trappers Lake Road. South .5 mile to trailhead. Take FDT 1821 3 miles to lakes.

5. Anderson Lake (Reservoir) (9,819 ft; 2.5 ac); Rated poor for brook and rainbow. From Meeker 1 mile east on Hwy 13 to County Road 8, east 39 miles to Trappers Lake Road. South approx. 3.5 miles to trail, short hike to lake on Picket Pin Trail.

6. Lake of the Woods (10,000 ft; 8 ac); Rated good for rainbow, brook and cutthroat. From Meeker 1 mile east on Hwy 13 to County Road 8, east 39 miles to Trappers Lake Road. South approx.6 miles to trail, short hike to lake.

7. Boulder Lake (9,790 ft; 4 ac); Doris Lake (10,010 ft; 5.5 ac); Rated good for rainbow. From Meeker 1 mile east on Hwy 13 to County Road 8, east 39 miles to

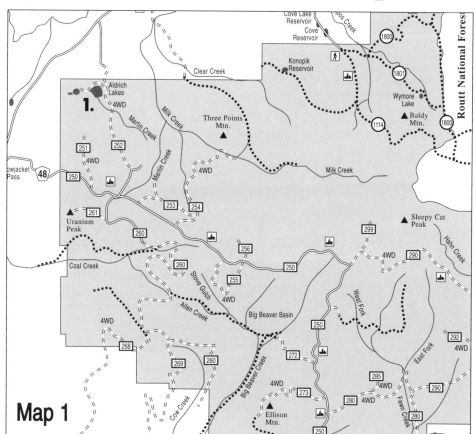

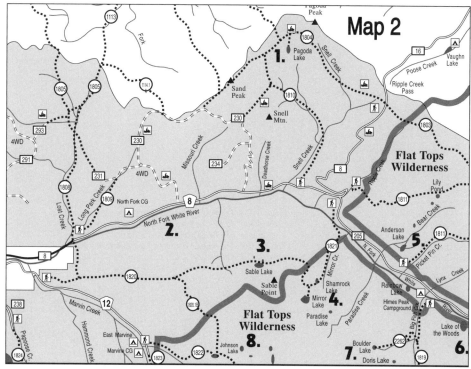

Trappers Lake Road. South approx. 6 miles to Himes Peak Campground. From Himes Peak Campground south on FDT 1819 1.25 miles to FDT 2262, west approx. 2 miles to lake. Doris Lake is south of Boulder Lake .25 mile.

8. Johnson Lake (9,020 ft; 2.5 ac); Rated fair for rainbow and brook. From Meeker 1 mile east on Hwy 13 to County Road 8, east approx. 29 miles to County Road 12, east 5 miles to Marvine Campgrounds. Approx. 2 miles east on FDT 1822.

White River National Forest Maps 3 & 4

1. Elk Lake (10,125 ft; 2 ac); Rated good for cutthroat. **McGinnis Lake (10,158 ft; 22.5 ac);** Rated good for cutthroat and rainbow. **Skinny Fish Lakes #1 (10,270 ft; 20 ac); #2 (10,270 ft; 3.8 ac);** Rated good for cutthroat, rainbow and brook. From Meeker 1 mile east on Hwy 13 to County Road 8, east 39 miles to Trappers Lake Road. South approx. 8 miles to trail. Approx. 2 miles to lake on FDT 1813.

Map 3

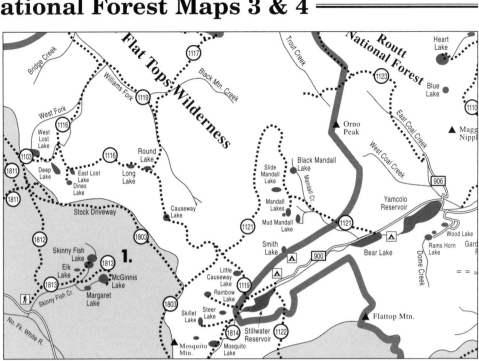

Map 4

1. Oak Ridge State Wildlife Area; Sleepycat Ponds (6,595 ft; 1.5 ac); Cutthroat. See page 94 for DOW information.

2. Miller Creek, Miller Creek, East; Miller Creek, Middle; Rated good for brook and cutthroat. From Meeker 1 mile east on Hwy 13 to County Road 8, east approx. 12 miles to County Road 57, south to Forest Boundary. Small streams with some beaver ponds. No public access lower section of Miller Creek, below Forest Boundary.

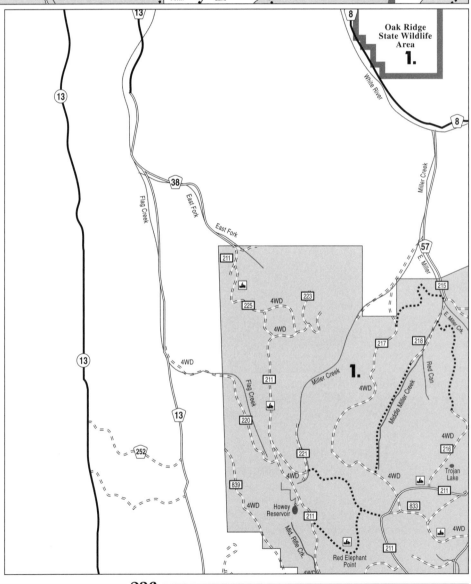

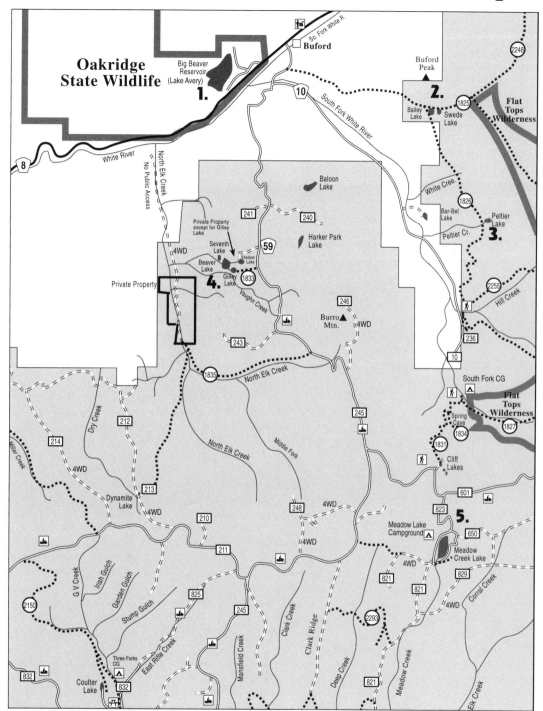

1. Oakridge State Wildlife Area, Avery Lake (Big Beaver Reservoir); (6,985 ft; 245 ac); Rated fair for rainbow and brook. See page 94 for DOW information.

2. Bailey Lake (8,790 ft; 10ac); Swede Lake (8,880 ft; 4 ac); Rated good for brook, rainbow. From Buford Community Center 4 miles east to Bailey Lake, .25 to Swede Lake. Strenuous hike.

3. Peltier Lake (8,892 ft; 13 ac); Rated good brook. South from Buford approx. 8 miles to Forest Boundary. North on FDT 1826 3.5 miles to lake.

4. Gilley Lake (8,305 ft; 9.5 ac); Rated good brook. South from Buford on County Road 59 approx. 6 miles to trail on right side of road. Short hike to lake. Nearby lakes are private.

5. Cliff Lakes (9,650 ft; 3 ac); Rated fair for brook. **Meadow Creek Lake (9,525 ft; 60 ac);** Rated fair for brook, and rainbow. From Buford south on County Road 59 (FDR 245) approx. 13 miles to FDR 601, east 2.5 miles to Cliff Lake, 1 mile to FDR 823, south 2 miles on FDR 823 to Meadow Creek Lake. Campground at Meadow Creek Lake.

White River National Forest Map 6

1. Guthrie Lakes #1 (9,280 ft; 1.5 ac); #2 (9,350 ft; 0.3 ac); Shallow Lake (9,560 ft; 2 ac); Rainbow Lake (9,520 ft; 2 ac); Rated good for brook rainbow, and cutthroat. From Meeker take Hwy 13 1 mile to County Road 8, southeast on County Road 8 28 miles to bridge, left on Marvine Creek road 6 miles to Marvin campgrounds and trailhead. Four miles on FDT 1822 to Rainbow Lake, Guthrie and Shallow Lakes are nearby.

2. Big Fish Lake (9,388 ft; 20 ac); Rated fair for cutthroat and rainbow. From Meeker 1 mile east on Hwy 13 to County Road 8, east 39 miles to Trappers Lake Road. South approx.6 miles to Himes Peak Campground. From Himes Peak Campground south on FDT 1819 3 miles to lake. **Gwendolyn Lake (9,960 ft; 3.8 ac);** Rated poor for cutthroat no designated trial to lake. **Fish Creek;** Rated good for rainbow. Public access from headwaters to Himes Peak Campground.

3. Slide Lake (8,650 ft; 5 ac); Pine Isle Lake (9,230 ft; 7 ac); Rated good for rainbow, brook, cutthroat. **Ruby Lake (9,080 ft; 5 ac);** Cutthroat. From Meeker on Hwy 13 east 1 mile to County Road 8, 28 miles northeast turn right on Marvine Creek Road, 6 miles to trailhead and campgrounds. Take FDT 1823, 3 miles to Slide Lake, 6 miles to Marvine Lakes.

4. Marvine Lake(Upper 9,317 ft; 88 ac, Lower 9,308 ft; 65 ac); Rated good for rainbow, brook and cutthroat. **Murphy Lake (9,350 ft; 4 ac);** Cutthroat. **Frosty Lake (9,850 ft; 16 ac);** Brook. **Mary Loch Lake (9,840 ft; 3 ac);** Rated good for cutthroat. **Trail Lake 10,500 ft; 3 ac);** Rainbow. **Ned Wilson Lake (11,075 ft; 3 ac);** Brook, cutthroat. See Slide

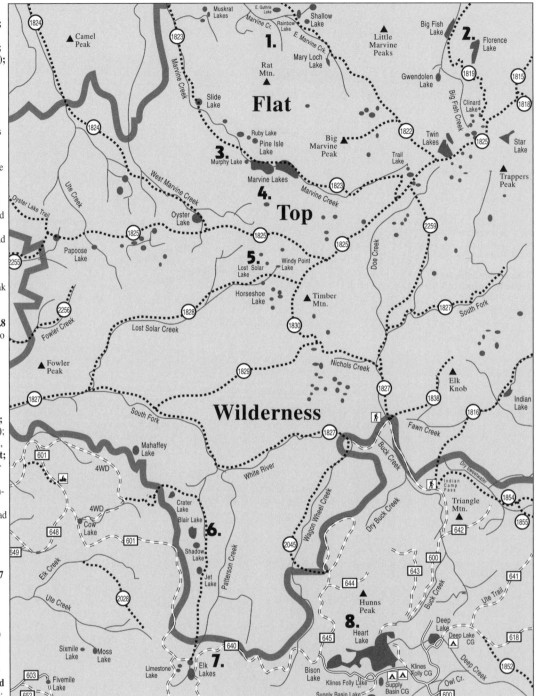

Lake. NOTE: Lakes on the Marvine Creek drainage are difficult to locate and identify, refer to topographic maps.

5. Lost Solar Lakes #1 (10,630 ft; 4 ac); #2 (11,100 ft; 1 ac); #3 (10,670 ft; 15 ac); Cutthroat.**Windy Point Lake(10,700 ft; 5.5 ac);** Cutthroat. From South Fork Campground east on FDT 1827 4 miles to FDT 1828, northeast on FDT 1828 approx. 6 miles. NOTE: Lakes are not named on Forest Service map, refer to topographic maps.

6. Crater Lake(10,263 ft; 16 ac); Cutthroat. **Blair Lake (10,466 ft; 27.5 ac);** Cutthroat, rainbow, brook. **Shadow Lake (10,456 ft; 5.7 ac);** Rainbow trout. **Jet Lake (10,335 ft; 7.5 ac);** Rainbow, brook. **Mahaffey Lake (9,783 ft; 10 ac);** Cutthroat. **Cliff Lakes (9,650 ft; 3 ac);** Rated fair for brook. **Meadow Creek Lake (9,525 ft; 60 ac);** Rated fair for brook, and rainbow. From Buford south on County Road 59 (FDR 245) approx. 13 miles to FDR 601, east approx. 8 miles to 4WD road northeast on road approx.1.5 miles to trail. Take trail east approx. 2

miles to Crater Lake. Travel south to reach lakes other than Mahaffey, no designated trail to lake.

7. Elk Lakes (10,660 ft; 4 lakes 1 to 14.3 ac); Rainbow, lakes have not been stocked recently. **Limestone Lake10,605 ft; 5 ac);** Brook. Located near wilderness boundary on FDR 601. West from Heart lake on 4WD road approx. 8 miles.

8. Heart Lake (10,708 ft; 480 ac); Rated good for brook, rainbow. Difficult bank fishing, non-motorized boats only. **Supply Basin Reservoir (10,780 ft; 18.5 ac);** Rated good rainbow. **Bison Lake (10,730 ft; 40 ac);** May contain some rainbow. **Deep Lake (10,470 ft; 37 ac);** Rated good for rainbow, brook, mackinaw trout. Special regulations for mackinaw. From Eagle 12 miles west on I-70 to Dotsero Exit. Follow signs for Sweetwater/Burns turning north onto Colorado River Road, 1.8 miles to Coffee Pot Road, FDR 600, 28 miles to turnoff, turn left at sign. Three campgrounds near lakes.

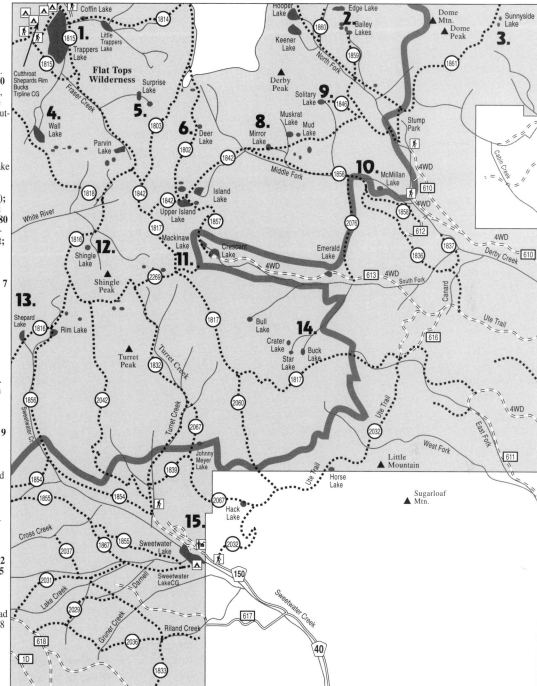

1. Coffin Lake (9,710 ft; 6 ac); Rated good for cutthroat. **Trappers Lake (9,627 ft; 270 ac);** Rated good for cutthroat, brook. **Little Trappers Lake (9,926ft; 20 ac);** Rated fair cutthroat. Special regulations apply for these lakes. **Little Trappers Creek** flows between Trapper and Little Trappers lakes. See Island Lake for directions.

2. Edge Lake (9,880 ft; 3 ac); Rated good for cutthroat and rainbow. **Keener Lake (10,780 ft; 12 ac);** Rated fair for rainbow. **Bailey Lakes (10,798 ft; 5 ac);** Rated fair for brook.

3. Sunnyside Lakes (#1 10,360 ft; 5 ac, #2 10,360 ft; 7 ac, #3 10,380 ft; 2.5 ac); Brook. From 2 miles east of Yamcolo Reservoir (Map 3), south on FDR 915 approx. 4 miles to FDT 1861, south approx. 2 miles to lake.

4. Wall Lake (10,986 ft; 45 ac); Rated good for cutthroat. From Trappers Lake south on FDT 1818 approx. 5 miles to lake. Strenuous hike.

5. Surprise Lake (11,128 ft; 9 ac); Rated fair for cutthroat and rainbow. From Trappers Lake south on FDT 1815 approx. 4 miles, no designated trail to lake.

6. Deer Lake (11,130 ft; 2.5 ac); Rated good for cutthroat. From Island Lakes north on FDT 1802 approx. 3 miles.

7. Island Lake (Upper 11,202 ft; 27 ac, Middle 11,180 ft; 15 ac, Lower 10,866 ft; 28 ac); Rated good for rainbow and cutthroat. From Meeker take Hwy 13 1 mile to County Road 8, southeast on County Road 8 39 miles to Trappers Lake Road, 10 miles to Trappers Lake trail FDT 1816. Take FDT 1816 5 miles to FDT 1836, FDT 1836 2 miles to lakes.

8. Muskrat Lake (10,220 ft; 5 ac); Mud Lakes #1 (10,300 ft; 3.5 ac); #2 (10,300 ft; 4 ac); #3 (10,260 ft; 1 ac); #4 (10,280 ft; 1 ac;) #5 (10,300 ft; 4 ac); #7 (10,056 ft; 4.5 ac); #8 (10,056 ft; 4.5 ac); Stocked rainbow, subject to winterkill.

9. Solitary Lake (10,638 ft; 12 ac); Rated fair for brook and rainbow. From trailhead at Stump Park approx. 4 miles on FDT 1846. Stump Park is reached from Burns on Cabin Creek Road 8 miles west to FDR 610. West on FDR 610 approx. 8 miles to trailhead. (FDR 610 is a 4WD road).

10. McMillan Lake (9,238ft; 10 ac); Cutthroat. From south of Stump Park on FDR 610 take FDR 612 to trailhead. Short hike to lake on FDT 1858.

11. Mackinaw Lake (10,766 ft; 30 ac); Cutthroat, mackinaw. **Crescent Lake (10,758 ft; 38 ac);** Rated fair for cutthroat and mackinaw. **Emerald Lake (9,598 ft; 10 ac);** Rated fair for brook. From Burns on Derby Road west approx. 9 miles to FDR 613. West on FDR 613 (4WD) approx 8 miles to Emerald, 12 miles to Mackinaw Lake.

12. Shingle Peak Lake (11,214 ft; 7 ac); Cutthroat. North from Rim lake on FDT 1816 approx. 3 miles.

13. Shepard Lake (10,762 ft; 30 ac); Rim Lake (10,804 ft; 14 ac); Rated fair for cutthroat and mackinaw. From approx. 3 miles north of Sweetwater Lake take FDT 1854 approx. 4 miles to FDT 1856, continue approx. 5 miles to lakes.

14. Buck Lake (11,040 ft; 4.3 ac); Cutthroat. No designated trail to lake. From FDR 613 near Emerald Lake follow stream to lake.

15. Sweetwater Lake (7,709 ft; 72 ac); Brook, brown, rainbow, kokanee. From Eagle on west on I-70 12 miles to Dotsero exit. Follow signs to Sweetwater turning north on Colorado River Road. Continue 7 miles turning left on Sweetwater Creek Road, 10 miles to Sweetwater Campground. Hand propelled boats allowed, no boat ramp.

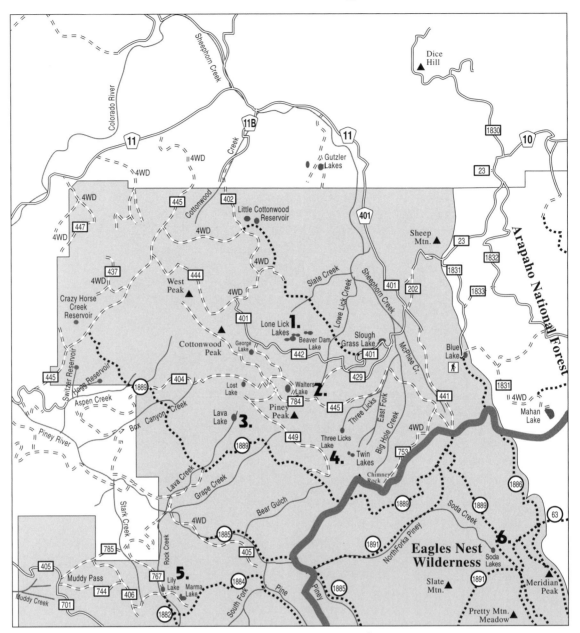

1. Lone Lick Lakes (9,780 ft; 1 ac); Rated fair for cutthroat and brook. **Beaver Dam Lake (9,560 ft; 0.3 ac);** Rated fair for cutthroat. From State Bridge northeast on County Road 11 20 miles to Forest Boundary, south on FDR 401 10 miles to lakes.

2. Walter Lake (10,360 ft; 8 ac); Rated fair for rainbow, brook and cutthroat. South of Lone Lick Lakes on FDR 442 approx. 2 miles.

3. Lava Lake (9,610 ft; 2.8 ac); Rated fair for brook. Southwest of Walters Lake approx. 2 miles, no designated trail to lake.

4. Three Licks Lake (10,030 ft; 5 ac); Rated fair for cutthroat. From Forest Boundary south on FDR 401 5 miles to

Three Licks Road south approx. 2 miles. No designated trail to lake.

5. Lily Lakes (#1 9,030 ft; 3 ac, #2 9,030 ft; 3 ac); Rated fair for brook. From Wolcott north on Hwy 131 2.5 miles to County Road 6, east on CR 6 5 miles to Forest Boundary. East On FDR 405 2 miles to FDR 406, approx. 4 miles to lake.

6. Soda Lake (10,160 ft; 2 ac); Rated fair for cutthroat. From Vail north on FDR 700 to Piney Lake, approx. 10 miles. Take FDT 1899 north approx. 7 miles, no designated trail to lake. Access from north on FDR 441.

7. Streams in the area are rated fair but are heavily fished.

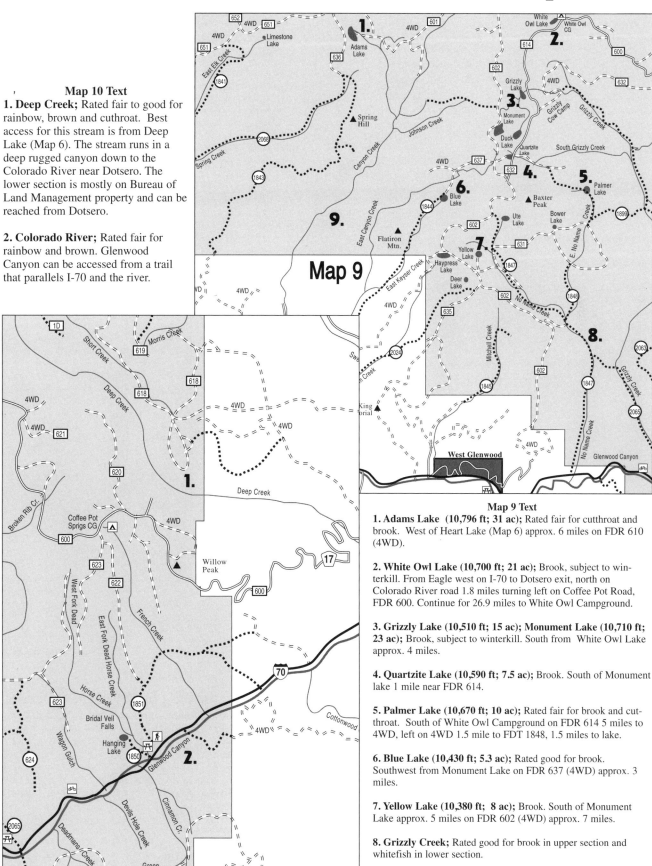

Map 10 Text

1. Deep Creek; Rated fair to good for rainbow, brown and cuthroat. Best access for this stream is from Deep Lake (Map 6). The stream runs in a deep rugged canyon down to the Colorado River near Dotsero. The lower section is mostly on Bureau of Land Management property and can be reached from Dotsero.

2. Colorado River; Rated fair for rainbow and brown. Glenwood Canyon can be accessed from a trail that parallels I-70 and the river.

Map 9 Text

1. Adams Lake (10,796 ft; 31 ac); Rated fair for cutthroat and brook. West of Heart Lake (Map 6) approx. 6 miles on FDR 610 (4WD).

2. White Owl Lake (10,700 ft; 21 ac); Brook, subject to winterkill. From Eagle west on I-70 to Dotsero exit, north on Colorado River road 1.8 miles turning left on Coffee Pot Road, FDR 600. Continue for 26.9 miles to White Owl Campground.

3. Grizzly Lake (10,510 ft; 15 ac); Monument Lake (10,710 ft; 23 ac); Brook, subject to winterkill. South from White Owl Lake approx. 4 miles.

4. Quartzite Lake (10,590 ft; 7.5 ac); Brook. South of Monument lake 1 mile near FDR 614.

5. Palmer Lake (10,670 ft; 10 ac); Rated fair for brook and cutthroat. South of White Owl Campground on FDR 614 5 miles to 4WD, left on 4WD 1.5 mile to FDT 1848, 1.5 miles to lake.

6. Blue Lake (10,430 ft; 5.3 ac); Rated good for brook. Southwest from Monument Lake on FDR 637 (4WD) approx. 3 miles.

7. Yellow Lake (10,380 ft; 8 ac); Brook. South of Monument Lake approx. 5 miles on FDR 602 (4WD) approx. 7 miles.

8. Grizzly Creek; Rated good for brook in upper section and whitefish in lower section.

9. Canyon Creek; East Canyon Creek; rated fair for brook and cutthroat. Small fast streams with lots of undergrowth.

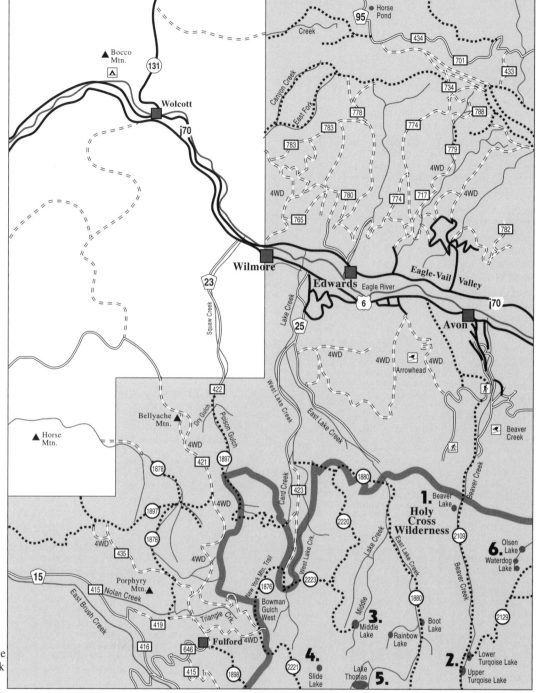

1. Beaver Lake
(9,746 ft; 7 ac); Rated good for brook and cutthroat. South of Avon on Beaver Creek Road to the trailhead in Beaver Creek ski area. Take FDT 2109 south approx. 4 miles.

2. Turquoise Lakes (#1 11,070 ft; 5.5 ac, #2 11,300 ft; 4.8 ac); Rated fair for cutthroat. South of Avon on Beaver Creek Road to the trailhead in Beaver Creek ski area. Take FDT 2109 south approx. 9 miles. Upper lake is considered better fishing.

3. Middle Lake (11,120 ft; 9.6 ac); Rated fair for cutthroat and rainbow. South from Edwards on County Road 25 to FDR 423 to trailhead (Baryeta Cabins site on Forest Service map) approx. 15 miles. Take FDT 2223 east approx. 1.5 miles to FDT 2220, south approx. 3 miles to lake.

4. Slide Lake (10,700 ft; 7.5 ac); Cutthroat. East from Fulford on 4WD road approx. 3 miles to FDT 2221, southeast approx. 3 miles to lake. Check with Forest Service about access from Polar Star Mine property.

5. Thomas Lake (12,675 ft; 14 ac); Rated good for cutthroat and rainbow. South from Edwards on County Road 25 approx. 8 miles to wilderness boundary. South approx. 9 miles on FDT 1880. Lake is west of trail approx. 2 miles, no designated trail to lake. Strenuous hiking, refer to topographic map.

6. Waterdog Lakes #1 (10,760 ft; 2 ac); #2 (11,130 ft; 0.3 ac); Cutthroat. **Olsen Lake (11,250 ft; 2 ac);** Southwest of Minturn approx. 6 miles on FDT 2129.

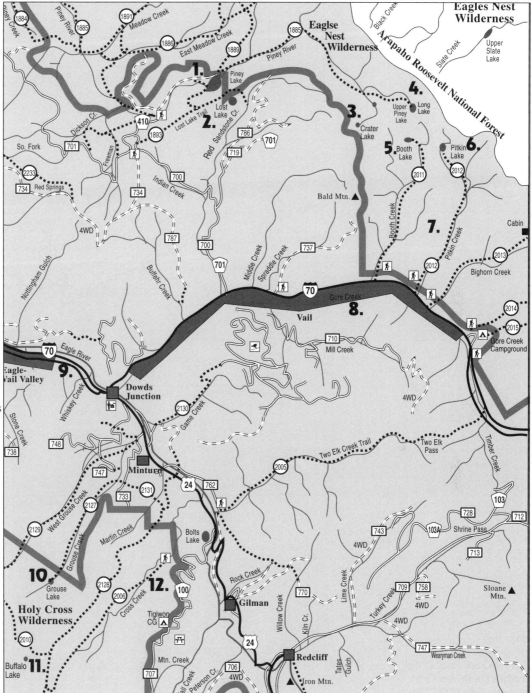

1. Piney Lake (9,342 ft; 45 ac); Rated fair for rainbow and brook. **Piney River;** Rated fair for brown, rainbow and cutthroat. North from Vail on FDR 700 approx.10 miles to lake. Heavy pressure.

2. Lost Lake (10,158 ft; 12.5 ac); Rated fair for rainbow and mackinaw. North from Vail on FDR 700 for 2.5 miles, right on FDR 786 approx. 3 miles to FDT 1893. A short hike to lake. Heavy pressure.

3. Crater Lake (11,300 ft; 8.8 ac); Stocked brook and rainbow. From Piney Lake take FDT 1885 east approx. 8 miles to Long Lake (Upper Piney). Crater lake is southwest approx 2 miles. No designated trail.

4. Long Lake (Upper Piney Lake); (11,100 ft; 7.5 ac); Rated fair for cutthroat. From Piney Lake take FDT 1885 east approx. 8 miles to Long Lake (Upper Piney).

5. Booth Lake (11,470 ft; 5 ac); Rated fair for cutthroat. From Vail east on I-70 approx. 2 miles to Exit 180, left to service road, west 1 mile to trailhead. Take FDT 2011 approx. 5 miles to lake.

6. Pitkin Lake (11,380 ft; 8 ac); Rated fair for cutthroat. From Vail east on I-70 approx. 2 miles to Exit 180, left to service road, to trailhead. Take FDT 2012 north approx. 6 miles to lake.

7. Booth Creek; Bighorn Creek; Pitkin Creek; Rated fair for brook and cutthroat. Fast small streams, best fishing in upper sections.

8. Gore Creek; Rated fair for rainbow, brown and cutthroat. Special fishing regulations. Check with Vail Visitors Center for public access information.

9. Eagle River; Rated fair for rainbow and brown. Intermittent public access. Approx. 2 miles of public access west of Dowd Junction.

10. Grouse Lake (10,690 ft; 5 ac); Rated fair for brook. Southwest of Minturn approx. 2 miles to FDT 2127, south approx. 5 miles to lake.

11. Buffalo Lake (10,910 ft; 2 ac); Cutthroat. From Minturn and Hwy 24 take FDT 2128 south for approx. 9 miles to lake.

12. Cross Creek; Rated good for brook. South of Minturn at Bolts Lake west approx. 1.5 miles to FDT 2006. Trail generally parallels stream to headwaters. Beaver ponds in upper section.

White River National Forest Map 13 & 14

1. Rollins Reservoir (10,070 ft; 4.5 ac); Stocked cutthroat trout. Southeast of Battlement Mesa on County Road 338 approx. 6 miles to 4WD road, turn right to trailhead. Take trail south for approx. 4 miles to lake.

2. South Mamm Peak Lake (10,550 ft; 3 ac); Stocked cutthroat trout. Southeast of Battlement Mesa on County Road 338 approx. 6 miles to 4WD road, continue 2 miles to trailhead. Take FDT 2160 approx. 5 miles, no designated trail to lake. Refer to topographic map.

Map 13

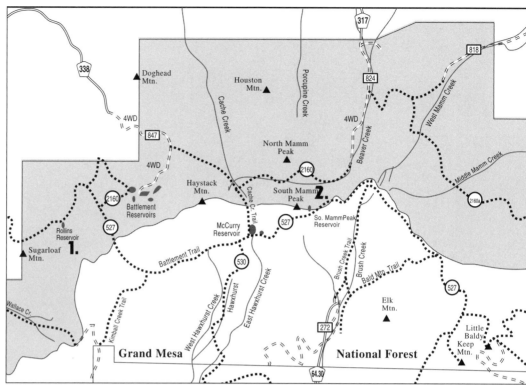

Map 14

1. Park Lake Reservoir (9,050 ft; 5.5 ac); Rainbow. From Silt exit on I-70 south 1 mile, east 1.5 miles to County Road 313, south on CR 313 19 miles to Forest Boundary. South on FDR 801 approx. 5.5 miles to lake.

2. Thompson Creeks; Rated fair for rainbow and cutthroat. West of Carbondale on County Road 108 approx. 9 miles to FDR 305. Refer to Forest Service map for public access in lower section of streams.

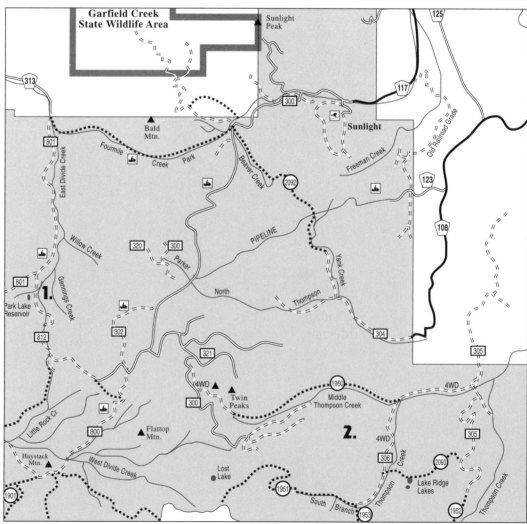

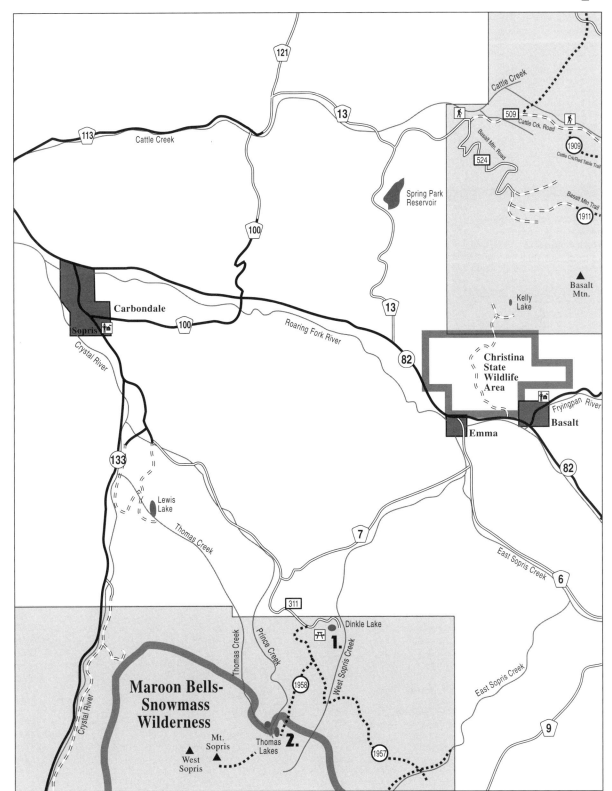

1. Dinkle Lake (8,580 ft; 9 ac); West Sopris Creek; Rated fair for rainbow and brown. South from Carbondale on Hwy 135 approx. 1.5 miles to Prince Creek Road, south on road approx. 14 miles to lake. Creek below lake is private, upper section is open to public.

2. Thomas Lakes (#1 10,200 ft; 9.2 ac, #2 10,200 ft; 9.8 ac, #3 10,200 ft; 0.9 ac); Rated good for cutthroat. South from Dinkle Lake on FDT 1958 approx. 4.5 miles to lakes.

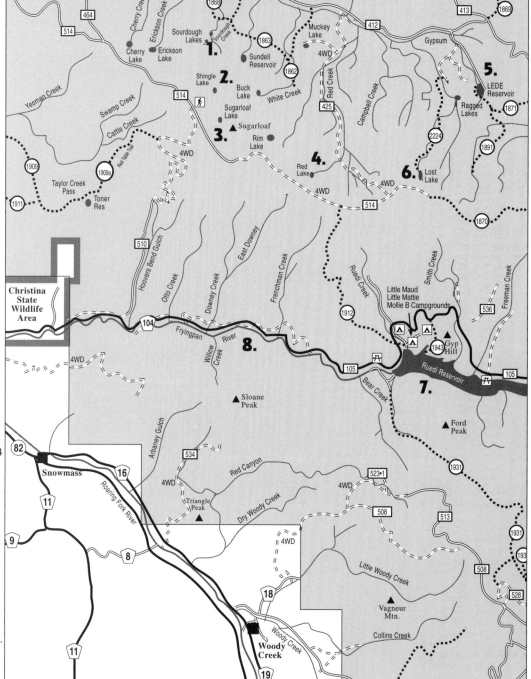

1. Sourdough Lakes (#1 9,380 ft; 0.4 ac, #2 9,450 ft; 0.3 ac, #3 9,500 ft; 0.3 ac); Rated fair for brook. South from Gypsum on FDR 412 (CR 102) approx. 14 miles to FDT 1862, 1.5 miles to Muckey Lake, 2.5 miles to end of designated trail. Sugarloaf and Rim Lakes are approx. 2 miles south of end of trail.

2. Shingle Lake (10,500 ft; 2.1 ac); Stocked cutthroat, rainbow and brook. From Cottonwood Pass southeast approx. 14 miles on County Road 79 (FDR 514). Lake is north of road approx. .25 mile, no trail.

3. Sugarloaf Lake (10,700 ft; 4 ac); Rainbow, brook and cutthroat. **Rim Lake (10,640 ft; 7 ac);** Rainbow, brook and cutthroat.

4. Red Lake (10,755 ft; 3 ac); Brook. Has not been stocked recently and tends to winterkill. South from Gypsum on FDR 412 (CR 102) approx. 15 miles to FDR 425. FDR 425 follows Red Creek south to lake. (4WD road.)

5. LEDE Reservoir (9,530 ft; 27.3 ac); Stocked rainbow. South from Gypsum on FDR 412 (CR 102) approx. 22 miles to lake. Irrigation reservoir that can draw down by late summer.

6. Lost Lake (10,860 ft; 5.1 ac); Rated fair for cutthroat and brook. Two miles north of LEDE reservoir turn west on rough road approx. 1 mile to trailhead. South on FDT 2224 approx. 4 miles to lake.

7. Reudi Reservoir (7,766 ft; 1,000 ac); Rated good for rainbow, brook, mackinaw and brown. East of Basalt 17 miles on FDR 105.

8. Fryingpan River; Rated good for rainbow, brown and cutthroat. Intermittent public access in this area. From Basalt east along County Road 104 (FDR 105). Special regulations.

Holy Cross Wilderness
Lakes numbered **1 through 5** are reached from the north from Edwards (See map 11). Numbers **7 and 8** are reached from the east from Minturn. (See map 12). Numbers **9 through 14** are reached from the west from Basalt (See map 15). Refer to the map to estimate distance of trails. Estimated Scale 1/2" = 1 mile. Numbers **10 through 22** are outside of wilderness.

1. Nolan Lakes (11,240ft; 7.2 ac, Upper 11,400 ft; 6 ac); Rated good for brook. Nolan Lake is the headwaters of Nolan Creek that is rated fair for brook and rainbow.

2. New York Lake (11,274 ft; 40 ac); Rated good for cutthroat.

3. Big Pine Lake (11,260 ft; 5 ac); Gold Dust Lakes (#1 11,522ft; 15 ac, #2 11,558 ft; 10 ac, #3 11,916 ft; 25 ac, #4 11,740 ft; 4.8 ac; #5 12,070 ft; 2 ac); Rated good for cutthroat.

4. Horseshoe Lake (11,580 ft; 10 ac); Big Lake (11,580 ft; 20 ac); Big Spruce Lake (11,600 ft; 30 ac); Rated good for cutthroat.

5. Mystic Island Lake (11,310 ft; 30 ac); Lake Charles (11,055 ft; 16.2 ac); Rated fair for brook and cutthroat.

6. Eagle Lake (10,067 ft; 9.6 ac); Halfmoon Lake (10,050 ft; 7.2 ac); Fairview Lake (10,684 ft; 17 ac); Rated good for cutthroat.

7. Cross Lakes, West (#1 11,670 ft; 5.5 ac, #2 11,790 ft; 4.8 ac, 11,835 ft; 4.8 ac,12,210 ft; 3.6 ac); Rated fair for cutthroat.

8. Blodgett Lake (11,665 ft; 25 ac); Cutthroat. **Harvey Lake (11,025 ft; 20 ac);** Brook, cutthroat. **Treasure Vault Lake (11,675 ft; 10 ac);** Cutthroat. **Missouri Lakes (#1 11,380 ft; 4 ac, #2 11,420 ft; 4 ac, #3 11,502 ft; 13 ac, #4 11,530 ft; 5 ac, #5 11,500 ft; 6 ac, #6 11,500 ft; 3 ac);** Cutthroat, brook. **Nancy Lake (11,370 ft; 7 ac);** Cutthroat.

9. Sherry Lake (11,000 ft; 7.7 ac); Strawberry Lake (#1 11,220 ft; 5 ac, #2 11,260 ft; 10 ac); Rated fair for brook.

10. Tellurium Lake (10,535 ft; 7.5 ac); Rated fair for stocked cutthroat.

11. Lake Josephine (10,000 ft; 4.1 ac); Rated fair for brook.

12. Savage Lake (Lower 11,044 ft; 22 ac, Upper11,140 ft; 12 ac); Rated fair for brook.

13. Mormon Lake (11,460 ft; 7.9 ac); Rated fair for brook.

14. Lyle Lake (11,369 ft; 10 ac); Rated fair for brook.
Outside wilderness area
15. Sylvan Lake State Park (8,510 ft; 42 ac); Rated good for rainbow and brook. See State Parks section. West Brush Creek feeds Sylvan Lake and is rated good for rainbow and brook, some beaver ponds.

16. Leeman Lakes (10,130 ft; 2 ac); Cutthroat. South of Sylvan State Park byway of Leeman Gulch approx. 2 miles. No designated trail.

17. Diemer Lake (9,519 ft; 11.5 ac); Rainbow, brook trout. East from Ruedi reservoir on FDR 104 approx.10 miles (1mile past Nast Turnoff) to FDR 105. Take FDR 105 northwest approx. 6 miles to lake. Refer to Forest Service map.

18. Sellar Lake (10,220 ft; 11.5 ac); Rated fair for rainbow. See Diemer Lake for directions.

19. Chapman Reservoir (8,560 ft; 25 ac); Rated fair for rainbow and brook. West from Ruedi Reservoir approx. 7 miles. **South Fork of the Fryingpan River** that enters the Fryingpan River near Norrie is rated good for rainbow and cutthroat.

20. Chapman Lake (9,850 ft; 23 ac); Rated fair for cutthroat, brook. From Ruedi reservoir east approx. 6 miles to Norrie. Southeast on FDR 504 approx. 6 miles to trailhead. Short hike on FDT 1923.

21. Nast Lake (8,710 ft; 8 ac); Rainbow. West of Ruedi Res. approx. 10 miles to Nast.

22. Ivanhoe Lake (10,929 ft; 72.6 ac); Rainbow. East of Ruedi Reservoir on FDR 105 approx. 20 miles to lake. **Ivanhoe Creek** is rated fair for brook and rainbow.

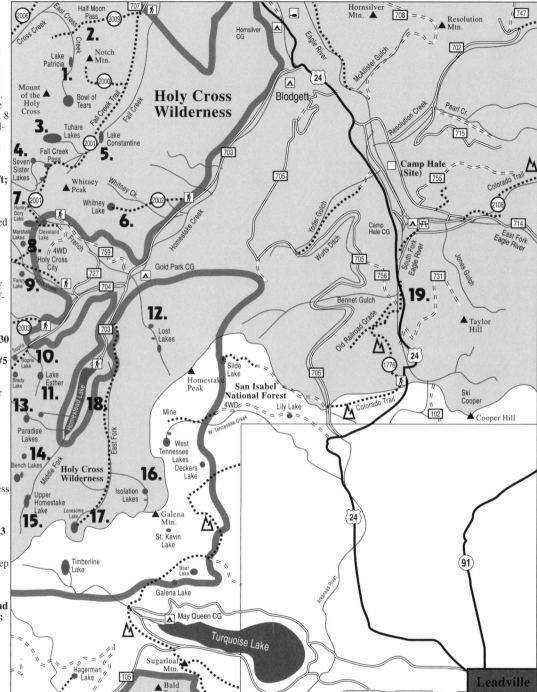

Holy Cross Wilderness
Lakes in the Holy Cross Wilderness can be reached from Minturn on the north on FDR 707 and FDR 703. Halfmoon Trailhead at the end of FDR 707 is approx. 8 west of Hwy 24, three trial-heads at Holy Cross City (Site) are approx. 14 miles west of Hwy 24

1. Lake Patricia (11,398 ft; 12 ac); Rated fair for cut-throat.

2. East Cross Creek; Rated fair for cutthroat.

3. Tuhare Lakes (Lower 12,090 ft; 12 ac, Upper 12,365 ft; 43 ac); Rated good for cutthroat. West of Lake Constitine .5 mile difficult climb.

4. Seven Sisters Lakes #1 (11,828 ft; 5 ac); #2 (12,330 ft; 2 ac); #3 (12,150 ft; 5 ac); #4 (12,300 ft; 5 ac); #5 (12,750 ft; 6.5 ac); Four lower lakes rated fair for cutthroat and brook. Upper lakes are barren.

5. Lake Constantine (11,371 ft; 13 ac); Rated fair for cutthroat, rainbow and brook. Five mile hike from Halfmoon Trailhead. Fall Creek below lake is rated good for brook. Access is difficult.

6. Whitney Lakes (#1 10,956 ft; 5.3 ac, #2 11,483 ft; 1.5 ac, #3 11,483 ft; 2 ac); Rated fair for brook, rainbow and cutthroat. Steep 3 mile climb.

7. Hunky Dory Lake (11,300 ft; 5 ac); Cleveland Lakes (11,820 ft; 12.9 ac); Rated fair for brook, cut-throat and rainbow.

8. Mulhall Lakes #1 (11,790 ft; 2.5 ac); #2 (11,960 ft; 6.3 ac); Rated fair for rainbow and cut-throat.

9. Fancy Lake (11,540 ft; 8 ac); Rated fair for brook.

10. Sopris Lake (11,030 ft; 1 ac); Brady Lakes #1 (10,850 ft; 1 ac); #2 (10,984 ft; 8.9 ac); Rated fair for cutthroat.

11. Esther Lake (11,310 ft; 2.4 ac); Rated fair for brook.

12. Lost Lakes (#1 10,756 ft; 2.5 ac, #2 10,990 ft; 2.5 ac, #3 10,993 ft; 10 ac, #4 11,180 ft; 7.5 ac); Rated fair for cutthroat.

13. Paradise Lakes (#1 11,230 ft; 7.4 ac, #2 11,190 ft; 12 ac, #3 11,560 ft; 2.4 ac, #4 11,590 ft; 4.2 ac, #5 11,500 ft; 1 ac); Rated fair for cutthroat.

14. Bench Lakes (#1 11,140 ft; 3 ac, #2 11,220 ft; 12 ac); Rated fair for cutthroat.

15. Upper Homestake Lake (10,925 ft; 23.3 ac); Rated good for cut-throat.

16. Isolation Lakes (#1 11,580 ft; 5 ac, #2 11,620 ft; 5 ac); Rated good for cutthroat.

17. Lonesome Lake (#1 11,160 ft; 6 ac, #2 11,350 ft; 10 ac); Rated fair for cutthroat, rainbow and brook.

Outside wilderness area
18. Homestake Reservoir; (10,260 ft; 210 ac); Rated fair for rainbow, brook and cutthroat. Steep banks. From Minturn, southeast approx. 9 miles to FDR 703, southwest approx. 14 miles to lake.

19. South Fork Eagle River; Rated fair for rainbow and brook in lower section, poor in upper section. Parallels Hwy 24.

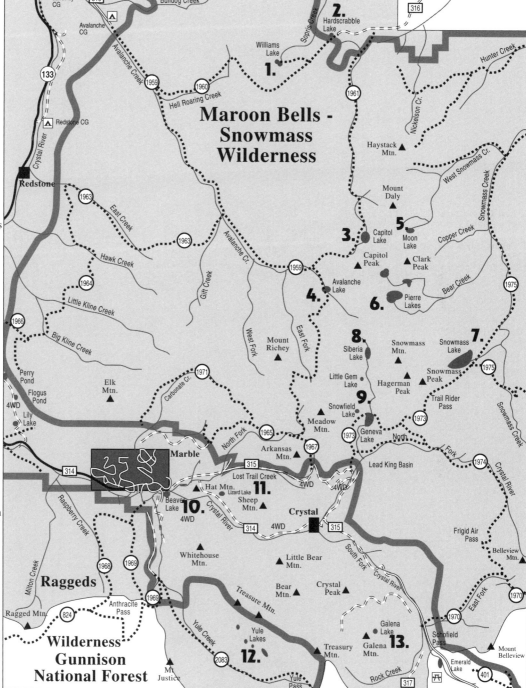

1. Williams Lake (10,815 ft; 11.6 ac); Rated fair for brook and cutthroat. From Carbondale south on Hwy 133 for 12.5 miles, left at Avalanche Creek, follow road 2.5 miles to Avalanche Campground and parking area. Take FDT 1959 3 miles to FDT 1960, approx. 8 miles to Williams Lake an 9.5 miles to Hardscrabble Lake. Lakes can be reached from the north. South from Snowmass on County Road 9 to FDR 316 (Last section 4WD).

2. Hardscrabble Lake (10,130 ft; 2.4 ac); Rated poor for cutthroat. See Williams Lake for directions.

3. Capitol Lake (11,590 ft; 21.7 ac); Stocked cutthroat. Irrigation lake that draws down in summer.

4. Avalanche Lake (10,695 ft; 8.5 ac); Stocked cutthroat. Avalanche Creek is rated poor for rainbow. From Carbondale south on Hwy 133 for 12.5 miles, left at Avalanche Creek, follow road 2.5 miles to Avalanche Campground and parking area. Take FDT 1959 11 miles to lake.

5. Moon Lake (11,720 ft; 9.9 ac); Stocked cutthroat. See Snowmass Lake for directions.

6. Pierre Lakes (#1 12,070 ft; 4.3 ac, #2 12,130 ft; 12.9 ac, #3 12,190 ft; 44.3 ac, #4 upper 12,340 ft; 15.7 ac); Rated good for cutthroat. Upper lake is considered best. See Snowmass Lake for directions.

7. Snowmass Lake (10,980 ft; 81.5 ac); Rated good for brook, rainbow and cutthroat. Snowmass Creek is rated good for brook, with beaver ponds. From Snowmass Village west to FDR 119 and trailhead. Take FDT 1975 approx. 9 miles to lake. Moon Lake and Pierre Lakes are reached from this trail, no designated trail to lakes. Refer to topographic maps.

8. Siberia Lake (11,860 ft; 3.3 ac); Cutthroat. **Little Gem Lake (11,660 ft; 3 ac);** Rated fair to poor for cutthroat and brook.

9. Snowfield Lake (11,480 ft; 3.0 ac); Geneva Lake (10,936 ft; 26.3 ac); Rated fair for brook. North Fork and South Fork Crystal River. Rated fair

for brook and cutthroat. Fast streams, snow can prevent access until mid-summer. From Crystal 4wd road north to Lead King Basin approx. 2 miles to trailhead. Take FDT 1973 approx. 2 miles to lakes.

10. Beaver Lake (7,956 ft; 25 ac); Rated fair for brook, and rainbow. See page 88 for DOW information.

11. Lizard Lake (8,715 ft; 1.5 ac); Rated fair for brook. East of Marble 2 miles.

12. Yule Lakes (#1 12,140 ft; 7 ac, #2 11,910 ft; 7.6 ac, #3 11,920 ft; 1.4 ac, #4 11,840 ft; 3.3 ac, #5 11,860 ft; 10 ac); rated poor for cutthroat.

White River National Forest Map 20

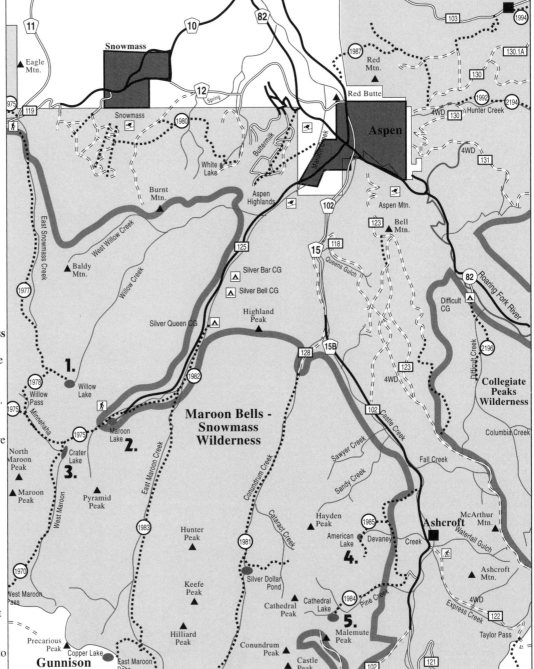

Maroon Bells-Snowmass Wilderness

Magnificent view and the ambiance make this area one of the most heavily visited areas in Colorado. All lakes and streams in this area receive heavy pressure. Reservations are required to camp.

1. Willow Lake (11,795 ft; 19.3 ac); Rated good for brook and cutthroat. Approx. 4 miles west of Maroon Lake. Difficult hike.

2. Maroon Lake (9,580 ft; 25 ac); Rated fair for rainbow and brook. From Aspen .5 mile west on Hwy 82 turn left on Maroon Creek Road at the stop light. 9.5 miles to Maroon Creek parking area. From mid-June through September the road is closed from 8:30 a.m. to 5 p.m. and you need to take a shuttle bus from Ruby Park in Aspen. Phone Roaring Fork Transit @ 970-925-8484 for information.

3. Crater Lake (10,076 ft; 16 ac); Rated poor, may be barren. Approx. 2 miles south of Maroon Lake. Camping in designated sites only.

4. American Lake (11,365 ft; 2.8 ac); Rated fair for rainbow. From Aspen west on Hwy 62 .5 mile to Maroon Creek road immediately turn left onto Castle Creek Road, travel 10 miles to parking area on right. A strenuous 3.2 mile hike on FDT 1985 to lake.

5. Cathedral Lake (11,866 ft; 16.8 ac); Rated fair for cutthroat, brook and rainbow. From Aspen west on Hwy 62 .5 mile to Maroon Creek road immediately turn left onto Castle Creek Road, travel 12.2 miles, turn right after passing through Ashcroft onto gravel road, .5 mile to trailhead. Difficult 3.2 mile hike on FDT 1984.

6. Streams in this area are rated fair to poor for rainbow, brook and cutthroat.

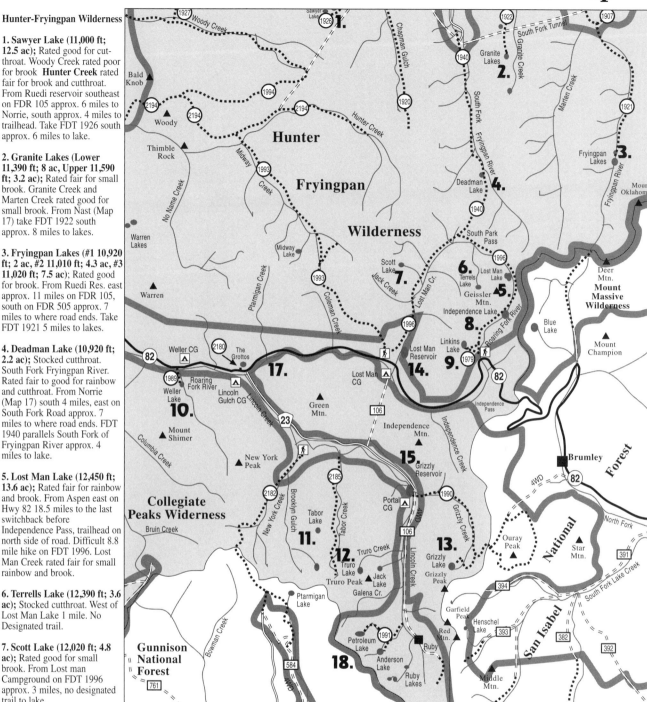

Hunter-Fryingpan Wilderness

1. Sawyer Lake (11,000 ft; 12.5 ac); Rated good for cutthroat. Woody Creek rated poor for brook **Hunter Creek** rated fair for brook and cutthroat. From Ruedi reservoir southeast on FDR 105 approx. 6 miles to Norrie, south approx. 4 miles to trailhead. Take FDT 1926 south approx. 6 miles to lake.

2. Granite Lakes (Lower 11,390 ft; 8 ac, Upper 11,590 ft; 3.2 ac); Rated fair for small brook. Granite Creek and Marten Creek rated good for small brook. From Nast (Map 17) take FDT 1922 south approx. 8 miles to lakes.

3. Fryingpan Lakes (#1 10,920 ft; 2 ac, #2 11,010 ft; 4.3 ac, #3 11,020 ft; 7.5 ac); Rated good for brook. From Ruedi Res. east approx. 11 miles on FDR 105, south on FDR 505 approx. 7 miles to where road ends. Take FDT 1921 5 miles to lakes.

4. Deadman Lake (10,920 ft; 2.2 ac); Stocked cutthroat. South Fork Fryingpan River. Rated fair to good for rainbow and cutthroat. From Norrie (Map 17) south 4 miles, east on South Fork Road approx. 7 miles to where road ends. FDT 1940 parallels South Fork of Fryingpan River approx. 4 miles to lake.

5. Lost Man Lake (12,450 ft; 13.6 ac); Rated fair for rainbow and brook. From Aspen east on Hwy 82 18.5 miles to the last switchback before Independence Pass, trailhead on north side of road. Difficult 8.8 mile hike on FDT 1996. Lost Man Creek rated fair for small rainbow and brook.

6. Terrells Lake (12,390 ft; 3.6 ac); Stocked cutthroat. West of Lost Man Lake 1 mile. No Designated trail.

7. Scott Lake (12,020 ft; 4.8 ac); Rated good for small brook. From Lost man Campground on FDT 1996 approx. 3 miles, no designated trail to lake.

8. Independence Lake (12,490 ft. 8.6 ac); Rated fair for brook. See Lost Man lake for directions.

9. Linkins Lake (12,008 ft; 11.4 ac); Rated fair for rainbow and brook. Short steep .6 mile hike on FDT 1979. From Aspen east on Hwy 82 18.5 miles to the last switchback before Independence Pass, trailhead on north side of road.
Collegiate Peaks Wilderness
10. Weller Lake (9,550 ft; 8.6 ac); Rated fair for rainbow. Short hike from Weller Campground on FDT 1989 to lake.

11. Tabor Lake (12,320 ft; 5.7 ac); Cutthroat. From Hwy 82 south approx. 4 miles on Lincoln Creek Road. Take FDT 2185 approx. 3 miles. No designated trail.

12. Truro Lake (12,190 ft; 6.7 ac); Jack Lake (12,240 ft; 2.4 ac); Rated good for cutthroat. Short steep hike to lakes. South from Grizzley Reservoir approx. 1.5 miles. No designated trail up Truro Creek.

13. Grizzly Lake (12,510 ft; 8 ac); Rainbow.

Outside Wilderness Area
14. Lost Man Reservoir (10,640 ft; 7.2 ac); Rated fair for rainbow and brook. North of Lost Man campground on Hwy 82.

15. Grizzly Reservoir (11,537 ft; 27.5 ac); Rated fair for rainbow. From Aspen east on Hwy 82 to Lincoln Creek Road, south 6.5 miles to Portal Campground.

16. Petroleum Lake (12,310 ft; 12.4 ac); Rated good for rainbow. **Anderson Lake (11,840 ft; 8.6 ac);** Rated fair for rainbow. Moderate 1. 8 mile hike on FDT 1991. **Lincoln Creek** rated fair for rainbow. From Aspen east on Hwy 82 to Lincoln Creek Road, south 6.5 miles to Portal Campground. From campground 4WD road 3.3 miles to trailhead.

17. Roaring Fork River; Rated good for rainbow, whitefish and brown. Gold Medal Waters special regulations.

Larimer County Parks - Carter Reservoir

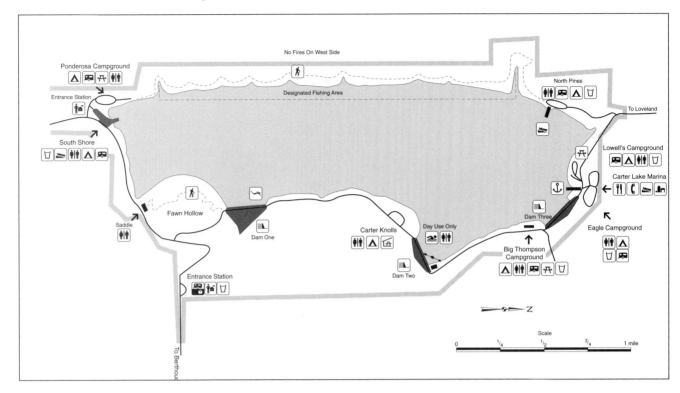

Directions: From Denver, take I-25 north to the Berthoud exit (Highway 56). Travel west on Highway 56 through Berthoud. Highway will take a northern turn, then turn west again. At that point, the road will take you along the east shoreline.

Fee: Daily pass or annual pass.

Size: 1,140 surface acres.

Elevation: 5,760 feet.

Maximum Depth: 100 feet.

Facilities: Marina, restrooms, water, dump station, restaurant.

Boat Ramp: Multi-lane concrete boat ramp available on the north end at the marina, South Shore Marina and at North Pine.

Fish: Trout, kokanee salmon, largemouth bass and perch. Boat fishing trolling flashers with bait and lures. Perch best along the west shore and in the coves. Largemouth bass in the cove areas.

Recreation: Sailing, water skiing, personal water craft, fishing, boating, wind surfing

Camping: Four campgrounds with 190 campsites. Picnic tables, fire rings. Overnight camping fee. Camping is on a first-come, first-served basis, no reservations. Camping units to 35 feet.

Information: Handicapped accessible restrooms located at South Shore and North pines boat launching areas. Eagle and Big Thompson Campgrounds.

Special Restrictions: Quiet hours 10 p.m. to 6 a.m. No fires on the west side of the lake. Swim beach is located at Dam #2. Swimming is prohibited elsewhere. Cliff diving and jumping into the water is prohibited.

Controlling Agency: Larimer County Parks Department. Lake office phone (970) 679-4570.

Carter Lake is part of the Colorado-Big Thompson Project which is operated by the United States Bureau of Reclamation and the Northern Colorado Water Conservancy District.

Carter Lake Reservoir is one of the two main project storage reservoirs in the east slope distribution system. It is filled by the pumping unit at Flatiron Power Plant which pumps from Flatiron Afterbay through a connecting pressure tunnel 1 1/3 mile long. The pumping life through this tunnel varies from a minimum of 162 feet to a maximum of 286 feet, depending on the water surface elevation in the reservoir. During peak power demands on the project system, the flow through this tunnel can be reversed and the pumping unit at Flatiron used as a generator.

The reservoir as constructed has a total capacity of 112,000 acre-feet of which approximately 109,000 acre-feet is active or usable. The partly natural site provides the cheapest storage per acre-foot of any project reservoir. The outlet, which is in the 285 foot high main dam on the southeast side of the reservoir, has a capacity of 625 cubic feet per second. In addition to the main dam, there are two smaller dikes across low saddles in the surrounding hills. Construction of Carter Lake Reservoir began in July 1950 and was completed in October 1952.

Carter Lake Reservoir is popular for fishing, sailing, camping and water skiing. The park is open year round.

Directions: From Denver north on I-25 to Fort Collins Harmony-Timnath exit. West on Harmony Road to a "T" in the road. Turn right (north) onto Taft Hill Road about one mile. Turn left (west) onto County Road 38E, which will take you to the reservoir.

Fee: Daily or annual park pass.
Size: 1,875 acres.
Elevation: 5,430 feet.
Maximum Depth: 180 feet.
Facilities: A service complete recreation area that includes a Marina and food store.
Boat Ramp: Two ramps are available at Satanka Cove on the north end, one at South Bay Landing on the south end and one at Inlet Bay Marina on the southwest side. All ramps are concrete.
Fish: Largemouth and smallmouth bass, rainbow trout, walleye and perch. Fair to good for trout either shore fishing or trolling. Fishing good for smallmouth bass and occasional largemouth. Most bass are 2-3 pounds, with some up to 4 pounds. Bass under 15 inches must be released. Walleye fishing can be great during the early spring. Trophy walleye up to 16 pounds, with many in the 10-12 pound range, are caught every year. Walleye restricted to an 18-inch minimum. Perch fishing is fair to good.
Recreation: All water recreation sports, scuba diving, fishing and camping.
Camping: There are 180 designated campsites between Satanka Cove, Soldier Canyon Cove, Eltuck Bay, Orchard Cove, Quarry Cove, Inlet Bay, South Bay and Turkey Point campgrounds. All campgrounds feature vault toilets, water, picnic tables and fire grates. Open camping also is allowed where access allows along shorelines of reservoir.
Controlling Agency: Larimer County Parks Department
Information: Park office (970) 226-4517. Handicapped accessible restrooms located at South Bay boat launch, Inlet Bay Marina, Turkey Point and North Inlet Campgrounds.

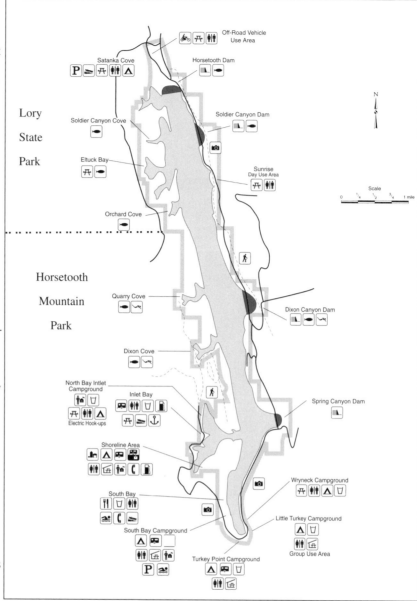

Horsetooth Reservoir, located just west of Fort Collins and adjacent to Lory State Park, was constructed as part of the Big Thompson Water Project. The reservoir is six and a half miles long and covers 1,875 surface acres. It was formed by the construction of four large earth-filled dams. Horsetooth, Spring Canyon, Dixon Canyon and Soldier Canyon Dams, each approximately 210 feet high, are built across openings in the long hogback forming the eastern side of the reservoir. Horsetooth Dam is constructed across the north end of the foothill "glade" formed by the uplift ridges.

The reservoir covers what once was an old quarry town named Stout. Stout was constructed by the Greeley, Salt Lake and Pacific Railroad, under the charter and making of the Union Pacific Railroad. The area had an almost limitless supply of high grade fine-grained sandstone; the variety of color and quality of the sandstone made it popular for use as building material in the late 1800's. Boats using sonar for fish-finding may locate some old structures left standing when Horsetooth Reservoir was filled. Other traces of the quarry activity may be found on the north end of the reservoir.

The scenic setting and the variety of recreation activities makes Horsetooth Reservoir one of the top recreation areas on the front range.

Wolford Mountain Reservoir

Directions: Take I-70 west to Silverthorne exit. North from Silverthorne on Colorado 9 for 38 miles to Kremmling. West on US 40 from Kremmling 5 miles to the Ritschard Dam and 2 miles farther to the Wolford Mountain Recreation Area. These are the only vehicular access roads to the reservoir.

Fee: Camping and day use fee required.

Size: 1,450 surface acres.

Elevation: 7,500 feet.

Maximum Depth: 110 feet.

Facilities: Picnic tables, shelters, fire grates, water, electricity, trash removal, dump station.

Boat Ramp: Concrete boat ramp available at the Recreation Area.

Fish: Initial stocking in 1995 with rainbow and cutbow.

Recreation: Camping, fishing.

Camping: One full service campground available, with 48 campsites, all with electricity. Restrooms with composting toilets and running water. Two group use sites by reservation only. Day use area with shelter, picnic tables and charcoal grills.

Controlling Agency: Colorado River Water Conservation District.

Information: The reservoir is located on Muddy Creek, about 5 miles northwest of the town of Kremmling. The reservoir extends up Muddy Creek a distance of 5.5 miles, and has a surface area of 1,450 acres. The dam site on the west flank of Wolford Mountain, a prominent local feature which consists of precambrian granite resting upon cretaceous shales. The shoreline of Wolford Mountain Reservoir consists of Pierre and Niobrara shales, with vegetation consisting of sage brush and dryland grasses.

Wolford Mountain Project Office.
(970) 724-9590.

The Wolford Mountain Reservoir has a capacity of 60,000 acre feet of water, 24,000 acre-feet is owned by the Denver Water Department for dry year water supply use. The balance of the water is split between Middle Park Water Conservancy District, general west slope demands, environmental and mitigation uses, and conservation pool. The main outlet capacity is 800 cubic feet per second, the service spillway capacity is 24,000 cfs, with an emergency spillway capable of passing an additional 20,000 cfs.

For information on Handicapped accessible facilities call the project office.

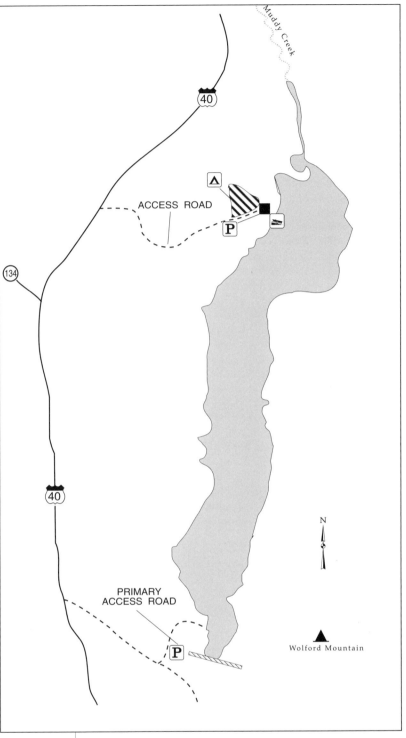

Abbreviation Key

ANF = Arapaho/Roosevelt National Forest
ANRA = Arapaho National Recreation Area
FRS = Front Range Section
GMNF = Grand Mesa National Forest
GNF = Gunnison National Forest
LCP = Larimer County Parks
PNF = Pike national Forest
RGNF = Rio Grande National Forest
RMNP = Rocky Mountain National Park
RMNP = Rocky Mountain National Park
RNF = Routt National Forest
SINF = San Isabel National Forest
SJNF = San Juan National Forest
SP = State Park
STL = Sate Trust Lands
SWA = State Wildlife Area
UNF = Uncompahgre National Forest
WRNF = White River National Forest

Name
Page No.

Abyss Lake (FR) 39
Abyss Lake (PNF)..172
Adams County Fairground Lakes (FR 12
Adams Fork (RGNF) 189
Adams Lake (WRNF)......................................241
Adobe Creek Reservoir(SWA) 86
Agate Creek (GNF)...167
Agate Creek (STL)...82
Agua Fria Lake (RNF) 98
Alamosa River (RGNF) 189
Alan Lake (SINF) 208
Albert Lake (RNF)..198
Alberta Park Reservoir (RGNF) 189
Alberta Park Reservoir (SWA) 92
Alder Creek (RGNF).......................................179
Alder Creek (RGNF).......................................188
Alder Lake (RNF)...200
Aldrich Lakes (WRNF)...................................235
Alexander Lake (GMNF) 129
Allen Basin Reservoir (RNF) 201
Alta Lakes (UNF) 231
Alver Jones Lake (RGNF) 191
American Lake (WRNF)..................................250
Anderson Lake (WRNF)..........................235, 251
Andrews Lake (SWA) 94
Andrews Lake (SJNF)......................................221
Anglemeyer Lake (SINF) 209
Annie Lake (SJNF) 222
Antero Reservoir (PNF) 176
Antero Reservoir (STL) 82
Antero Reservoir (SWA) 93
Anthracite Creek (GNF)..................................152
Anthracite Creek, East (GNF).........................153
Anthracite Creek, Middle (GNF) 153
Anthracite Creek, North (GNF) 153
Arapaho Creek (ANF)......................................118
Arapaho Lakes (FR) 33
Archuletta Lake (RGNF)..................................187
Arkansas River (SP) 58
Arkansas River (STL) 80
Arkansas River (SWA) 86, 93, 86, 94
Arkansas River, East Fork (SINF) 205
Arkansas River, South (SINF) 210
Armstrong Creek (RNF) 194
Arrowhead Lake (RMNP)................................101

Arvada Reservoir (FR) 14
Atkiinson Creek (GMNF)................................136
Atkinson Reservoir (GMNF) 136
Aurora Reservoir (FR)......................................23
Avalanche Lake (WRNF)................................249
Avery Lake (Big Beaver Res.) (WRNF)..94, 237
Badger Creek (STL) 80
Bailey Lakes (WRNF) 237, 239
Baldwin Lake (SINF) 210
Baldy Lake (GNF)...169
Balman Reservoir (SINF) 212
Balsam Park Pond (FR).....................................16
Banana Lake (ANF)..118
Banana Lake (FR)..31
Banjo Lake (SINF) 212
Banner Lakes (SWA)..95
Barker Reservoir (FR)..29
Barnes Meadow Reservoir (ANF)...................111
Barnum Park Lake (FR)......................................16
Baron Lake (GMNF) 130
Barr Lake (SWA)...86
Barr Lake SP 11
Battlement Reservoirs (GMNF) 149
Bear Creek (FR)..41
Bear Creek (GNF) 159
Bear Creek (RGNF) 184
Bear Creek (SJNF) 211, 218
Bear Creek (SWA)...86
Bear Creek Ponds (FR).......................................17
Bear Creek Reservoir (FR) 17
Bear Lake (RGNF) 189
Bear Lake (RNF)..202
Bear Lakes (SINF) 209, 215
Bear Lakes (RNF) 196
Beartrack Lakes (FR) 39
Beaver Brook Creek (STL)..................................80
Beaver Creek (ANF) 109, 112, 116
Beaver Creek (GNF) 164
Beaver Creek (PNF)..................................172, 174
Beaver Creek (RNF) 200
Beaver Creek (SWA)...........................88, 94, 95
Beaver Creek Reservoir (RGNF) 188
Beaver Creek Reservoir (SWA) 88
Beaver Creek, East (GNF) 162
Beaver Creek, Little (ANF)..............................112
Beaver Dam Lake (WRNF) 240
Beaver Flat Tops Ponds (RNF) 200
Beaver Lake (RNF)..196
Beaver Lake (RNF)..200
Beaver Lake (SWA)..88
Beaver Lake (UNF)..230
Beaver Lake (WRNF) 242, 249
Beaver Lake (GMNF).......................................127
Beaver Ponds (GNF)..159
Bell Roth Park Pond (FR)...................................13
Bellaire Lake (ANF)..109
Bellows Creek (RGNF).....................................183
Bellows Creek, East (RGNF)............................183
Bellows Creek, West (RGNF)............................183
Bench Lake (ANF) 111
Bench Lakes (WRNF)......................................248
Berkeley Lake (FR)..15
Betty Lake (FR)...32
Betty Lake (SJNF)..222
Big Buck Creek (RGNF)....................................181
Big Creek (GMNF)..136
Big Creek (RNF)...197

Big Creek Lake (RNF) 196
Big Creek Lake (RNF) 198
Big Creek Reservoir #1 (GMNF) 136
Big Creek Reservoir (UNF)..............................230
Big Dutch Creek (RMNP).................................101
Big Fish Lake (WRNF).....................................238
Big Lake (RGNF) 190
Big Lake (WRNF)..247
Big Meadows Reservoir (RGNF) 92,187
Big Pine Lake (WRNF)....................................247
Big Spruce Lake (WRNF)................................247
Big Thompson Ponds (SWA)..............................90
Big Thompson River (ANF).............................115
Big Thompson River (RMNP) 102
Big Thompson River, North Fork (SWA)........91
Bighorn Creek (WRNF)...................................243
Bighorn Lakes (RNF) 196
Bill Moore Lake (FR) 36
Birdland Lake (FR) 15
Bison Lake (WRNF)..238
Black Hollow Creek (ANF) 112
Black Lake (RMNP)...102
Black Lakes..122
Black Mountain Lake (RGNF).........................182
Blair Lake (WRNF)..238
Blodgett Lake (WRNF)....................................247
Blue Heron Pond (FR) 18
Blue Lake (ANF)..........................111, 114, 118
Blue Lake (GMNF)..147
Blue Lake (GNF)..153
Blue Lake (RGNF)...191
Blue Lake (RNF)..196
Blue Lake (SINF) 206, 215
Blue Lake (STL)..80
Blue Lake (WRNF)..241
Blue Lakes (SINF) 214
Blue Lakes (UNF)..231
Blue Mesa Reservoir (GNF) 165
Blue River (ANF)..................................120,122
Blue River (SWA) 95
Bob Lake (FR)...32
Boedecker Reservoir (SWA)..............................90
Bolam Pass Lake (SJNF)..................................220
Bonham Reservoir (GMNF)............................136
Bonita Creek (GMNF) 139
Bonita Reservoir (GMNF) 139
Bonny Reservoir (SP) 59, 95
Booth Creek (WRNF).......................................243
Booth Lake (WRNF)..243
Borns Lake (SJNF) 226
Boss Lake Reservoir (SINF)............................210
Boswell Creek (ANF) 106
Boulder Creek (ANF)......................................122
Boulder Creek, Middle (FR) 41
Boulder Creek, North (FR) 41
Boulder Creek, South (FR) 42
Boulder Lake (GNF) 162
Boulder Lake (WRNF) 235
Boulder Lakes (ANF) 122
Boulder Ponds (FR)...28
Boulder Reservoir (FR).....................................26
Bowen Lake (ANF)..114
Bowles Grove Pond (FR)...................................20
Bowman Creek (GNF)......................................155
Box Creek (RNF)..195
Box Creek (RNF) 196
Box Lake (RMNP) 104

Appendix

Boyd Lake (SP) 48
Brady Lakes (WRNF) 248
Brainard Lake (ANF) 29, 118
Branch Creek, South (SINF).........212
Brewery Creek (RGNF) 179
Brighton City Park Pond (FR) 12
Brim Pond (FR) 13
Brook Lake (RNF) 200
Broomfield Community Park Ponds (FR) 12
Brown Lakes (RGNF)..............89, 182
Browns Creek (SINF) 210
Browns Creek, Little (SINF).........210
Browns Lake (ANF) 112
Brush Creek (STL) 82
Brush Creek Lakes (SINF)..........212
Brush Creeks (GNF) 154
Brush Creeks (SINF) 212
Brush Hollow Reservoir (SWA) 88
Buchanan Creek (ANF)...............118
Buck Lake (WRNF) 239
Buckeye Lake (SINF) 205
Buckhorn Creek (ANF) 113
Buckles Lake (SJNF) 227
Buckskin Creek (PNF)................174
Buffalo Lake (WRNF) 243
Buffs Lake (GMNF) 133
Bull Creek Reservoir #1, 2, 5 (GMNF) 128
Bull Creek (GMNF) 128
Bullion King Lake (SJNF) 218
Bundy Lake (RNF) 200
Burn Creek (RNF).......................197
Burning Bear Creek (PNF) 172
Burns Reservoir (RNF)...............198
Bushnell Lakes (SINF) 211
Buzzard Creek (GMNF) 145
Byron Lake (FR) 37
Cabin Creek (ANF)......................116
Cabin Creek, Roaring Fork of (RMNP) 104
Cache la Poudre River (RMNP) 101
Cache le Poudre River (ANF).......113
Cache le Poudre River S.Fk.(ANF) 113
Cache le Poudre River, N. Fk. (ANF)......109
California Gulch (RGNF) 184
Camenisch Park Pond (FR)...........13
Camp Lakes (ANF) 111
Canadian River (STL) 81
Canyon Creek (GNF) 167
Canyon Creek (UNF) 232
Canyon Creek (WRNF)................241
Canyon Creek,East (WRNF)........241
Capitol Lake (WRNF)..................249
Carbon Creek (GNF)...................159
Carl Park Pond (FR) 15
Carmody Park Pond (FR) 18
Carp Lake (GMNF)......................129
Carson Lake (GMNF) 147
Cary Lake (ANF).........................111
Cascade Creek (GNF) 157
Cascade Creek (RMNP) 101
Cascade Creek (SJNF) 220
Castilleja Lake (SJNF).................221
Castle Creek (GNF)....................159
Catamount Reservoir, North (PNF) 177
Catamount Reservoir, South (PNF) 177
Cataract Lakes (ANF) 119
Cathedral Lake (WRNF)..............250
Causeway Lakes (RNF)...............202

Cave Creek (RGNF) 184
Ceanothuse Lake (RNF)..............198
Cebolla Creek (SWA)...................89
Cedar Mesa Reservoir (GMNF) 139
Cement Creek (GNF) 159
Centennial Park Lake (FR) 20
Central City Park Ponds (FR) 30
Chalk Lake (SINF) 210
Chambers Lake (ANF) 111
Chapin Creek (RMNP) 101
Chapman Lake (WRNF) 247
Chapman Reservoir (WRNF) 247
Chapman Reservoir (RNF) 201
Chartier Ponds (SWA) 93
Chasm Lake (RMNP) 102
Chatfield Reservoir (RNF) 202
Chatfield Reservoir State Park (FR) 21
Chatfield State Park Ponds (FR).....21
Chedsey Creek (RNF) 198
Cheesman Lake (FR)....................45
Cherry Creek State Park (FR) 23
Cherry Lake (RGNF) 180
Chicago Lakes (FR) 39
Chichuahua Lake (ANF) 123
Chicken Creek (SJNF) 224
Chinn's Lake (FR)........................36
Chipeta Lakes (SWA)...................93
Chopper Lake (SJNF) 221
Christina Lake............................87
Cimarron River (UNF) 230
Cimarron River (SWA)..................88
Cimarron River, East Fork (UNF) 230
Cimarron River, West Fork (UNF) 230
City Park Lake (FR)......................23
City Reservoir (SJNF)..................221
Clayton Lakes (FR) 34
Clear Creek (SINF) 208
Clear Creek (SJNF) 224
Clear Creek (STL)........................80
Clear Creek , South Fork (SINF) 208
Clear Creek ,North Fork (SINF) 208
Clear Creek Pond (FR) 14
Clear Creek Reservoir (SWA).......86
Clear Creek Reservoir (SINF).......207
Clear Creek (ANF) 123
Clear Creek (FR)..........................42
Clear Creek, North (RGNF) 181
Clear Creek, West Fork (ANF) 121
Clear Lake (FR)...........................38
Clear Lake (GMNF) 149
Clear Lake (SJNF).......................217
Clear Lake (SP)...........................53
Clear Lake (UNF)........................230
Cleveland Lakes (WRNF).............248
Cliff Creek (GNF) 157
Cliff Lake (ANF)..........................119
Cliff Lake (RNF) 200
Cliff Lakes (WRNF) 237
Cliff Lakes (WRNF) 238
Clover Creek (RGNF) 179
Coal Creek (GNF) 152
Coal Creek (GNF) 159
Coal Creek (SJNF) 217
Cochetopa Creek (GNF) 169
Cochetopa Creek (SWA)...............94
Coffin Lake (WRNF) 239
Coke Oven Creek (SJNF) 217

Colby Horse Park Reservoir (GMNF) 142
Cold Creek (SJNF) 217
Cole Reservoir #1 (GMNF) 141
Colorado River (SWA) 88
Colorado River (Glenwood Canyon) (WRNF)241
Colorado River (Lower) (SP) 66
Colorado River (SWA) 88
Colorado River (SWA) 92
Columbine Lake (ANF) 118
Columbine Lake (SJNF) 217
Columbine Lake (SJNF) 221
Comanche Lake (SINF) 212
Comanche Reservoir (ANF) 112
Community College Pond (FR) 12
Cone Lake (FR)...........................37
Conejos River (RGNF) 189
Conejos River (SWA)...................87
Conejos River, Middle (RGNF) 189
Conejos River, North Branch (SWA) 86
Conejos River, North Fork (RGNF) 189
Coney Lakes (ANF) 118
Continental Reservoir (RGNF) 182
Cony Creek (RMNP).....................104
Cooney Lake (PNF) 173
Cooper Lake (UNF) 233
Coot Lake (FR) 26
Copper Lake (GNF) 154
Copper Mountain Pond (ANF) 122
Cornelius Creek (ANF).................109
Corral Creek (ANF).....................111
Costo Lake (GNF) 159
Costo Reservoir (UNF) 230
Cotton Lake (RGNF)....................180
Cottonwood Creek (GMNF) 135
Cottonwood Creek (STL)...............81
Cottonwood Creek,s (SINF) 209
Cottonwood Lake (SINF) 209
Cottonwood Lakes (RGNF) 185
Cottonwood Park Pond (FR) 18
Cottonwood Reservoir #1 (GMNF) 135
Cottonwood Reservoir #4 (GMNF) 135
Cow Creek (UNF) 232
Cow Lake (GNF) 163
Cowdrey Lake (SWA)...................89
Craig Creek (PNF) 175
Crater Lake (ANF) 118
Crater Lake (RNF) 202
Crater Lake (SJNF) 227
Crater Lake (WRNF)....................238
Crater Lake (WRNF)....................243
Crater Lake (WRNF)....................250
Crater Lake (GNF) 151
Crater Lakes (FR) 34
Crawford Lake (ANF)...................118
Crawford Reservoir (GNF) 156
Crawford Reservoir (SP)...............67
Creedmore Lakes (ANF)..............109
Crescent Lake (WRNF)................239
Crestone Lakes (RGNF)..............180
Croke Reservoir (Carlson Res.) (FR) 12
Crooked Creek (PNF) 174
Crosho Reservoir (RNF) 201
Cross Creek (WRNF) 243
Cross Creek, East (WRNF)..........248
Cross Lakes (WRNF) 247
Crown Hill Lake (FR) 15
Crystal Creek Reservoir (PNF) 177

Crystal Lake (GNF)..................................162
Crystal Lake (RGNF) 182
Crystal Lake (RMNP)...............................102
Crystal Lake (SINF)..................................206
Crystal Lake (SJNF)..................................217
Crystal Lake (UNF)..................................233
Crystal Lakes (RGNF) 189
Crystal Lakes (SINF) 207
Curecanti Creek (GNF) 164
Deadman Creek (ANF)..............................107
Deadman Creek (SJNF) 223
Deadman Lake (WRNF).............................251
Deadman Lakes (RGNF)............................185
Deckers Lake (SINF) 205
Deep Creek (WRNF).................................241
Deep Creek (RGNF)..................................183
Deep Lake (FR)..31
Deep Lake (RNF)......................................200
Deep Lake (RNF)......................................202
Deep Lake (WRNF)..................................238
Deep Slough Reservoir (GMNF) 130
Deer Creek (PNF).....................................173
Deer Lake (WRNF)...................................239
Delaney Butte Lakes (SWA) 89
Deluge Lake (ANF)...................................122
Devil's Thumb Lake (FR) 32
DeWeese Reservoir (SWA) 87
Diamond Lake (FR) 31
Diamond Lake, Upper (FR) 31
Diana Lake (RNF).....................................196
Diemer Lake (WRNF)................................247
Dillon Reservoir (ANF)..............................122
Dines Lake (RNF).....................................202
Dinkle Lake (WRNF).................................245
Dinosaur Lake (RNF).................................198
Dirty George Creek (GMNF) 149
Disappointment Lake (RNF) 200
Divide Lake (SINF)...................................206
Divide Lake (SJNF)...................................222
Divide Lake Pothole (SJNF)........................222
Dogfish Reservoir (GMNF).........................144
Dollar Lake (GNF) 159
Dollar Lake (SJNF)...................................222
Dolores River (SJNF)................................217
Dolores River (SJNF)................................218
Dolores River (SWA)..................................87
Dolores River (SWA)..................................93
Dolores River 228
Dome Lake (RNF).....................................198
Dome Lakes (GNF) 168
Dome Lakes (SWA) 94
Donut Lake (RMNP)..................................101
Dora Lake (ANF)......................................119
Doris Lake (WRNF)..................................235
Dorothey Lake (SWA)..................................91
Doughspoon Res. #1 (GMNF) 148
Doughspoon Res. #2 (GMNF) 148
Doughty Creek (GMNF)............................144
Doughty Reservoir (GMNF)........................144
Douglas Lake (SWA) 91
Douglas Reservoir (SWA)............................91
Dowdy Lake (ANF) 109
Dowdy Lake (SWA) 90
Dream Lake (RMNP).................................102
Drink Creek (ANF)...................................107
Dry Creek (STL).......................................82
Dry Lakes (SINF) 212

Duck Lake (RGNF)...................................192
Dugger Reservoir (GMNF)..........................148
Dumont Lake (RNF)..................................199
Dunkley & Dubeau Reservoir (RNF) 201
Dyer Creeks (GNF)...................................164
Eagle Lake (WRNF)..................................247
Eagle River (SWA)......................................88
Eagle River (WRNF).................................243
Eagle River, South Fork (WRNF)................248
Eaglesmere Lakes (ANF)............................119
East Delaney Butte Lake (STL) 81
East Inlet Creek (RMNP)............................104
East Muddy Creek (GNF)...........................151
East Reservoir (FR).....................................17
East River (GNF) 154
East River (GNF) 159
East River SFU...89
Echo Canyon Reservoir (SJNF)...................227
Echo Canyon Reservoir (SWA) 86
Echo Lake (FR)..38
Edge Lake (WRNF)...................................239
Edward Lake (RNF)..................................197
Eggleston Lake (GMNF) 131
Eggleston Lake, Upper, Little (GMNF) 133
Elbert Lake (RNF)....................................198
Eldorado Lakes (SJNF)..............................221
Electra Lake (SJNF)..................................220
Eleven Mile Reservoir (SP)..........................60
Elk Creek (RGNF)....................................192
Elk Creek, (SJNF).....................................221
Elk Creek, South (RGNF)...........................192
Elk Lake (SJNF).......................................222
Elk Lake (WRNF).....................................236
Elk Park Reservoir (GMNF)........................134
Elk River (RNF).......................................197
Elk River, North Fork (RNF).......................195
Elkhead Reservoir (SP)...............................49
Elkhorn Creek (ANF).................................109
Elkhorn Creek (ANF).................................109
Elkhorn Creek (RGNF)..............................179
Elks Lakes (WRNF)..................................238
Elmo Lakes (RNF) 199
Emerald Lake (GNF).................................153
Emerald Lake (RMNP)..............................102
Emerald Lake (SJNF).................................221
Emerald Lake (WRNF)..............................239
Emerald Lake (SINF).................................206
Emerald Lakes (SJNF)...............................222
Emmaline Lake (ANF)...............................112
Empedrado Lake (RGNF)...........................190
Encampment River (RNF)...........................195
Encampment River, West Fork (RNF) 195
Engineers Lake (FR)....................................14
English Creek (RNF)..................................195
Envy Lake (ANF) 118
Estes Lake (ANF).....................................115
Esther Lake (WRNF).................................248
Ethel Lake (FR)..37
Eureka Lake (SINF)..................................212
Evergreen Lake (FR)...................................39
Exposition Park Pond (FR)...........................23
Fairgrounds Lake (FR)................................25
Fairview Lake (GNF) 162
Fairview Lake (WRNF) 247
Fall Creek (SJNF).....................................217
Fall River (RMNP) 102
Fall River Reservoir (FR)............................36

Fancy Lake (WRNF)..................................248
Farris Creek (GNF) 159
Faversham Park Pond (FR) 13
Fay Lakes (RMNP)...................................102
Fern Creek (RMNP)..................................102
Fern Lake (RMNP)...................................102
Fifth Lake (RMNP)...................................104
Finger Lake (RNF)....................................200
Finger Rock Ponds (SWA) 94
Finney Cut Lake #1 (GMNF) 140
Finney Cut Lake #2 (GMNF) 140
Fish Creek (ANF).....................................106
Fish Creek (SWA)......................................87
Fish Creek Reservoir (RNF)........................199
Fish Creek Reservoirs (UNF) 230
Fish Creek, (SJNF)...................................217
Fish Creek, Little (SJNF) 217
Fish Hawk Lake (RNF)..............................197
Fish Lake (SJNF)......................................227
Fishers Creek (RGNF)...............................187
Flagler Reservoir (SWA)..............................90
Flapjack Lake (ANF).................................119
Flint Lakes (SJNF)....................................222
Flint Lakes (SJNF)....................................222
Foose Creek (SINF) 210
Forbay Reservoir (Lake) (SJNF)...................220
Forest Lakes (FR)......................................33
Forester Creek (RNF).................................196
Fork Creek, South (RGNF).........................184
Forrest Lake (GMNF)................................133
Forty-Acre Lake (GMNF)...........................134
Four Mile Creek (SWA) 95
Fourmile Creeks (SINF)............................209
Fourmile Creek (PNF)...............................174
Fourmile Creek (SWA)................................93
Fourmile Lakes (SJNF)..............................226
Fourth Lake (RMNP).................................104
Frank Ponds (SWA)....................................91
Franz Lake (SWA).....................................86
Franz Lake (SWA).....................................86
Fraser River (STL).....................................81
Frazer River (ANF)...................................121
Freeman Reservoir (RNF)...........................194
French Creek (PNF)..................................171
Frenchman Creek (SINF) 209
Frosty Lake (WRNF).................................238
Frozen Lake (FR).......................................40
Fruita Reservoirs (UNF).............................230
Fryingpan Lakes (WRNF)...........................251
Fryingpan River (SWA) 95
Fryingpan River (SWA) 87
Fryingpan River (WRNF)...........................246
Fryingpan River, South Fork (WRNF) 247
Fuch Reservoir (RGNF) 189
Fuller Lake (SJNF)...................................217
Gardner Park Reservoir (RNF).....................202
Garfield Lake (FR).....................................16
Garfield Lakes (SJNF) 221
Garland Park Pond (Lollipop Lake) (FR) 23
Gem Lake (RNF)......................................196
Geneva Creek (FR)....................................42
Geneva Creek (PNF)..................................172
George Creek (ANF)..................................109
Georgetown Lake (FR)................................38
Ghost Lake (RGNF)..................................182
Gibson Lake (FR)......................................40
Gibson Lake (PNF)...................................172
Gilbralter Lake (ANF)..............................118

Appendix

Gilley Lake (WRNF)............................237
Glacier Creek (RMNP)........................102
Glacier Creek (SINF)..........................205
Glacier Lake (RGNF)...........................189
Glacier Springs Lake (GMNF) 127
Gold Dust Lakes (WRNF).....................247
Golden Gate State Park (FR)..................30
Golden Lake (GNF)..............................159
Golden Ponds (FR)................................25
Goodenough Reservoir (GMNF) 144
Goodwin Creek (SINF).........................212
Goodwin Lakes (SINF).........................212
Goose Creek (RNF)..............................196
Goose Creek (RGNF)...........................187
Goose Lake (RGNF).............................187
Gore Creek (WRNF).............................243
Gore Lakes (ANF)................................122
Gourd Lake (ANF)...............................118
Grace Creek (ANF)..............................106
Granby Lake (ANRA)............................99
Granby Reservoir #1 (GMNF)...............148
Granby Reservoir #12 (GMNF) 149
Granby Reservoir #2 (GMNF)...............148
Granby Reservoir #7 (GMNF)...............149
Granby Reservoirs #4, 5, 10, 11 (GMNF) 149
Grand Lake (ANRA)..............................99
Grandview Ponds (FR)...........................12
Granite Lake, Lower (SJNF)...................222
Granite Lakes (WRNF).........................251
Grape Creek (STL)................................80
Grass Lake (SINF) 210
Grays Lake (ANF)................................123
Green Creek (SINF)..............................210
Green Creek (RNF)..............................199
Green Gables Park Pond (FR)..................18
Green Lake (GNF)................................159
Green Lake (RGNF)..............................191
Green Mountain Reservoir (ANF) 119
Green River (SWA)................................92
Greenleaf Creek (SINF)........................212
Griffith Lake #1 (GMNF)......................128
Griffith Lake, Middle (GMNF).................128
Grizzly Creek (RNF)............................194
Grizzly Creek (STL)..............................81
Grizzly Creek (WRNF).........................241
Grizzly Gulch Lakes (SJNF)..................221
Grizzly Lake (SINF).............................210
Grizzly Lake (WRNF)..........................241
Grizzly Lake (WRNF)..........................251
Grizzly Reservoir (WRNF).....................251
Gross Reservoir (FR) 29
Groundhog Reservoir (SWA)...................87
Grouse Lake (WRNF)...........................243
Gunnison River (SWA)...........................87
Gunnison River (SWA)...........................88
Gunnison River, Lake Fork (UNF) 233
Guthrie Lakes (WRNF).........................238
Gwendolyn Lake (WRNF)......................238
Gypsum Ponds (SWA) 88
Hagerman Lake (SINF).........................205
Hague Creek (RMNP)..........................101
Hahns Peak Lake (RNF)........................195
Haley Reservoir (RNF)..........................201
Half Moon Lake (SJNF)........................222
Halfmoon Lake (WRNF)........................247
Halfmoon Lakes (SINF)........................206
Hampton Lakes (UNF)..........................230

Hancock Lakes (SINF)..........................210
Handcart Gulch (PNF) 172
Hang Lake (ANF).................................111
Hanson Reservoir (GMNF)....................144
Hardscrabble Creeks (SINF)..................213
Hardscrabble Lake (WRNF)...................249
Harper Lake (FR)...................................27
Harriman Lake Reservoir (FR) 18
Harris Lake (SJNF)..............................227
Harrison Creek (RNF)...........................199
Harrison Flats (SINF)...........................208
Hartenstien Lake (SINF)........................209
Harvey Gap Reservoir (SP).....................68
Harvey Lake (WRNF)...........................247
Harvey Park Lake (FR)...........................17
Hassel Lake (ANF)...............................123
Hassel Lake (FR)...................................37
Hatcher Lakes (SJNF)..........................226
Hatnach Lake (RMNP)..........................101
Haviland Lake 90
Haviland Lake (SJNF)..........................220
Hay Lake (UNF)...................................233
Hayden Creek (SINF)...........................212
Hazel Lakes (SJNF)..............................221
Heart Lake (FR)....................................34
Heart Lake (RGNF)..............................181
Heart Lake (RNF)................................202
Heart Lake (WRNF).............................238
Henderson Lake (SJNF) 221
Henry Lake (GNF) 162
Henson Creek (UNF)............................233
Hermit Lake (SINF)..............................212
Hermosa Creek (SJNF).........................220
Hermosa Creek (SJNF).........................224
Hermosa Creek, East Fork (SJNF).............220
Hidden Lake (SJNF).............................221
Hidden Lakes (SINF)............................206
High Creek (STL)..................................82
Highland Mary Lakes (SJNF)..................218
Highline Reservoir (SP)..........................69
Hine Lake Reservoir (FR).......................18
Hinman Creek and Scott Run (RNF) 195
Hog Park Creek, South Fork (RNF)............195
Hohnholtz Lakes (SWA)..........................91
Hohnholtz SWA (ANF) 107
Holbrook Reservoir (SWA).......................93
Hollenbeck Ponds (SINF)......................206
Home Lake (SWA) 94
Homestake Lake, Upper (WRNF) 248
Homestake Reservoir (WRNF)..................248
Hope Lake (UNF).................................233
Horn Lakes (SINF)...............................212
Horseshoe Lake (SINF).........................212
Horseshoe Lake (WRNF).......................247
Horseshoe Reservoir (SP)........................61
Horsethief Lake (GNF)..........................155
Hossick Lake (SJNF) 223
Hot Creek (SWA)..................................86
Hot Springs Reservoir (STL) 81
Hotel Twin Lake (GMNF)......................130
Howard Creek (SINF)...........................211
Hubbard Creek (GNF)...........................151
Huerfano River (SINF)..........................214
Huerfano River (SWA)...........................89
Hunky Dory Lake (WRNF).....................248
Hunkydory Lakes (SINF).......................210
Hunt Lake (SINF)................................210

Hunter Creek (WRNF) 251
Hunter Reservoir (GMNF)......................142
Hunter's Glen Lake(FR)..........................12
Hunters Lake (RGNF)...........................187
Hunts Lake (SINF)..............................211
Huston Park Lake (FR)............................17
Hutcheson Lakes (RMNP)......................104
Hyland Ponds (FR)................................13
Ice Lake (FR) 35
Ice Lakes (SJNF).................................217
Iceberg Lake (ANF)..............................111
Iceberg Lakes (FR)................................34
Idaho Springs Reservoir (FR)...................38
Illinois Creek (GNF).............................155
Illinois Lake (GNF)..............................156
Illinois River (SWA)..............................89
Independence Creek (RNF).....................195
Independence Lake (WRNF)....................251
Indian Creek (RGNF)............................179
Indian Creeks (SJNF)...........................223
Indian Creeks) (STL).............................82
Indian Run (RNF)................................200
Irving Lake (SJNF)..............................221
Island Lake (ANF)................................118
Island Lake (SJNF)..............................217
Island Lake (ANF)................................111
Island Lake (GMNF).............................129
Island Lakes (WRNF)...........................239
Isolation Lakes (WRNF)........................248
Italian Creek (GNF) 155
Ivanhoe Lake (WRNF)..........................247
Ivy Creek (RGNF)................................187
Jack Lake (WRNF)...............................251
Jackson Gulch Res. (SP).........................70
Jackson Lake (State Park) 50
Jackson Lake (SWA)..............................93
Jacobs Ladder Lake (SJNF)....................225
James Peak Lake (FR)............................34
Jasper Lake (FR)...................................31
Jefferson Lake (PNF).............................172
Jenny Lake (FR)....................................33
Jerry Creek Lakes (SWA)........................92
Jet Lake (WRNF).................................238
Jewel Lake (RMNP)..............................102
Jewell Lake (SJNF)..............................221
Jewell Park Pond (FR)............................18
Jim Baker Reservoir (FR)........................15
Joe Moore Reservoir (SWA)....................92
Joe Wright Reservoir (ANF)....................111
John Martin Reservoir (SWA)...................86
Johns Creek (RGNF)............................184
Johnson Creek (ANF)...........................106
Johnson Lake (WRNF)..........................235
Johnson Reservoir (Clement Park) (FR)........20
Jonah Lake (RNF)................................198
Jumbo Reservoir (GMNF).......................127
Jumbo Reservoir (SWA)..........................92
Jumper Lake (RNF)..............................186
Junction Creek (SJNF)..........................224
Karval Reservoir (SWA)..........................92
Kathleen Lake (RNF)............................200
Keener Lake (WRNF)...........................239
Kelly Lake (SP)....................................53
Kendrick Park Reservoir (FR)..................18
Kenney Creek (GMNF).........................142
Kenney Creek Res. (Kendall Res.) (GMNF) 141
Kerber Creek (RGNF)...........................179

Kerr Lake (RGNF) 189
Ketner Lake (FR) 13
Ketring Park Lake (Gallup Lake) (FR)............20
Keystone Creek (ANF) 123
Kidney Lake (RNF)........................200
Killarney Reservoir (RNF)..............202
Kilpacker Creek (SJNF) 217
King Creek (STL) 82
King Lake (FR) 32
King Solomon Creek (RNF) 195
Kinney Lake (SWA) 92
Kiser Creek (GMNF) 132
Kiser Creek (GMNF) 132
Kiser Slough Reservoir (GMNF) 131
Kite Lake (PNF) 173
Kitson Reservoir (GMNF) 135
Kitty Creek (RGNF) 181
Kiwanis Park Pond (FR) 13
Knox Reservoir (GMNF) 134
Kroenke Lake (SINF) 209
La Jara Creek (STL)........................80
La Jara Reservoir (STL)...................80
La Jara Reservoir (RGNF) 190
La Manga Creek (RGNF) 92
LaGarde Creek (ANF) 107
LaGarde Creek (STL) 81
Lagerman Reservoir (FR) 25
LaJara Creek (SWA) 86
LaJara Reservoir (SWA) 86
Lake Adams (RMNP)......................104
Lake Ann (RGNF)..........................189
Lake Ann (SINF)............................208
Lake Arbor (FR) 13
Lake Caroline (FR) 36
Lake Charles (WRNF) 247
Lake Constantine (WRNF) 248
Lake Dorothy (ANF).......................118
Lake Dorothy (FR) 31
Lake Eileen (RNF) 196
Lake Emma (PNF) 173
Lake Fork (SINF) 205
Lake Fork (RGNF) 187
Lake Fork Creek (RGNF) 189
Lake Fork of the Gunnison (SWA) 89
Lake Geneva (FR) 20
Lake Haiyaha (RMNP)....................102
Lake Henry (SWA) 87
Lake Husted (RMNP)......................104
Lake Irwin (GNF) 153
Lake Irwin (SWA) 88
Lake Isabel (SINF) 214
Lake Isabelle (ANF) 118
Lake Isabelle (FR) 29
Lake John (SWA) 89
Lake Josephine (WRNF) 247
Lake Katherine (RNF) 198
Lake Nanita (RMNP) 102
Lake Nokini (RMNP) 102
Lake of Glass (RMNP).....................102
Lake of the Clouds (RMNP).............101
Lake of the Clouds (SINF)...............212
Lake of the Crags (RNF)..................198
Lake of the Woods (WRNF) 235
Lake Patricia (WRNF) 248
Lake Verna (RMNP) 104
Lamphier Lake, Upper (GNF) 162
Lanning Lake (GMNF)....................142

LaPlata River (SJNF) 224
Larson Lake (UNF).........................233
Las Animas River (SWA) 90
Lava Lake (WRNF).........................240
Lawn Lake (RMNP) 102
LEDE Reservoir (WRNF).................246
Lee Creek (GNF) 152
Leeman Lakes (WRNF) 247
Lefthand Creek Reservoir (FR)..........29
Lemon Reservoir (SJNF) 225
Leon Creek (GMNF)........................143
Leon Creek, East (GMNF) 143
Leon Creek, Middle (GMNF)............143
Leon Lake (GMNF) 142
Leon Peak Reservoir (Sissie Lake) (GMNF) 140
Leroux Creek, East (GMNF) 144
Leroux Creek, West (GMNF) 144
Leviathan Lakes (SJNF) 221
Liitle Cochetopa (SINF) 211
Lillie Lake (SJNF)...........................221
Lily Lake (GMNF) 135
Lily Lake (WRNF) 240
Lily Lakes (SINF) 214
Lily Pond (RGNF) 189
Lime Creek (RGNF) 187
Limestone Lake (WRNF) 238
Lincoln Creek (WRNF)....................251
Lincoln Lake (FR)............................39
Link Creek (ANF) 107
Linkins Lake (WRNF) 251
Little Cimarron River (UNF) 230
Little Echo Lake (FR) 34
Little Gem Lake (WRNF) 249
Little Gem Reservoir(GMNF)............129
Little Grouse Reservoir (GMNF) 132
Little Gunnison (GNF) 157
Little Red Park Creek (RNF) 195
Little Rock Lake (RMNP)..................101
Little Sand Creek Lake (RGNF).........185
Little Snake (RNF) 194
Little Snake River (STL)....................82
Little Snake, Middle Fork (RNF) 194
Little Trappers Creek (WRNF) 239
Little Trappers Lake (WRNF)............239
Little's Creek Pond (FR) 20
Lizard Head Creek (SJNF) 217
Lizard Lake (WRNF) 249
Loc Amora Pond (Jacob's Pond) (FR) 12
Loch Lomond Lake (FR) 35
Lon Hagler Reservoir (SWA) 91
Lone Licks Lake (WRNF) 240
Lone Pine Creek (ANF) 109
Lone Pine Creek, N. Fork (ANF) 109
Lone Pine Creek, S. Fork (ANF) 109
Lone Pine Lake (RMNP) 104
Lonesome Lake (WRNF)...................248
Lonetree Reservoir (SWA) 91
Long Draw Reservoir (ANF) 111
Long Lake (ANF) 118
Long Lake (ANF) 118
Long Lake (FR)................................29
Long Lake (GNF) 159
Long Lake (RNF) 199
Long Lake (RNF) 200
Long Lake (RNF) 202
Long Lake (Upper Piney Lake) (WRNF)......243
Loomiller Pond (FR) 25

Loomis Lake (RMNP)......................102
Los Pinos Creek (GNF)....................168
Los Pinos Creek (STL).......................82
Los Pinos River (SJNF) 225
Los Pinos River (SJNF) 222
Lost Dog Creek (RNF) 195
Lost Lake (ANF) 111
Lost Lake (ANF) 114
Lost Lake (ANF) 122
Lost Lake (FR).................................32
Lost Lake (GMNF) 127
Lost Lake (GMNF) 142
Lost Lake (GNF) 159
Lost Lake (RGNF) 188
Lost Lake (RGNF) 192
Lost Lake (RMNP) 104
Lost Lake (RNF) 199
Lost Lake (SINF) 208
Lost Lake (SINF) 214
Lost Lake (SJNF) 221
Lost Lake (SJNF) 221
Lost Lake (WRNF) 243
Lost Lake (WRNF) 246
Lost Lake (WRNF) 248
Lost Lake Slough (GNF) 159
Lost Lakes (RNF) 202
Lost Man Lake (WRNF) 251
Lost Man Reservoir (WRNF) 251
Lost Solar Lakes (WRNF) 238
Lost Trail Creek (RGNF) 181
Lost Trail Creek, West (RGNF) 181
Lottis Creeks (GNF) 162
Love Lake (RGNF) 186
Lowell Ponds (FR) 15
Luna Lake (RNF) 198
Lyle Lake (WRNF) 247
Lynch Creek (PNF) 176
Macey Lakes (SINF) 213
Machin Lake (RGNF) 183
Mackinaw Lake (WRNF) 239
Mad Creek, Middle Fork (RNF) 197
Mad Creek, North (RNF) 197
Mad Creek, South Fork (RNF) 197
Mahaffey Lake (WRNF)...................238
Mahan Lake (ANF) 119
Main Reservoir (Osner Res.) (FR) 17
Manazanares Lake (RNF).................195
Mancos River, East (SJNF)...............224
Mancos River, Middle (SJNF) 224
Mancos River, West (SJNF) 224
Mandall Lake, Black (RNF) 202
Mandall Lake, Mud (RNF) 202
Mandall Lake, Rainbow Slide (RNF)...........202
Mandall Lake, Twin (RNF)...............202
Manitou Reservoir (PNF) 177
Marcott Creek (GMNF) 143
Margaret Lake (RNF) 197
Marie Lake (SJNF) 221
Maroon Lake (GNF) 154
Maroon Lake (WRNF) 250
Marshall Creek (GNF) 167
Marshall Creek (STL) 82
Martha Lake (RNF).........................198
Martin Reservoir (SP) 61
Marvine Lakes (WRNF) 238
Mary Loch Lake (WRNF).................238
Maxwell Lake (FR).........................27

Appendix

McDonough Reservoir (GNF) 168
McGinnis Lake (WRNF)............................236
McIntyre Creek (ANF) 107
McIntyre Lake (ANF) 111
McJunkin Creek (SJNF) 218
McMillan Lake (WRNF)...........................239
McPhee Reservoir 228
Meadow Creek (SJNF) 217
Meadow Creek Lake (WRNF) 237
Meadow Creek Lake (WRNF) 238
Meadow Park Lake (FR)..............................15
Medano Lake (RGNF) 185
Meredith Reservoir (SWA) 87
Meridan Lake (GNF)................................153
Mesa Creek (GMNF) 127
Mesa Creek (RGNF) 182
Mesa Lake (GMNF) 127
Mesa Lake, South (GMNF) 127
Mica Lake (RNF) 196
Michigan Creek (PNF) 171
Michigan Creek (SWA).............................93
Michigan Lake (PNF) 171
Michigan Reservoir (SP)............................53
Michigan River (SP)..................................53
Michigan River (STL).................................81
Michigan River (SWA)...............................90
Michigan River (SWA)...............................89
Middle Creek (RGNF) 179
Middle Creek, East (RGNF) 179
Middle Lake (WRNF) 242
Milavec Lake Recreation Area (FR)..............25
Miler Creek (WRNF) 236
Military Park Reservoir (GMNF) 133
Mill Creek (GNF) 159
Mill Lake (GNF) 162
Miller Creek, East (WRNF) 236
Miller Creek,Middle (WRNF) 236
Millions Reservoir (RGNF) 188
Mills Lake (RMNP) 102
Miners Creek (RGNF)...............................182
Miners Creek (RGNF)...............................184
Miramonte Reservoir (SWA) 95
Mirror Lake (ANF)...................................119
Mirror Lake (GNF) 163
Mirror Lake (RNF) 198
Mirror Lake (WRNF) 235
Missouri Lakes (WRNF)............................247
Mitchell Lake (ANF).................................118
Mix Lake (RGNF).....................................189
Molas Lakes (SJNF) 221
Monarch Lake (ANF)................................118
Monarch Lake (ANRA) 99
Montgomery Reservoir (PNF) 174
Monument Creek (GMNF) 143
Monument Lake (PNF) 177
Monument Lake (SWA)..............................88
Monument Lake (WRNF) 241
Monument Reservoir #1 (GMNF) 142
Moon Lake (SJNF) 222
Moon Lake (WRNF) 249
Moraine Lake (FR) 29
Mormon Lake (WRNF).............................247
Morris Reservoir (GMNF) 148
Morrison Creek (SWA)...............................87
Mosquito Creek (PNF) 174
Mosquito Lake (RNF)...............................202
Mount Elbert Forebay (SINF) 207

Mountain Home Reservoir (SWA) 87
Mud Lakes (WRNF) 239
Muddy Creek (STL) 81
Mulhall Lakes (WRNF).............................248
Murphy Lake (WRNF)..............................238
Murray Lake (FR)......................................40
Muskrat Lakes (WRNF).............................239
Mysterious Lake (GNF) 155
Mystic Island Lake (WRNF)......................247
Nancy Lake (WRNF) 247
Narraguinnep Reservoir (SWA) 92
Narraquinnep Reservoir 228
Nast Lake (WRNF) 247
Native Lake (SINF) 206
Navajo Lake (SJNF) 217
Navajo Reservoir (SP)................................71
Ned Wilson Lake (WRNF) 238
Nee Noshee Reservoir (SWA).....................90
Needle Creek (GNF) 168
Needle Creek (SJNF) 221
Needle Creek Reservoir (GNF)..................168
Neva Lakes (FR)...31
Neversweat Reservoir (GMNF) 134
New York Lake (WRNF)............................247
Newcomb Creek (RNF).............................198
Nichols Lake (PNF) 177
Nicholson Lake (GNF) 153
No Name Creek (STL)................................81
No Name Lake (RGNF) 192
No. Fork Big Thompson River (RMNP) 104
Nolan Lakes (WRNF)................................247
Noname Creek (SJNF) 221
Norris Creek (SWA) 89
North Colony Lakes (SINF) 213
North Fork Colorado River (RMNP) 101
North Fork Reservoir (SINF) 210
North Fork South Platte (PNF) 172
North Inlet Creek (RMNP) 101
North Lake (RNF) 198
North Lake (SINF) 215
North Lake (SWA) 92
North Platte River (STL)............................81
North Platte River (SWA) 89
North Platte River (SWA) 90
North Platte, North Fork (SWA) 89
North St. Vrain Creek (RMNP)...................104
North Sterling Reservoir (SP).....................51
Nunn Creek (ANF)...................................107
Oat Lake (RNF)..202
Odd Fellows (SWA) 90
Odessa Lake (RMNP) 102
Oh Be Joyful Creek (GNF)........................153
O'Haver Lake (SINF) 211
Ohio Creek (GNF)....................................159
Oliver Twist lakes (PNF) 173
Olney Reservoir (SWA) 87
Olsen Lake (WRNF) 242
Onahu Creek (RMNP)...............................101
Opal Lake (SJNF) 228
Ophir Creek (SINF)..................................213
Ordway Reservoir (SWA)............................87
Ouzel Creek (RMNP)................................104
Ouzel Lake (RMNP)..................................104
Overland Park Pond (FR) 17
Overland Reservoir (GNF) 151
Owens Creek (GMNF) 145
Pagoda Lake (WRNF)...............................235

Pagosa Creek (SJNF) 226
Palmer Lake (PNF) 177
Palmer Lake (WRNF)...............................241
Panhandle Creek (ANF) 109
Paonia Reservoir (GNF) 152
Paonia Reservoir (SP)................................72
Paradise Lakes (WRNF)............................248
Park Creek (GMNF) 143
Park Creek (RGNF) 188
Park Lake Reservoir (WRNF).....................244
Park Reservoir (GMNF) 133
Partorius Reservoir (SWA) 90
Parvin Lake (ANF) 109
Parvin Lake (SWA) 91
Pass Creek (GNF) 159
Pass Creek (GNF) 163
Pass Creek Lake (SINF) 211
Pass Creek, Little (GNF) 159
Pass Creeks (RGNF) 187
Pauline Creek (GNF) 169
Peacock Pool (RMNP)..............................102
Pear Reservoir (RMNP) 104
Pearl Lake (RNF) 195
Pearl Lake (SJNF) 221
Pearl Lake (SP) 54
Pedro Reservoir (GMNF) 131
Peeble Creek (ANF) 122
Peeler Lake (GNF) 153
Peggy Lake (RNF) 196
Peltier Lake (WRNF) 237
Pennock Creek (ANF) 112
Pennsylvanian Creek (PNF) 174
Percy Lake (RNF) 199
Peterson Lake (ANF)................................111
Petroleum Lake (WRNF) 251
Pettingell Lake (RMNP) 102
Piedra River (SJNF) 225
Piedra River, East Fork (SJNF)...................223
Piedra River, East, Middle Forks (SJNF) 226
Pierre Lakes (WRNF) 249
Pika Lake (ANF) 118
Pine Creek (GNF) 155
Pine Creek (RNF) 200
Pine Creek (SINF) 209
Pine Isle Lake (WRNF)............................238
Pine Valley Ranch Pond (FR) 40
Piney Lake (WRNF) 243
Piney River (WRNF).................................243
Pitkin Creek (WRNF) 243
Pitkin Lake (WRNF) 243
Platoro Reservoir (RGNF) 189
Plumtaw Creek (SJNF) 226
Poage Lake (RGNF) 189
Pole Creek (ANF) 106
Pole Creek (RGNF) 181
Pomeroy Lakes (SINF) 210
Pomona Lake (FR) 13
Poncha Creek (SINF) 211
Porcupine Lake (RNF) 198
Porter Reservoir #4 (GMNF) 148
Pot Hole Reservoirs (GNF).......................155
Potato Lake (SJNF) 220
Poudre Lake (RMNP) 101
Poudre River (STL)....................................81
Poudre River (SWA) 90
Poudre River (SWA) 91
Poudre River (SWA) 91

Poudre River SWA (ANF)............113
Poudre River, North Fork (STL) 81
Poudre River, North Fork (SWA) 90
Poudre, North Fork (STL) 81
Prewitt Reservoir (SWA)..............92
Price Lakes (SJNF) 228
Priest Gulch Creek (SJNF) 218
Pristine Lake (RNF) 198
Progress Park Pond (FR)..............20
Prospect Park Lakes (FR) 15
Ptarmigan Lake (GNF) 155
Ptarmigan Lake (RNF) 198
Ptarmigan Lake (SINF) 208
Ptarmigan Lake (UNF) 232
Pueblo Reservoir (SP)..............62
Pueblo Reservoir (SWA)..............94
Puett Reservoir (SWA)..............93
Purgatorie River (SWA)..............91
Purgatorie River, North Fork (SINF) 215
Purgatorie River, North Fork (SWA) 92
Quartz Creek SFU..............89
Quartz Creek (GNF)............166
Quartz Creek, Middle (GNF)............167
Quartz Creek, North (GNF) 163
Quartz Lake (SJNF) 226
Quartzite Lake (WRNF) 241
Quincy Reservoir (FR)..............23
Rainbow Lake (RNF) 198
Rainbow Lake (RNF) 202
Rainbow Lake (WRNF) 238
Rainbow Lake (SINF) 212
Rainbow Lake (SINF) 209
Rainbow Lakes (ANF)............111
Rainbow Lakes (FR)..............29
Ramah Reservoir (SWA)..............88
Rampart Reservoir (PNF)............177
Ranger Lake (RGNF) 189
Ranger Lakes (SP)..............53
Raspberry Creek (SWA)..............89
Rat Creek (RGNF) 183
Rawah Creek (ANF)............111
Rawah Lakes (ANF) 111
Razor Creek (GNF)............168
Razor Creek (SWA)..............88
Red Deer Lake (ANF) 118
Red Dirt Reservoir (RNF)............203
Red Lake (RGNF) 192
Red Lake (WRNF) 246
Red Mountain Creek (GNF)............155
Red Rock Lake (FR)..............29
Reed Reservoir (GMNF)............131
Regan Lake (RGNF) 182
Republican River, North Fork (SWA)..............95
Reynolds Lake (FR) 35
Ridgeview Park Pond (FR) 20
Ridgway Reservoir (SP)..............73
Rifle Creek, East..............88
Rifle Gap Reservoir (SP)..............74
Rim Lake (WRNF) 239
Rim Lake (WRNF) 246
Rim Rock Lake (GMNF) 129
Rio Alto Lake (RGNF)............180
Rio Blanco Lake (SWA)..............94
Rio Chama, West Fork (RGNF)............191
Rio Grand River (RGNF)............183
Rio Grande Reservoir (RGNF)............185
Rio Grande River (RGNF) 188

Rio Grande River (SWA) 92
Rio Grande River (SWA) 94
Rio Grande River (SWA) 94
Rito Azul (RGNF)............189
Rito Hondo Reservoir (RGNF)............182
Rito Hondo Reservoir (SWA)..............89
Road Canyon Reservoir (RGNF)............182
Road Canyon Reservoir (SWA)..............89
Roaring Fork River (SWA)..............89
Roaring Fork River (SWA)..............90
Roaring Fork River (SWA)..............88
Roaring Fork River (WRNF)............251
Roaring Forks Creek (SJNF)............218
Roaring Judy Ponds (GNF)............159
Robinson Creek (GNF)............157
Rock Creek (RGNF) 190
Rock Creek (SINF) 206
Rock Creek (SWA) 94
Rock Creek (RNF) 203
Rock Creek, North Fork (RGNF)............190
Rock Creek, South (ANF)............122
Rock Creek, South Fork (RGNF)............190
Rock Hole Lake (ANF)............111
Rock Lake (GMNF) 141
Rock Lake (RGNF) 192
Rock Lake (RMNP) 101
Rock Lake (SJNF) 222
Rocky Brook Creek (GNF)............162
Rocky Mountain Lake (FR) 15
Roeber Reservoir (SWA)..............87
Roger Pass Lake (FR) 34
Rollins Reservoir (WRNF) 244
Roosevelt Lakes (FR) 39
Rosa Lake (RNF)............198
Rosedale Lake (SINF)............210
Rosemont Reservoir (SWA) 95
Rotella Park Pond (FR) 13
Round Lake (RNF) 199
Round Lakes (RNF) 202
Round Mountain Lake (RNF) 198
Roxy Ann Lakes (RNF) 198
Ruby Anthracite Creek (GNF)............153
Ruby Creek (RGNF)............181
Ruby Jewel Lake (SP)..............53
Ruby Lake (PNF)............173
Ruby Lake (WRNF)............238
Ruby Lakes (SJNF)............221
Ruby Lakes(RGNF)............186
Ruedi Reservoir (WRNF)............246
Runyon/Fountain Lakes (SWA) 94
Ruybalid Lake (RGNF)............192
Ryman Creek (SJNF)............218
Sable Lake (WRNF)............235
Sackett Reservoir (GMNF)............140
Sacramento Creek (PNF) 174
Saguache Creek, South Fork (RGNF) 184
Saint Charles Creek, Little (SINF) 214
Saint Charles River (SINF)............214
Saint Mary's Lake (FR)..............36
San Cristobal Lake (UNF)............233
San Francisco Lakes (RGNF)............190
San Isabel Lake (RGNF)............180
San Juan River, East Fork (SJNF)............226
San Juan River, West Fork (SJNF)............226
San Luis Creek (RGNF)............179
San Luis Lakes (SP)..............63
San Luis Lakes (SWA)..............86

San Miguel River (SWA)..............95
San Miguel River (UNF)............231
Sanchez Lakes (RNF)............195
Sanchez Reservoir (SWA)..............87
Sand Creek (ANF)............107
Sand Creek Lakes (RGNF) 185
Sand Lake (RNF) 202
Sandbar Lakes (ANF) 111
Sandbeach Lake (RMNP) 104
Sands Lake (SWA) 86
Savage Lake (WRNF) 247
Sawmill Creek (RNF) 194
Sawmill Lakes (RNF) 198
Sawmill Ponds (FR) 27
Sawyer Lake (WRNF) 251
Sayers Gulch (SINF)............206
Scotch Creek (SJNF) 218
Scott Lake (WRNF) 251
Seaman Reservoir (STL) 81
Seeley Reservoir (SWA) 95
Sellar Lake (WRNF) 247
Seller-Crowell Reservoir (RNF) 201
Service Creek (RNF)............199
Service Creek (SWA) 94
Seven Lakes (RNF)............196
Seven Sisters Lakes (WRNF) 248
Seymore Lake (SWA)..............90
Seymore Reservoir (RNF)............200
Shadow Lake (WRNF) 238
Shadow Mountain Reservoir (ANRA) 99
Shaffer Creek (RNF) 196
Shaffer Reservoir (RNF)............201
Shallow Lake (WRNF) 238
Shamrock Lake (WRNF) 235
Shaw Lake (RGNF)............187
Sheep Creek (ANF)............109
Sheep Creek (GMNF)............147
Sheep Creek (RGNF)............192
Sheep Creek (ANF)............112
Sheep Creek (GMNF)............147
Sheep Creek (RGNF)............179
Sheep Lake(GNF)............159
Sheer Lake (FR)............36
Shelf Lake (FR)............40
Shelf Lake (PNF)............172
Shepard Lake (WRNF) 239
Sheriff Reservoir (RNF)............202
Sherry Lake (WRNF)............247
Sherwin Lake (FR)............36
Shingle Lake (WRNF)............246
Shingle Peak Lake (WRNF)............239
Shoestring Lake (RNF)............198
Siberia Lake (WRNF) 249
Silver City Creek (RNF)............195
Silver Creek (SINF)............211
Silver Dollar Lake (FR)............40
Silver King Lake (SINF) 209
Silver Lake (SINF)............212
Silver Lake (UNF)............231
Silver Lake (GMNF)............134
Silverjack Reservoir (UNF)............230
Simpson Ponds (SWA)..............91
Skaguay Reservoir (SWA)..............95
Skillet Lake (RNF)............202
Skinny Fish Lakes (WRNF)............236
Sky Pond (RMNP) 102
Skyscraper Reservoir (FR) 32

Appendix

Slack-Weiss Reservoir (RNF) 200
Slate Creek (SJNF) 217
Slate Lakes (ANF) 122
Slate River (GNF) 153
Slater Creek (RNF) 194
Slaughterhouse Creek (RGNF) 179
Sleepycat Ponds (WRNF) 236
Slide Lake 205
Slide Lake (WRNF) 238
Slide Lake (WRNF) 242
Slide Lakes (RNF) 196
Slide Lakes (RNF) 198
Sloan Lake (FR) 16
Smith Creek (RNF) 195
Smith Fork (GNF) 156
Smith Lake (RNF) 202
Smith Reservoir (FR) 18
Smith Reservoir (SWA) 87
Snake River (ANF) 123
Snow Creek (SJNF) 217
Snow Lake (RGNF) 189
Snowfield Lake (WRNF) 249
Snowmass Lake (WRNF) 249
Snowstorm Lake (RNF) 197
Soap Creek (GNF) 164
Soda Creek (RNF) 197
Soda Lake (WRNF) 240
Soda Lakes (FR) 17
Solitary Lake (WRNF) 239
Solitude Lake (RMNP) 102
Sopris Lake (WRNF) 248
Sourdough Lakes (WRNF) 246
South Colony Lakes (SINF) 213
South Fork (RGNF) 187
South Fork (RGNF) 191
South Mamm Peak Lake (WRNF) 244
South Platte Park Ponds (FR) 20
South Platte River (FR) 45
South Platte River (PNF) 176
South Platte River (STL) 82
South Platte River, Middle Fork (SWA) 93
South Platte River, South Fork (SWA) 93
South Platte, North Fork (FR) 45
Spectacle Lake (RGNF) 192
Spencer Lake (GNF) 154
Spencer Lake (RGNF) 190
Spinney Mountain Reservoir (SP) 64
Spinney Mountain Reservoir (SWA) 93
Spirit Lake (RMNP) 104
Sprague Lake (RMNP) 102
Spring Creek (GNF) 159
Spring Creek (RGNF) 179
Spring Creek (RGNF) 182
Spring Creek (SINF) 211
Spring Creek Pond (RGNF) 182
Spring Creek Reservoir (GNF) 162
Spring Creek Reservoir (SWA) 89
Spring Creek (SINF) 207
Spring Creeks (RNF) 197
Spring Lake (RNF) 202
Spruce Lake (RMNP) 102
Spruce Lake (RGNF) 187
Spur Creek (SJNF) 217
Square Top Lakes (FR) 40
Square Top Lakes (PNF) 172
Squaw Creek (STL) 80
Squaw Creek, Little (RGNF) 186

Squaw Lake (RGNF) 185
St. Kevin Lake (SINF) 205
St. Louis Creek (ANF) 121
St. Louis Lake (ANF) 121
St. Vrain State Park (FR) 25
Stagecoach Reservoir (SP) 52
Stalker Lake (SWA) 95
Stambaugh Reservoir (RNF) 198
Standley Lake (FR) 13
Stanley Reservoir (PNF) 177
Starvation Creek (SINF) 211
Steamboat Lake (RNF) 195
Steamboat Lake (SP) 54
Stearns Lake (FR) 28
Stell Lake (GMNF) 132
Stell Lake, East (GMNF) 133
Sterne Pond (FR) 20
Steuart Lake (FR) 35
Stillwater Reservoir (RNF) 202
Stone Lakes (ANF) 118
Stoner Creek (SJNF) 218
Storm Lake (FR) 31
Stout Creek Lakes (SINF) 211
Strawberry Creek (SINF) 214
Strawberry Lake (WRNF) 247
Strontia Springs Reservoir (FR) 45
Stub Creek (ANF) 107
Stuck Creek (ANF) 106
Sugarbowl Lake (ANF) 111
Sugarloaf Lake (WRNF) 246
Summit Lake (FR) 39
Summit Lake (RNF) 198
Summit Reservoir (SWA) 93
Sunnyside Lakes (WRNF) 239
Sunset Lake (GMNF) 127
Supply Basin Reservoir (WRNF) 238
Supply Creek (ANF) 114
Surprise Lake (ANF) 119
Surprise Lake (WRNF) 239
Swamp Lake (SINF) 206
Swede Lake (WRNF) 237
Sweetwater Lake (WRNF) 239
Swift Creek (SINF) 212
Sylvan Lake (SP) 75
Sylvan Lake State Park (WRNF) 247
Table Lake (SJNF) 227
Tabor Lake (WRNF) 251
Tarryall Reservoir (PNF) 175
Tarryall Reservoir (SWA) 93
Taylor Creek (SJNF) 218
Taylor Creek, Middle (SINF) 212
Taylor Creek, Middle (SWA) 87
Taylor Lake (GNF) 154
Taylor Reservoir (GNF) 162
Taylor River (GNF) 159
Taylor River (GNF) 155
Taylor River (SWA) 89
Teal Lake (RNF) 198
Teller Lake (FR) 27
Tellurium Creek (GNF) 155
Tellurium Lake (WRNF) 247
Ten Mile Creek (ANF) 122
Tenmile Creek (SJNF) 221
Terrace Reservoir (SWA) 87
Terrace Reservoir (RGNF) 190
Terrells Lake (WRNF) 251
Texas Creek (GNF) 162

Texas Creek (GNF) 163
Texas Creek (SINF) 212
Texas Creek (RGNF) 186
The Pecks Reservoir #1 (GMNF) 141
The Pecks Reservoir #2 (GMNF) 141
Thomas Lake (WRNF) 242
Thomas Lakes (WRNF) 245
Thompson Creeks (WRNF) 244
Thompson Lake (UNF) 233
Three Island Lake (RNF) 196
Three Lakes (SINF) 206
Three Licks Lake (WRNF) 240
Threemile Creek (PNF) 172
Thunder Lake (RMNP) 104
Thunderbird Lake (FR) 27
Thurston Reservoir (SWA) 94
Tiago Lake (RNF) 198
Timber Creek (RMNP) 101
Timber Lake (ANF) 111
Timber Lake (RMNP) 101
Timber Lake (RGNF) 191
Timberline Lake (ANF) 112
Timberline Lake (SINF) 205
Timpas Creek (SWA) 93
Tipperary Lake (ANF) 119
Tobacco Lake (RGNF) 189
Tomichi Creek (GNF) 167
Tominchi Creek (STL) 82
Tonahutu Creek (RMNP) 101
Torso Creek (RNF) 194
Totten Reservoir (SWA) 93
Trail Creek (RNF) 195
Trail Lake (RGNF) 191
Trail Lake (WRNF) 238
Trap Creek (ANF) 111
Trap Lake (ANF) 111
Trappers Lake (WRNF) 239
Treasure Vault Lake (WRNF) 247
Trinidad Reservoir (SP) 65
Trinity Peaks Lake (SJNF) 221
Trio Reservoir (GMNF) 139
Trout Creek (PNF) 174
Trout Creek (RGNF) 186
Trout Creek, East (RGNF) 186
Trout Creek, West (RGNF) 186
Trout Lake (GMNF) 134
Trout Lake (UNF) 233
Trout Lake (RGNF) 186
Trujillo Meadows Reservoir (RGNF) 192
Trujillo Meadows Reservoir (SWA) 87
Truro Lake (WRNF) 251
Tucker Ponds (RGNF) 189
Tuhare Lakes (WRNF) 248
Tumbling Creek (PNF) 176
Turkey Creek (SJNF) 224
Turkey Creek Lake (SJNF) 226
Turks Pond (SWA) 86
Turquoise Lake (SINF) 205
Turquoise Lakes (WRNF) 242
Twelvemile Lakes (PNF) 173
Twilight Lakes (SJNF) 221
Twin Crater Lakes (ANF) 111
Twin Lake #1 (GMNF) 140
Twin Lake #2 (GMNF) 140
Twin Lakes (ANF) 111
Twin Lakes (GNF) 154
Twin Lakes (RGNF) 185

Twin Lakes (RGNF) 189
Twin Lakes (RNF).............196
Twin Lakes (SINF) 207
Twin Lakes East (ANF).............111
Twin Lakes Park Ponds (FR) 14
Two Buttes Reservoir (SWA) 86
Two Ledge Reservoir (RNF) 200
Twobit Creek (SINF).............207
Uncompahgre River (UNF).............232
Union Creek (SINF).............207
Union Reservoir (FR).............25
Union Square Ponds (FR).............16
Urad Reservoir, Upper (FR).............37
Ute Creek (RGNF) 185
Ute Creek (RNF).............196
Ute Lake (RNF).............196
Ute Lake, Main (RGNF).............185
Ute Lake, Middle (RGNF).............185
Ute Lake, Upper (RGNF).............185
Ute Lake, West (RGNF).............185
Vallecito Creek (SJNF).............225
Vallecito Lake (SJNF).............221
Vallecito Reservoir (SJNF).............225
Vanderbilt Park Pond (FR).............17
Vaughn Lake (RNF).............200
Vega Reservoir (SP).............76
Vela Reservoir (GMNF).............134
Venable Creek (SINF).............212
Venable Lakes (SINF).............212
Verde Lakes (SJNF).............218
Vestal Lake (SJNF).............221
Victoria Lake (RNF).............198
Viele Reservoir (FR).............27
Wahotoya Lake Reservoir (SWA).............89
Walden Ponds (FR).............27
Wall Lake (WRNF).............239
Walter Lake (WRNF).............240
Walton Creek (RNF).............199
Waneka Lake (FR).............27
Ward Creek (GMNF).............130
Ward Creek Reservoir (GMNF).............130
Ward Lake (GMNF).............129

Ward Road Pond (FR).............15
Washington Creek (GNF).............153
Washington Park Lakes (FR).............23
Watanga Lake (ANF).............118
Water Point Pond (FR).............13
Waterdog Lakes (SINF).............210
Waterdog Lakes (WRNF).............242
Waterdog Reservoir (GMNF).............127
Watson Lake (SWA).............91
Webb Lake (SJNF).............221
Webster Lake (FR).............12
Weir and Johnson Reservoir (GMNF).............140
Weller Lake (WRNF).............251
Wellington Reservoir #4 (SWA).............91
West Branch Creek (ANF).............111
West Branch, North Fork (ANF).............111
West Creek Lake (SINF).............211
West Dolores River (SJNF).............218
West Fork Lake (RNF).............195
West Lake (ANF).............109
West Lake (SWA).............91
West Lake (SWA).............92
West Muddy Creek (GNF).............152
West Sopris Creek (WRNF).............245
West Tenneesee Lakes (SINF).............205
Westminster City Park Pond (FR).............12
Whale Lake (RNF).............198
Whalen Creek (RNF).............198
Wheat Lake (RNF).............202
Wheeler Lakes (ANF).............122
Wheeler Lakes (PNF).............173
Whiskey Creek (RNF).............195
Whiskey Creek (STL).............80
White Dome Lake (SJNF).............221
White Owl Lake (WRNF).............241
White River (SWA).............94
White River,North Fork (WRNF).............235
Whitney Lakes (WRNF).............248
Williams Creek (SJNF).............226
Williams Creek (SJNF).............223
Williams Creek Reservoir (SJNF).............223
Williams Creek Reservoir (SWA).............89

Williams Fork Reservoir (ANF).............116
Williams Fork River (SWA).............88
Williams Fork, South Fork (RNF).............200
Williams Lake (SJNF).............223
Williams Lake (WRNF).............249
Willis Lake (SINF).............206
Willow Creek (ANF).............116
Willow Creek (GMNF).............145
Willow Creek (GNF).............157
Willow Creek (PNF).............176
Willow Creek (RMNP).............101
Willow Creek (SJNF).............217
Willow Creek Lake (RGNF).............185
Willow Creek Reservoir (ANRA).............99
Willow Creek, West (RGNF).............183
Willow Creeks (GNF).............162
Willow Creeks (GNF).............163
Willow Lake (RNF).............200
Willow Lake (WRNF).............250
Windsor Lake (SINF).............206
Windy Point Lake (WRNF).............238
Wolf Lake (SINF).............215
Wolverine Lake (RNF).............198
Wonderland Lake (FR).............27
Woodland Lake (FR).............32
Woods Lake (ANF).............123
Woods Lake (SWA).............95
Woods Lake SWA (UNF).............231
Wrights Lake (UNF).............231
Yamcolo Reservoir (RNF).............202
Yampa River (SP).............55
Yampa River (STL).............82
Yampa River (SWA).............94
Yankee Doodle Lake (FR).............33
Yellow Lake (WRNF).............241
Youngs Creek (GMNF).............132
Youngs Creek Reservoir #1 (GMNF).............131
Youngs Creek Reservoir #2 (GMNF).............131
Youngs Creek Reservoir #3 (GMNF).............131
Youngs Lake (GMNF).............141
Ypsilon Lake (RMNP).............102
Yule Lakes (WRNF).............249
Zimmerman Lake (ANF).............111

Colorado National Forest Recreation Guide Series
Forest Service trail information for over 750 trails
The eleven National Forests located in Colorado attract over 32 million visitors annually and eighty percent of all Colorado recreation occurs within their boundaries. Describes and maps the best trails within each National Forest.

Arapaho and Roosevelt National Forests
Code CO-08 ....83 Trails ....ISBN 0-930657-08-X ....96 Pages $12.95
Grand Mesa and Uncompahgre National Forests
Code CO-09 ....53 Trails ....ISBN 0-930657-09-8 ....48 Pages $6.95
Gunnison National Forest
Code CO-10 ....72 Trails ....ISBN 0-930657-10-1 ....160 Pages $12.95
Pike National Forest
Code CO-11 ....71 Trails ....ISBN 0-930657-11-X ....64 Pages $12.95
Rio Grande National Forest
Code CO-12 ....137 Trails ....ISBN 0-930657-15-2 ....96 Pages $9.95
Routt National Forest
Code CO-13 ....62 Trails ....ISBN 0-930657-12-8 ....64 Pages $9.95
San Isabel National Forest
Code CO-14 ....68 Trails ....ISBN 0-930657-14-4 ....160 Pages $12.95
San Juan National Forest
Code CO-15 ....77 Trails ....ISBN 0-930657-13-6 ....72 Pages $9.95
White River National Forest
Code CO-16 ....150 Trails ....ISBN 0-930657-16-0 ....96 Pages $9.95